W9-CJI-166

MEXICANO POLITICAL EXPERIENCE IN OCCUPIED AZTLÁN

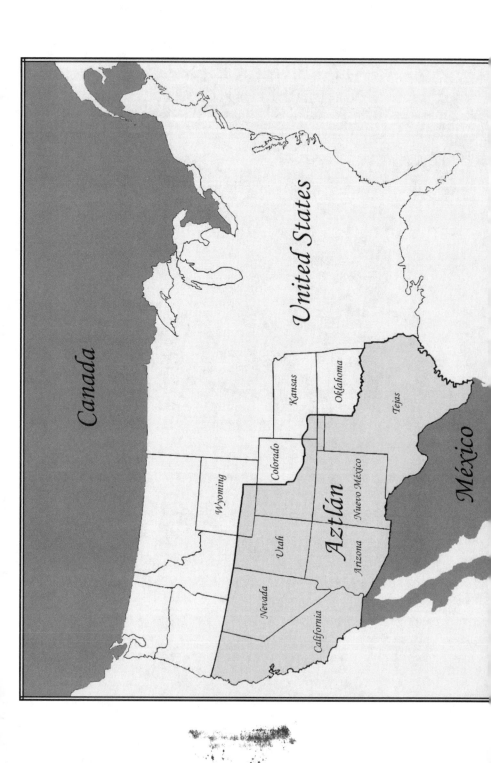

MEXICANO POLITICAL EXPERIENCE IN OCCUPIED AZTLÁN

Struggles and Change

ARMANDO NAVARRO

ALTAMIRA
PRESS

A Division of
ROWMAN & LITTLEFIELD PUBLISHERS, INC.
Walnut Creek • Lanham • New York • Toronto • Oxford

AltaMira Press
A division of Rowman & Littlefield Publishers, Inc.
1630 North Main Street, #367
Walnut Creek, CA 94596
www.altamirapress.com

Rowman & Littlefield Publishers, Inc.
A wholly owned subsidary of The Rowman & Littlefield Publishing Group, Inc.
4501 Forbes Boulevard, Suite 200
Lanham, MD 20706

PO Box 317
Oxford
OX2 9RU, UK

British Library Cataloguing in Publication Information Available

Library of Congress Cataloging-in-Publication Data

Navarro, Armando, 1941–
    Mexicano political experience in occupied Aztlán : struggles and change / Armando Navarro.
        p.   cm.
    Includes bibliographical references and index.
    ISBN 0-7591-0566-9 (cloth : alk. paper)—ISBN 0-7591-0567-7 (pbk. : alk. paper)
    1. Mexican Americans—Politics and government.   2. Mexican Americans—Ethnic identity.   3. Aztlán.   4. Mexico—History.   5. Mexico—Relations—United States.   6. United States—Relations—Mexico.   I. Title.
E184.M5N33   2005
973'.046872—dc22   2004026315

Printed in the United States of America

♾ ™ The paper used in this publication meets the minimum requirements of American National Standard for Information Sciences—Permanence of Paper for Printed Library Materials, ANSI/ NISO Z39.48-1992.

CONTENTS

Preface

A CCORDING TO HISTORIAN Rodolfo Acuña, "History can either oppress or liberate a people." Inspired by these words, this work is written in the spirit of contributing to the liberation of Aztlán's barrios and *colonias* from their oppressive colonial and occupied status. The book's purpose is to provide a comprehensive political-historical examination of the Mexicano political experience in occupied Aztlán from 1848 to 2003. It comes at an auspicious time when Mexicanos in Aztlán are in transition to demographically becoming the new majority within the region, which will occur within the next thirty to forty years or so. This means that whites will be relegated to a new minority status. Profound ramifications will occur not only politically, but economically, socially, and culturally as well. With the aforementioned in mind, I have written this work as a political historical "primer" to intellectually help Mexicanos, Latinos, and others as well to better understand Aztlán's past political history, its present, and its prospects and challenges for the future. Also, well documented and in order to broaden its reach, it is written in lucid and understandable language.

Quite appropriately, I have entitled this work, *Mexicano Political Experience in Occupied Aztlán: Struggles and Change.* I argue that as an occupied people, Mexicanos throughout Aztlán have politically resisted their oppression, exploitation, and marginalization. Secondly, today Mexicanos are in the midst of a critical political-historical juncture characterized by a severe and ominous "worst of times" crisis. Truly the work's uniqueness is its thesis, which propounds that Aztlán's barrios and *colonias* are "colonized" and that Aztlán as a region—the Southwest or the lands that once belonged to México—are "occupied" territories. Not since Rodolfo Acuña's first edition of *Occupied America* (published in 1972) has any work made this assertion so emphatically. I not only embrace Acuña's initial analysis, but also further expand on it. My justification is predicated on the notion that today's conditions impacting the Mexicano political experience are so deleterious and egregious that they warrant a return to such an analysis. This means that at this time no other existent work makes such arguments.

Because of these and other arguments made and the work's overall antiliberal capitalist posture, numerous Hispanic and non-Hispanic scholars as well as institutional politicians, leaders, and activists will probably consider the work controversial and anachronistic. They will categorically repudiate its arguments and conclusions. However, regardless of the intellectual and political flack and attacks I receive from either the ideological Right or Left or both, the work's paramount objective is to energize and reinvigorate the intellectual debate on the past, present, and especially the future of Aztlán's dialectically evolving Mexicano political experience.

Moreover, I do not purport that this is the definitive study on Aztlán's Mexicano political history. The fact is much more research needs to be conducted, and some topics are only briefly dealt with. Yet, notwithstanding, I contend, this work to date is by far the most current and comprehensive political historiographical work on the Mexicano in the United States. It encompasses the Mexicano's political history in the United States from the time of the arrival of the first migrants into the Western Hemisphere some 40,000 to 50,000 years ago to December 2003.

The work complements the excellent scholarship of political historian Juan Gómez-Quiñones's two works: *Roots of Chicano Politics, 1600–1940* (Albuquerque: University of New México Press, 1994) and *Chicano Politics: Reality & Promise, 1940–1990* (Albuquerque: University of New México Press, 1990). There are several other works currently available that provide a more comprehensive overall historical account of the Mexicano experience. One such excellent work is Rodolfo Acuña's fifth edition of *Occupied America: A History of Chicanos.* What I have sought to do, however, is to focus on the "political aspects" of the Mexicano historical struggle within the context of Aztlán. Only when absolutely necessary do I make reference to the Mexicano's political experience outside of Aztlán. Understanding the historical fact that the Mexicano political experience in the twenty-first century transcends Aztlán's geographical limits, another political historiographical work needs to be written that is truly national in scope. Furthermore, it is important to note that the cardinal emphasis is on Mexicanos and not on Latinos; yet, when necessary an appropriate reference is made to Latinos.

Another unique aspect of this work is that it combines political historiography with theory. None of the existent works on Mexicano political history in the United States have a theoretical framework to them. As a political scientist, I have sought to combine the factual richness of historiography with the explanatory virtue of theory. It is important to note that theory serves to describe in generalizations and seeks to explain what really happened. Theoretically, a set of four assumptions impels its analysis: one, the historiographical aspects and analysis are guided by "internal colonialism"; two, Aztlán's Mexicano politics since 1848 have been impacted by competing "subpolitical cultures"; three, changes within the Mexicano mode of politics and subpolitical cultures have fostered the rise of "political generations"; and four, for purposes of analysis, historiography can be examined as being "cyclical," meaning analytically political history can be broken down into somewhat distinct epochs or periods.

This work is my fourth in a five-work series that deals with Mexicano politics in the United States. My earlier publications include the *Mexican American Youth Organization: Avant-Garde of the Chicano Movement in Texas* (Austin: University of Texas Press, 1995); *The Cristal Experiment: A Chicano Struggle for Community Control* (Madison: University of Wisconsin Press, 1998); and *La Raza Unida Party: A Chicano Challenge to the U.S. Two-Party Dictatorship* (Philadelphia: Temple University Press, 2000). Originally, they were part of a four-volume interrelated series on the Chicano Movement, of which the fourth was to be tentatively entitled *What Needs to Be Done? The Building of a New Movement.* After completing two chapters, however, I realized that because of the scholarly dearth of current works on Mexicano political historiography and politics, I first needed to write a scholarly political historiographical work. I felt it would provide the requisite political historical foundation for what has now become my sixth book, which will provide a theoretical and futuristic look at Mexicano politics that will examine a number of strategic options. I say sixth book because I am currently working on my fifth book, which is tentatively titled, *The United States–México Border Crises: Militia Terrorism in Arizona.*

As to the book's organization, the introduction examines the work's theoretical framework. It provides a compendium examination and explanation of internal colonialism, political culture, political generations, and cyclical theory/ historical periodization. An explanation and brief analysis on each is provided. The first chapter provides the reader with the "historical antecedents" that impacted the genesis of the Mexicano political experience. This means that a historical synopsis of the myriad of antecedents that preceded it are examined— from the arrival of the first migrants to the Western Hemisphere to the conclusion of the United States War on México with the signing of the Treaty of Guadalupe Hidalgo (1848). This chapter sets the historical stage that is indispensable to understanding the historical forces that gave rise in 1848 to the Mexicano political experience in occupied Aztlán.

Chapters 2 through 8 correspond to the use of political historical periods or epochs. Using a "periodization approach," the work's historiographical body is broken down into several epochs that correspond to its chapters. While I recognize the intellectual dangers of breaking down a political history into arbitrary time periods, I find it useful in explaining and identifying the dominant forms of resistance and change that occurred within the political sphere of each epoch. Each epoch is marked by its own prevailing mode of politics. In turn, each epoch's salient issues, events, leaders; demographic/socioeconomic profile; subpolitical cultures; organizations; and electoral politics are carefully examined.

More specifically, from a historical perspective not "all" issues, events, or leaders are dealt with. Only those I feel were germane to the politics of the Mexicano experience. Each chapter provides a demographic/socioeconomic profile of the said epoch. The cardinal intent is to illustrate statistically that the demographic "re-Mexicanization of Aztlán" had its roots at the turn of the twentieth century. Moreover, with the exception of the Depression years of the 1930s, it has increased dramatically every decade hence. As to the socioeconomic part, it clearly records the "worst of times" reality created by the barrios and *colonias* colonization. The Mexicano's various subpolitical cultures are examined from the perspective of how they contributed to changes within each epoch's mode of politics, especially the rise of several political generations. The myriad types of organizations that have colored the Mexicano political experience from the epochs of resistance to transition are dealt with using an abbreviated case study format. Lastly, the diverse aspects of Mexicano politics via the ballot box are analyzed.

This work is a cumulative product of several years of research. It relies on a combination of both primary and secondary sources. An abundance of works, journal articles, reports, and newspaper and magazine articles embellish every chapter's documentation and research. In chapter 8, because of the unavailability of literature that covers the politics of transition (2000–2003), using content analysis, I rely on reports, newspaper and magazine articles, and lastly the Internet. In addition, when there were gaps in my research, such as in ascertaining the current status of certain organizations, in-depth interviews either in person or by phone were conducted with persons who played an important leadership role. Primary documents, such as reports and letters, were used in addition to demographic and socioeconomic data released by the Bureau of the U.S. Census and other sources.

Lastly, I rely on participant observation as a research tool. This is important since from 1968 to the present I have participated consistently in a leadership, organizer, or activist capacity in numerous struggles for social change, empowerment, and social justice both domestically and internationally. This has given me an opportunity to observe firsthand, both as a scholar and secondly as a participant, the issues, events, leaders, and organizations of the politics of the Mexicano experience over the last thirty-five years. From my perspective, my activist experience greatly enhances the quality of the work's political historiography and analysis. Even today, I strive to combine the power of scholarship and praxis with the intent of strengthening my role as a scholar activist.

Acknowledgments

I want to thank the people who assisted me in completing this arduous and voluminous work. First I want to graciously recognize the numerous contributions made by my *companera* Maria Anna Gonzales, who patiently and arduously spent numerous nights and days doing the painstaking final editing and formatting of the 1,000-page manuscript and who constructively gave me input vis-à-vis its content and analysis. Moreover, I also want to thank Rosalie Robertson, senior editor of AltaMira Press, for her initial editing that improved the style of the manuscript. In addition, I want to recognize the fine work done by Jean Middleton, who did the indexing. Unfortunately, time and circumstances, however, precluded me from having some of my peers examine the manuscript. I would be remiss if I did not also publicly thank my two student research assistants, Sonia Mariscal and Jose Lopez, who were instrumental in conducting library research. I also want to thank the University of California, Riverside Academic Senate, and the Ernesto Galarza Applied Research Center for providing me the grants that supported my research.

I also wish to thank the many people who I have organized with and have inspired me since 1968 in the numerous struggles for resistance and change. We won some battles for change and lost some, but the important thing is that we did not accept our oppression or subordination. We fraternally struggled righteously to improve the lives of our people with integrity and immutable commitment. To all of you too many to mention, *mis gracias*. As a token of my gratitude, I respectfully dedicate this work to you.

Introduction

THIS INTRODUCTION PROVIDES a theoretical framework,[1] presenting seven underlying premises of the work's political historical analysis. First, the Mexicano[2] political experience in the United States has been one of incessant struggles of resistance and change. Second, Mexicanos, particularly throughout Aztlán,[3] who reside in the barrios (enclaves) and *colonias* (unincorporated usually impoverished subdivisions)[4] are an occupied people who are undergoing a reoccupation of their conquered territory. Third, Mexicanos' political history in the United States has been predicated on oppressive and exploitive conditions resulting from U.S. imperialism and colonialism, which began as an internal phenomenon, but in the twenty-first century is evolving into a form of external colonialism. Fourth, the country's two-party dictatorship has thwarted Mexicanos' political progress. Fifth, the Mexicano political experience in occupied Aztlán evolved through several different political historical epochs, each with its own particular mode of politics. Sixth, because of their occupied status, Mexicanos as a people can be argued as tantamount to being the "Palestinians" of the United States, a people without a country. And finally, the Mexicano political experience in the United States could dialectically be altered to where Mexicanos and Latinos in the twenty-first century, especially in Aztlán, could well have the capacity to liberate themselves or dramatically alter their occupied and colonized status.

Mexicanos: A Colonized People

The Internal Colonial Model

During the tumultuous 1960s, some progressive intellectuals from across ethnic and racial lines began to identify with the rise of a new controversial theory: "internal colonialism." Its intellectual roots can be traced to the late 1950s when some scholars immersed in the study of oppressed and exploited third world peoples began to use the concept of "domestic colonialism" in their analyses of development and underdevelopment. By the early 1960s, black theorists in the United States began to apply the term to the study of the "black political experience in the United States." Harold Cruse in 1962 characterized race relations in the United States as "domestic colonialism."[5] Kenneth Clark, in his classic, *Dark Ghetto*, two years later alleged that the political, economic, and social structure of Harlem was essentially a colony. He wrote, "The dark ghettos are social, political, educational and—above all—economic colonies. Their inhabitants are subject peoples, victims of the greed, cruelty, insensitivity, guilt, and fears of their masters."[6] Likewise, Stokely Carmichael and Charles Hamilton, in *Black Power*, published in 1967, based their analysis on internal colonialism. In reference to the black experience in the United States, they argued that "black people in this country form a colony, and it is not in the interest of the colonial power to liberate them."[7]

During the 1960s third world scholars, such as Frantz Fanon and Albert Memmi, produced works on colonialism that inspired others to follow suit.[8] In particular, the works on internal colonialism by Rodolfo González-Casanova as they related to Latin America created great interest in the United States.[9] His work was further complemented by a number of other theorists, such as Andre Gunder Frank, who drew a theoretical nexus between colonialism, underdevelopment, and dependency theory.[10] Increasingly, by 1969, scholars and activists alike used internal colonialism in their analysis of oppression of black and other people of color in the United States. Particularly influential was sociologist Robert Blauner, who in his classic work *Racial Oppression in America* further refined the theoretical understanding of various aspects of internal colonialism by applying it to the experiences of not just blacks, but of Mexicanos and the indigenous people in the United States.[11] He makes an effective distinction between the "colonized" and "immigrant minorities." In the United States, the former are a result of forced entry into their homelands; the latter have a voluntary status.

Hence, because of the turbulent epoch of the 1960s and early 1970s, scholars and activists alike, in an effort to better understand the various aspects of racial oppression, utilized internal colonialism as a model. Michael Omi and Howard Winant identify the following as the salient elements of internal colonialism:

1. A colonial *geography* emphasizing the territoriality or spatial arrangement of population groups along racial lines;
2. A dynamic of *cultural domination and resistance*, in which racial categories are utilized to distinguish between antagonistic colonizing and colonized groups, and conversely, to emphasize the essential cultural unity and autonomy of each;

3. A system of *superexploitation*, understood as a process by which extra-economic coercion is applied to the racially identified colonized group, with the aim of increasing the economic resources appropriated by the colonizers;

4. Institutionalization of *externally based control*, such that the racially identified colonized group is organized in essential political and administrative aspects by the colonizers or their agents.[12]

Thus, various ethnic and racial groups in the United States adopted internal colonialism as a theoretical model and applied it to their particular and cultural nationalist agendas.

By the early 1970s, Mexicano activists and scholars increasingly jumped on the intellectual bandwagon of the internal colonial model. They were influenced by a growing radicalization of the country's political climate and a surge of cultural nationalism, which emphasized the cultural aspects of their experience: a sense of collective identity, community, and feelings of "people hood."[13] This spirit of cultural rebirth led to a rejection of assimilationist-reform accommodation politics. Many of them now preferred to identify their struggles with third world national liberation. In particular, within the activist sector, numerous leaders and organizations drew upon the cultural nationalist concept of Aztlán, calling for self-determination by building a "Chicano nation." The intellectual and activist climate was such that some equated the present status of the Southwest or Aztlán to that of an internal colony. Historian Rodolfo Acuña in his classic *Occupied America: The Chicano's Struggle toward Liberation*, published in 1972, based much of his historical analysis on internal colonialism. He wrote, "I have attempted to underscore my thesis that Chicanos are a colonized people in the United States."[14] At about the same time, political scientists Mario Barrera, Carlos Muñoz, and Charles Ornelas presented their concept of the "barrio as an internal colony."[15] They addressed the limitations of the older "assimilationist/accommodationist"[16] perspective, which alleged that U.S. society is comprised of diverse racial and ethnic groups integrated into an orderly, cohesive, "melting pot" of divergent interests where the ultimate fate is "assimilation," "integration," "consensus," and "cooperation."[17] Their perspective was based on the notion that the barrio was an internal colony and that the problem of Chicano politics was essentially one of powerlessness.[18] In 1975 sociologist Edward Murgia wrote a monograph in which he applied the models of assimilation and internal colonialism to the Mexican American experience, and in the end opted for a third model based upon "cultural pluralism."[19]

Other scholars, however, such as Tomás Almaguer, Guillermo Flores, and

Ronald Bailey, using a Marxist class analysis were hypercritical of internal colonialism.[20] They argued that the internal colonial model was "ideologically short-sighted" and "counterrevolutionary" and that its emphasis on race and cultural oppression erroneously missed the true culprit of oppression, which was liberal capitalism. From their Marxist perspective, there was a nexus between internal colonialism and cultural nationalism. Their criticism of internal colonialism was also based on the notion that Mexicanos, especially throughout Aztlán, were not a nation or a nation within a nation; rather they were an oppressed and exploited "national minority" that was a dependent labor force within the liberal capitalist economy. They also argued that Mexicanos were not a nation because of their linguistic, historical, and cultural diversity.[21]

Fred A. Cervantes challenged the adequacy of explaining the contemporary "Chicano situation" from an internal colonial perspective. His Marxist analysis rejected Barrera, Muñoz, and Ornelas's interpretation, which saw Mexicanos as powerless, enmeshed within a distinct system of exploitation, racism, and nationalism. Cervantes also criticized them for not making a clear distinction between an internal colony and an external colony, particularly as in defining the legal status of the colonized and in the conceptual difference between internal colonial and class "exploitation." From his class struggle perspective, he sees Mexicanos in the United States as a national minority that seeks "multicultural pluralism" instead of being an anticolonial force that struggles for national liberation.[22] This intellectual debate on the usage of internal colonialism revealed the ongoing ideological conflict waged by cultural nationalists and Marxists within the Movimiento (Movement).

With the end of the militant epoch of protest (1966–1974) the decline of the Chicano Movement and the rise of the Viva Yo Hispanic Generation, the intellectual political climate among Mexicano scholars was such that internal colonialism as a theoretical framework fell from intellectual grace. Even in the diminishing activist sector, few but the sectarian Left identified with the internal colony theory. In the ensuing years an incessant conservative political climate led to a reliance on system maintenance-oriented "mainstream scholarship." By 2003, within both the humanities and social sciences, internal colonialism was all but passé and considered by most Latino scholars as an anachronism, until the writing of this work.

A fundamental argument of this work is that the barrios and colonias of Aztlán, since the genesis of the "Mexicano political experience" in 1848, have and continue to be internal colonies. The internal colonialization of Aztlán's barrios and *colonias* contributed significantly to the liberal capitalist development of the United States via the exploitation of their cheap labor, loss of land and resources, control of the surplus value, and of their consumer markets. This means that today little has changed, even though the barrios and *colonias* are becoming bigger and more plentiful. The barrios and *colonias* of Aztlán today exist under the specter of "neocolonialism," which in turn continues to be fed by the exploitive nature of liberal capitalism. The truth is interdependence exists between the two, which fosters class cleavages both within and outside of the internal colony itself. As a result, the country's liberal capitalist system, economically insatiable, feeds, benefits, and prospers via the exploitation, subordination, and marginalization of the oppressed peoples of the internal colony.[23]

The present work will more than suffice to buttress the validity of the applicability of my internal colonial thesis via the analysis, data, and illustrations. I challenge readers to explain why is it that the country's barrios and colonias are underdeveloped, impoverished, and relegated to what appropriately can be described as a third world status within the geographical context of the richest country in the world. My intent within this introduction is not to review every criticism made against the internal colonial model. Instead, I have sought to provide the reader with an overview of internal colonialism as a theoretical framework, which is vital to this work's historiography of the "Mexicano political experience." My own perspective will become increasingly evident throughout the work.

Colonialism: External versus Internal

The political reality of Mexicanos and Latinos in the twenty-first century is that their barrios and *colonias* throughout Aztlán are dialectically in transition, from being internal colonies to external colonies. In order to understand the basis of this argument, it is imperative to examine what these two theoretical frameworks are and their individual differences. "External colonialism" is somewhat synonymous with the traditional concept of colonialism. To begin with, colonialism infers a particular form or pattern of exploitation and oppression. The paramount difference between the two interrelated concepts is that in external colonialism the colonizing power constitutes a minority of the population within the colonized periphery or territory; whereas, in internal colonialism, the opposite is the case. Robert Blauner defines colonialism as "the establishment of domination over a geographically external political unit, most often inhabited by people of a different race and culture, where domination is political and economic and the colony exists." He states, "Typically, the colonizers exploit the land, the raw materials, the labor, and other resources of the colonized nation; a formal recognition is given to the difference in power, autonomy, and political status and various agencies are set up to maintain this subordination."[24] In further making the distinction between external and internal colonialism, Blauner writes, "Traditional colonialism involves the control of the majority of a nation by a minority of outsiders."[25] Alfredo Mirandé makes the argument that Chicanos (Mexicanos in the United States) are a "defacto colony." In making the distinction between the two forms of colonialism he writes:

> Chicanos today are not colonized in the classic sense of the word, but they remain "internal colonized." Internal colonialism differs from the classic variety in that it entails not the subordination of a distant land but the acquisition of contiguous territory. Once the territory is acquired, local elites are deposed from power and indigenous institutions are completely destroyed. The "classic" colony is recognized formally and legally, while the "internal colony" has only an informal existence.[26]

Murgia explains, "In classical colonialism the colonized are in the majority in their own conquered country."[27] Therefore, colonialism historically was and is a system of political control forced upon conquered peoples.[28]

External colonialism continues to be a product of imperialism and for centuries has been its progenitor. During the last five hundred years, impelled by mercantilism, numerous European and non-European powers, such as Spain, Portugal, Great Britain, France, the Netherlands, the United States, Japan, Germany, Italy, and the Soviet Union, became colonial powers as a result of imperialism. What then is imperialism? Words that help us understand the politically loaded and controversial concept include, *expansion, imposition of power, use of force, control, domination,* and *exploitation*. Imperialism denotes one country's expansion of territory over another or others and the imposition of its power by the use of force in order to politically and economically control, dominate, and exploit its resources, labor, and market either formally or informally. Michel Beaud explains the nexus between what he calls "new capitalism" and imperialism in the context of the turn of the twentieth century:

> It included many factors, among which the following were prominent: concentration of capital, cartels, trusts, and monopolies; interpenetration of industrial capital and banking capital within the new reality of finance capital; the renewed role of the state, through social legislation, its major role in large public works projects, territorial expansion, and militarism; export of capital, colonization, and the dividing up of the world.[29]

From a colonial power perspective a colony is a geographical area maintained for political, strategical, and economic purposes. In another "de-colonization" point of view, Sukarno of Indonesia saw colonialism as "a situation in which a people are governed by other people politically, economically, intellectually, and physically."[30]

From a neo-Marxist perspective political scientist Michael Parenti defines "imperialism" as "the process whereby the dominant political-economic interests of one nation expropriate for their own enrichment the land, labor raw materials, and markets of another people."[31] In another of his works, he argues that an imperialist power "dominates through the use of economic and military power." He categorizes the United States as "the greatest imperialist power in history."[32] In the twenty-first century, capitalist imperialism differs from the earlier forms in the way it accumulates capital: through the organized exploitation of labor and penetration of foreign markets, which has fostered the globalization of capital. For any imperialist power, capital accumulation occurs by controlling the other country's substructures (economies) and integrating them into its productive structures and by dominating their political cultures and superstructure (governmental structures).[33]

During the past 500 years, colonialism and imperialism have appeared in various forms. One can deduce that essentially there have been three main types of colonies:

1. *Colonies of Settlement*: This form of colony results when persons from a foreign country migrate to and eventually take total control by use of force and dominate all aspects of the evolving social order, and in most cases substitute their culture for the existing native one. Colonizers usually exclude the native colonized from leadership in their society or all too often kill many of them in violent confrontations or by accidental or deliberate exposure to disease. Examples of settlement colonies include the United States, Canada, and Australia.

2. *Colonies of Exploitation*: In this form of colony the colonizer foreign power establishes political and economic control using force, if necessary, against colonial resistance. For all intents and purposes they do not eradicate or displace the native societies and tolerate their cultures. Exploitation of the labor force and of the colonized raw resources drives the colonial economy. The colonizer does not arrive in large numbers, but enter strategic segments of the society, as planters, administrators, merchants, and military officers. Colonies of exploitation include most of Latin America, Africa, and several other countries in Southeast Asia, such as India.

3. *Contested Settlement Colonies*: This form of colony tends to develop its own government, independent of or even in defiance of the parent colonizer

country. It forms its own cultural and political identity and dominates the native populations for purposes of exploiting their labor, which become the backbone of the colonized economy. The native peoples manage to maintain some control over their lives to where eventually they are able to contest the colonizer's control of the colony, both the control by the colonizing country and that of the minority colonizer settlers. Rhodesia, Algeria, and South Africa are contemporary examples of this form of colony.[34]

A fourth form of colonialism is internal colonialism. To Ramon Gutierréz internal colonialism is "a modern capitalist practice of oppression and exploitation of racial and ethnic minorities within the borders of the state characterized by relationships of domination, oppression, and exploitation."[35] Most of colonialism's salient characteristics are applicable to internal colonialism. Generally, internal colonialism can be characterized as involving exploitative relationships between a "metropolis and center" (the colonizer) and "periphery or satellite" (the colonized) within a single state or society.[36] In this case the metropolis core dominates an underdeveloped periphery politically and exploits it economically. Politically, the colonizer's superstructure and governmental machinery of control and power are located at the center where intensive economic development also takes place. As a result of the exploitation an acute disparity develops between the center and periphery: the center becomes increasingly wealthier, while the periphery faces the deleterious effects of underdevelopment and dependency-produced poverty. Cultural conflict between the colonizer and colonized is also an inherent attribute to the exploitive relationship.[37] Typically, the periphery is not formally or legally recognized as being colonized, but the oppressive and exploitative socioeconomic and cultural conditions and its political powerlessness and subordinated status are indicative of its colonized status.

Moreover, integral to internal colonialism as is also the case with traditional colonialism are several interrelated relationships of domination, oppression, and exploitation. Robert Blauner identified four such relationships: Forced Entry, Cultural Impact, External Administration, and Racism.[38] First, the colonies are conquered involuntarily by force. Two, there is a deliberate effort by the colonizer to destroy the colonized people's culture, heritage, and language. Three, the colonized are politically externally administered and manipulated by the colonizer and are relegated to a powerless and subordinated status. And four, the colonizer's political culture is permeated by a racism predicated on a form of social domination that perceives the colonized to be different, inferior, and the colonizer to be physically and mentally superior biologically (genetically) to the colonized. From my perspective, there are two additional aspects of internal colonialism that help explicate its insidious impact: the occupied internal colonies become a locus of cheap labor that fosters capitalist accumulation and the colonized land, wealth, and substructure are converted to a dependent consumer economy.

The study of neocolonialism is buttressed by "dependency theory," which from a Marxist perspective purports that the liberal capitalist development of the metropolis is predicated on unequal power relationships, which allows it to strip the periphery's resources and surplus. Liberal capitalism within the internal colonial context fosters underdevelopment in the periphery and an exploitive form of interdependency. As a result, underdevelopment occurs in the periphery from the loss of surplus that was expropriated and appropriated for investment in the metropolis's development.[39] A political, economic, social, and cultural relationship exists between the metropolis and periphery that serves and enhances the metropolis's development and progress at the expense of the periphery's development. Therefore, underdevelopment for the periphery in simple terms denotes monopoly by the metropolis over the periphery, a dependency of the periphery on the metropolis, and the creation of oppressive and exploitative conditions that are characterized by poverty and a plethora of social problems, culminating in the people's powerlessness and alienation.

Internal colonialism is reinforced by liberal capitalism. The colony is a vital source of capital and profit for the liberal capitalist metropolis. While the metropolis prospers economically, the colony or periphery faces growing poverty. This unequal relationship is characterized by an unequal distribution of wealth and power, and ultimately foments social stratification, class conflict, racial/ethnic antagonisms, and institutional racism. The underdevelopment created by internal colonialism also fosters a colonized economy that is "consumer" oriented. This means that the colonized become commodities of profit for the liberal capitalist metropolis, which controls the means of production and distribution, particularly the colony's raw material and labor. Workers in the colonies perform the least undesirable jobs, the "dirty and servile" jobs that colonizers avoid. Internal colonialism creates a permanent reservoir of subordinated and cheap labor, which satiates the demands of liberal capitalism.[40] In explaining the nexus between the two, David Brown writes:

> [It] becomes the means employed by the state to conserve the non-capitalist modes of production and social organization in the periphery, which are crucial for the development of capitalism in the core regions, but which are being undermined by that same capitalism.[41]

In sum, internal colonialism entails two inherent characteristics that stem from liberal capitalism. The first is economic, which focuses on the extraction of labor, wealth, and resources from the colonized peoples. This creates a colonized economy within the liberal capitalist economy that is underdeveloped, impoverished, and dependent, which as a result produces a stratified social structure. The second is cultural, requiring a close regulation of the colonized peoples' lives and dominance over their culture.[42] The net effect is the prevalence of institutional racism or even outright racism expressed as bigotry, prejudice, and discrimination against the colonized. Lastly, it is political in that the colonized are powerless, subordinated, and dependent on the metropolis, which means in effect the colonized had no real viable voice in their governance or access to power sharing. At best what the colonized exercise is indirect rule.

Mexicanos in Occupied and Colonized Aztlán

Since the occupation began in 1848, the Mexicano barrios and *colonias* of Aztlán have been relegated to internal colonies. Literally millions of Mexicano migrants throughout the decades have resettled in the barrios and *colonias* of Aztlán and beyond and have been victimized and subjected to the specter of a dehumanizing and oppressive internal colonialism. As previously stated, this thesis was first posited in 1972 by historian Rodolfo Acuña, who in his classic *Occupied America: Chicano's Struggle toward Liberation* wrote:

> [T]he conquest of the southwest created a colonial situation in the traditional sense—with the Mexican land and population being controlled by an imperialistic United States. Further, I contend that this colonization—with variations—is still with us today. Thus, I refer to the colony, initially, in the traditional definition of the term, and later as an internal colony. . . . The parallel is between Chicanos' experience in the United States and the colonization of other third world peoples too similar to dismiss.

Acuña was one of the first to apply the model of internal colonialism to the analysis of the "Mexicano political experience." His above definition provides the template by which the concept can be further elaborated. It is important to reiterate that at the core of internal colonialism is the notion that the colonizer constitutes the majority of the population while the colonized represents the oppressed and exploited minority.

As a result, the Mexicano political experience from 1848 to the present has been shaped within Aztlán's barrios and *colonias*: the United States internal colonies. Aztlán, geographically as a region, was forcibly and involuntarily taken from México first in the Tejas Revolt of 1836 and later as a result of U.S. imperialistic

War against México in 1846–1848. As the occupier of Aztlán, the United States sought to destroy the Mexicanos' culture, heritage, and language via a socialization process. This acculturation was predicated on the ethos of liberal capitalism, while paradoxically maintaining Mexicanos in a segregated, underdeveloped, and impoverished status. Since the start of the occupation in 1848, Mexicano labor has been used as a source of cheap labor in order to promote the capitalist development and capital accumulation. As a result, Mexicanos in the United States have been relegated to dependent, subordinate, and powerless economic consumers who have no control over the means of production and distribution. With the exception of Nuevo México, Mexicanos politically were relegated to a powerless and subordinated status while their barrios and *colonias* were externally administered and governed. In addition, the country's political culture continues to be permeated by a pervasive current of racism that stereotypes Mexicanos as being inferior to whites. As this work amply illustrates, the plethora of social problems that have pervaded the Mexicano political experience throughout Aztlán's barrios and *colonias* stem from their internal colonial status and the inherent contradictions of liberal capitalism.

The United States historically has maintained its colonizer hegemony over Aztlán by co-opting Mexicano elites and organizations that are willing to serve as gatekeepers or custodians of the liberal capitalist social order. Colonial white power elites have always buttressed their control by relying on two types of colonial agents: buffers and "want to be whites." In most cases, neither type is cognizant of the colonized oppression in the barrios and *colonias* or of their own colonial agent status. Furthermore, they do not entertain alternative ideological options because they are products of a ubiquitous socialization process that has converted them to purveyors of liberal capitalism, which makes them indispensable to the white elite plutocrats who continue the external and internal administration of Aztlán.

Buffers refer to those individuals or organizations that perpetuate the internal colonialism of Aztlán's barrios and *colonias* by not pressing for major change. They propose limited and nonthreatening reforms to the social order and do not challenge its authority or legitimacy. In most cases, they rely on conventional methods; however, on occasion some adhere to the use of militant methods.[43] Buffers also absorb or neutralize conflict, thwart the building of a social change consciousness among Mexicanos and Latinos, buttress the maintenance of the social order by not offering alternatives for social change, and act as a bridge between the colonizing authorities and the colonized. Ideologically, most espouse liberal capitalist beliefs and are critical of those who espouse an extreme Left or ultranationalist perspective. Some buffers, however, display cultural-nationalist propensities, which are manifested by their rejection of assimilation and adherence to acculturation or cultural pluralism. Occasionally buffers seek to represent the best interests of the colonized.

"Want to be white" applies to individuals and organizations that take on the characteristics of the colonial superstructure and are zealots of assimilation, integration, and accommodation. They may be referred to as "coconut" (brown on the outside and white on the inside) or *vendido* (sellout). Unlike some buffers, "want to be whites" personify the ethos of a conservative Horatio Alger of liberal capitalism and white culture. They scorn being identified as Mexicano or Chicano.

Conversely, the antithesis to the buffer and "want to be white" is the "advocate transformer." Dramatically smaller in number, they are anti-system and pro-social change–oriented. The scope of social change they propose varies from peaceful major reform to violent revolutionary transformation. The advocate transformer repudiates liberal capitalism and embraces either ultranationalism or socialism. More sectarian in their politics, they are cognizant of the plight of Mexicanos and Latinos in the United States. They seek to change the oppressive, exploitative, and marginalized status of Aztlán's barrios and *colonias*. Within the context of the Mexicano political experience, social advocate transformers represent the paragon of resistance to Aztlán's occupation and liberal capitalism.

Thus, the rise of *Pax Americana*[44] denotes a worldwide crusade for the globalization of liberal capitalism. This presages a renaissance of colonialism. This neo-colonialism, however, is taking on a new form but its exploitive nature still remains the same. Some sovereign countries in practice have exhibited an economic dependency syndrome.

Mexicano Evolving Political Culture

Theoretical Aspects of Political Culture

Although it is a debatable concept in political science,[45] "political culture" is important to the analysis of the Mexicano's political experience, especially of occupied Aztlán. Since the start of the occupation in 1848, the country's liberal capitalist-based "political culture" has helped maintain the occupation of Aztlán and the internal colonial status of its barrios and *colonias*. This has impacted significantly the Mexicano political experience. It is important to note that there is a clear distinction between culture and political culture. Roderic Ai Camp explains the difference between culture and political culture: "Culture incorporates all the influences—historical, religious, ethnic, political—that affect a society's values and attitudes. The political culture is a microcosm of the larger culture, focusing specifically on those values and attitudes having to do with an individual's political views and behavior."[46]

Since the time of Plato, Aristotle, and the Greek City states, political culture has played a key role in the study of societies' overall politics. Plato in his *Republic* argued "That governments vary as the dispositions of men vary, and that there must be as many of the one as there are of the other." Aristotle in his classic *Politics* stresses the importance of political cultural variables and their relationship to social stratification and political structural and performance variables. Major theorists like Machiavelli, Montesquieu, and de Tocqueville also dealt with diverse aspects of political culture. In the twentieth century, social psychologists and sociologists produced a number of studies on the political behavior of individuals and social groups during the rise of the Bolshevik Revolution, Italian Fascism, and German National Socialism.[47] It was not until 1963, however, with the publication of Almond and Verba's *Civic Culture*,[48] that political scientists began to focus on the study of political culture.

Most political scientists concur that political culture is not a theory and that it essentially refers to a set of variables that are conducive to the construction of theories. Political culture on the other hand, offers an empirical question, open to hypothesis and testing.[49] Political culture envelops people's political values, beliefs, and biases. It reveals people's behavior toward politics and political institutions and processes, and it is within this context that politics takes shape and direction. Political culture in essence revolves around two primary questions: What do people think politically? And, How do they see themselves within the political arena?

From birth to death, in any social order, people undergo a well-systematized socialization and conditioning process. Political culture, according to Gabriel A. Almond and G. Bingham Powell, Jr., consists of "attitudes, beliefs, values, and skills which are current in an entire population, as well as those special propensities and patterns which may be found within separate parts of the population."[50] For Walter A. Rosenbaum "those dimensions of an individual's thoughts, feelings, or behaviors that are linked to the creation and maintenance of a society's fundamental political order belong under the label political culture." He identifies several core components as orientations toward the governmental structures (e.g., regime and input and output orientations); the political system (e.g., political identifications, political trust, and rules of the game); and one's own political activities (e.g., political competence and political efficacy).[51]

Political culture, particularly in the United States, provides the boundaries of legitimacy based on liberal capitalist beliefs, values, and symbols, and defines the political possibilities for debate, action, and change. Such is the work of Almond and Verba, which, influenced by Talcott Parson's work, offers the proposition that there are three major intrinsic interrelated orientations to political culture: cognitive, affective, and evaluative. Cognitive orientations encompass knowledge, political beliefs, and objects; affective orientations foster feelings of attachment and involvement, about political objects; and evaluative orientations involve judgments and opinions of political objects.[52] They identify the ensuing three ideal types of political cultures:

1. *Parochial political culture*: Entails societies with little or no specialized political roles, meaning their internal political orientations are not separated from religious and social orientations. In addition, these societies lack an awareness of the political system and expect little or nothing from it. They have little or no knowledge of the workings of the political system; lack political organization; have low expectations for change; and politically are nonparticipatory. In short, parochial political cultures tend to be passive, traditional, and ostensibly apolitical from a participatory perspective.

2. *Subject political culture*: People in these societies have "a high frequency of orientations toward a differentiated political system and toward the output aspects of the system." In this case, the subject is cognizant of the political system; has some understanding of its workings; has some affective (dislikes or supports it) and evaluative (is able to ascertain its legitimacy) opinions of it; but "the orientations toward specifically input objects, and toward the self as an active participant, approach [is] zero." Thus, the relationship of the subject to the political system is largely passive.

3. *Participant political culture*: The members of the society are oriented toward participating politically. In other words, they are cognizant of the workings of government to where they participate in both the input and output aspects of the political system. They tend to be oriented toward an "activist" role of the self in the polity. In short, their level of cognitive, affective, and evaluative orientations in comparison to the subject and parochial are highest.[53]

Modern societies tend to be an admixture of all three ideal types. The United States and European countries, among a few others, claim that they incarnate a predominant "participant" political culture, while some societies such as in Africa, Latin America, and other underdeveloped regions of the world are said to have parochial political cultures.

Political culture can be understood in the context of a society's "collective political mentality or personality," which contributes to its political identity and ethos. Moreover, political culture is an extension of the society's ideology. The two concepts are interrelated and are inseparable. A political ideology is a belief system that explains and justifies a preferred political order for society, either existing or proposed, and offers a strategy (processes, institutions, programs) for its attainment.[54] Political culture provides a diffusion of the political ideologies into the society's collective psyche. In the case of the United States, its political culture is predicated on a liberal capitalist ideology.

Political culture also encompasses the people's emotional or psychic attachment to a society's political symbols, political parties, and laws that make up the political order. Hence, inherent to political culture are three basic dimensions: the individual perceives his or her role within the arena of politics; the political system is the framework for constructing the individual's attitudes toward their country, political system, and government officials; and public policy output reflects the political culture. Political scientist Almon Leroy Way, Jr., writes, "A society's political culture is the result of the entire society's past and present experience."[55] Thus, political culture is a broad term that encompasses the value and belief system of society, including people's perceptions of politics and government.

How is a political culture acquired? The political culture of a society like its general culture is the product of experience and learning. Integral to the transmission of political culture is the process of "political socialization," by which each individual of the social order acquires basic attitudes, values, beliefs, and norms. In other words, political socialization is "the process through which an individual acquires his [or her] particular political orientations—his [or her] knowledge, feelings, and evaluations regarding his [or her] political world."[56] Essential to understanding a society's political behavior, political culture denotes a learning process, which transfers political information, beliefs, values, opinions, and biases. from one generation to the next. It occurs through the use of both informal acculturation, which involves informal learning contexts, and formal acculturation that requires more of a structured or planned political education and indoctrination.[57]

Various agents of socialization transmit society's core political values both formally and informally. These socialization agents play a fundamental role in the transmission of values that create subgroups, hierarchies, and power relationships within the social order. Every organized society engages in some sort of political socialization;[58] it has to in order to regulate and maintain itself. In states with the greatest control over individuals, socialization is tantamount to indoctrination. Yet universally and regardless of the ideological inclination of the nation-state, as a process socialization proceeds via the following agents transmitting its ideology via its political culture: the family, media, education, religion, peer group, and workplace. The resilience, stability, or longevity of any political system is largely dependent on the degree to which the people believe in its political cultural ideology.[59] Therefore, agents of political socialization mold the country's political culture and influence the people's perspective on politics, government, and public policy. Thus, in the case of U.S. political culture, it is so ubiquitous that it is insulated and protected from any other form of ideological challenge.

United States Political Culture

In order to better understand the overall development of the politics of the Mexicano experience in occupied Aztlán it is imperative to briefly examine U.S. political culture and identify its core values and beliefs.[60] First of all, the country's political culture stems from its omnipresent liberal capitalist ideological framework. Politically, the use of *liberal* in this context refers to classical liberalism, which has its roots in the liberal theorists of the European Enlightenment, such as John Locke, Thomas Hobbes, and Jean-Jacques Rousseau, whose ideas found fertile political ground in the Thirteen Colonies. The liberal political creed is predicated on six core beliefs:

1. *Popular sovereignty*: At the core of liberalism is the belief of popular sovereignty, which denotes that political power radiates in its original form from the legitimacy and consent of the governed—the people.
2. *Individualism*: This belief accentuates the primacy of the individual in his or her right to pursue the ideals of Life, Liberty, and Pursuit of Happiness (property) unencumbered by society and the state.
3. *Freedom*: In order for the individual to realize his or her rights fully, he or she must have the freedom to make his or her own choices with a minimum of restraint.
4. *Private Property*: The individual must be allowed to accumulate private property, which is at the heart of individual freedom; one cannot survive without the other.
5. *Limited Government*: For individuals to maintain their individual freedom and private property government must be limited and constrained from enacting any abuses against the people's rights.
6. *Political Equality*: Systems of hereditary privilege are rejected and every individual has the inalienable right to equal opportunity and no more, and that in the eyes of the law everyone is politically equal.[61]

Thus, while in theory these six beliefs have characterized the nature of liberalism, in practice, it has historically been the opposite. The political reality of liberalism is that the U.S. superstructure at the national and state levels is, for all practical purposes, controlled by a plutocratic power elite.[62] Furthermore, the country is governed by a two-party dictatorship that obviates serious competition from other political parties within the electoral system.[63] With few exceptions the country's political party system functions more like a one-party dictatorship governed by two ideologically compatible parties—Republicans and Democrats—that are zealously committed to liberal capitalism. In theory both claim to represent the people, but in practice they represent the interests of the military industrial complex.[64]

Capitalism as an economic system was catalyzed by liberalism's above six salient beliefs. However, it is important to note that it rose out of the decline of mercantilism and the Industrial Revolution. What then is capitalism? In its classical form, the central features of the capitalist creed include the dominance of private property, the presence of competition, the dynamics of the private motive, and the existence of a free market. Inherent to these beliefs is the notion that private ownership of the means of production (e.g., land, industry, property, technology) and distribution will maximize people's self-interests, which in turn maximizes productive potentialities. The market system concomitantly plays multiple roles, that of the stimulator, regulator, coordinator, and harmonizer of people's pursuit for wealth. Other notions that have impelled capitalist development include: the presumptions that private property should not be regulated, decentralization of economic power is the best defense against its abuse, inequality of wealth is normal and a desirable state of affairs, the proper role for government is to keep its hands off of business (laissez faire), and the law of supply and demand is the basis of capitalist economy.[65]

As an economic system, capitalism is inherently oppressive and exploitive in nature. Howard L. Reiter explains, "Capitalism is intensely individualistic, based as it is on the assumption that the people share no fundamental interest and that the economic system functions best as 'every person for his or herself.' At the base of capitalism therefore is a social system in which inequalities are not only tolerated, but also essential. . . . This is one of the most important contradictions between American capitalism and democracy."[66] Capitalism is consequently plagued by a number of deleterious inherent contradictions: increasing chronic poverty and misery, stratification of society based upon an omnipotent ruling class and a subordinated and marginalized proletariat, massive income differentials and inequality, and a monopoly capitalism that fosters imperialism and wars due to the insatiable pursuit of capital accumulation and profit. Capitalism is also predicated on the prevalence of the economic exploitation and oppression of one class, the bourgeoisie, over another, the proletariat. By the early 1990s, with the decline of the Soviet Union, Marxism became a less appealing alternative and liberal capitalism became ideologically ubiquitous.

As a result, at the beginning of the twenty-first century, less than a handful of nation-states are Marxist, and monopoly capitalism has been redefined as the globalization of capital. This is occurring in the midst of a worldwide political, economic, and environmental crisis that threatens the very survival of the planet. The inherent contradictions of liberal capitalism are becoming increasingly evident both within its globalization and domestically. The gap between the rich and poor is widening dramatically, poverty is increasing, a plethora of social problems is becoming more acute, and interethnic/racial conflicts are worsening. From a cultural perspective this is worsened by the rise of cultural imperialism, driven by multinational corporations that threaten not only the underdeveloped nation-states, but seek economic hegemony over their markets and resources. Hence, the dangerous nature of the global crises is characterized by increasing terrorism and violence, political instability, oppression and exploitation of masses, and incessant wars, all of which are a result of the goals of liberal capitalism, and the ostensible rise of a new worldwide empire—the United States as *Pax Americana*.

The country's political culture and its all-encompassing socialization processes have contributed not only to the social order's perpetuation, but to the maintenance of Aztlán's occupation and internal colonization of its barrios and *colonias*. Concomitantly, it has been a major factor in the development of the various modes of Mexicano politics that have been integral to the Mexicano experience in the United States. Each political epoch examined in this work has dealt with the hegemony of the country's liberal capitalist-based political culture. Since the genesis of the Mexicano political experience, U.S. political culture predicated on liberal capitalist beliefs and values has significantly impacted the political development of the Mexicano in occupied Aztlán.

For purposes of analysis, a political subculture denotes an aggregation of individuals within a political system whose political orientation varies somewhat from the majority's political culture. Imbued with its own ethos, each subculture within a generational context may seek to define its own way of looking at politics and government, and their perspective has often complimented the country's political culture. It is important to note that political culture and subcultures can influence or induce generational change. During the period of occupation, Mexicanos have embodied seven political subcultures: Traditional Mexicano, Hispano, Mexican American, Chicano, Viva Yo Hispanic, Neo-Mex, and Latino (Lat). In the following chapters, I will provide a thorough explanation and analysis of each.

Generational Politics

Political Generations

The study of generational politics emanated from the social sciences during the nineteenth century. The first major theorist of generations was Plato in the fourth century B.C.E. in Greece. The Roman Empire used generations, and the closely related concept of cycles manifested themselves in Roman thought. From an evolutionary context, Auguste Comte, the founder of sociology, posited a "decisive element in the velocity of human evolution, and therefore the passing of one generation to another."[67] The study of generations, however, did not gain impetus until after World War I.[68] Historian Arnold Toynbee examined the role of generations in imparting rhythms to modern history.[69] In his book *The Theme of Our Time*, Ortega y Gasset argues that the motivating force behind history comes neither from the masses or individuals, but from generations. In explaining Ortega's usage of generation, Mexican philosopher Samuel Ramos states, "a generation is a kind of intermediate element between the mass and the individual; it is neither one nor the other, but nevertheless partakes to some extent of both."[70] Ramos defined generation:

> Generation does not mean merely those of similar age who perform simultaneously in different fields of endeavor. The unity, which converts a group of individuals into a "generation," comes from a mutual concept of life, even though life is expressed in many different forms and activities of culture. . . . Strong spiritual bonds must unite a generation, not simply by motives of expediency.[71]

Studies concerning generations with a focus on politics have been at best but a trickle.[72] Rarely do they appear in the political science literature. Sociologists such as Karl Mannheim, Kingsley Davis, Ralph Linton, and Joseph Gusfield have contributed significantly to the study of generations. According to Karl Mannheim, "The social phenomenon generation represents nothing more than a particular kind of identity of location, embracing related 'age groups' embedded in a historical-social process."[73] Only a few political scientists have ventured into the waters of exploring the application of generations to political science, particularly developmental studies.[74] Samuel Huntington is one political scientist who applied generations to his study on political development under the guise of "political generations."

Historian Mario Garcia, in order to study Mexicano politics in the United States, pioneered the use of political generations with his work *Mexican Americans*.

He examines the political and intellectual history of the leaders, organizations, and issues of Aztlán between the 1930s and 1960s. Other Mexicano scholars, such as historian Ignacio Garcia and political scientist Carlos Muñoz, also incorporate the use of political generations in their works.[75] For purposes of strengthening the work's overall analysis, I too incorporate its use.

Like so many other concepts in the social sciences political generations is problematic. As a concept, political generation is imprecise and vague, and a myriad of definitions and perspectives exist. Understanding this, my intent is not to provide an overall examination or critique of the literature on the subject, but to merely provide a terse analysis and a working understanding and definition of the concept. According to Richard J. Samuels, "Political generations involve the lives of individuals bound to each other through shared experiences of the passing of time alone."[76] To Marvin Rintala, political generations are "a group of human beings who have undergone the same basic historical experiences during the formative years."[77] Political generations are thus dynamic not static, heterogeneous not monolithic. Unlike class, political generations are not static. They are continually dialectically changing, which means they are an ephemeral phenomenon.[78]

Political generations differ ideologically and politically and compose what Mannheim calls "generation units." Ignacio Garcia further clarifies, "They still comprise a holistic political generation because their political responses emanate from the same source or foundation—their shared historical experience."[79] Political generations are largely predicated on the notion of time or to what some scholars refer to as the boundaries of a "generational age cohort." Most scholars agree that the longevity of a political generation cycle varies between twenty and thirty years. In some cases, an overlap might occur between political and biological generations. The age cohort can be liberally interpreted as long as it has been influenced by the same historical experiences and has politically reacted in a certain fashion that differentiates it from past actions. The political generational process suggests that the old generation transmits to the new generation its common set of political beliefs through a number of socialization agents. Each new generation may develop, however, their own political personality, which contrasts with that of the old or parent generation. Thus, each political generation leaves its historical imprint on society's greater culture.

Most scholars agree that the rise of a new political generation is shaped by shared historical changes or antagonisms convulsive in nature, for example, revolution or war, and is specific to a certain period of time. According to Mario Garcia these historical events "trigger a particular response or responses by a collection of individuals who come of political age during this time who concomitantly believe that their historical time or destiny has arrived." He further explains,

> A political generation is distinct from a biological generation in that while it possesses, like a biological generation, chronological or age-cohort boundaries . . . it is not age but politics that determines its character. A political generation consciously and politically reacts to its historical era.[80]

It is possible to have at least four concurrent biological generations within one political generation: children and adolescents, young people, mature adults, and elderly.[81] Throughout history it has been the young and mature adults who are the catalytic forces to the rise of political generations. This does not preclude, however, the existence of more than one political generation within one generational age cohort, which can foster political generational conflict.

A related aspect is that political generations are power- and social change-driven. The scope of change sought by political generations is determined by the social order's ideology and political culture and its ability to control the socialization agents. Studies of political generations suggest that they tend to represent the politics of an elite or vanguard. In examining the nexus between elites and masses, Julian Marías explains, "In any generation . . . we find a mass or multitude and a guiding minority in which the essence of the generation is revealed and which lends the generation its notoriety and historical relief."[82]

Richard J. Samuels discusses three models that explain generational activity and generational differences. One, the life cycle or maturation model, suggests that generational activity and differences are based significantly on age. In addition, that initial shared political orientations formed from youthful protest change as the person reaches adulthood, matures, and becomes part of society's mainstream.[83] In his view, a person's values change as they go through the life cycle. Their youthful rebelliousness is tempered by the demands of adult life, and in time their adult roles change and shape their social and political orientations.[84] Samuel Huntington further explains, "That as the young get older, they will become like what the older were previously. The cohort changes, but there is not much change in society." Conflict is moderate due to both generations being in a continuous state of change—the young grow old, and the old die[85]—this ensures that society's dominant values endure. Age as a predictive value suggests that under certain circumstances its role is to allocate values, and as individuals get older their roles change as a result of this process—serving to ensure macropolitical order and continuity.[86]

Huntington's second model, the interaction, proposes that one political generation reacts to another, suggesting that their differences are the product of sequence. He suggests that what identifies a generation's uniqueness is its "reaction" or "opposition" to the values of the previous political generation, suggesting that there is a cyclical nature to political development and social change. According to Huntington, "Change does take place in the society, and conflict will be brief but will recur with each new generation to a fairly intense degree." Huntington says that Plato, who in his *Republic* argues that the decay of the ideal polity was a result of one generation challenging the values and goals of the preceding generation, initially articulated the interaction model.[87] In reference to the politics of age, this model suggests that societies, according to Jorge I. Dominguez, "are also the most likely to experience bottlenecks caused by a generation that refuses to divest itself of its roles and may strike down younger challengers or harass them from retirement."[88]

In his third model, called the experiential, Huntington argues that the most decisive factor in the formation of political generations is "the shared experiences of an age cohort," particularly at the formative stage. This model accentuates that the enduring character of certain fundamental political orientations is shared historical experiences that become an enduring part of the young person's intellectual orientation. Identifiable age cohorts possess various orientations that are consistent over time and succeed each other; consequently, they create a change in society's distribution of values.[89] The model allows for variations in the intensity of generational conflict and in the degree of generational difference. From a predictive perspective, the shared experiences of an age cohort, especially at a person's formative years, may provide the basis for political consciousness, organization, leadership, and action.[90]

Throughout this study, *political generations* will denote a collection of individuals who are from a certain generational age cohort and have experienced either the same or similar socialization experiences and whose shared politics, including certain attitudes and behavioral patterns, have been shaped or impacted by historical events that are political, social, cultural, or economic in nature. Moreover, as stated by Rodolfo Alvarez, "each generation reflects a different state of collective consciousness concerning its relationship to the larger society."[91] In some cases, within a given biological generation or specific political historical cycle or epoch, multiple political generations coexist. In addition, existent political generations at times adhere to divergent forms of competing political subcultures that are products of sharp discontinuities.

As an analytic construct, the usage of political generations in this work is useful, for it complements the use of political culture and cyclical theory.

Historical Epoch Formation

Cyclical Theory

Complementing the use of political culture and generations is cyclical theory, which is compatible with historical periodization. Some political scientists interpret U.S. politics from a cyclical theoretical perspective. Cyclical theory is predicated on perpetual change, which denotes that change is endemic to the system.[92] In order to facilitate analysis, they separate political phenomena into specific time cycles or periods. For example, in examining liberalism and conservativism or party realignment and critical elections some political scientists have used cyclical theory.[93] A connection can be drawn between cycles and political generations, yet there are cycles that are not generational and political generations that are not cyclical. A relationship can be established between cycles and generational analysis. Some economists as well use cyclical theory in examining changes that occur within the economic marketplace; they refer to these changes as economic cycles. For instance, Marxist economics is predicated on dialectically driven historical materialism: primitive communal, slave, feudal, capitalist, socialist, and ultimately communist. All this said, within the field of political science there are those who give no credence to the role of cycles in politics. They see cyclical interpretations as being too mechanistic, primitive, and unsophisticated.[94]

Historical Periodization

Historians have used their own form of cyclical theory for years—historical periodization. According to William A. Green, "Periodization is both the product and begetter of theory. . . . Once firmly established, periodization exerts formidable, often subliminal, influence on the refinement and elaboration of theory."[95] In its simplest form, periodization entails the attempt to categorize or divide history into discrete time blocks or periods. Historians divide history into blocks of time so as to facilitate their analysis of the past and enhance their ability to articulate changes over time. Periodization blocks are not precise and sometimes there is overlap, which suggests that it is a highly subjective process to where designated periods are subject to scrutiny, challenges, and redefinition.

In this work, I argue that the Mexicano political experience in occupied Aztlán has been dialectically impelled by political cycles and what historians address as periods, and from my own perspective epochs. For purposes of analysis, the changes that were realized within Mexicano politics were the result of political, cultural, economic, and social antagonisms, which occurred within specified blocks of time. Thus, the subsequent chapters are framed within the political historical context of periodization: Resistance (1848–1916), Adaptation (1917–1945), Social Action (1946–1965), Militant Protest (1966–1974), Viva Yo Hispanic Generation (1975–1999), and Transition (2000–2003).

Notes

1. A more comprehensive expansion of this theoretical framework will be provided in my forthcoming book, *What Needs to Be Done? The Building of a Movement.*

2. Through the work *Mexicano* will be used to describe those who are of Mexican extraction who reside both in México and the United States or elsewhere. In chapters 6, 7, and 8, *Mexicano* is used interchangeably with *Chicano.* While the word *Chicano* has various connotations and is subject to debate, throughout this work *Chicano* is used to denote a Mexicano born in the United States.

3. *Aztlán* refers to the edenic place of origin of the Mexica (the Aztecs); supposedly it denotes either the "land of the herons" or "land of whiteness" (John R. Chavez, *The Lost Land: The Chicano Image of the Southwest* [Albuquerque: New México Press, 1984]). The term *Aztlán* is subject to much debate and intellectual speculation. Throughout this work, however, *Aztlán* is used to denote the geographical place of origin of the Aztecs, which some scholars propose was located somewhere within the five southwestern states: California, Arizona, Nuevo México, Colorado, and Tejas. Some say the real point of origin was near the Blythe area of the Arizona/California border; others argue it was somewhere in Utah or in northern present México. No one knows for sure. However, much more important to note is that *Aztlán* will be used to politically identify and include all the land—nearly one million square miles—located in the southwest regional part of the United States, which México lost as a result of the Tejas Revolt of 1836 and the imperialist War by the United States on México (1846–1848). Thus, when the term *occupied Aztlán* is used it means all the land within the region called the "Southwest" that belonged to México prior to 1848.

4. *Colonias* are unincorporated subdivisions characterized by poverty and the syndrome of social problems it creates. More specifically, the norm is unpaved roads, inadequate sewage and disposal system, and untreated water as well. They can be found in Tejas, Nuevo México, Arizona, and California, but Tejas has the largest number (some 1,400) and has the largest *colonia* population. They are predominantly Mexicano found mostly along the U.S./México border; have a limited tax base, and are usually located in isolated rural areas or outside city limits. See *Federal Reserve Bank of Dallas,* "Texas Colonias," No Date.

5. The article was not widely read until it was included in the publication of Harold Cruse, *Rebellion or Revolution* (New York: Morrow, 1968)

6. Kenneth Clark, *Youth in the Ghetto* (New York: Haryou Associates, 1964), 11.

7. Stokely Carmichael and Charles Hamilton, *Black Power* (New York: Random House, 1967), 5.

8. See Frantz Fanon, *The Wretched of the Earth* (New York: Grove Press, Inc., 1963), and Albert Memmi, *The Colonizer and Colonized* (Boston: Beacon, 1965).

9. Rodolfo González-Casanova, "Internal Colonialism and Development," in *Latin American Radicalism: A Documentary Report on Left and Nationalist Movements*, ed. Irving Louis Horowitz, Josué de Castro, and John Gerassi (New York: Vintage, 1969), 118–39.

10. Andre Gunder Frank, *Capitalism and Underdevelopment in Latin America: Historical Studies of Chile and Brazil* (New York: Modern Reader Paperbacks, 1969).

11. For an excellent scholarly work that brings together a synopsis of the research done on internal colonialism, especially the author's contributions to its study, see Robert Blauner, *Racial Oppression in America* (New York: Harper & Row, 1972).

12. Michael Omi and Howard Winant, *Racial Formation in the United States*, 2nd ed. (New York: Routledge, 1994), 44.

13. Omi and Winant, *Racial Formation*, 40.

14. Rodolfo Acuña, *Occupied America: The Chicano's Struggle toward Liberation* (New York: Canfield Press, 1972), 1.

15. Mario Barrera, Carlos Muñoz, and Charles Ornelas, "The Barrio as an Internal Colony," in *Urban Affairs Annual Reviews*, Vol. 6, ed. Harlan H. Hahan, 565–98. (Beverly Hills, Calif.: Sage).

16. For a comprehensive examination of the assimilation model see Nathan Glazer and Daniel Patrick Moynihan, *Beyond the Melting Pot* (Cambridge, Mass.: MIT Press, 1963), and Milton M. Gordon, *Assimilation in American Life* (New York: Oxford University Press, 1964).

17. For a comparative analysis of internal colonialism and the assimilation model see Alfredo Mirandé, *The Chicano Experience: An Alternative Perspective* (Notre Dame, Ind.: University of Notre Dame Press, 1985), 186–89.

18. For a further analysis see Barrera, Muñoz, and Ornelas, "The Barrio," 465–98.

19. Edward Murgia, *Assimilation, Colonialism and the Mexican American People* (Austin: Center for Mexican American Studies, University of Texas, 1975), 2.

20. For a Marxist critique on internal colonialism see Tomás Almaguer, "Historical Notes on Chicano Oppression: The Dialectics of Racial Class Domination in North America," *Aztlán-IJCSR* Vol. 5 (Spring/Fall 1974): 27–56, and Guillermo Flores and Ronald Bailey, "Internal Colonialism and Racial Minorities in the United States: An Overview," in *Structures of Dependency*, ed. Frank Bonilla and Robert Gerling (Stanford, Calif.: Institute of Political Studies, Stanford University, 1973), 149–60.

21. Mirandé, *The Chicano Experience*, 189–90.

22. For an excellent overview, especially a critique of internal colonialism, see Fred A. Cervantes, "Chicanos as a Post Colony Minority: Some Questions Concerning the Adequacy of the Paradigm of Internal Colonialism," in *Latino/a Thought: Culture, Politics, and Society*, ed. Francisco H. Vasquez and Rodolfo D. Torres (Lanham, Md.: Rowman & Littlefield, 2003).

23. I am cognizant of the conceptual and other intellectual pitfalls of making such a charge that Aztlán's barrios and *colonias* are indeed colonized. Time and space, however,

does not allow me within the context of this introductory chapter to theoretically eluci-date comprehensively. Yet, as mentioned previously, this will be done in my subsequent work.

24. Blauner, *Racial Oppression in America*, 83.

25. Blauner, *Racial Oppression in America*, 83.

26. Mirandé, *The Chicano Experience*, 4.

27. Murgia, *Assimilation, Colonialism and the Mexican American People*, 6.

28. Richard Peet with Elaine Hartwick, *Theories of Development* (New York: Guilford, 1999).

29. Michel Beaud, *A History of Capitalism: 1500–1980* (New York: Monthly Review Press, 1983), 141.

30. Robert Petersen, "Colonialism as Seen from a Former Colonized Area," *Arctic Anthropology* Vol. 32, No. 2 (1995): 118–26.

31. Michael Parenti, *Against Empire* (San Francisco: City Lights Books, 1995), 1.

32. Michael Parenti, *Democracy for the Few*, 6th ed. (New York: St. Martin's, 1995), 97.

33. Parenti, *Democracy for the Few*, 3.

34. This typology of colonialism was taken from an encyclopedia article from the Encarta website: encarta.msn.com

35. Ramon Gutierréz, "Chicano History: Paradigm Shifts and Shifting Boundaries," in *Voices of a New Chicana/o History*, ed. Refugio I. Rochín and Dennis N. Valdés (East Lansing: Michigan State University Press, 2000), 98.

36. Gordon Marshall, ed., *The Concise Oxford Dictionary of Sociology* (Oxford: Oxford University Press, 1994), 254.

37. Much of the above analysis is taken from the following work: Michael Hechter, *Internal Colonialism: The Celtic Fringe in British National Development* (New Brunswick, N.J.: Transaction, 1998).

38. Blauner, *Racial Oppression in America*, 84–85.

39. For an extensive examination of dependency theory and its effects on underdevel-opment see Andre Gunder Frank, *Capitalism and Underdevelopment in Latin America*.

40. See the article by Peter Bohmer entitled, "African Americans as an Internal Col-ony: The Theory of Colonialism," at academic.evergreen.edu.

41. David Brown, *The State and Ethnic Politics in Southeast Asia* (London: Routledge, 1994), 254.

42. Summary of these two characteristics was taken from the following website: www.class.uh.edu.

43. Conventional pressure methods include voting; circulating petitions; lobbying of sorts for example, writing letters, making calls, sending letters, and meeting with politi-cians, whereas unconventional methods include marches, picketing, sit-ins, confronta-tions, riots, etc.

44. The rise of *Pax Americana*, derived from the Latin phrase *Pax Romana*, which described the relatively peaceful state throughout Europe as a result of Roman power,

denotes a worldwide crusade for the globalization of capitalism or a reemphasis of colonialism.

45. Within political science, the concept of "political culture" is one that conjures up debate for a number of reasons. One was over the pervasive disillusionment in response to the focus and liberal capitalist bias of Gabriel A. Almond and Sidney Verba's *Civic Culture: Political Attitudes and Democracy in Five Nations* (Boston: Little, Brown, 1965) and microeconomic approaches that have become dominant in the field. Also, some are hypercritical because it does not effectively explain collective action. However, from my perspective, it is useful because in the case of the Mexicano political experience, it helps explain precisely how the liberal capitalist ethos within the country's political culture has served to impede collective action and struggles for change among Mexicanos and Latinos.

46. Roderic Ai Camp, *Politics in México* (New York: Oxford University Press, 1993), 55.

47. For an excellent work on political culture, its origins, development, and in particular on a critique on civic culture, see Gabriel A. Almond and Sidney Verba, ed., *The Civic Culture Revisited* (Newbury Park, Calif.: Sage, 1989).

48. Gabriel Almond and Sidney Verba's study *Civic Culture*, published in 1963, became one of the most influential works in the study of political culture. This study employed survey research to look at the political cultures of five countries—the United States, Great Britain, Germany, Italy, and México—by collating various individual responses to questions and organizing them into larger "aggregate" cultures.

49. Almond and Verba, *The Civic Culture Revisited*, 26.

50. Gabriel A. Almond and G. Bingham Powell, Jr., *Comparative Politics: A Developmental Approach* (Boston: Little, Brown, 1966), 23.

51. Walter A. Rosenbaum, *Political Culture* (New York: Praeger, 1975), 6–7.

52. Almond and Powell, *Comparative Politics*, 50.

53. Rosenbaum, *Political Culture*, 59. For a more extensive analysis, see Almond and Verba, *Civic Culture*, 14–20.

54. Reo Christenson et al., *Ideologies and Modern Politics*, 2nd ed. (New York: Dodd, Mead & Company, 1975), 6.

55. Almon Leroy Way, Jr., "Constitutional Democracy & Other Political Regimes," p. 2, www.poliedu.net.

56. Richard Dawson et al., *Political Socialization*, 2nd ed. (Boston: Little, Brown, 1977), 33.

57. Way, "Constitutional Democracy & Other Political Regimes."

58. Christopher J. Bosso, John H. Portz, and Michael C. Tolley, *American Government: Conflict, Compromise, and Citizenship* (Boulder, Colo.: Westview, 2000), 198.

59. Ideology is an extremely important concept to the understanding of political culture. It is the vision, the belief system of ideas that gives the political order its legitimacy, direction, and justification.

60. For a much more thorough examination on liberalism and its relationship to

capitalism and political culture see my book *La Raza Unida Party: A Chicano Challenge to the U.S. Two-Party Dictatorship* (Philadelphia: Temple University Press, 2000), 7–13.

61. Navarro, *La Raza Unida Party*, 51.

62. I prescribe to the C. Wright Mills and other elite theorists' theory that propounds that a power elite governs the United States. See C. Wright Mills, *The Power Elite* (New York: Oxford University Press, 1956).

63. For a comprehensive examination of this argument see Navarro, *La Raza Unida Party*, introduction.

64. Navarro, *La Raza Unida Party*, 12.

65. For an overview of the various aspects of liberal capitalism see Christenson et al., *Ideologies and Modern Politics*, chapter 7.

66. Cited in Navarro, *La Raza Unida Party*, 12.

67. Cited in George Modelski, "An Evolutionary Approach to World System History: The Problem of Periodization," faculty.washington.edu/modelski/WSHPERIOD.html, 5–6.

68. Samuel Huntington, "Generations, Cycles, and Their Role in American Development," in *Political Generations and Political Development*, ed. Richard J. Samuels (Lexington, Mass.: Lexington Books, 1977), 9.

69. Modelski, "An Evolutionary Approach to World System History," 6.

70. Samuel Ramos, *Profile of Man and Culture in México* (Austin: University of Texas Press, 1972), 147.

71. Ramos, *Profile of Man and Culture in México*, 146.

72. Ramos, *Profile of Man and Culture in México*, 146; Huntington, "Generations, Cycles, and Their Role in American Development," 9.

73. Karl Mannheim, *Essays on the Sociology of Knowledge* (New York: Oxford University Press, 1952), 292.

74. Mannheim, *Essays on the Sociology of Knowledge*; Richard J. Samuels, "Introduction: Political Generations and Political Development," in *Political Generations and Political Development*, ed. Richard J. Samuels (Lexington, Mass.: Lexington Books, 1977), 1.

75. Ignacio Garcia, *Chicanismo* (Tucson: University of Arizona Press, 1997), and Carlos Muñoz, *Youth, Identity, Power* (London: Verso, 1989).

76. Samuels, "Introduction: Political Generations and Political Development," 1.

77. Marvin Rintala, "Political Generations," in *International Encyclopedia of the Social Sciences*, ed. David L. Sills (New York: MacMillan, 1968), 6:92–96; also in *The Youth Revolution: The Conflict of Generations in Modern History*, ed. Anthony Esler (Lexington, Mass.: D. C. Heath, 1974), 15–20.

78. Huntington, "Generations, Cycles, and Their Role in American Development," 10.

79. Mario T. Garcia, *Mexican Americans: Leadership, Ideology & Identity, 1930–1960* (New Haven, Conn.: Yale University Press, 1989), 5.

80. Garcia, *Mexican Americans*.

81. Ramos, *Profile of Man and Culture in México*, 148.

82. Julian Marías, *Generations: A Historical Method* (Tuscaloosa: University of Alabama, 1970), 43–44.

83. Samuels, "Introduction: Political Generations and Political Development," 2.

84. Samuels, "Introduction: Political Generations and Political Development," 2.

85. Huntington, "Generations, Cycles, and Their Role in American Development," 11.

86. Jorge I. Dominguez, "The Politics of Age," in *Political Generations and Political Development*, 139.

87. Huntington, "Generations, Cycles, and Their Role in American Development," 11.

88. Dominguez, "The Politics of Age," 139.

89. Samuels, "Political Generations and Political Development," 2.

90. Dominguez, "The Politics of Age," 139.

91. Rodolfo Alvarez, "The Psycho-Historical and Socioeconomic Development of the Chicano Community in the United States," in *Beyond 1848: Interpretations of the Modern Chicano Political Experience*, ed. Michael R. Ornelas (Dubuque, Iowa: Kendall/Hunt, 1999), 3.

92. Sohail Inayatullah, "Transcending Boundaries: Positive Visions of the Future," www.ru.org/macrohistory.html, 3.

93. Arthur M. Schlesinger, *Paths to the Present* (Boston: Houghton Mifflin, 1964); and Walter Dean Burnham, *Critical Elections and the Mainspring of American Politics* (New York: Norton, 1970).

94. Huntington, "Generations, Cycles, and Their Roles in American Development," 15–16.

95. William A. Green, "Periodizing World History," in *World History: Ideologies, Structures, and Identities*, ed. Phillip Pomper et al. (Malden, Mass: Blackwell, 1998), 53.

Historical Antecedents to the Mexicano Political Experience in the United States (50,000 B.C.E. to 1848 C.E.)

I

I N ORDER TO UNDERSTAND the rise of the politics of the Mexicano experience in occupied Aztlán, it is important to have some insight into its historical antecedents. If Mexicanos in the United States are to understand their current political reality and their prospects for the future, it is imperative to comprehend the historical antagonisms that preceded its emergence in 1848. These antecedents go back some 40,000 to 50,000 years ago to the first migration or "exodus" into the Western Hemisphere, to the advanced Amerindian civilizations of Mesoamerica, to Spain's own historical and political experience, to the conquest of México by the Spaniards, to the Spanish colonization of México and Aztlán, to the struggle for México's independence from Spain, to the United States' imperialistic politics of Manifest Destiny, to the United States' expansionist war against México that resulted in the loss of Aztlán, and lastly, to the signing of the Treaty of Guadalupe Hidalgo, which precipitated the Mexicano political experience and the occupation of Aztlán.

The Amerindian Experience: The Pre-Colombian Civilizations

The First Migration: The Paleoindian Stage

The anthropological aspects of the Mexicano political experience in the United States can be traced to the Amerindian experience, which according to recent research goes back some 40,000 to 50,000 years ago when the first migrations from northeastern Asia to the Western Hemisphere are identified.[1] Anthropologists have labeled this stage of development as the Paleoindian (50,000–8,000) B.C.E.[2] Consequently, this unequivocally rejects the notion that Cristobal Colon (Christopher Columbus) discovered a New World in 1492. The historical reality is that all of the Western Hemisphere was initially inhabited by undocumented migrants who came from Asia, crossing the frozen Bering Strait via a land bridge at a time when the ocean levels were much lower than today into Alaska. The first migrants that came to the New World were part of the first diaspora and first migration to a new promised land that took over 40,000 years to inhabit from Alaska to the tip of the Tierra de Fuego in today's Argentina. It is believed that these original settlers reached the Tierra de Fuego about 11,000 B.C.E.[3] Anthropologist James Diego Vigil notes that the first migration "brought hordes of people whose descendents . . . established themselves throughout North and South America. They were the original Americans."[4]

During this first migration, numerous nomadic groups that relied primarily on hunting broke off and ventured into various parts of the Western Hemisphere. These immigrants brought with them their hunting cultures, shamanism, and ceremonialism.[5] Their survival was dependent on a perpetual search for game, edible plants and fruits, water, and warmer climates. Whenever possible, they lived in caves and temporary shelters and moved on as the food supply mandated. The earliest known villages appeared on the coasts of North America around 12,500 years ago. However, most anthropologists concur that some time between 8000 and 10,000 B.C.E. human populations began to settle in México and throughout Mesoamerica. Using Marx's dialectical materialist theory,[6] the mode of production and distribution was based on a primitive communism, meaning life was communal and the production of the hunts and plant and fruit gatherings were shared. At the end of the Paleoindian stage, these first immigrants began their transition from being hunters and plant and fruit gatherers to becoming sedentary farmers:[7] the rise of the next developmental stage, the Archaic.

The Archaic Period: Rise of Settlements and Agriculture

Most anthropologists concur that the Archaic period of the Amerindian experience in Mesoamerica[8] was from around 8000 to 2000 B.C.E. It was during these very important years that México's Amerindian experience went through some major changes in both the productive forces and productive relations.[9] Robert Quirk writes that "as the climate changed and became warmer and drier after 7500 B.C.E., México's lush grasslands disappeared, and the decreasing numbers of herding mammals were hunted to extinction." He further notes that the Amerindians were forced to depend on their immediate environment for their food supply. They moved short distances with the changing seasons, yet remained relatively sedentary. They initially lived in caves and ultimately constructed crude homes.[10] Sometime during 7000 to 5000 B.C.E., the early Amerindians settled in the Tehuacan Valley, located southeast of present-day México City, around 5000 B.C.E. Incipient communal agriculture occurred with the domestication of food plants such as maize (corn), beans, squash, cacao (chocolate), pineapples, peanuts, potatoes, avocados, tomatoes, pumpkins, strawberries, tapioca, quinine, maple syrup, vanilla bean, cashew nuts, peanuts, pepper, and chile peppers and the creation of complex irrigation systems. Quite appropriately, Michael D. Coe notes, "It is hard to conceive of European cuisine before the arrival of these plants."[11] The most important plant to be domesticated was maize, which became the major food source for the Amerindian. Domestication also included animals such as dogs, turkey, Muscovy duck, and the honeybee.[12] "By 1400 B.C.," according to Eric Wolf, "cultivation was no longer peripheral to Middle America but an integral aspect of its existence."[13]

The formation of villages with religious ceremonial centers and burial mounds and the rise of sacred or religious rulers particularly impacted their productive relations. The sedentary life acted as a catalyst for the development of tools, use of various metals, pottery, and art forms as well as religious rituals and beliefs. Farming villages became permanent and developed a higher form of tribal organization and infrastructure. As the population grew so did the surpluses. The division of labor and specialization became more complex,[14] as illustrated by the role of women. Anthropologist James Diego Vigil notes that women were primarily responsible for creating the agricultural revolution since they were the food gatherers and were instrumental in the development of cotton goods and artifacts, while men were busy hunting game.[15] The presence of pottery, for example, is dated back to 2400 B.C.E. With villages established, better shelters were built and trade centers were constructed. From the onset of the Amerindian experience, religion played a very significant role. Their concerns of an afterlife were evident in the erection of religious ceremonial centers and their use of human sacrifice to propitiate the capriciousness of nature.[16]

Amerindian political culture began to evolve based upon social class stratification—most importantly within the priestly castes that wielded great influence and power. Hence, political culture and governance was based upon a theocratic authoritarianism and elite rule. At the apex was the shaman priest who was supported by a warrior caste.[17] At the same time primitive forms of record keeping began to evolve. From a historical materialist perspective, between 3400 and 2500 B.C.E., significant changes occurred within the productive forces and productive relations to where a new stage developed. Qualitative changes occurred in the Amerindians' productive forces[18] and productive relations that gave rise to the next historical period.

The Formative Pre-Classic: An Epoch of Great Achievements

The third period, Formative Pre-Classic (2000 B.C.E. to 200 C.E.), served as the foundation for the great achievements of the subsequent Classic period. It was a period of acceleration within both the productive forces and productive relations, which represented an advance on its predecessor period. Furthermore, it was during this period that Mesoamerica as a distinctive cultural entity took form. Widely dispersed peoples throughout Mesoamerica spoke a variety of languages but were united by two cardinal traits: their reliance upon maize agriculture and their common participation in a religious tradition that accentuated the earth and fertility.[19] The intensification and further development of agricultural villages led to the rise of numerous chiefdoms throughout the region of Mesoamerica. No other region in North America matched Mesoamerica's level of development and complexity, from its political, social, and economic organization, and religious development that included the building of pyramids and the strengthening of the leadership role of priests.

The most sophisticated civilization to emerge during the Formative Pre-Classic period was the Olmeca. Although their origin is a mystery and their longevity debated, most scholars concur that the Olmeca culture was the "mother culture" for all of México's higher civilizations of the Classic period. It was a product of a cross-fertilization of regional cultures.[20] A review of the literature suggests that the Olmeca civilization emerged sometime between 1500 and 1000 B.C.E., flourished along the southern Gulf Coast of México, and declined sometime around 600 B.C.E. Initially, it was the area specifically around San Lorenzo that dominated the Olmeca heartland. Inhabited by thousands, San Lorenzo was an urban center with public buildings, a drainage system, a ball court, and large temples built on earthen mounds. But by 900 B.C.E. its importance began to fade with the emergence of other Olmeca centers, such as La Venta, followed by Laguna de los Cerros and Tres Zapotes.[21] It was in La Venta, however, where large quantities of sculpture, that is, giant stone heads, and other artifacts were found, identifying it as the largest population and religious ceremonial center of the Olmeca civilization.

Complex formal settlements were established by 1150 B.C.E., and Olmeca influence spread through a combination of proselytizing, trade, and military conquest: from La Venta to the Mexican southwest Gulf Coast of present-day Veracruz and Tabasco, into the highlands, and as far south as El Salvador and Costa Rica. Changes in the Olmeca production became evident in its expanding economy. The Olmeca economy developed to where raw materials were exchanged for finished products. Women were excluded from the production process.[22] Likewise, their social structure evolved into a hierarchical, patriarchal, and class-oriented society where slavery was practiced. The Olmeca governmental structure (superstructure) was the antithesis of democracy. Initially it was egalitarian; however, increasingly it took on a theocratic, authoritarian, and oligarchic form. Olmeca religion was polytheistic, with the proliferation of religious cults dedicated to gods of rain, fire, Plumed Serpent,[23] the earth, and the underworld,[24] and human sacrifice was practiced. At the center of power were the chiefs of chiefdoms, and as Olmeca society became more centralized emperors or kings evolved. They demanded unquestionable obedience, and a powerful priest-elite enforced their power. Political culture was parochial and its cognitive, affective, and evaluational orientations were limited and controlled. The Olmeca set the template for the mode of governance and political culture adopted by numerous subsequent Amerindian civilizations.

Many of the significant cultural achievements identified with ancient México stem from Olmeca innovations. As a civilization their sophistication was evident in their advanced artistic skills as well their construction of stone temples and pyramids, ornate dress, commercial networks, defense fortification, and sea travel. Olmeca carvings in basalt and jade were unsurpassed. Sculptors carved large stone heads of helmeted males, some nearly ten feet tall.[25] The Olmeca also developed the first hieroglyphic scripts and the foundation for the complex calendar of the Maya and Zapotec. The Olmecas developed three calendars. The first was a ritual calendar with a 260-day cycle. The second was a solar calendar for the agricultural cycle that had eighteen months of twenty days with five additional days, similar to the 365-day calendar used today. And the third was a combination of the two calendars in which religious events and days of birth determined functions such as the name of a newborn child.[26] The development of the calendars required a sophisticated understanding of mathematics and astronomy. There are some researchers who propound that the Olmeca were responsible for the discovery of the "zero."[27]

The mysterious demise of the Olmeca civilization occurred around 300 B.C.E. Its decline, however, began three hundred years earlier when La Venta was destroyed by either external forces or internal insurrection. Remnants of the Olmecas remained for a few hundred years and continued to influence other civilizations that were emerging regionally during the Classic period. The chief center of Olmeca culture during these years of the Formative Pre-Classic was Izapa, a large city near Tapachula on the México–Guatemala border. Monte Albán was another chiefdom arising inland, in present-day Oaxaca, and also had its genesis during the late Formative period, but blossomed along with the Mayas during the next period.

The Classic Period: The Golden Age of Mesoamerica

The Classic period existed from about 200 to 900 C.E.[28] and is described by some anthropologists as the "Golden Age of Mesoamerica." Major changes occurred within both the productive forces and productive relations that produced two advanced urban civilizations: one centered at Teotihuacán (City of the Gods) and the other at Monte Albán. The former emerged around 200 C.E.; the central city covered some eight square miles, and was located some thirty miles northeast of present-day México City. By 600 C.E., its population had grown to some 150,000 people, making it the largest city in the world outside China.[29] Its principal structures were used for religious purposes, such as the Pyramid of the Sun, which was the largest and most imposing; the Pyramid of the Moon; and the famous Pyramid of Quetzalcóatl, dedicated to the Feathered Serpent deity.

Significant changes occurred within its economic substructure, particularly in its commercial aspects. With its plethora of craftsmen, Teotihuacán became one of the most important manufacturing centers of the early Classic period. Politically, Teotihuacán had an authoritarian theocratic system of governance by priest-rulers, and as a society had a highly stratified and hierarchical social structure and a parochial political culture. Recent discoveries have revealed that the ruling aristocratic elite practiced mass human sacrifices. Such evidence suggests there was nothing egalitarian about Teotihuacán society.[30] Interestingly, however, the paintings in many of the ruins glorify nature and the supernatural and emphasize egalitarian rather than aristocratic values.[31] Teotihuacán's influence spread throughout the Mexican highlands and deep into the Mayan areas to the south. Yet by 600 C.E., it had adopted a more warlike political culture represented by the use of jaguars and coyotes as symbols of warrior knights.[32] However, between 700 and 850 C.E. Teotihuacán entered a state of decline. Scholars disagree about the reasons for and time of its decline, so we do not know if it was due to invasions or because of internal factors.[33] According to Acuña, "Even after its decline Teotihuacán continued to be a great city of 30,000 inhabitants (between 750 and 950 A.D.)."[34]

Existing about the same time as Teotihuacán was another advanced urban city-state, the great Zapotec citadel of Monte Albán. Its origins go back to the Formative period, between 500 and 100 B.C.E. Evidence exists that initially Monte Albán profited from commerce and a trading relationship with the Olmeca civilization. From 300 to 900 C.E. it was influenced as well by Teotihuacán and the Mayan city-states to the south. Monte Albán never reached the religious, commercial, or intellectual stature of Teotihuacán or of the Mayas, but without a doubt, it was an advanced civilization that experienced major changes in its productive relations. They wrote in hieroglyphics, were zealots of astronomical observations, and had their own calendar systems. The city contained plazas, pyramids, temples, a ball court, and underground passageways. Its political culture was parochial and its superstructure was theocratic, characterized by the presence of a centralized state, a socially stratified society with priests as the most powerful, nobility, and peasants who were the powerless workers. With an emphasis on trade and commerce, Zapoteca merchants built their economic substructure on tribute received from subject villages.[35]

By 900 C.E. Monte Albán fell to the rising power of the Mixteca from the north. Skillful in the art of war, the Mixteca increased their influence in the highlands and had intermarried with the Zapotec by 1100 C.E. They constructed their capital at Zaachila; built the religious center of Mitla, south of Oaxaca City; and established the center of Tutuepecon on the coast, where they extracted tribute from other kingdoms. After they captured Monte Albán, it was used to bury their dead. Monte Albán's influence was not as great as that of Teotihuacán, but spread along the Gulf Coast to the present state of Guerrero. Like the other Amerindian civilizations, the Mixteca experienced what scholars describe as "parallel evolution," that is they borrowed and were diverse in their development. Like some other previous Mesoamerica civilizations, the Mixteca too had a calendar (fifty-two-year cycle), used hieroglyphics, built temples, were excellent goldsmiths, excelled in ceramics, had their own art style of codex paintings, and used a vigesimal counting system. The Mixteca, like the Tolteca and Aztecas that followed, created strong bonds with other city-states both through intermarriage and military exploits.[36]

During the Classic period, the most advanced Amerindian civilization to emerge in Mesoamerica was the Mayas.[37] The Mayan civilization originated in the lowlands of México and in the Yucatan Peninsula around 300 C.E. and lasted until about 900 C.E. Initially, the Mayan civilization developed around centers such as Uaxactun, Bonampak, Copán, and Tikal. With the decline of the Olmeca, the Mayas absorbed the Olmeca/Izapan culture, forming an eclectic society.[38] At their apex of development, they occupied the present states of Yucatan, Campeche, Qunitana Roo, parts of Chiapas, Tabasco, all of Guatemala, Belize, and parts of Honduras and El Salvador.[39]

The Mayas reached levels of development in both the productive forces and productive relations not attained by previous Amerindian civilizations. The Mayan empire was organized into fifty or more independent city-states encompassing more than 100,000 square miles of highland forest and lowland plain.[40] There were centers of religion, government, trade, and learning, linked by a well-developed road system. Politically, the city-states had tenuous relationships with each other. The Mayan superstructure and the basis of governance within each center were based on the clan and tribe. Rulers were hereditary and closely allied to the priestly class that headed their polytheistic religion. Mayan political culture was like that of the Olmeca. As a society it was highly stratified; it included priests, nobles, feudal lords, warriors, freemen, and slaves. The economic substructure of Mayan society boasted a lucrative commercial trade and was based on high yields of corn, peppers, tomatoes, squash, and cacao.[41] Mayan privileged circumstances resulted in the construction of pyramids, temples, palaces, and commercial plazas in urban centers that were inhabited by thousands of people. The Mayas also made great strides in astronomy and mathematics, and improved upon the Olmeca calendrical system. Their amazing achievements were recorded in hieroglyphics, codices, paintings, and on sculpture.

Mayan civilization reached its apogee in about 700 C.E. and for unknown reasons, within the next two hundred years the Mayans abandoned the ceremonial centers and returned to the simple village life. Some speculate that the land had been exhausted due to the use of slash-burn cultivation methods, others believe it was due to the climatic changes, and still others attribute the cause to internal wars. Whatever the reason for their decline, in the words of Quirk, "the Mayan people broke off their march toward an even more advanced civilization."[42] However, "By 1441 the Mayan cities had exhausted themselves through constant warfare."[43] Yet Mayan settlements around the lake area of Petén and parts of Yucatan survived for at least one more century.[44] With the mysterious decline of the Mayan civilization, the stage was set for the emergence of another period.

The Post-Classic Period: The Militarist Epoch

The Post-Classic or the Militarist period as described by some scholars occurred from around 900 to 1519 C.E. This was a time of troubles for the Amerindians. It was a period of increased militarization and secularization, and of few intellectual and scientific advances. According to Quirk, "The priests were relegated to a secondary role in society, and the new age belonged to the professional soldiers, who could protect a city, destroy a neighbor, or keep a subject in check." It was an age of fortified cities, of barbarian invasions, and of frequent migrations of peoples. It was also the time when the Chichimecas (*barbarians*, in the Nahuatl tongue)[45] became the most powerful force in México. Two major clans of the Chichimecas were the Toltecas and Aztecas, and these became the two most dominant powers of the late Classic period. While religion was still very important to the various Amerindian civilizations, they became increasingly more secular. Hence, it was a period that witnessed changes in both the productive forces and productive relations in which civic and commercial aspects of their society became more important than they had been previously.[46]

The rise of the Toltecas occurred around 900 to about 1156 C.E.[47] As a sub-group or clan of the Chichimecas, they were from the northwestern desert areas of present-day México and the United States. The Toltecas were at first a semino-madic people who farmed when the climate permitted, but more often were food gatherers, communal hunters,[48] and fearsome warriors skilled in the art of war. As they migrated south, they absorbed the cultural, commercial, religious, and other practices of the Olmecas, Teotihuacános, and Mayas, and those they con-quered. With their arrival in the Valley of México, the Toltecas first served as mercenaries. James D. Cockcroft notes, "The Toltecs moved southward and grad-ually incorporated other peoples in central México into a tribute system, extend-ing their influence at least as far as Oaxaca and the Guatemalan highlands, either through conquest or alliance building."[49]

Their military prowess allowed the Toltecas to establish the first militarist state in Mesoamerica. By 968 C.E., Tula, located about forty miles north from present-day México City in the state of Hidalgo, became their locus of power and development. It was there that they fashioned a high culture that became one of subsequent admiration by scholars.[50] From Tula, they dispatched successful military expeditions and their hegemony extended deep into the Yucatán penin-sula and present-day Central America. In the last years of the tenth century, according to legend, there was a Tolteca leader called Quetzalcóatl. A rival faction drove the godlike hero from Tula. He fled to the coast where he took a raft to the east and promised that he would return to lead the people of Tula once again.[51] He was adopted as a god by the then Toltec king Topiltzin.[52] In Tula, the Great Temple of Quetzalcóatl was built with fifteen-foot columns in the form of stylized human figures.[53] New and ferocious gods were subsequently intro-duced into the Tolteca pantheon and human sacrifice became a central aspect of religious worship. Politically, like its predecessors, Tolteca political culture was parochial and theocratic and society was highly authoritarian and stratified. Yet as Acuña says, "Political power was less intertwined with supernatural power, and economic and commercial affairs became more independent of state control." He goes on to explain, "There was a marked expansion of market systems and long distance exchange. In short, there was an integration of not only commercial but cultural exchanges."[54] The Toltecas were known for their architecture, stone carv-ing, and metalwork. Their influence extended into Central America.

The reasons for the decline of the Toltecas by the late twelfth century are subject to speculation. Acuña argues that by "the mid-1100s the Tolteca col-lapsed, perhaps under attack by nomadic tribes, and Tula was abandoned."[55]

Some scholars argue that the Toltecs succumbed to other Chichimeca invaders;[56] others attribute their decline to abandonment because of drought and famine.[57] Yet the Toltecas created a military, political, religious, and artistic template for their successors, the Aztecas.

Like the Toltecas, the Aztecas or Mexica (hereafter used interchangeably with Aztecas) were Chichimecas ("the dog people") that originated from the area called Aztlán.[58] Scholars are in a perpetual debate as to its actual location. Some argue that it was somewhere in the present-day Southwest in the United States, but disagreements remain. Still others propose that it was somewhere in northern México. According to legend, the Aztecas left Aztlán in 1168 and journeyed into the interior of México. They were led by the Azteca warrior-god Mexitli, who claimed to be following a prophesy from heaven to find a new permanent settlement for the Mexica. For years they wandered, surviving as mercenaries. They found temporary refuge in Michoacán in western México, than settled near the Toltec city of Tula. In 1325 the Mexica entered the Valley of México, which they called Anáhuac, and encountered an auspicious omen, foretold in their prophecies: a royal eagle of extraordinary size was perched on a cactus plant with a snake in its talons, its broad wings opened to the rising sun.[59] It was at this location by Lake Texcoco that they settled, built their capital, and began to consolidate their power.[60]

As prophesized, their settlement on that barren island became their capital, Tenochtitlán, which is México City today (deriving its name from the Azteca war god, Mexitli).[61] By 1432, after numerous hardships and struggles, the Mexica succeeded in consolidating their power by forming the powerful Triple Alliance that included Tenochtitlán as well as the neighboring lakeside cities of Texcoco and Tlacopán. Through their military prowess, the Aztecas imposed their rule in 1473 on Tlatelolco and took control of the great market system. Within a few years, under the leadership of Tlacaelel, the Azteca reached their zenith with the reconstruction of the Templo Mayor in Tenochtitlán, celebrated with the human sacrifice of thousands. By the end of the fifteenth century, Tenochtitlán was the dominant city in central México.[62] The Azteca Empire stretched across the continent from the Pacific to the Atlantic to the south, into the farthest corners of Guatemala and Nicaragua. In the words of William H. Prescott, it resembled the Roman Empire.[63] Possessing the greatest military machine in Mesoamerican history, the Aztecas were proficient in the extraction of tribute from their conquered territories.

As was the case with previous Mesoamerican civilizations, the Aztec Empire precipitated changes within the productive forces and productive relations. As a large city of some 250,000 inhabitants,[64] Tenochtitlán contained pyramids, temples, royal palaces, and other large structures, homes for the social classes, canals that served as thoroughfares for canoes, botanical gardens and zoos, and causeways joining the island's city with the shores.[65] As a people, they synthesized the various technologies, knowledge, culture, and religious aspects of their predecessors, especially the Toltecas. The Aztecas, however, excelled as well in the area of astronomy, had their own calendar, were excellent architects and engineers, were productive farmers, and were quite knowledgeable in commerce and trade. From an economic perspective, Azteca society resembled that of a feudal society, where the concept of private property existed and was practiced and enjoyed by its aristocracy.

In comparison to other Amerindian civilizations in México, the Aztecas made few original contributions and could not match the sophisticated accomplishments of previous civilizations, such as those of Teotihuacán and America's "Greeks," the Mayas.[66] Their major strength was in the realm of productive relations, in their social, political, and especially military organizational abilities. They built an effective military apparatus that conquered and administered a large territory and a population of some nine to ten million people. Moreover, their elective monarchy was nearly absolute in power and was designated emperor and reigned over his confederated monarchies.[67] The head of the Azteca government was called the *tlatoani*, "he who speaks," or called "emperor" by the Spaniards. Beneath him was a well-defined caste system of priests, nobles, merchants, free peasants, and slaves.[68] The nobility was comprised mostly of warriors who formed the military aristocracy, which had a right to private ownership of land farmed by slaves and bondsmen. An inherent aspect of Azteca society, for religious and economic reasons, was the practice of slavery. As a military and commercial power, the Mexica never colonized or annexed alien territories, but did extract tribute from those within the imposed confederation.[69]

The Mexica adhered to a more efficient system of legal and political administration, and excelled in various branches of the arts.[70] One such unit of political governance was the *calpulli*, in its basic form a territorial unit corresponding to a village, a town, or a neighborhood within a city.[71] James Cockcroft further elucidates on the workings of the *calpulli*.

> Politically at the heart of the Aztec state was the calpulli. Translated literally, calpulli means "large house," an institution that antedated the Aztecs and was a community endowed with inalienable land that each member was obliged to work. Under the Aztecs, the calpulli became economic, religious, military, and (by the middle of the fifteenth century) administrative units. Community members elected the calpullec, or head of the cal-

pulli. He was always from the same family, so that there developed hereditary nobility. A council of elders supported the calpullec. The Aztec priesthood enjoyed economic power and independence ran the calpulli schools.[72]

The nobility or military aristocracy had the power to circumvent the authority of the representatives of the calpulli through their appointment of the chief speaker.[73]

Azteca society was patriarchal and highly moralistic, and demanded conformity.[74] Its religion was polytheistic, emphasized human sacrifice, and was tied to war. Though the Aztecas venerated the ancient gods Tláloc and Quetzalcóatl, the Toltec bringer of civilization, they also worshipped newer and fiercer deities, who demanded human blood. In their pantheon, these included the sun god of war Huitzilopochtli; Tezcatlipoca of the Smoking Mirror; Xipe Totec, Lord of the Flayed One; and Coatlicue, the Eater of Filth and the hideous mother of gods.[75] Atop the great pyramid at Tenochtitlán, Azteca priests sacrificed countless thousands of human victims in reverence to Huitzilopochtli, from captured war prisoners to slaves.[76] Hence, war and human sacrifice were interwoven and formed an integral part of Azteca religious practices.[77]

For the Azteca, human sacrifice was based on the belief that the sun and earth had been destroyed four times by wind, water, fire, and earth. They believed that they were living in the fifth world of creation, El Quinto Sol, which meant that final destruction of the world was imminent.[78] Only by placating Huitzilopochtli through daily offerings of human sacrifice during his daily rounds as the Lord of the Sun could they prevent the earth's destruction and maintain the orderly workings of the universe. With the rising of the sun atop the temple, each day the priests would cut out a living victim's heart and offer it to Huitzilopochtli. It was believed that the ritual of human sacrifice guaranteed the Sun's return each day and that without human sacrifice the entire world would be in chaos.[79] The Aztecas concluded that the calamitous droughts and famines in 1450 were caused by insufficient human sacrifices. This led to the Flowers Wars (*xochiyayotl*), whereby wars were arranged with the sovereigns of friendly states, and battles were fought to allow the Aztecas to take prisoners for sacrifice. Generally, their victims were carefully chosen and received special treatment and privileges for weeks prior to meeting their deaths.[80] The fact is that the Aztecas were a bellicose people who glorified war and aggression.

By the early part of the sixteenth century, the Mexica empire was at its height of power and glory. In 1502 Montezuma II was elected *tlatoani* and faced the awesome responsibility of holding a precarious empire together in the face of a new challenge—the arrival of the Spanish conquistadors to México in 1519.

The Hispano (Spanish) Experience

Genesis of the Hispano Experience

The Amerindian experience is only one side of the Mexicano experience. The other side is the Hispano (Spanish) experience. In most cases, when examining the historical experience of México, historians, especially Chicanos, stress the Amerindian side and treat the Spanish conquest and colonization in rather pejorative historical terms. The Spanish are depicted as intrusive and ruthless conquerors that imposed colonialism and forced the Amerindian into an oppressed and exploited status. They are absolutely right; nevertheless, the Hispano experience must be acknowledged for its undeniable impact in shaping the Mexicano political experience in both México and the United States. This argument was made by one of México's most prominent intellectuals, who wrote, "the footprints of Spain are present everywhere in our culture, we are so much alike."[81]

The Hispano geographical and historic roots derive from Europe's Iberian Peninsula—Spain. Located at the crossroads between Europe and Africa, Spain's history can be traced to the Upper Paleolithic period (35,000 B.C.E.–10,000 B.C.E.).[82] It was during this prehistoric time, that Cro-Magnon man decorated the walls of caves in Altamira, near the northern port of Santander, and elsewhere with ceremonial sketches, mostly abstract depictions of animal life. Like the Amerindian experience, the Hispano experience as well went through a primitive communist and subsequent slave stage of development. By the Neolithic age, about 3000 B.C.E. to 2000 B.C.E., the early peoples of Spain increased their productive capabilities by their knowledge of animal husbandry, some agriculture, the art of pottery making, basket manufacturing, cloth weaving, and soft metalworking. Trade with other parts of the eastern Mediterranean served to enhance their overall development.[83]

From the onset of the Hispano experience, Spaniards, like others in Europe, are products of a multiplicity of cultures and ethnic groups. As Manuel Gonzales explains, "The following millennia are shrouded in mystery but the Iberian Peninsula . . . must have attracted a variety of people." He describes Iberians, who were the "dwellers along the Ebro River" as they were called by the Greeks; the Basques, whose origin is still debated; the Celts, who dominated the region during the period 900 B.C.E.–650 B.C.E.; the Phoenicians, contemporaries of the Celts, who established colonies from their base in the eastern Mediterranean; and Greeks, who arrived in present Spain and settled along its coast about 600 B.C.E.[84]

Truly, however, of all the ancient peoples to settle in Spain, the Romans were the most influential contributors to the Hispanic experience. The Romans fought three Punic Wars against Carthage for domination of the Mediterranean, ending in 146 B.C.E. with the defeat of Carthage. The Roman legions then took over the Iberian Peninsula, which they named "Hispania." Between the second century B.C.E. and the end of the fifth century C.E., it became an integral part of the Roman Empire. Spain as a colony contributed economically to Rome's substructure. The Roman Empire brought development to the conquered and exploited land in the form of a network of roads, aqueducts, theaters, forums, and baths.[85] Rome imposed its authoritarian government, language, polytheistic religion, and culture on its new colonial subjects, the Celt-Iberians.[86] By the first century C.E., Hispania or Spain reached a cultural level that produced notables such as the Stoic philosopher Lucius Seneca (4 B.C.E.–65 C.E.) and Emperor Trajan (52–117 C.E.), who became one of Rome's most powerful caesars. Other Roman contributions included the introduction of their Latin language, which eventually gave rise to Castilian Spanish, as well as Catalán and Gallego. In the area of religion, it brought Catholicism by the middle of the third century C.E., which by the fourth century C.E. had become the official religion of Rome and ultimately had a profound impact on shaping the peoples' national character as well as their political culture.[87]

Beginning in the second century C.E., Spain was subjected to further waves of immigrants. Among them were Jews of the Diaspora. By the fifth century C.E., Europe as well as Spain fell to the barbarians. Germanic tribes consisting of the Visigoths, Vandals, Alani, Suevi, and Goths swept over the peninsula and imposed their way of life.[88] A cultural and religious metamorphosis occurred. These tribes combined their Germanic contributions with those of Rome and the evolving Catholic tradition. The dominant Visigoths assimilated the Roman religion, language, and government.[89] During this time, Spain's monarchial system developed with the major collaboration of the Catholic Church, signifying that the state and church had become united as a governing structure.[90]

The Moorish Invasion: Conquest of Spain

By the eighth century, the Hispano experience underwent another dramatic cultural and ethnic change. Led by Tarik ibn Zizad, an army of Moors from Africa, which had been recently converted to Islam, invaded Spain by crossing the Strait of Gibraltar in 711. The invasion was an unsuccessful military penetration into Europe, but was a great military success in Spain. By 719, much of Spain came under Moorish control. Islamic Spain came to be known as Al-Andulas and was occupied by the Moors for some 750 years. During this long occupation, Hispanos were locked into a perpetual state of war to oust the Moors.[91] As a result, they experienced prosperous commercial and cultural ties with Africa, the Near East, and Byzantium, and new cities like Sevilla, Córdoba, and Granada became centers of commerce and culture. In addition, the Moors introduced new crops like rice and sugar and new agricultural techniques, and created new industries.[92] Adding to the hybrid and evolving Spanish/Moorish culture was the Jewish presence in Spain. During the Moorish occupation of Spain, the Jewish community, especially those who were Sephardic, had grown in numbers and in prosperity. Unimpeded by the Moors, they made contributions in commerce, as well as in arts and letters.

Between the tenth and thirteenth centuries, the Moors developed a civilization that was the envy of their northern neighbors. Moorish scholars not only preserved Spain's classical heritage, but also made significant contributions of their own, especially in literature, arts, mathematics, and philosophy. One such scholar was Averroës (1126–1198), who as an authority on Aristotle became a powerful influence on Christian thinkers during the Middle Ages.[93] The Moors established academies in Barcelona, Cordoba, Granada, and Toledo and produced renowned scholars, who translated the Talmud into Arabic. A Sephardic Jewish scholar who perhaps stands as one of Spain's greatest philosophers is Maimonides, who lived in Córdoba, like his contemporary Averroës.[94]

Under the guise of La Reconquista, the first major battle was fought at Covadonga and won by the Moors in 718. In the subsequent seven centuries Spaniards were engaged in an incessant military struggle to oust the Moors from occupied Spain. La Reconquista came in cycles of military intensity and activity. At first the war went slowly; however, in the year 900, Spanish king Alfonso of Asturias discovered the purported tomb of Saint James the Apostle in the northeast of Spain,[95] and used this strategically to foment a sense of Spanish nationalism and a Catholic religious crusade against the so-called Moorish infidels. By the tenth century Moorish control was weakened. Catalona and Navarra, located in the northeast of Spain, became independent kingdoms, and by the next century, Aragón and Castilla also became independent kingdoms, adding impetus to La Reconquista.[96] With the famous Spanish victory by King Alfonso VIII of Castilla at Las Navas de Tolosa in 1212, the Moors controlled only the kingdom of Granada to the south.

By the second part of the fifteenth century, Los Reyes Catolicos (the Catholic Kings) dealt a mortal blow to the Moorish occupation of Spain. The kingdoms of Castile and neighboring Aragón united in 1479, when Isabella of Castile and Ferdinand of Aragón, who had been married since 1469, inherited the thrones of their respective kingdoms.[97] Their marriage and the unification of their kingdoms significantly contributed to the ultimate unification of Spain under their grandson, Charles V.[98] During the ensuing years the Spanish monarchs succeeded in consolidating their power, imposed law and order over an anarchic Spain, effectively suppressed banditry, reduced the power of the nobles and brought them under their control, established the basis of a feudal system, and effected major changes in a society that was socially hierarchical and highly stratified. Their governance was monarchical and authoritarian, predicated on repression of its conquered subjects, and its political culture was parochial.

Los Reyes Catolicos introduced economic, religious, and social reforms, and became patrons of the arts. It is at this time that Spain experiences Siglo de Oro (1492–1648), which was the great epoch of letters, arts, and economic enterprise. Politically, throughout Spain towns that participated in the struggle to oust the Moors were given charters (*fueros*) in which the monarchy guaranteed the people their possessions and rights. They were also permitted to regulate the election of their governing officials and established elected city councils, or Ayuntamientos. In order to maintain law and order, *hermandades* (brotherhoods) were also formed.[99] In addition, Los Reyes Catolicos renewed military efforts to remove the last Moorish bastion in Spain, Granada. However, it was not until January 1492 that the Moors were ousted from Spain. Thus, with the removal of the Moors and the consolidation of power by the new monarchs, Spain became the force in the conquest of México.

The Hispano Conquista of México

The Discovery of the Americas

With the defeat of the Moors, Spain became an evolving unified nation. Within a few decades, it emerged as a super power of the time, a great colonial and imperialist power. With Spain united and at peace, Los Reyes Catolicos turned their attention to commerce and trade. Recent advances made by both Spain and Portugal in the areas of map making, ship building, and explorations, for example, the discovery of the Canary Islands, facilitated Queen Isabella's decision to support Italian explorer Christopher Columbus. His proposal to sail in a westerly course in search of the East Indies was designed to open up for Spain a share of the lucrative trade monopolized by the merchants of Venice. Columbus was given command of three ships, *La Niña*, *La Pinta*, and *La Santa Maria*, and on August 3, 1492, he sailed from port of Palos de la Frontera. After several weeks at sea and with crews on the verge of a mutiny, Columbus sighted the Bahama Islands on

October 12, 1492, believing he had discovered the East Indies. He continued sailing southward until his naval expedition came upon the islands of Cuba and Espanola. He named the Amerindian peoples found in these islands, "Indians" and claimed them for Spain.[100]

Columbus returned to Spain with a small number of Amerindians and enough gold to convince Los Reyes Catolicos to support three subsequent expeditions to the so-called New World. None of his expeditions produced the anticipated amounts of treasure, especially gold; soon he resorted to the slave trade, beginning with the Arawaks (Tainos). In 1495, the Spaniards rounded up some 1,500 Tainos. Five hundred were sent to Spain to be sold as slaves, and many of them, rather than accept their servitude, committed mass suicide.[101] This historical reality cast Columbus as a controversial figure who has been demonized by many for his racist actions against Amerindians. Columbus, designated the Admiral of the Ocean Sea in Spain, had in reality discovered an Old World and not a New World, occupied by Amerindians some 40,000 to 50,000 years before his arrival.

Cortés's Conquista of the Aztecas

With the alleged discovery of the Americas by Columbus, the forces were unleashed that transformed the Amerindian experience throughout the Western Hemisphere, leading to the conquest of México. For twenty-seven years after 1492, Spaniards traveled throughout the Caribbean area and explored numerous islands, gathering information. It was not until 1511, however, that Spain established a colonial base in Cuba.[102] This process was fueled by the Spanish's ardent pursuit of the three G's (Gold, Glory, and God, in that order). Among those Spaniards who settled in Cuba was Hernán Cortés (1485–1547), who at the age of sixteen had come to Cuba in search of riches and adventure.[103] Given an administrative position in the Spanish colonial administration, he gained political prominence, and even served as mayor. Cortés was intrigued with stories and rumors of untold riches in other unexplored lands of the Americas.[104] His enthusiasm increased in 1518; he learned that a ship commanded by Juan de Grijalva sailed from Cuba and after skirting the coast of Yucatan landed near present-day Veracruz and became the first Spanish landing on mainland México. This reconnaissance mission was followed by a large naval armada under Cortés's leadership. The armada was not sanctioned or supported by Diego Velasquez, then governor of Cuba, but was financed by Cortés himself. On a shoestring budget, he gambled that the expedition would indeed be successful in finding and bringing back plenty of plundered goods.

On February 18, 1517, an invading force consisting of six hundred men, eighteen horses, a few artillery pieces, and a fleet of eleven ships set sail toward the Yucatan. It reached the island of Cozumel and found little more than tropical overgrowth. Disappointed, the armada followed the coast north and briefly landed in Tabasco.[105] It was here, that Chontal elders gave Cortés a young female slave named Malintzin Tenepal (later to be called La Malinche by the Spaniards). Of noble origins, after the death of her *cacique* father, she was sold into slavery by her mother and stepfather. She was highly intelligent and spoke both Aztec Náhuatl and Chontal Mayan and was familiar with their customs; she opened many doors for Cortés.[106] She learned quickly the language of the conqueror, Spanish. Because of her language skills, Cortés utilized her primarily as his interpreter, Amerindian envoy, strategist, and concubine, and named her Doña Marina. According to Michael Coe, "Much of his [Cortés] success in dealing with Aztecs must be attributed to the astuteness and understanding of this remarkable personage."[107]

Nevertheless, La Malinche, like Columbus and Cortés, became a controversial historical figure. As Cortés's concubine, she never married him, but bore him a son named Martín. Throughout México's political experience (1519–present), La Malinche has been portrayed controversially playing a variety of roles—that of the power behind Cortés, a victim of historical circumstances, and a traitor. John Ross is one scholar who argues that the persona of La Malinche is more loathed than loved in contemporary México. He writes:

> The bottom line is that Cortés's mistress betrayed her people and aided and abetted the most painful annexation of México on the books. La Malinche remains a supreme symbol of submission to forced domination. Whether this submission was consensual, or the most brutal rape in the nation's history is a question that continues to dog the Mexican psyche. Nonetheless, her myth has endured and even flourished, and, as the millennium closes down, La Malinche teaches us much about why México has survived intact as a culture.[108]

On Holy Thursday, April 21, 1519, the Spanish armada dropped anchor near what today is Veracruz and on Good Friday went ashore. Planting his sword and a cross in the sand, in the name of the Crown and Holy Mother, Cortés christened the landing site as La Villa Rica de la Vera Cruz and claimed it on behalf of Spain. With little organized Amerindian opposition to his expedition, Cortés convened an *ayuntamiento* and proclaimed himself captain general, allowing himself full rights to explore and reap the riches of the fruitful land that became known as New Spain.[109] To strategically ensure the fidelity of his men, Cortés ordered the burning of all the ships, leaving no avenue for escape. The historical significance of this expeditionary event was twofold: the second migration to the Western Hemisphere had begun, and the last Amerindian empire in México, the Azteca, was to become a casualty of Spanish imperialism and colonialism.

The conquest of the Azteca Empire began with the establishment of a base of operations in Veracruz where the preparations for a march into the Valley of Anahuac were made. From the onset, Cortés relied on the formation of alliances with neighboring Totonacos and Tlaxcaltecos, both of whom resented paying tribute to the Aztecas. These alliances demonstrated his divide and conquer tactics and were greatly facilitated by the translation and diplomatic skills of Doña Marina. He also relied on military force and superior armaments as a means of persuasion. Informed by Doña Marina that the Cholula tribe was plotting against the expedition, Cortés unleashed his military machine, slaughtering some three thousand of their warriors in the center of their city. As a result the Cholulans capitulated and brought with them the additional support of their allies, the Huejotzingos.[110] These military alliances proved invaluable to Cortés's expeditionary force. A series of pitched battles against both friendly and unfriendly tribes in turn served to enlarge the size and capability of his expeditionary force.

From both a political and military perspective, the Azteca response to the Spanish invasion was problematic and proved to be disastrous. Aztec emperor Montezuma II fatally miscalculated the intentions of the invading Spaniards. He relied upon a religious prophecy, which predicted that one day the bearded and fair-skinned Quetzalcóatl, the feathered serpent god, would return from the east. According to legend, the time of his return coincided with that of the arrival in México of Cortés's armada. The Azteca priests and Emperor Montezuma II were convinced that Quetzalcóatl was returning from the sun to cleanse México of it sins.[111] This view was further buttressed by the presence of the large naval vessels with huge sails; horses, which they had never seen; men in shining armor; artillery that made loud noises and demonstrated awesome destructive fire power; and conquistadors armed with shinning sabers and muskets. When the expedition arrived in Tabasco, Montezuma sent emissaries bearing gifts of gold, silver, jade, and feathers to the Spanish invaders. The rationale was twofold: if it were Quetzalcóatl, he would be appeased; but if not, the invaders would be satisfied and would depart. But the gifts to Cortés only served to further expand his and the expedition's voracious appetite for treasure. The Spanish superiority in weaponry, the religious beliefs of the Azteca leadership, and the use of the alliances formed with several Amerindian tribes gave Cortés the military edge.

Almost three months from the time they left Veracruz, on November 8, 1519, without a shot being fired, Cortés's expeditionary force of some ten thousand marched into Tenochtitlán, a city of over two hundred thousand inhabitants. Instead of a belligerent reception, Montezuma and the Aztec aristocracy greeted the Spanish invaders as honored guests. Fearing military retaliation from the apprehensive Aztec warriors, Cortés first courted the trust of Montezuma, but later made him a prisoner and a hostage in his own palace. For months, Cortés astutely ruled the Azteca confederation behind the scenes through Montezuma, collecting vast amounts of gold, silver, and precious stones, from all corners of the empire.[112]

By the spring of 1520, Cortés's lucrative exploits were threatened by the arrival in Veracruz of another Spanish expedition led by Panifilo Navarez. This expedition was sent by Governor Diego Velasquez with orders to arrest Cortés, as the governor had not sanctioned the expeditionary force. Aware of the threat, Cortés left Tenochtitlán and marched to Veracruz, where he successfully convinced Navarez to join his victorious expedition. Upon returning to Tenochtitlán, he found it in a state of rebellion. The Emperor Montezuma and some of the Azteca chiefs and warriors had been killed by elements of the Spanish force that had remained in Tenochtitlán. Facing imminent destruction and under siege, Cortés retreated from Tenochtitlán under the cover of darkness in the early hours of June 30, 1520. Described as La Noche Triste (The Sad Night), Cortés's expeditionary was decimated, and he barely avoided capture. His retreating force staggered back to Tlaxcala, whose inhabitants proved to be faithful allies.[113]

The final military phase to the conquest of the mighty Mexica Empire was begun in May 1521. Cortés's expeditionary army was reinforced by new troops from Veracruz, supported by thousands of Tlaxcalan warriors, and enlarged by new alliances. The attack on Tenochtitlán was initiated. The fighting on the plains near Otumba was so fierce on both sides that the siege to Tenochtitlán lasted some seventy-five days.[114] During the course of siege, Cuauhtémoc, the new Aztec emperor, failed to secure military support from other tribes within the Azteca confederation. In addition, the Mexica forces were decimated by hunger and a virulent smallpox epidemic that killed thousands. On August 13, 1521, Cuauhtémoc surrendered to the victorious Cortés. Estimates of casualties among Cortés's allies, the Mixtecs, in the recapture of Tenochtitlán ran as high as twenty thousand.[115]

What ensued was the total destruction of Tenochtitlán. Building after building was destroyed, and its beautiful canals were filled with rubble.[116] This was followed by a bloodbath at the hands of the revengeful Tlaxcallans that in the words of Michael Coe "sickened the most battled-hardened conquistador."[117] Cuauhtémoc was held captive for three years but refused to reveal the locations of alleged Aztec treasure. Cortés had Cuauhtémoc, the Descending Eagle, tortured and killed—a martyrdom exalted by David Alfaro Siqueiros's monumental mural enshrined in México City's Instituto de Bellas Artes.[118]

The literature suggests that the reasons why the Aztecas lost to the Spanish were several. One, the Azteca primitive weaponry was no match for the Spanish superior military technology that included the use of muskets, gunpowder, and cannons. Two, Cortés's strategic use of divide and conquer tactics coupled with his alliances with other Amerindian tribes overwhelmed the more numerous Aztecs. Three, the pervasiveness of acute divisions among the Amerindian tribes facilitated their political fragmentation. Four, the Azteca religious mythology and superstitions, especially of the return of Quetzalcóatl, were cleverly manipulated by Cortés to achieve his political ends. Sixth, the Azteca concept of war was different from that of the Spaniards. While strategically Aztecas waged ritual warfare to seek tribute or to capture sacrificial victims for their gods, the Spaniards waged war to destroy their enemy. And finally, one of the most important factors was the spread of infectious diseases, which decimated the Azteca population and weakened it militarily.[119]

With the recapture of Tenochtitlán and surrender and death of Cuauhtémoc, for the Aztecas, the Fifth Sun, El Quinto Sol, had perished.[120] A major chapter closed in the experience of the Amerindian and a new one commenced in the experiences of the Hispano and Mexicano.

The Colonization of México and Aztlán

The Rise of the Mexicano Experience

The Hispano conquest of the great Azteca civilization fostered the genesis of the Mexicano experience. Unlike other colonizing powers, the Spanish brought very few women with them to México and did not hesitate to mate with Amerindian women.[121] "Spaniards of widely diverse peninsular backgrounds," according to Meier and Rivera, "combined with Indians of varied Middle American societies to produce a new culture and its protagonist, the mestizo."[122] Symbolically speaking, it appeared that from the sexual union of Hispano Cortés and Amerindian Doña Marina, the first Mexicano mestizo[123] was conceived. The progress of miscegenation produced a new *raza* (race) as described some four centuries later by Mexican philosopher Jose Vasconcelos in his classic *La Raza Cosmica*. This genetic, cultural, and linguistic metamorphosis produced what I call the genesis of the Mexicano experience. Fathered by the Spaniard and mothered by the Amerindian, a mestizage was fostered, which created the Mexicano as a hybrid people and culture that gave rise to México as a distinct nation.

Historically the Mexicano political experience in the United States would have never arisen without the prior "Mexicano experience" in México. Explaining the impact on Chicanos (Mexicanos born in the United States), John Chavez writes, "Later this fact would lead to much uncertainty in the Chicano's image of themselves . . . for being descendents of both conquered Indians and conquering Spaniards and Indians, Chicanos would vacillate between a self-identity as foreigners and a self-identity as natives."[124]

The Spanish conquest of México became an inextricable factor in the development of the two experiences. After the conquest of the Aztecas, Spanish colonization continued from 1521 to 1821. The Spaniards adopted the name *México* for the new territory from the indigenous name for the Aztecas, the *Mexica*. There was a relentless effort to spread the conquest to other parts of México, but due to continued Amerindian armed resistance, it took the Spanish several years to complete their conquest and pacification. Initially, they found the Mayas difficult to subdue and for years made no effort to control the other seminomadic Chichimecas.

The Hispano Colonization of México

As a colony, México and the rest of Latin America for the next three hundred plus years entered into a feudal stage of development. The military conquest and political consolidation of México was buttressed by the Catholic Church's spiritual conquest of the Amerindians. Both the sword and cross became weapons of domination and control. This was evident in the methods used by the Spaniards to propagate their conquest. In a systematic fashion, they consolidated their control, supported by their Amerindian allies, and wrought destruction in the name of doing God's work. Robert Quirk explains, "Inspired by the missionary priests to eliminate the pagan cults, the conquering Spaniards demolished Indian religious centers throughout México. They leveled pyramids, broke apart the temples, and used the stone to construct their own buildings. They proscribed the priest class and killed or tamed the tribal rulers." The Spaniards came as conquerors and masters of a New World, "las Americas,"[125] supported by the power of Catholicism. Bloodshed and plunder marked the conquistadores' path throughout México[126] and most of Latin America. The one major exception was Brazil, colonized by the Portuguese, which suffered its own treacherous experience of colonization.

Religion became an especially powerful political instrument of governance and domination. This was enhanced by the apparition of the Virgen de Guadalupe at Tepeyac in present México City to an Amerindian, Juan Diego, on December 12, 1531. The "Brown Madonna" of the Americas reaped many Amerindian converts. In 1536 alone, five million were converted to Roman Catholicism from what church officials considered heathen idolatry, five times the number of conversions during the previous fifteen years of colonization.[127] In spite of the Spanish missionary zeal to convert the Amerindian masses to Catholicism and efforts to establish Spanish political and economic systems, life went on as before for most Amerindians.[128]

For Amerindians, the postconquest epoch was a holocaust of unprecedented proportions. Although there are numerous estimates of the number of Amerindians who perished, the exact figures are unknown: estimates of those who died in central México of disease, starvation, suicide, exposure, or brutal treatment range from fifteen to twenty million. Some nineteen epidemics swept México during the first one hundred years of Spanish colonization. Those diseases included smallpox, typhoid, measles, mumps, pneumonia, influenza, and the common cold and proved fatal for most since they lacked the immunological resistance.[129] The deadliest, however, was smallpox, killing 845,000 Amerindians in just a few weeks in 1545.[130] The total population in central México declined from twenty-five million in 1519 to about one million by 1630.[131] According to Eric Wolf, of those Amerindians that died between 1519 and 1650 probably two-thirds died of European-transferred diseases.[132]

From a political cultural perspective, the conquest and colonization of México gave rise to the "México political experience." After 1521 the Spanish colonial superstructure was structured in a pyramidal-hierarchical fashion with the king at the apex of power. Because the king was in Spain, the next most powerful authority directly under the king was the Council of the Indies, headquartered in distant Seville. In general, the council carried out the orders of the king and wielded executive, legislative, and judicial powers. When the king absented himself from Spain, the council assumed executive power over the colonial government. Moreover, its powers also included the appointment of viceroys, bishops, and other colonial officials, ensuring that laws were carried out.[133] It was also quite active in curbing the ambitions of colonists and maintained legislative control.[134] Finally, the council acted as a court of last appeal from decisions of royal courts abroad.

The king's authority, however, was vested with the viceroy, followed by a *audiencia* in México City and Guadalajara. Viceroys wielded great individual power and had discretion in enforcing the king and council's will in the colonies. To check the power of the viceroy, *audiencias* shared some power with the viceroy. They served primarily as courts of law; secondly, as local lawmaking bodies; and thirdly, as a check and balance to the viceroy. They had the authority go over the head of the viceroy and correspond directly with the council in certain matters. Led by a president, the decisions of the *audiencias* were subject only to the king's veto.[135] At the intermediate level of the power pyramid, under the viceroy and *audiencias* were *corregidores* or governors with authority over a certain geographical area or region. Beyond the enforcement of colonial policies, they collected tribute and were in charge of the work assignments of Amerindians.[136]

At the base of the pyramid were the town councils or *cabildos*, which were limited in their power. At the head of the *cabildo* was the municipal secretary. Amerindians were allowed to serve in a council of elders, and one was elected *alcalde* mayor. Other Amerindians filled lower positions as *aguaciles* (constables). They were allowed to participate at the lowest levels of governance, but ultimately the municipal secretary dictated policy and had veto power.[137] Under Spain's colonial system of government, the colonial political experience produced a political culture that was antidemocratic and predicated on elitism and authoritarianism. At the apex of the political hierarchy were the *gachupines* (Hispanos born in Spain), followed by the creoles (Hispanos born in México). Next were the mestizos (part Hispano and part Amerindian), who in most cases had little or no political clout. The powerless and exploited Amerindians were at the bottom, victims of an oppressive colonization.

A dialectical blending occurred of parochial and authoritarian political cultures—one theocratic and the other monarchical. At no time was there a presence of a civic culture that accentuated the people's democratic participation. The people's political input and output in their governance was limited. This ultimately would impact the Mexicano's political culture in occupied Aztlán. After some three hundred years of Hispano colonization, it engendered the ethos of México's evolving parochial political culture. Thus, intrinsic to its emergence was the absence of democratic values based on the people's political participation. Under Hispano colonialism, the reality was that the overwhelming majority of México's population, mestizo and Amerindian, alienated from the political process, were relegated to a powerless, subjugated, and oppressed group.

The oppressiveness of Spain's colonial substructure was exacerbated by mercantile economic policies that were buttressed at the beginning by the use of the *encomienda* system. This was a grant from the crown to those who had served Spain, providing them with free labor and tribute from the Amerindians. It was a form of trusteeship in which the *encomendero* (Spanish settler) was theoretically expected to take care of Amerindian medical and physical needs. It differed from slavery as the Amerindians were legally free and not property. In its application, the *encomienda* was so abused that Amerindians became victims of forced labor practices. These were so blatantly exploitive that the Catholic Church, represented by

Father Bartolomé de las Casas, intervened and brought the abuses to the attention of the Crown. In 1542, the Crown issued the New Laws, which abolished the *encomienda* and severely restricted the Spanish *pobladores'* (settlers) control over the Amerindians. By 1549 the *encomienda* was officially dead, but in some areas such as Yucatan, it survived until the last quarter of the eighteenth century. In place of the *encomienda*, in order to ensure the availability of a labor force, the Crown adopted the *repartimiento*. Under this new labor system, the Amerindians worked for a specified number of days on projects deemed important by the Crown and were paid wages, fed, and housed. But again abuse and corruption led to more exploitation, maltreatment, and abuse of Amerindians than under the *encomienda*. Amerindian forced labor, particularly in the mines and haciendas, was in practice another form of serfdom.

The Hispano Colonial Expansion into Aztlán

In the perpetual search for "gold, glory, and god," Spanish colonialism spread to other regions of México. Particularly, Spanish *pobladores* and Franciscan and Jesuit missionaries moved along the west coast, north to present-day Durango and Chihuahua and established presidios, missions, and pueblos. The demand for accessible labor for the new mines and haciendas followed. In place of the dying and diseased Amerindians, the Spaniards brought in thousands of African slaves from Gambia, Angola, and the Cape Verde Islands. The effects of their intermarriage were such that by 1819, Africans and Afro-Mestizos numbered 634,000, more than 10 percent of the total population.[138]

During the sixteenth century, numerous exploratory expeditions were sent into the southern and Aztlán (Southwest) regions of the present United States.[139] Motivated by the myth of the fabled Seven Cities of Gold (Cíbola), Hispano explorers made several expeditions into these two regions. As Juan Gonzales notes, these "Spanish conquistadors crisscrossed and laid claim to much of the southern and western parts of the United States nearly a century before the first English colonies were founded at Jamestown and Massachusetts Bay."[140] Ponce de Leon in his quest for a "Fountain of Youth" discovered present-day Florida in 1513. Unsuccessful the first time, eight years later he returned with a second expedition; this time he was killed in battle with the Calusa Amerindians. Panfilo de Navárez in 1527 led an unsuccessful expedition into Florida, attempting to complete its colonization. After landing, he lost his ships; hostile Amerindians killed him as well as most of the expedition. Only four survived. Among them were Alvar Nuñez Cabeza de Baca and a Spanish Moor named Estevancio. They spent the next seven years in captivity, escaped, and wandered through the wilderness of the south and into Tejas, Nuevo México, and Arizona as "medicine men," living among the Amerindians. Ultimately, they managed to cross the Rio Grande into México and the Spanish frontier town of Culiacán in the western province of Sinaloa.[141] Baca subsequently submitted a comprehensive report of their exploits to the Spanish Crown. Two other major expeditions followed in pursuit of riches. Explorer Francisco Vasquez de Coronado, starting from central México, led an expedition north in 1539 in search of the fabled cities of gold. The expedition traveled to Arizona and discovered the Grand Canyon, and then traveled to Nuevo México, Tejas, Oklahoma, and Kansas, claiming these new territories for the Crown of Spain, but returned without gold or treasure. In 1542 upon the return of the Coronado expedition to México, Hernando De Soto launched an expedition from Cuba into the present southern states of the United States and again found no gold and paid the price—half of his men perished.[142]

The actual Spanish colonization of Aztlán did not occur until 1598 with the establishment of the first settlements in Nuevo México. Nine years before the English established Jamestown, Juan de Oñate, son of a wealthy mine owner, led a large expedition that founded San Gabriel de los Españoles. In 1610, Oñate's successor founded the settlement of Santa Fe de San Francisco. After a century, twenty-five missions had been built in Nuevo México. In 1680 an Amerindian (Pueblo Indian) revolt led by Popé and other shamans occurred, costing the lives of hundreds of Spanish settlers. This forced a temporary withdrawal of Spaniards to the El Paso area of Tejas. However, by 1693, the Spaniards retook control and in 1706 founded the present city of Albuquerque.[143]

Nuevo México became the major buffer between the valuable mining region to the south and the marauding Amerindians of the north. Even though it was also a crossroad for Spain's colonization of the rest of the Southwest, for years Nuevo México remained an isolated colony. By the 1750s, however, with a new threat from French traders penetrating Nuevo México, Spanish officials began to increase the number of settlements to fourteen. By the end of the eighteenth century, Nuevo México was well established as a Spanish colony. Only sixty-eight of some sixteen thousand persons had been born outside of Nuevo México, with two born in Spain. Land grants were issued to elite families, such as the Archuletas, Bacas, Chávezs, Luceros, and Montoyas, all of who were related to Nuevo México's original settlers.[144] By the beginning of the nineteenth century, it was the most populated Spanish colony in Aztlán.

As in the case of Nuevo México, Amerindians from central México played a significant part in the colonization of Tejas. According to Carlos Vélez-Ibañez, the Tlaxcalán initially served in the capacity of scouts and auxiliary soldiers for several expeditions into the north of México. They played an important role in the establishment of the presidio of San Juan Baustista in 1688 near today's Eagle Pass.[145] Although some would argue that this area was part of Nuevo México, by 1680 Spanish *pobladores* established the Mission of Our Lady of Guadalupe El Paso, which became today's El Paso, Tejas.[146] The cardinal motivation for the Spanish colonization of the rest of Tejas was the fear of French encroachment, which had already established a settlement as a result of Robert La Salle's expedition down the Mississippi River in 1682.

Spanish colonization of Tejas evolved around three geographical areas: the San Antonio de Béxar central area, the La Bahia coastal area, and the Los Ades/Nacogdoches area of east Tejas.[147] In response to France's arrival into the Louisiana region, Spain established two missions on the Neches River in 1690.[148] The next year, Spain officially designated it as a frontier province and sent various expeditions into Tejas. Franciscan friars in 1690 established six missions along the present-day eastern Tejas border, which were vacated years later under French military pressure.[149] In June 1716, the area was reoccupied by a Spanish expedition under the command of Captain Domingo Ramon. A presidio was established at Los Adaes as well as several missions. By this time, the presidios (garrison forts) were vital in efforts to pacify the Amerindians, who were a serious ongoing security concern. Two years later, another expedition led by Martin de Alarcón established the presidio of San Antonio de Béxar and the Mission of San Antonio de Valero along the San Antonio River.[150]

The vast Spanish colonial lands of Tejas were incorporated in 1722 into the established Spanish colonial province of Coahuila. A civilian settlement, called San Fernando de Béxar, was founded in 1731 by a group of fifty-five persons from the Canary Islands, adding to the revitalization of the San Antonio presidio and mission. In 1731 the first town council was seated in San Antonio, which included two *alcaldes*, six councilpersons, one *aguacil*, and a secretary.[151] By the 1730s, San Antonio consisted of a presidio, a municipality, and five missions.[152] The issuance of land grants created large haciendas, and throughout the 1700s, Tejas's nascent economy was heavily dependent on ranching and farming. In the ensuing years, with the intention of winning Amerindian converts and averting their attacks, a number of other settlements and missions were established, for example, Goliad (1721), Laredo (1755), and Nacogdoches (1779). But at the turn of the eighteenth century, Tejas remained relatively unpopulated. According to Manuel G. Gonzales, "By 1800, there were only about 3,500 Tejanos in the neglected province."[153]

The colonization of present-day Arizona developed even more slowly than that of Tejas. According to Acuña, "During the colonial period, very few missions, presidios, and towns were established in what today is southern Arizona."[154] The hot and arid desert climate coupled with the presence of bellicose Amerindians was not conducive to any settlement formation. The few settlements that did develop were products of the zealous missionary work of Jesuit Father Eusebio Kino. Italian by birth, Father Kino traveled north in about 1687 and established a chain of missions from Sonora to southern Arizona. Kino was responsible for the establishment of three missions in Arizona, with the most successful being the mission San Xavier del Bac (near present-day Tucson), established on April 28, 1700, and also he founded the presidio at San Ignacio de Tubac. Prior to his death in 1711, he led a total of fourteen expeditions into various parts of Arizona, including the Grand Canyon. Because of his legendary exploits, some consider him the father of Arizona.[155] The discovery of silver by a Yaqui in 1736 had the effect of bringing some miners into the area. Yet the presidio towns of Tucson and Tulac were not formed until the second half of the eighteenth century. Troubled by a constant threat from the Apaches, the Spanish government succeeded in curbing their attacks for a brief time by providing them with rations.[156] By the turn of the eighteenth century, there were still only two thousand *pobladores* in Arizona.

The Spanish colonization of present-day California began in 1769. Yet the actual exploration of California occurred much earlier in 1602–1603 by explorer Sebastien Vizcaíno. He sailed along the Pacific coast of México all the way up to what is now Monterrey Bay and back. Although initially the Jesuits had sought to colonize Alta California, they were not able to do so since the Crown officially expelled them from the empire in 1767. The responsibility fell to the Franciscan order. Under the combined leadership of Captain Gaspar de Portolá and Franciscan missionary Father Junipero Serra, an expedition traveled from Baja California to present-day California. Father Serra in 1769 founded the mission of San Diego de Alcala, the first of twenty-one missions that were built stretching up to Sonoma, north of present-day San Francisco.[157] In 1770, Captain Portolá built the presidio of Monterrey, and Governor Phillipe de Neve, along with eleven families, founded the Pueblo de Los Angeles in 1781.

For the missionaries, California with its fertile land gave rise to an agricultural and ranching economy, making it one of the most prosperous colonizing regions. In part the success was ascribable to the pacification and incorporation of Amerindian tribes into the mission system. By 1823, Spanish colonizers in California had established the twenty-first mission in Sonoma, and three presidios and towns were founded. California's total population was about 3,500.[158] Most of it was concentrated in Los Angeles, San Diego, Santa Barbara, and Monterey, all of which were mission or presidio towns.

The Rise of the Mexicano Political Experience

México's Struggle for Independence

After some three hundred years of Spanish colonization, the Mexicano experience was once again historically and politically altered. The event that caused this transformation was México's struggle for independence, a product of a politically, militarily, and economically weakened Spain. By the early 1800s, Spain was weakened both domestically and internationally, setting the stage for the dismemberment of its empire and the emergence of struggles for independence. Growing discontent, instability, and conflict plagued Spain's colonial empire in the Americas, particularly México. For the next eleven years (1810–1821), the productive forces and relations of both Spain and the colonized Americas underwent major changes.

During the late eighteenth century and well into the early nineteenth century a number of antagonisms laid the foundation for the independence movement in México. In great part this was a historical product of the United States and French Revolutions of 1776 and 1889, respectively. The U.S. Revolution was a successful product of some eight years of revolutionary struggle by thirteen former British colonies, resulting in a liberal capitalist republic. The French Revolution of 1789 was equally significant as a revolutionary struggle that transformed the French social order. The propagation of the ideas of the European Enlightenment predicated on secular humanism, republicanism, and anticlericalism largely supported by Spain's Bourbon kings. The rise of liberal capitalism also added to a changing political and economic climate. A fervor for change developed in Spanish-colonized Latin America, and most particularly among México's restless and disenchanted elites.

By the early 1800s in México there were growing conflicts over political and economic control between contending *gachupines*, creoles (Spaniards born in México), and mestizos (mixture of Spanish and Amerindian). The oppressed and powerless Amerindians were not an intrinsic part of the political equation. However, in 1802 in the provinces of Tepic and Nayrit they mounted a rebellion against Spanish rule. Led by "el Indio Mariano" they sought to restore the empire of Montezuma II. After a prolonged armed struggle, Mariano was captured and executed by colonial authorities.[159] Among other segments of the population there was also growing discontent. The creole elites felt that they had been excluded from the highest positions of colonial governance including the church and economy, and that preferential treatment had been given to the *gachupines*.

As a result, the political climate in México and much of New Spain became increasingly permeated by discontent and animosity toward Spain. Spain's debilitated status as a major military power was illustrated by France's successful invasion by Napoleon Bonaparte's armies in 1808. The unpopularity and inherent weaknesses of the Bourbon monarchs led to the overthrow of Spain's king Charles IV by Napoleon and the accession of his brother Joseph I. These events severed the political ties between Spain and the colonies in the Americas.[160] Those loyal to Charles IV in Spain resisted the French occupation and developed a more liberal constitution in 1812; by 1814 the Bourbon rule was restored. With the return of Charles to the Crown, his regime suppressed the liberal measures of the new constitution. In the new colonies, according to John Ross, because of México's "mercantile successes, [it] had become a tinderbox of class and racial tensions."[161]

For Spain, it was too late. The colonies in the Americas had tasted reform and ardently resisted the Crown's attempts to suppress the constitution's liberal provisions. Disgruntled creoles and meztizos formed clandestine revolutionary societies like the Literary and Social Club of Querétaro and the Freemasons that plotted for México's independence from Spain.[162] On September 16, 1810, the actual struggle for México's independence began. Father Miguel Hidalgo y Costilla, a creole parish priest from Dolores who became the first practitioner of the theology of liberation, upon being notified that the plot for insurrection had been discovered by the Spanish authorities, promulgated his famous cry for México's independence, "El Grito de Dolores." In Dolores, Hidalgo, he proclaimed himself "Capitan-General of America." Hidalgo, supported by other creole elites, such as Ignacio Allende, was initially successful in mobilizing an army of some eighty thousand that included Amerindians, mestizos, and some creoles. The incipient military operations against the Spanish were successful, but the creole insurrection became increasingly enmeshed in a class struggle. Amerindians, who comprised the bulk of the insurgent army, relentlessly destroyed and killed the opposing Spanish *gachupines* and creoles. This created major concerns among the propertied creole. They feared that a violent social upheaval had been unleashed. Ultimately, however, Hidalgo halted the attack on México City, fearful of turning loose his undisciplined and vengeful Amerindian army on the viceregal capital. As a military leader, Hidalgo lacked the military decisiveness to attack the capital and his insurgent movement began to wither. Subsequently, Hidalgo was captured, stripped of his clerical status, tried for treason, and decapitated on July 30, 1811. As a warning to other insurgents, his head was put on display by Spanish authorities.

For the next ten years, what ensued was an interclass struggle for independence, which was vehemently anticolonial. It succeeded in fostering México's independence, but failed to extricate México from the clutches of feudalism and an emerging exploitive liberal capitalism and create a social revolution. In the words of James D. Cockcroft, a cardinal problem was that "no single class or class fraction was able to assert or maintain hegemony over the tide of rebellion that swept the land."[163]

Yet with Hidalgo's death, another priest, José María Morelos y Pavón, a mestizo, became the insurgency's new leader. Far more versed and competent in military and political matters, Morelos pursued an armed resistance. Ideologically, as a leader, he made pronouncements against all the rich, particularly the *gachupines* and creoles, and promised to redistribute half of all the wealth to the poor. His ideological proclivities, ostensibly liberal capitalist, became evident in 1813 at the Congress of Chilpancingo, when he promulgated to end slavery and all caste distinctions; initiate an income tax; abolish state monopolies; abolish sales taxes and tributes; guarantee private property; and provide for higher wages for the poor.[164] Meeting stiff Spanish resistance, Morelos was captured in 1815 and like Hidalgo was defrocked and executed, and his decapitated head put on display as a warning to others.

For the next six years, the struggle for independence continued under the leadership of Vicente Guerrero, the son of black slaves,[165] and Guadalupe Victoria, through the use of guerrilla warfare. In 1820, however, Spain's king Ferdinand VII was overthrown by a military coup d'etat, and a constitutional monarchy was established. This led to the reintroduction of the liberal Cadiz Constitution of 1812, which allowed the Spanish Cortes (parliament) to reenact certain laws that threatened the interests of creole, such as providing protection for Amerindian rights and property, eliminating ecclesiastical and military *fueros* (special privileges), and limiting the right of the Catholic Church to acquire property.[166] Apprehensive of the consequences of the liberal reforms, the creole elite in 1820 joined the struggle for México's independence under the leadership of General Agustín de Iturbide and promulgated his "El Plan de Iguala," which called for equality between creole and *gachupines* and the preservation of the Catholic Church's privileged position. By 1821, Iturbide succeeded in establishing a military alliance with Guerrero and Victoria. On September 27, 1821, his forces marched triumphantly into México City. As John Ross explains, this was "Precisely 300 years after Cortez had captured Cuauhtémoc and extinguished the Aztec sun."[167] Politically, Iturbide immediately proclaimed himself emperor of México (1821–1823). Major changes ensued in the country's productive resources, but México's productive forces for decades to come remained at the feudal stage of development. In 1824 México became a federal republic under the leadership of President Guadalupe Victoria, patterned very much on the model of the United States.

By the early 1820s, México's geographical northern region of Aztlán was to face a new threat: United States imperialism under the guise of Manifest Destiny.

The Rise of Manifest Destiny

A Guise for U.S. Imperialism

Manifest Destiny is a political doctrine deeply imbedded in both the political experiences of the United States and México. For some 225 years, Manifest Destiny has not only permeated and impelled United States foreign policy,[168] but the country's political culture as well. The origins of Manifest Destiny can be traced to the founding of the United States as a nation-state. Its basis was and continues to be predicated on Anglo-Saxon chauvinism[169] and imperialism. The cultural basis to its formulation was an Anglo-Saxon Protestant ethnocentric ethos, which subsequently evolved into a more inclusive Euroamerican ethos. Samuel Huntington, in describing the country's quest for national identity, alludes to the "American Creed," which he explains are the "political principles of liberty, equality, democracy, individualism, human rights, the rule of law, and private property."[170] From a political historical perspective, the validity of most of his preceding principles is questionable. But Huntington in his distorted and biased analysis excludes in his "Creed" the "bellicose" nature that is inherent to the country's political culture, which gave rise to Manifest Destiny. Thus, from the 1790s to the present, the doctrine of Manifest Destiny—a guise for U.S. imperialism—has permeated the people's political ethos.

Manifest Destiny has its roots in the late nineteenth century when the United States became a nation-state and began to enter the industrial capitalist stage of development. During the late 1790s, with an interest in expanding its influence to the Pacific Ocean, U.S. ships began to visit the California coast, where they carried on illicit trade. One such tradesman was Captain William Shaler. In 1805 he published a glowing description of California in which he praised its beauty and resources, but was hypercritical of the lethargy of the Spanish settlers: in his opinion this made progress relatively impossible. In ethnocentric terms Shaler felt that only American energy and diligence could develop the vast potential of California. This was, in the words of Manuel Gonzales, "one of the first expositions of a sentiment later labeled Manifest Destiny."[171]

Manifest Destiny was and continues to be linked to white nationalism and liberal capitalist imperialism. The historical fact is that most U.S. presidents during the nineteenth century supported the notion of U.S. expansionism. First this was at the expense of France and Spain, then México, and again Spain. The main proponents and beneficiaries were speculators, plantation owners, bankers, merchants,[172] and power-hungry politicians who pandered to the white masses. Inherent to Manifest Destiny is the ethnocentric belief in the superiority of the United States as a nation-state. It was predicated on the primacy of its Anglo-Saxon heritage, culture, language, and Protestant religious background. Frederick Merk provides a compendium of its fundamental aspects: "It [Manifest Destiny] meant expansion, prearranged by Heaven, over an area not clearly defined. In some minds it meant expansion over the region to the Pacific; in others, over the North American continent; in others, over the hemisphere."[173]

John L. O'Sullivan, an archexpansionist editor of the *Democratic Review*, illustrated the aforementioned mind-set when he wrote, "The whole boundless continent is ours."[174] Acuña explains, "Manifest Destiny had its roots in Puritan ideas, which continue to influence Anglo[175] thought to this day." He goes on to say, "Euroamericans believed that God had made them custodians of democracy and that they had a mission—that is, that they were predestined to spread its principles."[176] Inherent to Manifest Destiny was the belief that Anglos were the chosen people of God, that they were superior to all other races and ethnic groups, and that they were predestined to expand and control all of the land between the Atlantic and Pacific Oceans. Hence, non-Anglos who inhabited the North American continent were perceived as inferior peoples. As Gonzales argues, Manifest Destiny emerged "as the nineteenth-century code-phrase for racial superiority."[177] Moreover, U.S. liberal capitalism was considered to be superior to all other political and economic systems. At its core, Manifest Destiny is liberal capitalism's insatiable appetite for territorial expansion, capital accumulation, control of new resources, and new markets.

As previously stressed, from the onset, Manifest Destiny was deeply ingrained in the political culture of most of the founding fathers and elites of this country. According to Juan Gonzales, "Most U.S. leaders . . . coveted the Spanish colonies as targets for the nation's own expansion and held little regard for the abilities of the Latin American patriots."[178] Numerous historical examples can be found that clearly indicate the incipient belief in the doctrine of Manifest Destiny. One such colonial leader was Benjamin Franklin who openly proposed that both Cuba and México should be targeted for future annexation. James Monroe wrote to Thomas Jefferson in 1801, "Our present interests may restrain us within our limits, it is impossible not to look forward to distant times, when our rapid multiplication will expand beyond those limits, and cover the whole northern if not the southern continent."[179] Henry Clay as well dreamed as early as 1811 of the

United States expanding its control to all the Western Hemisphere from the Arctic to South America.[180]

During the early 1800s, John Quincy Adams was another U.S. leader who embraced the doctrine of Manifest Destiny. Particularly in reference to the annexation of Cuba, he wrote, "There are laws of political as well as of physical gravitation, and if an apple, severed by a tempest from its native tree, cannot choose but fall to the ground, Cuba, forcibly disjoined from its own unnatural connection with Spain, and incapable of self-support, can gravitate only towards the North American Union, which, by the same law of nature, cannot cast her off from its bosom."[181]

By 1803, this ethnocentric ethos produced an insatiable hunger for U.S. expansion. It was manifested in President Jefferson's "Louisiana Purchase" from France for the meager amount of $12 million.[182] The acquisition allowed the United States to extend its dominion over the area of Louisiana north to the Canadian border and to the west bordering New Spain. The political effect of the Louisiana Purchase was such that it further stimulated the insatiable appetite among ensuing U.S. administrations for expansion into Aztlán. "Thomas Jefferson," according to Rodolfo Acuña, "six years later, for example, enunciated that the Spanish borderlands 'are ours the first moment war is forced upon us.' The war with Great Britain in 1812 intensified [Anglo] designs on the Spanish territory."[183]

Prior to Spain's sale of La Florida to the United States, for nearly ten years, whites engaged in several expeditions both into La Florida and Tejas. Since 1810, the U.S. imperialist intentions had become evident as several U.S. armed incursions nibbled away at Spain's La Florida's territory. In 1818, General Andrew Jackson led a contingent of U.S. forces in an invasion of La Florida, where he occupied chunks of territory. These actions had been designed to pressure a weakened Spain into selling La Florida to the United States. As early as 1812, the Gutierrez-Magee Expedition, comprised initially of some 158 men, invaded Tejas and for a brief time occupied Nacogdoches, La Bahia, Salcedo, and San Antonio.[184] Their intent was to free Tejas from Spanish control. The Spanish forces regrouped and were able to defeat the invading army. Augustus Magee was killed and with dissension setting in among his troops, Jose Bernardo Gutierrez de Lara and the remnants of the invading army retreated to Louisiana.[185] While Gutierrez's intentions supposedly were to support the struggle for Mexican independence, they were questionable.

In 1819, the push for U.S. expansion became further evident with the U.S. purchase of La Florida from Spain. Under the threat of U.S. aggression, Spain in 1819 signed the Adams-Onis Treaty, culminating in the sale of La Florida to the

United States for the amount of $5 million.[186] Supposedly integral to the treaty was the U.S. agreement to renounce its claim to Tejas and establish a clear-cut boundary between Louisiana and the Spanish-controlled Tejas. Anglo jingoists did not support it and insisted that the boundary should be extended to the Rio Grande in Tejas.

While supposedly not sanctioned by the U.S. government because of ongoing diplomatic efforts to purchase La Florida, other filibustering expeditions were launched from Louisiana into Tejas.[187] In response to the Adams-Onis Treaty, in 1819, James Long, supported by Gutierrez de Lara, led an abortive foray for the purpose of establishing the Republic of Texas. Long's army occupied momentarily Nacogdoches, where he declared himself president. According to Acuña, "Long believed that Texas belonged to the United States and that 'Congress had no right to or power to sell, exchange, or relinquish an American possession.'"[188] As with previous expeditions, Long's army was defeated by the Spanish. He was captured and sent to México where he was executed. Gutierrez de Lara, however, managed to escape and subsequently settled in Tamaulipas, México, where he became its first governor.[189]

México's Tejas: A Victim of U.S. Manifest Destiny

The White Exodus into Tejas

After eleven years of insurrection, México in 1821 won its independence from Spain. Yet México as an emerging nation-state was plagued by regionalism and parochialism, inhibiting the emergence of a common national identity. Case in point was what happened in Tejas during the ensuing fifteen years. After México's independence, little changed in Tejas for the small Mexicano population that numbered a mere 2,240. San Antonio, Goliad, Nacogdoches, and Victoria were the main settlements, and society continued to be divided into two classes: the *rico* (rich) elites and *los pobres* (the poor).[190] The economy as during Spanish colonialism remained largely feudal, although there were certain characteristics of early capitalism present. Exploitation of the land still rested with the *ricos*, the small rich elite who controlled large tracks of land or haciendas. As was the practice before Mexican independence throughout the Southwest, some of these haciendas practiced the encomienda system (large grants of land given by the king of Spain to noblemen that allowed them to use Amerindian labor power to develop their land). The poor served as peons, exploited laborers who worked for subsistence wages and constituted the majority of the small Mexicano population.

Incessant political instability caused by internecine strife between conservatives and liberals from 1821 to 1835 weakened México's hold on Tejas. The conservatives or centralists defended the interests of the feudal landowners, the Catholic Church, and the military caste. This troika sought to perpetuate their power by means of a centralized government. The nascent bourgeoisie, liberal landowners, public functionaries, the body of military officers, and the vanguard intelligentsia, who supported increased autonomy of the states under a federalist governmental structure, on the other hand, supported the liberals or federalists. This meant restriction of the power of both the Catholic Church and military caste, and the application of bourgeois reforms.[191] The result was that for decades, frequent uprisings, rebellions, and chronic political instability plagued México's domestic politics.

The distance from Tejas to México City, the capital of México, became an impediment to governance. It created a habitual neglect that proved to be detrimental to México. Tejas in 1821 was designated as a section of the state of Coahuila. According to De León, "Political vicissitudes in México City did little to alter those affairs, and the transition to the state government of Coahuila y Tejas did not disrupt the people's daily lives. They enjoyed a salutary rule over themselves and exercised influence on issues at the state level."[192] Another related effect of this isolationism was that it nurtured a pronounced sense of regionalism not only in Tejas, but also throughout the rest of Aztlán. This sort of "salutary neglect," however, did not last long due to the influx of whites[193] into Tejas. Also, by January 6, 1824, Tejas and Coahuila were joined into a new state called "Coahuila y Tejas," with its capital in Saltillo.[194]

Just prior to México's independence, Spain, concerned about its increasingly precarious military situation, adopted an immigration policy designed to populate Tejas with white settlers. This exodus into Tejas began in 1821 when the Spanish government granted permission to Moses Austin, a Missouri entrepreneur, to settle some three hundred Catholic families from formerly Spanish Louisiana in exchange for free land.[195] The Spanish grant to Austin was honored by Coahuila governor Antonio Martinez, who argued that "admitting foreigners would be the easiest, least costly, and most expeditious method of enlarging the population."[196] That same year, however, Austin died, but the Mexican government then provided his son Stephen with a similar grant allowing him to bring white settlers into Tejas and establish the settlement of San Felipe de Austin,[197] which is today the Tejas capital. Unfortunately for México, these 300 families figuratively speaking became a "Trojan Horse," developing a base for white hegemony, subversion, and ultimately insurrection.

In 1824, José Erasmo Seguín, a close friend of Stephen Austin, was representing Tejas in México's national congress and worked to bring about the passage of the colonization law, which created an influx of white settlers into the eastern part of Tejas. According to this law, a foreigner who settled in Tejas received a land grant if the person was of good moral character, would develop the land, become a Mexican citizen, and Roman Catholic and agree to obey Mexican laws.[198] By the mid-1820s, too many Tejanos (Mexicanos born in Tejas) and Mexicanos welcomed the white settlers foolishly with open arms. Mexicano government officials perceived them to be indispensable to the growth and prosperity of the region[199] and out of political and economic expediency failed to recognize the potential threat they posed to themselves and México as a whole. White immigration into Tejas was driven by the pursuit for land, but it was also a characteristic of the pervasive Manifest Destiny ethos that motivated many of the white settlers to come and settle in Tejas.

Interventionist Antecedents to the Tejas Revolt

The growing threat of U.S. Manifest Destiny to México became increasingly apparent with the promulgation of the Monroe Doctrine. During the early 1800s, the United States began to prepare the political stage for intervention in Latin America by conquering markets and investments and by substituting itself whenever possible for British colonialism.[200] In 1823 President James Monroe's audacious foreign policy resulted in his infamous Monroe Doctrine, warning especially the European powers that Latin America was off-limits to any further colonization.[201] Essentially it declared the Western Hemisphere to be under the sphere of influence or hegemony of the United States. In explaining the rationale behind the Monroe Doctrine, Acuña argues, "Uppermost in the minds of the U.S. government, the military, and much of the public was the acquisition of territory."[202] The U.S. arrogance of power was further manifested in 1824, when President John Quincy Adams attempted unsuccessfully to pressure México to adjust its border to the river east of the Sabine. In 1826, Adams again pressured México, this time to sell Tejas to the United States for $1 million. President Andrew Jackson in 1830 again tried unsuccessfully; this time the offer was for $5 million.[203]

Manifest Destiny's imperialism against Mexicanos became blatantly evident in 1826 with the Fredonian Revolt. This revolt demonstrated the lack of respect for Mexican law, for many of the white settlers did not take the Mexicano nationality issue seriously. Impresario (businessman) Haden Edwards, from Nacogdoches, sought in a land dispute to evict Mexicano, Native American, and white settlers. In doing so he violated the legal process, which resulted in Mexican officials nullifying his land claim. This action infuriated Edwards and he and his band of some two hundred followers on December 21, 1826, declared the creation of the Republic of Fredonia. The Mexican military moved in and with some support from sympathetic whites in Austin and Dewitt, quickly put down the aborted insurgency. Much of the media in the United States, however, sided with the insurgents. "U.S. newspapers," writes Acuña, "played up the rebellion as '200 Men against a Nation!' and described Edwards and his followers as 'apostles of democracy crushed by an alien civilization.'"[204]

By 1828, México feared its immigration policy was out of control, as whites brought slaves into Tejas. México's president Guadalupe Victoria that year sent General Manuel Mier y Terán to Tejas to report on the deteriorating political and military situation. The report called for vigorous action to be taken before more serious problems arose. In 1829, newly elected Mexican president Vicente Guerrero implemented some of General Mier y Terán's recommendations, one of which was the abolishment of slavery. Threatened economically by this law, white landholders protested and the decree was suspended in Tejas.[205]

By 1830, whites numbered some twenty thousand, their slaves some two thousand,[206] and Mexicanos only four thousand. Gonzales writes, "Not only were they overwhelmed, but many of the newcomers, it seemed, had no intention of assimilating into Mexican society."[207] The initial trickle of white immigration by the late 1820s had become an invading horde.[208] Despite agreeing to abide by México's laws, these settlers insisted on preserving U.S. political traditions, homesteaded land illegally, engaged in land speculation, carried out contraband trade, and practiced slavery, which was still illegal.[209] Also contributing to the escalating tensions was a growing cultural and race conflict. Arnold De León argues that these two issues became the basis of growing conflict since "three-quarters of the Anglos in Texas were southerners committed to slavery."[210]

What occurred in Tejas between 1830 and 1836 was indicative of Manifest Destiny at work. The abolition of slavery in 1829 by México did not go into effect in Tejas until 1830, which served to aggravate whites' anger toward México's government. In 1830 México enacted legislation that significantly curtailed U.S. white immigration into Tejas and curbed the importation of blacks as indentured servants.[211] Of great concern to Mexican authorities was that many of the white settlers were undocumented. In 1831, in order to offset the majority white population that had its origins mostly from the southern states of the United States, México encouraged Mexicano migration and European immigration into Tejas. Moreover, México also adopted other very restrictionist measures, such as sending of troops into Tejas, establishing new presidios, adopting more stringent custom regulations, and mandating white settlers pay custom duties.

Disgruntled whites refused to abide by many of these actions and on December 1831 rioted at Anáhuac. One of their major leaders was Sam Houston, who was a strong supporter and friend of President Jackson. A year later in 1832, a group of whites unsuccessfully attacked a Mexican garrison and that same year, whites met in San Felipe and drafted resolutions demanding more autonomy from the Mexican government. Specifically, they sought the repeal of the 1830 immigration legislation and sought to separate Tejas from Coahuila. In 1833, a second convention was held and Stephen Austin was sent to México City to negotiate. Upon his arrival, he spoke to Mexican government officials regarding the lifting of restrictions on white immigration, separation of the state, and also about the slavery issue. While in México City, on October 22, 1833, Austin wrote a communiqué to the San Antonio *ayuntamiento* exhorting Tejas to declare it a separate state. Angered by the petitions, Mexican government officials had Austin incarcerated. The situation was further exacerbated by a scandal involving the U.S. minister to México, Anthony Butler, who made a crude effort to bribe Mexican officials into selling Tejas to the United States. One Mexican government official was offered $200,000 to "play ball." Upon his release in 1835, Austin openly advocated annexation of Texas to the United States.[212] Thus, by 1835 the stage was set for the next event that influenced both of the Mexicano experiences, the "Tejas Revolt."

The Tejas Revolt (1835–1836)

While some whites by the 1830s had ventured into California and Nuevo México, Tejas became the first Mexicano territory to succumb to Manifest Destiny's imperialism. The presence of this ethos was manifested in the racist attitudes most whites had toward Mexicanos, which exacerbated the precarious situation. Eugene Baker wrote that by 1835 "the Texans saw themselves in danger of becoming the alien subjects of a people to whom they deliberately believed themselves morally, intellectually, and politically superior. Such racial feelings underlay [Mexicano–U.S.] relations from the establishment of the first Anglo . . . colony in 1821."[213] Carey McWilliams likewise wrote that each group by 1834 had formed highly unfavorable and negative impressions of each other. He writes, "To the early [white] settlers, the Mexicans were lazy, shiftless, jealous, cowardly, bigoted, superstitious, backward, and immoral. To the Mexicans, on the other hand, the whites were 'Los diablos Tejanos': arrogant, overbearing, aggressive, conniving, rude, unreliable, and dishonest."[214] By this time, the white insurrectionist movement had built up momentum to where it grew to open defiance against México.

The struggle for Tejas independence was given further impetus in 1834 with the overthrow of the federalist government in México City. By 1835, General Antonio López Santa Anna had abolished the federalist constitution of 1824, dissolved the Mexican congress, held elections for a new congress controlled by conservatives, and audaciously declared himself dictator.[215] The actions by Santa Anna strategically played into the hands of the Tejas white insurgents who precipitated the Tejano Revolt of 1835–1836. Responding to reports that México was sending additional troops into Tejas, William Barrett Travis led a contingent of thirty insurgents in a successful attack on Anáhuac on June 30, 1835, and by September another skirmish occurred. Santa Anna responded by sending some four thousand troops under the command of General Martin Cos into Tejas. A two-month protracted battle was fought in October/November of 1835 where the insurgents laid siege to San Antonio, ultimately defeated the Mexicano troops,[216] and rallied for political independence.

On November 7, 1835, supported by a few co-opted Mexicanos, whites proclaimed conditional independence for Tejas. This was in response to General Santa Anna's centralist takeover and the escalating military situation. On March 2, 1836, the insurgents held a second convention at Washington-on-the-Brazos, at which fifty-nine delegates met and declared Tejas's independence from México. David Burnett was elected provisional president; Lorenzo de Zavala, a prominent Tejano land impresario, became vice president; and Sam Houston was designated to be head of the army.[217] Of the fifty-nine delegates only three were Mexicanos. Beyond Zavala, the other two *rico* oligarchs were José Antonio Navarro and José Francisco Ruiz; a fourth one who was unable to attend because of swollen streams was Jose Antonio Padilla.[218] The insurgent delegates audaciously declared the so-called Tejas Republic independent. The Mexican government responded to the insurrection by sending additional Mexican forces from México into Tejas under the command of General Santa Anna.

The four Mexicano *rico* elite, among others, who supported the Tejas Revolt, believed that they were going to benefit from their involvement in the struggle for independence. As history proved, most were naïve, self-interested, and some, I would argue, traitors. They were used and manipulated in order to advance white political and economic hegemony and to secure Tejas's independence. In the words of Carey McWilliams, it is a historical fact that many of the white delegates who attended the Tejas constitutional convention had "preyed upon Mexicans," and had "necessarily compelled [them] by force or otherwise to give up such property as they had."[219] This historical episode of white treachery and deceit against *vendido* (sellout) opportunistic *ricos* and especially the poor Mexicanos was only one of many more betrayals to come that permeated the Mexicano experiences in both México and in the United States.

In late 1835, General Santa Anna personally led an army of some six thousand conscripts to squelch the rising insurrection. The so-called Tejas Revolt was a brief episode with only three major battles fought at the Alamo, Goliad, and San Jacinto. On February 23, 1836, General Santa Anna committed 1,400[220] of his troops to the siege of the Alamo (the old Franciscan mission of San Antonio de Valero). Opposing the Mexican forces were 188 men led by Colonel William Barrett Travis. The Alamo was the most formidable fortress between New Orleans and Monterrey México. Equipped with twenty-one artillery pieces, with walls that were nine feet high, the defenders possessed long-range muskets and experienced frontier men like Davy Crockett and James Bowie. The Mexican troops were ill-equipped with muskets that had a range of only seventy yards and eight cannons; they laid siege on the Alamo for days. On March 6, the *deguello*, a bugle call used by the Mexican Army to signify that no quarter be given to the defenders, was played and the final assault was initiated. In hand-to-hand combat, after ninety minutes of carnage, all of the Alamo defenders were killed. Of the 188 defenders killed, eight were Mexicanos.[221] Despite the victory, Mexican losses were substantial: some four hundred to five hundred men were killed.[222]

While the Tejas defenders lost the battle, the loss became propaganda and a call to arms. "Remember the Alamo" became their rallying cry. As Acuña notes, "The Alamo battle did, nevertheless, result in massive aid from the United States in the form of volunteers, weapons, and money." Also important to note was that two-thirds of the 188 Alamo defenders had recently arrived to Tejas from the United States and only a half dozen had been in Tejas for more than six years, having come in the pursuit of riches and glory. Yet the loss of the Alamo became a call to arms to whites both in Tejas and United States.[223]

The Tejas Revolt's second major "battle of Goliad" occurred a month later, when General Santa Anna's army under the command of General Jose de Urrea routed the insurgent Tejas forces at Goliad. After fierce fighting, some 350 Tejas insurgents under the command of Colonel Fannin were killed. Urrea's forces also disposed of white resistance at San Patricio, Agua Dolce, and Refugio.[224]

The final and decisive battle of the insurgency was fought at "San Jacinto." On April 21, 1836, General Santa Anna's army of some fifteen hundred men, while taking a siesta, fell in a surprise attack by General Sam Houston's army of nine hundred. Captain Juan Seguin and his calvary troops spearheaded the attack. At the end of the battle over six hundred Mexicanos had been slaughtered and Santa Anna captured. In exchange for his life and freedom, General Santa Anna was forced to sign the illegitimate Treaty of Velasco. The conditions of the treaty included the recognition of a Texas Republic and the removal of Mexican troops south of the Rio Grande.[225] It is important to note that at no time did the Mexican congress or other military commanders ever recognize the legitimacy of the treaty. After it was signed, the Tejas insurgents ratified a constitution that legalized slavery and sent an envoy to Washington to demand annexation and recognition as an independent republic.[226] Sam Houston became president of the new "Lone Star Republic" and his adherence to Manifest Destiny became evident when he declared, "The Anglo-Saxon race must pervade the whole southern extremity of this vast continent. . . . The Mexicans are no better than the Indians and I see no reason why we should not . . . take their land."[227]

The United States War on México

The Post-Tejas Insurrection Years

The success of the Tejas Revolt gave further impetus to Manifest Destiny. As a historical fact, while the United States never officially took sides, unofficially men, weapons, and money were poured into the insurrection. The Jackson administration ignored the protests[228] and the result for Mexicanos in Tejas was disastrous. The "Remember the Alamo" ethos continued to mold white–Mexicano relations. Bitterness between the two groups intensified a thousandfold. From 1836 to 1845, a spirit of revenge by whites pervaded relations between the two peoples: for the whites, the memory of the slaughter at the battles of the Alamo and Goliad, and for Mexicanos the humiliating rout and massacre at San Jacinto.[229] For Mexicanos in Tejas, the situation deteriorated rapidly. They were treated as foreigners in their own land and were subjected to white racial and physical attacks, discrimination, and retribution.

Mexicanos were treated as a conquered people with few rights, including those of property. Many Mexicanos lost their lands through outright confiscation; this included some of the loyalists who had supported the cause for Tejas independence. Many of these families were compelled to vacate their lands at the point of a gun and became victims of white unbridled violence and destruction of their properties. In 1837, the Mexicano communities of Victoria, San Patricio, Goliad, and Refugio were the first to come under ravaging attacks. In 1839 in the community of Nacogdoches, in what is now East Tejas, some one hundred Mexicano families were forced to abandon their homes and lands.[230] The political alliance that existed between Mexicano elites and whites in Texas after 1836 quickly deteriorated. David Montejano further writes that the transient Tejano *rico*/white political alliance began to dissipate right after the Battle of San Jacinto.

> The alliance that made Lorenzo de Zavala the first vice-president of the republic, for a few days began unraveling soon after the route of Santa

Anna's army at San Jacinto. A spirit of revenge and abandon prevailed in the young republic, and many ex-Soldiers carried out raids that claimed the land, stock, and lives of Mexicans, ally and foe alike. Many of the victims had fought alongside the Anglo colonists against Santa Anna's dictatorship. . . . During the brief tenure of Texas Republic, Texas Mexicans suffered from forced marches, general dispossession, and random violence.[231]

In the San Antonio area the situation became untenable for most Mexicanos. The Tejano insurgent hero Juan Seguín, captain in Houston's Texas army, hero of San Jacinto, and the last Mexicano mayor of San Antonio (1840–1842), was one such loyalist who lost everything. In 1842 because of death threats made against him, he and his family were forced into exile in México, the motherland he had fought so valiantly against. At about the same time, some two hundred Mexicano families also moved away from San Antonio.[232] While the great majority of the Mexicano masses suffered greatly from white hatred and racism, a few of the Mexicano oligarchs, such as Zavala, Navarro, Garza, and a few others, did manage to do well economically if not politically.

A few Tejano elites, however, managed to benefit from the misfortune of other Mexicanos. They purchased thousands of acres at extremely low prices. This was insignificant compared to what the white elites purchased, using fraud, intimidation, and violence. In ensuing years, the Republic of Texas experienced Mexicano resistance to increasing violent and discriminatory actions. In describing the relationship between whites and Mexicanos, McWilliams writes, "Throughout the decade of the Texas Republic (1836–1845), the shooting war continued," especially along the disputed Texas/México border where he described the type of violence as being one of "uninterrupted guerrilla warfare."[233]

Tensions with México, however, increased. Between 1836 and 1845, despite the continued internecine conflicts between liberals and conservatives, México initiated several military forays into what it perceived as an occupied Tejas. For the next nine years, the Lone Star Republic and México were politically and militarily at odds. México never ratified the treaty and relations between both countries were precarious. From the out, the Lone Star Republic sought annexation to the United States, but since Texas practiced slavery, annexation posed a problem for the United States because of the growing conflict over the slavery issue.[234] In addition, the threat of war with México and fear of British intervention precluded annexation.[235] In 1839, Mexican general Don Antonio Canales launched a revolution on Tejas soil against Santa Anna and declared it the "Republic of Rio Grande." Of the 600 men that comprised his invading force, 180 were Texas whites. After a number of engagements along the border in which the Mexican forces had been victorious,[236] Canales withdrew from the venture after he realized that the white Texans eager to attack México were only using him.[237]

The spirit of Manifest Destiny again became evident in the ill-fated Santa Fe Expedition of 1841. Texas president Mirabeau Lamar wanted to gain from the Santa Fe trade in Nuevo México and having "Manifest Destiny," inclinations, which included annexation of California, gave the go-ahead to a new expedition. Lamar assembled a 320 armed men invasion force commanded by General Hugh McLeod that was organized into five companies for the campaign. Four commissioners representing the government were assigned to establish jurisdiction over Nuevo México. In September 1841, Lamar's armed invaders, after wandering for weeks and exhausted were intercepted and captured by Mexicano dragoons under the command of Nuevo México governor Manuel Armijo without a shot being fired.[238] They were bound and marched to Santa Fe and according to Meier and Rivera, "Some of the Texans were executed and the remainder sent on a grueling death march to México City. The survivors were eventually released only after strong [U.S.] and British protests."[239] Lamar was publicly censured by the Texas Congress for his failure and was threatened with impeachment. For the young and aggressive Lone Star Republic, the Santa Fe Expedition had turned into a military debacle.

Thus, bellicose tensions pervaded Texas–México relations throughout the brief duration of the Texas Republic. In retaliation of the ill-fated invasion of Nuevo México, in February 1842, President Santa Anna ordered Mexican forces under the command of General Vasquez to invade Tejas and for a time occupied Refugio, Goliad, and San Antonio. However, México's incessant liberal/conservative conflict prevented Mexicano forces from effectively reoccupying Tejas. A Lone Star Republic counterinvasion force of seven hundred armed men retaliated and went into México, briefly occupying the border towns of Laredo and Guerrero, and at Mier, Mexicano forces defeated them. Some 176 Texans were captured, one in ten was shot, and the rest were sent to México City for confinement.[240] In 1843, the Mexican government, concerned with further white encroachments into its territory, closed the Santa Fe Trail.[241]

Meanwhile, tensions between México and the United States worsened to where a military collision became inevitable. In 1836, México had warned the United States that any attempt to annex Tejas would be considered an act of war. One year before, President Jackson had made known the U.S. interest in acquiring California. México responded with concern and suspicion, since it had experienced U.S. unofficial support over the Tejas Revolt. This expansionist concern became evident in 1842 when Thomas Catesby Jones, commodore of the U.S.

Pacific squadron, prematurely occupied California's capital, Monterey, on the false assumption that the United States was at war with México.[242] Starting in 1843, Captain John C. Fremont, under the aegis of the U.S. Army's topographical engineers, and for military purposes, conducted three expeditions into the Southwest to illegally survey California.

Prior to formal hostilities with México, in March 1846, Captain John C. Fremont in his third expedition into California committed a military blunder. His expeditionary force had been in California since May 1845, reinforced by additional U.S. military personnel. Thinking a state of war existed between the two countries, Fremont prematurely marched his troops to Hawk's Peak and raised the U.S. flag. Mexicano general José Castro, commander of the Monterey garrison, ordered Fremont to leave or face the military consequences. At that critical juncture, a messenger from President Polk reported to Fremont that the war against México had not yet commenced, but that war with México was near and to wait. Fremont withdrew his forces and headed toward Sacramento. According to Rodolfo Acuña, "Thomas Oliver Larkin, the U.S. consul at Monterrey, served as an agent, reporting on conditions and fomenting discontent among Californios while President James K. Polk conspired to pull off another Texas adventure in California."[243] The historical stage was set for war between México and the United States that significantly altered the Mexicano experience in México.

México: A Victim of U.S. Aggression

The Democratic Party platform of 1844 and its presidential candidate, James K. Polk, a slaveholder, were committed to U.S. expansionism. Liberal capitalist land and banking interests desired ports in California in order to promote lucrative continental trade. México was seen as a hindrance toward these ends.[244] By March 1845, President Polk, by a joint resolution of Congress, moved to annex Tejas, knowing this could lead to war with México. Immediately, México broke off diplomatic relations with the United States. In August, Polk sent John Slidell to México with instructions to purchase California and Nuevo México for $25 million and resolve the México/Tejas border issue. Mexican government officials, embroiled in internal conflicts, refused to see him. Their attitude was that any attempt to negotiate at that juncture was tantamount to political suicide.[245]

With Slidell's failure to negotiate the purchase, Polk opted for the military action. U.S. forces under the command of General Zachary Taylor were ordered into the disputed Nueces River border area in southeastern Tejas. According to John Chavez, "What finally started the war was Taylor's crossing of the Nueces and his advance to the Rio Grande."[246] An armed clash occurred between U.S. and Mexicano forces, which produced several U.S. casualties and prisoners, whereupon Polk claimed that "American blood" had been shed on "American soil."[247] Polk's message, according to Michael C. Meyer and William L. Sherman, "was remarkable for its distortion and provocative to the absurd."[248] The clash provided Polk with the pretext needed to precipitate an imperialist war with México and on May 11, 1846, Congress declared war. Polk succeeded in baiting México into war over the Tejas boundary issue, in order to acquire California and Nuevo México.[249] The nation was caught up in the euphoria of unbridled ethnocentrism and nationalism. "Ultimately," writes Richard Griswold Del Castillo, "the popularity of the ideology of Manifest Destiny led the U.S. Congress to a near-unanimous declaration of war against México."[250]

Provoked into a war it did not seek, México became the victim of blatant U.S. imperialism. The focus of this work does not permit a detailed account of the numerous battles that were fought or an elaborate examination of the politics of the United States War on México. Suffice it to say, however, from a military perspective, this war was fought essentially on three fronts. General Zachary Taylor's army of 4,000 invaded México from the north and moved his troops south toward México City. Several major battles were fought, such as those of Matamoros, Monterey, and Buena Vista. Colonel Stephen Kearney with an army of 1,500 men moved west to Aztlán and captured Nuevo México encountering minor resistance. His conquest of California also met some resistance, where he lost the Battle of San Pascual to Mexicano dragoons led by Andres Pico. Kearney's forces suffered several casualties and Kearney himself was wounded in the battle. His beleaguered forces were reinforced by the arrival of Commodore Robert Stockton's Pacific naval squadron in northern California, and the dispatch of Captain Archibald Gillispie's naval flotilla into the southern part of the state. Captain John C. Fremont, in a diversion, initiated the Bear Flag Revolt, in which California's independence was declared and the Bear Flag Republic proclaimed. By January 1847, Kearney was successful in neutralizing the resistance in California culminating in the defeated Californios (Mexicanos who resided in California) signing of the Treaty of Cahuenga.[251]

On March 1847 General Winfield Scott's army of 10,000 landed in Veracruz. With the military objective to occupy México City, Scott's army fought successful battles at Cerro Gordo, Puebla, Contreras, and Churubusco. At Churubusco Scott's army suffered heavy casualties and stiff resistance by the "San Patricio Battalion," made up of some 250 Irish Roman Catholics and other deserters from the U.S. forces. This heroic battalion sided with the Mexicano forces because of U.S. atrocities, for example, the desecration of Catholic churches, killing of priests, and rape of nuns perpetrated by invading U.S. forces. In the end, the eighty survivors of the San Patricio Battalion were executed in San Angel, a suburb of México City. The execution was perceived by Mexican government officials to be a barbarous proof of Yankee cruelty.

On September 13, 1847, General Scott's marines entered México City and engaged Mexican troops at Molino del Rey. Five days later, they fought the famous battle of Chapultepec, courageously defended by some fifty "Los Niños Heroes" (the Heroic Children)—young Mexican military cadets from México's academy who were outgunned and outmanned but fought valiantly. After running out of ammunition, rather than surrender, six of the remaining cadets, in an incredible act of courage and patriotism wrapped themselves in the Mexicano flag and leaped to their deaths from the ramparts of the fortress to the rocks below yelling "Viva México!"[252] On September 17, the Mexican forces, under the command of General Santa Anna, who like a cat with several lives, retreated to Querétaro, had assumed leadership once again only to see México fall into the clutches of U.S. imperialism. México lost the military war due to a variety of reasons— chronic political internal divisions and military miscalculations being primary— but the terms of peace were so severe that it also lost the political war of maintaining its own territorial integrity.

Resistance to the U.S. War on México

Not everyone in the United States supported the U.S. war on México. Opposition came from elements of the Whig Party, as well as from antislavery proponents and abolitionists who regarded the war as part of an expansionist conspiracy of slave owners.[253] In fact, a peace movement emerged that adamantly opposed it on a variety of grounds. Senator Daniel Webster called the war against México "unconstitutional." The famous black abolitionist leader Frederick Douglass described it as a "disgraceful, cruel" war that was transforming México into "a doomed victim to Anglo Saxon . . . love of domination."[254] Henry David Thoreau, a famous writer and naturalist, protested against the war by refusing to pay his state poll tax and was jailed for it. His *Essay on Civil Disobedience*, which he wrote to justify his actions, became the best-known work of U.S. literature for those struggling throughout the world for freedom. Abraham Lincoln, a freshman congressman from Illinois, challenged President Polk's assertion that the "Rio Grande flowed through United States" and did not support the war against México. The Whig Legislature of Massachusetts declared that it was a war of conquest, a war to strengthen the "slave power," a war against the free states, and one that was unconstitutional.[255]

Moreover, then-congressman John Quincy Adams likewise perceived the U.S. invasion of México as a shameless act of aggression impelled by the South's "slavocracy," and publicly exhorted military officers and soldiers to desert. The peace movement's resistance to the war was such that some 5,331 enlisted men, some 13 percent of the army, deserted, as did thousands more draftees, and some mutinies occurred as well. It produced the highest desertion rate in the history of the United States.[256] Yet among most people, the war was popular and had their zealous support, which was fanned by yellow journalism and President Polk's foreign policy of Manifest Destiny and its by-product, imperialism.

A major aspect of the U.S. war on México was the high number of blatantly cruel atrocities perpetrated by U.S. military forces against Mexicanos, particularly civilians. Future U.S. president Ulysses S. Grant, who fought in the war as an army lieutenant, described "a great many murders" and other atrocities committed by U.S. troops, noting, "How much they (Texans) seem to enjoy acts of violence." Somewhat paradoxically, he strongly opposed the war on moral grounds and described it as "one of the most unjust ever waged by a stronger against a weaker nation." Later, Grant, wrote, "I had a horror of the Mexican War . . . only I had not moral courage enough to resign." General Zachary Taylor also reported a number of "shameful atrocities." Likewise General Winfield Scott who commanded the U.S. forces that captured México City acknowledged, "murder, robbery, and rape of mothers and daughters in the presence of tied-up males of the families have been common." In a book entitled *My Confessions*, a soldier described scenes such as entering a cave where U.S. soldiers scalped and butchered women and children.[257] Carey McWilliams noted, "A large part of our invading army was made up of volunteers who, by all accounts were a disgrace to the [U.S.] flag."[258] While U.S. forces advanced into México, Mexicano armed resistance to the invasion in Nuevo México was taking place as well.

The Taos and Mora Revolts in Nuevo México

Some Mexicanos in Nuevo México rejected the nonviolent accommodation politics of the *ricos* and opted to resist the U.S. military occupation via armed struggle. Two major revolts, involving both Mexicanos and Amerindians occurring in 1847, categorically repudiate the view of some historians that the occupation was bloodless. The Taos and Mora revolts also belie the passivity attributed to Nuevo Mexicanos.[259] Although the two uprisings did not materialize into full-scale revolutionary social movements because of the harsh and swift retaliation by the U.S. military forces, they were expressions of counterviolence and resistance by some Mexicanos against the U.S. occupation.

The Taos Revolt was spurred by discontent over rumors that land would be confiscated and that the Catholic clergy would lose its privileges under U.S. rule.[260] Colonel Diego Archuleta, Tomas Ortiz, and Antonio Jóse Martinez, among others,[261] mostly from the Santa Fe area, collaborated with the Taos indigenous to form a clandestine alliance that sought to oust all whites from Nuevo México. In October, the insurgents informed the Mexican government of their intentions. The group created its own government: Ortiz was named governor and Archuleta commander of the army.[262] The "December Plot" as it became known, was thwarted when news was leaked to Secretary Donaciano Vigil, who then had Colonel Sterling Price arrest some of the conspirators. Archuleta and Ortiz fled to México and Father Martinez at his trial was not charged for lack of evidence.[263]

Territorial governor Charles Bent declared in December that the planned insurrection had been squelched and that Nuevo México was under firm U.S. control and governance. He accused both Ortiz and Archuleta of being jealous men whose motivation for rebellion was based on resentment due to not receiving any positions within the new government. He exhorted people to not become engaged in rebellious activities; essentially it fell on deaf ears.[264] One month later (January 1847), Governor Bent, believing everything was under control, visited Taos to resolve some pressing political problems. In the end the problems were bigger than he thought they were. He was brutally killed and scalped by a band of Nuevo Mexicanos and Taos Amerindians led by Pablo Montoya, called the self-styled Santa Anna of the north, and Tomasito, the leader of the Taos indigenous.[265] The insurrectionists called for all Nuevo Mexicanos to arms and support the rebellion.[266] The December Plot was not directly connected to the Taos Revolt or massacre, but was part of continuing armed resistance directed at U.S. occupation forces.

A total of three battles were fought as part of the Taos Revolt. The first major military engagement occurred at the Battle of La Cañada, which occurred south of Taos, involving some fifteen hundred to two thousand Nuevo Mexicanos and Amerindians.[267] Although they outnumbered the U.S. forces commanded by Colonel Price, the resistance was unable to mount an effective offensive due to the powerful U.S. artillery. Resistance leader Tafoya was killed in action and the U.S. forces won the battle. The second battle was fought in February 1847 at El Embudo Pass. U.S. forces were routed into a hasty retreat toward Taos, which produced the only victory for the defending Nuevo Mexicano forces. The third and final battle was fought at the pueblo of Taos. Using the supremacy of artillery fire, Taos was bombarded for two days and the Nuevo Mexicano defenders were forced to withdraw into the pueblo church, which was breached by U.S. forces.

The resistance sued for peace by surrendering and handing over their leader, Pablo Montoya.[268] The Taos Revolt proved to be a costly unsuccessful armed struggle. In this final battle, some 150 resistant fighters were killed; the total casualties for all three battles were 282 with an undisclosed number of wounded. Pablo Chavez and Manuel Tafoya were two major resistance leaders killed in battle. Supposedly, U.S. casualties were extremely low: seven killed and fifty-five wounded.[269]

Pablo Montoya and other ringleaders of the revolt were brought to trial. As a result, as the *Missouri Republican* reported, fifty-five insurgents were found guilty of treason against the United States and were executed. Meier and Rivera note, "This hanging of these leaders for the crime of treason against a government which they did not accept deeply shook the entire New Mexican region and left a long heritage of ill-will and bitterness between Anglos and Nuevo Mexicanos."[270] During the trial, one of the insurgent defendants, Antonio María Trujillo, categorically denied the legitimacy of the trials and of the treason charge by declaring that the insurgents were Mexicano patriots and that the revolt was justified because they were defending their homeland. Because of political opposition in Washington, both on the issue of the illegality of the trials and the military occupational government itself, President Polk was pressured into intervening on the matter. As a result, Trujillo was acquitted on the charge of treason and the government of occupation was allowed to continue. Donaciano Vigil replaced Bent as governor, but the real power remained in the hands of the U.S. military occupation.

Beyond the Taos Revolt, a second revolt occurred in late January 1847 in Mora. Led by Manuel Cortez, the Mora Revolt, inspired by the Taos Revolt, sought to open a second armed front against U.S. military occupation in Nuevo México. The revolt began with the assassination of Lawrence Waldo and another white businessman. As a result of these killings, U.S. troops under the command of Israel R. Hendley were dispatched to the area to confront the insurgents. In a fierce battle, the insurgent forces scored a military victory. With Hendley killed in action, the U.S. forces retreated to the town of Las Vegas to regroup. On February 1, 1847, the U.S. forces were reinforced by some additional two hundred troops under the command of Nuevo Mexicano Jesse I. Morin. Rather than confront the superior U.S. forces in numbers and firepower, Cortez withdrew into the surrounding mountains for a while and resorted to armed resistance via guerrilla warfare. In retaliation, Morin ordered U.S. forces to burn Mora as well as the surrounding wheat fields.[271] Both the Taos and Mora revolts offer clear historical accounts that Mexicanos in Nuevo México did resort to armed resistance in their struggle against the U.S. military occupation. As the United States consolidated its military occupation of Aztlán, a defeated México was compelled to sign the infamous Treaty of Guadalupe Hidalgo.

The Treaty of Guadalupe Hidalgo

The hostilities between the two countries ended with the signing of the Treaty of Guadalupe Hidalgo[272]—a treaty that became known for its broken agreements and promises. Just before Scott's army entered México City, Polk dispatched Nicolas P. Trist to the Mexican capital to negotiate the peace treaty. After weeks of negotiations and political maneuverings, on February 2, 1848, at Guadalupe Hidalgo, a suburb of México City, the infamous Treaty of Guadalupe Hidalgo was signed. Some extreme nationalist politicians in Washington immediately began to demand the annexation of México as a whole. Secretary of State Buchanan unsuccessfully exhorted Polk to repudiate both Trist and the treaty.[273] The spirit of Manifest Destiny was such that these jingoists even suggested that Central America was ripe for the picking. Others advocated that U.S. hegemony should include South America.[274] Some Southerners especially opposed it for they feared that the acquisition of a large nonwhite, nonslave population would encourage black aspirations to freedom.[275]

México was militarily vanquished and badly divided. Yet even though anti-Mexicano views were prevalent in the United States, because of concerns about a growing military resistance to the U.S. invasion in México, México was spared from total annexation and the loss of additional territory. Speaking against the annexation of México before the U.S. Senate, Senator John C. Calhoun's racist sentiments became obvious: "I protest against such a union as that! Ours, sir, is the Government of a white race. The greatest misfortunes of Spanish America are to be traced to the fatal error of placing these colored races on equality with the white race."[276] Satisfied that the military objectives of acquiring California and Nuevo México were realized, President Polk sent the treaty to the Senate and on March 10, 1848, the treaty was ratified on a thirty-eight to fourteen vote. The negative votes followed geographic divisions with most northerners opposing it.[277] On May 26, 1848, the Mexican congress reluctantly ratified the treaty. However, the treaty ratified by the United States was not the one originally signed by México after its defeat, yet México had little choice but to accept the imposed terms.[278]

The old saying "to the victor go the spoils of war" became a truism. The territorial settlement imposed by the treaty was disastrous and humiliating for México. First, México was compelled to accept the loss of Tejas, and the Rio Grande became the borderline separating Tejas from México. Second, México lost what today are the states of California, Arizona, New México, Colorado, Utah, Nevada, and smaller sections of other contiguous states. And third, with Tejas included, México lost some 916,945 square miles (45 percent) of its territory, including the immense riches of Tejas's oil fields and California's gold.[279] These provisions caused great divisions in México. Several Mexicanos, such as Benito Juarez, spoke against the treaty and argued for a continuation of the war. Del Castillo writes, "The Mexican War (1846–1848) and the treaty that ended it were undertaken against the backdrop of Manifest Destiny."[280]

The Treaty of Guadalupe Hidalgo was a historical statement of the time. According to Armando Rendon, "The Treaty of Guadalupe Hidalgo climaxed the first of our imperialistic and declared wars against a people outside the boundaries of the United States."[281] The treaty as amended was comprised of some twenty-three articles. Articles V, VIII, IX, and X had the most impact in molding the character of the Mexicano political experience in the United States that was to ensue.[282] Article V defined the new boundary between the United States and México. Under Article VIII, Mexicanos in occupied México (those lands lost to the United States) had one year to decide whether to stay and become U.S. citizens or return to México. Under this article, property rights as well were to be protected. Specifically, the article reads,

> In the said territories, property of every kind, now established there, shall be inviolably respected. [Italics mine] The present owners, the heirs of these and all Mexicans who may hereafter acquire said property by contract, shall enjoy with respect to it the guarantees equally ample as if the same belonged to citizens of the United States.[283]

Article IX was equally important in that it addressed the issue of civil and religious rights. Specifically, it guaranteed Mexicanos "the enjoyment of all the rights of citizens of the United States according to the principles of the Constitution; and in the mean time shall be maintained and protected in the free enjoyment of their liberty and property, and secured in the free exercise of their religion without restriction."[284]

Article X, which in strong and clear language delineated protections for existing land grants, but was deleted by the U.S. Senate, stated, "All grants of land made by the Mexican Government or by the competent authorities, in territories previously appertaining to México, and remaining for the future within the limits of the United States, shall be respected as valid, to the same extent that the same grants would be valid, if the said territories had remained within the limits of México."[285] This article was strongly opposed by white land speculators and barons because it would interfere and impede the land grabbing that had already taken place in Tejas and would occur as well in Nuevo México and California. Furthermore, the United States threatened to restart the war if México insisted on keeping Article X.[286] Mexicano officials protested and U.S. emissaries drafted a Statement of Protocol, which promised that the deletion of Article X did not mean that the United States sought to annul the land grants and that they would be respected. Acuña argues, "The importance of the Statement of Protocol was that it proved the bad faith of Polk and U.S. authorities." He goes on to explain "even as the statement was being sold to Mexican authorities, it was called worthless in the United States because Trist did not have the authority to sign the treaty."[287]

And lastly, Articles XII, XIII, XIV, and XV dealt with the indemnity aspects of the treaty. In exchange for the land, the United States agreed to pay México $15,000,000 and to assume Mexican debts to U.S. citizens to the amount of $3 million.[288] None of the articles addressed the political, civil, or property rights of the Amerindian peoples, who at least on paper had been given citizenship by the Mexican government.[289] With regard to territorial acquisition, the Treaty of Guadalupe Hidalgo became one of the harshest treaties concluded between two countries.[290] Like other treaties signed by the U.S. government, especially with the indigenous peoples, it became a "Treaty of Broken Promises."

Some scholars quite erroneously have said that the Treaty of Guadalupe Hidalgo also provided explicit provisions for the protection of the culture and language. The fact of the matter is this was not the case. On the contrary, none of the treaty articles provide any explicit mention of this. McWilliams, for example, incorrectly wrote, "The treaty also provided specific safe guarantees for the property and political rights of the 'native' population and attempted to safeguard their cultural autonomy, that is, they were given the right to retain their language, religion, and culture." Chicano scholars Rendon and Vigil incorrectly also make this claim.[291] The Treaty of Guadalupe Hidalgo, writes Chavez, "officially separated the first Mexicano in the U.S. or Chicanos from their motherland country, it permanently changed their image of the homeland." He concludes by saying quite appropriately, "Mexicans in the southwest were now a conquered people in a conquered land."[292] "Despite the treaty's guarantees of property rights and equality of citizenship," explains Meier and Rivera, "bitterness and conflict grew between the Anglos and the [Mexicanos] during the latter half of the nineteenth century."[293]

Thus, the official signing and ratification of the Treaty of Guadalupe Hidalgo gave rise to the Mexicano political experience in occupied Aztlán, which is the paramount focus of this book.

Notes

1. Who the original peoples are is a subject of inquiry and debate; nevertheless, the radiocarbon (C-14) method of dating among other innovative research procedures has fostered a scholarly general consensus as to the time of arrival and settlement of said immigrants to México.

2. For a comprehensive examination of these evolutionary historical development periods, see Robert M. Carmack, Janine Gasco, and Gary H. Gossen, *The Legacy of Mesoamerica: History and Culture of a Native American Civilization* (Upper Saddle River, N.J.: Prentice Hall, 1996), 48–49.

3. Victor Barnouw, *An Introduction to Anthropology, Vol. 1: Physical Anthropology and Archaeology*, the Dorsey Series in Anthropology, 3rd ed. (Homewood, Ill.: Dorsey Press, 1978), 128, 139, and 186; and Richard E. Leaky, *The Making of Mankind* (New York: Dutton, 1981), 6 and 213.

4. James Diego Vigil, *From Indians to Chicanos: The Dynamics of Mexican-American Culture* (Prospect Heights, Ill.: Waveland Press, Inc., 1998), 14.

5. David Carrasco, *Religions of Mesoamerica* (San Francisco: Harper, 1990), xxi.

6. Dialectical materialism—the Marxist theory that maintains that the basis of a reality constantly changes in a dialectical process and the primacy of matter over mind. A term used by both Hegel and Marx to denote a process of change. Hegel argues that all of life is in a constant state of flux, that from the time of creation begins a changing process that eventually leads to death. His logic posited that every idea takes the form of a thesis, which inevitably is opposed to another, antithesis. Moreover, inherent to the struggle a synthesis occurs, a combination and higher form of the two opposing ideas. Marx borrowed Hegel's dialectic and added a materialist basis, meaning matter over mind, under the rubric of dialectical materialism.

7. Robert J. Sharer, *The Ancient Mayan*, 6th ed. (Stanford, Calif.: Stanford University Press, 1994), 4.

8. While the concept of Mesoamerica is a subject of much debate by scholars, in this work it is being used to geographically describe what scholars call "Middle America." Specifically, it refers to the area from around present México City to the coasts of both the Gulf of México and Pacific and south into present-day Guatemala, El Salvador, Belize, Honduras, and Nicaragua. For an extensive examination of the diverse aspects that the concept denotes see Carmack, Gasco, and Gossen, *The Legacy of Mesoamerica*, chapter 1.

9. The basis of historical materialism can be understood in the context of Marx's dialectical materialism, which posits the view that the ultimate determinant of social change is not predicated on ideals or ideas of eternal truth or social justice but changes that occur in mode of production and exchange.

10. Robert E. Quirk, *México* (Englewood Cliffs, N.J.: Prentice Hall, 1971), 6.

11. Michael D. Coe, *America's First Civilization* (New York: American Heritage Publishing Co., Inc., 1968), 26.

12. Coe, *America's First Civilization*, 26.

13. Eric Wolf, *Sons of the Shaking Earth: The People of México and Guatemala—Their Land, History, and Culture* (Chicago: University of Chicago Press, 1959), 54.

14. Rodolfo Acuña, *Occupied America: A History of Chicanos*, 4th ed. (New York: Longman, 2000), 4.

15. Vigil, *From Indians to Chicanos*, 16.

16. Quirk, *México*, 7.

17. Louis K. Harris and Victor Alba, *The Political Culture and Behavior of Latin America* (Kent, Ohio: Kent State University Press, 1974), 19.

18. From the Marxist perspective, productive forces and productive relations are integral to the materialist interpretation of history. Productive forces denote the people's relation to nature in the context of changes effectuated due to technological, scientific know-how, and expansion of knowledge. Productive relations, on the other hand, involve relations among people, meaning the rise of social institutions. When they contradict, they come into conflict, especially with the productive forces.

19. Carmack, Gasco, and Gossen, *The Legacy of Mesoamerica*, 41–42.

20. William F. Rust and Robert J. Sharer, "Olmec Settlement Data from La Venta, Tabasco, México," *Science* Vol. 242, No. 4875 (October 7, 1988): 102ff.

21. Carmack, Gasco, Gossen, *The Legacy of Mesoamerica*, 50–51.

22. Acuña, *Occupied America*, 4th ed., 4–5.

23. According to Toltec legend, the Plumed Serpent or Quetzalcóatl was a tall and light complexioned ruler elevated by the Toltec to god-like status. They considered him master of their universe. With the Toltec Empire in crisis, he left the Valley of México, promising one day to return to rule again. Later, Aztecs adopted Quetzalcóatl into their pantheon of gods.

24. Carrasco, *Religions of Mesoamerica*, xxiii.

25. Quirk, *México*, 10.

26. Carmack, Gasco, and Gossen, *The Legacy of Mesoamerica*, 53.

27. Acuña, *Occupied America*, 5.

28. Carmack, Gasco, and Gossen, *The Legacy of Mesoamerica*, 60–69.

29. Carmack, Gasco, and Gossen, *The Legacy of Mesoamerica*, 57.

30. Mark Stevenson, "Pre-Aztec México Likely No Bed of Roses," *Los Angeles Times*, October 12, 2002.

31. See Ester Pasztory, *Teotihuacan, An Experiment in Living* (Norman: University of Oklahoma Press, 1997).

32. Quirk, *México*, 12–14.

33. Quirk, in his work *México*, posits the argument that it fell to invading forces, probably from the south. On the other hand, Acuña in *Occupied America* (4th ed.), without going into any detail, explains that the decline was due to "internal convulsion."

34. Acuña, *Occupied America*, 4th ed., 11.

35. Quirk, *México*, 14, and Acuña, *Occupied America*, 4th ed., 12–13.

36. Acuña, *Occupied America*, 4th ed., 12–13.

37. Matt S. Meier and Feliciano Rivera, *Mexican Americans, American Mexicans: From Conquistadors to Chicanos*, rev. ed. (New York: Hill & Wang, 1993), 12.

38. Quirk, *México*, 11.

39. Acuña, *Occupied America*, 4th ed., 6.

40. Acuña, *Occupied America*, 4th ed., 6.

41. Meier and Rivera, *Mexican Americans, American Mexicans*, 13

42. Quirk, *México*, 15.

43. Quirk, *México*, 17.

44. Carmack, Gasco, and Gossen, *The Legacy of Mesoamerica*, 64.

45. Charles C. Cumberland, *México: The Struggle for Modernity* (New York: Oxford University Press, 1968), 18.

46. Acuña, *Occupied America*, 4th ed., 13.

47. Acuña, *Occupied America*, 4th ed., 13.

48. For an examination of the various ancient Amerindian civilizations to impact México see Michael D. Coe, *México: From Olmecs to Aztecs* (New York: Thames and Hudson, Inc., 1994)

49. James D. Cockcroft, *Mexico's Hope: An Encounter with Politics and History* (New York: Monthly Review Press, 1998), 15.

50. For an analysis on this aspect of the Toltecs see F. J. Mathien and R. H. McGuire, *Ripples in the Chichimec Sea: New Considerations of Southwestern–Mesoamerican Interactions* (Carbondale: Southern Illinois University Press, 1992).

51. Quirk, *México*, 17.

52. Cottie Burland, Irene Nicholson, and Harold Osborne, *Mythology of the Americas* (New York: Hamlyn Publishing Group, 1970), 145.

53. Cited by Acuña, *Occupied America*, 4th ed., 13.

54. Acuña, *Occupied America*, 4th ed., 13.

55. Acuña, *Occupied America*, 4th ed., 13.

56. Scholars who identify with this position include Quirk, *México*, 17; Meier and Rivera, *Mexican Americans, American Mexicans*, 14; and Acuña, *Occupied America*, 4th ed., 13.

57. Two scholars who identify with this position are Robert A. Calvert and Arnoldo De León, *The History of Texas* (Arlington Heights, Ill.: Harlan Davidson, Inc., 1990), 2.

58. According to historian John Chavez, Aztlán denotes either the "land of herons" or "land of whiteness." Chavez argues that Aztlán was more than likely located in the present state of Nayarit in México, located some four hundred miles from present-day México City. See *The Lost Land: The Chicano Image of the Southwest* (Albuquerque: New México Press, 1984), 8.

59. William H. Prescott, *History and Conquest of México* (New York: Modern Library, 1843), 15–16.

60. Manuel G. Gonzales, *Mexicanos: A History of Mexicans in the United States* (Bloomington: Indiana University Press, 1999), 21.

61. Vigil, *From Indians to Chicanos*, 26.

62. Meier and Rivera, *Mexican Americans, American Mexicans*, 15.

63. Prescott, *History and Conquest of México*, 18.

64. Quirk, *México*, 18.

65. Calvert and De León, *The History of Texas*, 2.

66. Juan Gonzales, *Harvest of Empire: A History of Latin America* (New York: Penguin, 2000), 5.

67. Prescott, *History of the Conquest of México*, 20–21.

68. Meier and Rivera, *Mexican Americans, American Mexicans*, 15.

69. Ramón Eduardo Ruiz, *Triumphs and Tragedy: The History of the Mexican People* (New York: Norton, 1992), 23.

70. Calvert and De León, *The History of Texas*, 21

71. Carmack, Gasco, and Gossen, *The Legacy of Mesoamerica*, 476.

72. Cockcroft, *México's Hope*, 16.

73. Cockcroft, *México's Hope*, 16.

74. Acuña, *Occupied America*, 16.

75. Quirk, *México*, 18–19.

76. Quirk, *México*, 18–19.

77. Acuña, *Occupied America*, 4th ed., 16.

78. For a comprehensive work on the Aztecas' polytheistic gods see Burr Cartwright Brundage, *The Fifth Sun: Aztec Gods, Aztec World* (Austin: University of Texas Press, 1979).

79. Vigil, *From Indians to Chicanos*, 40–41.

80. For an examination of the particulars of the ritual of human sacrifice see R. C. Padden, *The Hummingbird and the Hawk: Conquest and Sovereignty in the Valley of México, 1503–1541* (Columbus: Ohio University Press, 1967), and Vigil, *From Indians to Chicanos*, 39–42.

81. Cited in Ruiz, *Triumphs and Tragedy*, 26.

82. Meier and Rivera, *Mexican Americans, American Mexicans*, 16.

83. Meier and Rivera, *Mexican Americans, American Mexicans*, 16.

84. Gonzales, *Mexicanos*, 10.

85. Gonzales, *Mexicanos*, 10.

86. Meier and Rivera, *Mexican Americans, American Mexicans*, 17.

87. Gonzales, *Mexicanos*, 10.

88. Meier and Rivera, *Mexican Americans, American Mexicans*, 17.

89. Calvert and De León, *The History of Texas*, 7.

90. Arnoldo Carlos Vento, *Mestizo: The History, Culture and Politics of the Mexican and the Chicano* (Lanham, Md.: University Press of America, 1998), 44.

91. Gonzales, *Mexicanos*, 11.

92. Meier and Rivera, *Mexican Americans, American Mexicans*, 17.

93. Gonzales, *Mexicanos*, 11.

94. Gonzales, *Mexicanos*, 12.

95. Calvert and De León, *The History of Texas*, 8.

96. Meier and Rivera, *Mexican Americans, American Mexicans*, 17–18.

97. Calvert and De León, *The History of Texas*, 8.

98. Meier and Rivera, *Mexican Americans, American Mexicans*, 18.

99. Calvert and De León, *The History of Texas*, 8.

100. Julian Samora and Patricia Vandel Simon, *A History of the Mexican American People* (Notre Dame, Ind.: University of Notre Dame Press, 1977), 14.

101. Acuña, *Occupied America*, 4th ed., 21.

102. Acuña, *Occupied America*, 4th ed., 22.

103. Samora and Simon, *A History of the Mexican American People*, 15.

104. Samora and Simon, *A History of the Mexican American People*, 14.

105. Gonzales, *Mexicanos*, 22.

106. John Ross, *The Annexation of México: From Aztecs to the I.M.F.* (Monroe, Me.: Common Courage Press, 1998), 12.

107. Coe, *México*, 198.

108. Ross, *The Annexation of México*, 13.

109. Ross, *The Annexation of México*, 13.

110. Ross, *The Annexation of México*, 9.

111. Samora and Simon, *A History of the Mexican American People*, 16–17.

112. Meier and Rivera, *Mexican Americans, American Mexicans*, 19.

113. Gonzales, *Mexicanos*, 23–24.

114. Coe, *México*, 199.

115. Coe, *México*, 199.

116. Meier and Rivera, *Mexican Americans, American Mexicans*, 19.

117. Coe, *México*, 199.

118. Ross, *The Annexation of México*, 11.

119. For an analysis on the manifold factors that led to the defeat of the Aztecs see Coe, *México*, 197–200.

120. Coe, *México*, 199.

121. Julian Nava, *Viva La Raza: Readings on Mexican Americans* (New York: D. Van Nostrand Co., 1973), 26–27.

122. Meier and Rivera, *Mexican Americans, American Mexicans*, 16.

123. *Mestizo* labels a person who is a hybrid Spanish and Amerindian and mixed ancestry.

124. Chavez, *The Lost Land*, 10.

125. It is important to note that the so-called New World was named the *Americas* after explorer Amerigo Vespucci, a Florentine merchant and navigator, who made two important voyages of exploration along the north and east coasts between 1499 and 1502 of what today is considered South America. Upon his return, he announced the existence of a new continent that formed a "fourth part of the world." This was important because during this time, Columbus was still adamant that he had reached the mainland of Asia.

126. Calvert and De León, *The History of Texas*, 10.

127. Ross, *The Annexation of México*, 17.

128. Quirk, *México*, 19–20.

129. Richard Griswold del Castillo and Arnoldo De León, *North to Aztlán: A History of Mexican Americans in the United States* (New York: Twayne Publishers; London: Prentice Hall International, 1996), 6.

130. Ross, *The Annexation of México*, 15.

131. Colin M. MacLachlan and Jaime E. Rodríguez O., *The Forging of the Cosmic Race: A Reinterpretation of Colonial America* (Berkeley: University of California Press, 1980), 201–2.

132. Wolf, *Sons of the Shaking Earth*, 30.

133. Quirk, *México*, 28.

134. Vigil, *From Indians to Chicanos*, 95.

135. Samora and Simon, *A History of the Mexican American People*, 28–29.

136. Vigil, *From Indians to Chicanos*, 95.

137. Vigil, *From Indians to Chicanos*, 95; Quirk, *México*, 28.

138. Ross, *The Annexation of México*, 20.

139. Acuña, *Occupied America*, 4th ed., 31.

140. Gonzales, *Harvest of Empire*, 8.

141. Calvert and De León, *The History of Texas*, 10.

142. Gonzales, *Harvest of Empire*, 9.

143. Meier and Rivera, *Mexican Americans, American Mexicans*, 21.

144. Acuña, *Occupied America*, 35.

145. Carlos Vélez-Ibáñez, *Border Visions: Mexican Cultures of the Southwestern United States* (Tucson: University of Arizona Press, 1996), 47–48.

146. Samora and Simon, *A History of the Mexican American People*, 52.

147. Juan Gómez-Quiñones, *Roots of Chicano Politics: 1600–1940* (Albuquerque: University of New México Press, 1994), 44.

148. Gómez-Quiñones, *Roots of Chicano Politics*, 43–44.

149. Acuña, *Occupied America*, 4th ed., 36

150. Cited in Arnoldo De León, *Mexican Americans in Texas: A Brief History* (Arlington Heights, Ill.: Harlan Davidson, Inc., 1993), 8.

151. Cited in Gómez-Quiñones, *Roots of Chicano Politics*, 47.

152. Calvert and De León, *The History of Texas*, 20.

153. Gonzales, *Mexicanos*, 39.

154. Acuña, *Occupied America*, 4th ed., 37.

155. Gonzales, *Mexicanos*, 41–42.

156. Acuña, *Occupied America*, 4th ed., 37.

157. Samora and Simon, *A History of the Mexican American People*, 54.

158. Meier and Rivera, *Mexican Americans, American Mexicans*, 24.

159. Meier and Rivera, *Mexican Americans, American Mexicans*, 24.

160. Quirk, *México*, 42–43.

161. Ross, *The Annexation of México*, 20.

162. Cockcroft, *México's Hope*, 54.

163. Cockcroft, *México's Hope*, 54.

164. Cockcroft, *México's Hope*, 56.

165. Ross, *The Annexation of México*, 23.

166. Cockcroft, *México's Hope*, 56.

167. Ross, *The Annexation of México*, 23.

168. For an excellent contemporary examination on the historical aspects of Manifest Destiny see Anders Stephanson, *Manifest Destiny: American Expansion and the Empire of Right* (New York: Hill & Wang, 1995).

169. Gómez-Quiñones, *Roots of Chicano Politics*, 184.

170. Samuel Huntington, *Who Are We? The Challenges to America's National Identity* (New York: Simon & Schuster, 2004), 46.

171. Gonzales, *Mexicanos*, 55.

172. Gonzales, *Harvest of Empire*, 28.

173. Frederick Merk, *Manifest Destiny and Mission in American History* (New York: Knopf, 1963), 24–25.

174. Peter N. Carroll and David W. Noble, *The Free and the Unfree: A History of the United States*, 2nd ed. (New York: Penguin, 1988), 167.

175. *Anglo* will be used as a generic term to describe non-Mexicano whites from the United States that are of European extraction.

176. Acuña, *Occupied America*, 4th ed., 49.

177. Gonzales, *Harvest of Empire*, 28.

178. Gonzales, *Harvest of Empire*, 32.

179. Gonzales, *Harvest of Empire*, 32.

180. Gilberto López y Rivas, *The Chicanos: Life and Struggles of the Mexican Minority in the United States* (New York: Monthly Review Press, 1973), 16.

181. Louis A. Pérez, Jr., *Cuba: Between Reform & Revolution* (New York: Oxford University Press, 1995), 108.

182. Samuel Eliot Morison and Henry Steel Commager, *The Growth of the American Republic* (New York: Oxford University Press, 1962), 381.

183. Cited in Acuña, *Occupied America*, 43.

184. Gómez-Quiñones, *Roots of Chicano Politics*, 81–85.

185. Meier and Rivera, *Mexican Americans, American Mexicans*, 37.

186. Morison and Commager, *The Growth of the American Republic*, 454.

187. Matt S. Meier and Feliciano Rivera, *The Chicanos: A History of Mexican Americans* (New York: Hill & Wang, 1972), 34–35.

188. Acuña, *Occupied America*, 43.

189. Meier and Rivera, *Mexican Americans, American Mexicans*, 38.

190. Arnoldo De León, *The Tejano Community, 1836–1900* (Albuquerque: University of New México Press, 1982), 4.

191. Cited in López y Rivas, *The Chicanos*, 21. See A. Balenki, *La Intervencion Extranjera en México, 1861–1867* (México: Fondo de Cultura Popular, 1966).

192. De León, *The Tejano Community*, 4–5.

193. Hereafter *white* is more applicable since not all who came from U.S. territories were of Anglo-Saxon stock.

194. Gómez-Quiñones, *Roots of Chicano Politics*, 132.

195. De León, *Mexicans Americans in Texas*, 27.

196. Quoted in Eugene C. Barker, "Native Latin American Contributions to the Col-

onization and Independence of Texas," *Southwestern Historical Quarterly* Vol. 46, No. 3 (January 1943): 325.

197. Del Castillo and De León, *North to Aztlán*, 16.

198. David J. Weber, *Foreigners in Their Native Land: Historical Roots of the Mexican Americans* (Albuquerque: University of New México Press, 1973), 58.

199. Weber, *Foreigners in Their Native Land*, 58.

200. López y Rivas, *The Chicanos*, 20.

201. Morison and Commager, *The Growth of the American Republic*, 459.

202. Acuña, *Occupied America*, 4th ed., 51–52.

203. Acuña, *Occupied America*, 4th ed., 44.

204. Acuña, *Occupied America*, 44.

205. Meier and Rivera, *Mexican Americans, American Mexicans*, 57.

206. Andres Tijerina, *Texanos under the Mexican Flag, 1821–1836* (College Station: Texas A&M University Press, 1994), 3–24.

207. Gonzales, *Mexicanos*, 70.

208. Leobardo F. Estrada, F. Chris Garcia, Reynaldo Flores Macias, and Loniel Maldonado, "Chicanos in the United States: A History of Exploitation and Resistance," *Latinos in the Political System*, ed. F. Chris Garcia (Notre Dame, Ind.: University of Notre Dame Press, 1988), 29.

209. Del Castillo and De León, *North to Aztlán*, 16.

210. Arnoldo De León, *They Called Them Greasers: Anglo Attitudes toward Mexicans in Texas, 1821–1900* (Austin: University of Texas Press, 1983), 1–13.

211. De León, *Mexican Americans in Texas*, 28.

212. For an interesting depiction of these and other events see Acuña, *Occupied México*, 4th ed., 44–45; and Meier and Rivera, *Mexican Americans, American Mexicans*, 2nd ed., 57–58.

213. Eugene Baker, *México and Texas, 1821–1835* (New York: Russell and Russell, 1965), 52.

214. Carey McWilliams, *North from México: The Spanish-Speaking People of the United States* (New York: Greenwood, 1968), 99. This was the first major historical work, originally published in 1948, done on the Mexicano in the United States. Even though several others have been written on the subject, it remains today as one of the best works.

215. Calvert and De León, *The History of Texas*, 63.

216. Calvert and De León, *The History of Texas*, 64.

217. Meier and Rivera, *Mexican Americans, American Mexicans*, 58.

218. Weber, *Foreigners in Their Native Land*, 92.

219. McWilliams, *North from México*, 101.

220. A major discrepancy exists among historians as to the size of General Santa Anna's army. Consequently, the number of Mexican troops that participated in the attack on the Alamo is open to debate. Historian Acuña cites a figure of 1,400, which is a figure based upon Mexican sources. Historians Calvert and De León cite a figure of 1,800. De León himself in his own work used the figure of 2,400. Historian Manuel Gonzales uses the general figure of 5,000.

221. Gonzales, *Mexicanos*, 73. Gonzales lists the names of the eight: Juan Abamillo, Juan Antonio Badillo, Carlos Espalier, Gregorio Esparza, Antonio Fuentes, Galba Fuqua, Jose Toribio Losoya, and Andres Nava.

222. Calvert and De León, *The History of Texas*, 68–69.

223. Acuña, *Occupied America*, 4th ed., 47.

224. Calvert and De León, *The History of Texas*, 69–70.

225. Calvert and De León, *The History of Texas*, 69–70.

226. Morison and Commager, *The Growth of the American Republic*, 599.

227. Cited in Cockcroft, *México's Hope*, 65.

228. Acuña, *Occupied America*, 4th ed., 48.

229. McWilliams, *North from México*, 100.

230. David Montejano, *Anglos and Mexicans in the Making of Texas, 1836–1986*, 1st ed. (Austin: University of Texas Press, 1987), 26–27.

231. Montejano, *Anglos and Mexicans*, 26.

232. Montejano, *Anglos and Mexicans*, 27.

233. McWilliams, *North from México*, 101.

234. Meier and Rivera, *Mexican Americans, American Mexicans*, 2nd ed., 59.

235. Carroll and Noble, *The Free and Unfree*, 174.

236. Gómez-Quiñones, *Roots of Chicano Politics*, 148.

237. McWilliams, *North from México*, 101.

238. Calvert and De León, *The History of Texas*, 91.

239. Meier and Rivera, *Mexican Americans, American Mexicans*, 61.

240. Calvert and De León, *The History of Texas*, 91.

241. Weber, *Foreigners in Their Native Land*, 94.

242. Weber, *Foreigners in Their Native Land*, 94.

243. Acuña, *Occupied America*, 4th ed., 136.

244. Gómez-Quiñones, *Roots of Chicano Politics*, 184.

245. Gonzales, *Mexicanos*, 75.

246. Chavez, *The Lost Land*.

247. Gene M. Brack, *México Views Manifest Destiny, 1821–1846: An Essay on the Origins of the Mexican War* (Albuquerque: University of New México Press, 1975), 116–17.

248. Michael C. Meyer and William L. Sherman, *The Course of Mexican History* (New York: Oxford University Press, 1979), 345.

249. Morison and Commager, *The Growth of the American Republic*, 611.

250. Richard Griswold Del Castillo, *The Treaty of Guadalupe Hidalgo: A Legacy of Conflict* (Norman: University of Oklahoma Press, 1990), 4–5.

251. Meier and Rivera, *Mexican Americans, American Mexicans*, 62–65.

252. Samora and Simon, *A History of the Mexican American People*, 97.

253. Morison and Commager, *The Growth of the American Republic*, 612.

254. Cockcroft, *México's Hope*, 66–67.

255. Morison and Commager, *The Growth of the American Republic*, 612.

256. Cockcroft, *México's Hope*, 67.

257. Above citations and quotes are taken from Cockcroft's study, *México's Hope*. He provides an excellent historical analysis of aspects of the U.S. War against México that few U.S. historians, including some Mexicanos, have admitted occurred. For an overview of this aspect see pages 66–68.

258. McWilliams, *North from México*, 102–3.

259. For an excellent historical analysis on various aspects of the Chicano experience in Nuevo México see Erlinda Gonzales-Berry and David R. Maciel, ed., *The Contested Homeland: A Chicano History of New México* (Albuquerque: University of New México Press, 2000), 13.

260. For a thorough examination of the various social conflicts that Nuevo Mexicanos faced between 1810 and 1910 see Tobías Durán, *We Come as Friends: Violent Social Conflict in New México*, PhD dissertation, University of New México, 1985.

261. Alvin R. Sunseri, *New México in the Aftermath of the Anglo American Conquest*, dissertation, Louisiana State University and Agricultural and Mechanical College, May 1973, 131.

262. Carlos Herrera, "New México Resistance to U.S. Occupation during the Mexican-American War of 1846–1848," in Gonzales-Berry and Maciel, *The Contested Homeland*, 31.

263. Meier and Rivera, *Mexican Americans, American Mexicans*, 89.

264. Herrera, "New México Resistance to U.S. Occupation during the Mexican-American War of 1846–1848," in Gonzales-Berry and Maciel, *The Contested Homeland*, 31–32.

265. Michael McNierney, ed., *Taos Revolt: The Revolt in Contemporary Accounts* (Boulder, Colo.: Johnson, 1980), 4.

266. Sunseri, *New México in the Aftermath of the Anglo American Conquest*, 133.

267. Sunseri, *New México in the Aftermath of the Anglo American Conquest*, 133.

268. Herrera, "New México Resistance to U.S. Occupation during the Mexican American War of 1846–1848," 33.

269. Sunseri, *New México in the Aftermath of the Anglo American Conquest*, 134.

270. Meier and Rivera, *Chicanos*, 98–99.

271. For an examination of the Mora Revolt see James W. Goodrich, "Revolt at Mora, 1847," *New México Historical Review* Vol. 47 (1972): 52–57.

272. For an extensive examination of the politics and particulars of the Treaty of Guadalupe Hidalgo see Del Castillo, *The Treaty of Guadalupe Hidalgo*; Fernando Chacon Gomez, *The Intended and Actual Effect of Article VIII of the Treaty of Guadalupe Hidalgo: Mexican Treaty Rights under International and Domestic*, dissertation, University of Michigan, 1977; and Armando Rendon, *Chicano Manifesto: The History and Aspirations of the Second Largest Minority in America* (New York: Collier Books, 1971).

273. Morison and Commager, *The Growth of the American Republic*, 616.

274. Gonzales, *Mexicanos*, 79.

275. John D. P. Fuller, "Slaveholder Opposed Conquest of México," in *The Mexican War: Was It Manifest Destiny?* ed. Ramon Ruiz (New York: Holt, Rinehart and Winston, 1963), 29–38.

276. Weber, *Foreigners in Their Native Land*, 135.

277. Del Castillo, *The Treaty of Guadalupe Hidalgo*, 46.

278. Samora and Simon, *A History of the Mexican American People*, 99.

279. López y Rivas, *The Chicanos*, 24.

280. López y Rivas, *The Chicanos*, 4.

281. Rendon, *Chicano Manifesto*, 71.

282. For an excellent examination on the history to the Treaty of Guadalupe Hidalgo and particularly the articles and Queretaro Protocol see Del Castillo, *The Treaty of Guadalupe Hidalgo*.

283. Del Castillo, *The Treaty of Guadalupe Hidalgo*, 189–90.

284. Del Castillo, *The Treaty of Guadalupe Hidalgo*, 190.

285. Del Castillo, *The Treaty of Guadalupe Hidalgo*, 180–81.

286. López y Rivas, *The Chicanos*, 26.

287. Acuña, *Occupied America*, 4th ed., 54.

288. Gonzales, *Mexicanos*, 79.

289. Meier and Rivera, *Mexican Americans, American Mexicans*, 67.

290. Gómez-Quiñones, *Roots of Chicano Politics*, 188.

291. See McWilliams, *North from México*, 51; Rendon, *Chicano Manifesto*, 71; and Vigil, *From Indians to Chicanos*, 161.

292. Chavez, *The Lost Land*, 41–42. From my perspective, this is a serious misrepresentation of history since it impacts many of the arguments that Chicano activists have used in the promotion of bilingual/bicultural education and Chicano Studies.

293. Meier and Rivera, *The Chicanos*, 73.

Epoch of Armed and Political Resistance (1848–1916)

2

THIS UNPRECEDENTED PERIOD of armed and political resistance commenced in 1848 with the signing of the Treaty of Guadalupe Hidalgo, and ended about 1916. These sixty-eight years gave birth to the Mexicano political experience in the United States and to the occupation of Aztlán by the United States. As a political epoch, it was characterized by significant historic events and memorable leaders, organizations, and struggles, which demonstrated that indeed Mexicanos resisted their internal colonial conditions of oppression, exploitation, and subordination. The stereotype perpetuated by some white historians that Mexicanos were submissive or obsequious is erroneous and a racist myth. On the contrary, the Mexicano resistance to their occupation came in two basic forms—armed struggle and ballot box politics—in spite of their limited population and resources. Hence, the political landscape of occupied Aztlán evolved through a myriad of brushfire conflicts between Mexicanos and whites and ultimately impacted the politics, economics, culture, language, and religion of both groups. With the occupation of Aztlán, the Mexicano was relegated to an internal colonial status, one characterized by socioeconomic oppression and exploitation, political powerlessness and subordination, and cultural subjugation.

Expansion of Manifest Destiny

The Gadsden Purchase (1853)

Manifest Destiny did not stop with the ratification of the Treaty of Guadalupe Hidalgo. The U.S. expansionist appetite again became evident in 1853 with the Gadsden Purchase. The purchase was driven by four principle historical antagonisms. First, perhaps the most important was the desire by the United States to acquire a more direct railroad route from Tejas to California. Second, from a security perspective, the United States was increasingly concerned about the volatility of the United States/México border. Third, the United States had both economic and military concerns to obtain rights of transit across the Isthmus of Tehuantepec. And fourth, the United States desired to be released from the obligations of the Treaty of Guadalupe Hidalgo's Article XI. As a result, the United States pressured México diplomatically as well as militarily into selling the land in the Mesilla Valley and south of Gila. James Gadsden was sent to México as an envoy to negotiate the purchase of this additional territory.

Again, Mexican general Santa Anna[1] was back in power in spite of defeat. México, in dire financial straits and under pressure to sell, agreed to what became known as the Gadsden Purchase for the amount of $10 million.[2] Santa Anna signed the Gadsden Treaty (Tratado de Mesilla) on December 30, 1853, and the U.S. Senate ratified it during the spring of 1854. It abrogated Article XI of the Treaty of Guadalupe Hidalgo, the article making the United States financially liable for indigenous raids on México. In addition, some 29,142,000 acres of land, which translated to some 45,000 square miles of which 35,000 were in southern Arizona and the rest in Nuevo México, were ceded to the United States.[3] México's political and military reality was such that it had little choice but to sell. Because of intense U.S. military pressure, demonstrated by the sending of 2,000 troops to Nuevo México, México acquiesced. Rejection would have likely led to another war, which México could ill afford. The United States continued imperialist adherence to Manifest Destiny was evident from the onset of United States/México negotiations. Initially, the United States unsuccessfully had sought the purchase of México's five northern states as well as Baja California. Some of México's leadership alleged that U.S. motivation was predicated on the acquisition of the port of Guaymus.[4] The Gadsden Purchase proved to be a lucrative sale for the United States as the territory was found later to contain some of the world's richest copper deposits.[5]

A Profile of a Conquered People

Mexicano's Demographic/Socioeconomic Profile

In politics, demographic numbers constitute an important variable in the equation of power and influence and provide significant insight into the socioeconomic status of a people. As a result of the ratification of the Treaty of Guadalupe Hidalgo in 1848 and the U.S. occupation, with the exception of Nuevo México, Mexicanos throughout Aztlán were relegated to a minority status in their own land. At the beginning of the nineteenth century, the population of Aztlán was a mere 25,000. However, according to Oscar Martinez, Aztlán's Mexicano population in 1850 ranged somewhere between 86,000 and 116,000. Aztlán's population based on the present states was Nuevo México, between 62,000 and 77,000; California, 9,100 to 14,300; Tejas, 13,900 to 23,200; and Arizona 1,000 to 1,600.[6] Yet some scholars, such as McWilliams, cite a lower total figure of around 75,000.[7] Due to the enforcement of the treaty's Article VIII only two thousand or so decided to return to México; consequently, no massive exodus occurred. Right after 1848, Aztlán succumbed to a demographic "whiteanization" of its territories.

Aztlán's population did not begin to appreciably increase until the 1890s when the migrant exodus from México into the United States began. The Porfiriato's rampant political repression and wretched poverty "pushed" the migration. At the other end, the United States' demand for cheap labor was a driving "pull" factor. Carey McWilliams writes, "Prior to 1900 there had been a trickle of Mexican migration to the borderlands: In 1900, Tejas had an immigration population of 71,062; Arizona, 14,172; California, 8,096; and New México, 6,649." Due to México's worsening political and economic conditions in 1910, the migrant population in the following four states increased: Arizona's increased to 29,987; California's to 33,987; Nuevo México's to 11,918; and Tejas's to 125,016.[8] According to Oscar Martinez, the Mexicano population grew to somewhere between 381,000 and 562,000. Aztlán's overall population in 1900, including whites and Mexicanos, was 5,358,000. Some 98 percent of the Mexicano population resided in Aztlán.[9] Due to the scarcity of census data, but based upon available research, the estimated Mexicano population in 1900 was around 500,000, which translated to less than 1 percent of the country's population. Moreover, one can also postulate that based on qualitative analysis available for that period, the great majority of Mexicanos were lower class, meaning that along with blacks and indigenous peoples they were poor.

Mexicanos: Relegated to an Internal Colonial Status

Joan Moore and Harry Pachon write, "the years after the treaty saw the rapid loss of most Mexican property interests in Texas and the slippage of Mexicans (as an economic group) into a segregated and despised working class."[10] As a conquered and occupied people, Mexicanos were subjected to physical attacks and violence, were segregated and impoverished, became victims of shootings and lynching, and were denigrated by a white cultural imperialism that considered them "greasers" and an inferior people.

The Mexicano masses became victims of incessant racism, poverty, and powerlessness and were relegated to a segregated existence. Politically, in the Nuevo México experience, the Mexicano elite struggled somewhat effectively against the "external administration" aspects of internal colonialism, primarily due to their majority status and political skill. In all other parts of Aztlán, this was not the case. At the local level, the Mexicano poor were required to live in barrios that were segregated from the rest of white society. Inherent to internal colonialism is the concerted effort by the colonizer to destroy or assimilate the colonized culture. This became the historical and cultural reality Mexicanos faced as their culture came under white vicious attack. In writing about the cultural impact of the conquest on Mexicanos, Carey McWilliams notes:

> Mexicans are a "conquered" people in the Southwest, a people whose culture has been under incessant attack for many years and whose character and achievements, as a people have been consistently disparaged. . . . Having been subjected, first to a brutal physical attack, and then to a long process of economic attrition, it is not surprising that so many Mexicans should show evidences of spiritual defeatism, which so often arises when a cultural minority is annexed to an alien culture and way of life. More is involved, in situations of this kind, than defeat of individual ambitions, for the victims suffer from defeat of their culture and of the society of which they are part.[11]

Hence, white authorities made a deliberate effort to destroy the Mexicano's culture. Under segregation the U.S. educational system sought to inculcate the white liberal capitalist ethos in the minds of Mexicano children, while denying them the retention of their language, culture, and heritage. Ironically, however, its effect was limited since few finished school. Their overriding economic role was nothing more than a source of cheap labor for both whites and the few Mexicano middle-class business elites. Yet because of segregation, barrios became self-contained communities. This meant that the Mexicano worker and *campesino* had little or no social and cultural interaction with whites outside their work time. Camarillo explains, "The segregation of Mexican residents in their communities reinforced the use of the Spanish language, religious practices, cultural and social activities, and family ties."[12] Thus, segregation, instead of destroying the Mexicano's culture, acted as a cultural preservative.

White adherence to ethnocentrism and racism was manifested by the practice of overt segregation, discrimination, and prejudice; cruelty and violence; and lynching of Mexicanos. According to Del Castillo and De León, "Anglos also considered the natives a decadent folk with treacherous and criminal propensities."[13] Mexicanas in some white circles were looked upon as being promiscuous and lascivious. Yet paradoxically, in spite of the prevalence of these racist attitudes, Acuña documents that some white males relied on intermarriage with Mex-icanas as a way of securing property and getting rich.[14] Horace Bell described whites who engaged in such practices as "matrimonial sharks" marrying "unso-phisticated pastoral provincials." To the parents it was a form of protection; to the daughter it was a way to acquire prestige by marrying into the dominant race.[15] In the end, this practice proved to be disastrous: many land grants were lost to whites through the vehicle of intermarriage.

The effects of internal colonialism also became evident economically vis-à-vis the pervasiveness of poverty and myriad of social problems that permeated the barrios and *colonias* of Aztlán. From a class perspective, it was also evident that most Mexicanos were relegated to an exploited working-class status. There was, however, an emergent bourgeoisie that benefited economically from the occupa-tion, and these individuals were manipulated politically to maintain control over the impoverished masses. Internal colonialism was also effective in exploiting Mexicano labor for the economic development of the region's substructure. In the areas of agribusiness, mining, railroad construction, and ranching, there was a gradual but increasing demand for Mexicano labor and expertise. Mario Barrera explains that overall under the new economic order, "the fortunes of Chicanos of all classes" relatively declined.[16]

In the agribusiness sector, Mexicano labor proved indispensable to the har-vesting of cotton in Tejas and Arizona and vegetables of all sorts, including grapes, in California. In mining Mexicano labor became particularly important in Arizona and Colorado. With the passage of the Chinese Exclusion Act in 1882, the demand increased dramatically for Mexicano labor in laying rail lines. Since 1880, Mexicanos made up 70 percent of the section crews and 90 percent of the extra gangs on the principal railroad lines.[17] Mexicano labor also played a signifi-cant role in the development of cattle and sheep herding in Tejas and Nuevo México. Hence, during this epoch, along with other oppressed ethnic groups, Mexicanos were the "beasts of burden" that contributed significantly to the capi-talist development of occupied Aztlán. Mexicanos were devalued as a people but welcomed for their cheap labor. For several decades Mexicanos were customarily paid about half of what whites were paid for doing the same job.[18] Relations between whites and Mexicanos were predicated on a "conqueror verses con-quered" relationship.

The Rise of an Epoch of Resistance

The Politics of Armed Resistance

Few of the armed struggles for resistance that emerged between 1847 and 1916 became viable revolutionary social movements. However, three insurgencies of significant political historical value were the Cortina rebellion, the Magónista Mexican Liberal Party, and the separatist El Plan de San Diego. The Cortina rebellion and the separatist struggle of the Plan of San Diego were armed insurgencies that for various reasons failed to become full-fledged insurgent or revolutionary movements. Only the Magónistas blossomed to become an integral part of a revolutionary social movement—México's Revolution of 1910. The historical significance of these three insurgencies among other events is that they demonstrate that some Mexicanos were not passive or obsequious, but rather resisted the occupation of their territories through armed struggle. The political struggles of resistance and change dealt with below illustrate the preceding argument.

Filibustering Expeditions of the 1850s

After the United States war against México, the spirit of Manifest Destiny expansionism continued via several filibustering expeditions. While most did not have the official blessing of the U.S. government, most were given covert support or were tolerated. In 1848 and again in 1849, former Spanish officer Narciso López, supported by publisher William O'Sullivan, led a small invading force, mostly of mercenaries from the United States, into Cuba. It proved to be a military disaster, particularly since López was captured and executed by Spanish forces.[19]

William Walker led a filibustering expedition from California in 1853. With the Gadsden Purchase, Walker, a southerner who was a doctor, journalist, and lawyer, felt that México was weak and vulnerable. Walker's plan was to create an independent empire, a third republic between México and the United States with himself as the founder and chief of state. He invaded Baja California for the purpose of using it as a base of operations for invading Sonora. His small army of mercenaries occupied La Paz for a few days, but was chased out by Mexican forces. Next his forces momentarily occupied Ensenada then proceeded to invade Sonora in order to incorporate it into his promulgated new Republic of Lower California. Without supplies and plagued by desertion, his small force was beaten back by Mexican forces. He retreated north toward Tijuana, crossed the U.S. border, and surrendered to U.S. army officials. Thomas Torrans explains what happened when Walker went to trial: "when one considers the cavalier attitude long espoused by the United States toward México, he was acquitted."[20]

The next expedition into México occurred in 1857, this time led by Henry Alexander Crabb, who like Walker was from Tennessee. A year before, motivated by internal rivalries and divisions among the Mexicano elite in Sonora, Crabb formed the Arizona Colonization Company and enlisted about one hundred men with the objective of annexing Sonora. His small army sailed from San Francisco to San Pedro, California, where they then marched into Arizona. Their ethnocentric attitude was that Sonora belonged to them or the United States. Crabb was cognizant of the mineral riches of Sonora and an integral part of his imperialistic design was the securing of Guaymus, one of México's finest ports on the Pacific Coast. Crabb's invasion of Sonora proved to be a military disaster. The expedition met strong resistance and surrendered to Mexican forces. As a warning to others, Mexican commander Hilario Gabilondo had fifty-eight of Crabb's followers executed, and Crabb himself was shot and decapitated and his head was preserved in alcohol. According to Thomas Torrans, "the grim trophy [was] exhibited for some time as a symbolic warning of the fate any would-be insurrectionists might expect."[21] Several U.S. jingoistic newspapers described the executions as "brutal," called for "retributions," and equated them to another "Alamo."[22]

Prior to the U.S. Civil War, expansionist politicians and newspapers in Washington, D.C., were active in proposing that México be made a protectorate of the United States. Senator Sam Houston from Tejas introduced such a resolution and President Buchanan's administration contemplated orchestrating a series of events that would give the United States control of Sonora. In 1859 President Buchanan went so far as to send a U.S. warship to Guaymas, Sonora, to precipitate a war with México. The provocation was to be similar to the earlier events in Tejas and California. As in California, the United States sent in Charles P. Stone to survey Sonora on behalf of a group of capitalist interests, but Sonoran governor Ignacio Pesqueria ordered Stone to leave. Stone recommended annexation to the Buchanan administration. Captain William Porter of the *St. Mary*, already in Mexican waters off the port of Guaymus, protested the expulsion of Stone to where he threatened to bombard it. Some U.S. forces from Fort Buchanan concomitantly entered Sonora, further exacerbating the explosive situation.[23]

Governor Pesqueria retaliated with a threat of his own: if the attack occurred, U.S. economic interests throughout Sonora would be in jeopardy. The U.S. warship left Guaymas, but the incident did not end there. In November 1859, President Buchanan, irate over the expulsion of Stone and the forced departure of the U.S. warship, requested approval from the U.S. Congress for the occupation of Sonora as well as Chihuahua, México. As Rodolfo Acuña notes, "sectional differences and the pending Civil War prevented Buchanan from waging yet another unjust war."[24] The above events clearly indicate that the expansionist spirit of Manifest Destiny continued after the U.S. war against México. However, the various filibustering expeditions into México were unsuccessful, due in great part to México's effective military and political resistance and U.S. bad timing. Because of its preoccupation with the pending Civil War, the United States did not follow through with its imperialist design to swallow up more of México's territory; otherwise, perhaps México today would have been a much smaller country. The expeditions, however, did engender a more volatile relationship between the conqueror whites and conquered Mexicanos, especially all along the precarious U.S./México border.

Guerrilleros *or* Bandidos?

From the early 1850s to the 1870s, from California to Tejas, a rebellious spirit of resistance existed among some Mexicanos in response to the U.S. occupation of Aztlán. Several were categorized as advocate transformers, not because they were ideologues for social change, but because they resisted the occupation with violence and did not recognize the governing white colonial authorities. These social bandits, as some scholars have described them, resisted the occupation by resorting to armed struggle. The term *social bandit* is borrowed from Eric J. Hobsbawm, who in his study of peasant movements regarded social banditry as a primitive form of social protest. He defines it as "a universal and virtually unchanging phenomenon, is little more than endemic peasant protest against oppression and poverty: a cry for vengeance on the rich and the oppressors, a vague dream of some curb upon them, a righting of individual wrongs."[25] To many whites of the time, these bandits were categorized as ruthless and murderous outlaws. Yet as Hobsbawn explains, many Mexicanos considered them "as heroes, as champions, avengers, fighters for justice, perhaps even leaders for liberation, and in any case men admired, helped, and supported."[26] In similar analysis, Eric Wolf argues that the bandit in addition to being a popular hero is also a primitive revolutionary, a political leader who articulates the aspirations of the peasantry.[27] Yet at no time did these social bandits evolve into viable revolutionary or insurgent social movements. They lacked most of the ingredients that make up a social movement. Suffice it to say that their armed struggles were not collective actions oriented toward social change or liberation, but in fact were individual armed actions that sought material rewards and vengeance, and were largely retaliatory in nature.

Some Mexicano historians in the United States agree with Hobsbawn's interpretation of social banditry. They explain that while some Mexicanos acquiesced to their occupied status and sought to accommodate the new U.S. social order; others categorically refused to do so. Their cardinal thesis is that some Mexicanos resisted their occupation and internal colonized status with counterviolence, in short, armed resistance. Alfredo Mirandé writes, "The truth, however, is that the history of the Mexican and Chicano people is replete with examples of active resistance to economic, political, and legal oppression."[28] Julian Samora and Patricia Vandel Simon note, "Both Mexicans and Anglos turned to violence to vent their anger—violence directed against their own groups as well as against each other." Two other Chicano historians concur. Richard Griswold Del Castillo and Arnoldo De León write, "While some native residents accepted American rule, other segments of the population spurned it."[29] Rosenbaum further agues, "The fact that Mexicanos violently resisted Anglo-American domination may come as a surprise. Resistance does not fit the myth of the speedy conquest; neither does it square with stereotype of neither cowardly and inferior 'meskins' nor the comforting belief in the benevolence and general attractiveness of the American way of life."[30]

During the next thirty years, the politics of armed resistance found its impetus in California, picked up momentum in Tejas, and continued to Nuevo México. Why? The answer in great part lies in the understanding that it was a direct response to the white brutality, violence, and racism directed at Mexicanos. Whites and Mexicano *ricos* and *politicos* saw those who resorted to violence as bandits who needed to be dealt with harshly. Some Mexicanos, however, saw them as *guerrilleros* (warriors) determined to resist the white occupation of their lands. Other Mexicanos, especially the poor at times, accepted them as heroes, like Robin Hoods, often abetting and aiding their activities.[31]

The Politics of Armed Resistance in California

California produced a major share of these Mexicano *guerrilleros*. Carey McWilliams writes that many of them "contained a hundred or more men and were well organized for guerrilla fighting." He also identifies those he considered to be the most important, which includes Joaquin Murrieta, Tiburcio Vasques, Louis Bulvia, Antonio Moreno, Procopio, Soto, Manuel Garcia, Juan Flores, Pancho Daniel, and many others.[32] According to Gómez-Quiñones, "During the 1870s, a few relatives of elite families such as the Lugos, Carrillos, Sepúlvedas, Castros, and Vallejos also took to banditry."[33] They were the product of a climate of change during and after the gold rush of 1849.[34] A heavy influx of white miners into California turned Mexicanos not only into a minority, but into targets of indiscriminate violence. As a result of this pervasive violence and racism and an economic depression that reached its apogee by the mid-1850s,[35] growing Mexicano frustration turned into outright anger and aggression. López y Rivas adds, "Fired with the spirit of revenge and the thirst for justice, Mexican miners and displaced property owners rose-up."[36] Some Mexicanos took up arms in retaliation and their resistance took on violent proportions. Of the several alleged *guerrilleros* that emerged during these years, Murrieta, Vasques, and Flores became

California's most legendary. All three were historical participants in what some historians describing the 1850s in California labeled as the "race wars."[37]

Of the three, Joaquin Murrieta became the most notorious during his own lifetime. His legendary exploits, however, were imbued with controversy. He is perhaps the least understood of all the California *guerrilleros*. His insurgency lasted a mere two years (1851–1853). Much has been written on Murrieta;[38] however, much is still unknown about who he really was and numerous other aspects of his life and death. Nevertheless, it is important to note that he was a product of an intolerable situation in which violence became his only recourse. Some scholars venture to say that Murrieta was more a myth than reality. Leonard Pitt writes, "Joaquin Murrieta became California's foremost folk legend; the truth may be doubtful but the myth is real."[39] Murrieta was born in Sonora, México, and in 1850 at the age of eighteen he migrated to northern California, where he became a miner in search of gold. For the next two years, according to John Rolling Ridge, a half Cherokee who called himself Yellow Bird, Murrieta suffered a number of denigrating experiences at the hands of white miners, which caused him to take up arms against whites. He was forced to move from his mining claim by whites on at least two occasions and was severely beaten up by whites; his girlfriend was raped and murdered in his presence; and finally his half brother was lynched by whites.[40] What happened to Murrieta was not unique. Violence was persistently directed at Mexicanos and other Latinos by white miners who were jealous of "foreign" miners getting so-called American gold. Perceived as competitors, up to the mid-1850s, notes Rosenbaum, "lynch and mob justice, directed particularly at Latin Americans—greasers—and Orientals, characterized the California camps."[41]

For the next two years (1851–1853), Murrieta and his trusted lieutenant Three-Finger Jack and their band of *guerrilleros* terrorized the countrysides of central and northern California, particularly Calaveras County. Cattle rustling and horse stealing, robbery, and killing (according to some accounts, some twenty-four to twenty-nine were killed by his band) were exploits that turned him into notorious and legendary figure. As a social bandit, Murrieta did not see his armed struggle as a viable social movement. While he and his small band of followers did have leadership skills, they had little or no organization beyond the immediate band, and possessed no ideology other than motives of vengeance, anger, and material reward. While adulated by some Mexicanos, Murrieta never came close to developing a power capability that threatened physically the survival of the occupying white social order.

For months Murrieta and his band appeared to be everywhere and yet were nowhere to be found. His stature grew to where whites feared him and his "Robin

Hood" bandit image was catapulted nationally by a profiteering press. To some Mexicanos his image was romanticized; he was a hero, a legend, a "Robin Hood" who sought vengeance for white atrocities perpetrated against Mexicanos, but especially against him. Others saw it as a war on terror that he launched against the white oppressors. Del Castillo and De León note that Murrieta and his band "audaciously avenged injustices perpetrated on the Spanish-speaking with selective strikes on Anglo ranches, settlements, and other symbols of white domination." And they further argue, "poor folks vicariously identified with his war of reprisal."[42]

The state's political climate became increasingly polarized because of the so-called Joaquin scare. As a result, some whites retaliated by violently attacking innocent Mexicanos to where their hatred reached an all-time high. Also, a special ranger force led by Captain Harry Love was created by the California state legislature for the capture of Murrieta. A $1,000 bounty was offered for his apprehension, "dead or live." What actually happened afterward is the subject of scholarly debate and controversy. Some scholars (e.g., Del Castillo and De León) postulate that Murrieta was indeed killed in an ambush in 1853 by Captain Love and his Rangers.[43] Furthermore, Captain Love ordered the decapitation of Murrieta and had Three-Finger Jack's hand severed, and both the head and hand were pickled in whisky. This account persisted and for years both Murrieta's head and Three-Finger Jack's hand were displayed in numerous bars and fairs throughout California until the San Francisco earthquake of 1906, when both were destroyed.[44]

Remi Nadea is one among several who disputes this conclusion to the Murrieta saga. He argues, "From the record, Harry Love's claim is very difficult to credit, and it is more likely that he brought back the head of another person."[45] Likewise, David Weber writes, "There were widespread rumors that the rangers had killed an innocent Mexican in order to collect the reward."[46] Another version is that Murrieta left California in 1853 and settled in Sonora, México, and led a prosperous life.[47] Still others would argue that Murrieta was a myth and in reality there were several so-called bandits with the same surname of Murrieta. Nevertheless, after his alleged death, the legend of Murrieta grew dramatically until it became a romanticized myth that grew bolder with each newspaper or book account.[48] Murrieta's mythology has been one of historical debate and speculation. For many Mexicanos, Murrieta became a symbol of the armed resistance that occurred against the U.S. occupation of California and Aztlán.

The epoch's second most notorious and popular symbol of armed resistance in California was Tiburcio Vásquez. Born in Monterey, California, on August 11, 1835, he came from a lower middle-class background, had an above average education for the time, and never married.[49] Vásquez's entry into the world of social banditry occurred under violent circumstances. In 1851, while attending a dance, he and two others got into an altercation over a white man dancing and courting a Mexicana. Vásquez had a reputation for being a lady's man and had a pronounced hatred for whites, and during the scuffle, pistols were drawn and shots fired by both parties. As a result of the gun battle, Monterey's Constable Hardmount was shot and killed, allegedly by Vásquez; two of his friends were wounded as well. Vásquez and a friend, Anastasio Garcia, fled Monterey pursued by white vigilantes, who had just lynched Vásquez's other wounded friend José Higuera.[50]

At the young age of sixteen, Vásquez's defiant social banditry career had begun. From 1851 to 1857, he spent most of his time robbing stagecoaches and stealing cattle. In 1857, he was captured and sent to San Quentin prison, where with the exception of 1859, when he briefly escaped, he remained until his release in 1863. Vásquez returned to a life of obscure banditry, and in 1867 he was again captured and sent to the penitentiary for three years (1867–1870). In 1873 he gained statewide notoriety for the first time with the robbery and murders at Tres Pinos. A reward of $3,000 was placed on his head and a manhunt for his capture was initiated.[51] In 1874 Vásquez was captured, tried, and convicted, and was hung on March 19, 1876.[52]

Pedro Castillo and Albert Camarillo describe his legacy as that of "a symbol to the Chicano community as someone who resisted the conquest and who created fear in the Anglos because of his revolutionary potential." These two scholars go so far as to describe him as a "quasi-bandit revolutionary."[53] Yet there is no evidence as with Murrieta that Vásquez ever came close to developing an insurgent movement. One cardinal reason was that he had no revolutionary ideology. Vásquez's hatred for what he described as the "Yankee invaders of California" is what motivated his banditry. Yet he stated, "Given $60,000 I would be able to recruit enough arms and men to revolutionize Southern California."[54] Another comment he made illustrates his defiance toward whites: "A spirit of hatred and revenge took possession of me. I had numerous fights in defense of what I believed to be my rights and those of my countrymen. I believed that we were unjustly and wrongfully deprived of the social rights which belonged to us."[55] Some Mexicanos in California, especially the poor, idealized him and supported him as well. Like Murrieta, he too enjoyed great notoriety and subsequently gained legendary status, becoming a symbol of Mexicano resistance to Aztlán's occupation. In both cases, their actions were responses to individual or collective acts of violence against them as Mexicanos.[56]

The brazen Juan Flores was another alleged social *bandido* who garnered widespread notoriety, especially in southern California. While less famous than those of Murrieta and Vásquez, Flores's armed resistance activities were described by some writers as the "Juan Flores Revolution." Leader of a much bigger band of followers, he demonstrated potential for creating an insurgent social movement. Flores's short-lived outlaw career began at the age of twenty-one when he escaped from San Quentin, where he was serving a sentence for horse stealing.[57] He returned to the San Juan Capistrano area where, with the assistance of his lieutenant, Pancho Daniel, in the words of Pitt, he "assembled the largest bandit aggregation ever seen in California." Some fifty men came from San Luis Obispo to join his ring, which operated out of the San Juan Capistrano area.[58] When Los Angeles sheriff James Barton went into the area to investigate the Flores Ring, he was killed. As a result of the incident, rumors were rampant that Flores and his band intended to kill whites.[59]

When the news reached Los Angeles, the white political elites assumed that a full-fledged political rebellion had started.[60] Vigilante committees were formed and many whites flooded into Los Angeles seeking protection. This led to a split along class lines among Mexicanos: the few buffer *ricos* (rich) backed the white, while the poor majority supported Flores. The *ricos*, led by Andres Pico, joined in with the white El Monte Gang (a vigilante group) in the pursuit of Flores and his ring, and martial law was declared in Los Angeles. Nine of Flores's men were captured and hung; the El Monte Gang and Pico hung two.[61] With the exception of one Mexicano, Flores and his band were captured. Del Castillo and De León explain, "Whites responded to the 'Flores Wars' with ruthlessness. They rounded up suspects and summarily hanged many of them, including Flores,[62] who was hung on February 14, 1857.

Tomás Sanchez and Andres Pico were two of the prominent *rico* Mexicanos who participated in the vigilante actions against Flores and his men. According to Pitt, both of these men "won the gringos' everlasting gratitude," and were "among the few [Mexicanos] ever to reach positions of armed power in gringo government, Sanchez became sheriff, while Pico assured himself a brigadiership in the California militia and election as state assemblyman."[63]

The Decline of Armed Struggle in California

Violence in the form of lynching and murders of Mexicanos by whites and Mexicano *rico* vigilantes continued for years, and banditry was not sufficiently neutralized in California until the 1880s. The decline of Mexicano armed resistance to the occupation can be ascribed to the dramatic increase in the white population concomitant with the major decrease of the Mexicano population, the growth of repressive law enforcement agencies, and the expansion of written and telegraphic communication. Robert Rosenbaum notes, "Violent resistance in California never expanded beyond basic outrage."[64] This simply meant that the armed resistance to the occupation in California ended before ever developing into a viable insurgent movement.

The Armed Struggle in Tejas

Social banditry or *guerrillismo* in Tejas did not surface until the latter part of the 1850s. It was rooted in the dramatic political, economic, social, and demographic changes that occurred after 1836. The overwhelming majority of Mexicanos politically lived in a state of siege. From 1836 to the late 1850s, Mexicanos in Tejas suffered the most severe violence of any in the former Mexicano territories.[65] With Mexicanos relegated to a powerless minority, whites consolidated their power and landholdings. Walter Prescott Webb writes that after 1848, "the old landholding families found their titles in jeopardy and if they did not lose in the courts they lost to their American lawyers."[66] Through the use of adverse court rulings, chicanery, and exorbitant legal fees, Mexicanos lost their landholdings. Further exacerbating the conflict was the role of the Texas Rangers in enforcement of the law. Formed in 1836, they served much like a Gestapo police force for the white business and political elites of Tejas. Many times they acted as prosecutor, judge, jury, and executioner in their treatment of Mexicanos. In several towns of central Tejas, Mexicanos were banished by the Rangers on grounds that they had assisted black slaves in their escape into México.[67] For decades the Rangers were notorious if not infamous for their violence and blatant racism directed at Mexicanos.[68]

THE CART WAR OF 1857   The Rangers' Gestapo tactics became evident during the "Cart War" of 1857. This conflict developed between Mexicano and white teamsters who sought to drive the Mexicanos out of business by force. For years, Mexicanos had profited from lucrative overland trade between San Antonio and the Gulf area. However, because Mexicano teamsters charged less than their white competitors, they became the focus of the latter's retribution.[69] For some six months, the conflict escalated and so did the killings on both sides. In what became known as the Cart War, numerous *arrieros* (muleteers) lost their lives until the Mexican government, the U.S. secretary of state, and the Texas Rangers interceded to restore order.[70] By 1859, resentment was running high on both sides. "Here indeed," wrote Webb, "was rich soil in which to plant the seed of revolution and race war."[71] Thus, by 1859, the stage was set in Tejas for the rise of a Mexicano *guerrillero* insurgency that lasted several years.

THE CORTINA INSURGENCIES   The Cart War and other conflicts fostered a climate of change that was conducive to the rise of Juan Nepomuceno (Cheno) Cortina,[72] who embodied the spirit of an advocate transformer. He was born in Camargo, Tamaulipas, on May 16, 1824, to an affluent family that owned over one thousand acres of land and livestock. His father died when he was young. Cortina was raised by his mother, Estefana Cavazos, described by Larralde and Jacobo as "a strong and fearless woman who possessed a keen interest and great acumen in business and politics."[73] Although provided with numerous opportunities to get an education, Cortina was never in school very long because of his bad temper and a tendency to get in fights; he was often expelled from school.[74] Throughout much of his life, Cortina displayed exceptional military and political leadership qualities that were instinctive rather than learned.[75] In describing Cortina's flair for leadership, Walter Prescott Webb wrote, "the disposition of a gambler, an eye for the main chance, and a keen intuitive insight into the character of the Mexicans, made him a man of destiny."[76] The Red Robber of the Rio Grande became the most infamous of all the *guerrilleros* or social *bandidos* that pervaded the historical landscape of this epoch of resistance. Like Murrieta, he too became a symbol of Mexicano resistance to the occupation with a reputation for heroic leadership during a time of "racism, propaganda, and journalistic excess."[77]

Cortina's notorious career as a *guerrillero* began on July 13, 1859, as a result of an armed confrontation with Brownsville city marshal Bob Shears. Shears precipitated the incident over the pistol-whipping of a Cortina former ranch hand. Cortina interfered and a fight ensued. He fired a warning shot in the air, demanding that Shears release the ranch hand. When Shears refused, Cortina shot him, took the ranch hand, and rode out of town to his mother's Rancho El Carmen, located west of Brownsville.[78] Although white authorities filed charges of attempted murder, according to Goldfinch, "no one seemed to have the courage to arrest him."[79] This incident precipitated the "Cortina Insurgency," which lasted a mere two years (1859–1860), but Cortina's political career as an adversarial "political gadfly" to the United States did not end until sixteen years later. In comparison to the armed struggles of Murrieta, Vásquez, and Flores in California, the Cortina insurgency possessed some of the requisite ingredients for a full-fledged insurgent social movement. Larralde and Jacobo describe it as such:

> Cortina's struggle was more than just a reactionary act. It was part of a larger movement seeking justice for those Mexicanos in the lower strata of the socio-economic lower order. . . . Juan Cheno Cortina was a liberator, not a thief or an assassin; rather, [he] represented a collective ideology that fought against injustice. . . . He believed that justice, civil rights, and

economic power for the Mexican people could only be achieved through insurrection.[80]

Enraged by the incident, whites initiated a reign of terror against so-called greasers. Cortina responded by forming an insurgent army of one hundred supporters. On September 28, 1859, Cortina's forces raided Brownsville with shouts of *"Viva Cortina! Mueran Los Gringos!"* (Long Live Cortina! Death to the Gringos [racist whites])! They occupied the town, freed the prisoners, killed three whites accused of mistreating Mexicanos, and raised the Mexican flag.[81] Cortina was persuaded to leave Brownsville by Mexican political and military authorities that had crossed from Matamoros to speak with him.[82] "Within a month," writes Montejano, "Cortina had organized an irregular force of five to six hundred men."[83]

Shortly thereafter, he issued two major proclamations from Rancho Del Carmen, which justified the reasons for his fighting. For too long, Cheno proclaimed, "Whites had been despoiling Mexicanos of their land and prosecuting and robbing them for no other crime . . . than that of being of Mexican origin."[84] Neither proclamation, however, offered a clear ideological rationale. On the contrary, they were primarily grievances and did not delineate clear-cut goals such as an alternative to the white occupation of Tejas or to the Mexicanos' treacherous and oppressive internal colonial status. Yet, according to Gómez-Quiñones, disputed by some historians, Cortinas allegedly "proposed rejoining the Texas side with México"[85] during the course of his military campaign.

On October 24, Cortina's forces, using conventional military strategy and tactics, defeated the Brownsville militia and a party of Texas Rangers.[86] In early November, white authorities apprehended a friend of his, Tomas Cabrera, who had participated on the raid on Brownsville. Even though Cortina threatened serious consequences if Cabrera was not released, on November 10, 1859, Cabrera was taken out of jail and hung by what Goldman describes as "an unknown and lawless mob."[87] Cortina retaliated by ambushing a party of Rangers; three were killed and one captured. A few days later, Cortina defeated another Ranger force that had retreated to Brownsville.[88]

In their pursuit of Cortina, the Texas Rangers were reinforced by U.S. Army troops under the command of Major S. P. Heintzelman. By this time, as Montejano reports, "There remained no property belonging to [whites] that had not been destroyed."[89] Cortina's small band was outgunned and outmanned. After an unsuccessful clash with U.S. troops and Rangers in January 1860, he strategically retreated to México where he continued to make sporadic guerrilla attacks across the border.[90] Unsuccessful, he was forced to flee the border area and took refuge in the Burgos Mountains. By 1861 Texas was engaged in the Civil War; Cortina reinvaded Tejas on May 23 but once again was driven out by confederate troops. Many lives were lost, especially noncombatant Mexicanos, who got caught up in the crossfire during the insurrection. According to Gonzales, "Border lynching and other atrocities became commonplace throughout the 1860s."[91]

By 1862 Cortina adopted a Machiavellian political strategy and entered into a number of transitory alliances. At the beginning of the U.S. Civil War, he collaborated with the North and South by signing a treaty that allowed both sides to move supplies from México into South Texas and was able to secure concessions from both.[92] This gave him and his forces access to badly needed resources and additional manpower. For a short period of time, out of economic expediency, Cortina supported the Confederates in Tejas and became temporarily an ally. In return, Confederate officials abolished the Committee of Safety, which had the responsibility in Nueces County to combat "predatory bands of Cortina Mexicans" and Indians.[93] Supposedly, he was also offered the rank of general in the Confederate Army and was given 400 bales of cotton. By 1864, Cortina and his forces shifted their military support to the Union forces in exchange for providing his troops with arms and supplies in South Tejas. Concurrently, however, Cortina issued orders to his men that Confederate forces under the command of Mexicanos should not be attacked, such as those under the command of Colonel Santos Benavides.[94]

During this same time, for reasons again of political convenience, Cortina sided with the French intervention of México (1862–1867). Emperor Maximilian offered him a knighthood, but Cortina turned it down; instead he accepted the title of honorable officer in Maximilian's army. Yet in 1863, Cortina reversed himself again; this time he supported President Benito Juarez by allowing arms and supplies to reach Juarez's Liberal Army. For his support and effort, he was granted the rank of lieutenant colonel.[95] Later that year, he proclaimed himself governor and military commander of the state of Tamaulipas. His forces proved to be vital to Juarez's defeat of the French and conservative armies that supported Maximilian in the north of México. Cortina was rewarded again by being promoted to brigadier general in the Mexican Army and in 1870 became governor of the Mexican state of Tamaulipas.

Until 1876, Cortina continued to be a persistent thorn in the side of whites in South Tejas. Regardless of whatever rank and position of power he held in México he continued to support cattle rustling forays into South Tejas. Historians debate the impact of his efforts; nevertheless, for many Mexicanos in both South Tejas and northern México, Cortina was a folk hero, a legend who left his imprint on history as one who dared resist the white injustices of the occupation. Because of his numerous exploits, he has been immortalized in a number of *corridos* (folk ballads). Literally, for nearly twenty years, he dominated the history of the Tejas/México border. In 1875, due to U.S. pressure on México, Cortina was briefly arrested on trumped-up charges of cattle rustling by Mexican government officials. He was again arrested in Matamoros and turned over to the new Díaz regime. Cortina was brought to México City, where he remained under house arrest until 1890; after two years of freedom, he passed away in 1892.[96]

Thus, of all the *guerrilleros* who resisted the occupation of Aztlán through armed struggle, Cortina came close to building a viable insurgent social movement. Yet in the end, his struggle left a historical legacy of a leader who led an insurgency against the U.S. occupation in the defense of his people that will not be forgotten.

THE SALT WAR OF 1877   While *guerrillero* armed struggles ended by the 1870s, numerous other incidents occurred that could also be characterized as armed resistance. One such incident was the Salt War of 1877 that occurred near El Paso, Tejas. Violent resistance to white hegemony, persecution, and repression did not depend solely upon charismatic personalities such as Cortina. During the course of this conflict, the entire Mexicano community took action when its collective interests were threatened. The core issue behind the Salt War of 1877 was the free access by Mexicanos to the Guadalupe salt lakes, which were located some one hundred miles east of El Paso, Tejas. Since the Spanish colonization, the salt lakes had been available for public use and were considered community property.

However, with the arrival of more white settlers to the area, the use of the salt beds became contentious and violent. For ten years, white business interests first headed by Samuel Maverick in 1866 and then Charles H. Howard in 1877 sought to monopolize the salt deposits by charging a fee for their use.[97] When Howard did this, the reaction of the Mexicano community for the next three months was one of open defiance. According to Weber, Howard had "aroused Mexicans on both sides of the border into a well organized revolt. . . . The war over the salt turned into a race war with rumors spreading that all gringos would die."[98] The conflict intensified until Howard was captured and detained by a small Mexicano armed band led by Chico Barela.[99] After three days, he was forced to sign an agreement renouncing his claim to the salt beds.

Angered over his humiliation, Howard killed a Mexicano, Don Luis Cardis, who was his strong political opponent on the issue. "In retaliation," according to Meier and Rivera, "a mob of [Mexicanos] executed Howard, killed other Anglos, and inflicted considerable property damage in El Paso,"[100] Their collective actions also sought to regain public use of the salt beds. The Salt War came to an end with the brutal intervention of the Texas Rangers, who in the words of De León, "committed wanton outrages" against Mexicanos.[101] In the end, however, the salt beds were privatized.

Armed Resistance in Nuevo México: The Lincoln County Wars (1876–1879)

Nuevo México was not exempt from the violence of armed resistance. Several incidents occurred that were illustrative of this. One such incident was the Lincoln County Wars, which occurred during the early 1870s. It was an armed conflict between Mexicanos and newly settled white settlers from Tejas that reached a violent stage to where it became commonplace. Beyond the white racial hatred factor toward Mexicanos, economic competition between cattlemen and sheepherders also fueled the growing conflict. By 1874 the situation deteriorated to where *The Sante Fe New Mexican* in an article wrote that Lincoln County had exploded into "an unfortunate war between the Texans and Mexicans."[102]

Lincoln County's political climate was further exacerbated in 1876 by a major political and economic struggle for control involving two rival white cattle barons, Republican Laurance Gustave Murphy and Democrat John P. Chisum. Mexicanos became caught up in the strife, since they comprised a great number of the *vaqueros* (ranch hands). During the course of the three-year conflict, Mexicanos sided with Chisum and several became casualties of the range war. Both sides hired gunslingers and known outlaws such as Billy the Kid, among others. After much bloodshed and pressure, President Rutherford B. Hayes appointed Republican general Lew Wallace as territorial governor with the directive to bring an end to the range war. Wallace ordered the formation of a militia led by Mexicano Juan Patrón and peace was finally restored in 1879.[103]

Las Gorras Blancas (The White Caps)

Armed resistance by Mexicanos continued well into the 1880s, this time in Nuevo México with the emergence of Las Gorras Blancas.[104] As advocate transformers, driven by the discontent over land grabbers who took their lands, Juan José Herrera and his younger brothers, Pablo and Nicanor, with support from numerous other poor people from San Miguel County, formed Las Gorras Blancas in April 1889. His followers called Herrera "El Capitán" (The Captain), as he had been commissioned as a captain with the union forces during the Civil War.[105] "On the night of April 26, 1889," Rosenbaum writes, "masked and armed horsemen rode toward a ranch near the village of San Geronimo in San Miguel County, New México territory." The ranch, owned by two whites, became the target of this group of hooded, night-riding Mexicano gunmen, who leveled the ranch's entire wire fence.[106]

This type of clandestine guerrilla action was typical of the Las Gorras Blancas, who for years to come carried out similar raids in Mora, Sante Fe, and San Miguel counties. They destroyed wire fences and railroad ties, severed telegraph lines, burned ranches to the ground, and relied on the use of armed intimidation in their struggle against mostly white "land grabbers."[107] According to Alfredo Mirandé, "Most of their attacks were directed against large landholders who had appropriated communal lands."[108] Railroads and ranchers in particular suffered severely from their vigilante attacks. In 1889, the Atchison, Topeka, and Santa Fe Railroad had some nine thousand ties cut in half in an attack involving some three hundred men. A year later, nine miles of barbed wire fence were destroyed in a single night.[109] Some whites perceived these actions as a prelude to a war of independence.

Like the earlier armed struggles, Las Gorras Blancas were also a product of a climate of change laden with discontent. Del Castillo and De León describe those who were part of Las Gorras Blancas "as poor people [who] sought to retain the rights to their common lands from new claimants, the Las Vegas Land Company."[110] Gómez-Quiñones elucidates on the conditions that lead to their formation.

> By the mid-1880s economic conditions for the Mexicano in Nuevo México had deteriorated considerably. Furthermore, politically targeted violence was becoming a practice on many sides. Through a variety of legal and illegal means, Mexicans increasingly were losing their communal and private lands; and large land companies, cattlemen, and the railroads were stepping up their demands for access to both land and water rights held by Mexicans.[111]

By 1890, the ranks of Las Gorras Blancas had reached some fifteen hundred men. They were comprised of poor landholders, railroad and lumber workers, and local political leaders. While they relied on armed self-defense methods, they also had linkages to the Knights of Labor, and politically to El Partido del Pueblo Unido (The United People's Party).[112]

Between the years 1889 and 1891, Las Gorras Blancas were effective in slowing down the land grabbing of Mexicano land. Their relentless attacks were directed at both whites and *rico* Nuevo Mexicanos who had engaged in land grabbing schemes. Not equipped with an explicit ideology, Las Gorras Blancas formed a clandestine armed protest movement that sought retribution against usurper land grabbers. Early in March 1890, three hundred Gorras Blancas entered Las Vegas and posted copies, in leaflet form, of their "Platform and Principles." Written in Spanish and quite lengthy, it was signed, "The White Gaps, 1,500 Strong and Growing Daily." The following are four of its salient points:

- Our purpose will be to protect the rights of all people in general, and especially the rights of the poor people.
- We want the Las Vegas Land Grant to be adjudicated in favor of all those it concerns, and we maintain that it belongs to all the people who reside within its boundaries.
- We want no more land thieves, or any obstructions that might want to interfere. WE ARE WATCHING YOU.
- The people are now victims of partisan politics, and it would be best if politicians quietly maintain their peace; the people have been persecuted and mistreated in one thousand ways to satisfy the whims of politicians. They persist that their acts are customary. RETRIBUTION will be our reward.[113]

They became such a threat that Governor L. Bradford Prince of Nuevo México issued a proclamation calling on Las Gorras Blancas to disband and threatened to call out the militia and, if necessary, federal troops.[114] White paranoia was such that in 1889 twenty-six indictments were made against forty-seven persons suspected of being members of the group. In 1890, because of lack of evidence, charges against the forty-seven were dismissed.[115] According to Arellano, "By July 1890, according to a letter submitted to the Secretary of the Interior, some twenty-five acts of violence had been committed, hundreds of miles of fences cut, homes and haystacks sacked and burned, and agricultural implements broken and destroyed. Furthermore, railroad bridges and ties contracted for the railroad had been burned and destroyed. The letter also charged that people had been shot to death and many more had been wounded."[116]

By 1891, under increasing governmental pressure, the focus of Las Gorras Blancas shifted to electoral and union politics, yet their use of guerrilla tactics continued. In 1903, some three hundred riders rode through the community of Anton Chico destroying white fences on Mexicano land. According to Gómez-Quiñones, "Intermittent violent activity lasted until 1926."[117]

Other Episodes of Armed Resistance

From the 1870s to the early 1900s, several other violent incidents occurred that involved Mexicanos. Some, enacted by such as Elfego Baca, Sostenes L'Archeveque, and Gregorio Cortez, were not so much struggles of resistance, but individual conflicts that led to violent altercations with whites. In the case of Catarino Garza armed violence was directed at Porfirio Díaz's repressive regime in México. Elfego Baca, who was a sheriff in Nuevo México during the 1880s, became famous as a result of an armed confrontation with an armed mob of Texan white settlers as a result of a fracas in which he shot a Texan.[118] A mob of some eighty whites unsuccessfully sought to lynch Baca, who was charged with murder by the mob. For thirty-six hours he successfully held them off in a small adobe house, killing four and wounding several. He finally surrendered after being promised a fair trial. Baca was subsequently acquitted and went on to become sheriff of Socorro County.[119]

Another legendary figure from Nuevo México who resorted to armed self-defense from that same period was Sostenes L'Archeveque. He was born in Santa Fe, New México, of Mexicano-French parents. After whites killed his father, he went on a killing rampage. Within a very short time, he killed some twenty whites in retaliation for his father's murder. Ironically, Mexicanos admired his bravery, but fearing retaliation from whites, his own people, according to Meier and Rivera, "ambushed and killed him."[120]

In Tejas, Catarino Garza, a journalist and advocate transformer, also became a symbol of Mexicano resistance. Born in México but raised in Brownsville, Garza developed a reputation for being a defender of Mexicano rights in South Tejas and a strong adversary of Mexican dictator Porfirio Díaz. In 1891, hoping to precipitate an uprising against the despot Díaz, Garza formed a small army in South Tejas. It crossed into México and successfully captured the Mexican town of Guerrero.[121] However, a contingent of United States Army troops successfully intercepted Garza's forces. Garza was forced to retreat into Texas to regroup and plan another invasion; it never materialized.[122] His brief military incursion into México failed to topple the Díaz regime. Harassed by U.S. authorities for the next few years, the hapless crusader eventually fled to Cuba, then to Colombia on a filibustering expedition, where he was killed.[123]

Gregorio Cortez became another historical personality who embodied the spirit of armed resistance.[124] Like Baca in Nuevo México, he too was catapulted into fame by unusual circumstances. He was born in México in 1875 and moved with his family to Tejas in 1877. He did not have a record of criminal activity.[125] Yet on June 12, 1901, an armed incident occurred that turned him into a legendary figure. In an attempt by Sheriff Harper Morris to arrest Gregorio's brother Romaldo for alleged horse stealing, the sheriff shot his brother then fired at Gregorio and missed. Gregorio returned fire and killed the sheriff. This was the beginning of one of the most famous manhunts in Tejas history. Cortez escaped by walking some eighty miles and hid at a ranch owned by a friend of his, Martin Robledo.

While at the ranch, Cortez was ambushed by Sheriff Robert M. Glover and a posse. After the exchange of gunfire was over, Sheriff Glover had been shot dead by Cortez, a deputy shot by a member of the posse, and Robledo's wife and son wounded.[126] For days, Cortez successfully eluded posse after posse. After an exhaustive ten-day manhunt and a five hundred-mile chase toward Laredo, he was finally captured at the small ranch village of El Sauz. Rosenbaum writes, "The lone Cortez almost made it; a vaquero betrayed him to the Texas Rangers as he rested, preparing to cross the Rio Grande at night."[127] He was tried for the murder of Sheriff Morris and was found not guilty, but was found guilty of the murder of Sheriff Glover. He was sent to the state penitentiary at Huntsville and after twelve years was pardoned by Governor Oscar B. Colquitt.[128] He died of natural causes in 1916. In death, Cortez has lived not only in the literary works written about him, but more importantly, in the people's folklore and *corridos*.

The Politics of Armed Insurgencies: The Magónista Revolutionary Movement

At the turn of the century, armed resistance was reinvigorated by the Magónista Revolutionary Movement. The Mexican Revolution of 1910 was the twentieth century's first major social revolution. From 1910 to 1920, México was in an incessant state of turmoil and conflict. During these years, the U.S./México border became increasingly volatile. Over one million Mexicanos died in this unprecedented revolutionary struggle. Numerous leaders and armies fought in the pursuit of social change in México, and some of them inspired Mexicanos in the United States. Two leaders who helped revitalize the struggle of armed resistance by Mexicanos in the United States were syndicalist leaders Ricardo and Enrique Flores Magón, who because of their advocating revolutionary change were advocate transformers. Their struggle to topple the Díaz regime can be traced to 1900 with the founding of *Regeneración* (Regeneration), at first a law review, subsequently a revolutionary newspaper. Ricardo was jailed in 1901 and again in 1903 with Enrique, for "insulting" and distributing propaganda against Díaz, leading both brothers and a companion to leave México and go into political exile in the United States.

In January 1904, the Magón brothers came to Laredo, Tejas, and set up an office for their revolutionary organizing efforts against Díaz. Two years later they founded the Partido Liberal Mexicano (PLM—the Mexican Liberal Party) with Enrique as its main leader. For the next few years, the Magón brothers and others waged a relentless revolutionary struggle against the despot Díaz and were forced to move their political operation to San Antonio, Tejas. Magónistas (supporters of the PLM) in cooperation with the Western Federation of Miners initiated a labor strike against a U.S. mining company in 1906 that led to violence in Cananea, Sonora, México. The strike was precipitated by the prevailing two-wage policy (i.e., whites earned double than the wages of Mexicanos, while performing the same type of work). Pressured by the Díaz regime, U.S. officials arrested, tried, and jailed both of the Magón brothers in 1909 for some eighteen months. Persecuted by U.S. officials for violating neutrality laws, the Magón brothers and other PLM leaders fled first to St. Louis, Missouri, then in 1910 to Los Angeles, California.

In 1911, the Magónistas gathered an army in California and invaded and militarily occupied parts of North Baja California, México, for a short time. Before long, they were forced to withdraw to the United States by Mexicano federal forces. That same year, Ricardo was again arrested for revolutionary activities and sentenced to three years' imprisonment. He was again released in 1914, but then rearrested in 1918 for promulgating a manifesto calling for a world anarchist revolution. By this time U.S. and Mexican government officials believed that the PLM was nothing more than an extension of the International Workers of the World (IWW).[129] Ricardo Magón was sentenced by the courts in 1918 to twenty years for violation of U.S. neutrality laws. When Mexican president Alvaro Obregón finally succeeded in persuading U.S. officials to release him and have him returned to México, he mysteriously died in his jail cell on November 21, 1922.[130] The contribution of the Magónistas to the Mexicano political experience of both occupied Aztlán and México was significant. Scores of progressive activists participated in social change struggles on both sides of the border.[131]

El Plan de San Diego

In 1915, in the midst of México's Revolution and while most of Europe was engaged in World War I, a Mexicano irredentist struggle emerged in South Tejas under the guise of "El Plan de San Diego." With a precarious U.S./México border, the political climate was one of discontent and even violence among some Mexicanos toward whites. James Sandos argues that the bitter character of white–Mexicano relations of the time was "an authentic product of the border region."[132] Montejano further adds, "Most U.S. military observers stationed in Tejas recognized that a basic condition making for the rebellion was the prejudice and contempt that Mexicans in the region were subjected to."[133] Throughout the course of the Mexican Revolution, banditry had increased and tensions between the two countries had deteriorated as well. The resurgence of the doctrine of U.S.

Manifest Destiny became evident with the naval occupation of Tampico and the bombardment and occupation of Veracruz in 1914. Some two hundred Mexican naval cadets were killed in the fighting in Veracruz alone. Conflict was commonplace along the U.S./México border. Anticipating a possible war with México, the United States stationed thousands of army troops along the precarious border. War was averted only through the diplomatic intervention of the ABC Powers—Argentina, Brazil, and Chile. Within such a volatile political climate, an unprecedented Mexicano insurgency emerged in South Tejas.[134]

In response, frustrated and alienated, Mexicanos from both South Tejas and México organized a separatist revolutionary movement. The insurgent leadership included Luis de la Rosa, who was a former deputy sheriff in Cameron County and Ancieta Pizaña, a Carrancista (a loyalist to General Carranza).[135] They were advocate transformers because they advocated insurrection and separatism. In February 1915, Basilio Ramos, a Mexicano national, was arrested and taken to jail in Brownsville by Starr County sheriff Deodoro Guerra for having in his possession a copy of El Plan de San Diego.[136] While in jail, Ramos told authorities that the document was given to him by a friend during a stay in jail in Monterrey, México. He was accused of conspiracy against the U.S. government, but the charges were subsequently dismissed.[137]

El Plan de San Diego called for a combination revolution, race war, and separatist insurrection.[138] It was to occur on February 20, 1915, the day when Mexicanos were to initiate an armed struggle to reconquer all of the lands México had lost to the United States in 1836 and 1848. On that day, however, nothing happened; but a revised version of the plan appeared, "Manifesto to the Oppressed Peoples of America," which promulgated the following:

> On the 20th day of February 1915, at two o'clock in the morning, we will rise in arms against the government and country of the United States of America. ONE FOR ALL AND ALL FOR ONE, proclaiming the liberty of the individuals of the black race and its independence of Yankee tyranny which has held us in iniquitous slavery since remote times; and at the same time and in the manner we will proclaim the independence and segregation of the States bordering the Mexican nation, which are: TEXAS, NEW MÉXICO, ARIZONA, COLORADO, AND UPPER CALIFORNIA, OF WHICH states the Republic of MÉXICO was robbed in a most perfidious manner by North American Imperialism.[139]

As an irredentist revolutionary document, El Plan de San Diego promulgated a call for independence from "Yankee tyranny" via the formation of an armed insurrection movement. Strategically, the plan called for the establishment of a revolutionary military alliance with blacks, Japanese, and indigenous people who shared a history of white oppression.[140] In return, blacks were to be given six southeastern states to form their own republic; indigenous people, specifically the Apaches of Arizona, would likewise be given back their land.[141] A new independent Mexicano republic would be created from the above-named five southwestern states. The new southwest republic would have the option of reunification with México or of total independence. A race war was envisioned, with every white male over the age of sixteen to be shot, as well as all traitors who had collaborated with the white enemy.[142] Structurally, power was to be vested in a Supreme Revolutionary Congress, which would designate a supreme chief for the armed forces and issue commissions. In an interim basis, a Provisional Directorate would exercise the power of governance.[143] The revolutionary forces were to be called the "Liberating Army for Races and Peoples" and its rallying cry was "Equality and Independence."[144]

During the ensuing four months the white authorities did not take the plan's call for an uprising seriously, since there had been no insurgent activity. Shortly after Ramos's arrest, a junta was allegedly formed in Laredo between July and December 1915. Led by de la Rosa and Ancieta Pizaña, the insurgents, according to Juan Gomez-Quiñones, "directed armed organized bands of from 25–100 men in a series of actions in the Lower Rio Grande Valley."[145] In addition, they called for Mexicanos in Tejas to take up arms against white authorities. According to Robert J. Rosenbaum, "*los sediciosos* burned railroad trestles, stopped passenger trains, raided the Norias Ranch that was part of the King Ranch holdings, and fought a number of skirmishes with U.S. Army detachments and Texas Ranger patrols."

Initially a rural struggle, due to growing support, it soon spread to some of the urban areas. On August 30, 1915, in San Antonio a riot occurred between Mexicanos and police. With shouts of "kill the Anglos," some twenty-eight Mexicanos were arrested and charged with treason. Among whites, the incident created fear of a Mexicano uprising.[146] The raids ceased during the winter, but then began once again during the summer of 1916.[147] Acuña argues that "White authorities used the Plan of San Diego to step up a reign of terror along the border."[148] In response to the insurgent raids, the size of the Texas Rangers was increased to fifty. In addition, on June 18, President Wilson federalized the National Guards of Tejas, Nuevo México, and Arizona, creating a force of some one hundred thousand to patrol the U.S./México border.[149]

The military response to the alleged insurgency resulted in a dramatic increase of white brutality and repression, that is, lynchings, killings, and economic reprisals against Mexicanos, especially under the aegis of the Texas Rangers and vigilante "Law and Order Leagues." Some three hundred "suspected" Mexicano insurgents were shot, hung, or beaten to death by U.S. authorities, while the insurrectionists killed twenty-one whites.[150] Rosenbaum, however, puts the number of insurgent deaths much higher: from 300 to 5,000 that were summarily shot or hanged without a trial.[151] George Marvin in *World's Work* magazine wrote in January 1917:

> The killing of Mexicans . . . along the border in these last four years is almost incredible. . . . Some Rangers have degenerated into common man killers. There is no penalty for killing, no jury along the border would ever convict a white man for shooting a Mexican. . . . Reading over Secret Service records makes you feel as though there was an open gun season on Mexicans along the border.[152]

The militarization of the U.S./México border was a response to the great fear that federal and Tejas state authorities had over the particulars of El Plan de San Diego. The atrocities perpetrated against Mexicanos were so egregious that a U.S. Senate investigating committee documented the terror as did a state legislative investigation led by the Brownsville representative J. T. Canales. This latter investigation resulted in the implication of the Texas Rangers in the atrocities. As a result, a law was passed in 1919 reducing the size of the Texas Rangers.[153]

It is important to note that the true origins of El Plan de San Diego remain unknown. At the time, many U.S. officials, including the FBI, alleged that the insurrection was German-inspired. However, research suggests that the plan's zealots initially were Huertistas (supporters of Mexican president Victoriano Huerta). Yet the political reality suggested that the writers may have come from the ranks of both Huerta and his nemesis, General Venustiano Carranza,[154] who was México's president from 1914 to 1920. According to Acuña, "De La Rosa and Pizaña recruited freely in northern México and Carrancista general Emiliano P. Nafarratte gave the rebels carte blanche. And although Carranza called publicly for the arrest of the two recruiters, he allowed them to operate unimpaired."[155] The accusation that foreign agents, either German or Japanese, had influenced the Plan of San Diego was never proven by U.S. security agencies. The squelching of the insurgency brought to an end the politics of armed resistance leading to a dialectical shift during the next epoch to political accommodation.

The Politics of Accommodation (Ballot Box Politics)

While some Mexicanos resorted to the use of violence to resist the occupation of the United States, others resisted not by the power of the gun, but by accommodation.[156] In the political context, accommodation denotes a preference to adjust, adapt, reconcile, and compromise rather than resist, reject, and oppose by violence the political, social, and economic order. From 1848 to 1916, some Mexicanos, especially members of the old entrenched *rico* class (the oligarchs), unequivocally rejected violence. Instead they embraced accommodation, adaptation, and integration and willingly accepted the occupation as a fait accompli. Their political roles under the internal colonial system varied from in some instances acting as buffers to "want to be whites." In explaining the motivation of the Mexicanos elite in espousing accommodation politics, Del Castillo and De León note, "Several elites responded to the new politics with accommodation—a decision attributable to disillusionment with previous Mexican rule, admiration for the American union, desire to form convenient political and economic partnerships with newcomers (some of who adapted themselves to native ways), or callous opportunism."[157]

Mexicano Political Culture in the United States

Mexicano political culture began to change after 1848 with the United States' occupation of Aztlán. After nearly 330 years of evolution and as a result of the U.S. War on México, Mexicano political culture throughout Aztlán was altered. The inherent values and traditions of U.S. Anglo-Saxon political culture were predicated on liberalism, Protestantism, and mercantilism, which induced the rise of liberal capitalism in the United States; these beliefs were ostensibly nonexistent in México. Instead, México's politics developed through a metamorphosis of Hispano or Spanish and indigena political cultures both of which were based on authoritarian, nonegalitarian, and nonparticipatory values within the context of a feudal society.

Hence, from its conquest in 1519 to its loss of Aztlán in 1848, México's political culture was not conducive to the political and economic development of liberal capitalism in México. In simple terms, there was nothing democratic about Spain's colonial empire or México's independence after 1821. For the masses of people, colonialism fostered a system of political oppression, subordination, and powerlessness. Starting in 1824 when México became a republic and through the end of this epoch (1916), there was experimentation with representative democracy, but it never materialized. Instead, México was plagued by internal political strife, instability, and dictatorship. The perennial political and military conflicts between liberals and conservatives made representative democracy and liberal capitalism as practiced in the United States unattainable in México.

From 1821 to 1848, México's political culture was "parochial," essentially authoritarian permeated by a thin veneer of liberalism. More specifically, it was plagued by chronic political instability, militarism, *caudillismo, caciquismo*, and regionalism. It was not the epitome of a vibrant participatory civic-culture. The people's cognitive, affective, and evaluative orientations were extremely limited. México's politics was more oligarchical than democratic and permeated by nationalism. In fact, it can be argued, it was the antithesis of a participatory democratic-based political culture. Thus, during this epoch, México's political culture, which was parochial in nature coupled with the people's colonization in Aztlán, did not provide the requisite viable civic-democratic experiences.

What ensued after 1848 was the imposition of internal colonialism in U.S. politics, which sought to supplant the Mexicano's own political culture. Throughout the epoch, Mexicanos in general were denied the benefits of representative democracy, which for some still remained an intangible reality. To most Mexicanos the basic freedoms expressed in the spirit of the U.S. Constitution— "life, liberty, and the pursuit of happiness"—were abstractions. For the overwhelming majority of Mexicanos, they were unobtainable. Instead, the imposition of internal colonialism imbued the Mexicano Generation throughout Aztlán with another cultural layer of cynicism and alienation toward politics. The oppression and exploitation endemic to internal colonialism led to a political subordination that suppressed the Mexicano's political development. This was exacerbated by the rise of a "culture of poverty in the U.S.,"[158] which fostered a complex set of values, attitudes, and beliefs that were not conducive to Mexicano political participation. These included authoritarianism, personalism, machismo, acute individualism, mimicking, apathy, cynicism, suspicion, fatalism, self-denigration, alienation, inferiority complex, and distrust of authority.[159] With few exceptions, most Mexicanos during this epoch continued to adhere to México's political culture.

Moreover, the people's colonized and impoverished status and condition further supplanted their essentially apolitical attitudes and values. In spite of attempts to resocialize the colonized masses by the national, state, and local colonial governments, the conditions caused by their colonized status and liberal capitalism's exploitive nature, namely racism and segregation, contributed to the preservation of their ostensibly based Mexicano political culture. Hence, most Mexicanos during the epoch maintained a strong cultural affinity with their "Méxicanidad." By and large, Mexicano's affinity with México's political culture meant that within the context of occupied Aztlán they adhered to a political subculture that existed within the confines of the country's ubiquitous Anglo-Saxon Protestant-oriented liberal capitalist political culture. Yet, during this epoch, not all Mexicanos subscribed to the existent Mexicano-oriented political subculture. Those that did were essentially the poor, who were the majority. For the most

part, the *ricos* (rich), and the small emergent middle class sought either to acculturate or assimilate.

Most of the *rico* class for reasons of political and economic expediency
embraced the U.S. liberal capitalist political culture and sought to assimilate into
white society.[160] Most adopted political roles of being either buffers or "want to
be whites." In most cases, especially in Nuevo México, they practiced a politic
based on accommodation and pragmatic adaptation. Their level of cognitive,
affective, and evaluative orientations allowed them to benefit and in some cases
participate politically in the colonial governance of Aztlán's various territories,
barrios, and *colonias*. From a cultural perspective, these Mexicanos could be called
"cultural pluralists" who acculturated by adapting to some of the values, beliefs,
norms, and even symbols of white society; while they culturally sought to retain
some of their Mexicanidad, such as their language, customs, food, music. On the
other hand, the assimilationists, the "want to be whites," basically sought to integrate themselves into white society and adopted its superstructure, for example,
institutions, laws, and political practices. Among the *rico* class the cultural pluralists were the most dominant, especially in Nuevo México. However, with the
colonial system's control over the socialization processes, the "assimilationists"
gained ground by the turn of the twentieth century.

This political dichotomy within the *rico* class also applied to the emergent
small middle-class bourgeoisie who adjusted pragmatically to the changing overall
environment. From an internal colonial perspective, the white authorities as part
of their economic control, governance, and political stabilization used both the
ricos and middle class as buffers. Among poor Mexicanos, the "want to be whites"
were perceived as being "house Mexicans." Although relatively powerless, they
did the political and economic bidding of the white ruling elites at the expense
of the impoverished workers. Consequently, in one way or another both protected
the white elites' colonial interests.

Overall, the Mexicano's political ethos was shaped by the grim existence of
internal colonialism's poverty, segregation, and political powerlessness. The small
rico and middle classes were molded by their need for survival, which made it
expedient to collaborate with white elite rancheros, businessmen, professionals,
and politicians. They assumed a subservient political relationship. "Only a small
number of the once wealthy Spanish-speaking," according to Albert Camarillo,
"escaped the subsequent social and geographic segregation and were effectively
assimilated into American society, largely through intermarriage."[161] Richard Del
Castillo and Arnoldo De León write:

> These and others came to accept the many tenets of American life so that
> varying degrees of Americanization within communities evolved. Numer-

ous other things changed, albeit moderately—family structure, religious instruction, fashions and dress, and even ways of working the range. The direction Anglos came to give specific regions, the demographic ratios, prevailing between Anglos and Mexicans, and the intensity of racism in a particular environment all determined the newer life for Mexicans.[162]

Their adoption of the white liberal capitalist ethos ultimately meant that they adopted its values of individualism, private property, laissez-faire economics, and the "do unto others before they did unto you" type of mentality. In exchange, increasingly they had to divest themselves of certain aspects of their culture, language, heritage, and rituals, and embrace "whiteness," which was racist and perceived all Mexicanos as being inferior.

The racism directed at Mexicanos by whites was part and parcel of the liberal capitalist Protestant Anglo-Saxon ethos. The literature on the Chicano's history of Aztlán is replete with illustrations of the pervasive racism that permeated the emerging Mexicano political experience in the United States. The bottom line was that Mexicanos as a people were seen as inferior to whites. Carey McWilliams writes about the birth of the Mexicano stereotype and states "the first impressions which Anglo Americans formed of the native element were highly unfavorable." Then he cites a perception of a certain white author, Marmaduke, who wrote, "The greater part of them are the most miserable, wretched poor creatures that I have ever seen, poor, petty, thieving, gambling, bullbaiting." McWilliams explains that unfortunately this was the prevailing observation of many whites.[163]

The historical roots of such racism run deep in the political experience of the United States. Carlos Vélez-Ibañez suggests that "one stereotype of Mexicans stems in part from the Black Legend in which Spaniards were depicted as cruel, indolent, and rapacious." He cites Thomas Jefferson Farnham, a successful Maine lawyer, who wrote the following about Mexicanos: "The half breed, as might be expected, exhibits much of the Indian character; the dull suspicious countenance, the small twinkling piercing eye, the laziness and filth of a free brute, using freedom as a mere means of animal enjoyment." To Farnham, the Mexican was cowardly, intellectually limited, slothful, dishonest, and linguistically disabled because Mexicans spoke both native languages and Spanish. Furthermore, he explains, Mexicanas were depicted as being persons of questionable character, in short of being prone to infidelity.[164] Such were the negative stereotypes of many whites toward Mexicanos, which added to their burden of living under the specter of internal colonialism.

Thus, the Mexicano's political subculture did not encourage civic participation among the impoverished masses. It was largely constrained by their internal colonial status that fostered values of fatalism, resignation, apathy, and alienation vis-à-vis politics in general. This was not the case, however, with all Mexicanos, for some resisted their occupation via ballot box politics.

The Rise of Ballot Box Politics

The Mexicano's internal colonial status created a unique political environment. From the economic perspective, it was the *rico* class, and some of the middle class, that prospered politically from the occupation. In Nuevo México some Mexicanos embraced a buffer role and profited by the growing commerce fostered especially by the opening of the Santa Fe Trail. They adhered to the belief that the U.S. conquest and occupation would increase their wealth by the expansion of economic markets and better communications. Other Mexicano elites likewise saw the political situation from a pragmatic perspective: in order to advance their own individual interests, they needed to work within the parameters of the new political order. Their pragmatism was based on the white monopoly of power, that is, political, military, and economic wielded by the new white social order that controlled and occupied Aztlán. They believed, quite erroneously, that by forming alliances with the new white oligarchs they could protect their political, economic, and social interests and cultural way of life. In reality, however, the Mexicano elites were seldom unified on the issues impacting Mexicanos as a whole. They rarely spoke out as a class against the iniquities being perpetrated against the poor, who were the majority of the Mexicano population. Foremost on their political agenda was the advancement of their own individual interests and secondly their class interests. This elitist and *vendido* (sell-out) mentality was particularly pervasive in Nuevo México. Thus, as a result of the conquest and occupation of Aztlán what ensued was a master–servant colonial relationship— whites the masters, Mexicanos by and large the servants.

Despite their resistance to growing political oppression, Mexicanos were relegated into a state of political powerlessness within a very short time. In examining the status of Mexicanos in California from the 1850s to the 1880s, Albert Camarillo notes that these overall patterns were reflected: "(1) racial partisan politics; (2) political accommodation by the elite ranchero class; (3) political harassment and ostracism by neighboring white communities; and (4) adoption of methods to ensure Mexican voter powerlessness—gerrymandering, racial exclusion from political parties, and elimination of Mexican political representatives."[165] Mexicanos loss of political power, accompanied by their relative numerical decline in California, Tejas, and Arizona, resulted in a threat to their civil liberties. With such a small almost inconsequential population base few who were eligible to vote for reasons that will later be examined participated politically. Without political power, Mexicanos in the United States could not hope to protect themselves from capricious laws, or from the wrath of Yankee nativists.[166] This was evident during this epoch of resistance—few reforms materialized, except those in labor.

Tejas: The Politics of Racism

For Mexicanos in Tejas, politically the years preceding 1848 were contradictory. The cardinal reason for this was that some of the Mexicano *ricos*, the "want to be whites" such as Lorenzo Zavala, José Antonio Navarro, José Francisco Ruiz, and Juan Seguín, among others, profited from the conquest at the expense of the majority of the poor Mexicano population. As Gómez-Quiñones explains, "The overwhelming majority of Mexican Tejanos remained loyal to Mexican sovereignty; hence, the bitter conflict of generations."[167] These and other individuals who sided with the white insurrectionists were traitors to their people in that their sole intent was to advance their own selfish political, economic, and social interests. This mold of "traitorous politics" was first cast in Tejas and spread to the other territories, becoming an inherent part of the Mexicano's subpolitical culture in occupied Aztlán. Rodolfo Acuña is one historian who described them as "a bunch of *cabrones* that sold out their own people."[168]

From 1836 to 1848 a handful of "want to be white" and buffer *rico* Mexicanos participated in ballot box politics. Overall, however, Mexicanos were at a major disadvantage, as they constituted demographically a small minority. In addition, most were not fluent in English, yet business and politics were conducted in English. Also, in some cases, their cognitive orientations of the U.S. political system were rather limited. Robert A. Calvert and Arnoldo De León state, "Despite the guarantees in the Constitution of 1836, Tejanos seemed defenseless against a people who freely expressed their dislike for them and openly desired retribution for Santa Anna's carnage at the time of the Alamo and Goliad."[169] Yet some *ricos* who supported the Texas Revolt were given political and economic rewards. "Between 1836 and 1845," according to Gómez-Quiñones, "four Mexicanos, all from San Antonio served in the Texas Congress: Juan N. Seguín, José Antonio Navarro, and José Francisco Ruiz as senators; and Rafael de la Garza in the House." Initially, Navarro and Seguín prospered because of their political influence. Both received large land grants from the Tejas government.[170] Years earlier Navarro was a pro-slave landholder, who was the chief architect of a law that allowed whites to bring slaves into Tejas as permanently indentured servants.[171] While some of the *ricos* reaped the benefits of their politi-cal status, other Mexicanos, loyalist and not, lost their lands to whites and after 1836 some of them left Tejas and returned to México. Montejano cites that by 1840 some two hundred families had left San Antonio alone.[172]

As Chicano historians have aptly documented, the traitorous acts of many of these Mexicano *rico* elites backfired on them a few years later. The alliance between the Mexicano *ricos* and white oligarchs unraveled soon after the rout of General Santa Anna at San Jacinto.[173] Indicative of this demise: in 1837 some forty-seven Mexicanos ran for the city election in San Antonio; ten years later only five ran. Mexicanos maintained control of San Antonio's local politics until 1845, even though the white population has steadily increased. In 1839, Mexi-canos comprised the majority of San Antonio's population, but by 1846 the pop-ulation was evenly divided with each group having 750 each.[174] From 1848 to 1866, the aldermanic council included one or two Mexicanos.[175] Up to this point political expediency on both sides had allowed for token Mexicano political rep-resentation.

Initially, as part of San Antonio's governing elite, Juan Seguín served as a councilperson during the late 1830s and as mayor, 1840–1842. His years in public office, especially as mayor, proved to be both bitter and conflictive. His political situation worsened with the invasion of South Tejas and the capture and occupation of San Antonio by Mexican army forces under the command of Gen-eral Rafael Vasquez. During the occupation, General Vasquez exhorted all Mexi-canos to return with him to México and proclaimed that Juan Seguín was a loyal Mexican, which was interpreted by some as an action designed to discredit him among whites. It worked: white power holders accused him of being an accom-plice in a plot by México to reconquer Tejas.[176] They were suspect of his loyalty and threatened to indict or murder or even lynch him. Hence the political climate became so dangerous that Seguín resigned as mayor and along with his family was forced to go into exile in 1842 to the country he had fought against—México.[177] The Mexican government allowed him and his family exile status in Tamaulipas. Pardoned by México, he sought to redeem himself by volunteering to fight for México against the United States. In 1849, he was pardoned by Sam Houston and returned briefly to Tejas to regain his property, but because of the pervasive anti-Mexicano political climate, he returned again to Tamaulipas.[178]

By the time the Texas constitutional convention took place in 1845, José Antonio Navarro was the only Mexicano delegate to participate.[179] Like Seguín, Navarro's political adventures served the interests of the white power holders. Both in 1838 collaborated with whites in a filibustering secessionist expedition into the area of Tamaulipas, México, with the intent of establishing the "Republic of the Rio." Fortunately for México, the Texan expedition was defeated by Mexican forces. Navarro again in 1842 participated in another unsuccessful filibustering secessionist expedition: this time to Nuevo México. He was captured by Mexican forces and sentenced to death, but instead only served two years in prison and was released.[180] Upon his release, he returned to San Antonio where he became even wealthier, served in Congress from 1846 to 1849, and supported the Southern Confederacy.[181]

The convention took a definite anti-Mexicano posture, in which many delegates propounded the view that Mexicanos should not be allowed to vote in Tejas. Weber documents one delegate's words: "I fear not the Castilian race, but . . . those who, though they speak the Spanish language, are but the descendents of that degraded and despicable race which Cortez conquered." Another delegate said that it was long the tradition in Tejas to deny Mexicanos the vote even though many of them had taken the oath of allegiance, simply because "they could not be considered white persons; they were Mexicans." Yet in the end, Navarro argued effectively against the anti-Mexicano measure at the end of the convention.[182]

For several years afterward in San Antonio, "want to be whites" José Antonio Navarro, Alejo Ruiz, Vicente Martines, Jon Barrerea, and Rafael Ytúrris sided with ultraconservative and racist Southern Democrats who espoused white supremacy. They and a few others brokered the Mexicano vote, oblivious to the persecution and repression of poor Mexicanos.[183] Whites, to maintain control over the impoverished Mexicano masses, used these co-opted elites. One such politician was Santos Benavides from Laredo, who occupied various elected positions from the 1840s to the 1880s. He assisted in the suppression of insurgent Juan Cortina, fought for the Confederacy, and received high marks from his white colleagues in the legislature.[184]

Between the 1840s and the early 1900s, Mexicanos in Tejas were politically conspicuous by their absence at both the state and federal levels of government. An impeding factor contributing to their political powerlessness was the smallness of their population base. It was not until the early part of the twentieth century that at the state level that a Mexicano by the name of J. T. Canales distinguished himself as a state representative. He served from 1909 to 1911, in 1917, and in 1919 for the areas of Cameron, Hidalgo, Starr, and Zapata counties. In between terms, in 1914, he served as a county judge.[185] As a state representative, he voted for numerous progressive measures, among them education, judicial reform, modernization of irrigation laws, and the creation of a state Department of Agriculture.[186]

For the Mexicano elite, politics remained a local enterprise. During these years a number were elected to various local offices ranging from city councilpersons to county commissioners, assessors, and treasurers.[187] They were politically active in cities such as San Antonio, Laredo, Brownsville, El Paso, and in other areas in South Tejas where they constituted a substantial part of the population.[188] Yet in most cases, they had no reform agenda other than perpetuating their own self-interests. On some occasions, however, they did seek to protect the people's collective interests as an ethnic community. Some spoke out against slavery and against the nativist and anti-Catholic politics of the Know-Nothing Party during the 1850s. Other Mexicano politicians still adapted to a racist political climate. They chose the colonial role of "want to be whites," more concerned about being accepted by whites and securing concessions for themselves or the *rico* class than addressing the plight of the poor.

Regardless of Tejas's racist and violent anti-Mexicano political climate and culture, Mexicano political elites embraced accommodation, and with few exceptions, most danced to the political tune of the dominant white political elite interests. In De León's own words, "What they could carry out . . . depended on the limitations allowed by white society."[189] One can deduce that their low level of resistance could be ascribed to their colonized mentality. This situation became clearly evident in the role of the Mexicano poor in Tejas's machine and party politics.

As a people, Mexicanos became pawns of competing white political bosses. The few that voted went to support the political machines of Jim Wells of Brownsville and Bryan Callahagan and his son, "King Bryan II." Historian David Weber describes the latter as "a two-generation dynasty," which took over San Antonio in 1846 and ruled it until 1912.[190] These machines handed out patronage, that is, jobs and contracts, but in reality the major benefactors were the minority Mexicano elite, not the poor. Seldom did the elite side with interests of the Mexicano poor. Their political job was to turn out the Mexicano vote and in some cases, as Arnold De León explains, whites employed Mexicanos in the border areas to cross into México and recruit voters. They would first be naturalized and given the modest sum of 25 cents for their vote.[191] These cooperative alliances with white politicians were driven by the need to maintain their semblance of leadership, keep portions of their land, and secure valuable contracts or other material incentives. Del Castillo and De León state, "These relationships also permitted elites to integrate themselves into the realm of bossism, many times as members of local subrings that answered to the more powerful Anglo nabobs."[192] In spite of a hostile political climate, Mexicanos at the local level formed Democrat and Republican Party clubs. Several of these clubs organized conventions and engaged in state and presidential politics seeking strategically a broker role. Thus, some of the Mexicano political elite did participate in the politics of both major political parties.

Overall, however, political participation was impeded by the Mexicano's internal colonial status. White colonialism relied on a number of factors. One, on numerous occasions, whites sought to deliberately disfranchise Mexicanos. For example, the Reform Club in San Antonio, during the late 1880s seriously discussed disenfranchising Mexicanos.[193] Two, poverty was widespread; caught up in the syndrome of economic survival few had the time or know-how to become involved. Three, few had the right to the franchise, since they were not U.S. citizens. As an illustration of this point, in 1896–1897, Ricardo Rodriguez filed papers for naturalization before the U.S. Circuit Court in San Antonio. Two white politicians, T. J. McMinn and Jack Evans, went before the court and argued that Rodriguez did not qualify for citizenship on the grounds that he was not "a white person, nor an African, nor of African descent, and therefore [was] not capable of becoming a [U.S.] citizen."[194] Their motivation was to disenfranchise not only newly arrived Mexicanos, but others as well. The hostility of the political climate was reflected in the use of white primaries, and by 1902, the poll tax.[195] These measures, approved by the state Democratic executive committee, according to Calvert and De León, "eliminated many Texas-Mexican voters."[196] And four, physical and economic intimidation and at times violence were used to control the small Mexicano vote.

Thus, by the 1880s, not much was left of Mexicano efforts at ballot box politics. Accommodation politics, however, continued in the forms of organization formation and labor organizing.

California: The Decline of Mexicano Politics

Like in Tejas, Mexicano politics remained local and active only in a handful of communities, such as Los Angeles, Santa Barbara, and San Jose.[197] Some Mexicanos used armed resistance to hold off the U.S. invasion of California, as they did in Tejas and Nuevo México, but with the signing of the Treaty of Cahuenga in 1847, the *rico* class quickly shifted their mode of politics to one of accommodation. For the next two years, acting as buffers, they collaborated with U.S. military authorities in the transfer of political control to the United States. During this time, as Leonard Pitt explains "the new army was attempting to preserve the status quo instead of wrecking it. . . . Military governors treated [Mexicanos] with kid gloves and at the same time kept those Yankees who might have harmed them firmly in check."[198]

Colonel Stephen Kearney court-marshaled John Charles Fremont for claiming the title of military governor and in an effort to consolidate his power in California, he sought to recruit as interim governor or secretary of state Juan Baustista Alvarado, who declined both positions. Between 1847 and 1849, of those who made up the military administration, seventy-four were born in the United States or Great Britain; five were born in continental Europe; and forty-eight were born in California or México. During the occupation's first two years, Mexicano elites were not excluded from the politics of the territory. Yet Mexicanos kept dropping out of the political process. According to Pitt, too many of them preferred the "quietude of rancho life."[199] Unfortunately for Mexicanos, these two years proved to be the calm before the political storm.

By 1849 demographically whites constituted California's majority. With the discovery of gold on January 24, 1848, at Sutters Mill (only a week prior to the signing of the Treaty of Guadalupe Hidalgo), the gold rush of 1849 drew some one hundred thousand people into California.[200] According to Weber,[201] California's population increased to 380,000 in 1850, 15 percent of which was Mexicano. Thoroughly outnumbered, the Mexicano population and its influence declined rapidly as California's white population increased dramatically. In 1849, the military governor, General Bennett Riley, concerned about the great influx of people, called for a state constitutional convention. The convention was held at Monterey in June of that year. Of the forty-eight delegates elected to participate at the convention, eight were Mexicanos:[202] José A. Carrillo, Mariano Vallejo, Pablo de La Guerra, José M. Covarrubias, Miguel de Pedrorena, Don Antonio Pico, Jacinto Rodríguez, and Manuel Domínguez. Other notable *rico* leaders who played a significant role until 1847 were Juan Bandini, Juan Alvarado, and Pio Pico. Contrary to expectations, writes Pitt, "the Californios (Mexicanos born/raised in California) did not always act as a bloc; in thirty-five important roll calls, they broke ranks seventeen times."[203]

When some white racist delegates introduced a measure that suffrage should be limited only to white males, the delegates led by de La Guerra closed ranks to defeat the measure, arguing that it went against the provisions of the Treaty of Guadalupe Hidalgo. The final agreement was that any man previously considered a Mexican citizen, regardless of race, would be considered a citizen under California's Constitution. A related issue was also defeated: some of the white delegates had targeted Manuel Domínguez for removal because in the words of Gómez-Quiñones, he "possessed too much Indian blood to be allowed to participate in the convention." This issue was indicative of the zeal of white chauvinists who sought to deny nonwhites their full civil rights and basic legal protections.[204]

On the issue of dividing California into two political entities—the north into a state and the south below San Luis Obispo or Santa Barbara, into a territory—the eight Mexicano delegates divided their vote on geographical lines. The delegates from the south voted yes on the measure; whereas those from the north, who prevailed, voted to make California as a whole into a state. On the issue of the admittance of free blacks into California, only Carrillo of the eight delegates voted against the measure.[205] This was indicative of the political alliance some had forged with white Democrats who had strong views against black exclusion.[206] On the positive side, Mexicano delegates were able to secure agreements on the right of women to own property; for all state laws to be printed in Spanish,[207] and for biculturalism and bilingualism in California public schools, courts, and public administration.[208] Overall, the Mexicano delegates resisted by their willingness to play the political game of accommodation in the midst of a growing anti-Mexicano political climate characterized by white racism, hate, and violence.

From the eight delegates who attended the constitutional convention, only seven served in the state legislature during the 1850s (first three legislative sessions)—five in the Assembly and two in the State Senate. Their political efficacy proved to be rather limited. In 1850 the state legislature passed the highly discriminatory "Foreign Miners Tax Law," sending a request from the U.S. Congress that all foreigners be barred from the mines. Prior to its passage Mexicano and Latino miners were terrorized and became victims of white vigilante miners who perceived them as competitors. The legislation was directed specifically at Mexicanos and in general Latinos, which included those that were indigenous to California as well as those who had arrived from Sonora, México, and Latin America. Mexicanos had to pay a tax of $20 per month for the right to mine for gold.[209] Although it was repealed in 1851, the tax and exclusions caused scores of Mexicanos and Latinos to be terrorized, lynched, murdered, and extorted; their mining claims were jumped; and their property was stolen or destroyed by white xenophobic vigilantes. It served to effectively remove Mexicanos and Latinos from mining.[210] This piece of legislation had the effect of worsening the political climate between Mexicanos and whites. Resistance to the tax was intense. It acted as a catalyst for the emergence of Murrieta and other social *bandidos* (bandits) in California.

Other legislation both at the federal and state levels was passed that negatively impacted Mexicanos. At the federal level, the U.S. Congress passed the Land Act of 1851. The law specifically required Mexicanos to prove ownership of their properties. Anglo squatters believing in a "right of conquest," challenged the validity of Spanish and Mexican land grants.[211] According to Gonzales, "Essentially, this piece of legislation placed the burden of proof on the grantee, not the government, a notable exception to the American legal tradition." Furthermore, he notes, "In the case of Mexican claimants, it was also a clear violation of both the spirit and the letter of the Treaty of Guadalupe Hidalgo."[212] In the end, Mexicanos who were unfamiliar with the laws, chicanery, and outright use of intimidation and violence lost their properties to whites.

These pieces of legislation coupled with a racist hatred and prejudice toward Mexicanos led not only to armed resistance but also nonviolent protest. In Los Angeles, in spite of the fact that Mexicanos had a political presence in local government, the community became increasingly outraged over the prevailing double standard of justice—one for whites, another for Mexicanos. One such protest emanated from Francisco P. Ramirez, the young editor of the Los Angeles Spanish-language newspaper, *El Clamor Publico*. During the 1850s, through editorials, Ramirez had supported the actions taken by white vigilantes against some of the Mexicano *guerrilleros*, such as Juan Flores. This all changed when the lynching of Mexicanos became more commonplace and went unchallenged by public officials. With the conditions so deplorable for Mexicanos, he went through a major change—from an ardent assimilationist to a zealous nationalist.[213] In a scathing editorial written in 1856, he lamented, "Mexicans alone have been the victims of the people's insane fury! Mexicans alone have been sacrificed on the gibbet and launched into eternity! California is lost to all Spanish Americans. This is the liberty and equality of our adopted land!"[214] Ramirez continued publishing the newspaper until 1859 when he unsuccessfully ran for the Assembly. That same year he shut down the newspaper and left for Sonora, México.[215]

The pervasiveness of the anti-Mexicano ethos was demonstrated in 1856 when the legislature refused to pass legislation to fund translations of laws into Spanish, and when it passed an antivagrancy act, which, according to Acuña, "was commonly referred to as the 'greaser act' because section two specified "all persons who are known as 'Greasers' or the issue of Spanish or Native Blood."[216] In 1858 and 1859, a second unsuccessful attempt was made by Mexicano and white legislators from southern California to divide the state. Assemblyman Pico was successful in getting the state legislature to adopt a statewide referendum asking the voters to approve the creation of a southern "Territory of Colorado," which included San Luis Obispo, Santa Barbara, Los Angeles, San Diego, and San Bernardino counties. On this issue, nativism against Mexicanos was open and explicit. The newspaper, the *San Francisco Herald*, in opposing the measure wrote,

> [Mexicanos] are a degraded race; a part of them are so black that one needs much work to distinguish them from Indians; there is little difference between them and the Negro race; in the event a Territorial government would be established in the south very soon they would establish

friendship with the Negro slaves, would be united with one another, until all would be amalgamated and all would be slaves![217]

Although the referendum passed in 1859, it became entangled in the congressional quagmire over slavery and the pending civil war crisis. "Despite a popular mandate," according to Pitt, "the legislature balked at state separation and killed the idea."[218]

Only at the local level did Mexicanos exert a semblance of political power during this transitional time. During the 1850s through the early 1870s, Mexicanos in Los Angeles periodically held the offices of school superintendent, mayor, city council, county supervisors, sheriff, and district judge. During these years, two Mexicanos served as mayor of the city of Los Angeles: Antonio Coronel and Cristobal Aguilar. Both were born when California was ruled by Spain; both grew up under México's law; and both became mayors of Los Angeles after the occupation of California by the United States. Coronel was first elected mayor in 1853, served in the city council for twelve years, and was state treasurer from 1866 to 1870. He served as superintendent of schools and county assessor, became known as the "boss" of the Mexicano vote in Los Angeles, and championed indigenous rights. When Coronel left the city council in 1866, after serving four terms, Aguilar became mayor of Los Angeles. Previously he had served as a county supervisor, and served two one-year terms as mayor in 1866 and 1867 and a two-year term in 1870–1872, the last time a Mexicano served as mayor of Los Angeles. With Mexicano voter registration at only 22 percent, Aguilar lost his bid for reelection as mayor to a white, but he continued to wield political influence due to his position as director of waterworks.[219]

In Santa Barbara, Mexicanos maintained political control of local governmental structures from 1849 to about 1871. As Camarillo points out, "When the need arose, the Californios and their mestizo campaign managers could muster a solid Mexican voting bloc to defeat Anglo candidates who split the non-Mexican votes." Interestingly, during the Civil War some of the Mexicano political elites manifested Confederate tendencies due to bad feelings over the U.S. invasion of California. Local elites, such as Pablo de La Guerra, switched in their political party affiliation—from Democrat to Republican. By 1869, the balance of political power began to shift to whites as a result of increased migration. Whereas during the mid-1860s, Mexicano voters were 62.7 percent of the registered voters in Santa Barbara, by 1873 they constituted only 34.2 percent of the electorate, marking the end of their political power.[220]

In the pueblo of San Diego, Mexicano *ricos* lost political control of the local government to whites by the early 1850s. In order to protect their economic interests, they opted to accommodate the takeover.[221] Santa Barbara became the last bastion of Mexicano political and social influence. It was during the early 1870s that the Mexicano *ricos* lost their power base. By the 1870s, Mexicanos, a mere 4 percent of the state population, were relegated to a powerless and subordinated status.[222] The years 1880 to 1900 were the low point of the Mexicano political experience in California. The proportion of Mexicanos in Los Angeles during these years shrunk from 19 percent in 1880 to 6 percent in 1900. Statewide, the Latino population was a mere 50,000 of whom 90 percent were Mexicano.[223]

Geographically, whites very quickly became the overwhelming majority in the north and central parts of California; the Mexicano limited power base remained mostly in southern California, that is Los Angeles and Santa Barbara. The one exception in the north was San Jose. Even though they had become a small minority, Mexicanos continued to struggle politically. Increasingly the few existent *rico politicos* assumed a "want to be white" political role. Most were Republican and overwhelmingly identified as Californios rather than Mexicanos, and most espoused a form of accommodation politics largely based on assimilation. They rejected what was Mexicano and adhered to the so-called Spanish myth, claiming rather to be descendants from Spain.

At the state level, Mexicanos had few political triumphs. As previously examined, one such victory was the passage of the referendum initiated by Assemblyman Andres Pico, which called for the conversion of central and southern California into the "Colorado" territory.[224] However, the apogee of Mexicano political success at the state level was in 1873 when during a time of waning Mexicano influence, "want to be white" Republican Romualdo Pacheco of Santa Barbara was elected in 1871 to the office of lieutenant governor. In 1875 when California's governor was appointed U.S. senator, Pacheco served as interim governor from February to December. That year, however, he was not renominated for governor by the Republican Party. However, his political career was not over: between 1878 and 1882, Pacheco served two terms in Congress.

Moreover, the last Mexicano to serve both in the state legislature and Congress during this epoch was Reginaldo Del Valle. He was elected to the Assembly in 1880 and became its presiding officer in 1881. In 1882, he was elected state senator, in 1884 was elected to Congress, and in 1888 served as the chairperson for the Democratic Party state convention.[225] According to Antonió Ríos-Bustamante, "The last elected representative of a Mexican descent in the state legislature (until the early 1960s) served in 1909."[226] Thus, a political chapter in California's Mexicano politics came to a close and another began.

While Mexicano politicos from the *rico* class did participate in ballot box politics and did face a hostile political climate, their agenda was never one of defending the colonized interests, who were in the majority. They sought to advance their own self-interests by accommodating the new white power elite. In the words of Del Castillo, "not surprisingly, there is no evidence of any effort on their part to ameliorate the pressing social and economic ills that plagued the barrio."[227] Most of the *rico politicos* acquiesced to and even supported the segregation of Mexicanos in the schools and to vigilantism, which led to lynching, repression, and violence perpetrated against Mexicanos. They seldom spoke out against the Mexicanos' growing poverty, discrimination, and colonization.

Thus, by the early 1900s, the struggle in California via accommodation politics shifted from the ballot box to the labor politics arena. Although there were few victories garnered, Mexicano involvement in various labor struggles and movements were indicative of their commitment to resist their economic exploitation and oppression.

Nuevo México: The Exception to the Rule

Of the Mexicano territories occupied by the United States in 1848, Nuevo México was the exception to colonization. "In no other region in the country," according to Erlinda Gonzales-Berry and David Maciel, "has a Chicano elite wielded as much power and influence as in Nuevo México."[228] The political aspects of internal colonialism, especially the existence of an external administration, did not apply to Nuevo México simply because Mexicano elites from the onset were direct and viable participants in "ballot box" politics—from the local to state/federal levels of government. Nuevo México was subjected to the vices of internal colonialism, yet the role of the Mexicano political elite was much more substantial. Initially most who assumed the role of buffers wielded much more influence than anywhere else in occupied Aztlán. This was primarily due to two salient factors: their demographic majority and their political adroitness.

During the years of this epoch, Mexicanos in Nuevo México comprised the majority of the territory's population. White immigration into the territory remained sparse for decades. According to John Chavez, the major reasons were "because it had little gold, less arable land than neighboring areas, problems with Apaches, and a native Mexican population about ten times that of either Tejas or California."[229] Mexicanos in major parts of the territory outvoted and out registered whites politically.[230] Moreover, they also dominated the key elective office of territorial delegate from 1850 to 1911; controlled the territorial legislature up to the early 1880s; and remained a significant force until 1912, when Nuevo

México became a state. Up until 1859, all the territorial legislative sessions were conducted in Spanish. In no other territory and later state in Aztlán did Mexicanos politically excel and adapt so efficaciously to the U.S. occupation as they did in Nuevo México.[231] Weber writes, "Having numerical superiority in the territory would have been of little consequence for [Mexicanos] had they not proved adept at playing the Anglo political game."[232] W. H. H. Hunt, a former governor, also described Nuevo México politicians as keen, cunning men in politics who were a match to whites.[233]

Rather than resist whites from outside of the political system, those of the *rico* class adapted and participated by working from within. López y Rivas further explains, "The old dominant class allied itself with the newcomers in common exploitation of the downtrodden."[234] Rosenbaum argues that the *rico* class of Nuevo México preferred accommodation as a form of cultural resistance. This was also evident in the political and economic arenas, to protect their wealth and social status in the new territorial social order. The *rico* class participated and collaborated in the governance of the territory from the beginning. Donaciano Vigil was appointed interim territorial secretary, and briefly served as interim governor. In addition, Antonio José Otero was appointed one of three territorial judges. Father José M. Gallegos, one of the alleged leaders of the Taos Revolt, was acquitted of charges of treason and from 1852 to 1855 served as territorial delegate to Congress.[235] Other Mexicano elites served as well, such as Miguel Antonio Otero, Sr. (1855–1861), Francisco Perea (1863–1865), and J. Francisco Chaves (1865–1871). Later in 1861, Miguel Antonio Otero, Sr., was appointed secretary of the territory by then-President Lincoln. According to Gómez-Quiñones, "Members of the Pino, Chávez, Chaves, Ortiz, Baca, and Armijo families who had sought to resist U.S. forces were active in post-1846 politics. Former resistance and advocate transformer leaders Diego Archuleta and Antonio José Martínez honorably served fourteen years in the territorial Assembly." What ensued politically was the establishment of a "patron system," comprised of some twenty competing elite Mexicano families who shared power based upon a "practical exchange arrangement."[236]

For the next thirty years or so, Mexicano elite *politicos* (politicians), regardless of their political affiliation, wielded considerable clout over policy issues, particularly in the Territorial Assembly, which they controlled. During the 1860s and beyond, three major issues surfaced that illustrated the power wielded by them: control of Nuevo México's educational system, the maintenance of the indigenous slavery and peonage institution, and opposition to statehood. On the former, Mexicano *politicos* were successful until 1890 in opposing a plethora of legislation that called for public education for the territory. In 1891, they passed legislation for public education only because Congress was about ready to do so.[237] According to Weber, they opposed public education "in large part because they opposed the Americanizing effect of public schools and preferred parochial schools where lessons would be taught in Spanish and Roman Catholic principles would be transmitted to the next generation."[238]

On the second issue, the Territorial Assembly successfully resisted the repeal of indigenous slavery and peonage until 1867 when Congress passed an act out-lawing such a practice, which supposedly was indifferently observed for years after.[239] Prior and during the Civil War, Nuevo México allowed the practice of slavery. The Territorial Assembly in 1859 passed legislation protecting slave property. When the Emancipation Proclamation was promulgated in 1863, it was reported that there were some six hundred indigenous slaves in Nuevo México.[240]

On the third issue, involving statehood, most Mexicano *politicos* were against it because it threatened the parochial school system. But most of the white elite were against statehood because they feared a complete Mexicano political take-over. As the *Chicago Tribune* reported in 1889, Nuevo México's population was not "American," but "Greaser" persons ignorant of county's laws, manners, customs, language, and institutions.[241] In 1890, Mexicano *politicos* were instrumental in defeating the movement for statehood. Because they were committed to maintain-ing control of the territory's educational system, according to Gonzales-Berry and Maciel, "[Nuevo Mexicanos] held the office of state superintendent of schools until 1905."[242]

Acting primarily as buffers, Mexicano *politicos* were pragmatic in that they aligned themselves with both of the major parties, Democrat and Republican. Yet during the early 1890s, some Nuevo Mexicanos alienated from the two major party monopoly challenged it by concomitantly forming a union and a third party. This struggle was considered to be an intrinsic part of the "People's Move-ment," which included Las Gorras Blancas led by Juan José Herrera.[243] In order to advance their organizing efforts of the poor on the issues of property rights and land grant titles, Herrera and others combined armed resistance tactics by joining the labor organizing efforts of Los Caballeros del Trabajo (Knights of Labor).[244]

As a union, Los Caballeros del Trabajo was a strong advocate of poor farmers, ranchers, and the working man. It was committed to challenge the oppressive economic conditions of the poor, particularly in San Miguel County. On July 3 and 4, 1890, it held a large procession of some one thousand men led by a twenty-five-member string band playing Mexicano music through the streets of Las Vegas. As the support of the activities of the union grew so did that of Las Gorras Blancas as well as their political activities. That same year, 1890, Los

Caballeros del Trabajo acted as an organizing catalyst for the formation of El Partido del Pueblo Unido (The United People's Party), patterned to that of the national People's Party. The editors of the newspaper *La Voz del Pueblo* (The Voice of the People) became the party's official mouthpiece. On September 4, sixty-three precinct representatives met and formed the Executive Central Committee. Subsequently, its platform, which embodied many of the land issue concerns of the Los Caballeros del Trabajo and Las Gorras Blancas, was developed at a three-day convention.[245] In San Miguel County, El Partido del Pueblo ran a successful slate of candidates against the Republican Party machine during the November elections. The majority of its candidates in San Miguel County were Nuevo Mexicanos. Lead by Herrera and six marshals, some five hundred men on horseback carrying torches held a nighttime procession through town. Republicans and some newspapers alleged that El Partido del Pueblo, Los Caballeros del Trabajado, and Las Gorras Blancas were part of the same "People's Movement." The former as a third-party struggle was short-lived, but it demonstrated the political protest aspects of a reform-oriented movement.[246]

Mexicanos in Nuevo México were never politically unified or homogenous or voted as a bloc as illustrated by their participation in both major political parties. Especially the elites were astute wheeler-dealers: they formed alliances and cut deals with the emergent white political elite in order to advance their own political and economic interests. The most notorious of such alliances was the "Santa Fe Ring." Led by Thomas Benton Catron and Stephan B. Elkins, it was comprised of mostly Republicans and a few Democrats and cliques of Mexicano *rico politicos*. As a corrupt political machine, the Sante Fe Ring dominated much of Nuevo México's politics from the mid-1860s to the early 1890s.[247] Carey McWilliams describes the Santa Fe Ring, as "a small compact group of Anglo-American bankers, lawyers, merchants, and politicians who dominated the territory through their ties with the ricos who in turn controlled the votes of the Spanish-speaking."[248] The members of the ring amassed literally millions of acres of choice land. Catron, a Republican and lawyer, amassed two million square miles in property and was part owner in four million more. In 1869, as a group, the Santa Fe Ring secured the Maxwell Land Grant that ultimately included some 1,714,765 acres.[249]

This "unscrupulous and ruthless alliance"[250] Santa Fe Ring became notorious due to their numerous financial schemes involving cattle, mining, and public land stealing. Miguel A. Otero was one such Mexicano *politico* who was a major player in the various schemes the ring was engaged in. The existence of the ring contributed to the breakdown of law and order that was rampant from the 1870s to the late 1880s. One such episode was the Lincoln County range wars (1876–

1878).[251] A prominent opponent who thwarted the Santa Fe Ring's expansion during the 1880s was Francisco Chavez. Opposing Chavez was Amado Chaves, who was speaker of the legislature in 1884, and who in 1891 became the first superintendent of schools, and mayor of Santa Fe between 1901 and 1903.[252]

Finally, Mexicano *politicos* in Nuevo México as buffers continued to play a significant political role from 1890 to 1912 with the struggle to make Nuevo México a state. Miguel Antonio Otero was the territorial governor from 1897 to 1906. By the turn of the twentieth century, the issue of statehood had wide political support, including from Mexicano *politicos*, who felt they could protect their interests because of the majority population status. In 1906 an unsuccessful effort was made to join Arizona and New México as one state. Whites from Arizona, fearing political control by Mexicanos from Nuevo México overwhelmingly defeated the referendum.[253]

By 1910, however, interest grew from both Mexicanos and whites for Nuevo México statehood. Of the one hundred delegates who participated in 1910 at the constitutional convention, thirty-five were Mexicanos, under the leadership of Solomon Luna, and finally formed an effective political bloc. The state constitution that went into effect in 1912 followed the spirit of the Treaty of Guadalupe Hidalgo. All the protections enunciated in the treaty were included. Nuevo México officially became a bilingual state, putting English and Spanish on an equal basis with the intent of safeguarding their Nuevo Mexicano culture. A provision was included for the training of bilingual teachers and against school segregation, and Spanish was recognized as an official language.[254] Thus, by the end of the epoch of resistance (1916) only in Nuevo México did Mexicanos via ballot box politics enjoy representation and were active politically.

Arizona: Victims of Colonization

Mexicanos in Arizona from the time that it separated from Nuevo México as a territory in 1863 was politically relegated to an internal colonial status. The cardinal motivation behind whites' efforts to separate Arizona from Nuevo México and form their own separate territory was attributable to their fear of being under the political control of Mexicanos from Nuevo México. This preceding became apparent in that after 1863 whites dominated all aspects of political, economic, and social life in Arizona. Yet around Tucson, the area of highest Mexicano population concentration, from 1863 to about 1880, a semblance of parity did exist between the white and Mexicano *rico* elites, some of which took on both buffer and "want to be white" political roles. During these years because of the small white population intermarriage between the elite families and whites became commonplace.[255] Both populations were relatively small: Mexicanos numbered a mere 1,716; and whites accounted for 168 of which 160 were males.[256] A factor contributing to the small population was the persistent Apache threat to the small number of inhabitants, which created a precariousness that proved conducive to fostering up to the 1880s cooperative interethnic relations between both groups. Also during this time, Tucson's economy, because of its location and substantial trade with Sonora, México, up to the 1870s, utilized Mexican currency. By the late 1870s, however, for Mexicanos things began to change. Tucson's population by 1870 grew to some eight thousand as a result of the establishment of several army forts. Their purposes were to pacify the area of Apaches and allow trade to expand and mining industry to develop. The advent of the railroad by the early 1880s changed dramatically the demographic profile of both Tucson and the rest of the Arizona territory.

As to the politics of Arizona outside of Tucson, few Mexicanos participated in ballot box accommodation politics. Like Tejas, California, and Nuevo México, Mexicano politics were under the control of a small number of *rico* elites. In the case of Arizona there were three prominent buffer elites, Juan Elias, Pedro Aguire, and Estevan Ochoa, who participated in July and August of 1856 in the early conventions to organize the territory.[257] The first Territorial Assembly counted twenty-two whites and only three Mexicanos. According to Meier and Rivera, "During the entire territorial period the Arizona legislature at no time had more than four [Mexicano] members, and not a single appointed official was of Mexican decent."[258] In 1865, Francisco S. León and Estevan Ochoa were both elected to the Territorial Assembly. Ochoa was subsequently elected mayor of Tucson in 1875, the only Mexicano to hold this position during Arizona's territorial status (1863–1912). He developed a reputation for being a prominent leader who spoke out on behalf of Mexicanos.[259] Another political leader was Mariano Samiengo, who during those years served in various political positions in city, county, and Territorial Assembly. He was the first Mexicano to be appointed to serve as a member of the University of Arizona's first Board of Regents in 1886. Don Mariano was the acknowledged political *patron* or boss of the Mexicanos in Tucson.[260]

Only one Mexicano, Carlos C. Jacome, from the Tucson and Yuma areas in 1910 was elected to participate at the constitutional convention. The convention was held during a period of increasing white anti-Mexicano sentiment. This hostility and agitation became evident at the convention with two efforts: the attempt to enforce English language and civic requirements, which sought to disenfranchise many Mexicanos, and the elimination of foreigners from certain categories of employment. According to Gómez-Quiñones, "both declarations were passed, but they were stated in such a way that protected native-born Mexicans." Another provision that passed that impacted Mexicanos directly was the vote prohibiting formal segregation.[261] Thus, by 1916 Mexicanos were not an intrinsic political force in the governance of the new state.

Colorado: The Forgotten Territory

With their emphasis on Tejas, Nuevo México, California, and Arizona, Mexican historians have not written much on the Mexicano political experience of Colorado. Perhaps because Spain or México never really settled Colorado in sufficient numbers, during this epoch, it remained largely a forgotten territory. Yet there is some historical evidence that documents the presence of a small Mexican population clustered in southeastern Colorado, which today is Pueblo and Trinidad and indeed practiced ballot box politics. In 1849, the first permanent colony was established in Costilla Valley, and in 1851 the town of San Luis was founded, making it the oldest in the state.[262] In the next few years, other settlements were founded in San Pedro, San Acacio, and Guadalupe.[263] This migration into southeastern Colorado was part of a colonization effort initiated by settlers from Nuevo México, especially from the Taos/Santa Fe area, and during the 1850s remained an integral part of the Nuevo México territory.[264] For a few decades after Colorado became a territory in 1861, Mexicanos in southeastern Colorado remained the majority of the population.[265] Yet at no time did they opt for armed resistance; instead the *ricos* adhered to accommodation ballot box politics.

Ethnic relations between Mexicanos and whites were precarious. This was due to the prevalence of white racist attitudes directed toward poor Mexicanos. William E. Pabor explains, "To American observers . . . Mexican farmers were 'shiftless' members of a 'degraded' race, their methods of agriculture "slovenly and without signs of thrift."[266] Illustrative of the tensions between the two peoples, an incident occurred on Christmas Day in 1867 when a white shot a Mexicano and was jailed for the shooting. A group of whites in Trinidad attempted unsuccessfully to rescue the accused killer from jail. On January 1, according to Carl Abbott, "they found themselves besieged by scores of [Mexicanos] led by Sheriff Gutierrez of Las Animas County. It took the arrival of United States troops on January 5 before the Americans thought it was safe to surrender."[267] As was the pattern throughout Aztlán, during the ensuing three decades most Mexicanos lost their lands to whites and were relegated to an internal colonial status.

Their regional majority status contributed to a few Mexicano *rico* elite who as buffers and "want to be whites" became engaged in ballot box accommodation

politics based on the *patron* system. In explaining the patron system, Carl Abbott
writes,

> Contact with the Anglo world [was] funneled through a patron. In small
> settlements the patron might be the family patriarch, in other areas a large
> landowner who provided jobs for farm hands and tenants. The *patron* took
> the responsibility for selling local produce, supplying goods for the com-
> munity, solving local disputes, acting as political spokesperson, maintain-
> ing a limited standard of living and doing small favors.[268]

Most of the Mexicano elites politically identified as Democrats, but a few did
affiliate with the Republican Party. According to Gómez-Quiñones, "From 1861
to 1876 and through statehood, Las Animas, Costilla, and Consejos counties had
more than one or more representatives. Although several financial crises affected
the Mexican elite, particularly the crash of 1893 their representation endured."
In 1861, two Mexicanos were elected to the first Territorial Assembly, Jesús Barela, from San Luis, and Victor García, from Pueblo. Jesús María Garcia in 1875
participated in the constitutional convention and remained as secretary of the
Democratic Party in Las Animas County for more than two decades.[269]

During the course of the epoch of resistance, three Mexicano legislators, José
Urbano Vigil, Casimiro Barela, and Felipe Baca, as buffer *patrones* exercised some
regional political influence. All three were educated and combined their ranching
and business interests with their politics. These *politicos* exchanged Mexicano votes
for personal political and economic concessions, although at times they sought to
protect the community's general welfare.[270] Vigil was active in Democratic politics from the 1880s to 1915, when he died; served as Las Animas County chair
of the Democratic Party; and was a member of the state central committee. The
most famous of the *patron* Democrat politicians was Barela, originally a migrant
from Nuevo México. Prior to being elected to the Territorial Assembly in 1871,
Barela had been elected to various county offices. In 1875 he was a delegate to
the territorial constitutional convention held in 1876 when Colorado became a
state.[271] That same year, Barela was elected to the Colorado State Senate, holding
that office until 1912. He attended two national Democratic Party conventions
and because of his land, railroads, ranching, banking, and urban real estate interests became one of the most affluent elites of southern Colorado.[272]

None of the other *politicos* in Colorado of the epoch matched Barela's buffer
record and commitment to protect the rights of the poor Mexicano. As a centrist
and pragmatist *politico*, he always tried, according to Abbott, "to guard the interests
of the Spanish-speaking Coloradans from the strange bureaucracy of the Anglos.

In doing so, he helped to cushion the village of Hispano Colorado from the changes being forced on it."[273] He was able to persuade the Colorado legislature to have all the laws published in Spanish, German, and English until 1900; blocked a proposal to disenfranchise Mexicanos by delaying its enforcement until 1890; and in 1912 succeeded in creating a land court to adjudicate land claims. Barela also proposed unsuccessfully that Mexicano children be instructed in their native language, Spanish, and learn English as a second language. He also tackled problems faced by Mexicanos, such as land grant disputes, prejudiced courts, gerrymandering, discriminatory election laws, and interracial violence.[274]

Up to the early 1900s, a semblance of ballot box politics was still practiced by Mexicanos. Teodoro Abeyta from Trinidad held local offices between 1885 and 1902. His brother, Vivian, during the 1890s was elected as a state legislator and county commissioner, as was José R. Aguilar, while J. M. Madrid was also elected to the state legislature, county superintendent of schools, and as late as 1932, state senator. Yet from 1901 to 1904, some Mexicanos did participate in various labor struggles in Colorado, particularly those in the mining industry. Thus, lacking a significant population base, only a semblance of Mexicano political influence existed by 1916 in the southeastern portion of Colorado.[275]

Organizational Development and Politics

During the epoch of resistance, organizational development and politics began to take root. During the early years of the occupation little organizational formation occurred. The rise of organizations began during the 1870s and accelerated by the turn of the twentieth century. Without protection from innumerable problems and a hostile political climate, Mexicanos began to form organizations for self-support, protection, and social and cultural purposes. From an organizational perspective, adaptation became apparent in the formation of two types of organizations: mutual benefit and protective societies and union formation and activism. The former as organizations were committed largely to purely social, cultural, and mutual benefit activities; whereas the latter were buffer-oriented "interest groups" that sought to organize workers. "An interest group," according to Jeffrey M. Berry, "is an organized body of individuals who share some goals and who try to influence public policy."[276] From an advocacy change perspective, unions were the first form of interest or pressure group to permeate the Mexicano political experience in occupied Aztlán. Moreover, unions at times during this epoch as proponents of change functioned either as buffers or advocate transformers.

Mutualistas

Within the "Mexicano political experience in the United States, mutual benefit or *mutualista* organizations are the oldest form of organization."[277] Their origin can be traced to 1598 with the Spanish colonization of Nuevo México with the formation of *cofradias* or *confraternidades* (lay brotherhoods)—the basic institutions out of which evolved the numerous lodges, fraternal orders, livestock associations, health cooperatives, and other specific-purpose organizations in Mexicano communities.[278] Mutual aid societies, however, were also active in México. The first to be formally formed was in 1853 and was called the *Sociedad Paticular de Socorros Mutuos* (Private Society of Mutual Benefits). During much of the 1800s, newly arrived immigrants, for example, Germans, Jews, and Irish, also formed immigrant aid and benevolent organizations.

Mutual aid societies within the Mexicano communities in the United States developed out of a profound need for mutual assistance and support. They became vital "voluntary" mechanisms of self-help, civic participation, and union organizing. While it can be argued that they played an adaptation buffer role, in most cases, because of their strong Mexicano nationalist propensities, they did not seek acculturation but rather were "culture preservationists." According to Jose Hernandez, "as the need arose, they became a fundamental expression of dissatisfaction with the manner in which the Anglo society treated Mexican Americans. To them, government represented repression and fear as well as special interests, and it could not be counted on to protect the Chicano people."[279] From the resistance aspect, Carlos Vélez-Ibañez argues, "These functioned as the most important organizationally resistant forms to economic exploitation, civil discrimination, and educational inequality."[280]

Without the presence of governmental assistance (welfare and access to a myriad of social service programs), like other ethnic groups, working-class Mexicanos pooled their meager resources, and in order to help each other out they formed these self-help and self-reliant types of organizations. By collecting monthly dues, these fraternal mutual benefit organizations (*mutualistas*) provided their members with low-cost funeral and insurance benefits, low-interest loans, and other forms of social and economic assistance.[281] When a family whose *mutualista* member for example got sick or faced a crisis situation and was in need of assistance, members would provide the family in need some form of assistance or loan or donate money. In response to internal colonialism's segregation, *mutualistas* also provided cultural, social, and recreational activities, which included dances, dinners, sponsored weddings and baptisms, and patriotic celebrations, within their *colonias* and barrios.

Many of the *mutualistas*, especially those of the early twentieth century, had an ardent nationalist and patriotic affinity to México—their names, rituals, songs, were indicative of their continued loyalty to México. They categorically rebuked cultural assimilation and practiced a form of "Mexicanismo," which laid the cultural foundation for the rise during the next epoch of the "Mexicano Generation." This denoted a cultural attachment and affinity to what was Mexicano, including preservation of the culture, heritage, and Spanish language, which fostered a perception of being an extension of an informal kinship system. Structured as lodges with a hierarchy of leaders, members paid monthly dues. For many years, women were excluded from membership; consequently, they formed their own auxiliaries. Lastly, as Paul Taylor notes, *mutualistas* also provided "a forum for discussion and a means of organizing the social life of the community."[282]

Mutual benefit societies first formed during the 1870s in Tejas. As a result of increasing white colonial repression, ethnic segregation, and poverty, Mexicanos in Tejas "resisted" their internal colonized status through the formation of *mutualistas*, which formed the social nucleus of the Mexicano barrios and *colonias* and became the sole basis for community organizing and self-help.[283] One such *mutualista* was the Club Recíproco, founded in Corpus Christi, Tejas, in 1873, which had as its stated purpose "the protection of the poor and the mutual benefit of its members, calculated to assist society and elevate all who may wish to associate with the members of the club." From the late 1870s to the early 1900s, various types of *mutualista* were formed throughout Tejas. The most prominent during these years were the Sociedad Mutualista Benito Juarez (1879), the Sociedad Mutualista Miguel Hidalgo, and the Sociedad Ignacio Zaragoza (1881). In Brownsville, the oldest *mutualista* founded in 1881 was the Sociedad Mutualista Miguel Hidalgo.[284] Some twelve such groups existed by 1910 in Corpus Christi alone. A plethora of these self-help associations or societies had formed, most independent from each other. By the early 1900s, La Orden de Caballeros de Honor (The Order of Knights of Honor) was formed and had several lodges throughout the state. According to Weber," Most of these organizations were seen to have been exclusively male"; the one exception was the all-women Sociedad Beneficencia, founded in Corpus Christi in 1890.[285]

Because of the deplorable social and economic conditions Mexicanos faced in Tejas and the racial hatred and discrimination, in 1911 an unsuccessful attempt was made to unite all the *mutualistas*. On September 14, 1911, a number of *mutualistas* sent delegates to the historically unprecedented Primer Congreso Mexicanista de Tejas (the First Mexican Congress of Texas) with the intent of building a union of associations. Attended by some four hundred delegates, the agenda addressed the need for unity and citizen participation and action on labor exploitation, segregation and exclusion of Mexicano children from the schools, lack of criminal justice, and social discrimination in general. The delegates were concerned about seeking ways of Mexicanos protecting themselves from such white injustices, such as lynching, being burned at the stake, and persecution by the Texas Rangers.[286] As has been an on-going organizational pattern within the Mexicano political experience, efforts to unify a diversity of organizations into a permanent alliance, confederation, or federation largely met in total failure. El Primer Congreso Mexicanista de Tejas 1911 was no exception, but became a template for other subsequent efforts.

In Arizona, one of the most powerful buffer *mutualistas* to emerge was La Alianza Hispana Americana (the Hispanic American Alliance or hereafter La Alianza).[287] Formed in 1894, originally it was a statewide mutual benefit society subsequently evolving into a regional (Southwest) civil rights interest group that assumed a degree of political awareness and commitment for social action and advocacy.[288] Mexicanos in Tucson concerned by the economic downturns of an economic depression, coupled with the formation of a chapter of the nativist American Protective Association, formed La Alianza. Like many of the *mutualistas* that were formed during this epoch, La Alianza was a product of a small buffer elite group. The key leaders were Velasco Samiengo, Manuel Samaniego, and Ignacio Calvillo, but some thirty-six other economic and political elites also participated in its founding. Since it was to be nonpolitical, the Tucson chapter of La Alianza formed the Mexican Democratic club as its political action front.[289]

Oriented toward self-help efforts, La Alianza was established to protect the threatened rights of Mexicanos in Arizona. According to one of its founders, Calvillo, it was formed to "protect and fight for the rights of Spanish Americans in Tucson, for at that time there was a lot of strife and ill-feeling between us and the Anglo Saxon element caused in great part by prejudice, misunderstanding and ignorance."[290] At first, it was formed as a local organization, but quickly expanded its base throughout the state with lodges established in several communities and outside of Arizona as well, and by 1897, held its first national convention.[291]

By 1910, La Alianza had over three thousand members in Arizona, Tejas, Nuevo México, California, and even México.[292] According to Del Castillo and De León, "Its appeal spread first throughout Arizona and then California by the early 1900s, primarily among middle class, leaders who desired to see sickness and unemployment insurance benefits applied to the Mexican community." Yet in Nuevo México, it was not until 1906 that the first lodge of La Alianza was formed. This was because Nuevo México did not have a rich history of mutual assistance and support entities. David Weber writes that this "may indicate that the Hispanos there had less need to form an exclusive club until the turn of the century."[293]

Politically, La Alianza in its buffer organizational colonial role steered a centrist course emphasizing fraternity, brotherhood, and cultural pride.[294] Manuel Gamio further added, La Alianza's "aims were very clearly political" since its objective was to replace the white Texan residents in control of Tucson politics with Mexicanos.[295] From its inception, La Alianza struggled against discrimination and promoted candidates for office in local and state races in Arizona. During the 1890s and early 1900s several of its members were elected to local positions in Tucson. This was characterized by some observers as the "the golden age" for all local Mexicano politicians.[296] Influenced by the women's suffrage movement, in 1913 they voted to admit women to full membership.[297] Even though La Alianza was the largest and most influential, by the early 1900s, several other *mutualistas* were formed in Arizona, such as La Sociedad Mutualista Porfirio Díaz, Los Leñadores del Mundo, La Sociedad Mexicana-Americana, and La Liga Protectora Latina. The latter in particular, formed in 1914 in Phoenix, also stands out as a *mutualista* whose strategic agenda changed to one of acting like a traditional interest group. It openly lobbied against discriminatory legislation and opposed political candidates.[298]

During the epoch of resistance, Nuevo México, California, and Colorado also experienced some *mutualista* organizational development, but not at the same scope as Tejas and Arizona. In California, during this epoch, mutual benefit societies were not the prevalent form of organizational formation. They did not begin to proliferate in California until the early 1900s. One such *mutualista* was La Sociedad Zaragoza formed in 1911 in San Bernardino. The need for burial assistance was the catalyst issue that led to its formation. Another was the Hidalgo Society that was established in 1912 in Brawley, which provided its members with the benefits of family conviviality, disability and sick benefits, unemployment compensation, and protection against injustices. Still another was La Sociedad Hispano-Americana de Benéfica Mutua, established in Los Angeles, which provided similar services.

Complementing the formation of *mutualistas* were numerous cultural and patriotic clubs. Most of these entities were in a state of flux: they formed, disbanded, and at times regrouped. These included the Hispano-American Society of Los Angeles, the Mexican Progressive Society, and the Juarez Patriotic Society, which held patriotic and cultural celebrations in commemoration of important holidays such as Mexican Independence Day (September 16th).[299] A number of other cultural and social groups were formed as well as a few political clubs, such as San Francisco's Spanish American Independent Political Club.[300]

During this epoch, other types of non-interest groups were active, especially within the religious sector of the community, which acted essentially as buffers In Nuevo México; one such religious organization was the Holy Brotherhood of Penitentes. According to Acuña, "Descended from the Third Order of St. Francis of Assisi, it practiced public flagellation and, during Holy Week, initiated the ordeals of Christ."[301] Los Penitentes, a lay religious (Roman Catholic) brotherhood, whose genesis is obscure, is imbedded in the history of the colonization of Nuevo México. One account is that they emerged during the late eighteenth century.[302] It addressed the poor people's deep-seated spiritual and social needs. After 1846, when some of the Spanish priests had died or were exiled during the occupation of Nuevo México, members of Los Penitentes took over some of their religious functions.[303] In reaction to attempts to restore the Church's authority, Bishop Jean Lamy, appointed in 1853, and his successor, Jean-Baptiste Salpointe, in 1885 disdainful of Penitente's mystical brand of religious zeal and perceiving it as a threat to the institutional Church, sought unsuccessfully to abolish them.

As a result, the Penitentes were slandered and libeled and were even denied the sacraments. In response to their persecution, they operated clandestinely and were influential in the villages of northern Nuevo México and southern Colorado. In particular, by the 1880s and well into the early part of the twentieth century, they became a strong force in politics at all levels of government. Hernandez writes that most were Republican and were "members of the state legislature, sheriffs, county assessors, surveyors, and other public elected and appointed officials belonged to a local Penitente organization."[304] By the end of the epoch of resistance, they were still religiously functional and politically influential.

Uniones: *Vehicles of the Working Class*

By the latter part of the nineteenth century, integral to the organizational development aspects of the Mexicano political experience was the incipience of union organizing among Mexicanos. Resistance to their repressive working conditions became evident in the Mexicanos' active participation in various labor unions, which as previously mentioned became the first type of "interest group" to emerge. This is important because particularly many of the unions were not buffers; essentially some pursued an advocate transformer political role. Because of either their socialist or syndicalist ideological perspectives they were considered to be radical forms of social change worker's organizations. Unions in general struggled to ameliorate the worker's wages, working conditions, and benefits through the use of organized pressure against employers via negotiations or strikes.

Starting in the 1880s, Mexicano workers beleaguered by internal colonialism began to join unions in order to improve their economic lot. What encouraged their involvement in labor struggles? The expansion of capitalist economic development into Aztlán and the relegation of Mexicanos to an internal colonial status created a political climate that was propitious for Mexicano workers to join labor struggles and movements. Like in other areas, Mexicano workers, especially in the mines, were victims of crass exploitation and harsh abuse and were subjected to the worst of discriminatory working conditions. Commonplace throughout "occupied" Aztlán was the operation of a wage double standard, which meant that whites in most cases received double the wages and got the best jobs. In Nuevo México during the 1890s, Mexicanos were involved both as leaders and members in the Knights of Labor.

By the turn of the century, some Mexicanos in Tejas turned to labor organizing. In Tejas and the nation as a whole, U.S. labor unions, such as the American Federation of Labor (AFL), did not promote or seek and often impeded Mexicano labor organizing efforts. As Acuña explains, "North American unions often perceived Mexicans as enemies and made little effort to organize them."[305] In Tejas, the AFL openly discriminated against Mexicano workers and efforts to unionize them and at times joined management to defeat Mexicano strikes. The lack of support from white unions did not deter Mexicanos from striking for better wages and working conditions. One such strike occurred twice, in 1901 and again in 1905, in El Paso. During the 1901 strike, some two hundred Mexicano construction workers struck the El Paso Electric Street Car Company for higher wages. The police provided strikebreakers with protection and broke the strike. The company agreed not to employ outsiders, but refused the wage demands. Not satisfied, workers again struck unsuccessfully in 1905. During the ensuing years, Mexicano labor organizing activity increased. In 1907 in Laredo, Mexicanos joined the Federal Labor Union, of which two-thirds were Mexicanos, and successfully struck the Mexican Railway company shops in the city for a 25-cent a day increase. After the strike, although unsuccessful, the same union sought to organize miners. That same year, chiefly Mexicano workers in El Paso and in Thurber, Tejas, carried out two other strikes.[306] Further adding to the incipient labor movement in Tejas and elsewhere were the organizing activities of the Magónista Mexican Liberal Party and that of the IWW (International Workers of the World).

By the turn of the twentieth century, ballot box politics had all but disappeared for Mexicanos in California. Resistance by the early 1900s came in the form of increased labor organizing activity. Some Mexicano workers responded to deplorable colonial oppressive working conditions and low wages and joined unions and participated in strikes. In 1903 Mexicano and Japanese sugar beet workers formed the Japanese-Mexican Labor Association of Oxnard and initiated a strike that resulted in armed conflict with one Mexicano worker killed. The strike produced a partial victory in slightly higher wages, more equitable recruitment practices, and more favorable policies at the company store, and as a result of the strike the Sugar Beet and Farm Laborers Union was formed. About the same the time in Santa Barbara, Mexicano packers and sheepshearers struck their respective industries for higher wages and shorter hours. That same year (1903), Mexicano lemon workers in Santa Barbara successfully initiated a strike against the Johnston Fruit Company for higher wages and shorter hours. Between 1901 and 1903, Mexicano agricultural workers were also engaged in other strikes around Fresno, San Francisco, and Redlands. In 1903 and again in 1910, in an urban area of Los Angeles, Mexicano track workers formed La Unión Federal Mexicana (the Mexican Federal Union) and initiated two unsuccessful strikes against Pacific Electric railway.[307]

In Arizona by the turn of the century Mexicanos became engaged in union politics and organizing. Suffice it to say that Mexicanos participated in numerous labor struggles, such as the Clifton-Morenci Strikes of 1903 and 1915. During the first strike, some twelve hundred to fifteen hundred workers participated of which 80 to 90 percent were Mexicanos. Many of the strike leaders and workers as well came from membership ranks of *mutualistas*, such as Abraham Salcido, who was president of a Mexican society. In June 1903, opposed by Arizona Rangers, some two thousand Mexicanos marched through the streets of Morenci in torrential rains in support of the strike, dispersing only after serious flooding had occurred. The strike ended with arrests of the leaders, of which two were Mexicano.

Salcido was released from prison two years later, and joined the Magónista Partido Liberal Mexicano (PLM-Mexican Liberal Party), which adhered to an advocate transformer role. It became involved along with others from Arizona with the "Cananea, Sonora strike" in 1906.[308] On the evening of May 31, Mexicano miners under the aegis of the La Union Liberal Humanidad, an affiliate of the PLM, struck for equitable wages. Mexicano miners were paid half of what their white counterparts were paid. Whereas whites worked eight hours Mexicanos were compelled to work ten- to twelve-hour days. This situation led to some two thousand miners walking out and what ensued left a trail of conflict, violence, and death. Mexican federal troops were called in and were supported by Arizona Rangers. The strike was squelched: three miners were killed and scores injured.[309] However, the significance of the Cananea strike was the involvement of the Magónista PLM and the apparent transnational capitalist interests at play as suggested by the intervention of the Arizona Rangers.

Thus, by the end of the epoch of resistance in 1916, the Mexicano political experience in occupied Aztlán had experienced both armed struggles and ballot box politics. Moreover, it had been subjected to the insidious political, economic, cultural, and social aspects of internal colonialism. However, with the dramatic increase in the Mexicano population coupled with a growing volatile political climate both in the United States and México, the political stage was dialectically set for the next epoch, the "Politics of Adaptation."

Notes

1. I would argue that Santa Anna, despite the many negative aspects of his character and leadership, was inept and "México's worst real estate agent." From my perspective, he did not sell parts of México. I would argue that for all intents and purposes, he gave México away considering the relative value of the one million square miles of territory today. One can easily deduce that the value of México's lost lands in the context of the twenty-first century is worth trillions of dollars. This is providing that it is possible at all to put a price on these lands.

2. Samuel Eliot Morison and Henry Steel Commager, *The Growth of the American Republic* (New York: Oxford University Press, 1962), 645.

3. Richard Griswold Del Castillo, *The Treaty of Guadalupe Hidalgo: A Legacy of Conflict* (Norman: University of Oklahoma Press, 1990), 59–60.

4. Rodolfo Acuña, *Occupied America: A History of Chicanos*, 5th ed. (New York: Pearson and Longman, 2002), 102.

5. Leobardo F. Estrada, F. Chris Garcia, Reynaldo Flores Macias, and Lionel Maldonado, "Chicanos in the United States: A History of Exploitation and Resistance," in *Latinos in the Political System*, ed. F. Chris Garcia (Notre Dame, Ind.: University of Notre Dame Press, 1988), 31.

6. Oscar J. Martinez, "On the Size of the Chicano Population: New Estimates, 1850–1900," *Aztlán* Vol. 6 (Spring 1975): 50–56.

7. Carey McWilliams, *North from México: The Spanish-Speaking People of the United States* (New York: Greenwood, 1968), 52.

8. McWilliams, *North from México*, 163.

9. Oscar J. Martinez, *Mexican-Origin People in the United States: A Topical History* (Tucson: University of Arizona Press, 2001), 6–7.

10. Joan Moore and Harry Pachon, *Hispanics in the United States* (Englewood Cliffs, N.J.: Prentice Hall, 1985), 19.

11. McWilliams, *North from México*, 132.

12. Albert Camarillo, *Chicanos in California: A History of Mexican Americans in California* (San Francisco: Boyd & Fraser Publishing Co., 1984), 26.

13. Richard Griswold Del Castillo and Arnoldo De León, *North to Aztlán: A History of Mexican Americans in the United States* (New York: Twayne Publishers; London: Prentice Hall International, 1996), 30.

14. Acuña, *Occupied America*, 4th ed., 143.

15. Horace Bell, *On the Old West Coast* (New York: Morrow, 1930), 5–6.

16. Mario Barrera, *Beyond Aztlán: Ethnic Autonomy in Comparative Perspective* (New York: Praeger, 1988), 9.

17. Barrera, *Beyond Aztlán*, 168.

18. Acuña, *Occupied America*, 4th ed., 109.

19. Juan Gonzales, *Harvest of Empire: A History of Latinos in America* (New York: Penguin, 2000), 38.

20. Thomas Torrans, *Forging the Tortilla Curtain: Cultural Drift and Change along the United States–México Border, From the Spanish Era to the Present* (Fort Worth, Tex.: TCU Press, 2000), 80–81.

21. Torrans, *Forging the Tortilla Curtain*, 85.

22. Leonard Pitt, *Decline of the Californios: A Social History of the Spanish Speaking Californians, 1846–1890* (Berkeley: University of California Press, 1966), 209.

23. Acuña, *Occupied America*, 5th ed., 104

24. For an excellent brief account of U.S. filibustering expeditions, particularly on the Guaymas, Sonora, incident see Acuña, *Occupied America*, 4th ed., 109–12.

25. Eric J. Hobsbawm, *Primitive Rebels: Studies in Archaic Forms of Social Movements in the 19th and 20th Centuries* (New York: Praeger, 1959), 5–13.

26. Hobsbawm, *Primitive Rebels*, 5–13.

27. Eric Wolf, *Peasants* (Englewood Cliffs, N.J.: Prentice Hall: 1966), 107.

28. Alfredo Mirandé, *Gringo Justice* (Notre Dame, Ind.: University of Notre Dame University Press, 1987), 50.

29. Del Castillo and De León, *North to Aztlán*, 33.

30. Robert J. Rosenbaum, *Mexicano Resistance in the Southwest* (Dallas, Tex.: Southern Methodist University Press, 1998), 15.

31. Estrada et al., "Chicanos in the United States," 37.

32. McWilliams, *North from México*, 130.

33. Juan Gómez-Quiñones, *Roots of Chicano Politics: 1600–1940* (Albuquerque: University of New México Press, 1994), 203.

34. Camarillo, *Chicanos in California*, 18.

35. Acuña, *Occupied America*, 4th ed., 150.

36. Gilberto López y Rivas, *The Chicanos: Life and Struggles of the Mexican Minority in the United States* (New York: Monthly Review Press, 1973), 32.

37. Camarillo, *Chicanos in California*, 22.

38. There are numerous works on the life and escapades of Joaquin Murrieta. The following are but a few: John Rolling Ridge [Yellow Bird, pseud.], *The Life and Adventures of Joaquin Murrieta: The Celebrated Bandit*, reprint (Norman: University of Oklahoma Press, 1854); James F. Varley, *Joaquin Murrieta: California's Gold Rush Bandit* (Twin Falls, Idaho: Big

Lost River Press, 1995); Walter Noble Burns, *The Robin Hood of El Dorado: The Saga of Joaquin Murrieta, Famous Outlaw of California's Age of Gold* (Albuquerque: University of New México Press, 1999); Don Gwaltney, *The Bandit Joaquin* (Northbrook, Ill.: Apple Core Press, 1997); and Remi Nadeau, *The Real Joaquin Murrieta: Robin Hood or Gold Rush Gangster?* (Corona Del Mar, Calif.: Trans-Anglo Books, 1974).

39. Pitt, *The Decline of the Californios.*

40. Ridge, *The Life and Adventures of Joaquin Murrieta*, 9–13. It is important to note that other writers and scholars as to particular aspects of the life and death of Murrieta have challenged Ridge's account, written in 1854.

41. Rosenbaum, *Mexican Resistance in the Southwest*, 58.

42. Del Castillo and De León, *North to Aztlán*, 34.

43. Julian Samora and Patricia Vandel Simon, *A History of the Mexican American People* (Notre Dame, Ind.: University of Notre Dame Press, 1977), 115.

44. Richard Gerald Mitchell, *Joaquin Murrieta: A Study of Social Conditions in Early California*, master's thesis, Department of History, University of California, Los Angeles, 1927.

45. Nadeau, *The Real Joaquin*, 146.

46. David J. Weber, *Foreigners in Their Native Land: Historical Roots of the Mexican Americans* (Albuquerque: University of New México Press, 1973), 206.

47. Interview, Alfredo Figurora, May 8, 2001. Figurora has written a book on Murrieta, which is soon to be published. He claims to be a relative of his.

48. For an analysis on the mythology aspects see Varley, *Joaquin Murrieta*, chapter six.

49. Mirandé, *Chicano Justice*, 78.

50. Dominga L. Gestetner, *Tiburcio Vasquez* (Puyallup, Wash.: Historic Memories Press, 1964), 13–14.

51. Weber, *Foreigners in Their Native Land*, 226.

52. Mirandé, *Gringo Justice*, 79.

53. Pedro Castillo and Albert Camarillo, *Furia y Muerte: Los Bandidos Chicanos*, Monograph No. 4, Aztlán Publications, Chicano Studies Center, University of California, Los Angeles, 1973, 15.

54. Castillo and Camarillo, *Furia y Muerte*, 15.

55. Weber, *Foreigners in Their Native Land*, 227.

56. Estrada et al., "Chicanos in the United States," 36.

57. Rosenbaum, *Mexican Resistance in the Southwest*, 63.

58. Pitt, *The Decline of the Californios*, 167.

59. Acuña, *Occupied America*, 4th ed., 149.

60. Pitt, *The Decline of the Californios*, 168.

61. Pitt, *The Decline of the Californios*, 168.

62. Del Castillo and De León, *North to Aztlán*, 34.

63. Pitt, *The Decline of the Californios*, 173–74.

64. Rosenbaum, *Mexicano Resistance in the Southwest*, 66.

65. Samora and Simon, *A History of the Mexican American People*, 115.

66. Walter Prescott Webb, *The Texas Rangers: A Century of Frontier Defense* (Reprint, Cambridge: Houghton Mifflin, 1935), 132–33.

67. Robert A. Calvert and Arnoldo De León, *The History of Texas* (Arlington Heights, Ill.: Harlan Davidson, Inc. 1990), 107.

68. For a historical analysis from a Mexicano perspective on this theme see Julian Samora, Joe Bernal, and Albert Peña, *Gunpowder Justice: A Reassessment of the Texas Rangers* (Notre Dame, Ind.: University of Notre Dame Press, 1979).

69. Matt S. Meier and Feliciano Rivera, *Mexican Americans, American Mexicans: From Conquistadors to Chicanos*, rev. ed. (New York: Hill & Wang, 1993), 82.

70. Calvert and De León, *The History of Texas*, 107.

71. Webb, *The Texas Rangers*, 176.

72. For works that examine the life, adventures, and various other pertinent aspects of his life see Carlos Larralde and Jose Rodolfo Jacobo, *Juan N. Cortina and the Struggle for Justice in Texas* (Dubuque, Iowa: Kendall/Hunt, 2000); Jerry D. Thompson, ed., *Juan Cortina and the Texas–México Frontier, 1859–1877* (El Paso, Tex.: Texas Western Press, 1994); Carlos E. Cortés, ed., *Juan N. Cortina: Two Interpretations* (New York: Arno Press, 1974); Charles W. Goldfinch, *Juan N. Cortina, 1824–1892: A Re-Appraisal*, master's thesis, Department of History, University of Chicago, June 1949; and *Juan N. Cortina: Bandit or Patriot?*, an address by J. T. Canales given to the Lower Rio Grande Valley Historical Society, at San Benito, Texas, October 25, 1951.

73. Larralde and Jacobo, *Juan N. Cortina*, 4.

74. Goldfinch, *Juan N. Cortina*, 19–20.

75. Larralde and Jacobo, *Juan N. Cortina*, 4.

76. Webb, *The Texas Rangers*, 177.

77. Larralde and Jacobo, *Juan N. Cortina*, 7.

78. Arnoldo De León, *Mexican Americans in Texas: A Brief History* (Arlington Heights, Ill.: Harlan Davidson, Inc., 1993), 38.

79. For a comprehensive examination of the life and history of Juan Cortina see Goldfinch, *Juan N. Cortina, 1824–1892: A Re-Appraisal*. Arno Press, New York, published the dissertation in 1974.

80. Larralde and Jacobo, *Juan N. Cortina*, 47, 37.

81. Samora, Bernal, and Peña, *Gunpowder Justice*, 34.

82. Thompson, *Juan Cortina*, 12.

83. David Montejano, *Anglos and Mexicans in the Making of Texas, 1836–1986* (Austin: University of Texas Press, 1987), 32.

84. Arnoldo De León, *The Tejano Community, 1836–1900* (Albuquerque: University of New México Press, 1982), 18.

85. Gómez-Quiñones, *Roots of Chicano Politics*, 205.

86. Weber, *Foreigners in Their Native Land*, 207.

87. Goldfinch, *Juan N. Cortina*, 46.

88. Goldfinch, *Juan N. Cortina*, 47.

89. Montejano, *Anglos and Mexicans*, 33.

90. Mirandé, *Gringo Justice*, 92.

91. Gonzales, *Mexicanos*, 109.

92. Goldfinch, *Juan N. Cortina*, 66.

93. Larralde and Jacobo, *Juan N. Cortina*, 76.

94. Larralde and Jacobo, *Juan N. Cortina*, 76–83.

95. Larralde and Jacobo, *Juan N. Cortina*, 65.

96. Larralde and Jacobo, *Juan N. Cortina*, 65.

97. Meier and Rivera, *Mexican Americans, American Mexicans*, 83–84.

98. Weber, *Foreigners in Their Native Land*, 207–8.

99. Acuña, *Occupied America*, 1st ed., 51.

100. Meier and Rivera, *Mexican Americans, American Mexicans*, 84.

101. De León, *The Tejano Community*, 21.

102. Rosenbaum, *Mexican Resistance in the Southwest*, 93.

103. Acuña, *Occupied America*, 4th ed., 94–95.

104. For an excellent examination of the rise of La Gorras Blancas see Rosenbaum, *Mexicano Resistance in the Southwest*, chapters 7–9; and Andrew B. Schlesinger, "Las Gorras Blancas, 1889–1891," *Journal of Mexican American History* Vol. I (Spring 1971); Anselmo Arellano, "The People's Movement: Las Gorras Blancas," in *The Contested Homeland: A Chicano History of New México*, ed. Erlinda Gonzales-Berry and David Maciel (Albuquerque: University of New México Press, 2000), 63.

105. Arellano, "The People's Movement: Las Gorras Blancas," 63.

106. Rosenbaum, *Mexicano Resistance in the Southwest*, 99.

107. Weber, *Foreigners in Their Native Land*, 208.

108. Mirandé, *Gringo Justice*, 97.

109. Matt S. Meier and Feliciano Rivera, *The Chicanos: A History of Mexican Americans* (New York: Hill & Wang, 1972), 105.

110. Del Castillo and De León, *North to Aztlán*, 51.

111. Juan Gómez-Quiñones, *Roots of Chicano Politics*, 278–79.

112. For the political relationship between these entities see Armando Navarro, *La Raza Unida Party: A Chicano Challenge to the U.S. Two-Party Dictatorship* (Philadelphia: Temple University Press, 2000), 175–76. Also, in the following section on accommodation politics, an expanded analysis will be provided.

113. Arellano, "The People's Movement," 66.

114. Meier and Rivera, *The Chicanos*, 105.

115. Mirandé, *Gringo Justice*, 99.

116. Reference to letter cited in Arellano, "The People's Movement," 67.

117. Gómez-Quiñones, *Roots of Chicano Politics*, 283.

118. Meier and Rivera, *The Chicanos*, 102.

119. For a historical overview on the history of this defiant historical moment see Castillo and Camarillo, *Furia y Muerte*, 52–83.

120. Meier and Rivera, *The Chicanos*, 103.

121. Gonzales, *Mexicanos*, 109.

122. De León, *Mexican Americans in Texas*, 63.

123. Gonzales, *Mexicanos*, 109.

124. For a literary account of the life of Gregorio Cortez see Américo Paredes, *With His Pistol in His Hand: A Border Ballad and Its Hero* (Austin: University of Texas Press, 1958).

125. Samora, Bernal, and Peña, *Gunpowder Justice*, 58.

126. Castillo and Camarillo, *Furia y Muerte*, 130–33.

127. Rosenbaum, *Mexicano Resistance in the Southwest*, 47.

128. Samora, Bernal, and Peña, *Gunpowder Justice*, 61.

129. James A. Sandos, *Rebellion in the Borderlands: Anarchism and the Plan of San Diego, 1904–1923* (Norman: University of Oklahoma Press, 1992), 125–26.

130. Sandos, *Rebellion in the Borderlands*, 125–26.

131. Acuña, *Occupied America*, 5th ed., 155–56.

132. For an extensive examination of the Plan de San Diego see Sandos, *Rebellion in the Borderlands*, 10, 24; also, Juan Gómez-Quiñones, "Plan de San Diego Reviewed," *Aztlán: Chicano Journal of the Social Sciences and the Arts* Vol. I, No. I (Spring 1970), UCLA, Mexican American Cultural Center: 124–32.

133. Montejano, *Anglos and Mexicans in the Making of Texas*, 118.

134. Samora and Simon, *A History of the Mexican American People*, 129.

135. Acuña, *Occupied America*, 177.

136. Sandos, *Rebellion in the Borderlands*, 83.

137. Gómez-Quiñones, *Roots of Chicano Politics*, 348.

138. Calvert and De León, *The History of Texas*, 271.

139. Gómez-Quiñones, *Roots of Chicano Politics*, 348.

140. Rosenbaum, *Mexicano Resistance in the Southwest*, 50.

141. Sandos, *Rebellion in the Borderlands*, 81.

142. Mirandé, *Gringo Justice*, 95–96.

143. Sandos, *Rebellion in the Borderlands*, 81.

144. Gómez-Quiñones, "Plan de San Diego Reviewed," 125.

145. Gómez-Quiñones, "Plan de San Diego Reviewed," 125.

146. Gómez-Quiñones, "Plan de San Diego Reviewed," 126.

147. Cited in Rosenbaum, *Mexicano Resistance in the Southwest*, 51.

148. Acuña, *Occupied America*, 5th ed., 167.

149. Acuña, *Occupied America*, 5th ed., 168.

150. Don M. Coerver and Linda B. Hall, *Texas and the Mexican Revolution: A Study in State and National Border Policy, 1910–1920* (San Antonio, Tex.: Trinity University Press, 1984), 85–108.

151. Rosenbaum, *Mexicano Resistance in the Southwest*, 51.

152. Cited in Acuña, *Occupied America*, 4th ed., 177.

153. Calvert and De León, *The History of Texas*, 271.

154. Coerver and Hall, *Texas and the Mexican Revolution*, 87.

155. Acuña, *Occupied America*, 4th ed., 177.

156. Some aspects of this analysis are derived from an article of mine published in 1974 entitled "The Evolution of Chicano Politics," *Aztlán: Journal of the Social Sciences and the Arts* (Spring/Fall 1974): 57–82.

157. Del Castillo and De León, *North to Aztlán*, 32.

158. The "culture of poverty" posits the argument that poverty begets its own value and belief system or mind-set. Furthermore, this mind-set is characterized by such values as indifference, apathy, suspicion, fatalism, present orientation, and ultimately alienation. The end result is that this mind-set is politically detrimental: it fosters nonparticipation and a cynical perspective toward politics. For reference, see the following two works of Oscar Lewis: *Pedro Martinez* (New York: Vintage, 1964) and *The Children of Sanchez* (New York: Random House, 1961).

159. Two major works that characterize the Mexicano psyche by the use of such a cultural value complex, especially alleging that Mexicanos suffer from an inferiority complex, are Samuel Ramos, *Profile of Man and Culture in México* (Austin: University of Texas Press, 1962); and Octavio Paz, *The Labyrinth of Solitude: Life and Thought in México* (New York: Grove Press, 1961).

160. Weber, *Foreigners in Their Native Land*, 209.

161. Camarillo, *Chicanos in California*, 25.

162. Del Castillo and De León, *North to Aztlán*, 37–38.

163. McWilliams, *North from México*, 131.

164. Carlos G. Vélez-Ibáñez, *Border Visions: Mexican Cultures of the Southwest United States* (Tucson: University of Arizona Press, 1996), 72–73.

165. Albert Camarillo, *Chicanos in a Changing Society: From Mexican Pueblos to America's Barrios in Santa Barbara and Southern California, 1848–1930* (Cambridge, Mass.: Harvard University Press, 1996), 110.

166. Weber, *Foreigners in Their Native Land*, 150.

167. Gómez-Quiñones, *Roots of Chicano Politics*, 147.

168. Cited in Gonzales, *Mexicanos*, 91.

169. Calvert and De León, *The History of Texas*, 87.

170. Gómez-Quiñones, *Roots of Chicano Politics*, 147.

171. Calvert and De León, *The History of Texas*, 55.

172. Montejano, *Anglos and Mexicans*, 27.

173. Montejano, *Anglos and Mexicans*, 27.

174. Weber, *Foreigners in Their Native Land*, 177.

175. Acuña, *Occupied America*, 4th ed., 65–66.

176. Weber, *Foreigners in Their Native Land*, 177.

177. Montejano, *Anglos and Mexicanos*, 57.

178. Montejano, *Anglos and Mexicanos*, 57.

179. Montejano, *Anglos and Mexicanos*, 57.

180. Gómez-Quiñones, *Roots of Chicano Politics*, 148–49.

181. De León, *Mexican Americans in Texas*, 47.

182. Weber, *Foreigners in Their Native Land*, 145.

183. Acuña, *Occupied America*, 4th ed., 66.

184. De León, *Mexican Americans in Texas*, 47

185. Acuña, *Occupied America*, 4th ed., 67.

186. De León, *Mexican Americans in Texas*, 57.

187. De León, *Mexican Americans in Texas*, 47–48.

188. For an overview of the political participation of Mexicanos in Texas during this period see De León, *The Tejano Community: 1836–1900* (Albuquerque: University of New México Press, 1982), 23–49.

189. De León, *The Tejano Community*, 45.

190. Cited in Weber, *Foreigners in Their Native Land*, 146–47.

191. Cited in Acuña, *Occupied America*, 4th ed., 66.

192. Del Castillo and De León, *North to Aztlán*, 32.

193. Arnoldo De León, "In Re Ricardo Rodriguez: An Attempt at Chicano Disfranchisement in San Antonio, 1896–1897," in *En Aquel Entonces: Readings in Mexican American History*, ed. Manuel G. Gonzales and Cynthia M. Gonzales (Bloomington: Indiana University Press, 2000), 57–63.

194. Arnoldo De León, "In Re Ricardo Rodriguez," 57–63.

195. De León, *The Tejano Community*, 23–24.

196. Calvert and De León, *The History of Texas*, 241.

197. For an excellent and comprehensive study on the Chicano historical experience in California from 1848 to 1930 see Albert Camarillo, *Chicanos in a Changing Society*. See also his major work titled *Chicanos in California: A History of Mexican Americans in California* (San Francisco: Boyd & Frazer Publishing Company, 1984).

198. Pitt, *The Decline of the Californios*, 37.

199. Pitt, *The Decline of the Californios*, 35.

200. Camarillo, *Chicanos in California*, 14.

201. Weber, *Foreigners in Their Native Land*, 148.

202. Meier and Rivera, *Mexican Americans, American Mexicans*, 71.

203. Pitt, *The Decline of the Californios*, 43.

204. Gómez-Quiñones, *Roots of Chicano Politics*, 226.

205. Pitt, *The Decline of the Californios*, 45.

206. Gómez-Quiñones, *Roots of Chicano Politics*, 226.

207. Gómez-Quiñones, *Roots of Chicano Politics*, 228.

208. Meier and Rivera, *Mexican Americans, American Mexicans*, 72

209. Gonzales, *Mexicanos*, 86.

210. Gonzales, *Mexicanos*, 71.

211. John R. Chavez, *The Lost Land: The Chicano Image of the Southwest* (Albuquerque: New México Press, 1984), 49.

212. Gonzales, *Mexicanos*, 86–87.

213. Gonzales, *Mexicanos*, 150.

214. Camarillo, *Chicanos in California*, 20.

215. Pitt, *The Decline of the Californios*, 193–94.

216. Acuña, *Occupied America*, 4th ed., 144.

217. Cited in Pitt, *The Decline of the Californios*, 204–5.

218. Cited in Pitt, *The Decline of the Californios*, 204–5.

219. For an excellent newspaper article on the political careers of Coronado and Aguilar see Cecilia Rasmussen, "Latino Mayors in a Yankee Town Bridged Two Cultures," *Los Angeles Times*, May 27, 2001.

220. Camarillo, *Chicanos in a Changing Society*, 41–44.

221. Camarillo, *Chicanos in California*, 21.

222. Camarillo, *Chicanos in California*, 14.

223. Antonió Ríos-Bustamante, "The Barrioization of Nineteenth-Century Mexican Californians: From Landowners to Laborers," in *En Aquel Entonces: Readings in Mexican American History*, 74, 78.

224. Gómez-Quiñones, *Roots of Chicano Politics*, 230.

225. Gómez-Quiñones, *Roots of Chicano Politics*, 255.

226. Ríos-Bustamante, "The Barrioization of Nineteenth-Century Mexican Californians," 78.

227. For an elucidation of this analysis see Richard Griswold Del Castillo, *The Los Angeles Barrio, 1850–1890* (Berkeley and Los Angeles: University of California Press, 1979).

228. For an excellent anthology on the historical Chicano experience, including some of its political aspects, see Gonzales-Berry and Maciel, *The Contested Homeland*, 1.

229. Chavez, *The Lost Land*, 54.

230. Gómez-Quiñones, *Roots of Chicano Politics*, 236.

231. Weber, *Foreigners in Their Native Land*, 214.

232. Weber, *Foreigners in Their Native Land*, 214.

233. For an analysis on the ethnic conflict and resolution aspects related to relations between Nuevo Mexicanos and Anglos see Carolyn Zelany, *Relations between the Spanish-Americans and Anglo-Americans in New México: A Study of Conflict and Accommodation in a Dual-Ethnic Relationship*, PhD dissertation, Yale University, 1944.

234. López y Rivas, *The Chicanos*, 30–31.

235. Gómez-Quiñones writes that Father Gallegos did not have the support of the *rico* elite, that in essence he was an outsider from leadership of the patron system.

236. Gómez-Quiñones, *Roots of Chicano Politics*, 240.

237. Acuña, *Occupied America*, 4th ed., 89.

238. Weber, *Foreigners in Their Native Land*, 214.

239. Weber, *Foreigners in Their Native Land*, 214.

240. Acuña, *Occupied America*, 4th ed., 89.

241. Weber, *Foreigners in Their Native Land*, 215.

242. Gonzales-Berry and Maciel, *The Contested Homeland*, 19.

243. For an excellent examination of Las Gorras Blancas see Anselmo Arrellano, "The People's Movement: Las Gorras Blancas," in Gonzales-Berry and Maciel, *The Contested Homeland*, 59–82.

244. For analyses on the political connection between the two struggles see my book *La Raza Unida Party*, 174–76.

245. For background information on formation of El Partido del Pueblo in San Miguel County, see my book *La Raza Unida Party*, 173–74.

246. For more information of the makeup and workings of this third-party effort see Robert Johnson Rosenbaum, *Mexicano versus Americano: A Study of Hispanic-American Resistance to Anglo-American Control in New México Territory, 1870–1900*, dissertation, University of Texas at Austin, December 1972.

247. Gonzales, *Mexicanos*, 104.

248. McWilliams, *North from México*, 122.

249. For an excellent overview of the workings of the Santa Fe Ring see Acuña, *Occupied America*, 4th ed., 91–94.

250. Gonzales-Berry and Maciel, *The Contested Homeland*, 15.

251. Gonzales-Berry and Maciel, *The Contested Homeland*, 15.

252. Gómez-Quiñones, *Roots of Chicano Politics*, 258.

253. Chavez, *The Lost Land*, 61.

254. Chavez, *The Lost Land*, 61.

255. Weber, *Foreigners in Their Native Land*, 211.

256. Acuña, *Occupied America*, 4th ed., 112.

257. Gómez-Quiñones, *Roots of Chicano Politics*, 267–68.

258. Meier and Rivera, *Mexican Americans, American Mexicans*, 100–101.

259. Del Castillo and De León, *North to Aztlán*, 32.

260. Gonzales, *Mexicanos*, 95.

261. Gómez-Quiñones, *Roots of Chicano Politics*, 326.

262. McWilliams, *North from México*, 94.

263. Carl Ubbelohde, Maxine Benson, and Duane A. Smith, *A Colorado History: Revised Centennial Edition* (Boulder, Colo.: Pruett Publishing Co., 1976), 55.

264. Chavez, *The Lost Land*, 54.

265. Gómez-Quiñones, *Roots of Chicano Politics*, 263.

266. William E. Pabor, *Colorado as an Agricultural State* (New York: Orange Judd Co., 1883), 117–18.

267. Carl Abbott, *Colorado: A History of the Centennial State* (Boulder: Colorado Associated University Press, 1976), 44–48.

268. Abbott, *Colorado*, 44–48

269. Gómez-Quiñones, *Roots of Chicano Politics*, 264.

270. Gómez-Quiñones, *Roots of Chicano Politics*, 265.

271. For a comprehensive biography on this colorful and very pro-Mexicano politico see Jose Emilio Fernandez, *Cuaranta Años de Legislador: Biografia del Senador Casimiro Barela* (New York: Arno Press, 1976).

272. Abbott, *Colorado*, 47.

273. Abbott, *Colorado*, 49.

274. Chavez, *The Lost Land*, 62.

275. Gómez-Quiñones, *Roots of Chicano Politics*, 266.

276. For a comprehensive examination on the makeup and politics of interest groups in U.S. politics see Jeffrey M. Berry, *The Interest Group Society*, 3rd ed. (New York: Longman, 1997); H. R. Mahood, *Interest Groups in American National Politics: An Overview* (Upper

Saddle River, N.J.: Prentice Hall, 2000). Interest groups are distinguishable from other forms of organization in that they make some specific claim or demand on society or on governmental policies. In short any organized group that makes demands or uses conventional or unconventional pressure and uses the political process can be defined as an interest group.

277. For an extensive examination on the development of mutual benefit organizations see Jose Amaro Hernandez, *Mutual Aid for Survival: The Case of the Mexican American* (Malabar, Fla.: Robert E. Krieger Publishing Co., 1983).

278. For an examination on the development of these early forms of mutual benefit organizations see Nancie L. Gonzales, *Spanish-Americans in New México* (Albuquerque, N.M.: University of Albuquerque Press, 1967), 86–92.

279. Hernandez, *Mutual Aid for Survival*, 9.

280. Vélez-Ibáñez, *Border Visions*, 122.

281. Miguel David Tirado, "Mexican American Community Political Organization: The Key to Chicano Political Power," *Aztlán: Chicano Journal of the Social Sciences and the Arts* Vol. I, No. I (Spring 1970): 55.

282. Paul Taylor, *Mexican Labor in the United States* (Berkeley: University of California Press, 1928), 45.

283. Hernandez, *Mutual Aid for Survival*, 65.

284. Paul S. Taylor, *An American-Mexican Frontier, Nueces County, Texas* (Chapel Hill: University of North Carolina Press, 1934), 173–74.

285. Weber, *Foreigners in Their Native Land*, 216–17.

286. Hernandez, *Mutual Aid for Survival*, 61–62.

287. For a comprehensive examination on the history and development of La Alianza Hispana American see Kay Lysen Briegal, *Alianza Hispano-Americana, 1894–1965: A Mexican American Fraternal Insurance Society*, PhD dissertation, University of Southern California, 1974.

288. Tirado, "Mexican American Community Political Organization," 55.

289. Weber, *Foreigners in Their Native Land*, 217.

290. Weber, *Foreigners in Their Native Land*, 217.

291. Gonzales, *Mexicanos*, 97.

292. Briegal, *Alianza Hispano-Americana*, 51

293. Weber, *Foreigners in Their Native Land*, 217.

294. Del Castillo and De León, *North to Aztlán*, 55.

295. Manuel Gamio, *Mexican Immigration to the United States: A Study of Human Migration and Adjustment* (Chicago: University of Chicago Press, 1930), 45.

296. Martinez, *Mexican-Origin People in the United States*, 165.

297. Briegel, *Alianza Hispana-Americana*, 64.

298. Martinez, *Mexican-Origin People in the United States*, 165–66.

299. Pitt, *The Decline of the Californios*, 266.

300. Camarillo, *Chicanos in California*, 27.

301. Acuña, *Occupied America*, 4th ed., 97.

302. Gonzales, *Mexicanos*, 105.

303. Meier and Rivera, *Mexican Americans, American Mexicans*, 98–99.

304. For an overview of the Penitentes see Hernandez, *Mutual Aid for Survival*, chapter 1.

305. Acuña, *Occupied America*, 4th ed., 167–68.

306. Acuña, *Occupied America*, 4th ed., 167–68.

307. For an overview analysis on early labor organizing in California see Acuña, *Occupied America*, 4th ed., 167–68; and Del Castillo and De León, *North to Aztlán*, 51–52.

308. Acuña, *Occupied America*, 4th ed., 125–26.

309. Acuña, *Occupied America*, 5th ed., 151.

Epoch of Adaptation Politics (1917–1945)   3

OUT OF THE DIALECTICAL TENSIONS that pervaded the previous epoch of resistance, a new epoch of adaptation politics emerged by 1917 and lasted until 1945. This was an important political period in that it witnessed the end of armed resistance as the predominant mode of politics and the beginning of the hegemony of accommodation politics. While some radicalism emerged because of Marxist, anarchist, and Mexicano nationalist unions, politically the response by most Mexicano organizations and *politicos* to the U.S. occupation was adaptation, integration, and accommodation. As a result of México's Revolution of 1910 there was a massive migrant exodus, and generational politics emerged within the Mexicano Generation. The new Mexicano politics in occupied Aztlán was challenged by the rise of powerful nativist forces against Mexicanos. As a result of the devastating Depression in the United States, hundreds of thousands of Mexicanos were singled out, repatriated, and deported to México.

External Influences on U.S. Mexicano Politics

The Mexican Revolution

The Mexicano Revolution of 1910 became the most important historical antagonism to influence the Mexicano political experience in occupied Aztlán. It was the twentieth century's first major social revolution. For Mexicanos in the United States, the Mexican Revolution profoundly affected their political course. As a historical event, it bridged both the previous and present epoch. From 1910 to 1920, revolutionary movements permeated México's political landscape. They were led by *caudillos* whose struggles for power and control brought massive destruction and the death of some two million people, who died in one of the century's bloodiest revolutions. Its impact was felt in México and in the United States, and resulted in the exodus of hundreds of thousands of Mexicano migrants into the United States. Their journey north led to the incipient phase of the reoccupation of Aztlán, and was an important step in the evolution of Mexicano

politics in the United States. In order to understand the significance of the Mexicano Revolution it is important to examine its historical antecedents.

Historical Antecedents to Revolution

The origins of the Mexican Revolution are deeply imbedded in México's turbulent political history. Although México was blessed with an abundance of wealth
from the time it secured its independence from Spain in 1821, much of it was
squandered over nearly one hundred years of chronic political instability. Conservative and liberal forces produced unbridled militarism. Hundreds of armed
uprisings disturbed the internal order of the republic during her initial century of
nationhood.[1] This internecine political warfare robbed México of its potential
greatness, as greedy and inept politicians and *caudillos* relentlessly struggled for the
spoils of power at the expense of the people. Debilitated by these wars, México
became prey to U.S. imperialism, which led to the U.S. War on México in 1846–
1848.

In spite of the War of the Reform (1857–1861), which involved an armed
struggle between liberals and conservatives, México was denied peace. Under the
leadership of Benito Juarez the Liberals had won by 1861 and had adopted the
Liberal Constitution of 1857. However, in October of 1861, Spain, France, and
Great Britain met in London and agreed to a tripartite military mission to México, to remedy México's failure to make payment on its foreign debts. Once again,
México fell victim to imperialism. Spain was the first to land some four thousand
troops at Veracruz in December 1861, and was subsequently joined by a contingent of British troops. After the withdrawal of Spanish and British forces from
Veracruz in 1862, French troops invaded under the leadership of Napoleon III,
and with the support and invitation of conservative forces they remained. The
invading French forces were temporarily routed on May 5 at Puebla by the ill-
equipped Mexican forces under the leadership of General Ignacio Zaragoza.

From 1862 to 1867, Juarez's forces assembled into guerrilla units, struggling
to remove the French from México and defeat the conservative forces. With the
end of the Civil War, France was pressured into leaving México. During the years
1867–1876, Juarez and the liberal political forces moved México closer to
embracing liberal capitalism. Juarez served as president until his death in 1872.
The political situation worsened with Juarez's death in 1872 when Sebastian
Lerdo de Tejada was designated as Juarez's replacement. In 1876, Porfirio Díaz
made a successful bid for power by overthrowing Sebastian Lerdo de Tejada.[2]
With México in a state of political instability, the spirit of Manifest Destiny was
rekindled by U.S. president Rutherford Hayes who "stoked-up the war chant"
with his revival of the protectorate concept of annexation.[3]

For the next thirty-four years, Díaz created the Porfiriato (period of Díaz rule, 1876–1910), a dictatorship that ruled México with an iron hand, through the use of his ruthless *rurales* (his personal police force comprised of mostly former criminals)[4] and the military. Relative peace, stability, and political order were restored and capitalist development occurred with the influx of numerous foreign companies that Díaz allowed to exploit México's rich mineral and oil resources at the expense of its downtrodden masses. A group of positivists, the Científicos, who were technocratic Social Darwinists who sought to transform México into a modern nation using scientific principles, drove Díaz's policies. Positivist José Ives Limontour, in an address to the National Science Conference in 1901, said, "The weak, the unprepared, those who lack the necessary tools to triumph in the evolutionary process, must perish and leave the field to the strongest."[5]

The positivists believed that México's indigenous were inferior because nature willed it, and furthermore, the future and salvation of México lay in transforming it from an indigenous and mestizo country to a white majority, one oriented by European values and customs.[6] Ideas contrary to positivism were not permitted to circulate. Relations with the Catholic Church were precarious and contradictory. At times, church properties were confiscated and distributed among the oligarchy; at other times the church was allowed to buy new property.

During the Porfiriato, much of México's means of production and distribution were controlled by foreign enterprises. They had a powerful hold over rural lands and dominated mining, railroads, utilities, industry, and commerce. As a result, there was a pronounced disparity of wealth among the millions of Mexicanos that lived in impoverished and repressive conditions. "Left landless," according to Meier and Rivera, "many former small land owners were forced into peonage. While debt peonage among day laborers increased rapidly, domestic and foreign investors prospered as never before."[7] While the poor became poorer and were farmers without farms, Díaz and his friends became richer and controlled much of the farmland.[8]

Politically, the Díaz legacy was a full measure of blood and brutality at the expense of political freedoms for the masses.[9] México was governed by a dictatorship and a plutocracy that enjoyed strong political and economic support from the United States and numerous European countries. By the early 1900s, México began to experience a change. Opposition to the Porfiriato increased under the liberals, although they were fragmented and forced to operate underground. A growing discontent against the Díaz regime resulted. Initially, the liberals' ideological program was dedicated to putting into effect the provisions of the Mexican Constitution of 1857. These included: Díaz should honor his commitment not to run again; military conscription should be abolished; freedom of the press should be restored; increased budget outlays for education and school construction should be made; anticlerical provisions of the constitution of 1857 should be enforced; land reforms should be enacted; and, generally, the wealthy oligarchy should be deprived of its influence.[10]

Under the leadership of Ricardo Flores Magón, who was the publisher of the fledgling liberal newspaper, *Regeneración*, the liberals shifted to an anarchist or syndicalist's posture calling for the total destruction of the Porfiriato and the formation of a worker-state. Jailed in 1901, both he and his brother Enrique went into exile in the United States by 1903, where he and others forged El Partido Liberal Mexicano (PLM—the Mexican Liberal Party) and formed an alliance with the anarchist International Workers of the World (IWW) in 1906. Through the agitation of the *Regeneración* and the labor organizing of the PLM, the Magónistas waged their revolutionary struggle from the United States against the despotic Díaz regime. From St. Louis, Missouri, the PLM promulgated its social change manifesto in 1906, which included a call for a general distribution of land by breaking up the large haciendas. For the industrial workers, the PLM proposed minimum wage and maximum hour legislation, an end to child labor, outlawing of company stores, and payment of wages in cash, not chits. In the area of education, the PLM demanded the closing of Catholic schools and replacement with lay institutions.[11] Up to 1910, Magón and the PLM played a significant role in engendering a climate of change for revolution in México. The PLM was a major factor in fostering the growing discontent of the Mexican masses against the Porfiriato.

The Mexican Revolution: A Decade of Upheaval (1910–1920)

Liberal Francisco Madero, a wealthy *hacendero* from Coahuila who had studied in the United States, had broken earlier with the Magónistas because of their adherence to violence. As a leader he inspired many to rebel against the Porfiriato. Feeling omnipotence, the aging Díaz was interviewed in March 1908 by U.S. journalist James Creelman. Díaz boasted of the political maturity México had achieved under his leadership, but made the political mistake of stating that the presidential elections of 1910 would be unencumbered, allowing for the rise of opposition parties. Inspired by the Creelman interview, Madero wrote a politically innocuous treatise entitled *The Presidential Succession of 1910* in which he mildly proposed that if Díaz ran for reelection, the people should be free to elect their own vice president. As a result, liberals had rising political expectations. Madero himself was pressured into running against Díaz and formed the Anti-Reelectionist Party, whose motto became "effective suffrage and no-reelection."[12] By 1910, Madero's electoral challenge fostered the rise of a reform political movement.

As a result of Magónistas revolutionary activities and the Madero presidential bid coupled with profound economic problems, class antagonisms were also exacerbated. Frank R. Brandenburg explains, "A psuedoaristocratic society prevailed in which the rich, the foreigner, and the select politician denigrated the lower classes. The middle-class professional and intellectual was little better off unless they worked for a foreign concern, where they also felt shackled by a superiority-conscious employer."[13] The economic reality was that México under Díaz had sold its economic sovereignty to foreign enterprises.

Yet in his efforts to offset U.S. hegemony or possible further annexation of Mexican territory, Díaz sought diversification of foreign enterprises and capital. Ross writes, "the 'axiom Poor México, so close to the United States and so far from God' may be the Dictator's most lasting contribution to Mexican nationalist thought."[14] México by 1910 had become known as "the mother of foreigners and the stepmother of Mexicanos."[15] Brandenburg provides a specific profile of the aforementioned:

Americans seized the cement industry. The French monopolized large department stores. The Germans controlled the hardware business. The Spanish took over the foodstores and, together with the French, controlled the textile industry. The Canadians, aided by Americans and Englishmen, concentrated on electric power, trolley lines, and water companies. The Belgians, Americans, and English invested heavily in the railroads. And what ultimately shook the roots of revolutionary ideology was the American and British exploitation of minerals, especially oil.[16]

The spark that lit the fire of the Mexican Revolution was Madero's arrest on charges of sedition. Initially, Díaz had felt unfazed by the Madero electoral challenge. By June 1910 Madero won his party's nomination. His campaign had been successful in galvanizing support among the masses. Díaz felt politically threatened by Madero's surge in popularity; consequently, he had him arrested and incarcerated on false charges of sedition. Madero escaped from prison, fled México, and went into exile to El Paso, Tejas. Meanwhile, in what has been historically recorded as a fraudulent election, Díaz won reelection. This served to further solidify opposition and raised the level of discontent against his regime. On October 25, 1910, Madero and his supporters promulgated El Plan de San Luis Potosi, an antimilitaristic plan that promised a return to the provisions of the Constitution of 1857. Strategically, it called for an internal war against the Díaz regime and for the uprising to start on November 20. As planned, Madero crossed into México on the date designated and minor insurrections broke out in a dozen states. Lacking coordination, the insurgencies were effectively put down by the *federales* (federal troops). A dejected Madero returned to Tejas to regroup his forces.[17]

In February 1911, Madero reentered México to lead the revolution against Díaz. By this time, the winds of revolution permeated much of México. In northern México, around Chihuahua and Coahuila, Doroteo Arango (a former bandit who became known as Pancho Villa) and Pascual Orosco had joined the struggle against Díaz. In the south, Emiliano Zapata and Juan Andreu Almazán joined the insurrection in support of Madero's cause. Meanwhile, in Coahuila, Madero's home state, Venustiano Carranza also organized revolutionary forces against Díaz.[18] On May 10, 1911, Ciudad Juarez fell, and shortly thereafter on May 25, 1911, Díaz, fearing for his life, capitulated to Madero's "Ejercito Libertador" (Liberation Army). In actuality, the first phase of the Mexican Revolution lasted less then seven months. Díaz's thirty-five years of dynasty came to an end. That May, at the age of eighty-one and forced into exile, he sailed on the ship *Ypiranga* to Paris, France, where he lived another four years and died a bitter and broken man.[19] As the ship departed, he had made the following warning, "The wild beasts have been loosed. Now let us see who can cage them."[20] His prophetic words came true.

With the successful overthrow of the Porfiriato and the rise to power of Madero, the second phase of the Mexican Revolution began. Instead of taking power immediately at the height of his popularity, Madero made the political mistake of allowing Díaz's former minister of foreign relations, Francisco León, to become interim president until elections were held in October 1911.[21] In November, the interim president turned over the reigns of power to Madero in the midst of growing instability and counterrevolutionary activity. Madero, who became known as the "Apostle of Democracy," proved inept at governing México. Politically, Madero was an idealist who was naïve in the art of revolutionary governance. He made blunder after blunder; in particular, he kept intact Díaz's military apparatus and bureaucracy. Lieuwen argues, "It is generally futile for a ruler to attempt to control, by gentle tactics, a praetorian army."[22] One of the Mexican Revolution's most prominent intellectuals, Luis Cabrera in a journal article expands on this theme:

> This revolution had as its portent the political insurrection of Madero. But Madero saw no more than the political side of the Méxican situation. He professed that a change of government was sufficient to bring about a change in the general conditions of the country. Madero compromised with the Díaz regime, acquiesced in taking charge of the government, and

ruled the country with the same laws, the same procedures, and even with the same men, with which General Díaz had ruled. The logical consequence was that Madero had to fail, because he had not destroyed the old nor attempted to build a new regime.[23]

Equally as bad, Madero failed to control the revolutionary *caudillos*. Madero's *federales* faced the Magónista invasion of northern Baja California. By the time Madero took power on November 1911, Emiliano Zapata had openly broken with him over the issue of land reform and had promulgated the famous Plan de Ayala that same year under the slogan of Tierra y Libertad (Land and Liberty). Beyond these uprisings, he faced two others: Oroszco in Chihuahua, and Felix Díaz (nephew of the exiled dictator) in Veracruz. During his sixteen months of governance, Madero's regime accomplished little and México continued to be swept by the turbulent winds of revolution.

Madero's end came in February 1913, after the "Tragic Ten Days" when federal General Victoriano Huerta tried to subdue the insurrectionist forces of Felix Díaz, who were stockaded inside an old military garrison in México City known as the Cuidadela. William Johnson described the "Tragic Ten Days" as part of a plot between Huerta and Díaz to reap the spoils once Madero was overthrown. He wrote, "As a battle it was spurious, fraudulent, a grand deception."[24] After ten brutal days, Huerta in collaboration as well with U.S. ambassador Henry Lane Wilson engineered a coup d'etat against Madero. This led to his arrest and execution as well as that of his brother Gustavo, Vice President Jóse María Pino Suarez, Chihuahua governor Abraham González, and a few other lesser officials.[25]

The third phase of the Mexican Revolution began with Huerta's dictatorship, which was supported by U.S. ambassador Wilson. The revolution intensified to where once again, México was immersed in a violent upheaval. Huerta was doomed from the start, unable to control the tigers (*caudillos* and *caciques*) that rebelled against his illegitimate authority. During his brief tenure as dictator of México, Huerta faced the combined revolutionary armies of Pancho Villa, Emiliano Zapata, Venustiano Carranza, and Magónistas, among others. To make things worse, Huerta engaged in an exchange of insults with President Wilson over the U.S. naval blockade of Mexican ports, that is, Tampico and Veracruz, in order to curb the flow of arms from Germany. An incident occurred that led to bombardment and capture of Veracruz on April 1914 by U.S. Marines. War between the United States and México was averted through the diplomatic intervention of Argentina, Brazil, and Chile.[26]

Huerta's *federales* proved to be no match for the combined might of the revolutionary armies. On March 26, 1913, Carranza promulgated the Plan de Guadalupe, which called for the overthrow of the Huerta regime and recognition of Carranza himself as *primer jefe* (first chief) of the Constitutionalist Army. Moreover, the plan provided for the occupation of México City by Constitutionalist forces. Carranza would become interim president and would call for general elections of federal officials. Subsequently, state provisional governors recognized by the *primer jefe* were to call elections for selecting state officials.[27] In the armed struggle to overthrow Huerta, Carranza's Constitutionalist Army, for a brief time, was able to unite most of the tigers, except Zapata, under a unified command.

The armed struggle against Huerta took eighteen months. On July 15, 1914, Huerta fled México to Europe with a generous part of the Mexican treasury. A few months later, he returned to El Paso, Tejas, to organize a rebellion against Carranza, and was arrested for violating the Neutrality Act. He was jailed at Fort Bliss, and cirrhosis of the liver claimed his life on January 15, 1916.[28] On August 14, 1914, Carranza's Constitutionalist Army of 40,000 descended on México City. By early August of that year, all the *federales* unconditionally surrendered with the signing of the Treaty of Teoloyucan.[29] Still, no leader was able to tame the *caudillo* tigers that the revolution had unleashed.

The fourth phase of the Mexican Revolution began that August of 1914 with Carranza's rise to power as de facto president of México. Carranza placed command of his Constitutionalist Army under the leadership of General Alvaro Obregón. With the oustering of Huerta, the power struggles between Villa and Zapata on one side and Carranza on the other became more acute. After a series of confrontations, both camps agreed to meet in the neutral city of Aguascalientes on October 10, 1914. The so-called Aguascalientes Convention concluded on November 10, 1914, and produced a further polarization. After the Carrancista delegates walked out, the Villa/Zapata delegates held Carranza in contempt. In addition, they adopted the main articles of El Plan de Ayala; disavowed Carranza as the interim president of México; appointed Villa as Chief of the Division del Norte; and named Eulalio Gutiérrez, a *caudillo* from San Luis Potosi, as interim president.[30] The lines were drawn in the sand and *caudillos* and *caciques* from throughout México chose sides. In a show of force and power, Villa and Zapata's armies marched into México City in December 1914, but vacated the capital in early January 1915. Soon thereafter, México City was reoccupied by Obregón's forces.

Militarily, the Mexican Revolution reached its apogee in 1915. Internecine warfare engulfed much of the country, especially the central part. The year of the *chinga* (turmoil) proved lucrative for Carranza. Obregón's tactical adroitness became evident in the battles the Constitutional Army won against the Villa and

Zapata armies. Camín and Meyer argue that essentially four major battles won by Obregón's forces turned the military tide against the Villa and Zapata insurrections: "The two Celaya battles in April, the battle for positions in Trinidad during the month of May, and the Battle of Aguascalientes at the beginning of June." Because of food shortages, the latter battle forced Obregón to launch a sudden offensive that caught the Villista lines off guard.[31] By early August, after control of México City had changed hands several times, Constitutionalist forces under the command of General Pablo González retook México City. By October 1915, Carranza had the upper hand militarily and politically. The decisive defeat of Villa's Division del Norte occurred at the battle of Agua Prieta, near the Sonora/Arizona border area, by the Constitutionalist Army, under the command of General Plutarco Elías Calles.[32]

By 1916, Villa's forces were on the defensive, and in retaliation over the recognition of Carranza by the United States, he attacked Columbus, Nuevo México, causing seventeen U.S. casualties. President Wilson then ordered General John J. Pershing to organize a military expedition into México to capture Villa. The Pershing Punitive Expedition, as it became known, was comprised of some ten thousand U.S. troops, and proved to be a military fiasco for the United States. Villa successfully eluded capture and inflicted casualties on Pershing's forces, which turned Villa into a folk hero in México.[33] Relations between the two countries further deteriorated as a result of the interception of the "Zimmerman Note" by the United States. A telegraph from German foreign minister Arthur Zimmerman to his ambassador to México, to be delivered the day the United States entered the war in Europe, read: "We make México an offer of alliance on the basis of make war together, make peace together. We guarantee generous financial support (To be conveyed through a Japanese conduit) and the understanding that México is to recoup its lost territories."[34] Earlier in 1915, the insurrectionist Plan de San Diego had been intercepted and squelched by Texas Rangers and U.S. Army troops in Tejas (see chapter 2).

The fifth phase to the Mexican Revolution began in September 19, 1916, with Carranza's call for a constitutional convention in Querétaro. During the previous months, Obregón's forces had continued their effective military offensive against the debilitated Villa and Zapata forces. The convention proved to be historical in that it produced México's present constitution. Initially, the 221 delegates in attendance were introduced to Carranza's moderate social reform program. By January 1917, after holding a number of sessions at Querétaro, the socialist delegates, some of whom were considered military by the United States, such as Generals Francisco Mujica and Heriberto Jara, opposed several of Carranza's recommendations and pursued their own. Most of the military delegates were representatives of General Obregón.[35]

Under the intellectual leadership of Francisco J. Mujica, the delegates introduced several important articles to the new constitution. México's Constitution of 1917 embraced many of the liberal tenets of the 1857 constitution. However, as explained by Quirk, "In the Constitution of 1917 the basic principles of the Magónistas and of Villa and Zapata won a victory denied the convention's troops on the battlefield."[36] The uniqueness of the new constitution was its eclectic mix of socialist, nationalist, and liberal capitalist ideas. This was illustrated by the approval of several new articles: Article 3 prohibited the Catholic Church from participating in elementary public education; Article 27 provided the basis for agrarian reform and for nationalization of México's natural resources; Article 33 opened the door for the Mexican president to expel foreign companies and personnel from the land; Article 123 gave workers the right to collective bargaining, allowed for hours and wages legislation, and for the protection of women and children in industry; and Article 130 was a grab bag of restrictions directed at the Catholic Church, which prohibited or curtailed many of its activities.[37]

The years between 1917 and 1920 were the sixth phase to the Mexican Revolution. While turmoil and political instability plagued México, Carranza reluctantly accepted the new constitution but did little to enforce it. Few changes were implemented during the remaining years of Carranza's administration, which contributed to discontent among the masses. Villa and Zapata continued their guerrilla activities against the Carranza regime. Zapata was betrayed by Pablo González, who had allegedly agreed to provide him with a load of ammunition. Zapata was asked to come to the hacienda of Chinameca on the morning of April 10, 1919. *Federales* riddled him with bullets after first saluting him.[38] Without his leadership, the Zapatista insurgency was neutralized.

Zapata's fate became Carranza's as well. By 1919, México was economically on the threshold of collapse. Carranza refused to support Obregón politically and attempted to curb his power during the 1920 presidential election by fronting his own candidate, Ignacio Bonilla. With his life in jeopardy, Obregón consolidated his control over the military and in April 1920, his generals and supporters forged the "Plan of Agua Prieta," which disavowed the Carranza regime. With the loss of the military's support, Carranza intended to reorganize his forces and loaded up the treasury on a twenty-one-car train bound for Veracruz.[39] Pursued by Obregón's forces, however, Carranza abandoned the train and took refuge in an indigenous village of Tlaxcalantongo. On May 21, 1920, he was assassinated while he slept by forces loyal to General Manuel Paez.[40] Thus, the turbulent decade that produced the Mexican Revolution came to an end and another began.

The Post-Mexican Revolution Years: A Decade of Instability

For the next nine years or so, México was marked by political instability and counterrevolutionary struggles. Adolfo de la Huerta served as interim president until the election of General Obregón in 1920. Obregón governed México from 1921 to 1924 and implemented a number of reforms, especially in public education. In his efforts to consolidate his power in 1920 he convinced Pancho Villa to retire from his revolutionary activities by offering him amnesty and a lucrative package of material incentives. Three years later, Villa was assassinated in an ambush. From 1921 to 1923, Obregón successfully crushed several conspiracies. The most serious was the three-month rebellion (1923–1924) led by General Adolfo de la Huerta that nearly toppled his government, at a cost of 100 million pesos and seven thousand lives.[41]

In 1924, Obregón turned over the presidency to General Plutarco Elías Calles, who served as México's president until 1928. Calles focused particularly on implementing the anticlerical provisions of the Constitution of 1917. With the government confiscating church properties, abolishing religious instruction in public school, deporting priests, and expelling foreign priests, México experienced another unsuccessful armed rebellion, this time from rightist and clerical fanatics[42] who called themselves Cristeros. From 1926 to 1929, the so-called Cristero Rebellion involved some twenty-five thousand insurgents. Their battle cry was "Viva Cristo Rey!" (Long Live Christ the King), and they fostered an armed struggle and unrest throughout the states of Jalisco, Michoacán, Durango, Guerrero, Colima, Nayarit, and Zacatecas. The Cristeros were militarily no match for Calles's federales. When the rebellion was concluded in 1929, some ninety thousand people had been killed.[43] After lengthy negotiations that were brokered by U.S. ambassador Dwight Morrow, the Cristero Rebellion came to an end in 1929. Catholic Church officials agreed to register priests as demanded by Calles. In return, Calles allowed religious classes to be taught within the churches. Overall, Calles was the victor and the Church the loser—he succeeded in neutralizing both the political influence of the Catholic Church and relegating it to a subordinate status.

In 1928, while campaigning for the presidency for a second term, Obregón was assassinated by a religious fanatic. After 1929, Calles, El Jefe Máximo (Maximum Leader), maintained his political control behind the scenes by fronting a number of presidential puppets, for example, Emilio Portes Gil, Pascual Ortiz Rubio, and Abelardo Rodriguez.[44] It was not until the election of General Lazaro Cárdenas in 1934 that the spirit of the Mexican Revolution, incarnated in the various articles to the Constitution of 1917, becomes institutionalized. This was made possible in 1929 by the formation of the one-party dictatorship under the aegis of the Partido Nacional Revolucionario (National Revolutionary Party).

In the end, the paramount impact of the Mexican Revolution on the Mexicano political experience in occupied Aztlán was such that it unleashed the "Migrant Exodus," which in turn gave rise to the incipience of the demographic "re-occupation of Aztlán."

The Migrant Exodus: Return to the Promise Land (Aztlán)

Even though the migrant exodus can be traced to the 1890s, it was during the critical years from 1910 to 1929 that over one million Mexicanos left México and migrated to the United States. More specifically, the pervasive violence, chronic instability, immense poverty, governmental fiscal chaos, and general economic ruin throughout the Porfirato and Mexican Revolution were catalysts for the exodus. Mario Garcia describes the historical impact of the migrant exodus: "At no other time in Chicano history have Méxican immigrants and refugees so totally dominated the Spanish-speaking Méxican condition in the Southwest and elsewhere."[45] This unprecedented migration served as a safety valve for both political and economic pressures on México's regimes during this epoch. Thus, years before the Mexican Revolution, the seeds to the reoccupation of Aztlán were planted.

Much of the literature on Mexicano migration into the United States concurs that the Great Migration, as some Chicano historians have labeled it, or as I refer to it, the Migrant Exodus, had its genesis in the 1890s. This could be attributed to the rising demand by U.S. employers for inexpensive labor[46] and to the multiplicity of political, economic, and social problems permeating México. It is important to note that the Migrant Exodus came in the form of three major waves: the Genesis Wave (1890–1910), the Mexican Revolution Wave (1910–1920), and the Post-Mexican Revolution Wave (1921–1929).[47] It was during the years of the three migrations that México lost about 10 percent of its population to the United States.[48]

The First Migrant Wave

The first wave (1890–1910) occurred at a time when the Mexicano population in the United States was small, if not insignificant. According to David Weber, "The Mexican born population of the United States increased rapidly from 1870 on, more than doubling by 1900 when some 103,000 Mexican born were recorded as living in the United States."[49] This occurred during a time when México's population between 1875 and 1910 increased by some 50 percent.

However, the population growth was still at this point insignificant. The massive influx of immigration from southern and eastern Europe began with the gold rush in 1849 and further accelerated during the subsequent five decades. European immigration into the United States between 1881 and 1890 alone was 5,246,613.[50] During this phase, the Mexicano population in the United States, with the exception of parts of Nuevo México and south Tejas, lacked significant numbers or concentrations. According to David Gutierrez, "Ethnic Mexicans had become a tiny fraction of the total population of the region that had once been their domain." He goes on to explain, "Indeed, for most Americans living in the Southwest in the last decades of the nineteenth century, the Méxican presence in the region seemed a distant memory."[51] However, during 1900–1910, México's political, economic, and social conditions had deteriorated to where there was growing discontent among various sectors of Mexican society. The impoverishment of the Mexicano masses and the emergence of various political struggles, for example, the Magónistas, and Madero's presidential bid against the repression of the Porfiriato laid the groundwork for the "push" of the Migrant Exodus.

On the "pull side" of the exodus equation, the United States was experiencing rapid economic expansion. This was evident in the growing agricultural, mining, transportation, and manufacturing sectors of the Southwestern economy, which fostered an insatiable demand for a source of cheap labor.[52] From 1875 to 1900, there was a strong demand for unskilled workers who could be hired cheaply and dismissed freely. The great majority of European immigrants flowing into the United States through New York were being absorbed into the industrial economies of the Northeast and Midwest; the colonized Mexicanos became the main available source of exploitable labor in the development of the Southwest and beyond.[53]

A second major pull factor in the exodus was the laxity of the immigration laws as applied to Mexicanos. Prior to 1875, there had been federal statutes regulating immigration.[54] For the next one hundred years, U.S. immigration laws became highly exclusionary. Indicative of this was the treatment of Chinese, with the passage of the Chinese Exclusionary Acts in 1882 and later with the exclusion of the Japanese with the Gentleman's Agreement of 1907. Both sought to curb further Chinese and Japanese immigration into the United States on racial grounds. By the early 1900s, southern and eastern European immigrants who had served as the U.S. labor reservoir for over fifty years[55] became targets of nativism.

By 1900, the country's population had reached nearly one hundred million, and Mexicanos constituted less than 1 percent.[56] It is important to note that prior to 1900, no precise numbers existed on the number of Mexicanos who migrated into the United States. At times the available data on the migration exodus is contradictory. For example, some scholars reveal that the number of Mexicanos migrating into the United States prior to 1900 was relatively small. They state that in 1880 the number of Mexicano immigrants who had been born in México was no more than 68,000 and that by 1890 the figure increased slightly to 78,000. During the 1890s, the number increased appreciably by some 50,000.[57] Yet Carey McWilliams cites different statistics: for example, Tejas in 1900 had a Mexicano migrant population of 71,062; Arizona 14,171; California, 8,086; and Nuevo México, 6,649. He goes on to explain that the bulk of these migrants settled in the borderlands.[58] However, in 1908, economist Victor S. Clark, alluding to a report submitted to the U.S. Department of Labor, noted that an increasing number of Mexicanos were living outside of the Southwest.[59]

The Second Migrant Wave

The Migrant Exodus reached its zenith during the Mexican Revolution (1910–1920). It was during this phase that the Mexicano population throughout Aztlán underwent a major population surge.[60] At the start of the Mexican Revolution of 1910, the total number of Mexican born in the United States had increased to 221,915. The Mexican Revolution's violence, destruction, and impoverished conditions were the "greatest early stimuli" impelling the migrant exodus.[61] Adding to migrant influx in the United States was the Temporary Admissions Program of 1917, a guest worker program that was in effect until 1921 and brought more than eighty thousand Mexicanos to work in agriculture, on the railroad, and in the mines.[62] The fact is that many of those migrants remained and did not return to México. In addition, the number of undocumented migrants that came into the United States during this period reached some one hundred thousand.[63]

By 1920, the total number of Mexicanos born in the United States dramatically increased to 486,418. Tejas enjoyed the highest increase, from 125,016 in 1910 to 251,827 ten years later, followed by California, which went from 33,694 to 88,771.[64] In Tejas the Mexicano-born population in the Lower Rio Grande Valley more than doubled by 1920.[65] However, Colorado had the highest percent growth: it went from 2,602 in 1910 to 11,037 in 1920. Arizona also showed a substantial increase, from 29,987 to 61,580.[66] Meier and Rivera write, "The volume of the second wave provided the matrix for most present day [Mexican] communities, except in New México, which attracted few from this wave."[67]

The Third Migrant Wave

The third wave between 1920 and 1930 was the second largest population surge of Mexicanos in the United States. With the exception of the brief U.S. Depression of 1921–1922, which produced a temporary slowdown in Mexicano migration into the United States, the influx of migrants continued throughout the decade. It is important to note, however, that during this Depression thousands of Mexicanos were repatriated to México. To aid in the return of migrants, México spent some $2.5 million for food and transportation. Meier and Rivera explain, "This large sum indicates heavy repatriation during this period."[68] As to the lessons of the 1921 Depression, Lawrence A. Cardoso writes, "many braceros that toiled in the United States became helpless in times of economic crises. Their value was only in times of prosperity; in periods of retrenchment it was minimal. Ethnocentrism and the needs of employers and U.S. citizens at large dictated that Méxicans lost their jobs first."[69] The Depression of 1921 was but an omen for a more devastating depression (1929) to come, which would create a reverse Migrant Exodus to México.

In spite of the short-term economic depression, México's continued conflict and violent politics continued to push migrants north to the United States. The preceding was illustrated by two major events: the unsuccessful revolt of 1923 led by General Adolfo de la Huerta and the Cristero Rebellion of 1926–1929. Moreover, during these years, the earlier migration patterns shifted to a Mexicano diaspora. Mexicanos began to migrate and settle in other states outside Aztlán, particularly in the Midwest region of the country and even the Northwest. The result was the emergence of new barrios (enclaves) and *colonias* in both rural and urban areas in the United States.

By 1924, immigration from southern Europe had a catalytic effect of heightening the demand for Mexicano workers. Congress had passed several draconian immigration laws, (e.g., the 1917, 1921, and 1924 Immigration Acts), which relied on the use of a head tax, literacy requirements, quotas, and prohibition of contract workers, in order to restrict southern and eastern European immigration.[70] They excluded people largely on pseudoracial grounds; but immigrants from México and the rest of Latin America were largely "exceptions to the rule." According to Joan Moore and Harry Pachon, "Entry was increased or decreased by changes in law enforcement rather than by changing a policy."[71] In fact, great efforts were made by growers and railroad magnates to prevent any quota restrictions against Mexicano migrant workers, because their labor was in such demand.[72]

Statistically, the third immigrant wave showed a net increase of 152,599 over the total of the earlier period. The overall, Mexicano-born population increased from 486,418 in 1920 to 639,017 in 1930. Of all of the states, California outpaced Tejas and enjoyed the greatest growth of Mexicano immigrants. The numbers increased from 88,771 in 1920 to 191,346 in 1930. In total numbers, Tejas still had the largest Mexicano-born population in the country: from 251,827 in 1920 to 262,672 in 1930. However, during the ten-year period some states lost México-born population. Arizona went from 61,580 in 1920 to a low of 47,855. Nuevo México experienced a decline as well from 20,272 in 1920 to 15,983 in 1930.[73]

Impact of the Exodus: A Demographic Profile

The Migrant Exodus symbolized one of the twentieth century's greatest mass movements of humanity. This was evident in the dramatic population growth of Mexicanos in the United States. Most historians and demographers concur that the total Mexicano population in the United States by 1930 reached 1,449,295[74] and that 10 percent of México's entire population resided in the United States.[75] According to Balderrama and Rodríguez, "Research indicates that in all probability more than one million Méxicans entered the United States before the advent of the Great Depression."[76] During this thirty-year period, the number of Mexicanos born in the United States nearly tripled. The 1930 Census revealed that the Mexicano population in Tejas was 683,681; California, 368,013; Arizona 114,173; Colorado, 57,676; and New México 59,340. In the count of the Mexicano population, inaccuracies permeated the 1930 Census process for a number of reasons.[77] For example, Nuevo México's population of 59,340 was wildly inaccurate and victim of a major undercount; this was corroborated by a local report on school population that concluded that New México's "Spanish" population was 202,709.[78]

By 1930, 10 percent of the Mexican origin population in the United States lived outside Aztlán: Illinois had a Mexicano population of 28,906; Kansas, 19,150; Michigan, 13,336; Indiana, 9,642; Oklahoma, 7,354; Wyoming, 7,174; Nebraska, 6,321; Missouri, 4,989; Iowa, 4,295; Ohio, 4,037; and Utah, 4,012.[79] By 1930 the Mexicano population also became increasingly urbanized. According to Rodolfo Acuña, "The move to cities by Méxicans was significant; by 1930, 51 percent of the Méxican population was urban (as was 56 percent of the population at large)."[80] The significance of this thirty-year period is that 94 percent of the foreign-born Mexicano population in the United States arrived after 1900 and some 62 percent arrived after 1915.[81] Indicative of the rapid slowdown of the migrant exodus after 1930: only 38,980 Mexicanos migrated legally into the United States. The following year, it decreased to 11,915. Between 1931 and 1941, the number fluctuated between a high of 2,627 in 1932 to a low of 1,232 in 1935.[82]

The demographic impact of the Migrant Exodus was felt in numerous cities and locales throughout the Southwest and Midwest as well. The first three decades of the twentieth century witnessed the migration of some 728,000 legal immigrants and thousands of undocumented workers into the United States.[83] Gómez-Quiñones explains, "Increased migration, combined with the rapidly expanding economy of the Southwest, led to the expansion of large urban concentrations of Méxicans in the Southwest's major cities." Numerous barrios developed within many of these urban areas. This proved to be the beginning of the urbanization of Mexicanos in the United States. Census data shows that by 1930 more than half of the Mexicano-origin population resided in cities.[84]

"By the 1920s," writes Juan Gonzales, "the Rio Grande Valley was as segregated as apartheid South Africa."[85] The population of south Tejas at the turn of the century was 79,934. By 1920 it was recorded at 159,822, and by 1930, it reached 322,845. During this same period, the Winter Garden area grew from 8,401 to 36,816.[86] Montejano explains, "In the new era of commercial agriculture, South Tejas remained basically Méxican."[87] South Tejas cities such as Corpus Christi, Laredo, and Brownsville were major recipients of the influx of new migrants. Outside of South Tejas, migrants settled in cities like Austin, Houston, Dallas, and Lubbock. The city of Houston, for example, went from a few hundred Mexicanos in 1900 to over fifteen thousand by 1930.[88] In the early decades of the twentieth century, El Paso and San Antonio also experienced growth, becoming transient stopping-off places for the migrants. Yet of all the border cities, El Paso served as the major distribution point for Mexicano migrants, in some months processing more than five thousand persons.

In another part of the Southwest, the city of Los Angeles experienced a population explosion. It grew from 5,600 in 1910 to 97,000 in 1930[89] with a larger population than any city in México except México City. Although the Mexicano populations were small, other California cities affected by the migrant exodus were Santa Barbara, San Diego, San Francisco, San Jose, Fresno, Brawley, El Centro, Calipatria, and Calexico, among others. In the Midwest, Chicago between 1920 and 1930 went from four thousand to nearly twenty thousand Mexicanos. Almost 70 percent of the Mexicano population in Illinois lived in Chicago. In Wisconsin, some 60 percent of the Mexicanos lived in Milwaukee.[90] The Mexicano population in Detroit in 1926 was 5,000 and two years later it increased to fifteen thousand.[91] Additionally, some migrants also settled in western states such as Nevada, Utah, Wyoming, Oregon, and Washington.[92] Even Alaska experienced Mexicano migration. These are but a few illustrations of the "diaspora" that occurred as a result of the migrant exodus.

Implications of the Migrant Exodus

During the first thirty years of the twentieth century as well as before, what existed between México and the United States was an open border with few restrictions for entry into the United States. Even after the establishment of the U.S. Border Patrol in 1924, there was minimal effort to enforce existing immigration regulations that required Mexicanos to pass a literacy test and pay a head tax of $8. It was well understood and accepted by white economic, political, and immigration interests and by U.S. officials along the U.S./México border that cheap labor was crucial to the success of their large-scale capitalistic enterprises.[93] As a result, Mexicanos became the new coveted source for satisfying the U.S. demand for access to exploitable labor, particularly from farmers and ranchers.

The class and occupational composition of these new migrants was diverse. Included in the three waves of migration were workers, peasants, professionals, merchants, intellectuals, former soldiers, and political refugees. More specifically, however, according Del Castillo and De León:

> For the most part, the large percentage of immigrants who came north during the early twentieth century descended from the ranks of the lower class. Some 80 percent to 90 percent of them had experience in nothing other than agricultural work or unskilled occupations. The rest were clerks, craftsmen, and other types of skilled workers. The latter groups encompassed elites escaping the wrath of compesinos or revolutionary armies bent on retaliation for past injustices and oppression.[94]

Several states in México significantly contributed to the Migrant Exodus. The lure of jobs brought Mexicanos from México's border states of Tamaulipas, Nuevo León, and Coahuila, particularly into Tejas. Those from Guanajuato, Michoacán, Jalisco, and San Luis Potosí migrated mostly to California; although some also migrated to states in the Midwest region of the United States.[95] Most new migrants found work mainly in the expanding agricultural, mining, and railroad construction and maintenance sectors. According to Gonzales, they also "found work as laborers on construction sites, public works systems, service and food establishments, lumbering camps, and ranches."[96]

A very significant aspect of the exodus was the negative reaction the new migrants received from white immigration restrictionists, racists, and nativists. They publicly attacked and condemned the influx of Mexican migrants and demanded a halt to the migration. This was evident during the second wave in a warning by Samuel Bryan, a professor at Stanford University:

The evils to the community at large, which their presence in large number almost invariably brings, may more than overbalance their desired qualities. Their low standards of living and of morals, their illiteracy, their utter lack of proper political interest, the retarding effect of their employment upon the wage scale of the more progressive races, and finally their tendencies to colonize in urban centers, with evil results, combine to stamp them as a rather undesirable class of residents.[97]

It was during the third wave that the nativist forces accelerated their attacks. During the debate of the immigration acts of 1921 and 1924 nativists groups sought to include Mexicanos in the quota provision. Organized labor alleged that Mexicano migrants were taking jobs from domestic workers, were depressing wages, and degrading working conditions. Other nativists with their inflammatory racist rhetoric alleged that Mexicanos could not be assimilated because of their biological "mestizo mixture." Even politicians like Congressman John Box of Texas warned about the threat Mexicanos posed to the United States by describing them as "illiterate, unclean, peonized" and warned about the consequences of fostering a "distressing process of mongrelization."[98] In the end, Southwestern corporations and growers and their need for a source of cheap labor proved successful in lobbying Congress in fending off the nativist anti-Mexicano attacks.[99] Yet the nativists prevailed in influencing Congress to establish the U.S. Border Patrol in 1924 with an appropriation of $1,000,000 and the hiring of 450 men to patrol both the 2,000-mile-long U.S./México and 4,000-mile-long U.S./Canadian border.

From 1926 to 1928, nativists once again sought unsuccessfully to limit Mexicano immigration by including México in the quota system. Understanding the significant contributions made by Mexicano workers, once again, powerful white rancher and grower interests lobbied Congress to again defeat the nativist efforts. Among them was Fred H. Bixby, a prominent Southwesterner who owned some 100,000 acres in California and 250,000 acres in Arizona. In justifying the need for Mexicano labor, he said, "We have no Chinamen, we have no Japs. The Hindu is worthless, the Filipino is nothing, and the white man will not do the work."[100] As the Mexicano population increased during the third wave, so did the nativist activity and racism. By 1929 the Migrant Exodus came to abrupt end as the result of the calamitous economic impact of the Depression.

The Great Depression: Mexicano Repatriation and Deportations

The Great Depression of 1929 unleashed the fury of unemployment, economic dislocations, and a nativist resurgence that quickly halted the migrant exodus flow down to a trickle. From 1929 to 1941, Mexicanos were subjected to repatriation and deportations.[101] The depression years of the 1930s marked the first time in the history of international migration between the United States and other countries that the federal government sponsored and supported the mass expulsion of immigrants. Initially, repatriation was directed at all immigrants, but according to Camille Guerin-Gonzales, "became, within a matter of a few months, one that singled out Méxicans."[102] Government at all levels and nativists alike overtly proposed, "Mexicanos Go Home!" "You are not needed any longer!" During the duration of the Depression, Mexicanos were subjected to a flagrant and discriminatory double standard.

The Great Depression

What were the effects and implications of the Great Depression? Since World War I and into the 1920s, the United States enjoyed a period of great economic prosperity that was interrupted only briefly in 1921 by a short depression. However, generally speaking, the rest of the 1920s continued to be prosperous. This period ended abruptly in 1929 with the stock market crash that marked the beginning of the Great Depression.[103] In explaining its horrendous impact, Mario Barrera explains, "The economic dislocations of the Depression are well known: a substantial drop in the level of economic activity, dramatic declines in wage rates in industry and agriculture, and decline in the length of the average workweek."[104] With masses of workers unemployed, the federal government was compelled to develop social welfare programs designed to meet the urgent needs of the millions of impoverished people. The number of unemployed increased from four million in 1930 to more than thirteen million in 1933, 25 percent of the U.S. labor force. Wages dropped from 35 cents an hour to 14 and 15 cents, and in some instances down to 10 cents, and weekly wages of $1.50 were commonplace throughout the Southwest.[105] The economic crisis worsened even further when the mechanization of agriculture, displaced many workers, particularly Mexicanos.[106] The massive economic crises paralyzed the country from 1929 until the U.S. entry into World War II in late 1941.

What specifically were the effects of the Great Depression on Mexicanos in the United States? The Depression for the country as a whole was devastating, but for Mexicanos in particular, was even worse[107]—it brought acute economic misery. Many Mexicanos could not get jobs while others were fired to make room for non-Mexicanos such as whites escaping the poverty of the Dust Bowl in Kansas and Oklahoma.[108] As a result of layoffs and existing poverty, Mexicanos in the thousands lost everything, including their homes. Francisco E. Balderrama writes, "Many families not only lacked food but also shelter because they were unable to pay rent or mortgages."[109] Numerous Mexicanos, like others, found themselves on the rolls of the welfare agencies. The bad economic situation was exacerbated by a rise in white nativism. Increasingly, Mexicanos lived in a state of insecurity and trepidation due to the relentless nativist xenophobic attacks. They were singled out as "scapegoats" for the serious socioeconomic ills that the country faced.[110] The Great Depression served to reinforce the already existing discrimination, especially in the workplace. Mexicano workers quickly realized that there was no need for them to apply for work, because the jobs were reserved for whites.[111]

A Decade of Betrayal: Repatriations and Deportations

The impact of the Great Depression produced what scholars Francisco E. Balderrama and Raymond Rodríguez describe as the "Decade of Betrayal." This betrayal became blatantly clear in the federal government's scapegoating and massive efforts to return Mexicanos back to México. New restrictions on immigration to the United States were adopted not through legislation, but rather through federal administrative regulations.[112] Forced return took two forms: deportations and repatriation drives. Deportation was a formal procedure by the Immigration and Naturalization Service used to remove a person from the country on the grounds that he or she was illegally residing in the United States in violation of the country's immigration laws.[113] There were some twenty-six reasons for a deportation—from being in the country illegally to advocating the overthrow of the U.S. government.[114] Deportation proceedings were based on formal deportation hearings under warrant proceedings and voluntary departures without warrant proceedings. The former was discouraged because of hearing and transportation costs. The latter was more commonly used. The voluntary deportation process offered advantages to both the government and undocumented worker. The government saved money by paying for his or her transportation to the border; in turn, the undocumented person was able to enter the United States illegally once again. Most apprehended undocumented workers chose the option of "voluntary deportation."[115]

During the early 1930s, the federal government carried on highly publicized "deportation roundups" in numerous large cities both in the Southwest and Midwest. During the first two years of the Great Depression, deportations and threats of deportations coupled with nativist hostile attacks convinced thousands of Mexicanos, especially from Tejas, to voluntarily return to México. While deportation drives began on more of a regional basis in 1929 by 1931 they had spread nationally. From 1929 to 1935, the U.S. government utilized both formal deportation and voluntary departure processes to remove (deport) some eighty thousand Mexicanos to México.[116] From 1930 to 1939, Mexicanos comprised 46.3 percent of all the people deported and yet ironically, they only constituted 1 percent of the country's population.[117] At this time no other ethnic immigrant group in the United States suffered such racist and humiliating treatment. Tragically, over four hundred thousand Mexicanos were repatriated from Aztlán to México during the Depression years, many of them with their U.S.-born children.

Massive deportations engendered a climate of fear throughout the *colonias* and barrios. Under the auspices of the Department of Labor's Bureau of Immigration, most of the deportation roundups resembled full-fledged paramilitary operations. They were conducted in numerous large cities, but southern California was a focal point of the deportation frenzy. One of the most famous roundups was that of La Placita in Los Angeles, which occurred on February 26, 1931. Some four hundred Mexicanos were herded together like animals in spite of protests from México's vice consul to Los Angeles.[118] One could argue that it was reminiscent of the persecution actions against Jews in Hitler's Nazi Germany with the attacks by the storm troopers. In the United States, the Mexicano was the Jew and the Bureau of Immigration, Border Patrol, and local law enforcement agencies were this country's storm troopers.

The barrios of Aztlán and beyond were under a state of siege not only by government agencies and nativist organizations, but also by so-called reputable white organizations and unions. Patriotic organizations such as the Veterans of Foreign Wars and the American Legion and the American Federation of Labor spearheaded many of the anti-Mexicano and anti-migrant attacks. They were joined by a plethora of newspapers (e.g., *Chicago Tribune*) and magazines (e.g., *Saturday Evening Post*) that fanned the racist fires against the Mexicano and other so-called aliens.[119] They alleged that Mexicanos in particular were taking jobs away from white workers. Politically, few non-Mexicanos, specifically whites, came to Mexicanos' aid or spoke out against the double standard of the nativist attacks. The Depression clearly revealed that Mexicanos had few allies or friends. Some foreign consulates, however, in the major cities that contained numbers of Mexicanos did come to the defense of the migrant.[120]

Repatriation drives were far more effective than deportations in returning migrants to México. The heaviest years of repatriation occurred from 1929 to 1932, with 1931 being by far the highest. The number of those who were repatriated during this three-year period is as follows: 1929, 79,419; 1930, 70,127; 1931, 138,519; and 1932, 77,453. In 1931 alone, during the month of November 20,756 Mexicanos were repatriated. From 1933 to 1937, the numbers dramatically declined. In 1933, the total number of repatriations was 33,574; 1934, 23,943; 1935, 15,368; 1936, 11,599; and 1937, 8,037.[121] With the introduction of President Roosevelt's New Deal in 1933, Mexicanos started to shy away from voluntary repatriation. Mexicanos who were not U.S. citizens were not eligible to work on Works Progress Administration (WPA) projects.[122] Some of those repatriated had children who were born in the United States, which made them U.S. citizens. To them México, not the United States, was a foreign land.[123] Yet some Mexicanos chose to return to México voluntarily without the assistance of anyone. Still others were encouraged to repatriate by local welfare bureaus and private charitable organizations that sponsored city or county repatriation drives. Indigence, not citizenship, was the criteria used to ascertain which Mexicanos were subject to repatriation.[124] The methods of persuasion for voluntary repatriation included inducements of free food, clothing, medical aid, and free transportation to the border and into México as well. This meant that counties paid for rail transportation to México's border. From the border to the interior of México, the Mexican government provided gratuitous rail passage. Balderrama and Rodríguez explain that "trains with hundreds, sometimes over a thousand, repatriates aboard regularly left collection centers such as Detroit, Chicago, St. Louis, Denver, Phoenix, Oklahoma City, and Los Angeles."[125] Once in México, the Mexican government set up new *colonias* and offered some of the returnees free land and assistance.

Thus, for Mexicanos the decade of the 1930s truly proved to be a "Decade of Betrayal." With Europe and Asia in a state of war by 1939, the U.S. economy began to gradually improve. As the United States prepared for its entry into World War II, the Mexicano population in 1940 witnessed a slight increase.

Mexicano Demographic Profile of 1940

The Mexicano population in the United States was still relatively small in 1940. According to the U.S. Census Bureau the country's total Mexicano population was 1,624,733. This meant that during the turbulent decade of the 1930s, the population only grew by 175,438. Some historians allege that due to a major undercount, the actual figure was much higher, more like 2,125,000.[126] Considering that nearly five hundred thousand Mexicanos were repatriated and thousands more deported during the previous decade, the Mexicano population increase was significant. The urbanization of the Mexicano continued with some 60 percent living in the cities.[127] Cities offered greater work opportunities and generally better quality education, even though the schools were segregated.[128] David Gutierrez points out that the 1940 Census showed there were 377,000 resident Mexicanos undocumented in the United States, while nearly seven hundred thousand Mexicanos born in the United States had at least one parent born in México.[129] In great part the slight increase over the 1930 figure of 1,449,295 was essentially attributable to the restart of the migrant exodus.

In spite of the repatriations and deportations, the 1940 U.S. Census reported that the population of Mexicano ancestry was 1,075,653. Approximately 377,433 or 35.1 percent were Mexican born and 698,220 or 64.9 percent were U.S. born. Moreover, 90 percent of the Mexican origin population resided within the Southwest and only 10 percent lived outside of the region.[130] The data suggested that as the economy began to improve and demand for labor rose by the late 1930s, many of those who had been repatriated or deported began to return to the United States. The federal government adamantly discouraged illegal entrance into the United States.[131] From 1930 to 1940 only about twenty thousand Mexicanos immigrated to the United States legally. The recovering Mexicano population growth was a result of slight improvements in the U.S. economy due to President Roosevelt's New Deal policies and the beginning of World War II in Europe in 1939. Labor shortages began to occur both in resuscitating factories (e.g., packinghouses, foundries, canneries, and the like) and fruit and vegetable fields, particularly in the Midwest. This served to further strengthen the migrant stream, which included migrant workers from states like Tejas, who worked for a few months as seasonal workers then returned to their respective state; others, however, stayed.[132] High birthrates among Mexicanos also contributed to the population increase. Prior to World War II, only 10 percent lived outside Aztlán.

World War II: A Paradoxical Era

With the bombing of Pearl Harbor by the Japanese on December 7, 1941, the United States became engaged in World War II against the Axis powers of Japan, Germany, and Italy. The Great Depression came to an end by 1942 as a result of World War II and the New Deal economic policies.[133] For the Mexicano experience, World War II proved to be an era of political contradictions. As a people, Mexicanos were ethnically victimized, kicked out of the country during the decade of betrayal, and attacked as being inferior to the U.S. standard. Yet with the beginning of World War II, all of these previous racist actions and attitudes by whites were supposedly forgotten merely because the country was at war. All of a sudden, out of economic, military, and political expediency the nativist attacks shifted away from the Mexicano to the so-called Japs. Japanese Americans who lived in the United States were put in "detention camps," in reality concentration camps. The national propaganda proclaimed that all "Americans," including blacks and Mexicanos should join the war effort to defeat Hitler, Mussolini, and Emperor Hirohito whose totalitarian and tyrannical forces sought the annihilation of democracy worldwide. In short, after being repatriated and deported, Mexicanos were reinvited back to participate in "their" war effort.

Adding to the paradox was the deleterious political, social, and economic conditions endemic to internal colonialism. Segregation, discrimination, prejudice, poverty, exploitation, disenfranchisement, and a plethora of social problems still permeated the Mexicano experience during the early 1940s. Yet in spite of these contradictory realities, Mexicanos responded to World War II with great sacrifice, valor, and commitment to a country that had recently rejected them and categorized them as undesirables and inferiors. Mexicano labor was invaluable both in the factories and in the fields since once again a shortage of workers existed in both the industrial and agricultural sectors of the economy. Because of wartime manpower needs, numerous Mexicanos left the rural areas and agricultural work and sought employment in the cities' numerous defense factories.

The Bracero Program: A Provider of Cheap Labor

By 1942, desperate for manpower, the United States once again turned to México as a cheap supplier of labor.[134] A demand for Mexicano labor was rising prior to the entry of the United States into World War II. Between 1940 and 1942, growers petitioned the U.S. government for permission to use foreign labor, and pressured the Roosevelt Administration for an open border policy. This allowed growers, as had been the case during World War I, to simply hire individual Mexicanos who crossed the border. México's response to growing pressure for some sort of an informal labor agreement was not enthusiastic. Juan Ramon García writes, "Méxicans still recalled the deportation of their compatriots during the Depression; they were aware of the mistreatment suffered by United States citizens of Méxican descent; and they knew of the long history of cultural conflict between Méxicans and Americans, especially in the state of Texas."[135] México's declaration of war against the Axis powers of June 1942 expedited discussions over establishing a guest worker program of some sort.[136] However, not everyone in México was supportive of such an idea. Various organizations and minor political parties opposed a guest worker program and the exodus of their countrymen based on a profound sense of Mexicano nationalism.[137]

After a few months of negotiations, on August 4, 1942, a labor accord was concluded and signed by both the United States and México.[138] The preliminary labor agreement was called the Mexican Farm Labor Supply Program and informally became known as the "Bracero[139] Program."[140] It was a takeoff from an earlier bilateral accord that had been in effect during most of World War I, specifically between 1917 and 1920, which had supplied temporary Mexicano workers for U.S. agriculture. Established by executive order, under the terms of the agreement, México permitted its nationals to come and work in the United States for temporary periods under stipulated conditions. As initially agreed upon, the Bracero Program was supposed to last only for the duration of the war.[141]

Though amended several times, the 1942 Bracero Program agreement remained essentially unchanged and was the basis for the importation of guest workers from México from 1942 through 1947, when it expired.[142] Ernesto Galarza provides a summary of the principal provisions of the agreement:

> Mexican workers were not to be used to displace domestic workers but only fill proved shortages. Recruits were to be exempted from military service, and discrimination against them was not to be permitted. The round trip transportation expenses of the worker were guaranteed, as well as living expenses en route. Hiring was to be done on the basis of a written contract between worker and his employer and the work was to be exclusively in agriculture. Braceros were to be free to buy merchandise in places of their own choice. Housing and sanitary conditions were to be adequate. Deductions amounting to 10 percent of the earnings were authorized for deposit in a savings fund payable to the worker on his return to México. Work was guaranteed for three-quarters of the duration of the contract. Wages were to be equal to those prevailing in the area of employment, but in any case not less than 30 cents per hour.[143]

Employers were required to post a bond for every guest worker and had to abide by the agreement. Women were excluded because the Mexican government felt that they would be subjected to unacceptable treatment and abuse at the hands of greedy employers and sundry predators.[144] As Acuña points out, "Neither nativist groups, nor organized labor, not even the Communist party objected to the admission of seasonal agricultural laborers under the terms of the agreement."[145]

It was not until seven months later in early 1943 that President Roosevelt received formal congressional approval for the Bracero Program. Yet as early as September 27, 1942, the first installment of *braceros* arrived in El Paso, Texas, followed by the second two days later in Stockton, California.[146] Records show that from 1942 to 1945, some 167,925 *braceros* worked in the United States and the highest number was in 1944 with a total of 62,170.[147] Hence, under the guise of Public Law 45, the terms of the Bracero Program allowed Mexicano workers from México to work in the United States for temporary periods primarily in agricultural-related labor. It was in effect a federal subsidy for satisfying the agricultural labor demands.[148] Under the circumstances it was mutually economically beneficial to both countries. For México it acted as a "safety valve" alleviating its high levels of unemployment and poverty and for the United States, plagued by a chronic shortage of agricultural workers, it provided a steady flow of temporary cheap labor.

As will be examined in the next chapter, the Bracero Program faced some serious difficulties in its implementation due to the prevalence of racism against Mexicanos, such as in Tejas. Yet with Mexicanos joining the war effort and World War II's chronic need for additional labor, the Bracero Program profoundly impacted the Mexicano political experience by reigniting the migrant exodus.

Mexicanos Join the War Effort

During World War II some 375,000 to 500,000 Mexicanos joined the various branches of the U.S. armed forces, especially the army and marines.[149] Even though Mexicanos were often treated worse than second-class citizens, they responded with valor in the defense of the country. With México's declaration of war on the Axis powers on June 1, 1942, President Avila Camacho exhorted Mexicanos in the United States to forget about lingering animosities and support the war efforts. Thousands of Mexicano citizens who resided in the United States enlisted in the U.S. armed forces. In great part this came about as a result of wartime legislation that stipulated that in exchange for service, they were entitled to U.S. citizenship. Also, many Mexicanos born in the United States enlisted because of limited economic opportunities in their respective barrios and colonias. Many of them viewed the armed forces as a ticket to new opportunities, an escape from the drudgery of poverty, and a means of proving themselves by serving in defense of the country. Although some were drafted, the majority enlisted in either the army or marine corps. Most were between the ages of seventeen and twenty-one; some were as young as sixteen. Based on their percentage of the total population, more Mexicanos served in combat divisions than any other ethnic group. In addition, a high percentage of Mexicanos volunteered for the more hazardous duties, such as the paratroopers and marines.[150]

Mexicanos fought with gallantry on every war front—from the jungles of the South Pacific to the deserts of North Africa to the invasion of Italy and Europe itself. Raul Morín, in his work *Among the Valiant*, documented their valor and the numerous military contributions made in the defense of the United States. He explains that some Mexicanos in the armed forces felt a sense of betrayal because of the prevalence of racism at home. Nevertheless, Morín reminds his readers that 25 percent of the U.S. military personnel who were captured and forced to participate in the infamous Bataan Death March in the Philippines were Mexicanos. Important to note is that Mexicanos were killed or wounded in greater numbers than in proportion to their population in the United States. As Carlos Vélez-Ibañez points out, Mexicanos "over participated in combat units and suffered casualties in inordinate numbers."[151] Because of their gallantry they garnered proportionately more military honors than any other ethnic group. By the end of the war, seventeen Mexicanos had received the Medal of Honor of which five were awarded posthumously.[152] Equally important, none faced charges of desertion, mutiny, or treason.[153]

Thus, for the Mexicano in the United States, World War II became a paradox. Thousands of Mexicanos were killed and wounded in the battlefield allegedly in defense of democracy, yet at home democracy was largely denied to them, where they endured egregious racist attacks.

The Rise of Pachuquismo: *Mexicanos Come under Attack*

During World War II, while Mexicanos were dying in the battlefields, at home they continued to be victimized by the segregation, poverty, and racism engendered by their continued internal colonial status. Specifically, a cultural rebellion known as *pachuquismo* (zoot suiterism) emerged during the late 1930s in urban areas such as El Paso, Los Angeles, and Tucson, in the form of a gang subculture. Young Mexicanos in the barrios joined the gangs and wore faddish tapered suits with large lapels; padded and pointed shoulders; lengthy draped pegged pants; flat crowned, broad-brimmed hats with a feather; and long chains hanging from the belt to the pant pocket. They wore their hair in a long duck-tailed fashion, and used tattoos, especially a cross in the hand. Likewise, Mexicanas associated with the gangs wore short skirts and blouses, and their hair was combed in a high roll style. They spoke slang called *caló*, which was an admixture of English and Spanish and were also zealots of swing music, or jitterbug. Integral to their subculture was the adherence by some to violence and criminal activity, which ranged from petty harassment to murder.[154]

The first major wartime incident involving the formation of *pachucos* (gangs) was the Sleepy Lagoon Case.[155] The incident occurred on August 1, 1942, in Los Angeles and involved Henry Leyva and several other youths from the 38th Street gang. After altercations with another rival gang, Leyva allegedly killed a Mexicano teenager, José Díaz, at a swimming hole called the Sleepy Lagoon. Díaz's body was discovered along a dirt road and the police investigation revealed that he had met his death as a result of a fracture at the base of the skull. According to McWilliams, "It is not surprising that the Los Angeles press welcomed the death of Díaz like manna from the skies. Around the essentially bare facts of the case, they promptly proceeded to weave an enormous web of melodramatic fancy." A total of twenty-four members of the 38th Street gang were indicted for the murder of Díaz on the basis of highly circumstantial evidence.[156] During the course of the investigation, the police severely beat up two of the young men that had been arrested. On August 10 and 11 the police conducted raids of Mexicano barrios around Los Angeles. Some six hundred young people were arrested on suspicion of robbery, auto theft, and assault.[157]

These young Chicanos, as many identified themselves, became victims of "Mexicano baiting" by the well-organized efforts of the white press and police. The Sleepy Lagoon trial lasted several months, and on January 13, 1943, three of the twenty-four were found guilty of first-degree murder, nine guilty of second-degree murder, and five guilty of assault. The other five were found not guilty.[158] Hence, seventeen of the twenty-four were convicted in what was, up to that time, the largest mass trial for murder ever held in the country. During the course of the trial, alleged experts ascribed gang warfare and bloody killings to their Mexicano ancestry. Particularly, Captain E. Duran Ayres of the Los Angeles Sheriff's Department argued that the Mexicano's Indian blood predisposed them to a life of delinquency, crime, and wretchedness.[159]

As a result of the convictions a Sleepy Lagoon Defense Committee was formed. Chaired by Carey McWilliams, it came to the aid of the young Chicanos by raising sufficient resources to appeal the case. On October 4, 1944, after the case received national attention, the District Court of Appeals reversed the convictions of all the defendants in a unanimous decision and the case was later dismissed. This was the first time in the history of Los Angeles that Mexicanos had won such an organized victory in the courts.[160] The Sleepy Lagoon Defense Committee was recognized by then-Mexican president Lazaro Cardenas. Mexicanos in the armed forces also sent the Defense Committee innumerable letters of support. Decades later, Luis Valdez's well-known play and film Zoot Suit was a tribute to the Sleepy Lagoon incident.

The press sensationalism led by the Los Angeles Times and Hearst newspapers nurtured an anti-Mexicano sentiment that stereotyped pachucos as criminals or "sordid Méxican hoodlums." Concurrently, police departments harassed Mexicano youth, especially pachucos, and typically overpoliced the barrios. Literally, while Mexicanos were overseas dying in the battlefields, many of the segregated barrios in urban areas were under a state of siege by police and a racist press.

During World War II, a second major incident, "Zoot Suit Riots," occurred in 1943 involving *pachucos* and this time U.S. sailors. A few months after the convictions in the Sleepy Lagoon case the notorious Zoot Suit Riots also got national and international attention. During April and May of 1943 in the cities of Los Angeles and Oakland, California, several altercations occurred between *pachucos* and white sailors. They were the culmination of the anti-Mexicano *pachuco* crusade initiated by the police and hostile press. However, the altercations by June escalated into tumultuous riots in Los Angles when sailors invaded East Los Angeles en masse. The sailors literally attacked, beat up, stripped, and cut the hair of suspected *pachucos*, while the police looked the other way. To add insult to injury, after the beatings, the police moved in and had the victimized *pachucos* arrested for disturbing the peace. For one week, incident after incident occurred, inflamed by a sensationalist anti-Mexicano *pachuco* crusade by the press, particularly by the *Los Angeles Times* and *Herald Examiner*, both of which condoned and supported the sailors' violent and illegal actions. Rioting also broke out in Pasadena, San Diego, and Long Beach, and other similar confrontations occurred in other U.S. cities such as Chicago, Detroit, and Philadelphia during the summer months of 1943. Throughout the country there were strong reactions to the Zoot Suit Riots. *Time* magazine called them "the ugliest brand of mob action since the coolie race riots of the 1870s."[161]

The Zoot Suit Riots ended because diplomatic pressure was exerted on the United States by the Mexican government and because the Axis powers were using them as effective propaganda. The navy was compelled to cancel overnight passes and instituted strict controls before order was reestablished. However, they left a residue of anger and frustration in a Mexicano community that had been victimized again yet had an emergent leadership and capacity to organize and to effectively defend itself from such racist practices.

The Politics of Accommodation

The Rise of the Mexicano Generation

The hundreds of thousands of Mexicanos that came into the United States during this epoch as a result of the Migrant Exodus brought with them México's political culture. Historian Juan Gómez-Quiñones explains, "For the Mexican people of the Southwest, increased economic migration represented a numerical, cultural, and ideological strengthening of the population, as already existing transborder contacts and influences were increased and expanded."[162] The new migrants constituted the overwhelming majority of the Mexicano population throughout Aztlán and the country as a whole.[163] From a cultural perspective, they supplanted the existent Mexicanos and gave rise to a neo–Mexicano Generation, which served to buttress the existent and old Mexicano culture of the past epoch. They rebuked the idea of severing their political cultural ties with México and sought to culturally preserve their Méxicanidad.

The Mexicano Generation was a product of México's political culture, politics, and history. During this epoch, its ethos was permeated by a strong dosage of authoritarianism.[164] Power was in the hands of the few. Although it adhered to some democratic beliefs, strong authoritarianism characterized by the presence of a centralized government embodied it. This was evident with the Porfiriato (1876–1910), the turbulent and violent decade of the México's Revolution (1910–1920), the politically unstable decade of the 1920s, and the rise of the one-party dictatorship in 1929 that would govern México with an iron fist for decades to come. From the 1930s to the 1940s, México's political system gave rise to corporatism, meaning the political system created formal relationships between selected groups and institutions. President Lazaro Cardenas (1934–1940) applied Spain's system, which allowed his administration to bring numerous interest groups, for example, unions, business, *compesinos*, and military under its control by creating a sector structure within the one-party dictatorship.[165] Wayne A. Cornelius states, "Since the late 1930s, México has had a corporatist system of interest representation in which each citizen and societal segment should relate to the state through a single structure licensed by the state to organize and represent that sector of society."[166] Nevertheless, before the eyes of the world, México was projected as a representative democracy.

Personalismo has historically been part of México's political culture fabric, which means that political authority and loyalty are given to an individual person rather than an institutionalized office held by a leader.[167] Its politics has also been driven by *caudillismo*, which is derived from the Arabic term meaning leader. According to Floyd Merrell, a "caudillo is a charismatic, physically impressive, strong willed, domineering individual, often of military background, whose rule is marked by populist tactics."[168] México's politics have also been driven by powerful individuals, such as Madero, Magón, Zapata, Villa, Carranza, Obregón, de la Huerta, Calles, and Cardenas.

México's political culture has been permeated by patriarchy, paternalism, and parochialism and regionalism. In spite of the progressive nature of México's Constitution of 1917, patriarchy was rampant politically. Men dominated politics—women took on a subordinate political role. Those who governed provided the governed with some of their needs and allowed them a minimal responsibility, and in return the government expected their loyalty.[169] Parochialism was particularly evident during the years 1910 to 1929 with an excess of *caudillos* and *caciques* (local chieftains) whose political perspectives were often narrow in scope and were influenced by their local or regional geography.

Regarding regionalism, Lesley Byrd Simpson wrote the classic *Many Méxicos*, which referred to the major influence religion played on México's political values.[170] It was only after the revolution and the improvement of México's communications and transportation systems that regional differences began to decline, and increasingly most of the governed perceived themselves as Mexicanos first.

Many Mexicanos who migrated to the United States during this epoch brought with them México's political culture, which clashed with the U.S. political culture: Anglo-Saxon, Protestant, and liberal capitalist-oriented beliefs. With their migration to occupied Aztlán most Mexicano migrants were not willing to give up their patriotism or sense of Mexicanidad.

Mexicanos faced a culture of poverty both in México and the United States. The culture of poverty embodied negative political values, such as fatalism, apathy, distrust, and alienation, all of which were barriers to fostering civic participation. Samuel Ramos and Octavio Paz categorized the Mexicano ethos as riddled by an "inferiority complex."[171] Most migrants had a negative perspective toward politics because in most cases in México they had had a bad political experience. After all, many had come to the United States fleeing from the horrors of politics gone mad—a bloody revolution that produced massive destruction and death.

They did not embrace the notion that they were "Spanish," nor were they interested in acculturation, of fostering a hybrid culture or of assimilating into white society. While to some, the term *Mexicano* was negative, if not pejorative, to the new migrant it inspired nationalist feelings of pride (*orgullo*), patriotism (*patrotismo*), and love (*amor*) for the motherland. The newly migrated were hypercritical of those Mexicanos who had assimilated and had lost their ability to speak Spanish, viewing them as *pochos* or *agringados*.[172] Many of the migrants believed that their stay in the United States was temporary. They believed that when their own socioeconomic situation or that of México bettered, they would return, but in most cases they did not.

Participation in U.S. ballot box politics was not a major priority for those of the Mexicano Generation. Their residence in colonized, segregated, and impoverished barrios and *colonias* fostered political alienation, which served to reinforce their existent skepticism and cynicism toward politics. Attitudinally, they brought with them México's essentially "parochial" political culture. This meant that in most cases their cognitive, adaptive, and evaluative orientations toward politics and the workings of the country's political structures were weak and lacked specialized political roles. Yet a few did possess the three ideal types of orientation as illustrated by their involvement in labor organizing efforts as well as with a number of *mutualista* organizations. "The presence of immigrants," according to James Diego Vigil, "reinvigorated the Mexicano culture in the United States and added a more determined, militant element to the labor struggle."[173] Their ostensibly apolitical roles—a product of internal colonialism—was evident within the country's ballot box arena and was one of subordination and powerlessness.

Politically, many Mexicanos chose to remain apolitical and essentially detached from the politics of the United States. They tended to be distrustful of government and *politicos*. Because they did not understand the inner workings of government and politics in the United States, they were not interested in becoming engaged. Most, if not all, however, understood the pain, exploitation, and oppression that pervaded their colonized "occupied" barrios and *colonias*.

For reasons of survival, they adapted to some aspects of white society, but the Mexicano Generation's colonized segregation and the pervasiveness of racism, bigotry, and prejudice directed at them by whites became powerful stimuli that reinforced their Mexicano culture, in particular the use of Spanish. Most refused to give total political loyalty to the United States, to its white Anglo-Saxon-dominated culture and language, and remained largely estranged from the country's political process.

The new migrants developed their own cultural maintenance. Their segregated barrios and *colonias* were the foremost socialization agent. They formed scores of *mutualista* organizations that culturally and politically identified with México's political past and present. These organizations organized numerous cultural and religious events, for example, Cinco de Mayo (5th of May) and 16 de Septiembre (16th of September), Dia de la Virgin de Guadalupe (December 12). The Roman Catholic Church also became a socialization agent with its masses and deep religious experiences of México. Numerous cultural and musical events also acted as socialization agents. Most Mexicanos remained nationalistic and proud of their heritage, and language. They did not denigrate their mestizo or indigenous ethnicity. With this ingrained sense of nationalistic pride, the cultural seed of Chicanismo was planted and later flourished during the epoch of the Chicano Movement (1966–1974).

During this epoch, throughout Aztlán there were also Mexicanos who did not identify with the politics or ethos of the Mexicano Generation. As will be examined in the subsequent chapter, another subculture based upon a generational politic began to emerge as early as the 1920s, but flourished during the next epoch—the Mexican American Generation.

The Second Organizational Renaissance

The politics of the Mexicano experience underwent its second major organizational renaissance. As the population increased and the political, economic, and social conditions changed both in México and United States, the need for organization grew. Organization became their most powerful weapon of resistance to the continued internal colonial oppression and exploitation. With the exception of several unions and one progressive interest group that was an advocate transformer, the new organizations were "want to be white"-oriented. Older existent organizations such as *mutualistas* continued to play essentially a buffer political role. The organizational renaissance was a result of several specific historical antagonisms that produced a propitious climate for change. One such antagonism was the growing discontent and rising expectations among Mexicanos vis-à-vis their socioeconomic status. Secondly, within the migrant exodus there were those who were political refugees and intellectuals from México who had some degree of organizational and political experience. Third, the absence of governmental social assistance and programs coupled with the prevalence of segregation and prejudice encouraged the formation of self-help mutual benefit organizations. Fourth, as a result of their World War I experiences, some returning Mexicano veterans were no longer willing to accept the status quo and were eager for change. Lastly, the need for Mexicanos to resist the exploitive and change their segregated and impoverished status quo also created the conditions that were conducive to forming new organizations.

Michael de Tirado explains that the Mexicano during the early part of the twentieth century established "undifferentiated multipurpose organizations which not only served his political needs but also his economic, social and cultural ones as well."[174] The organizations can be basically broken down into three types: mutual benefit organizations, Mexicano advocacy–oriented interest groups, and the trade union movement and in the formation of their own Mexicano unions. Using an abbreviated case study format, all three ideal types of organizations are examined.

Mutual Benefit Organizations

Mutual benefit organizations or *mutualistas* continued to flourish during the epoch of accommodation politics. Henry Santiestevan notes, "mutualist organizations were characteristic of an era of adaptation and accommodation."[175] As previously mentioned, the socioeconomic conditions that helped induce their formation became more acute during this period. Wherever Mexicanos settled some form of mutual benefit society or fraternal organization was formed. People's need for burial insurance, mutual assistance, and social and cultural activities, and a pervading sense of Mexicano nationalism continued to facilitate their formation. Although some *mutualistas* functioned as buffers, they were also powerful instruments in helping migrants adapt to their new homeland. Many *logias* (lodges) served as launching vehicles for union formation. They also fostered a sense of community in a hostile white environment that practiced segregation, bigotry, and discrimination toward Mexicans. Hence, protection was another great incentive for cooperation. A universal tenet of all *mutualistas* was the aim of Union y Protección.[176] Structurally, they were comprised of lodges or logias; elected officers; a central body, usually a congress of some sort; a governing board or executive committee; and a number of standing committees.

Many of the *mutualistas* formed during the previous epoch of resistance continued to function and grow, while others proved to be transitory. According to Ricardo Romo, after 1918, they primarily performed three major functions: to meet the migrant families' basic needs, to maintain their Mexicano culture, and to defend Mexicanos against injustices and violations of their civil rights.[177] This does not mean that every *mutualista* formed prior to 1918 performed all three functions. But when existent ones did not, usually new ones tended to form. As self-help or mutual assistance organizations, they were historically significant because Mexicanos organized them wholly for Mexicanos within a hostile white-dominated political climate. As organizational buffers, they proved to be effective instruments of adaptation, integration, and survival, but not of assimilation, which was categorically rejected.

During the epoch of adaptation throughout the Southwest and Midwest, several new *mutualistas* were formed. Many adopted the motto Patria, Union y Beneficiencia, a unifying symbol that continued to propagate throughout numerous *colonias* and barrios. Some were apolitical and adaptation-oriented, while others were reformist and some even radical in their ideology and politics. In most cases, *mutualistas* of this period were more nationalistic than those formed during the previous epoch. "These organizations," according to Arnoldo Carlos Vento, "were numerous representing both moderate/middle class activities as well as activist-radical pursuits."[178] Some acted as catalysts in the formation of other organizations, particularly unions. However, a detrimental form of parochialism haunted Mexicano *mutualistas* and other forms of organizations. Efforts to integrate them into a viable unified network or a larger organizational effort proved unsuccessful. Typically, lack of resources, lack of expertise, and distrust and petty jealousies hindered such efforts and impeded unity of action.

La Alianza Hispana Americana

The second organizational renaissance in great part was induced by the expansion of the previously formed *mutualistas* and by the formation of new ones. In Arizona, the Alianza Hispana Americana (hereafter called La Alianza), formed in 1894, became the largest and most successful fraternal *mutualista*. Within a generation of its birth, it became the first regional (Southwest) Mexicano *mutualista*. "By 1929," according to Oscar Martinez, "It had 13,459 members, and ten years later that number had risen to 17,366,"[179] with lodges from San Diego, California, to Brownsville, Texas, and as far north as Cheyenne and Chicago.[180] Moreover, starting in 1924, La Alianza started organizing lodges in México. By 1936 it had established forty-four lodges in various cities in México with a membership of two thousand, most of which were formed during the early 1930s by Mexicanos who had been repatriated or deported. Differences over management led to a schism that in 1936 resulted with the separation of the lodges in both countries. In spite of its loss of membership in México, La Alianza in 1940 reached 18,000 dues-paying members.[181] The dire effects of the Depression were such that it served to fuel La Alianza's growth. By 1942, La Alianza had grown to where it had a total of some 373 lodges and became the largest regional (Southwest/ Midwest) Mexicano organization in the country.[182]

Throughout the twenty-nine years of this epoch, La Alianza's growth both in the United States and México was a result of its change from providing simple death benefits to a diversified life insurance system. The difficult socioeconomic conditions became the basis for La Alianza's organizational success. The fact that the overwhelming number of Mexicano families lacked the financial means to bury their family members made La Alianza's death benefit plan appealing. Moreover, its social and cultural activities provided another incentive for people to join,[183] especially when social activities were rather limited in a segregated society. One successful social activity was the creation of its youth program in 1924. Juvenile lodges, *legiones juveniles*, were established and provided their own educational services, rituals, and life insurance protection. By 1931 its youth membership had grown to 1,500.[184] During the Depression, La Alianza lodges collaborated with other self-help associations to provide immediate relief to the needy, particularly in seeking employment.[185] In general, most of its services were directed at its lower middle- and working-class paid membership, and not the poor.

As the country's economy began to recover by the late 1930s Mexicanos felt the effects of World War II, particularly in new job opportunities in the war industries, enlistment in the armed forces, and opportunities in the Bracero Program. These events served to undermine La Alianza's activities and organizing efforts. Many Mexicanos were no longer in need of its life insurance or social support.[186] But more detrimental to the organization were the increasing leadership power struggles, issues of financial solvency, increasing competition from commercial insurance companies, and the availability of other social activities, all of which by the early 1940s contributed significantly to its gradual decline.

La Liga Protectora Latina (La Liga)

In Arizona, La Liga accelerated its lobbying efforts against discriminatory practices toward Mexicanos. By 1919, La Liga had increased its membership to some five thousand in Arizona and had over thirty lodges, principally in Arizona, California, Nuevo México, and Tejas. Paid members were entitled to employment and financial assistance and received a newsletter, La Justicia. For several years, La Liga held conventions and pursued numerous legislative remedies related to education, bilingual curriculum, and teachers; efforts to increase naturalization and voting; fair treatment of workers and wages; and the defense of accused or prison inmates.[187] At times when necessary, it played the game of politics. During the 1916 and 1918 state elections in Arizona, La Liga campaigned against two white gubernatorial candidates because their support of legislation would negatively impact Mexicano workers. In addition, it fought relentlessly against the discriminatory treatment of Mexicano prison inmates, who were often framed, unjustly convicted, tortured, and executed at much higher rates than white prison inmates.[188] Moreover, it was at the forefront of many labor-related issues and struggles. Plagued by power struggles, differences over its service verses advocacy role, and faulty finances, La Liga began to decline during the 1920s and became moribund by the 1930s.

Mutualistas in California

During this epoch, several new mutualistas were established in California. During the 1920s mutualistas were organized in Bakersfield, Fresno, and adjoining communities by former members of the Hidalgo Society.[189] Plagued by parochialism, little was done to integrate them into one unified mutualista or to set up a viable network. Typically, some mutualistas—due to distance, lack of resources, lack of expertise, power struggles, and plain distrust of each other—added to a fractious organizational pluralism that impeded unity of action. One such example was the formation in 1929 of La Sociedad Progresista Mexicana, around the San Bernardino area. It emerged as a result of internal disagreements over the type of burial insurance La Sociedad Zaragoza was providing to its members. On October 16,

1929, it was incorporated in California as a nonprofit beneficial society.[190] During the Depression, numerous lodges or *logias* of La Progresista Mexicana were established in communities throughout the state. With members paying a minimal monthly amount, its low-cost burial insurance provided a lump sum that would cover most of the burial expenses. Hernandez notes that "during the economic difficulties of the 1930s lodge members of the society cooperated with other California fringe benefit associations by providing services and relief to the needy families of barrio residents."[191] In addition, the various *logias* took on the names of prominent political and military leaders from México. From the start they were committed to the preservation of their Mexicano cultural roots. By the mid-1940s, La Sociedad Progresista was the largest *mutualista* in California.

A number of other buffer-type *mutualista* organizations were formed, such as La Union Patriótica Benéfica Mexicana Independiente, which had several lodges throughout southern California. Besides providing death insurance and other support activities to its members, it sponsored numerous social and cultural events, for example, *fiestas patrias* (patriotic festivities) such as México's El Dia de la Independencia (Independence Day). The Mexican consulates also assisted in the formation of self-help organizations that did charitable work in the barrios. Two such organizational examples formed by México's consul Eduardo Ruiz in Los Angeles were La Cruz Azul (for women) and La Comisión Honorífica (for men).[192] Both grew as lodges were formed in various parts of the country. They were active in providing a number of relief services during the 1920s and the repatriations of the 1930s. Women also formed their own *mutualista* auxiliaries and at times also participated jointly with men. One such women's *mutualista* among several was the Unión Femenil Mexican.[193] In addition to *mutualistas*, Comites Patrioticos were formed in numerous communities throughout Aztlán and beyond. Their cardinal purpose was to organize cultural events around México's holidays, especially Mexican Independence Day. Although they did not provide services or assistance, they served as a socializing agent that kept the Mexicano culture alive and vibrant.

Mutualistas *in Other Parts of Aztlán*

As was the case in Arizona and California, numerous *mutualistas* also emerged throughout Aztlán and the Midwest. States such as Tejas, Nuevo México, and Colorado experienced major organizing efforts by *mutualistas*. Particularly, La Alianza Hispana Americana was the most prominent of all. In the Midwest, likewise, numerous *mutualistas* and patriotic groups of various sorts were usually formed wherever *colonias* and barrios of Mexicanos existed. La Liga Protectora Mexicana in Kansas City was at the forefront of defending Mexicanos from the threat of expatriation after World War I. It was formed at the height of the post-Depression years, and after two years of providing assistance such as, jobs, food, and clothing to the poor, it was dissolved in 1923.[194] In Chicago, several *mutualistas* were established: the Club Atlético y Social Cuauhtémoc, Sociedad Obreros Libres, Sociedad Caballeros de Nuestra Señora de Guadalupe, Sociedad Miguel Hidalgo y Costilla, and Sociedad Benito Juarez. Likewise, women's associations also proliferated, which included the Sociedad Femenil Mexicana, Sociedad Recreativa Femenil Guadalupana, Sociedad Josefa Ortíz Domínguez, Hijas de Maria, and Cruz Azul. In the Midwest, the latter became one of the most influential women-led groups.[195] Thus, by the close of 1945, *mutualistas* were the largest Mexicano organization and the most dynamic in growth and membership.

New Interest Groups

The 1920s experienced the rise of a new form of organization—interest groups.[196] Interest groups were a relatively new form of organization for Mexicanos. Among the ranks of emerging middle class some Mexicanos realized that there was a need to establish new forms of organizations, which were advocacy- and change-oriented for purposes of influencing public policy.[197] Jeffrey M. Berry defines: an "interest group is an organized body of individuals who share some goals and who try to influence public policy."[198] Another political scientist, David Truman, essentially defined interest groups as groups based on one or more shared attitudes and making political claims on other groups or organizations in society.[199] From Truman's definition one can assume that interest groups have two salient characteristics. One, interest groups are comprised of individuals and in some cases other organizations that share some common interest or agenda. Two, interest groups tend to become involved in the political process with the cardinal intent of influencing public policy. Interest groups adhere to either conventional methods, for example, lobbying or campaigning, or to unconventional protest tactics, such as marches, strikes, and boycotts, in their efforts to influence governmental public policy.[200] Also, interest groups come in various forms and types. Within the totality of the Mexicano political experience, interest groups have been: traditional, union, social action, political pressure, protest, sectarian, community power, and Mexicano-based.

During this epoch, however, the types of interest groups that emerged were traditional and union types, and "want to be white"-oriented. In Aztlán's barrios and *colonias*, the dominant organizations up to the 1920s were *mutualistas*. Although some *mutualistas* participated in various aspects of politics, by design they were apolitical and their nonprofit status prohibited them from doing so. As a result, a small number of middle-class Mexicanos in Tejas felt that in order to advance their interests a new form of organization was needed. They disagreed with the *mutualista's* Mexicano nationalist posture and orientation. In addition, they embraced a "want to be white" political role, meaning they were assimilationists and sought to reach some form of political accommodation with the dominant white society.[201] As the initial participants in Tejas in interest groups, they contributed significantly to the emergence and sustenance of the epoch's "politics of adaptation."

LA ORDEN DE LOS HIJOS DE AMERICA   By 1921, a group of thirty-seven men from San Antonio, under the leadership of Professor J. Luz Sáenz and Santiago Tafolla, a lawyer, met and formed La Orden de Los Hijos de America (The Order of the Sons of America), which became the first major "want to be white" interest group. They were middle-class and mostly white-collar workers and professionals and returning war veterans. Most had been members of the defunct Liga Mexicanista de Beneficiencio y Protección and had become disgruntled over its inability to move faster toward recognition of constitutional rights for Tejas Mexicanos and in general over their relative lack of political and economic influence.[202] Moreover, they were hypercritical of the traditional *mutualistas* for not pressing for full political participation and equality. However, a schism developed among the group concerning who was going to lead it. James Tafoya was elected as its first president, but Feliciano Flores, who had campaigned for the position and lost, walked out of the meeting with seven other members, splintering the nascent organization. Growing rivalries led to the formation of other groups. The defectors divided again in 1922 to form two separate organizations: the Order of Sons of Texas and the Knights of America, led by M. C. González.[203] Former members of La Orden in 1927 founded still another group in San Antonio, La Orden de Caballeros de America (the Order of Knights of America). Later in 1927 in the Rio Grande Valley, another civic group was formed, the League of Latin American Citizens, by war veterans J. Luz Sáenz and Alonzo S. Pearles.[204]

With its organizational role of "want to be white," La Orden internalized the politics of adaptation with an emphasis on accommodation and assimilation.[205] With its middle-class orientation its membership policy was predicated on "exclusion by citizenship." This meant that only citizens of the United States who were of Mexicano or Spanish extraction or who were naturalized would be eligible to join. Moore and Cuéllar write, "This exclusion by citizenship was meant—and used—as an exclusionary mechanism. The implication was that Mexican Americans were more trustworthy to whites than Mexican nationals and also more deserving of the benefits of American life."[206] In essence, La Orden wanted to demonstrate to whites that its membership was different from the other "troublemaking" lower-class Mexicanos. Furthermore, its "want to be white" orientation was based on the notion that in order to survive and progress, it needed to be as noncontroversial as possible, and openly and zealously promulgated declarations of loyalty to the United States.[207] Meier and Rivera summarize La Orden's rather conservative political cultural posture:

> The basic objectives of this organization were to enable Mexican Americans to achieve acculturation and integration, principally through political action. Ultimately, the Order sought to end prejudice against Mexican Americans, to achieve equality before the law, to acquire political representation at all levels and to obtain greater educational opportunities, restricting membership to United States citizens of Mexican or Hispanic background. It strongly emphasized that its members learn English and work toward gaining citizenship. Concerned about the widespread exclusion of Mexican Americans from jury duty service and firmly committed to the goal of political power, it stressed voter registration.[208]

At its height of development during the mid-1920s La Orden was comprised of seven councils throughout Tejas. The two most influential and active ones were in Corpus Christi and San Antonio.[209] The councils were semiautonomous and varied in philosophy, interests, and focus. Yet in its brief nine-year existence, La Orden was successful in achieving three major victories: the right for Mexicanos to serve on juries, the right for a Mexicano to sue a white, and the right for a Mexicano to use the public beaches along the coast of Corpus Christi. Understanding that internal colonialism and segregation plagued Mexicanos in Tejas, these achievements were considered milestones in the pursuit for their full citizenship.[210]

In 1926, Ben Garza of La Orden's Council No. 4, a prominent leader from Corpus Christi, and Manuel C. González of the Knights were both concerned about growing schisms among the various groups, so they took the lead in advocating for a merger of organizations.[211] Other leaders such as Alonzo Pearles, Louis Wilmont, Joe Garza, Andres Luna, Manuel Gonzales, James Tafolla, Sr., J. T. Canales, and Eduardo Idar also figured prominently in the negotiations to form a new unified organization. In August 1927, a conference was held in Harlingen, Texas, at which time a consensus was reached to reorganize.[212] A year and a half later on February 17, 1929, a unification conference was held under Garza's leadership, at the Obreros Hall in Corpus Christi, to launch a new organization.

In attendance were some 25 delegates and 150 nonvoting representatives from La Orden, Latin American League, the Sons of America, and the Order of Knights.

LEAGUE OF UNITED LATIN AMERICAN CITIZENS (LULAC)   The end result of the conference proved to be historical; a new "want to be white" organization was formed: the League of United Latin American Citizens (LULAC).[213] A supreme council was formed, and Ben Garza was elected as its first president general.[214] At a subsequent conference held in May of that same year, again in Corpus Christi, LULAC adopted a constitution that was compatible with its precursor, La Orden. LULAC's constitution clearly illustrated a major shift away from that of the *mutualista* viewpoint. It adopted what was unique for the time, a "want to be white" orientation, meaning it accentuated a greater concern for assimilation, integration, and the pursuit for full civil rights.[215] According to Michael Tirado, "While framing its first Constitution on the general model of the Orden de los Hijos de America, LULAC's placed more emphasis on absorption into American society and on their commitment to improving the political and economic position of the Mexican American community."[216] Yet it was not until 1933 that LULAC allowed women to become voting members.[217] Along with the drafting of the constitution was a formal statement of principles called "The LULAC Code," which came to define the organization's basic philosophy and political program for the next sixty years.[218]

The theme of unity was imbedded in the name, and once again membership was restricted to native-born or naturalized citizens of "Latin" extraction, who were over the age of eighteen. The use of the term *Latin* rather *Mexicano* was strategic and was indicative of its dissociation with the Mexicano migrant population. Nine months after its founding, LULAC supported restrictive immigration toward Mexicano nationals. On the issue of the deportations and repatriations of Mexicanos, Acuña points out that LULAC "was mute."[219] During the Great Depression, various LULAC leaders made disparaging anti-Mexicano remarks, which revealed their "want to be white" colonial role. Judge J. T. Canales, in an interview conducted by the newspaper *El Comercio*, was quoted as saying, "this organization should be integrated by Mexican Americans exclusively, since Mexicans from MÉXICO are a PITIFUL LOT who come to this country in great caravans to retard the Mexican Americans' work for unity that should be at the Anglo Saxon's level."[220] According to Benjamin Márquez, LULAC's leadership and membership disapproved of the increasing number of Mexicano migrants. He explains that they did not want to be identified or associated with migrants or the social stigma they brought with them.[221] The usage of *Latin*, like *Spanish*, evoked European rather than indigenous ancestry and was perceived to be less offensive than *Mexican*.[222] It was also more inclusive and more palatable to U.S.-born middle-class Mexicanos who were ardent proponents of assimilation and integration into U.S. society. Thus, LULAC sought reform by becoming a mainstream-oriented organization that was acceptable to whites and did not present a threat to the social order. Yet paradoxically, LULAC members, during its infancy as they organized to fight prevalent injustices, used to meet in secrecy, fearful of being accused of having ties with communists.[223]

In its initial constitution, LULAC made it explicitly clear that it espoused total assimilation of its members. Tirado in citing the constitution states, "in order to claim our rights and fulfill our duties it is necessary for us to assimilate all we can that is best in the new civilization amidst which we shall have to live." Yet Garcia takes a slightly different view; he argues that LULAC did not reject its Mexicano heritage, but that essentially it sought a balance between the two opposing cultures.[224] In the final analysis, however, LULAC's paramount mission was to inculcate into its membership the virtues and values of "American society."[225] Toward this end, the constitution stipulated that English would be the official language of LULAC and each member must pledge himself to teach others, especially children, to speak and read English.[226] Further, their patriotic fervor was evident with the adoption of the U.S. flag as its official emblem and the George Washington Prayer.[227]

LULAC's commitment, however, to advocacy became evident in its fight against discrimination wherever it encountered it. Strategically, however, it maintained a conservative political orientation as evident in Article III, Section 7, which categorically rebukes the use of "violent demonstrations or other acts that defy constituted law and authority, desecrate the symbols of our nation, and threaten the physical and spiritual welfare of individuals and institutions."[228]

LULAC's adherence to adaptation and accommodation politics was reflected in one of its aims, listed in its first article, which was to "develop within the members of our race the best, purest and most perfect type of a true and loyal citizen of the United States of America."[229] Ideologically, it adamantly opposed communism, fascism, and any form of totalitarianism and embraced liberal capitalism. The first constitution also made it clear that LULAC was "not a political club." However, Article II defends the right of its members to become involved in politics by advocating: "With our vote and influence we shall endeavor to place in public office men who show by their deeds, respect and consideration for our people."[230] Members, however, according to Acuña, "used fronts such as the *Club Democratico* and the League of Loyal Americans for their political activities."[231] LULAC's leadership zealously embraced the notion of the Puritan work ethic.

They believed that only through hard work and discipline could Mexicanos in the United States achieve integration. Furthermore, they identified with liberal capitalism's idea of progress: everything was possible if one worked hard.[232]

By the 1940s LULAC's structure had evolved to where it was a regional social action organization. Incorporated as a nonprofit, it was hierarchically structured, consisting of a regional or national assembly and a supreme council. At the state level, it was comprised of a state assembly, state council, district councils, and local councils. For purposes of broadening its organizational and membership base, women's auxiliaries were incorporated into LULAC in 1933 and later in the decade a Junior LULAC that was youth-based was formed. According to Garcia, "LULAC expanded throughout the 1930s. By the commencement of World War II, it included more than 80 councils in Tejas, Nuevo México, Arizona, California, and Kansas." Tejanos (Mexicanos born in Texas), however, dominated LULAC with their more numerous councils and assertive leadership.[233]

Throughout the epoch of adaptation LULAC got involved in a number of civil rights issues, such as the betterment of schools and voter registration efforts. In this pursuit, it was very much influenced by the strategies of the National Association for the Advancement of Colored People (NAACP). LULAC's political activities varied from council to council according to local circumstances. News of its activities was disseminated through its newsletter, the "LULAC News." However, during the 1930s and 1940s, in general, LULAC adhered to a three-pronged plan of attack that strongly accentuated the desegregation of public schools; encouraged its membership and citizens to register to vote, pay their poll taxes, and vote; and supported local legal campaigns to combat discrimination against Mexicanos in public facilities and on juries.[234] As Mario Garcia argues, through its actions and orientation, LULAC contributed significantly to the emergence of the Mexican American Generation.[235]

During World War II, LULAC as an organization was a strong and patriotic supporter of the U.S. war effort. Because many of its members served in the armed forces, a decline in its membership occurred. LULAC members sold war bonds, participated in civil defense, and worked in defense plants. Regardless of its preoccupation with the war effort, it still found the time and energy to continue its educational struggle against segregation. As the war was coming to an end in 1945, as will be examined in the next chapter, LULAC in California initiated a historic lawsuit, *Méndez v. Westminister School District*, against four Orange County school districts, claiming de facto segregation of Mexicano students. As the war ended, LULAC was the most prominent civil rights interest group in the Mexicano communities of the country.

MEXICAN AMERICAN MOVEMENT (MAM)   A "want to be white" social action type of interest group also formed during the epoch was the Mexican American Movement (MAM). In Los Angeles during the Depression, Mexicano youth from various local youth organizations such as the Catholic Youth Organization and Young Men's Christian Association (YMCA) formed MAM. After attending several conferences and meeting on issues pertinent to youth for some six years, in 1938 a small, energetic group of mostly Mexicano college and high school students met and formed MAM.[236] Originally it was called Mexican American Conference but later went through a name change.[237] Among some of the most prominent youth leaders were Paul Cornel, Felix Gutiérrez, Stephan Reyes, Manuel Ceja, Juan Acevedo, Arthur Casas, Angelo Cano, Mary Escudero, Mary Ann Chavolla, and Rebecca Muñoz.[238]

The students' emphasis on their Mexican American heritage was unprecedented and acknowledged their cultural bifurcated Mexicano and white roots. Ideologically, like LULAC, MAM embraced a "want to be white" perspective in that it espoused a "pro-system, integration and assimilation" orientation based on adaptation and accommodation. In fact, MAM complemented LULAC in that its leadership believed that they were of the same white race that segregated them as a people.[239] On the issue of Mexicano migration into the United States, they were hypercritical and very much against it. David Gutiérrez explains that they perceived it as being "at the very heart of most of the social problems facing Mexican Americans in the southwest." He further says, "MAM, like other contemporary Mexican American civil rights and service organizations adhered to a stridently assimilationist political philosophy." As to its general purpose, MAM pledged "to improve conditions among our Mexican American and Mexican people living in the United States" and to "promote citizenship, higher education . . . and a more active participation in civic and cultural activities by those of our national descent."[240] MAM sought to foster leadership in education, business, and social work, and among other professions, but education was its cardinal focus; this was illustrated by its motto, "Progress through Education."[241] Strategically, MAM was a proponent of reform and sought to effect change by working within the system without resorting to militant protest activities.

During the years leading up to 1945, MAM sought to organize the growing number of Chicano youth around Los Angeles. In 1938 it began publication of its newspaper, *The Méxican Voice*, which was published until 1944. In 1939 it established a leadership institute for youth and held its first major conference in Santa Barbara. MAM sponsored a Mexican American Girl's Conference, organized a Mexican American Teachers' Association, and networked with other similar organizations in Arizona and Tejas in 1940.[242] During the late 1930s, Bert Corona participated in the organization, as well as Ernesto Galarza, who served on its advisory board.[243] During World War II many of its leaders and members went into the armed forces, which caused its membership to decrease and reduced its activities. Yet in 1944 MAM had its first convention in Los Angeles, which was attended by some one hundred members and supporters. The convention's agenda focused on ways to strengthen its organizational base, and plans were formulated for MAM's expansion throughout Aztlán. Shortly afterward, MAM chapters were established in Los Angeles, Santa Barbara, San Bernardino, Anaheim, and Placentia. In spite of its pro-system politics, MAM came under attack during World War II, by right-wing groups that alleged it was a communist organization, and the FBI conducted an investigation to ascertain if it was a subversive group. Concerned about these allegations, MAM's leadership spent a great deal of time repudiating them and accentuated to its membership and supporters that it was committed to democratic principles.[244] When World War II ended, and some of its former members returned from military service, MAM sought to reorganize itself.

MEXICANO *SINARQUISTAS*   Another development in the Mexicano political experience was the rise in the United States of *sinarquista* interest groups from México. Founded in Leon, Guanajuato, in 1937 by Oskar Hellmuth Schreiter, José Antonio Urquiza, and Trueba Olivares,[245] the *sinarquistas* adhered to an advocate transformer role, which adulated the Spanish Falange (Spanish fascist movement founded in 1933 and dissolved in 1977. It was the official ruling party of Spain under Francisco Franco).[246] Their ideological posture is a matter of some debate among Chicano historians. Some claim that they were pro-fascist; others describe them more as Mexicano ultranationalists. John Chavez is one historian who alleges they were fascists. He writes, "Since they regarded Franco's Spain as a model Christian State, which México should emulate, the sinarquistas sympathized with the fascist powers that supported Franco and had, moreover, never harmed México."[247] Mario Garcia describes *sinarquismo* as being opposed to both fascism and communism. He notes that they "claimed to be the true Mexican nationalists."[248] One aspect on which historians concur is that their ultranationalism reflected their "irredentist" position: after the Axis powers triumphed, the Southwest would be returned to México. This proposal, write Meier and Rivera, "was consonant with the way some Mexicanos viewed the Southwest."[249] *Sinarquistas* categorically opposed México having any form of alliance with United States.

Shortly after the *sinarquista* movement emerged in México, the first regional *sinarquista* committee was organized in Los Angeles on November 1, 1937.[250]

Using the slogan of "Patria, Justicia, y Libertad" (Country, Justice, and Liberty), there was a concerted effort to propagate *sinarquismo* throughout the many *colonias* and barrios of the Southwest and Midwest. The propaganda appeared in the weekly newspaper *El Sinarquista* and a monthly magazine, *Orden.*[251] Regional centers or committees were established, each comprised of several local cells. The Los Angeles regional center alone had some twenty-one municipal cells.[252] Although cells were established throughout the Southwest and parts of the Midwest, California and Tejas witnessed the most active and strongest *sinarquista* movements. The *sinarquistas* claimed a membership of some fifty thousand in California. In reality their membership in the United States was around three thousand to four thousand.[253] Its membership was mostly working-class Mexicano nationals from the rural and urban areas. They were cognizant of their exploitation and oppression as Mexicanos both in the United States and México. From Los Angeles, Pedro Villaseñore and Martin Cabrera published the newspaper *El Sinarquista*. The first major national meeting of the *sinarquista* leadership in the United States was held in El Paso, Tejas, on September 27, 1942.[254]

Throughout much of 1942 and 1943, *sinarquistas* in the United States capitalized on a variety of issues that impacted Mexicanos. Perceived as a security threat, *sinarquista* members in 1942 were required to register with the Department of Justice under the Foreign Agents Restoration Act and came under surveillance by the FBI.[255] Hence, both the United States and México maintained vigilance over the organization's activities, and México, in particular, spoke out against them. In California, *sinarquistas* used the Sleepy Lagoon Case in 1942 and the Zoot Suit Riots in 1943 as part of their propaganda to agitate the Mexicano masses. The war effort by the United States and its allies was depicted as being part and parcel of "Yankee Imperialism" and aggression.[256] But by 1944 when the Axis powers began to lose the war and as a result of counterorganizing efforts by both governments as well as other Mexicano organizations in the United States, *sinarquismo* failed to take a strong hold among Mexicanos and soon faded.

Labor Organizations and Struggles

During this epoch's organizational renaissance Mexicanos continued to be involved in the general labor movement. From 1915 to the beginning of World War II in 1941, Mexicanos throughout Aztlán and the Midwest played a pivotal role in numerous labor struggles. In the years that followed 1917, three labor types of interest groups led the union movement in the West: the Industrial Workers of the World (IWW), the Western Federation of Miners (WFM), and the American Federation of Labor (AFL). All three played to some degree an advocate transformer role. The IWW was ideologically anarchist and had established a collaborative relationship with the Magónistas. It had been sympathetic to the plight of the Mexicano and sought unsuccessfully to organize them but by 1920 had disappeared. Likewise, Mexicano miners since the 1890s, eager to ameliorate their economic lot, participated in numerous strikes through the WFM. In 1903, government troops were called in to suppress the first major strike at the Clifton, Morenci, and Metcalf mines. In October 1915, three unions of Mexicano miners, numbering some five thousand men, went on strike again. The mine was sealed with cement and workers were told to go back to México. The strike was broken when hundreds of workers were arrested by National Guard troops. In 1917, Arizona copper miners, Mexicano and non-Mexicanos alike, went on strike. The strike was broken by a vigilante anti-union mob, which rounded up 1,186 strikers, shipped them in boxcars, and released them in the desert near Columbus, Nuevo México.[257]

Even though the politics of the AFL was more conservative than that of the IWW and AFM, it made a concerted effort to organize Mexicanos. AFL affiliates were active both in the rural and urban areas around cities such as El Paso and San Antonio, Tejas. Del Castillo and De León summarize the labor struggles of the AFL:

> On the farms Mexicans found the AFL appealing, despite its ethnocentrism and its disinterest in organizing agricultural hands. In Texas and parts of the Southwest, Tejano Clemente Idar succeeded to some extent in organizing diverse elements. Within the Mexican American agricultural and urban force during the late 1910s and early 1920s sugar beet-field workers in Nebraska, Wyoming and Colorado joined AFL's Beet Workers Association in 1929. Generally, however, Mexicans still felt suspicious toward the AFL and joined it only after having organized their own locals.[258]

In 1927, the AFL held its national conference in Los Angeles, and members debated the issue of immigration and openly took an anti-immigrant position by supporting exclusionist legislation; it made no effort to prioritize the organizing of Mexicanos.[259]

THE RISE OF MEXICANO *UNIONES* IN THE UNITED STATES   During the 1920s a number of Mexicano-based unions were established in Aztlán. In great part they were influenced by the formation in México of the Confederación Regional de Obreros Mexicanos (Regional Confederation of Mexican Workers) in 1918 and later the Confederación de Trabajadores de México (Confederation of Mexican Workers or CROM). Mexicanos in the United States formed their own unions, which in most cases adopted a buffer-type colonizing role.[260] Most could well be described as playing advocate transformer political roles. Motivated by horrendous working conditions and low wages, the leadership for these efforts largely came from the *mutualistas*. For example, in November of 1927, members of the Federation of Mexican Societies supported by CROM representatives from México came together in Los Angeles and took the unprecedented step in forming the Confederación de Uniones Obreras Mexicanas (CUOM). A constitution was adopted, and among its objectives was the organization of all Mexicano workers in the United States. Other goals included achieving wage parity with white workers, ending labor discriminatory practices against Mexicanos, and restricting of immigration into the United States by the Mexican government. They also proposed that México better assist economically repatriated workers by establishing agricultural colonies in México.[261] In April of 1928 CUOM held a general convention attended by delegates from twenty-two unions, which represented some three thousand agricultural and industrial workers.[262] Emilio Mujica, a CROM representative, participated and remained to assist in CUOM's organizing efforts.[263]

The first CUOM-called strike was in 1928 in Imperial Valley by one of its affiliate unions, La Unión de Trabajadores del Valle Imperial. The affiliate was comprised of melon workers who with the support of the Mexican consul formed a *mutualista*, the Mexican Mutual Aid Society of the Imperial Valley, which became La Union de Trabajadores.[264] The union was demanding a better wage, better working conditions, and improved housing, but the strike was broken by massive arrests. Two years later, five thousand cantaloupe workers struck again unsuccessfully. The failure was due in great part to an internecine power struggle between La Union de Trabajadores and a Communist Party-supported union, the Agricultural Workers Industrial League (AWIL). By the 1930s, without any major victories on its scorecard, CUOM became moribund.

In July of 1933, former leaders of CUOM held a convention and formed another Mexicano union, Confederación de Uniones Campesinos y Obreros Mexicanos (CUCOM). They became involved in various strikes involving some five thousand to seven thousand agricultural workers from Southern California. The most notable strike was the one that occurred in El Monte in May 1933.[265] In 1934, with a membership of some ten thousand workers, CUCOM again participated in orange picker strikes in San Bernardino and Riverside counties. During the ensuing three years it was active in a number of other strikes.

In 1935, the Roosevelt administration passed the National Labor Relations

Act (the Wagner Act). It guaranteed urban workers the right to organize, to engage in collective bargaining, and to strike, but excluded farmworkers. In the following years CUCOM cooperated in the formation of the Federation of Agricultural Workers of America, which included eleven locals and comprised various nationalities other than Mexicanos. That year in Los Angeles County CUCOM led a walkout of some twenty-six hundred celery workers.[266] However, by 1937, CUCOM was stricken by internal power struggles between moderates and radicals and rapidly declined.

Remnants of CUCOM's leadership along with other union leaders collaborated in the formation of the United Cannery, Agricultural, Packing, Allied Workers of America (UCAPAWA),[267] a Congress of Industrial Organizations (CIO) affiliate.[268] According to Vicki Ruiz, UCAPAWA made a concerted effort to recruit people of color from both genders as organizers. One such Mexicana was Luisa Moreno, who was the first Mexicana to serve on UCAPAWA's executive committee.[269] Although numerous unions consolidated with UCAPAWA during 1937 and 1938, its record was not highly successful, due to strikebreakers. One such strike was that of the pecan workers in San Antonio, Tejas, that affiliated with UCAPAWA in 1938. Workers, most of them women, abandoned some 130 plants, which led to the arrest of one thousand workers. This contentious strike was not successfully settled until 1939, but out of the struggle emerged a young woman, a progressive labor leader, Emma Tenayuca. She became known as La Pasionaria, after the communist passionflower, Dolores Ibarrui, of the Spanish Civil War. The union won the strike only to lose it later: the workers were replaced by machinery.[270]

MEXICANO INVOLVEMENT IN OTHER UNIONS   Concomitantly, Mexicanos were involved in numerous other labor efforts throughout the 1930s, especially those organized from a sectarian Marxist perspective. The Communist Party abandoned its working from within strategy and formed its own union, the Trade Union Unity League (TUUL). Their mission was to establish militant trade union organizations but tactically also relied on the infiltration of existing unions. One of the unions TUUL organized was the Agricultural Workers Industrial League (AWIL), which became embroiled in the Imperial Valley Strike of 1930. In a strategic maneuver, the AWIL in 1931 changed its name to the Cannery and Agricultural Workers Industrial Union (CAWIU), and from its inception to 1933 it participated in over twenty-five strikes that involved some 32,800 workers.[271] Mexicanos were also involved in several organizing efforts of the two large rival unions—the American Federation of Labor (AFL) and Congress of Industrial Organizations (CIO). Another group that also targeted Mexicanos was the International Longshore and Warehouse Union (ILWU). Founded in 1937, it recruited Mexicano labor organizers such as Bert Corona to conduct their campaigns, especially in the warehouse industry.[272] What is important to note is that Mexicanos played a significant organizing role in many of the country's labor struggles.

EL CONGRESO DE LOS PUEBLOS DE HABLA ESPAÑOLA (CONGRESS OF SPANISH-SPEAKING PEOPLES OR EL CONGRESO)   For Mexicanos, the labor movement acted as a catalyst for the formation of El Congreso de Los Pueblos de Habla Española (Congress of Spanish-Speaking Peoples—El Congreso).[273] El Congreso, because of its sectarian orientation, adhered to advocate transformer role. It was formed at a conference held in Los Angeles in 1938, and its first scheduled National Congress was held in Albuquerque, Nuevo México, in March 1939. According to Acuña, "Because of redbaiting it was moved to Los Angeles when Drs. George Sanchez and Arthur L. Campa, professors at the University of New México, had to resign because of pressure."[274] Luisa Moreno, who was an organizer for the UCAPAWA at the time, provided much of its initial organizational leadership. Attended by some 126 delegates, the National Congress finally met in April 1939 in Los Angeles. Actual representation of non-Mexicano Latinos was sparse. In attendance was the Mexican consul from Los Angeles and union representatives from México. Ed Quevedo was elected president and Josefina Fierro de Bright became executive secretary.[275] Other key persons that emerged out of the National Congress and subsequently provided leadership were Lisa Moreno, Bert Corona, and Emma Tenayuca.

Based on the notion of building a "popular front," El Congreso was active between 1939 and 1942, a mere three years. Structured as a confederation, it was successful in bringing together numerous unions and activist organizations[276] and at its peak had a membership of some of six thousand. El Congreso's general purpose was to work for "the economic and social and cultural betterment of the Mexican people, to have an understanding between Anglo-Americans and Mexicans, to promote organizations of working people by aiding trade unions and to fight discrimination actively."[277] Ideologically, El Congreso was leftist-oriented in its politics, unlike the earlier buffer-oriented organizations. Their ideology was ascribable to the pervasive influence of the Communist Party U.S.A. in its leadership and membership ranks. Ultimately, El Congreso's demise was a result of redbaiting, harassment of its leaders by the FBI, and the start of World War II, all of which produced an antithetical climate for radical politics. However, internal divisions over its orientation and functions as an organization as well as its radical ideological posture contributed to its decline.

Thus, in the context of the Mexicano political experience in occupied Aztlán, the epoch of adaptation proved to be a fertile period of organizational formation and development. It yielded a number of new organizations, and some existent ones flourished.

The Politics of Adaptation

The epoch of adaptation was not a prolific period in ballot box (electoral) politics for Mexicanos. The general internal colonial pattern established during the previous epoch of resistance continued. The external administrative control of internal colonialism was the political reality of the barrios and *colonias* of Aztlán. As was the case during the previous and present epochs, Nuevo México was the exception to the political rule. In this state, Mexicano politicians continued to play an admixture of buffer and "want to be white" political roles, the former being the most numerous. In every other state in the country, however, Mexicanos were relegated to a subordinate and powerless status. The U.S. occupation of their lands had cast them into an essentially apolitical role, where they were subjected to the manipulation of white politicians and an unresponsive two-party system. With the exception of Nuevo México, Mexicano activists seldom saw the value of organizing politically the small Mexicano vote. For most Mexicanos, representative democracy was largely an unattainable ideal and abstraction. The barrios and *colonias* were impoverished, segregated, and oppressed internal colonies that continued to serve as reservoirs of exploitable cheap labor.

Obstacles to Political Empowerment

During the epoch general efforts to enfranchise Mexicanos were unsuccessful. Politically, Mexicanos by and large continued being disenfranchised and administered externally by white politicians and bureaucrats. The white political establishment relied on a multiplicity of devices or political weapons to maintain their hegemony over the occupied Mexicanos. For purposes of governance control, this meant as previously mentioned the deliberate utilization of a few Mexicanos as either political buffers or "want to be whites." In addition, there were numerous citizenship restrictions that impeded Mexicano's participation in the political process. Oscar Martinez points out that "usually only those Mexicans who had a white appearing complexion could be accorded the privilege of citizenship."

The impediments to political participation in great part had their historical genesis in the Naturalization Law of 1790, which barred nonwhite immigrants from becoming U.S. citizens, voting, and running for public office. The law helped legitimize the political exclusion of many Mexicanos and reinforced segregation and dispossession of property. This was in violation of the Treaty of Guadalupe Hidalgo, which implicitly recognized Mexicanos as white and granted them citizenship rights and protection under the country's constitution. A number of other practices were used to effectively maintain the Mexicano's political powerlessness. By the epoch of adaptation these practices included English-only laws, literacy tests, the poll tax, single locations for voter registration, white only primaries, rigid voter registration guidelines, congressional and state gerrymandering of electoral districts, and at-large elections.[278]

Beyond internal colonialism, Mexicano political development was hampered by its small population base. With the exception of a few counties in South Tejas and Nuevo México, the Mexicano population had few large concentrations wielding some political clout. In South Tejas some concentrations existed, but were largely controlled by white political machines that were detached from the concerns of the Mexicano masses. Other impediments to political participation included the people's low levels of education, rampant poverty, a small middle class, and an internal colonial syndrome that was characterized by racism and xenophobia. The Mexicano's political efforts also lacked explicit ballot box-oriented organizations. None of the existing groups, for example, OSA, LULAC, *mutualistas*, were explicitly political organizations. And like LULAC, those that did dabble into politics took on mostly a "want to be white" perspective. They were more concerned about assimilating into white-dominated society. They did not address the inherent ideological contradictions of liberal capitalism and only dealt with a few of the social problems that were endemic to the barrios and *colonias'* colonized status. Some Mexicanos formed their own political partisan clubs, but lacked a social change agenda and did not appeal to the masses. Beyond the *sinarquistas* and leftist labor unions, no major Mexicano political movement developed during this epoch. Overall, the politics of the Mexicano experience were still internal colonial domination, and powerlessness.

Nuevo México's Electoral Politics: One of a Kind

Ballot box politics in Nuevo México developed unlike that of any other state. Politics was still a game played by essentially a buffer-oriented elite who did little to upset the mode of liberal capitalist politics. Mexicano elites and *politicos* played both sides of the partisan game. As Republicans or Democrats they adapted and helped maintain the status quo. None of the *politicos* in Nuevo México or anywhere else sought to alter the Mexicanos' internal colonial status, nor were they hypercritical of liberal capitalism. The criticisms against the system came primarily from the unions and sectarian third parties, not from those who were in power or aspired to power.

In the years that followed 1912, after Nuevo México became a state and World War I commenced, Mexicano elites continued to participate in the process of political governance. With a strong footing in both the Democrat and Republican Parties, Mexicanos adopted what Juan Gómez-Quiñones calls a "native son" movement. In essence they pushed for their cultural and political rights as natives with historical claims. A major show of political strength occurred in 1916 with election of Democrat Ezequiel Cabeza de Baca as governor of Nuevo México, who benefited from the native son effort. Previously, de Baca had been in 1912 Nuevo México's first lieutenant governor, serving from 1912 to 1916.[279]

Again, the 1918 gubernatorial election became pivotal for the native son movement with both Republicans and Democrats nominating Mexicanos. The Republican Party nominated Octaviano Larrazolo for governor, while the Democratic Party nominated Félix Garcia. After a hard-fought campaign, Larrazolo was elected, and during that same year, a Mexicano, Benigo Hernández, was elected to the U.S. Congress. As the native son movement declined between 1921 and 1932 so did the level of Mexicano political representation. For the next fifty years the governorship was in the sole possession of whites. Up to the 1940s, twelve whites served as lieutenant governors versus seven Mexicanos. While Mexicanos controlled the office of secretary of state, whites held the posts of treasurer. Also, during this time there was a scarcity of Mexicanos in the judicial branch of government. In general, even though Mexicanos constituted a majority of the state population, in state elective and appointive offices whites constituted the overwhelming majority.[280]

The ethnic distribution of legislative and county offices was more mixed than state offices. Up to 1938 whites constituted a majority in the State Senate. In the state House of Representatives, Mexicanos were occasionally in the majority, but in most cases, whites held a tenuous majority there and in county offices as well. Table 3.1 shows the percent of Mexicano elected officials in Nuevo México from 1918 to 1938 according to State Senate, State House, and county offices.[281]

It is important to note that between 1930 and 1945 during the depression

Table 3.1   Mexicano Political Representation in Nuevo México, 1918–1938

	State Senate %	State House %	County Offices %
1918	29	53	37
1928	21	43	31
1938	25	39	31

years, five Mexicanos served in the state House of Representatives.[282] At the local level, city council and school boards, Mexicanos did well, especially in those counties with concentrations of Mexicanos. At the federal level, from 1919 to 1923 and 1931 to 1935, Oscar Martinez documents that Mexicanos continued to elect their own to the U.S. Congress.[283] In 1931, Dennis Chavez, a Georgetown University Law School graduate, was elected to Congress and in 1935, he was appointed to the U.S. Senate, and retained his Senate seat until 1962.[284] Truly, Nuevo México remained the one exception throughout Aztlán where Mexicanos participated and benefited from ballot box politics. Thus, by the close of 1945, the racial antagonisms in most areas of the United States were such that the stage was set for the emergence of the "Epoch of Social Action Politics," which was characterized by a more assertive spirit toward activism.

Notes

1. Edwin Lieuwen, *Mexican Militarism: The Political Rise and Fall of the Revolutionary Army, 1910–1940* (Albuquerque: University of New México Press, 1968), xi.

2. Matt S. Meier and Feliciano Rivera, *Mexican Americans, American Méxicans: From Conquistadores to Chicanos* (New York: Hill & Wang, 1993), 104.

3. John Ross, *The Annexation of México: From the Aztecs to I.M.F.* (Monroe, Maine: Common Courage Press, 1998), 50.

4. Ernest Gruening, *México and Its Heritage* (New York: Appleton-Century, 1928), 301–2.

5. Cited in Ross, *The Annexation of México*, 52.

6. Frank R. Brandenburg, *The Making of Modern México* (Englewood Cliffs, N.J.: Prentice Hall, 1964), 37–42.

7. Meier and Rivera, *Mexican Americans, American Méxicans*, 104.

8. Julian Samora and Patricia Vandel Simon, *A History of the Mexican American People* (Notre Dame, Ind.: University of Notre Dame Press, 1977), 121–22.

9. Kenneth Johnson, *Mexican Democracy: A Critical View* (Boston: Allyn and Bacon, Inc., 1971), 18.

10. Johnson, *Mexican Democracy*, 18–19.

11. Robert E. Quirk, *México* (Englewood Cliffs, N.J.: Prentice Hall, 1971), 79–80.

12. Johnson, *Mexican Democracy*, 19–21.

13. Brandenburg, *The Making of Modern México*, 37–42.

14. Ross, *The Annexation of México*, 52.

15. Meier and Rivera, *Mexican Americans, American Mexicans*, 104.

16. Brandenburg, *The Making of Modern México*, 37–42.

17. Lieuwen, *Mexican Militarism*, 9.

18. Johnson, *Mexican Democracy*, 20–21.

19. Samora and Simon, *A History of the Mexican American People*, 124.

20. Jonathan Kendall, *La Capital* (New York: Random House, 1988), 404.

21. William Johnson, *Heroic México* (New York: Doubleday, 1968), 73.

22. Lieuwen, *Mexican Militarism*, 17.

23. For an examination on the etiology of the Mexican Revolution from a Mexicano intellectual perspective see Luis Cabrera, "The Mexican Revolution—Its Causes, Purposes, and Results," *The Annals of the American Academy of Political and Social Science*, Supplement to LXIX (January 1917): 1–17.

24. Johnson, *Heroic México*, 101.

25. Charles Cumberland, *México: The Struggle for Modernity* (New York: Oxford University Press, 1968), 241.

26. Johnson, *Mexican Democracy*, 25.

27. Lyle C. Brown, "The Politics of Armed Struggle in the Mexican Revolution, 1913–1915," in *Revolution in México: Years of Upheaval, 1910–1940*, ed. James W. Wilkie and Albert L. Michaels (Tucson: The University of Arizona Press, 1984), 62.

28. Ross, *The Annexation of México*, 70.

29. Lieuwen, *Mexican Militarism*, 24.

30. Héctor Aguilar Camín and Lorenzo Meyer, *In the Shadow of the Mexican Revolution: Contemporary Méxican History, 1910–1989* (Austin: University of Texas Press, 1993), 48–49.

31. Camín and Meyer, *In the Shadow of the Mexican Revolution*, 60.

32. Ross, *The Annexation of México*, 73.

33. Samora and Simon, *A History of the Mexican American People*, 128.

34. Ross, *The Annexation of México*, 78.

35. Lieuwen, *Mexican Militarism*, 42.

36. Quirk, *México*, 94.

37. Quirk, *México*, 93–94.

38. Camín and Meyer, *In the Shadow of Mexican Revolution*, 65.

39. Camín and Meyer, *In the Shadow of Mexican Revolution*, 65.

40. Ross, *The Annexation of México*, 80.

41. Lieuwen, *Mexican Militarism*, 78.

42. See Quirk, *México*, 94–102.

43. Camín and Meyer, *In the Shadow of the Mexican Revolution*, 86.

44. Quirk, *México*, 101.

45. Mario Garcia, *Mexican Americans: Leadership, Ideology & Identity* (New Haven, Conn.: Yale University Press, 1989), 14.

46. James D. Cockcroft, *Outlaws in the Promised Land: Mexican Immigrant Workers and America's Future* (New York: Grove Press, 1986), 36.

47. For major works on the migrant exodus see Manuel Gamio, *Mexican Immigration to the United States* (Chicago: University of Chicago Press, 1930); and Lawrence A. Cardoso, *Mexican Emigration to the United States* (Tucson: University of Arizona Press, 1980).

48. Ricardo Romo, "The Urbanization of Southwestern Chicanos in the Early Twentieth Century," in *New Directions in Chicano Scholarship*, ed. Ricardo Romo and Raymund A. Paredes (La Jolla: University of California, San Diego, 1978), 194.

49. David Weber, ed., *Foreigners in Their Native Land: Historical Roots of the Mexican Americans* (Albuquerque: University of New México Press, 1973), 222.

50. Leonard Dinnerstein, Roger L. Nichols, and David M. Reimers, ed., *Natives and Strangers: Blacks, Indians, and Immigrants in America*, 2nd ed. (New York: Oxford University Press, 1990), 127

51. David Gutiérrez, *Walls and Mirrors: Mexican Americans, Mexican Immigrants, and the Politics of Ethnicity* (Los Angeles: University of California Press, 1995), 39.

52. For an excellent examination of the economic developmental conditions that induced the migration exodus see Gutiérrez, *Walls and Mirrors*, chapter 2.

53. Leobardo F. Estrada, F. Chris Garcia, Reynaldo Flores Macias, and Loniel Maldonado, "Chicanos in the United States: A History of Exploitation and Resistance," in *Latinos in the Political System*, ed. F. Chris Garcia (Notre Dame, Ind.: University of Notre Dame Press, 1988), 38–39.

54. See Maldwyn Jones, *American Immigration* (Chicago: University of Chicago Press, 1960).

55. James Diego Vigil, *From Indians to Chicanos: The Dynamics of Mexican-American Culture* (Prospect Heights, Ill.: Waveland Press, Inc., 1998), 188.

56. Juan Gómez-Quiñones, *Roots of Chicano Politics, 1600–1940* (Albuquerque: University of New México Press, 1994), 297. It is important to note that prior to 1900, no precise numbers exist as to the number of Mexicanos who migrated into the United States from México.

57. See Cockcroft, *Outlaws in the Promised Land*, 49. See also Oscar J. Martinez, "On the Size of the Chicano Population New Estimates, 1850–1900," *Aztlán* Vol. 6 (Spring 1975): 43–67.

58. Carey McWilliams, *North from México: The Spanish-Speaking People of the United States* (New York: Greenwood, 1968), 163.

59. Cited in Francisco E. Balderrama and Raymond Rodríguez, *Decade of Betrayal: México Repatriation in the 1930s* (Albuquerque: University of New México Press, 1995), 6.

60. For a thorough analysis on Mexican immigration into the United States from 1897 to 1931 see Cardoso, *Mexican Immigration to the United States*, 52–53.

61. David E. Lorey, *The U.S.–Mexican Border in the Twentieth Century* (Wilmington, Del.: Scholarly Resources, 1999), 69.

62. Oscar J. Martinez, *Mexican-Origin People in the United States: A Topical History* (Tucson: University of Arizona Press, 2001), 28.

63. Cardoso, *Mexican Immigration into the United States*, 52.

64. Arthur F. Corwin, ed., *Immigrants—and Immigrants: Perspectives on Mexican Labor Migration to the United States* (Westport, Conn.: Greenwood, 1978), 110, 116.

65. Lorey, *The U.S.–México Border in the Twentieth Century*, 67–68.

66. Corwin, *Immigrants—and Immigrants*, 110, 116.

67. Meier and Rivera, *Mexican Americans, American Mexicans*, 120.

68. Meier and Rivera, *Mexican Americans, American Mexicans*, 128.

69. Cardoso, *Mexican Immigration to the United States*, 103.

70. For an extensive examination on each one of the immigration acts cited see Jones, *American Immigration*, 231, 237, 240, 249.

71. Joan Moore and Harry Pachon, *Hispanics in the United States* (Englewood Cliffs, N.J.: Prentice Hall, 1985), 135.

72. Dinnerstein, Nichols, and Reimers, *Natives and Strangers*, 248.

73. Corwin, *Immigrants—and Immigrants*, 110, 116.

74. Corwin, *Immigrants—and Immigrants*, 116.

75. Richard Griswold Del Castillo and Arnoldo De León, *North to Aztlán: A History of Mexican Americans in the United States* (New York: Twayne Publishers; London: Prentice Hall International, 1996), 60.

76. Balderrama and Rodríguez, *Decade of Betrayal*, 7.

77. A major problem existed in that it was impossible to know in accurate terms the size of the Mexicano population during the first half of the twentieth century either on a regional or national basis simply because the U.S. Census Bureau collected and published very limited data pertaining to Mexicanos. See Martinez, *Mexican-Origin People in the United States*, 11.)

78. Martinez, *Mexican-Origin People in the United States*, 13.

79. Martinez, *Mexican-Origin People in the United States*, 11–13.

80. Rodolfo Acuña, *Occupied America: A History of Chicanos*, 4th ed. (New York: Addison Wesley, 2000), 187.

81. Ricardo Romo, "The Urbanization of Southwestern Chicanos in the Early Twentieth Century," in *En Aquel Entonces: Readings in Méxican American History*, ed. Manuel G. Gonzales and Cynthia Gonzales (Bloomington: Indiana University Press, 2000), 130.

82. Leo Grebler, *Mexican Immigration to the United States: The Record and Its Implications* (University of California Los Angeles: Mexican American Study Project, 1966), 16.

83. Martinez, *Mexican-Origin People in the United States*, 26.

84. Martinez, *Mexican-Origin People in the United States*, 8.

85. Juan Gonzales, *Harvest of Empire: A History of Latinos in America* (New York: Penguin, 2000), 102

86. Acuña, *Occupied America*, 4th ed., 165.

87. David Montejano, *Anglos and Mexicans in the Making of Texas, 1836–1986* (Austin: University of Texas Press, 1994), 109–10.

88. Emilio Zamora, *The World of the Mexican Worker in Texas* (College Station: Texas A&M Press, 1993), 12.

89. Martinez, *Mexican-Origin People in the United States*, 9.

90. Martinez, *Mexican-Origin People in the United States*, 11.

91. Meier and Rivera, *Mexican Americans, American Mexicans*, 120.

92. Martinez, *Mexican-Origin People in the United States*, 9.

93. Manuel G. Gonzales, *Mexicanos: A History of Mexicans in the United States* (Bloomington: Indiana University Press, 1999), 126.

94. Del Castillo and De León, *North to Aztlán*, 60.

95. Del Castillo and De León, *North to Aztlán*, 60.

96. Gonzales, *Mexicanos*, 121.

97. Samuel Bryan, "Mexican Immigrants in the United States," *Survey* Vol. 28 (September 7, 1912): 730.

98. Mark Reisler, "Always the Laborer, Never the Citizen: Anglo Perceptions of the Mexican Immigrant during the 1920s," *Pacific Historical Review* Vol. 45, No. 2 (1976): 243.

99. Martinez, *Mexican-Origin People in the United States*, 27.

100. Balderrama and Rodríguez, *Decade of Betrayal*, 17.

101. For two excellent studies on the repatriation and deportation efforts directed at Mexicanos see Abraham Hoffman, *Unwanted Mexican Americans in the Great Depression: Repatriation Pressures, 1929–1939* (Tucson: University of Arizona Press, 1974), ix; and Balderrama and Rodríguez, *Decade of Betrayal*. For a study on the impact of repatriation on California see Camille Guerin-Gonzales, *Mexican Workers & American Dreams: Immigration, Repatriation, and California Farm Labor, 1900–1939* (New Brunswick, N.J.: Rutgers University Press, 1994).

102. Cited in Guerin-Gonzales, *Mexican Workers & American Dreams*, 77.

103. Samora and Simon, *A History of the Mexican American People*, 36.

104. Mario Barrera, *Race and Class in the Southwest: A Theory of Inequality* (Notre Dame, Ind.: University of Notre Dame Press, 1979), 104.

105. Meier and Rivera, *Mexican Americans, American Mexicans*, 147.

106. For an examination of economic dislocations created by the Great Depression see Barrera, *Race and Class in the Southwest*, chapter 5.

107. Estrada et al., "Chicanos in the United States," 46.

108. Dinnerstein, Nichols, and Reimers, *Natives and Strangers*, 249.

109. Francisco E. Balderrama, *In Defense of La Raza: The Los Angeles Méxican Consulate and the Méxican Community, 1929–1936* (Tucson: University of Arizona Press, 1982), 2.

110. Estrada et al., "Chicanos in the United States," 46.

111. Balderrama, *In Defense of La Raza*, 2.

112. Robert Divine, *American Immigration Policy, 1924–1952* (New Haven, Conn.: Yale University Press, 1957), 77–84.

113. Hoffman, *Unwanted Mexican Americans in the Great Depression*, 166.

114. Balderrama and Rodríguez, *Decade of Betrayal*, 50.

115. For an excellent study on both the repatriation and deportation movements against Mexicanos during the Depression years see Hoffman, *Unwanted Mexican Americans in the Great Depression*, 166.

116. Barrera, *Race and Class in the Southwest*, 105–6.

117. Cited in Balderrama and Rodríguez, *Decade of Betrayal*, 53.

118. Balderrama and Rodríguez, *Decade of Betrayal*, 57–58.

119. Balderrama and Rodríguez, *Decade of Betrayal*, 57–58.

120. For an in-depth examination of the involvement of México's consulates around the Los Angeles area, see Balderrama, *In Defense of La Raza*.

121. Record Group 59, 811.111 México Reports/59, 80, 99, 122, 141, and 142,

National Archives, Washington, D.C. The Mexican Migration Service collected these figures. Cited in Hoffman, *Unwanted Méxican Americans in the Great Depression*, 174–75.

122. Balderrama and Rodríguez, *Decade of Betrayal*, 74.

123. Balderrama and Rodríguez, *Decade of Betrayal*, 2.

124. Estrada et al., "Chicanos in the United States," 46.

125. Balderrama and Rodríguez, *Decade of Betrayal*, 101.

126. Del Castillo and De León, *North to Aztlán*, 85.

127. Acuña, *Occupied America*, 4th ed., 263.

128. Joan Moore and Alfredo Cuellar, *Mexican Americans* (Upper Saddle River, N.J.: Prentice Hall, 1970), 28.

129. Gutiérrez, *Walls and Mirrors*, 122.

130. U.S. Bureau of the Census, Census Population, 1910–1940.

131. Meier and Rivera, *Mexican Americans, American Mexicans*, 153.

132. Del Castillo and De León, *North to Aztlán*, 85.

133. Acuña, *Occupied America*, 4th ed., 263.

134. Samora and Simon, *A History of the Mexican American People*, 138.

135. Juan Ramon García, *Operation Wetback: The Mass Deportation of Mexican Undocumented Workers in 1954* (Westport, Conn.: Greenwood, 1980), 25.

136. García, *Operation Wetback*, 23.

137. Ernesto Galarza, *Merchants of Labor: The Mexican Bracero Story: An Account of the Managed Migration of Mexican Farm Workers in California, 1942–1960* (San Jose, Calif.: Rosicrucian Press, 1964), 61.

138. Kitty Calavita, *Inside the State: The Bracero Program, Immigration, and the I.N.S.* (New York: Routledge, 1992), 19.

139. The term *bracero* comes from the Spanish word *brazo* or literally in English "armman." Here it is used in the context of referring to essentially farm and railroad workers that participated in the Bracero Program.

140. There are a few excellent works on the history of the Bracero Program. Beyond Calavita's *Inside the State* see also Galarza, *Merchants of Labor*; Richard B. Craig, *The Bracero Program: Interest Groups and Foreign Policy* (Austin: University of Texas Press, 1974).

141. Samora and Simon, *A History of the Mexican American People*, 138.

142. Craig, *The Bracero Program*, 37.

143. Galarza, *Merchants of Labor*, 47–48.

144. Martinez, *Mexican-Origin People in the United States*, 34.

145. Acuña, *Occupied America*, 4th ed., 286.

146. There are some disagreements among some scholars as to when and where the first contingent of *braceros* arrived in the United States. Calavita, in her book *Inside the State*, argues that Stockton, California, was the first recipient with some five hundred *braceros* arriving in September 29, 1942. Juan Ramon Garcia, in his book *Operation Wetback: The Mass Deportation of Mexican Undocumented Workers in 1954* (Westport, Conn.: Greenwood, 1980), propounds that the first contingent arrived on September 27, 1942, at El Paso, Texas.

147. Samora, "Mexican Immigration," in *Mexican Americans Tomorrow*, ed. Gus Tyler (Albuquerque: University of New México Press), 72.

148. Estrada et al., "Chicanos in the United States," 48.

149. Acuña, *Occupied America*, 4th ed., 264.

150. Meier and Rivera, *Mexican Americans, American Mexicans*, 159–60.

151. Carlos G. Vélez-Ibáñez, *Border Visions: Mexican Cultures of the Southwest United States* (Tucson, Ariz.: University of Tucson Press, 1996), 200.

152. Meier and Rivera, *Mexican Americans, American Mexicans*, 160.

153. Del Castillo and De León, *North to Aztlán*, 102.

154. Del Castillo and De León, *North to Aztlán*, 88.

155. For an extended examination on the particulars of this incident see McWilliams, *North from México*, 228–33.

156. Gutiérrez, *Walls and Mirrors*, 124.

157. Arnoldo Carlos Vento, *Mestizo: The History, Culture and Politics of the Mexican and Chicano* (Lanham, Md.: University Press of America, 1998), 185–86.

158. Meier and Rivera, *Mexican Americans, American Mexicans*, 162.

159. Vento, *Mestizo*, 185.

160. Vento, *Mestizo*, 185.

161. Meier and Rivera, *Mexican Americans, American Méxicans*, 164.

162. Juan Gómez-Quiñones, *Roots of Chicano Politics, 1600–1940* (Albuquerque: University of New México Press, 1994), 297.

163. For an elaboration of the tensions that surfaced between the two Mexicano cultural groups see Gutiérrez, *Walls and Mirrors*, chapter 1.

164. Authoritarianism denotes a style of government in which the rulers demand unquestioning obedience from the governed. Traditionally an authoritarian government power rests with the government and not the people, yet some individual choice can exist. See Iain McLean and Alistair McMillan, *Oxford Concise Dictionary of Politics* (New York: Oxford University Press, 2003), 30.

165. For a more thorough analysis of corporatism see Roderic Ai Camp, *Politics in México: The Democratic Transformation*, 4th ed. (New York: Oxford University Press, 2003), 11–13.

166. Wayne A. Cornelius, *Mexican Politics in Transition: The Breakdown of a One-Party-Dominant Regime* (La Jolla, Calif.: Center for U.S.-Mexican Studies, U.C.S.D., 1996), 51.

167. Ai Camp, *Politics in México*, 29.

168. Floyd Merrell, *The Mexicans: A Sense of Culture* (Boulder, Colo.: Westview, 2003), 242.

169. Merrell, *The Mexicans*, 248.

170. Ai Camp, *Politics in México*, 92–95.

171. For an extended analysis on this argument by two of México's best scholars on the topic see Samuel Ramos, *Profile of Man and Culture in México* (Austin: University of Texas Press, 1962); and Octavio Paz, *The Labyrinth of Solitude*, trans. Lysander Kemp (New York: Grove Press, 1985).

172. *Pocho* is a term with negative connotation used in México to describe a Mexicano born in the United States who is not fluent in Spanish and has become assimilated into U.S. culture. *Agringado* is an expressive term used to describe a Mexicano who is Anglicized. For an extensive explanation of these two terms see Reynoldo G. Castro, *Chicano Folklore* (New York: Oxford University Press, 2001), 6–7, 189–90.

173. Vigil, *From Indians to Chicanos*, 188.

174. Michael de Tirado, *The Mexican American Minority's Participation in Voluntary Political Associations*, PhD dissertation, Claremont Graduate School, 1970, 11.

175. Henry Santiestevan, "A Perspective on Mexican-American Organizations," in *Mexican Americans Tomorrow: Educational and Economic Perspectives*, ed. Gus Taylor, Jr. (Albuquerque: University of New México Press, 1975), 176.

176. Jose Amaro Hernandez, *Mutual Aid for Survival: The Case of the Mexican American* (Malabar, Fla.: Robert E. Krieger Publishing Co., 1983), 88.

177. Cited in Acuña, *Occupied America*, 4th ed., 199.

178. Arnoldo Carlos Vento, *Mestizo: The History, Culture, and Politics of the Mexican and the Chicano* (Lanham, Md.: University Press of America, 1998), 179.

179. Martinez, *Mexican-Origin People in the United States*, 165.

180. Taylor, *Foreigners in Their Native Land*, 217.

181. Gómez-Quiñones, *Roots of Chicano Politics*, 362.

182. For an extended examination into the development and growth of La Alianza see Kaye Lynn Briegel, *Alianza Hispano-Americana, 1894–1965: A Méxican Fraternal Insurance Society*, PhD dissertation, Department of History, University of Southern California, June 1974, chapters 3 and 4.

183. Briegel, *Alianza Hispano-Americana*, 50.

184. Briegel, *Alianza Hispano-Americana*, 88.

185. Briegel, *Alianza Hispano-Americana*, 48.

186. Briegel, *Alianza Hispano-Americana*, 143–45.

187. Briegel, *Alianza Hispano-Americana*, 143–45.

188. Martinez, *Mexican-Origin People in the United States*, 166.

189. Hernandez, *Mutual Aid for Survival*, 76.

190. Hernandez, *Mutual Aid for Survival*, chapter VII.

191. For a case study on La Sociedad Progresista Mexicana see *Hernandez, Mutual Aid for Survival*, chapter VII.

192. Acuña, *Occupied America*, 4th ed., 199.

193. Camarillo, *Chicanos in California*, 37.

194. Miguel David Tirado, "Mexican American Community Political Organization," *Aztlán: Chicano Journal of the Social Sciences and the Arts* I, no. I (spring 1970): 55.

195. Martinez, *Mexican-Origin People in the United States*, 164–65.

196. For an overview of interest groups see Ronald J. Hrebner, Matthew J. Burbank, and Robert C. Benedict, *Political Parties, Interest Groups, and Political Campaigns* (Boulder, Colo.: Westview, 1999), chapter 10.

197. Tirado, "Mexican American Community Political Organization," 56.

198. Jeffrey M. Berry, *The Interest Group Society* (Glenview, Ill.: Scott, Foresman, 1989), 4.

199. David Truman, *The Governmental Process* (New York: Knopf, 1971).

200. Cited in Hrebner, Burbank, and Benedict, *Political Parties, Interest Groups, and Political Campaigns*, 269.

201. Santiestevan, "A Perspective on Mexican American Organizations," 176.

202. Hernandez, *Mexican Aid for Survival*, 72.

203. For an extensive analysis on the development and formation of LULAC see Mario T. Garcia, *Mexican Americans: Leadership, Ideology, & Identity, 1930–1960* (New Haven, Conn.: Yale University Press, 1989), see particularly chapter 2.

204. Cited in De León, *Mexican Americans in Texas*, 93.

205. Armando Navarro, "The Evolution of Chicano Politics," in *Aztlán* Vol. 5, No. 1 and 2.

206. Moore and Cuéllar, *Mexican Americans*, 143.

207. Santiestevan, "A Perspective on Mexican-American Organizations," 176

208. Meier and Rivera, *Mexican Americans, American Mexicans*, 200.

209. Gómez-Quiñones, *Roots of Chicano Politics*, 365.

210. Hernandez, *Mutual Aid for Survival*, 73.

211. Garcia, *Mexican Americans*, 29.

212. Santiestevan, "A Perspective on Mexican American Organizations," 178.

213. For an examination of the development of LULAC see Benjamin Márquez, *LULAC: The Evolution of a Mexican American Political Organization* (Austin: University of Texas Press, 1993).

214. Garcia, *Mexican Americans*, 30.

215. Meier and Rivera, *Mexican Americans, American Mexicans*, 201.

216. Tirado, "Mexican American Community Political Organization," 57.

217. Acuña, *Occupied America*, 4th ed., 193.

218. Gutiérrez, *Walls and Mirrors*, 76.

219. Acuña, *Occupied America*, 4th ed., 195.

220. Cited in Acuña, *Occupied America*, 4th ed., 195.

221. Márquez, *LULAC*, 29

222. John R. Chavez, *The Lost Land: The Chicano Image of the Southwest* (Albuquerque: New México Press, 1984), 113.

223. Sonia Melendez, "LULAC Celebrates 75 Years of Progress," *Hispanic Link Report* Vol. 22, No. 7 (February 16, 2004).

224. Garcia, *Mexican Americans*, 43.

225. Gonzales, *Mexicanos*, 180.

226. Gutiérrez, *Walls and Mirrors*, 76.

227. Mario Barrera, *Beyond Aztlán: Ethnic Autonomy in Comparative Perspective* (Notre Dame, Ind.: University of Notre Dame Press, 1988), 24.

228. LULAC, "The Constitution, By-Laws, and Protocol," 1973, 3.

229. Cited in Tirado, "Mexican American Community Political Organization," 57.

230. Cited in Tirado, "Mexican American Community Political Organization," 58.

231. Acuña, *Occupied America*, 4th ed., 259.

232. Garcia, *Mexican Americans*, 36.

233. Garcia, *Mexican Americans*, 33.

234. Gutiérrez, *Walls and Mirrors*, 77–78.

235. Garcia, *Mexican Americans*, chapter 1.

236. For a brief examination of MAM's developments as a youth organization see my book *Mexican American Youth Organization: Avant-Garde of the Chicano Movement in Texas* (Austin: University of Texas Press, 1995), 48–51.

237. David Gutiérrez also provides a brief overview on MAM's formation; particularly, he focuses in on its assimilationist orientation. See his book *Walls and Mirrors*, 136–38.

238. Gómez-Quiñones, *Roots of Chicano Politics*, 387.

239. Gómez-Quiñones, *Roots of Chicano Politics*, 388.

240. Gutiérrez, *Walls and Mirrors*, 136.

241. Navarro, *Mexican American Youth Organization*, 49.

242. Acuña, *Occupied America*, 4th ed., 255.

243. Acuña, *Occupied America*, 4th ed., 255.

244. Navarro, *Mexican American Youth Organization*, 50.

245. McWilliams, *North from México*, 264.

246. Garcia, *Mexican Americans*, 118.

247. Chavez, *The Lost Land*, 119.

248. Garcia, *Mexican Americans*, 168.

249. Meier and Rivera, *Mexican Americans, American Méxicans*, 166.

250. McWilliams, *North from México*, 264.

251. Gómez-Quiñones, *Roots of Chicano Politics*, 378.

252. Garcia, *Mexican Americans*, 168.

253. Meier and Rivera, *Mexican Americans, American Mexicans*, 166.

254. McWilliams, *North from México*, 264.

255. Gómez-Quiñones, *Roots of Chicano Politics*, 378.

256. Gómez-Quiñones, *Roots of Chicano Politics*, 378.

257. McWilliams, *North from México*, 197.

258. Del Castillo and De León, *North to Aztlán*, 74.

259. Meier and Rivera, *Mexican Americans, American Mexicans*, 139.

260. Gómez-Quiñones, *Roots of Chicano Politics*, 381.

261. Santiestevan, "Perspective on Mexican American Organizations," 184.

262. McWilliams, *North from México*, 191.

263. Gómez-Quiñones, *Roots of Chicano Politics*, 381.

264. Meier and Rivera, *Mexican Americans, American Mexicans*, 140.

265. Santiestevan, "A Perspective on Mexican American Organizations," 186.

266. Acuña, *Occupied America*, 4th ed., 234.

267. Acuña, *Occupied America*, 4th ed., 229.

268. Martinez, *Mexican-Origin People in the United States*, 100.

269. Vicki Ruiz, *UCAPAWA, Chicanas, and the Food Processing Industry, 1937–1950*, PhD dissertation, Stanford University, 1982, 127.

270. Acuña, *Occupied America*, 4th ed., 244.

271. For an excellent historical overview of the labor organizing efforts of the AWIL and ACWIU, among other Marxist oriented unions, see Acuña, *Occupied America*, 4th ed., 228–33.

272. Acuña, *Occupied America*, 4th ed., 247–48.

273. For an extensive examination on various aspects of the *El Congreso* see Garcia, *Mexican Americans*, chapter 6.

274. Acuña, *Occupied America*, 4th ed., 256.

275. Gómez-Quiñones, *Roots of Chicano Politics*, 384.

276. Martinez, *Mexican-Origin People in the United States*, 173.

277. Cited in Tirado, "Mexican American Community Political Organization," 59.

278. Martinez, *Mexican-Origin People in the United States*, 152–53.

279. Gómez-Quiñones, *Roots of Chicano Politics*, 328–33.

280. Gómez-Quiñones, *Roots of Chicano Politics*, 328–33.

281. Cited in Martinez, *Mexican-Origin People in the United States*, 163.

282. Del Castillo and De León, *North to Aztlán*, 91.

283. Martinez, *Mexican-Origin People in the United States*, 163.

284. Del Castillo and De León, *North to Aztlán*, 91.

The Epoch of Social Action Politics (1946–1965)

4

MEXICANOS IN OCCUPIED Aztlán accelerated their struggle for change during the epoch of social action. In the barrios and *colonias* they still lived under the specter of internal colonialism, but from 1946 to 1965 significant political developments occurred as a result of several historical antagonisms. The dominant mode of politics continued to be adaptation and accommodation, giving rise to the Mexican American Generation. Mexicanos made greater progress than during the previous epoch in both ballot box and organizational politics. There was an air of activism in both arenas, driven by social action politics. Mexicanos from throughout Aztlán engaged in running candidates and made electoral politics a priority. They increasingly became better organized, resulting in the formation of several new organizations. Demographically there was an increase due to intensification of the migrant exodus, which of all the issues would become the greatest wedge issue.

Historical Forces Impacting the Mexicano Experience

World War II: Antagonism for Change

World War II brought death, destruction, and extreme suffering to millions upon millions of people in various parts of the world. Yet out of the horrors of war, a climate of change began to permeate the United States and the Mexicano political experience. The country's economy was rescued from the Depression. A new era of affluence and economic growth pervaded the country's postwar economies. For Mexicanos as well as for other oppressed minority groups, World War II created new employment opportunities.[1] "The booming wartime economy," David Gutiérrez writes, "had opened up to allow Mexican Americans and other minority groups unprecedented access." He further explains, "Although the federal government had consistently dragged its feet in implementing anti-discrimination policies, discrimination in many sectors of American life including the military, defense industries, and some branches of the government seemed to decrease during the 1940s."[2] Thus, the impact of World War II on Mexicanos was significant: new job opportunities were created, their isolation was reduced,[3] and the new climate of change gave rise to a period of social action politics.

Simply put, Mexicanos' wartime experiences in the armed forces and in the factory workforce proved to be beneficial for some. Even though it was not effectively enforced during World War II, President Roosevelt issued Executive Order 8802 that expressly forbade discrimination against workers in defense industries. Although it failed to deter discrimination, it did manage to assist in opening the door to employment opportunities for Mexicanos. At Kelly Air Force Base, for example, out of the thirty-five thousand workers some ten thousand were Mexicanos. However, they held the lowest positions and received the lowest pay.[4] For Mexicanos, wartime employment opportunities rarely led to promotions and career enhancement. Employers generally directed them into the lower-paying jobs, paid them less for similar work done by whites, and often segregated them in their job assignments.[5] Even though the country's economy reached a level of full employment during the war, Mexicanos still remained at the bottom of the segregated socioeconomic pyramid.

In order to ensure against racial discrimination in defense plants, the Federal Employment Practices Commission (FEPC) was established in 1941.[6] According to Rodolfo Acuña, the FEPC itself "followed a policy of avoiding the presidential executive order, entangling and delaying enforcement in a bureaucratic web." He goes on to explain, "Even the State Department got involved in evading the executive order." In order to accumulate data on discrimination toward Mexicanos in employment, the FEPC scheduled hearings in El Paso, Tejas, but the State Department cancelled them.[7] However, according to Matt S. Meier and Feliciano Rivera, the FEPC was strongly supported by U.S. senator Dennis (Dionisio) Chavez of Nuevo México, and did in fact undertake a number of investigations of discrimination in the workplace that resulted in Mexicanos obtaining industrial employment. In order to strengthen the FEPC's efforts President Franklin D. Roosevelt appointed historian Carlos E. Castañeda as special assistant on "Latin American" (the Texas euphemism for Mexican) problems. Castañeda also served as assistant to the chairman of the FEPC. Due to his leadership within the FEPC, the Shell Oil Company was ordered to revise its work contracts in 1945 so it would be in compliance with the Fair Employment Practices Act.[8]

During World War II many Mexicano agricultural workers left the rural areas and *colonias* of Aztlán and the Midwest. They sought new employment opportunities in the urban centers due to the rapidly expanding war industries. Urban workers acquired new skills and made better wages. Overall, their working conditions were better than those of rural workers. Many were to leave the impoverished socioeconomic conditions of low wages, substandard working conditions, racism, and poverty of the rural economies. As difficult as the situation was for Mexicanos in the urban areas, they were dramatically worse in the rural areas. Their migration to the cities was impelled by hope for a better future. Thus, the limited change realized by urban employment served to heighten the Mexicano's expectations for even more change in spite of the ongoing reality of multifarious social problems.

The Post-War Years: A Best of Times, Worst of Times Scenario

What ensued during the post–World War II years (1946–1950) was a "best of times, worst of times" scenario. Even though the majority of Mexicanos continued to be relegated to an internal colonial status, some Mexicanos were better off as a result of the war. The former was evident in that some jobs and industries that had been closed to Mexicano workers prior to World War II afterward continued to provide employment for some.[9] In great part this was a result of the "cold war" rivalry between the liberal capitalist powers and Communist bloc led by the Soviet Union. The U.S. war economy continued to create job opportunities in both the industrial and agricultural sectors. The passage of the G.I. Bill of Rights also contributed to rising expectations, and Mexicanos found new opportunities to finish their high school education and acquire a college education, job training, business and home loans, and desegregated housing.[10] Particularly in education, the benefits helped them enormously in transforming their newly found aspirations into reality.[11] Because of the G.I. Bill of Rights, some veterans improved their level of education and were able to purchase new modest homes outside the barrios in suburbia, causing cracks in the walls of segregation. For the next two decades, the G.I. Bill became an effective instrument of upward mobility into the embryonic middle class for some Mexicanos.

After World War II, however, most Mexicanos who were not veterans experienced the "worst of times." According to Meier and Rivera, "At the end of the fighting some of the gains made during the war years were lost. Wartime jobs disappeared, some social advances were not retained, and many Chicano veterans returned to find little, if any, increase in acceptance."[12] They were still subjected to the acute social, economic, and political discrimination. There was increasing discontent among many Mexicanos, especially returning war veterans, over their segregated, impoverished status and limited job opportunities. Infused with a passion for change in their condition, they were unwilling to accept the status quo.

In the military they had had a taste of integration. Unlike Blacks or Japanese Americans, they were not placed in segregated units.[13] Their wartime experiences gave them direct contact with whites, and at least in the battlefield, in fighting and dying, they were treated as equals, not as second-class citizens. In other words, they experienced a semblance of what it meant to be equal to whites. They also experienced new places and new people within and outside the country and became more cognizant of their oppressed conditions at home.

The wartime integration proved to be ephemeral. Overshadowing their return was the reality of once again living under segregation and impoverished conditions. Many of these veterans realized that they had to do something at this critical juncture. They felt they had served their country well and were entitled to the same rights and benefits enjoyed by whites in general. Many veterans and workers alike became active in dealing with social issues via existing and new organizations that they helped establish. One such issue was the Westminister Case in Orange County, California. Led by the League of United Latin American Citizens (LULAC), it resulted in a major legal victory for the desegregation of the schools.

Thus, Mexicanos understood that they had fought valiantly, were killed and wounded by the thousands in battle, had contributed significantly to the war effort by working in the defense factories, and had picked the crops that fed a nation. In spite of innumerable social problems at home, by 1950 once again, Mexicanos were called upon to participate in another war—the Korean Conflict.

The Korean Conflict: A Continued Military Paradox

As a result of the growing cold war between the United States and Russia, the United States became engaged in what was called by some as a "police action," precipitated by the invasion of Communist South Korea by North Korea. The nascent United Nations intervened and sent in hundreds of thousands of troops, including U.S. troops, to stop the invasion. This so-called Korean Conflict did not end until an armistice was signed on July 1953. In his one of a kind book *Among the Valiant*, Raul Morin writes the following: "The 'Police Action' (term applied by the UN) was just as ghastly and horrible as all other modern wars and came close to precipitating World War III." In November 1950, the People's Republic of China entered the war. They had warned the United Nation's forces, under the command of U.S. general Douglas MacArthur, not to cross the 38th Parallel and occupy North Korea. Nearly two hundred thousand Chinese troops crossed into North Korea and drove the UN's forces southward. The United Nations retreated and was held at the 38th Parallel. Due to major policy and individual differences, President Truman replaced General MacArthur as commander of UN troops in Korea early in the conflict. General MacArthur had advocated the possible use of nuclear weapons against the Chinese. Up to the signing of the armistice, the police action became a military stalemate involving trench and guerrilla warfare in which an estimated three million people were killed.[14]

Paradoxically, once again, Mexicanos responded to the patriotic call for military service. As was the case during World War II, Mexicanos died in disproportionate numbers. According to Mario Garcia, while Mexicanos were 10 percent of the state's population in Colorado, they represented 28 percent of the state's casualties. In Arizona, Mexicanos were 20 percent of the population and 44 percent of the casualties. In Nuevo México the ratio of population to casualties was 49 to 56 percent, and in Texas it was 17 to 30 percent.[15] According to Carlos Vélez-Ibañez, a disproportionate number of Mexicans fought and died during the Korean Conflict. He cites the "E" Company of the 13th Infantry Battalion, United States Marine Corps Reserve of Tucson, Arizona. It was composed of 237 men of whom 80 percent were Mexicans when it was called up to active duty on July 31, 1950. Two months later, they landed as part of an invasion force in Inchon, Korea. Most were untrained and inexperienced and had received only two weeks of military training in Japan. Many of them first learned how to fire their weapons onboard ship while in route to Korea.[16]

The valor and sacrifice displayed by Mexicanos in the Korean Conflict again was exemplary. A total of six Mexicanos received the Congressional Medal of Honor and all six were from working-class families with limited educational backgrounds. Born in Los Angeles, California, Marine private first-class Eugene A. Obregon, was twenty years of age when killed in action. Army sergeant Joseph C. Rodriguez was born in San Bernardino, California. Army corporal Rodolfo P. Hernandez was born in Colton, California. Marine private first-class Edward Gomez was born in Omaha, Nebraska. Born in Texas, army corporal Benito Martinez was twenty-one years of age when he was killed in action. And marine sergeant Ambrosio Guillen, born in La Junta, Colorado, was twenty-four when he was killed in action.[17]

Unlike World War II, the Korean Conflict did not act as a catalytic agent for economic change, especially for Mexicanos at home. About the only positive result of the conflict was the continuation of the G.I. Bill of Rights, which continued to provide veterans with educational and housing benefits. Politically, economically, and even psychologically, this police action did not effect a national mobilization or general support that the world war did. It was not a popular conflict and occurred during the cold war "red scare" era, during "McCarthyism," which was an out and out hunt for persons accused of being communist or having communist leanings. While Mexicanos died defending the interests of the United States on the frozen hills of Korea, the Mexicano community came under severe nativist attack with the passage of the Walter McCarran Act and implementation of Operation Wetback. The regional and state Mexicano interest groups did not oppose the Korean Conflict. La Alianza, LULAC, and the newly formed American G.I. Forum zealously supported it. However, progressive labor Asociación Nacional México-Americana protested both the Korean Conflict and the loss of Mexicanos in battle.[18] At the end of the Korean Conflict a nativist political climate proved to be increasingly inimical toward Mexicanos.

The Bracero Program (1946–1964): A Guest Worker Program

Under the aegis of Public Law 45, the Bracero Program continued after World War II until its formal expiration in 1947.[19] During its first five-year period, some 220,000 *braceros* participated.[20] In 1942 only 4,203 *braceros* were admitted, while the highest number reached was 62,170 in 1944, and by 1947, during its last year, the number declined to only 19,632. More than half of the *braceros* contracted to work in the United States were employed in California agriculture. In 1945 alone, California growers employed 63 percent of the total *bracero* workforce. During the off-season months, from January to April, 90 percent of the *braceros* went to California. As an agricultural workforce, *braceros* were used to pick cotton, sugar beets, fruits, and vegetables, and in some areas comprised the bulk of the unskilled labor for these crops.[21]

Beyond California, some 46,972 *braceros* were sent to Washington, Oregon, and Idaho. The remainder worked mostly on southwestern railroads and agribusiness farms. As to the former, in 1941 the Southern Pacific Railroad requested permission to bring in workers from México for track-maintenance work. The U.S. government took no action until 1943 when some thirty-two railroads requested and secured *braceros* under an agreement that included a minimum wage and a guarantee of 90 percent employment during the six-month contract period. Ultimately about eighty thousand Mexican *braceros* worked for railroads, over half of them for two companies: the Southern Pacific and Santa Fe lines.[22] However, by 1946 their use in railroad maintenance work was terminated when political pressure was generated by the major railway workers union.[23]

During its first five-year period, the Bracero Program encountered a number of problems. Tejas did not participate in the wartime Bracero Program due to the lack of support from growers and ranchers. They favored an "open border" policy that allowed Mexicano migrants to come into Tejas when their labor was needed, which was contrary to the Bracero Program. They argued that for years it had functioned very well for them. In May 1943, the Immigration and Naturalization Service (INS) authorized one-year work permits, which in effect sanctioned an open border. Some two thousand Mexicanos entered Tejas before the border was shut down because of protests from the Mexican government.[24] By the summer of 1943, Tejas growers finally requested the use of *braceros*. Much to their chagrin, the Mexican government refused to issue permits on the grounds that discrimination against Mexicanos in Tejas was brutal and intolerable. According to Nelson Gage Copp, the Mexicano weekly *Mañana* wrote, "The Nazis of Texas are not political partners of the Fuhrer of Germany, but indeed they are slaves to the same prejudices."[25]

In an attempt to placate the Mexican government, Tejas governor Coke Stevenson pushed through the so-called Caucasian Race Resolution, which affirmed the rights of all Caucasians to equal treatment in public places of business and amusement. This proved to be a major political mistake since most whites in Texas did not consider Mexicanos Caucasians.[26] On September 4, 1943, Governor Stevenson established the Good Neighbor Commission of Texas in another effort to appease the concerns of the Mexican government. Funded with federal money, it sought to end discrimination against Mexicanos through better understanding, but it was not until October 1947 that México agreed to issue permits to Tejas.[27]

The Bracero Program was plagued by shortcomings and was not uniformly implemented. The typical *bracero* was an unmarried male, came from a rural working environment, was barely literate, and spoke little or no English. México's chronic poverty, low wages, and unemployment raised Mexicanos' expectations of improving the quality of their lives and drove many of them to endure the hardships of being a *bracero*. These included harsh working conditions, prejudice, substandard housing, poor quality food, physical mistreatment, undue exposure to pesticides, unjust wage deductions, unreasonable charges for room and board, and low net earnings. The housing issue was slightly improved by late 1943 with the construction of ninety-five labor camps by the federal government. A *bracero's* weekly earnings were at times below the cost of shelter and board. Average annual income did not exceed $500, but increased by the 1950s, reaching a level of $900 by 1960.[28] During the first five years, 10 percent of the *bracero's* wages were deducted and were to be returned as part of their social security retirement in México.

With the termination of World War II in 1945, the demand for continued use of *braceros* came into question. On November 15, 1946, the U.S. Department of State notified the Mexican government of its desire to terminate Public Law 45. Growers, who had profited greatly from the Bracero Program, lobbied for its continuation. They argued that the need for agricultural workers had not yet diminished and they required more time to replenish their former labor sources. In January 1947, legislation was introduced to Congress calling for an extension of the Bracero Program until the end of June 1948. The bill on April 28, 1947, was amended and passed as Public Law 40, which provided for an extension of the Bracero Program until December 31, 1947, upon which time it was to be liquidated within thirty days.[29] It also stipulated that the remaining *braceros* had to depart from the United States by no later than January 30, 1948.

With Congress's final termination of the Bracero Program, agricultural employers of *braceros* mounted a concerted campaign that swamped INS offices with petitions. They warned of continued labor shortages and demanded to extend the stay of their *braceros* and to allow for additional admissions. On February 21, 1947, the State Department negotiated a new accord with México that allowed for the continued importation of *braceros*. Seven months later, Congress passed Public Law 893, which fostered little discussion and no public hearings. One year later, the law expired and left the Bracero Program to operate outside of any formal congressional oversight or legislation. During this phase, according to Rodolfo Acuña, "Growers were permitted to hire undocumented workers and certify them on the spot." He further notes, "Between 1947 and 1949, 142,000 undocumented workers were certified, whereas only 74,600 braceros were hired by contract from México."[30] Between 1948 and 1951, a total of 401,845 *braceros* worked in the United States. The highest number was in 1951, when some 192,000 participated. By the end of 1950, over six hundred thousand guest workers had participated in the Bracero Program.[31]

The years between 1947 and 1951 constituted the second phase of the Bracero Program, which operated under negotiated administrative agreements with México. Because of continued abuses of *braceros*, the Mexican government became increasingly dissatisfied with the way it was being administered. An incident occurred on October 1948 in Juarez when the Mexican government denied thousands of frantic workers access to the program. Pressured by Tejas growers the INS opened the gates at the border on October 13, 1948, allowing the unencumbered entrance of Mexicano undocumented migrants into the United States. Three days later, after some four thousand undocumented workers had crossed into the United States, the gates were once again closed. In response to the incident, México abrogated the 1948 agreement on October 18, 1948. "In a diplomatic face-saving effort," according to Richard B. Craig, "Washington denied having sanctioned the action and apologized for the entire incident. México accepted the apology but did not sign another agreement until August 1949."[32]

In the words of Juan Ramon Garcia, "The bracero program deteriorated as legislation governing its operation removed much of the previous governmental supervision and placed the contracting of Mexican workers into the hands of private employers, which gave rise to many problems and abuses."[33] The government-to-government contracts that México had insisted on during the war were replaced by direct grower–*bracero* work agreements.[34] "Between 1947 and 1951," as Meier and Rivera point out, "workers continued to be brought across the border as agribusiness returned to prewar practices. Labor contracting was undertaken directly by agricultural organizations and farmers without any arrangements between the two governments and with extremely limited supervision, México only."[35]

The passage of Public Law 78 by Congress marked the beginning of the third phase of the Bracero Program. The Korean Conflict broke out in 1950 and acted as a catalyst for its renewal. The country's manpower needs led to stricter controls over the importation of Mexican labor. President Truman that same year appointed a Commission on Migratory Labor, which included Archbishop Robert Lucey of San Antonio, Tejas, to study the problem.[36] The Korean Conflict strengthened the negotiating hand of México. A conference was held in México City during January and February 1951 involving U.S. and Mexican delegates where the Migrant Labor Agreement was concluded to extend the Bracero Program until July 1, 1951.[37]

With the intent of implementing the various points agreed upon at the joint U.S./México conference, on February 27, 1951, Senator Allen J. Ellender submitted S984 as an amendment to the Agricultural Act of 1949. The spirit of the proposed legislation was to curb the influx of undocumented workers.[38] After going through an arduous congressional hearing process, floor debate, and conference negotiations and compromises, the Ellender legislation passed Congress and was signed by President Truman on July 13, 1951, as a temporary two-year measure. Known as Public Law 78, it was the new legal framework by which the Bracero Program was administered.

With its passage, once again the U.S. government assumed responsibility to recruit *braceros* and the role of government guarantor of individual work contracts.[39] It also provided for reception centers near the border, housing, subsistence, and transportation for contracted laborers. Recruitment and management of the Bracero Program fell under the auspices of the Department of Labor. The INS was responsible only for the entry and departure aspects of the Bracero Program,[40] whereas the Mexican government was responsible for the recruitment of workers and for making sure the contract was honored on both sides.[41] A quota system per state was used. However, because of the great number of applicants a lottery system for selection was developed. In México processing centers were established in Hermosillo, Chihuahua, and Monterrey. Once processed, successful applicants were taken across the border into U.S. recruitment centers and given medical examinations. Employer representatives then made their selection. After one week, those that were not picked were sent back across the border to fend for themselves. There was no provision for transportation support for their return to their respective villages, towns, or cities. Selected workers signed contracts and were than transported to their work sites. The farmer provided the transportation, housing, and work; the *bracero* was responsible for his health insurance, Mexican social security, and food, and all costs were deducted from his check. Certain conditions of employment, such as basic living and health needs and the protection of the worker's civil rights, were an integral part of Public Law 78 and the length of tenure was usually from three to six months.

With its main base of support coming from a coalition of conservative Republicans and southern Democrats, Public Law 78 was extended for two-year intervals in 1954, 1956, and 1958. During these periods, the number of *braceros* who entered the United States increased dramatically—from a low of 187,894 in 1952 to a high of 450,422 in 1957, while the average number between 1955 and 1959 was 400,000 per year. By 1956, there were approximately 193,000 *braceros* in Texas; 151,000 in California; 30,000 in Arizona; 20,000 in Nuevo México; 7,000 each in Colorado and Michigan; and 15,000 elsewhere.[42] From 1952 to 1960, the number of *braceros* who worked in the United States reached a total of 3,276,303.

The Bracero Program continued with extensions until May 1963 when the 88th Congress voted down a bill to extend it for another two years. The highest recorded number of *braceros* that came to the United States occurred during the late 1950s, specifically in 1955, 390,846; 1956, 444,581; 1957, 450,422; 1958, 418,885; 1959, 447,535. By 1964, when the Bracero Program expired, the number had dropped to 181,738.[43] According to official estimates, during its twenty-two years, the Bracero Program employed approximately some 4.8 million workers from México.[44] When their contracts expired, many of the *braceros* returned to the United States as undocumented migrants and remained permanently. In 1960 Public Law 78 came up for renewal and was subjected to continued controversy and debate. Earlier in 1958, legislation that sought its termination was defeated and that same year President Eisenhower called for a two-year study to be conducted.

Ultimately, the demise of the Bracero Program could be ascribed to the U.S. political and economic climate. From 1946 to 1964, numerous labor, religious, and civic organizations protested and pressured Congress for its termination.

Throughout its duration, various Mexicano organizations, such as the National Congress of Spanish-Speaking People, the California Federation of Spanish-Speaking Voters, the Bishop's Committee on the Spanish-Speaking, LULAC, the American G.I. Forum, and the newly formed Mexican American Political Association in California were all categorically against it.[45] A number of middle-class Mexicano organizations opposed the Bracero Program on the grounds that it also thwarted their organizing efforts and the overall progress of the community.

Labor unions were particularly against the Bracero Program since they saw that it allowed growers to effectively use *braceros* to break labor strikes. Undercutting farm unionization efforts was particularly evident in California, especially those of the National Farm Labor Union (NFWA) and its successor, the National Agricultural Workers Union (NAWU).[46] Organized labor charged that *braceros* displaced U.S. workers and depressed wages and working conditions.[47] Of the *politicos*, the most vociferous critic of the Bracero Program was Nuevo México U.S. senator Dennis Chavez. Reactions from the Mexicano community were mixed; however, Manuel Gonzales notes, "Those Mexicans living in the United States, regardless of class, who felt a strong sense of Mexican nationalism (*Mexicanidad*) were more likely to identify with the newcomers and accept them, especially if they themselves were immigrants." He further adds, "On the other hand, native born Mexicans with weak sentimental ties to the Old country were likely to reject the guest worker program."[48] With the emergence of the Civil Rights Movement and the election of President John F. Kennedy, a Democrat-controlled 88th Congress in May 1963 voted down a bill to extend it for another two years. At the expiration of the last extension, the Bracero Program in 1964 became moribund.

The Bracero Program left a legacy of prosperity for agribusiness, which it sought to continue in a modified form after the program's termination. In 1965, for example, a facsimile of the program was enacted as Section H-2 of the McCarran-Walter Act. The Johnson administration allowed some twenty thousand temporary workers to be brought in from México.[49] Furthermore, that same year, the Border Industrialization Program was established, allowing U.S. industries (*maquiladoras*), located along the U.S./México border in México, to hire thousands of workers. It also allowed the importation of finished manufactured goods from México into the United States duty free.[50] In the final analysis, the Bracero Program contributed significantly to the Mexicano political experience by reigniting the migrant exodus. As a result, millions of undocumented Mexicanos migrated from México and settled in the sprawling barrios and *colonias* of the United States.[51]

The Migrant Exodus Revitalized: The Diaspora Continues

The Bracero Program significantly impacted the migrant exodus.[52] "The bracero program acted as a magnet," writes Mario Barrera, "drawing Mexican workers into northern México. When many were not accepted as braceros, they crossed the border anyway."[53] In particular from 1946 to 1955, this situation fostered a steady flow of undocumented workers that paralleled the importation of *braceros*.[54] The Bracero Program itself was as much a product of "push and pull" factors as was the diaspora of the undocumented migrant. The salient push factors included México's pervasive poverty that produced unemployment, underemployment, and internal migrations from the rural to the urban areas and its burgeoning population growth.[55] In México, also acting as a push factor was the country's improved transportation system, which facilitated mass migrations from the interior to the border. In 1940 all-weather roads covered a mere two thousand miles. However, by 1950 they had increased to fifteen thousand, and there were also fifteen thousand miles of railroad lines.[56] Capital intensive, irrigated cash crop farming in northern México brought large numbers of workers from central México to the north and border areas.

The cardinal pull factor continued to be the U.S.'s insatiable demand for cheap labor, which was the result of a rapidly expanding economy. Between 1945 and 1955 alone some 7,500,000 acres of newly irrigated farmland came into production in seventeen southwestern states.[57] Demand for farmworkers skyrocketed during harvest time. In the United States also, the absence of legal penalties, insufficient border control, a heavily populated Mexicano Southwest, the presence of border and transborder recruiters, and widespread lack of concern at least until 1951 all contributed to the migrant exodus. The impact was so great that Ciudad Juarez's population increased from 48,881 in 1940 to 121,903 in 1950.[58] Once the undocumented migrants reached the U.S./México border, the motivation for crossing into the United States to make U.S. dollars became their driving incentive. Their impact on the workforce was such that during the postwar years, they began replacing Mexicanos born in the United States, particularly in Tejas. This was due to the acute labor shortage that existed in the agricultural sector of the U.S. economy. As previously described, many of the returning Mexicano veterans were not willing to go back to the rural areas and work; consequently, agribusiness resorted to the use of Mexicano undocumented migrants to satisfy their labor demands. Yet some of these new arrivals did not remain in agricultural-related work, but went into the urban areas and worked in service, light manufacturing, and construction-related jobs.

Even though the Bracero Program provided agribusiness with thousands of contracted temporary guest workers, the hunger for additional exploitable labor could not be satisfied. "Mexicans entered the United States illegally," according to John Chavez, "when the bracero program failed to accept them or because they wished to avoid the bureaucratic difficulties involved." He further explains, "They were hired by employers who were unable to obtain braceros or who wished to avoid the minimum wage and other restrictions imposed under the program."[59] Hence, undocumented migrants were usually hired for wages substantially below the modest levels that agribusiness established for *braceros*.[60] Unlike *braceros*, they did not have to secure a permit, nor did employers have to abide by contractual agreements. In differentiating between *braceros* and "wetbacks," Julian Samora writes, "Wetback labor is even cheaper—no need for contracts, minimum wage, health benefits, housing, transportation, etc. Since the workers are illegal aliens, they have few rights before the law and can be dismissed at a moment's notice."[61] Undocumented migrants integrated themselves much better into the *colonias* and barrios than did *braceros* since that is where they resided. Some married Chicanas and started families, adding incentive for them to remain, and many did so.

Early on they were designated quite inappropriately as "wetbacks"—in Spanish, *mojados* or *alambristas*. The former referred to those undocumented migrants who had allegedly swum or waded across the Rio Grande River from Brownsville to El Paso, Texas, into the United States. The irony was that many of the so-called wetbacks who came into the United States without legal documents did not swim or wade across a river.[62] An *alambre* or *alambrista* was an undocumented migrant who crossed the border illegally by presumably climbing over or cutting through a fence.[63] Others simply walked or rode across into the United States from various border points located from Brownsville, Texas, to San Ysidro, California. The smuggling of undocumented migrants became a lucrative business all along the U.S./México border, especially for those known as "coyotes," who arranged the illegal crossing and provided whatever was needed to make the crossing across the often perilous border—from guides called *polleros*, to transportation or counterfeit papers.[64] Their fees varied from one hundred to three hundred dollars, which included transportation costs.[65]

Braceros and undocumented workers often worked side by side on the same crews. Right after World War II, growers played an administrative game that reached levels of absurdity. Undocumented migrants caught by the U.S. Border Patrol were sent back across the Mexican border, and when growers experienced a shortage of workers they were readmitted as "legally contracted" workers. It was a process called "drying out" the so-called wetbacks.[66] Rodolfo Acuña explains:

> Collusion between the Immigration and Naturalization Service (INS) and the growers was a fact. For instance, the INS rarely rounded up undocu-

mented workers during harvest time, and it instructed its agents to with-hold searches and deportations until after the picking season. A rule of thumb was that when sufficient numbers of braceros or domestic labor worked cheaply enough, agents enforced the laws; when a labor shortage occurred, they open the doors, regardless of international or moral law.[67]

From 1946 to 1951, this was a common practice. In spite of agreements con-cluded between both governments to curb the influx of undocumented migrants, several such incidents occurred. One such agreement was concluded in early 1947 that included the legalization of undocumented workers. However, due to a reces-sion in 1949, massive roundups of undocumented workers were initiated by the INS.[68] An accord ratified in August 1949 emphasized the suppression of illegal entry. Growers who were caught hiring undocumented workers were denied access to *braceros*. As a result of this new agreement, 87,220 undocumented work-ers were legitimated in 1949 as *braceros*. An estimated sixty thousand were legal-ized in 1950 as they continued to cross the border in increasing numbers. With the start of the Korean Conflict, México became increasingly unhappy with the "drying out" arrangements and complaints of worker ill treatment, but to no avail; México's complaints went unanswered.

By 1951, the Bracero Program intended to control illegal immigration from México into the United States was a resounding failure. From 1940 to 1950 some eight hundred thousand undocumented workers were apprehended.[69] Even during World War II, from 1943 to 1945, some 98,480 undocumented workers were reported to have crossed into the United States. During 1950, the number of *braceros* was 67,500, compared to 458,215 undocumented workers.[70] The truth of the matter is that the Bracero Program was not successful in curbing the dias-pora of undocumented workers into the United States. So the number increased exorbitantly between 1946 and 1951 to a total of 1,690,580.[71] Thus, as the dec-ade of the 1950s began, the political stage was set for an acceleration of attacks on undocumented workers under the guise of "nativism."

The McCarthy Era: A Resurgence of Nativism

As a result of the dramatic increase in the number of undocumented workers that occurred during the early 1950s, the political climate became anti-immigrant and anti-Mexicano. The cold war's red scare politics of McCarthyism led to nativist and xenophobic reactions. The cold war was not one of battling armies but one of contentious and battling ideologies. It pitted the Marxist Soviet Union and its eastern bloc against the liberal capitalist United States and its allies in Europe.

It was a struggle for world hegemony between these two diametrically opposed ideological blocs. McCarthyism took the fears of the cold war to an extreme; it became an inquisition in which many individuals and organizations were accused of being communist sympathizers or fronts.

Even prior to World War II, the United States was leery of so-called communist subversion and in 1940 passed the Smith Act. This act made it a criminal offense to advocate the violent overthrow of the government or to organize or be a member of any organization or group devoted to such ends. The result was that numerous Left-oriented organizations and leaders came under its vicious scrutiny. FBI director J. Edgar Hoover played on the growing paranoia by postulating that the so-called Free World was in a do-or-die struggle against communism. Numerous politicians, such as Richard Nixon, Pat McCarran, and Joseph McCarthy, pandered to the ideological fears of the people, which were exacerbated by the country's propaganda machinery.[72] The red scare politics were further buttressed by world events, such as the Berlin Crisis (1948), the success of the Maoist Revolution in China (1948), the Korean Conflict (1950–1953), and the Soviet Union's transformation into a nuclear super power by the early 1950s.

"McCarthyism" described the efforts of Senator Joseph McCarthy, who used investigative hearings to accuse numerous individuals and groups that he suspected of being communist or communist sympathizers. The McCarthy era produced a reactionary political climate predicated on fear, repression, and witch hunts. As Juan Ramon Garcia notes, "The times were not conducive to protest and resistance."[73] The country's political culture was such that dissension or criticism of the system that was based on social injustices was easily misconstrued as being part of communist infiltration and activity.

Indicative of this political climate was the passage of restrictive laws. The internal Security Act of 1950 and the McCarran-Walter Act of 1952 both reflected this red scare mentality or mind-set. They provided the mechanism for political control of naturalized citizens and in the words of Rodolfo Acuña, "laid the foundation for a police state."[74] David G. Gutiérrez, notes, "The Internal Security Act was passed as a means for prosecuting anyone who had ever been even nominally affiliated with a Communist, Socialist, or other organizations deemed subversive."[75] In particular, the latter piece of legislation had a powerful impact on "Operation Wetback." Its architect was Senator Pat McCarran from Nevada, who saw himself as the chief guardian in Washington of maintaining the country's racial (white) purity. He was not only against admitting more foreigners into the country, but perceived it as a dangerous threat to the country's security. In 1950, he introduced the McCarran Act to the Senate, seeking to tighten immigration laws and exclude subversive elements. By 1952 this omnibus legislation had a coauthor, Congressman Francis Walter of Pennsylvania. Designated the McCarran-Walter Act, it passed Congress over the veto of President Harry S. Truman,[76] who felt that it created a group of second-class citizens. Truman also opposed the provision that naturalized citizens could have their citizenship revoked and that they were subject to deportation on political grounds.[77]

Briefly, the McCarran-Walter Act had other insidious provisions, which directly affected Mexicanos in the United States. As described by Rodolfo Acuña, it specifically

> provided for (1) the codification of previous immigration acts, relating to national origins; (2) the abolition of racial bars to entry and citizenship; (3) the establishment of a complicated procedure for admitting Asians; (4) the inclusion of a long list of grounds on which aliens could be deported or excluded; (5) the inclusion of conditions under which naturalized citizens could be denaturalized; and (6) the granting of power to the INS to interrogate aliens suspected of being illegally in the country, to search boats, trains, cars, trucks, or planes, to enter and search private lands within 25 miles of the border, and to arrest so-called "illegals" and also those committing felonies under immigration laws.[78]

Moreover, under Title I of the act, a Subversive Activities Control Board was established to investigate suspected subversion. Title II was equally as pernicious in that it authorized the construction of several camps to intern suspected subversives without a trial or hearing if either the president or Congress called for a "national emergency." Two years after its passage, some six camps were built.[79] Although it was not aimed primarily at Mexicanos, it had a tremendously negative impact on community leaders and organizations. Many of those leaders perceived as leftist now risked deportations and denaturalization if they were found guilty of activities deemed subversive. Organizations became subject to investigation as well. Passage of the act served to reveal the fears and biases of the country's governing leadership by defining very specifically the parameters of who was or was not eligible for citizenship. With few exceptions most Mexicano middle-class organizations supported its passage, but when implemented some spoke out against it. Thus, the cold war and the rise of McCarthyism set the stage for the rise of Operation Wetback.[80]

Operation Wetback: A Nativist Crusade

Operation Wetback and the nativist crusade it engendered against the so-called wetbacks can be traced to 1951 with the release of a report by the president's

Commission on Migratory Labor. It sounded an alarm over the rise in illegal immigration, warning ominously, "The magnitude of the wetback traffic has reached entirely new levels in the past 7 years. . . . In its newly achieved proportions, it is virtually an invasion." It further concluded, "The wetback traffic has reached such proportions in volume and in consequent chaos, it should not be neglected any longer." Growers and their allies in Congress attacked the essence of the report as being biased by union sympathies and reformist in nature. The fact was the release of the report acted as a catalyst for mobilizing anti-immigrant nativist sentiments among the populace and served to open debate on the issue, which in time the media picked up on.[81]

Upon release of the commission's report, the New York Times ran a five-part series on the alleged "illegal aliens," blaming southwestern growers as responsible for bringing them into the country then treating them as peons who depressed wages and contributed to crime. The series served to whet the appetite of a politicized and biased press, which was quick to sensationalize the issue. With the dramatic increase in the number of undocumented migrants during the early 1950s, even radio stations reacted by pandering to the whites' fears. A New York Times service broadcast from Los Angeles alleged that illegal immigration from México had reached such overwhelming proportions that INS officers had admitted candidly that there was nothing to stop the whole nation of México from moving into the United States. It was also argued that 10 percent of México's population was in the United States already.[82] Much of the media depicted undocumented migrants as dangerous "aliens" who could pose a security threat to the country. This effectively aroused anti-immigrant sentiments and ignited nativist calls for their prompt expulsion and return to México.

Further adding to the media frenzy against undocumented migrants was the release of another report that same year (1953) entitled "What Price Wetbacks?" and prepared by the American G.I. Forum in collaboration with several labor unions. Written in vitriolic language much like that of reactionary Right politicians McCarthy and McCarran and others, it concluded that the so-called wetback problem was the fundamental problem facing Mexicanos of the Southwest. The report ardently supported the Border Patrol's efforts to curb illegal immigration, calling for additional resources and facilities and the passage of stronger immigration laws.[83] The American G.I. Forum was one of several other middle-class Mexicano organizations that vehemently opposed both the Bracero Program and the diaspora of undocumented migrants. As an organization, it took the position that both were major obstacles for Mexican Americans in their struggle to achieve their civil rights and economic objectives.[84] Mexicano migrants had met the enemy and the enemy in part was their own: assimilation-oriented Mexicanos had become zealots of liberal capitalism. Others, however, were in opposition for a number of reasons; among these were two prominent scholars, Ernesto Galarza and George Sanchez.

With the United States plagued by an economic recession in 1953, widespread alarm grew about the so-called wetback invasion. Nativist activists and politicians recommended to Congress that the U.S. Army should be utilized to "stem the tide."[85] In Washington, D.C., the politicians were under tremendous pressure, especially by labor, to do something about the influx of "wetbacks." With the appointment of retired Lieutenant General Joseph M. Swing as INS commissioner by newly elected president Dwight Eisenhower, the stage was set for the creation of Operation Wetback. Swing's background, says Rodolfo Acuña, was that of "professional longtime Mexican hater." He explains, "Swing had been a classmate of President Dwight Eisenhower at West Point in 1911, and had been on General Pershing's punitive expedition against Pancho Villa in 1916."[86] With Swing's appointment, the INS became more assertive in its tactical efforts to deport undocumented migrants and increasingly took on a more military posture. INS commissioner Swing, in his determination to flush out undocumented Mexicanos, requested $10 million to build a 150-mile-long fence along the border and set a quota for those to be deported from each target area. In 1953, the INS deported some 875,000 Mexicanos. Of those, 20,174 were airlifted into México from Spokane, Chicago, Kansas City, St. Louis, and other cities.[87] Named by Swing, Operation Wetback was not officially launched until 1954.

In June 1954, U.S. attorney general Herbert Brownell, Jr., ordered a massive deportation drive that put Operation Wetback into a full-speed mode. He cited the possible illegal entrance of political subversives into the United States as the rationale for launching the drive.[88] California became the first target and then Texas, but within weeks it was extended to several Midwest cities.[89] In subsequent months, throughout the country, especially in the Southwest, *colonias* and barrios came under a state of siege. Undocumented workers lived under the constant fear of deportation both at their residences and at workplaces. With the implementation of Operation Wetback, the civil liberties and human rights of deportees were often callously ignored. Simply "looking Mexican" was often sufficient reason for official scrutiny. In fact, just because a person "looked Mexican" and did not have the appropriate legal documentation when questioned, he ran the risk of arrest. The physical treatment of deportees at times was marked by the use of intimidation, harshness, and contempt.[90]

Buttressed by a high-profile media campaign, mobile armies of U.S. Border patrolmen conducted military-type sweeps, deporting thousands of undocumented migrants annually. By 1954 the number deported dramatically increased to 1,075,000; and in 1955 with the economy beginning to improve, the number decreased to 242,608. With the country no longer in a recession and the demand for cheap labor rising, the number in 1956 decreased even further to 72,442. The number deported again decreased but in 1964 gradually increased to 43,844 and in 1965 to 55,349.[91] The total deported from 1950 to 1955 was 3,675,309 (this figure includes multiple counts of men who had entered and been expelled more than once).

What ensued after 1955 was a dramatic decline in deportations that continued in relatively low numbers until the slight increase in 1964 when 43,844 were deported. When the Bracero Program terminated the next year, the number increased to 55,349. Of those deported only 63,515 went through formal proceedings. The others were simply removed under the threat of deportation. Most were not merely sent across the border, but with the cooperation of the Mexican government were sent to points designated near their homes in México.[92] It is important to note that the highest number deported occurred during the country's years of economic recession, while the lowest number occurred during those years the economy was stable and relatively healthy. Moreover, the low number of undocumented migrants was compensated by a dramatic increase in the number of *braceros* who were contracted—from a low of 398,650 in 1954 to a high of 437,643 in 1959.[93] The federal government essentially guaranteed the growers access to a source of cheap labor.

The duration of Operation Wetback was relatively short. INS commissioner Swing announced its termination in 1955 calling it a great success. Juan Ramon Garcia notes, "Operation Wetback marked the end of the wetback decade. However, it did not mark the end of the illegal. The mass deportation of undocumented workers was only a temporary stopgap measure, designed to quell critics and assuage an aroused public. For the moment employers had to content themselves with contracting braceros."[94] Because of its large scale, the use of military tactics in its implementation, and rough treatment given to those apprehended, Operation Wetback became one of the most traumatic experiences endured by Mexicanos in the United States in their dealings with the federal government.[95] No barrio or *colonia* in Aztlán remained untouched; neither did those in the Northwest and Midwest.

Yet, paradoxically, while the growers sought access to a cheap source of labor and spoke out against Operation Wetback, the overwhelming number of middle-class Mexicano organizations, such as LULAC and American G.I. Forum, supported it. One of the few organizations to ardently speak out against it was La Asociacíon Nacional México Americana.[96] Unlike most other Mexicano organizations that were middle class, its leadership and membership was working-class based and committed to protecting the interests and rights of undocumented migrants. Thus, Operation Wetback contributed to the widening chasm between Mexicanos from México and Mexicanos born in the United States.

The Mexicano's Changing Demographic Profile (1950 and 1960)

The Bracero Program and burgeoning numbers of undocumented migrants created a significant increase in the Mexicano population in the United States. Due to economic reasons, many *braceros* returned to the United States and established residence in *colonias* and barrios throughout Aztlán, the Midwest, and Northwest. Although the United States was no Shangri La, in comparison to México, to some migrants it was the promised land. For all the inequities Mexicanos faced in the United States, socioeconomically they were better off than living under the impoverished conditions of México. In other words, it was much better to be poor in the United States than in México. Both illegal and legal immigration contributed to the maintenance and continuation of the migrant exodus. Legal immigration also contributed to the Mexicano's demographic growth. Immigration on permanent visas began to accelerate during the early 1950s. There was an appreciable increase in legal immigration from 6,372 in 1951 to over 65,000 in 1956. During the decade as a whole, nearly 293,500 were recorded, which meant that during the second half of the 1950s, some 15 percent of the total legal immigration into the United States were Mexicanos. The increased volume did not reflect a relaxation of the law or its administration, but merely indicated the changes introduced by the McCarran-Walter Act of 1952. This recoding of existing status affected mainly Europeans, but left the status of Mexicano immigrants essentially unchanged. The number decreased in 1960 to 30,000; by 1963 increased to 55,000; and by 1964 due to new administrative restrictions decreased to 33,000.[97]

The Mexicano population increase was also due to high birthrates. Above any other ethnic or racial group in the United States, Mexicanos had by far the largest families. Joan W. Moore noted that no other category of people in the United States except the Native American matched their typical family size of 4.8 persons. Whites in Aztlán averaged 3.4 persons per family in 1960, and the nonwhites in the same region, 4.5 persons.[98] Thus, about 31 percent of all Spanish-surname families, over one-fifth of nonwhite families, and only one-tenth of white families had six or more persons. In particular, Mexicanos living in the rural areas had larger families than those living in urban areas.[99] The median age of the entire

Mexicano population was 19.6 in 1960—a full ten years lower than for whites and four years lower than for nonwhites. Some 40 percent of the Mexicano population was younger than fifteen years of age; whereas for whites only about 30 percent were under fifteen.[100]

Hence, the Mexicano population witnessed an appreciable increase after 1950. According to the U.S. Census, the country's population in 1950 was 150,216,110. The Spanish-surname population in Aztlán reached 2,289,550, which by 1960 increased to 3,464,999 nationally. Although the majority of the Mexicano population was native-born in 1950, by 1960, the number of foreign-born had increased. These later represented the largest portions of the population in California, Tejas, and Arizona, in that order. In contrast, fewer economic inducements were available, and fewer foreign-born resided in Colorado or Nuevo México.[101]

The most dramatic population shift for Mexicanos occurred in California. In 1950 California's Spanish-surname population was 760,453; by 1960 it increased dramatically to 1,426,538. Numerically, California had the largest concentration of Mexicanos in the country, followed by Tejas, which had a population in 1950 of 1,033,768 and by 1960 increased to 1,417,810. Nuevo México's Spanish-surname population went from 248,880 in 1950 to 269,122 in 1960; Arizona's increased from 128,318 in 1950 to 194,356 in 1960; and finally, Colorado's went from 118,131 in 1950 to 157,173 in 1960.[102] Thus, in spite of the great population increases that occurred during this epoch of social action politics, Mexicanos were still numerically not a significantly large population, but socioeconomically their status as a people was changing.

Socioeconomic Profile (1950 and 1960)

The Mexicano population's growth changed their socioeconomic profile. Particularly, the trend toward urbanization increased as many left the rural colonias believing that there were greater opportunities in the urban areas for improving their standard of living and general quality of life. Urban life offered new job opportunities, improved working conditions, and higher wages. In Nuevo México alone around a fifth of the rural Mexicano population left the state.[103] The impact of urbanization was such that by the 1950s two-thirds of all Mexicanos lived in towns and cities, and during the 1960s that figure continued to grow. The demand for labor and new technology in an expanding postwar economy allowed more Mexicanos to enter skilled and semiskilled positions.[104] Employment opportunities increased in construction, building maintenance, trucking, refineries, smelters, the garment industry, assembly-line work, hotels and restaurants, retail clerking, gardening, and domestic service.[105]

Large cities throughout Aztlán like Los Angeles, San Diego, San Francisco, San Antonio, Houston, Dallas, Phoenix, Tucson, Denver, Pueblo, Colorado Springs, and numerous smaller cities experienced the migrant exodus of Mexicanos from the rural areas into the urban cities. In the Midwest, cities like Chicago, Kansas City, Toledo, and Detroit, among others, also felt the impact, especially from those who came from Tejas to be part of the seasonal "Migrant Stream." In the northwest, cities like Seattle and Portland also experienced this rural to urban exodus.[106] The rapid growth of the country's interstate highway system connecting the major job centers contributed to increased migration, both seasonal and permanent.[107]

While Mexicanos became more urbanized, they were confronted with a myriad of social problems and new challenges. In most cases, barrios continued to be internal colonies, islands of poverty, surrounded by a white ocean of relative prosperity. The barrios and *colonias* were segregated enclaves that provided the country's liberal capitalist system with a constant source of cheap and exploitable labor, both in the urban and rural areas. Throughout Aztlán no other ethnic group, except the indigenous people, says Joan W. Moore, were "so severely pinched economically."[108]

The impact of the country's liberal capitalist system left Mexicanos at the lowest level of the economy. According to the 1960 Bureau of the Census, about 35 percent of all Spanish-surname families lived below the poverty line of $3,000 annual income, although they comprised less than 10 percent of all the families in Aztlán. Mexicanos were overrepresented among the country's poor, particularly among poor children, of whom 29 percent in Aztlán were Mexicano. By contrast, only 22 percent of poor children, many of them afflicted by malnutrition, were black and slightly less than half were white.[109] Joan Moore writes, "By any yardstick, especially measuring housing, health, and community services, Mexican American poverty is oppressive. In some respects American citizens of Mexican descent are poorer than any other sizable minority in modern America, though this fact has been largely unnoticed."[110] As Oscar Lewis argues, poverty begets poverty, which creates a social and economic web difficult to escape from.[111]

In 1960, Mexicanos only earned $.47 per person for every dollar of white income earned per person. At this time, the median income of Mexicano males in the Southwest was $2,768, which was only 57 percent of that earned by a white male. Most urban Mexicano males were employed as semiskilled workers and laborers. Only 19 percent worked in white-collar occupations (professional, managerial, clerical, and sales) compared to nearly half of the whites. The Mexicano's dismal economic picture was further exacerbated by high unemployment rates, roughly twice those for whites.[112]

The detrimental impact of the poverty syndrome in 1960 was particularly evident in education. Statistics clearly showed the inferior colonized educational status of Mexicanos. That year, it was reported that Mexicanos attained a median of 7.1 years of schooling as compared with 12.1 for whites and 9.0 for nonwhites (adults of twenty-five years or older). California had the highest with 8.6 years, while Texas had the lowest with 4.8 years or only slightly better than functional illiteracy. In every state in the country, blacks were better educated than Mexicanos. The high incidence of functional illiteracy (zero to four years of elementary education) among Mexicano children was seven times that of the white population and nearly twice that of nonwhites as a whole.[113] Further indicative of the educational crises was the low number of Mexicanos who graduated from college. Only 5.6 percent of those aged fourteen or over had "some college," while four times as many whites had some college and twice as many nonwhites attended college.[114]

These problems were further exacerbated by the omnipresence of segregation, another by-product of internal colonialism. From the beginning of the epoch in 1946 to 1954, when the Supreme Court decision of *Brown v. Board of Education* ruled that segregation was unconstitutional, Mexicanos, like blacks, suffered from the pernicious effects of de jure segregation predicated on the "separate but equal doctrine." Hence, for numerous decades, Mexicanos were subjected to an inferior and racist education. Mexicano children, especially in the barrios and *colonias*, had their own separate schools where white racist teachers and administrators deliberately sought to educate them, but only enough to where they would be valuable contributors to the country's cheap labor. Pedagogically, the white educational system sought to systematically destroy the Mexicano's culture and heritage, and the use of the Spanish language. As a result, Mexicano's culture and history were denigrated and the speaking of Spanish was prohibited via spankings or washing the mouth with soap.

Although segregation began to gradually diminish by the late 1950s, its de facto practice continued into the early 1960s. Often in a barrio, a railroad track or road or street was the boundary separating whites from Mexicanos. Local governments were discriminatory in their delivery of services, and employment opportunities were few. In most cases, the white sector of a community was the recipient of resources, often excluding the barrios from water, sewer, paving of roads, or sewage collection services. Even in communities where Mexicanos were in the majority, such as in Tejas, whites held all the "good paying" jobs. Police and sheriffs often abused their authority by brutalizing Mexicanos; they were seen as an "occupation force" by barrio residents. Segregation in public facilities was illustrated by various discriminatory practices. Mexicanos had separate seating areas in movie theaters, usually in the balcony, and were not served in white restaurants located outside the barrios. Access to city-operated swimming pools was limited usually to the end of the week, only after whites had dirtied the water and it was about to be changed. Lastly, especially in Tejas, parks located outside the barrios and white cemeteries were off-limits to Mexicanos. Even in death, Mexicanos were subjected to segregation.[115]

Pachuquismo and *cholismo*, both synonymous with gang formation and violence, were major social problems that plagued most barrios. Their subculture was a "cultural metamorphosis" that utterly rejected white assimilation and distanced themselves from their Mexicanidad by opting to be identified as "Chicanos." *Pachuquismo* as a cultural phenomenon did not end with the Zoot Suit Riots of 1943. Actuated by poverty, racism, and cultural conflict, it grew to where it became a major problem in many of the *colonias* and barrios of both urban and rural areas. A by-product of internal colonialism, gangs acted as if they were armies protecting the nation-state (barrio) from other nation-states. As Frantz Fanon described the allure of violence as a "cleansing force," such was the case with gang violence.[116] Frequently, not recognizing whom the real enemy was, they violently fought with other gangs over control of turf (territory) and over what gang was the most *chingon* (most powerful). With internal colonialism producing a form of tribalism and acute alienation, *pachucos* embraced a subculture of violence, often drugs and alcohol. Young Chicanos died or were wounded in meaningless battles that produced prisoners of poverty. They were sent to state or federal penitentiaries in disproportionate numbers or to the local hospitals, or worse, cemeteries.

However, by the 1950s, *pachuquismo* began to give way to *cholismo*. Culturally, while the latter drew significantly from its Mexicano "mother" culture, the former was less dependent. In essence, both formed and represented a subculture of their own. Where *pachucos* had resorted to *caló*, an admixture of Spanish and English slang where Spanish was more dominant, *cholos* spoke a more English-dominated slang influenced by black vernacular. Caught between two cultures, *cholos* were products of an acculturation process that fostered alienation. While they still sought to maintain a hybrid subculture of their own, as had their predecessors, *los pachucos*, many *cholos* leaned much more toward the white side of the cultural spectrum. Most of the attire of *pachucos* was gone, as well as their lifestyle. Instead of the zoot suits and plumed hats, *cholos* kept the ducktail hairstyle of *pachucos*, used pegged pants, wore gang jackets displaying their colors, and instead of swing became immersed in rhythm and blues. *Cholas* also went through a change as well. Gone were the short skirts and use of the pompadour hairstyle. They still used heavy makeup and wore longer skirts, but now their hair color was heavily peroxided or blonde. With the contradictions of internal colonialism becoming more acute by the 1960s, the *cholo* gangs throughout Aztlán became more numerous and territorial and increasingly more violent than their predecessors, especially because of the rise of the barrio's illegal drug economy.

The detrimental effects of poverty were apparent in other areas of the Mexicano socioeconomic experience. In 1960, one-third (34.6 percent) of Mexicano families suffered from overcrowded housing, while for whites it was a mere 8 percent and for nonwhites 22 percent.[117] The housing crisis in the county's *colonias* and barrios was further intensified by dilapidated or substandard housing, unpaved roads, no sidewalk curb or gutters, no street lights, and general deterioration and decay. Poverty also created deplorable health conditions. Even though the use of the *curanderas* (health practitioner who healed the physical as well as the spiritual) and *parteras* (midwives) was declining in the urban areas by 1960, nevertheless, in the rural areas, this type of Mexicano folk medicine was still in use. The lack of viable medical care was a major problem. Mexicano infants were three times as likely as white babies to die at birth.[118] These socioeconomic conditions intensified the Mexicano's organizational development and participation in ballot box politics.

The Politics of Social Action

Generational Politics: The Mexican American Generation

The epoch of social action politics experienced an intensification of generational politics. Mexicanos identified with two distinct political generations: the Mexicano Generation and the Mexican American Generation. The Mexicano Generation with its genesis in the past epoch, crossed over into the new epoch. The continued influx of Mexicano migrants served to reinforce the growth of the Mexicano Generation. The segregated barrios and *colonias* of Aztlán grew due to the increased exodus. While the new Mexicano migrants brought with them México's parochial political culture, the level of cognitive, affective, and evaluative orientations increased to a hybrid level where the subject and participant categories of political culture increased. The people's political orientation was based upon a socialization process that indoctrinated them with an admixture of values, beliefs, and symbols predicated on nationalism, the Constitution of 1917, and México's semiauthoritarian/democratic political system. Lucian Pye described México's political system as one that belonged to an expanding category of hybrid, part free, part authoritarian systems that did not conform to classical typologies.[119] Wayne A. Cornelius writes:

> On paper, the Mexican government appears to be structured much like the U.S. government: A presidential system, three autonomous branches

of government (executive, legislative, judicial) with checks and balances, and federalism with considerable autonomy at the local level (municipal) level. In practice, however, México's system of government was far removed from the U.S. model. Decision making has been highly central-ized. The president, operating with relatively few restraints on his author-ity, completely dominated the legislative and judicial branches.[120]

México's political system continued to be governed by a one-party dictatorship under the aegis of the Partido Revolucionario Institucional (PRI).

Politically, however, the epoch of social action was driven by the ethos of the Mexican American Generation (MAG).[121] It was during this epoch that the MAG reached its apogee. Historian Mario T. Garcia places the MAG from 1930 to the early 1960s. However, its historical roots go back to the 1920s to when La Orden de los Hijos de America and LULAC were formed. Most of the Mexicano political elites, especially politicians, that preceded its emergence, were middle-class rather than lower-class or poor. They embraced either a buffer or "want to be white" colonizing role. In general, they espoused the same political attitudes of accommodation, adaptation, and acculturation, if not assimilation. While some minor differences existed, they all adhered to the ideal of struggling for the Mexi-cano's integration into the country's liberal capitalist system.

Proponents of the MAG's ethos were adamant in their pursuit of the alleged "American Dream." While some were bilingual, most advocated that their pri-mary language should be English. Carlos Muñoz explains, "In their minds, politi-cal accommodation and assimilation was the only path toward equal status in a racist society. Integration in education and at all levels of society would result, they believed, in the acceptance of their people as first-class citizens."[122] Their zeal for integration was such that they had absolutely no interest in going back to México. Their allegiance was unequivocally to the United States. Garcia fur-ther notes, "Coming of political age during the reform period of the New Deal and experiencing the patriotic idealism generated by World War II, Mexican Americans expected more from American life than immigrants." He explains:

This was a generation, certainly in its manifestation as a political genera-tion, which sought its place in American history. Mexican Americans, like other descendents of the new immigrants, came of political age by the Great Depression and World War II. Unlike the nineteenth-century Mex-ican Americans or the previous generation of immigrants from México, Mexican Americans by the 1930s and 1940s recognized themselves as U.S. citizens knew that their country was the United States and not México, had become increasingly socialized to U.S. norms, ideologies, and mass culture, and they expected to be treated like other Americans. At the same time they were not ashamed of their ethnic cultural backgrounds. . . . Faced with dualities and paradoxes as Mexican Americans, this generation actively sought the meaning of being American and its place in U.S. society.[123]

While the leadership of the MAG was essentially middle class, there was some inclusion of the working class. Although both women and men were intrinsic parts of this unique leadership, Garcia explains, "It was mostly dominated by men." Ideologically, most within its ranks were liberals, although there were some radicals. However, the bottom line was that none were revolutionary in their politics. At best, a few intellectuals were reformers who believed in the virtues of liberal capitalism. Hence, many were willing to acculturate to white values and sought integration into a liberal capitalist system that still practiced the use of an "apartheid system" that shut them out.[124]

Politically the MAG generally espoused what Ignacio Garcia refers to as the "liberal agenda," which meant "the traditional manner by which immigrants and minorities were supposed to integrate into the American mainstream. This would include education, good citizenship, patriotism, alliances with liberal groups, faith in government, and cultural assimilation."[125] They advocated social change predicated on inclusion, integration, and on making Mexican Americans viable political participants. Few identified or subscribed to the politics of confrontation, protest, or unbridled militancy. Change was to be brought about by working within the existing social order and its electoral and pressure group politics. In the words of Mario Barrera, "World War II was a watershed for Chicano political and community organizations. Chicanos who fought in the war were from a political generation."[126] Because of the MAG, new social action organizations were formed and some existing ones revitalized. Increasingly, Mexicanos beyond Nuevo México became more engaged in electoral or ballot box efforts. While most *colonias* and barrios were still internal colonies, there was a growing sense or *conciencia* (consciousness) that something needed to be done to alter their political and socioeconomic status.

This sense of consciousness was also attributable to the rise of what Manuel G. Gonzales calls the "Mexican American Intelligentsia." Those who could be categorized as intellectuals included Ernesto Galarza, PhD, from Colombia University, an educator, union organizer, and specialist in labor history; Américo Paredes, PhD, from the University of Texas, folklorist, poet, and novelist; and Jovita Mireles Gonzales, a folklorist and historian. Three others, however, particularly influenced and helped shape the MAG. These were Carlos Eduardo Castañeda (1896–1958), Arthur Campa (1905–1978), and George Sanchez (1906–1972). Castañeda obtained his PhD from the University of Texas, wrote a dozen major historical works, and was the first historian to write about the history of Mexicanos in the Southwest. Campa received his PhD from Colombia University in languages and achieved intellectual prominence as a folklorist. Sanchez got his EdD in education administration and became known for his writings, particularly the *Forgotten People*, an impressionist history of Mexicanos. He was a pioneer in bilingual education and was politically active as a civil rights leader in various organizations and causes.[127] These scholars and a few others, through their writings, teaching, and activism, were purveyors of the MAG ethos.

Thus, the MAG had a tremendous impact in the politics of existing organizations as well as in the creation of new ones.

The Third Organizational Renaissance

While Mexicano politics in the United States was still predicated on resistance, accommodation, and adaptation, a vigorous new spirit committed to social and political action permeated the epoch. Influenced by the ethos of the MAG, Mexicanos were more cognizant of the injustices confronting them and resolute in their efforts to seek redress. This was particularly true of returning war veterans and urban factory workers who were more assertive in their pursuit of civil and human rights than in the two previous epochs. Impelled by growing discontent, Mexicanos adopted a mode of politics that was more social action-oriented, which meant it was characterized by more civic participation through both organizational advocacy and ballot box politics. Overall, however, it was a time when Mexicanos devoted their energies to personal economic and social betterment.[128] The MAG contributed significantly to the rebirth of political activism by the formation of new organizations. Some became the training ground for the next generation of activists.[129] Driven by this more change-oriented ethos, and rising expectations, some Mexicanos chose to deal with social problems plaguing the *colonias* and barrios via organizational politics. Organizations became the quickest and most efficient means to challenge existing policies and propose social change. With one exception, the overwhelming establishment of new interest groups adhered to a buffer political role.

Mutual Benefit Organizations

During this epoch, *mutualistas* continued to grow. As buffers, they provided burial insurance, self-help assistance, and social and cultural outlets for those who continued to cling tenaciously to the heritage of the mother country, México. In particular, *logias* (local fraternal lodges) would sponsor dances, dinners, and fiestas throughout the year. While extremely well organized and generally well led, the *mutualistas* continued to maintain an apolitical position. This meant that they did not become involved in controversial issues or electoral politics. However, Miguel Tirado indicates that due to their size and popularity they offered "a potential source of great political strength in the Mexican community."[130] While the *mutualista* membership ranks were getting older and grayer they were still being replenished by the influx of documented and undocumented workers from México who settled in the countless *colonias* and barrios. Thus, while *mutualistas* remained active throughout Aztlán, in California, La Sociedad Progresista Mexicana was still the strongest, largest, and by far the most influential.[131]

Older Existent Interest Groups

LA ALIANZA HISPANA AMERICAN   During this epoch, La Alianza was a *mutualista* that had evolved into a more traditional interest group. Growing administrative and membership problems riddled its development, however. Newly elected supreme president Candelario B. Sedillo was able to resolve them by 1941. During the next five years, he initiated other reforms that positively impacted its faltering membership. While its membership in 1940 reached some 17,000, by 1946, it had declined to 11,486; but because of Sedillo's instituted reforms, the membership increased to 12,906 by 1947. These reforms were called the "21 Point Fraternal Service Program," which expanded the *mutualista* type of services offered and gave it much more of a civil rights focus. One of the most controversial reforms was Sedillo's push for assimilation, which introduced discord among some of the leadership and membership. This "want to be white" role was a contradictory new direction for La Alianza. From its inception it had followed a course of development based on what Briegel describes as "on the idea of separation."[132] Sedillo's reelection bid in 1948 met stiff opposition by Gregorio Garcia, La Alianza's supreme attorney. Sedillo won the alleged rigged election, and Garcia challenged the results. For the next two years, Garcia litigated the matter before Arizona's courts—from Maricopa's County Superior Court to the State Supreme Court. Because of the power struggle, its membership by 1951 decreased to 11,595.[133]

During his three-year tenure as supreme president, Garcia shifted the emphasis of La Alianza to a civil rights agenda in which the struggle against school segregation was prioritized. In 1950 leaders from within La Alianza collaborated with others from throughout Aztlán to form a new organization, the American

Council on Spanish-Speaking People. Committed to eliminating segregation, this new organization assisted La Alianza's leadership in its first major desegregation case against the Tolleson School District in Arizona. Filed in 1951 in the federal court, their suit was successful in ending the practice of the segregation of Mexicano children, however, only in that particular school district. The federal court agreed with La Alianza's legal arguments that the Tolleson School District was not equal for Mexicanos when it came to buildings, teaching equipment, and teacher preparation.[134]

La Alianza made an unsuccessful attempt in 1952 to desegregate all the schools in Arizona. Yet in a subsequent case, La Alianza filed a successful suit desegregating the swimming pool of Winslow, Arizona, that was settled out of court. According to city ordinance, Mexicanos were allowed use of the pool only one day out of the week, on Wednesday. The day after, the pool's water was drained and disinfected prior to being used by whites of the community. After initiating various other suits and discrimination struggles, in 1955 La Alianza created the Civil Rights Division. Ralph Guzman, an East Los Angeles activist, who later became a professor of political science, headed it. With a focus on coordinating the legal efforts against violation of Mexicanos' civil rights, it joined the NAACP in a case involving the desegregation of the El Centro School District, in California. After going through some legal maneuverings, the suit was settled out of court in 1956, producing a victory for both black and Mexicano students.[135]

During Operation Wetback, La Alianza's leadership protested against the decline of civil and constitutional rights of innocent Mexicanos and asked the federal government to respect the human rights of undocumented migrants. Legal redress and publicity were the two major weapons used by La Alianza leaders in their struggle against discrimination. In the arena of immigration, it also dealt with cases involving alleged violations of civil rights, especially of the right of some people to be in this country.[136] Although nonpartisan, La Alianza in Arizona acted similar to a political machine. According to Hernandez, "Senators and members of the House of Representatives, ambassadors, state legislators, sheriffs, county assessors, mayors, and members of the judiciary, all belonged to the [Alianza]." He further explains that white politicians, such as Senator Barry Goldwater, were members.[137] Yet by 1956, La Alianza's leadership developed a close working relationship with the Democratic Party. That year, Estrada was a delegate to the 1956 National Convention, and in 1960 La Alianza's leadership joined other organizations in support of Democrat presidential candidate John F. Kennedy in forming the "Viva Kennedy Clubs." With Kennedy's election, several of La Alianza's leaders were rewarded with appointments, including its Supreme President Ralph Estrada and Ralph Guzman.

With the appointment of Estrada, Carlos McCormick, who had an appointment with the State Department, left this position and was elected as La Alianza's supreme president in 1963. That same year, he was forced to resign due to a lien placed on all insurance certificates.[138] McCormick was indicted in 1965 on eleven counts of embezzling a total of $169,000 from La Alianza. The supreme vice president, J. M. Romero, replaced McCormick and found himself leading an organization about ready to collapse. Thus, the indictment forced the organization into receivership, and by 1965, for all intents and purposes, little was left of the once influential *mutualista* turned civil rights organization.

LEAGUE OF UNITED LATIN AMERICAN CITIZENS (LULAC)   Another earlier organization, LULAC, experienced revitalization. In 1930 LULAC entered the arena of education reform by initiating the first legal challenge to segregation in Tejas. It filed the class action suit *Independent School District v. Slavtierra*. The courts, however, ruled in favor of the school district, stating that it did not violate the Mexicano children's constitutional rights. The decision was a major blow to LULAC's efforts to end segregation in Tejas.[139] As a consequence, during World War II, it experienced a decline in membership. But beginning in 1944, LULAC once again became increasingly active, especially in the struggle to end segregation in the schools. That year, it set new goals for itself: to eradicate discrimination and realize equal protection under the law. LULAC sought political unification and involvement from the local to national levels.[140] Its new agenda was presented at the First Regional Conference on Education of the Spanish-Speaking People in the Southwest at the University of Texas, Austin on December 13–15, 1945. Academicians George I. Sanchez of the University of Texas and A. L. Campa of the University of New México took an active role in the proceedings, which produced a condemnation of segregation.[141]

After World War II, while it continued to support the notion of ardent assimilation, LULAC took on the challenge of desegregation and antidiscrimination. Benjamin Marquez further elucidates, "As in the 1930s, LULAC would reiterate its attachment to United States society and its long standing goal to integrate Mexican Americans into that society. The campaign it waged against discrimination carried also the ideological combination of conformity, patriotism, and free market capitalism."[142] However, it perceived education pragmatically as a means of promoting upward mobility and better jobs.

In 1946 LULAC supported a successful desegregation class suit filed by Gonzalo and Felicitas Méndez against four school districts in Orange County, California: Westminster, Garden Grove, El Modeno, and Santa Ana. The suit alleged that their policies of segregating Mexicano students throughout most if not all of the elementary grades were discriminatory and in violation of the Fourteenth Amendment. The plaintiffs, numbering some five thousand, charged that the school districts discriminated against Mexicano students, who were not permitted to attend other schools in their districts, composed predominantly of white students. Attorney David C. Marcus of Los Angeles, representing the National Lawyers Guild and the American Civil Liberties Union, argued the case.[143] In 1946 Judge Paul J. McCormack in the U.S. District Court in southern California heard the unprecedented *Méndez v. Westminister School District* case and ruled in favor of the plaintiffs by declaring that segregation was unconstitutional. Consequently the affected districts were enjoined to discontinue their practice of segregation. On April 14, 1947, the U.S. Court of Appeals for the Ninth Circuit Court affirmed the decision, stating, according to Acuña, "that Mexicans and other children were entitled to equal protection of the laws, and that neither language nor race could be used as a reason to segregate them." The *Méndez* suit became one of the most important of the Mexicano political experience for it accelerated the end of de jure segregation in California.[144]

Because of the suit, the Associated Farmers of Orange County initiated a "red baiting" campaign against Mexicanos. LULAC responded in late 1946 by launching its own countercampaign. Assisted by Industrial Areas Foundation organizer Fred Ross, LULAC pushed for support of Proposition 11, the Fair Employment Practices Act, which prohibited discrimination in employment. LULAC chapters conducted a door-to-door voter registration campaign and unsuccessfully ran a candidate for the segregated El Modena School District Board. In 1947, the district attorney alleged that LULAC in Orange County had been infiltrated by communists and specifically demanded that LULAC's leadership be dismissed. LULAC's leadership, choosing not to alienate the district attorney, capitulated. As a result, lacking sufficient support, Ross left for Los Angeles.[145]

Encouraged by its success of the Westminster Case, LULAC in 1948 moved aggressively in Tejas to desegregate the schools. Although the state attorney general had issued an opinion forbidding racial segregation in the schools, it continued to be practiced. That year, LULAC filed a desegregation suit, *Minerva Delgado v. Bastrop Independent School District*, which sought to put an end to the school segregation practices in four Tejas counties. As in the *Westminster* Case, the federal court ruled that the segregation of Mexicano children violated the Fourteenth Amendment. Mario Garcia points out that the *Delgado* case "went one step further and specifically declared unconstitutional the segregation of Mexican Americans in separate class rooms within integrated schools."[146] Both of these suits proved to be invaluable precedents for the National Association for the Advancement of Colored People in the landmark case of *Brown v. Board of Education* (1954), which ruled that the "separate but equal doctrine" was unconstitutional.

While de facto segregation continued until the 1960s to be LULAC's priority issue, in 1954 with the collaboration of the American G.I. Forum it sent attorneys to argue the *Hernandez v. the State of Texas* case before the U.S. Supreme Court. The case was an important step toward ending legal discrimination against Mexicanos. It cleared the way for Mexicanos in Tejas to serve on trial juries.[147] During the rest of the 1950s, LULAC's councils continued to accentuate various aspects of the education agenda. In 1957, LULAC initiated a preschool English-language program called the "Little School of the 400." According to Garcia, "These preschools for Mexican American children sought to teach them 400 basic English words. The hope was that this would lessen the cultural and linguistic shocks that Spanish-speaking children generally experience as they began their education."[148] The program proved to be so successful that it became the model for the federally funded Project Head Start during the early 1960s.[149]

By the end of the epoch in 1965, LULAC had grown into a national organization, with numerous councils throughout the Southwest and Midwest. In 1960, LULAC reported it had a total of some 150 councils in comparison to 46 in 1932.[150] By 1965, LULAC had already replaced La Alianza as the leading organization within Mexicano communities. Yet because of its middle-class base and ardent espousal of integration and assimilation, it failed to connect with many of the interests and aspirations of the working-class Mexicanos. David Gutiérrez writes, "LULAC was the foremost opponent of the Bracero Program and the use of wetback labor." He explains that if anything, LULAC's long-standing positions stressed the need for Mexican Americans to assimilate on the one hand and to support restrictive immigration policies toward México on the other.[151] This was further evident in its zealous conservative posture and in its patriotic support of Operation Wetback. Instead of speaking out against its inequities, LULAC joined the political chorus of right-wing nativist groups in support of it and failed to speak out or organize on the issue of McCarthyism. Thus, as an interest group, LULAC continued to be steadfast in its espousal of liberal capitalism and refused to become involved directly in electoral politics or in direct action struggles that appeared militant or radical.

MEXICAN AMERICAN MOVEMENT (MAM)   As an organization, MAM did not survive the epoch of social action politics. From its inception MAM was a youth-oriented organization that subscribed to essentially a buffer colonizing role, but World War II took a toll on its development. Despite plans, meetings, and additional conferences, after World War II, MAM was not able to galvanize its membership or support base. Few of MAM's members who had served in the armed forces during the war resumed their participation. For the next five years, with very few members, MAM struggled to stay afloat. Periodically, it became involved in some issues impacting the Mexicano communities in southern California. One such issue was the *Méndez* suit in 1946–1948 where it joined LULAC and others to litigate the case. Some of its members also played key organizing roles in the formation of the Community Service Organization in 1947–1948 and collaborated closely on various activities with LULAC. Thus, lacking resources and a membership base, the leadership became disillusioned, and by 1950 the organization became defunct.[152] It left a legacy as a precursor to many of the Chicano Movement's student organizations that emerged during the next epoch.

New Social Action Interest Groups

Indicative of this period's political renaissance was the formation of several new interest group-types of social action organizations. They shared a number of common characteristics: adhered to a buffer colonizing role, were advocacy change-oriented, strategically relied on use of service, were voluntary membership-based, were liberal capitalist ideologically, identified with the liberal agenda and ethos of the Mexican American Generation, and overall, most were lower to middle class in membership. In essence, they approximated the role of traditional interest groups in that they sought to influence policy and advance the interests of their particular constituents. The word *approximate* is used because none possessed the resources, professional staff, and lobbyists that typified many white or black interest groups. Unlike previous Mexicano social action organizations, like LULAC and La Alianza Hispano-Americana, these new social action organizations were more assertive in their politics and less assimilation oriented.

COMMUNITY SERVICE ORGANIZATION (CSO)   The first such social action organization to be established after World War II was the CSO. On September 7, 1947, the CSO was founded by an energetic group of Los Angeles businessmen, unionists, workers, and veterans.[153] Formed in California in 1947, the CSO emerged out of the Committee to Elect Edward Roybal to the Los Angeles city council. Although Roybal lost the election, the campaign provided the organizing impetus that led to the CSO's formation. In the aftermath of the election, the committee met and developed future plans, wrote a constitution and bylaws, raised funds, and held open community meetings to discuss a variety of issues.

Initially, due to their agenda being political, they named it the "Community Political Organization." Acuña explains, "Not wanting to be confused with the Communist Party (CP) or partisan politics, the emerging organization changed its name in 1947 to the Community Service Organization (CSO)."[154]

That same year, the fledgling organization caught the attention of Saul Alinsky's Industrial Areas Foundation (IAF), which earlier had sent community organizer Fred Ross to assist in the organizing of the Unity Leagues in neighboring San Bernardino and Riverside counties. Ross was sent to Los Angeles and assisted CSO founders and leaders Antonio Rios and Gilbert Anaya in the CSO's development. By 1948, the IAF was the main source of funding for the new barrio-based social action organization. According to Gutiérrez, "Although the IAF grant to CSO prohibited direct participation in partisan politics, CSO—like so many other Mexican American organizations—were inherently political from the outset."[155] As a prelude to another Roybal city council bid in 1949, the CSO mounted an unprecedented grassroots voter registration drive that produced some fifteen thousand new voters, mostly Mexicanos. This time, Roybal won a resounding victory due to the well-organized CSO get-out-the-vote drive. His victory was a major political achievement for the CSO, since Roybal was the first Mexicano to be elected to the city council in Los Angeles since 1888.[156]

From 1949 to 1965, the CSO shifted to a more social service agenda that in some aspects resembled a *mutualista*. Miguel David Tirado notes, "This change in approach, however, did mean that CSO would never again publicly support a candidate for political office even though unofficial fundraising functions continued to be held for those candidates responsive to the problems of the Mexican American minority."[157] With its office and small organizing staff in Los Angeles, it developed a number of service programs. Gutiérrez writes that with the Roybal election, the "CSO concentrated its community service efforts on nonpartisan voter registration drives, neighborhood improvement, legal advice, youth activities, health screening and referral, and legislative advocacy at the local and state levels."[158] In 1950, with the assistance of 150 voter registrars, the CSO registered 32,000 new Mexicano voters within three months, which in San Fernando contributed to the election of businessman Ernesto Padilla to the San Fernando city council.[159] The CSO also developed a store cooperative, death benefit insurance, consumer complaint center, credit union, pilot housing, leadership training, and ongoing citizenship training. The latter was successful in producing forty thousand new citizens by 1960.[160] During these years, CSO was active in dealing with a variety of issues such as police brutality, gang violence, housing discrimination, and school segregation.

Initially, with its strong barrio focus, the CSO was less assimilation-oriented

than LULAC and La Alianza. By the early 1960s, however, its membership base
had changed and was more middle class, included whites, and had become
increasingly accommodation-oriented. It also embraced a much more social service posture rather than a political one. While CSO did not support the Bracero
Program and avoided taking a stand on the controversy of Operation Wetback,
it pushed for making the undocumented migrants citizens. However, some of its
leadership and members did join coalitions that categorically opposed Operation
Wetback. Unlike most other Mexicano organizations in California, for a time, in
dealing with issues, it had the capacity to lobby in Sacramento. By the early
1960s, CSO had a total of thirty-four chapters in California and Arizona and
membership of ten thousand.

By the early 1960s, however, the CSO began to decline. With the loss of IAF
funding, for its sustenance, the CSO relied on federal, state, and foundation
grants. This transition stifled its advocacy role to where it was almost totally
service-oriented. Internally, power struggles over direction and focus engendered
schisms, such as the one in 1962 when CSO state director Cesar Chavez resigned
when the CSO would not initiate a program to organize farmworkers. Concomitantly, difficulties arose when incorporating the various state chapters due to
localism and parochialism. By 1965, the CSO had lost much its unique organizing thrust.

AMERICAN G.I. FORUM (AGIF)   Faced with innumerable problems, returning
war veterans in Tejas formed AGIF. This motivation was the pervasive discrimination Mexicano veterans experienced, especially in Tejas, in the areas of education, employment, medical attention, and housing. Under the able leadership of
Dr. Hector P. García, a former World War II surgeon with a distinguished military record, and attorney Gustavo (Gus) García, the developing Mexicano veterans' organization was given impetus at a meeting attended by some seven hundred
veterans, on March 26, 1948. The meeting produced a consensus to form a permanent social action group with the capacity to lobby on behalf of veterans, and
Hector García was elected to lead it. Henry A. J. Ramos explains why they
decided to select a name that did not include the group's ethnic identity:

> The absence of direct ethnic identification with the Mexican American
> community was intentional and largely the result of Garcia's thinking.
> That they had served their nation honorably in the military on the front
> lines of combat accounted for the use of GI in the organizational title. . . .
> Finally, the term Forum was chosen to connote the group's commitment
> to open discourse and to the principles and ideals of democracy.[161]

Soon thereafter, a logo and an official constitution were developed, which accentuated AGIF's patriotic character. The logo showed the U.S. flag complete with red, white, and blue coloring, and thirteen stars representing the original thirteen colonies. The thirteenth star appeared in the middle of the logo above the organizational design. Ramos notes, "Symbolizing the Star of David, this star conveyed the organization's religious conscience." Like LULAC and La Alianza, the AGIF ideologically embraced accommodation, adaptation, and the liberal capitalist system. According to Mario Barrera, "Not unexpectedly, given changing circumstances, it did not place the same heavy stress on assimilation" as did LULAC.[162] A cardinal objective was to "secure the blessings of American Democracy" through strictly nonviolent means. AGIF expressed a strong loyalty to the United States and the constitution and a commitment to defend the country from all its enemies. The core of its objectives was to "aid needy and disabled veterans."[163]

AGIF's formation, however, was originally expedited by the refusal of a white-owned mortuary to bury a Mexicano war veteran named Private Felix Longoria, at their cemetery at Three Rivers, Tejas.[164] Longoria had been killed in action in the Philippines, and when his body was returned home, the local mortuary, Rice Funeral Home, refused to bury him at the segregated cemetery on the grounds that whites would object to having a Mexicano buried in their cemetery. García turned the issue into a crusade with national visibility. He was able to secure the support of newly elected U.S. senator Lyndon B. Johnson, who defused the issue by having Private Longoria's remains buried with full honors in 1949 at Arlington National Cemetery in Virginia.

The fact that Private Longoria could not be buried in the white cemetery was illustrative of the continued military paradox Mexicanos faced: they were good enough to die for a country that even in death segregated them and did not consider them equal to whites. Not everyone was happy with the compromise; some believed Longoria should have been buried in his hometown, and vowed to continue the struggle against discrimination. Yet for García and others in the fledging AGIF, the Longaria issue was used strategically for its effective expansion. In Tejas, AGIF took the issue of discriminatory practices against Mexicanos in white cemeteries before the state's Good Neighbor Commission but were unsuccessful.[165] About the same time, García was successful in eliminating discriminatory practices at the Corpus Christi Hospital.[166] Thus, the Longoria issue proved to be politically lucrative in that it helped build AGIF into a regional organization with numerous chapters and a membership that demanded justice.[167] AGIF's expansion was so rapid that by 1949 some one hundred chapters were formed in Tejas alone.

Throughout the 1950s and early 1960s, AGIF chapters throughout Aztlán and the Midwest were grouped within geographical districts. These districts in turn were placed under a state Board of Directors.[168] Women and youth were encouraged to become auxiliary members. A "Ladies Auxiliary" was formed, and the youth had the "Junior GI Forum." According to Ramos, both were accorded "full voting power equal to that of senior male members." Numerous women, such as Nellie Navarro from Kansas, Faid Galván of Colorado, Dominga Coronado and Margarita Simón of Tejas, and Isabelle Télles of Nuevo México, distinguished themselves as leaders and organizers.[169]

From 1949 to 1965, AGIF's social action activities were multi-issue oriented. With its emphasis on patriotic symbols and rhetoric, it was able to effect changes during the "red baiting" era of McCarthyism. During this difficult and precarious time, AGIF made a strong commitment to the attainment of civil rights and an end to segregation. Several class action suits were filed by AGIF aimed at desegregating schools, recreational facilities, and transportation.[170] Some of these suits were filed in collaboration with LULAC, such as *Hernandez v. the State of Texas*, which was argued before the U.S. Supreme Court, and cleared the way for Mexicanos to serve on trial juries. AGIF's commitment to education was reflected in its motto, "Education is our freedom, and freedom should be everybody's business"[171] and as a result, many of its chapters developed scholarship projects.

AGIF categorically opposed the Bracero Program and strongly supported Operation Wetback. The organization believed that both the *bracero* and undocumented worker impinged upon the welfare and interests of the Mexicano born in the United States. David Gutiérrez notes, "Forum members insisted that much of the poverty, ill health, under-employment, and low educational attainment was tied at least indirectly to the adverse impact of Mexican immigration."[172] Driven by their adherence to the Mexican American Generation ethos, AGIF's leadership, namely García, failed to recognize that it was liberal capitalist forces that were creating the Mexicano's socioeconomic plight, not Mexicano *braceros* or undocumented workers. Both AGIF and LULAC's conservative posture on immigration served to buttress the nativism that pervaded the McCarthy era.

Politically, AGIF remained more moderate than LULAC. Although it was officially nonpartisan, AGIF's members were encouraged to become involved in politics. For example, AGIF promoted with some success the "pay your poll tax" and "get out the vote" drives[173] to improve the political impact and posture of the Mexicanos. With most of AGIF's membership and leadership registered as Democrats, AGIF played a very prominent organizational leadership role during the 1960 presidential election. Its 150 chapters collaborated with other organizations in the formation of the "Viva Kennedy Clubs," which are examined later in this chapter. In 1964 once again, AGIF's leadership established the "Viva Johnson" network. By 1965, AGIF's political clout along with LULAC's was such that both were awarded by the Johnson administration a $5 million grant to fund a job-training program called Service, Employment, and Redevelopment (SER). In addition, AGIF was instrumental in establishing the Inter-Agency Committee on Mexican American Affairs.[174]

Other New Interest Groups

In 1963, two new social action organizations emerged that will be examined in the next chapter. In Nuevo México, a charismatic preacher, Reies Lopez Tijerina, created La Alianza Federal de Mercedes. As an interest group, initially it adhered to a buffer role, committed to the recovery of land grants. For the next two years it concentrated on building up its grassroots membership and conducted lobbying efforts to advance its land grant agenda. Meanwhile, in Colorado, Rodolfo "Corky" Gonzales, a former boxer, poet, and businessman, formed Los Voluntarios, a Denver-based interest group that dealt with a variety of local issues, especially police brutality. Both entities played important and significant organizational leadership roles during the subsequent "epoch of protest."

FORMATION OF ORGANIZATIONS WITHIN ORGANIZATIONS   Activists of the Mexican American Generation also made several attempts to unify individual organizations under one structure. One such effort was the formation of the American Council of Spanish-Speaking People (ACSSC), which was a result of a national convention held in El Paso, Tejas, on May 18–19, 1951. Called by Dr. George Sanchez, leaders of various organizations met and decided to form the ACSSC. It became a national coalition of Mexicano organizations, primarily including AGIF, LULAC, the CSO, and La Alianza Hispano-Americana. Tibo J. Chavez, lieutenant governor of Nuevo México, was elected as its first president, and Dr. Sanchez served as its executive director.[175]

The ACSSC's general purpose was to coordinate the various efforts dealing with desegregation cases. Its five cardinal objectives included bringing closure to segregation in the schools, ending discrimination in housing, fostering participation of Mexicanos in juries and in public office, having equal access to public facilities, and ending discrimination in employment of Mexicanos in government agencies.[176] With a grant from the Robert Marshall Foundation in 1952, the council worked during the ensuing years on a number of desegregation cases. In 1955, La Alianza developed a civil rights department headed by Ralph Guzman, who became its director and collaborated with the NAACP in dealing with a number of cases. Without a continued source of funding, the ACSSC became defunct by the late 1950s, but its former member organizations continued their struggles against segregation and discrimination.

At the local level, a second effort to foster social action collaborations was initiated in 1953 in Los Angeles, under the auspices of the Council of Mexican American Affairs (CMMA). Organized by a few professionals, the CMMA sought to unify and coordinate the activities on community issues.[177] Comprised of forty-four member organizations, the CMMA started with a small staff, office, and budget that in great part derived from organizational membership dues. As a nonpartisan, nonsectarian, and nonprofit organization, it promoted leadership formation and sought to coordinate the various groups concerned with the betterment of the Mexican American in the Los Angeles region.[178]

From its inception, the CMMA took an elitist middle-class orientation, which meant that lower-class Mexicanos in the barrios of Los Angeles failed to identify with its efforts. As an umbrella group, the CMMA also failed to develop the grassroots power base needed to deal with the community issues in part because of its buffer role. Its professional and business leadership spent most of its time holding political banquets and community forums.[179] With a refusal by some of the organizations to pay their dues and a lack of sufficient resources, the CMMA declined within a few years. After several years of dormancy, there was an attempt to revitalize it in 1963, which ended in failure.[180]

Political Pressure Interest Groups

During the epoch of social action politics, several political pressure organizations (PPOs) were formed, which adopted a buffer political colonizing role. While social action organizations such as LULAC, La Alianza, the CSO, and AGIF dabbled in electoral or pressure group politics, none were explicitly partisan or totally committed to advancing a political agenda for Mexicanos. PPOs were interest groups that sought not only to influence public policy, but elections as well. They sought to register and politically educate voters, conduct get-out-the-vote drives, and endorse candidates. Strategically, while adhering to an accommodation approach, PPOs were more assertive in their use of pressure tactics than the typical issue-oriented social action interest group.

THE UNITY LEAGUES   The first Mexicano PPOs were the Unity Leagues formed after World War II. Spawned in southern California, specifically in San Bernardino and Riverside counties, the Unity Leagues were active from 1946 to 1948. They were the creation of Ignacio Lopez, editor of the Spanish language weekly newspaper *El Espectador*, and Fred Ross, organizer for the Industrial Areas Foundation.[181] Richard A. Ibañez, an aggressive attorney in the area who later became a judge, was also one of its leaders. In explaining their genesis, Mario Garcia writes, "In February 1946 *El Espectador* reported that a group of fifty young Mexican Americans, many of them World War II veterans, had met in Pomona and organized the Pomona Unity League for the purpose of aiding the Mexican American community by engaging in civil-political affairs."[182] They were formed because World War II veterans felt they had sacrificed and risked their lives for the defense of democracy while it was paradoxically denied to them at home.[183] Unity Leagues were established in Pomona, Chino, Ontario, San Bernardino, and Redlands,[184] and sought to break out of their politically powerless syndrome.

Unlike existing organizations of the time, the Unity Leagues were explicitly political in their focus. They did not promote radical revolution or confrontation politics, but appealed to Mexicanos to become engaged in ballot box politics. In fact, Garcia notes, "In an editorial entitled Democracy lives, Lopez encouraged Mexican Americans to rally behind the American way of life, which was rooted in the basic dignity of the individual, regardless of race, nationality, religion, or social background." Lopez ardently believed that Mexicanos essentially had two choices: they could either accept their second-class citizenship, as many had done for generations, or they could struggle by getting organized for equality. For him, with a growing Mexicano population, the time was propitious to demand the Mexicano's rightful place in U.S. society.[185] Thus, ideologically the Unity Leagues were liberal capitalists and sought political integration via political action and change.

The leagues organized massive voter registration and political education drives and encouraged Mexicanos in the barrios to run for office. Under the organizing leadership of Fred Ross, they perceived the vote and organizing as powerful mechanisms for change. In the words of Acuña, "They emphasized mass action, bloc voting, and neighborhood protests."[186] Strategically, their candidates stressed "good citizenship" and "honorability." In addition, they ran grassroots political campaigns based on block committees and made appeals to the people's sense of nationalism and loyalty, and their Mexicano identity.[187] As early as 1946, politically organized in "squadrons," Unity Leagues mounted grassroots efforts for get-out-the-vote drives that stressed "elect one of your own." Within San Bernardino and Riverside counties, they proved effective in helping elect in 1946 the first Mexicano to the Chino City Council, Andrew Morales. During their brief two-year existence, the Unity Leagues supported a number of Mexicanos for local offices.

The Unity Leagues were also unique in their social action orientation. In unprecedented fashion, they campaigned vigorously against the blatant discrimination that was evident in housing, restaurants, theaters, schools, cemeteries, police services, and public accommodations.[188] They initiated lawsuits and organized to create the requisite pressure to achieve change. Their grassroots orientation meant that they were barrio-based and were comprised mostly of middle-class and lower-class Mexicanos, including some undocumented workers. While they practiced an assertive-type accommodation to achieve reform, they did not press the agenda of assimilation. In fact, one can describe them as precursors to the "cultural nationalists" in that they accentuated ethnic pride and solidarity.

With the defeat of Samuel Calderon to the Chino City Council in 1948 and the presence of infighting, the Unity Leagues disbanded, with most of the membership joining other organizations such as the CSO. By this time, divisions had developed in Chino over the lack of leadership by Councilman Andrew Morales, who had lost favor with Lopez and others within the Unity Leagues. In the end, the ephemeral Unity Leagues left a political legacy through their unique combination of political and social action. This made them a model of community organization that was emulated subsequently by other organizations, such as the CSO.

THE MEXICAN AMERICAN POLITICAL ASSOCIATION (MAPA)   The second political pressure organization to emerge was the Mexican American Political Association (MAPA). Until the late 1950s no distinctly Mexicano political organization existed across Aztlán. The genesis of MAPA as a buffer political entity can be traced to the California Democratic Council convention held in 1959, where Edward Roybal convoked a meeting of Mexicano delegates. As a result, a call was made to establish a Mexicano political organization.[189] Their rational was a growing dissatisfaction with the Democratic Party's lack of support for Mexicano candidates. Specifically their dissatisfaction was due to the lack of financial support for Edward Roybal's campaign for lieutenant governor in 1954 and again for Henry (Hank) Lopez, a Harvard-trained attorney, who ran for state treasurer in 1958. In both cases, the two received the Democratic Party nominations, but failed to secure strong organizational support from the party's white leadership. Lopez was given a mere $1,500 by the Democrats to run a statewide campaign, and Edmund G. Pat Brown, who was running for governor, refused to appear on the same platform with Lopez and did not endorse him. Much of the Democratic Party's leadership felt that a Mexicano was not electable statewide. The election results were such that all Democrats that ran for statewide offices were victorious, except Lopez, who lost by less than 1 percent of the vote.[190] Further exacerbating the frustration of Mexicano leaders like Roybal was his unsuccessful bid for Los Angeles county supervisor in 1958, when he again failed to garner strong support from the Democratic Party's white leadership.

Hence, on the weekend of April 22–24, 1960, some 150 Mexicanos from throughout California, representing various communities and organizations, for example, the CSO, AGIF, and former members of the Asociación Nacional México-Americana (ANMA), met in Fresno, California, and formed MAPA.[191] Bert Corona, one of MAPA's founders and major leaders, elucidates on the rationale used by the delegates to form MAPA:

> Following the Lopez campaign, we felt that the only answer was to form our own Mexican American political organization in order to mobilize broad sections of the Mexican community to register to vote, to participate in political campaigns, and to encourage those Mexicans who were not citizens to become citizens in order to vote. We felt that the time had come to organize an independent electoral organization that could take up questions pertinent to the Mexican communities without having to compromise itself with other groups inside the Democratic Party. It would be an organization based on the needs of the community and not on the electoral needs of the Democratic Party. This was a significant step forward in the political thinking of the Spanish-Speaking in California and the Southwest.[192]

After considering several ethnic labels by which to call this new organization, the delegates opted for the usage of "Mexican American," instead of "Latin American." This was indicative of a reemerging sense of cultural nationalism that was beginning to challenge the earlier assimilation orientation of the Mexican American Generation. Secondly, they decided on defining MAPA as a "political association" because they wanted to send a clear message of its explicit political aspirations. Gómez-Quiñones explains, "MAPA declared, from the first, that its basic aspiration was to become the political voice of the state Mexican community."[193] In sum, MAPA was organized "to be the active, hell-raising arm of the Mexicano community."[194]

MAPA's politics were based on accommodation and adaptation, and were reform-oriented. Unlike other existent interest groups, it was determined to be active in both the pressure group and electoral arenas. While the CSO had politically functioned as an interest group with strong linkages to the Democrat Party, MAPA declared its independence from both major parties. It did not go to the extreme of creating a new party, but instead sought to establish itself as a political interest group working for the advancement of the interests of Mexicanos through both the Democrat and Republican Parties.[195] The following six general aims or objectives were approved by the delegates: MAPA was to be a nonpartisan organization that would seek the social, economic, cultural, and civic betterment of Mexicanos through political action; MAPA would seek the appointment and election of Mexicanos and others sympathetic to its aims; MAPA would encourage its membership to become engaged with both Democrats and Republicans; MAPA would take a stand on public issues and would endorse candidates for public office; MAPA would publish a bimonthly newsletter; and MAPA would forge constructive alliances with other groups that had compatible aims.[196]

The delegates also elected MAPA's first slate of statewide officers, which included Edward Roybal, as state president, from Los Angeles; Hector Moreno, as state vice president, from San Jose; Juan Acevedo, as state secretary, from Montebello; Julius Castelan, as state treasurer, from Daly City; Andrew Barragan, as northern California director, from Sacramento; Louis Garcia, as northern California vice director, from San Francisco; Hank Lopez, as southern California director, from Los Angeles; and Augustine "Teen" Flores, as southern California vice director from Riverside.[197] From a class perspective, MAPA's early leadership and membership was mostly middle class; yet by 1965, its leadership was still heavily middle class, but its ranks had begun to include working-class Mexicanos.

MAPA's political activities from 1960 to 1965 were extensive. While still in the embryonic stage of developing its structure of chapters, MAPA joined in the formation of Viva Kennedy Clubs during the 1960 presidential campaign. Hank Lopez, MAPA southern California director, was selected at the National Democratic Convention to organize Viva Kennedy Clubs in thirteen states. In California, many of the newly formed MAPA chapters became Viva Kennedy Clubs. The motivation behind the Mapistas' (MAPA members) involvement with the Viva Kennedy Clubs was ascribable to the traditional Mexicano support for the Democratic Party; the charisma of Kennedy and the fact that his wife, Jacqueline spoke Spanish; and the religious factor that Kennedy was Catholic. That same year, motivated by MAPA's formation, a major voter mobilization effort resulted in the successful election of Leo Sanchez for East Los Angeles municipal judge.

However, it was not until 1962 that MAPA demonstrated its voter mobilization capacity with the election of Edward Roybal to Congress and John Moreno and Phil Soto to the State Assembly. These electoral victories were unprecedented, since no Mexicano from California had served in Congress since the 1880s, and none had served in the California state legislature since 1909. For the first time, Mexicanos had their own representatives in both Sacramento and Washington, D.C. At the local level of electoral politics, MAPA activist John

Sotelo became the first Mexicano elected to the Riverside City Council, while Augustine "Teen" Flores was defeated for a second seat. But because of increasing factionalism, MAPA's efforts to elect a Mexicano to fill Congressman Roybal's former city council seat in Los Angeles failed.[198]

During the 1964 presidential and state elections, MAPA continued to flex its fledgling political muscle. At the national level, MAPA endorsed Johnson for president and supported his Viva Johnson campaign.[199] Congressman Roybal opted instead for the "Californians for Johnson." Various MAPA leaders were recruited into Johnson's campaign, such as Louis Garcia of San Francisco and Hector Abeytia of Sanger. MAPA mobilized its chapters in support of the "Californians for Johnson" campaign and also endorsed Democrat Alan Cranston for the U.S. Senate. Instead of forming Viva Cranston committees or clubs, new MAPA chapters were formed and existing ones revitalized. The various campaigns were increasing MAPA's membership and number of chapters. While in 1960 MAPA's membership was a mere 292, by 1964 its membership increased to 3,700 in 36 chapters.[200]

During 1965, MAPA's leadership sought to cash in on Johnson's landslide victory. Under the able leadership of MAPA President Eduardo Quevedo, some seventy-five MAPA leaders met in Sacramento with Governor Pat Brown to discuss a variety of issues, one in particular being the Bracero Program. Although it had already expired nationally in December 1964, California had obtained an exemption. MAPA's leadership pressed the governor to end the Bracero Program and succeeded in convincing him to renew a statewide anti-Bracero campaign out of his office. Hector Abeytia was appointed by the governor to direct the campaign, while MAPA state president Eduardo Quevedo, Bert Corona, and two others from AGIF were appointed as consultants. At this time, MAPA hoped to expand into a regional or national organization and sought to form chapters outside of California, but regionalism and parochialism were difficult to overcome.[201]

None of the other state organizations, such as the CSO, LULAC, or AGIF, wielded MAPA's political influence. Yet it must be noted that for all the talk of its leaders MAPA was neither nonpartisan nor bipartisan but in actuality was partisan Democrat. Moreover, its chapters were often divided internally over issues. There were power struggles among competing leaders, and a fluctuating membership increased momentarily during election time then subsided afterward. Gómez-Quiñones further notes, "It was often accused of not having a sharply informed and well-reasoned position, of reacting too late and too ineffectively to issues, of uninformed spokespersons, and of a leadership that diverted the voiced populist concerns of the membership to the careerist interests of officials."[202] Still as 1965 came to a close, MAPA was at its pinnacle of influence and political clout.

THE VIVA KENNEDY CLUBS   An unprecedented political coalition emerged during this epoch, the Viva Kennedy Clubs. The presidential candidacy of Democrat John F. Kennedy, who in 1960 ran against Republican Richard Nixon, became the catalyst for their formation. As buffer political entities, hundreds of them were organized, chiefly among Mexicanos throughout the country, to foster a voter mobilization for Kennedy's presidential bid. The movement to organize them began after the Democratic Party Convention. With a commitment to secure the Mexicano vote, the Kennedy campaign hired Carlos McCormack, a native of Santa Barbara and resident of Tucson, Arizona, who moved expeditiously to line up support for the Kennedy campaign. One of the first Mexicano leaders in Tejas to propose a voter mobilization drive among Mexicanos was Bexar County commissioner Albert Peña from San Antonio. McCormack convinced AGIF, particularly its leader Hector P. García, and LULAC's leadership, to support the idea. From the leadership ranks of LULAC, Tony Bonilla was designated as director of the Tejas Viva Kennedy effort. However, in Tejas as well as in some other states, AGIF became the backbone of the Viva Kennedy Club movement. Interestingly, the name actually came from the Nixon camp, where Latino supporters had urged the Republicans to make a strong appeal to Latinos. After it was rejected because of its ethnic focus, the Kennedy campaign zealously adopted it.[203]

Within a matter of weeks, through McCormack's negotiations and persuasive skills, the Viva Kennedy Club movement secured support from a number of Mexicano organizational and political leaders across the Southwest, Midwest, and beyond. Senator Dennis Chavez and Congressman Joseph Montoya, both of Nuevo México, were appointed as honorary chairmen. In those states targeted for organizing, McCormack appointed cochairpersons. The appointed included Henry "Hank" Lopez and Edward Roybal, California; Jose Alvarado of Illinois; John Mendoza of Nevada; Filo Sedillo of Nuevo México; Stanley Valadez of Pennsylvania; and Henry B. Gonzalez, Albert Peña, and Hector P. García of Tejas. Additional appointments were Ricard Rucoba and Joe Maravilla of Indiana; Frank Rubi of Arizona; Vicente Ximenes of Nuevo México; Jesse Alvarado and David Vega of Kansas; Mrs. Augustine Olvera of Iowa; and several others from Minnesota, Nebraska, Colorado, Michigan, La Florida, Ohio, and New York.[204] While AGIF and LULAC were strongly in support of the effort, other organizations, such as La Alianza Hispano-Americana, MAPA, the CSO, among others, also participated in the Viva Kennedy Clubs.

The Viva Kennedy Clubs came together without a prescribed strategy. They were spontaneous, having no ideological foundation except to work for the election of Kennedy. Their quick formation was ascribable to the stature of the leadership and their ability to persuade others to participate. An unprecedented organizing effort directed by Mexicanos for Mexicanos developed. Although relatively autonomous, many of these clubs held fund-raisers, conducted voter registration, offered political education, and ran get-out-the-vote drives. In some states, such as Indiana and Illinois, women's auxiliaries were formed or else were incorporated into the club hierarchy.[205] Never before had *colonias* and barrios participated in such an unprecedented presidential voter mobilization effort.

Buttressed by the hard work of the Viva Kennedy Clubs, Kennedy received approximately 85 percent of the Mexicano vote nationally. In Tejas, Kennedy won an impressive 91 percent of the Mexicano vote, which allowed him to win the state and the presidency. He also carried Nuevo México with 70 percent of the Mexicano vote; it narrowly allowed him to carry the state by a mere two thousand votes. Although Kennedy lost California, Arizona, and Colorado to Nixon by margins ranging from 35,000 to 71,000, in all three states, he carried about 75 percent of the Mexicano vote.[206] The political effectiveness of the Viva Kennedy Clubs demonstrated the growing political capacity and pivotal significance of the Mexicano vote.[207] They demonstrated the potential for Mexicanos to affect the balance of power and play a swing vote political role.

During its post-election years, the Kennedy administration made a few middle-range appointments of Mexicanos, but none at the cabinet level. The lack of Mexicano appointments fostered a growing rancor toward the Kennedy administration by former Viva Kennedy Club leaders such as Roybal and García, who felt slighted and used politically.[208] The reality was that for all the rhetoric of the Kennedy campaign and the expectations it fostered, the Kennedy administration produced few rewards for the Viva Kennedy Club leadership and in particular for the Mexicano community. It was the Johnson administration (1963–1968) with passage of its civil rights agenda and its war against poverty programs that positively impacted Mexicanos, particularly the passage of the Civil Rights Act (1964) and Voting Rights Act (1965).[209] Out of the political experience of the Viva Kennedy Clubs, a national effort emerged for the establishment of a national PPO.

POLITICAL ASSOCIATION OF SPANISH-SPEAKING ORGANIZATIONS (PASO)   The Viva Kennedy Clubs became the springboard for the formation of PASO. After the election, the Viva Kennedy Clubs disbanded, but from their ashes an effort was created to build a permanent national political organization.

Driven by the interest of consolidating their efforts, the Viva Kennedy Club leadership in Tejas came together in March 1961 in Victoria and formed a new political organization, Mexican Americans for Political Action (MAPA), which had no connection to MAPA in California. Albert Peña, Jr., was elected state chairperson and AGIF leader Hector P. García national organizer.[210] Attending delegates endorsed district judge E. D. Salinas for the federal bench vacancy in South Tejas and agreed to support Henry B. Gonzalez's run for the U.S. Congress. Even though there was already an ongoing organizing effort to form MAPA in California, the MAPA leadership of Tejas sought to consolidate the efforts of the Viva Kennedy Clubs and to transform its MAPA into a national political organization by calling for a national meeting to be held that same month in Phoenix, Arizona.[211]

At the conference, numerous leaders and persons who had participated in the Viva Kennedy Clubs were in attendance. McCormack presided as chairman pro tem and opened the conference with an assessment of the status of Mexicanos in politics. Other speakers accentuated the great political successes of the Viva Kennedy Clubs. Edward Roybal and Hector P. García were particularly incensed over the lack of Mexicano appointments by the Kennedy administration. After much debate, the delegates agreed to form a new organization and selected Hector P. García as president and Roybal as vice president, both leaders of the two separate MAPAs. Conflict developed over what to call the new political organization. García writes, "The delegates could not agree on an organizational name because they could not agree on what to call themselves." This was due to the diversity of the historical, cultural, economic, and immigration experiences of the delegates present. Many of the delegates clung to their regional identities. Some from Colorado identified themselves as Spanish Americans; those from Tejas, Latin Americans or Spanish Speaking; from Nuevo México, Hispanos; from California, Mexican American; and from other areas, Latinos or Americans of Spanish descent.[212] There were also disagreements as to whether the new organization was to be inclusive of all Latinos or whether it should be exclusively Mexicano-oriented.[213] Further complicating the debate was California MAPA's leadership, which refused to subordinate itself to the new organization. Roybal and others argued that California had the largest number of Mexicanos and that the new organization should be called MAPA. After much rankling debate, the delegates tentatively agreed to the name of PASO.

Intended to be a national buffer-type political confederation of organizations, PASO never achieved such a status. After the Phoenix meeting, a second meeting was held in Las Vegas, Nevada. Few of the principal leaders who attended the previous conference and many representing the various states failed to show up. Those that did attend became embroiled in endless debates over structure, the name of organization, bylaws, and differences over strategy and organizing approaches. A pivotal problem was the lack of financial resources available to establish and organize PASO. Without a strong commitment and participation of state leaders like McCormack, García, and Roybal, debilitated by feuding over the name of the new organization and funding, the dream of building a Mexicano national political confederation faded rather quickly.

PASO in Tejas replaced in name the Mexican Americans for Political Action. From 1961 to 1965, PASO functioned solely in Tejas. During those four years, it was plagued by disagreements over endorsements, ideology, and leadership. Albert Peña, a liberal in politics with strong connections to labor, primarily the Teamsters, was the main leader of the liberal PASO forces. On the conservative side, Hector P. García and the Bonilla (William and Tony) brothers, who were more business-oriented, led the opposing forces. The ideological chasms became more evident at PASO's statewide convention held in San Antonio on February 9, 1962. Some twenty-four Democrat and Republican candidates sought PASO's endorsement. The endorsement for governor became a divisive issue that split the delegates into three camps: those for incumbent Democrat Price Daniel, those for liberal Republican Don Yarborough, and those for Democratic challenger John Connally. After much wrangling, the final convention vote favored Daniel, 51-1/ 2 votes to Yarborough's 41-1/2. The endorsement had little political value since those who were committed to their respective candidates continued to work with them after the convention. The split was so severe that PASO was not able to mount a unified effort in support of Daniels.[214]

PASO's internal schisms became more apparent by 1963 with the political takeover by five Mexicanos (Los Cinco) in the Crystal City (Cristal) town council.[215] Led by Juan Cornejo, a Teamster business agent, the takeover was a result of a massive grassroots effort organized by the local PASO chapter, supported by the Teamsters Union. The cardinal theme of the PASO campaign was that the time had come for Mexicanos to unite and empower themselves.[216] Cristal was a farming/ranching community in South Tejas with a population of some nine thousand people. With Mexicanos comprising about 80 percent of the town's population, the political victory was unprecedented in Tejas history. The gringo (Anglo racists) governing elite was badly beaten by the power of the ballot box. For the first time, Mexicanos were in total political control of the governance of a small South Tejas city and the victory served to put PASO on the political map in Tejas. In describing the impact of the initial PASO victory, Robert A. Calvert and Arnoldo De León wrote, "The victory was both symbolic and very important, because it notified Anglos that no longer could the minority population rule unchallenged. Crystal City portended the passing of the old order."[217] That same year, PASO leaders boasted that they had some twenty thousand dues-paying members and chapters in seventy counties.

The so-called PASO revolution in Cristal proved to be transitory. During its short two years, divisions developed within Los Cinco as well as among Mexicanos in Cristal. The victory also intensified the existing divisions statewide within PASO's leadership and membership ranks. At the 1963 PASO convention held in Waco, Tejas, the internecine conflicts between PASO leaders became deleterious. The moderate faction of Hector P. García of AGIF and William and Tony Bonilla from LULAC, among others, walked out, protesting the liberal faction's association with the Teamsters Union. During its 1964 convention, in order to recruit youth into its ranks, PASO's membership age requirement was lowered from twenty-one to eighteen. PASO student chapters were subsequently formed in various community colleges and universities. However, without the support of AGIF and LULAC, PASO was dramatically weakened to where by 1965 it was barely politically alive.

AMERICAN COORDINATING COUNCIL ON POLITICAL EDUCATION (ACCPE)   Out of the Viva Kennedy Clubs and during efforts to form PASO, a new PPO, the ACCPE, was formed in Arizona. The bickering and infighting that had occurred at the Phoenix PASO convention coupled with the tendency toward localism or parochialism, convinced the Viva Kennedy Club leadership and supporters in Arizona to form their own political organization, the ACCPE. As with PASO, the terms *Mexicano* and *Mexican American* were omitted, even though its membership was exclusively that.[218] Its leadership was committed to building a PPO that was mainstream and not solely ethnic-oriented, which gave it more of a buffer orientation. ACCPE was the embodiment of a mode of politics predicated on accommodation, adaptation, assimilation, and liberal capitalism. The key to their politics was inclusion. It was not focused on major reforms but on citizenship programs, voter registration drives, and support for Mexicano candidates.[219]

The ACCPE spread quickly throughout various counties of Arizona, particularly where there were large pockets of Mexicanos. By 1962, with membership of some 2,500 members, it succeeded in establishing chapters in ten of Arizona's fourteen counties.[220] That year it made political history by helping elect five Mexicanos to the Miami city council.[221] By 1965, the ACCPE was barely hanging on. This was by now a characteristic pattern in Chicano political organizations: their transitory or ephemeral nature. In the words of Meier and Rivera, the ACCPE "remained a fairly lusterless reflection of PASO."[222]

Labor Organizations and Organizing

ASOCIACIÓN NACIONAL MÉXICO-AMERICANA (ANMA)   Beyond the formation of social action and PPOs, the epoch of social action politics experienced continued labor organizing among Mexicanos. A progressive social action organization, which adhered to an advocate transformer role, emerged out the ranks of labor: the Asociación Nacional México-Americana (ANMA). Almost a decade after the formation of El Congreso del Pueblo de Habla Española in 1938, ANMA was founded in 1949 in Grant County, Nuevo México, by liberals and leftists who had participated in the "Amigos de [Henry] Wallace" 1948 presidential election. ANMA was formed as a result of a clash that occurred between Mexicano miners and police in the village of Fierro in Nuevo México. At a meeting held in Albuquerque on August 14, 1949, the decision was made to transform it into a national organization.[223] Efforts to organize ANMA were supported by the International Union of Mine, Mill, and Smelter Workers, which in turn had political backing from the Communist Party.[224] ANMA also had direct links with the Independent Progressive Party (IPP).[225] It was progressive and Left-orientated, and it sought to engender major social change within the existent liberal capitalist order.

At the national level, Alfredo Montoya became ANMA's first and only president and Virginia Ruiz its secretary-general; it operated administratively out of Denver, Colorado. According to Del Castillo and De León, "Two of its most influential leaders were the aforementioned Josefina Fierro de Bright and Eduardo Quevedo. Quevedo was a New Deal Democrat originally from New México but very active in Mexican Los Angeles's political life."[226] From the onset, ANMA was inclusive of women within its leadership ranks. In the Los Angeles area alone, Grace Montañez, Mary Jasso, Amelia Camacho, Virginia Montoya, and Julia Mount were all active in some leadership capacity.[227]

Although it claimed to be national in scope, in reality, ANMA was primarily an Aztlán-based regional social action organization. Committed to the attainment of democratic and economic rights, ANMA pursued a rather pragmatic Marxist agenda that adjusted to the organizing circumstances within the United States. This meant that it was international and progressive and oriented toward trade union issues. Using a popular front organizing approach, it stressed unity based on class—the working class—as well as ethnicity.[228] Between 1949 and 1954, ANMA confronted a number of issues such as police brutality, housing discrimination, Operation Wetback's deportation raids, and media stereotyping of Mexicanos and other Latinos. Between 1950 and 1952, ANMA was deeply involved in a fifteen-month copper miners' strike at Bayard, Nuevo México, made famous by the classic film *Salt of the Earth*.[229] In 1954, while some of the leading Mexicano organizations lined up in support of Operation Wetback, ANMA was one of the few organizations to strongly protest against it.[230] Internationally, ANMA opposed the Korean Conflict, U.S. support for right-wing dictatorships in Latin America, and the interventions in Guatemala and the Middle East.[231]

With a membership of some four thousand and some thirty chapters, ANMA strategically sought to advance its progressive labor agenda by forming coalitions. Although its organizing focus was directed at the Mexicano communities, because of its class emphasis, coalitions were formed with non-Mexicano entities, such as the Committee for the Protection of the Foreign Born, the Progressive Citizens of America, and the Civil Rights Congress. In a significant ANMA effort, Josefina Fierro de Bright, a veteran of the former defunct Congreso, ran unsuccessfully for Congress in 1951 under the aegis of the Independent Progressive Party.[232] Through its actions and organizing newspaper, *Progreso*, it addressed cold war issues within and McCarthyism in a political climate that ultimately contributed to its demise. In 1954, the U.S. attorney general added ANMA to its list of subversive organizations. Meier and Rivera conclude, "Harassed throughout its life by the FBI, which labeled it a communist-front organization, ANMA lost community support and became a casualty of the Red scare and the Cold War."

NATIONAL FARM WORKER UNION (NFWU)   In California in 1947, a union-organizing effort was begun under the aegis of the NFWU, which that year had become an affiliate of the American Federation of Labor (AFL). The NFWU's paramount focus and constituency was California's farmworkers, who became quickly engaged in a power fight with agribusiness. Aggressive in pursuit of its labor agenda, it functioned as a buffer-style union. That same year, under the leadership of Ernesto Galarza, a well-known scholar activist, and Henry Hasiwar, the NFWU local 218 led a strike against the Di Giorgio Corporation in Arvin, a small farming town in the San Joaquin Valley, California.[233] Its demands included a ten-cent an hour increase, seniority rights, a grievance procedure, and recognition of the NFWU as the sole bargaining agent.[234] During its anti-NFWU campaign Di Giorgio used the power of its political connections in Washington, D.C. The Senate Un-American Activities Committee conducted hearings on the matter, and the Di Giorgio Corporation produced a statement allegedly signed by most Di Giorgio farmworker employees rejecting Local 218's efforts to represent them. In 1949 congressional hearings were held in Bakersfield and further dramatized Di Giorgio's $2 million libel suit against the union and the Hollywood Film Council for the controversial film *Poverty in the Land of Plenty*, which had been produced by Galarza, who was the NFWU's director of research and education.[235] The basis of the suit was that the controversial film depicted Di Giorgio's treatment of farmworkers in a negative and libelous manner. On March 9, 1949, Di Giorgio commissioned Congressman Thomas H. Werdel from Kern County to read a damaging report into the Congressional Record, which concluded that it would be against the public interest to introduce new laws or to extend present laws to protect farmworkers.[236]

After two years of struggle, the strike ended in failure. Contributing to the failure was the strong anti-union campaign and lack of sufficient support from its parent union. The fledgling NFWU paid a heavy price: Di Giorgio agreed to settle the suit for $1 on the conditions that the NFWU plead guilty to the judgment, admitting libel. The film was removed from circulation with a recall of all the prints, the NFWU reimbursed Di Giorgio for attorney fees, and the strike was called off.[237] Galarza and the rest of the NFWU leadership vowed to continue the struggle to organize farmworkers. In 1952 another strike was called, this time against Schenley Corporation, a major San Joaquin grape grower. Still with little support from the parent union and the use of *braceros* to break the strike, once again the strike collapsed.[238] From 1953 to 1960, the NFWU altered its organizing tactics from conducting strikes to working for the termination of the Bracero Program by alerting the public on its abuses and mistreatment of workers. By 1960, it lost its charter and autonomy after being absorbed by another AFL-sponsored trade union, the Agricultural Workers Organizing Committee (AWOC).

Throughout the organizing history of both the NFWU and AWOC, the usage of undocumented workers as strikebreakers and the availability of farmworkers via the Bracero Program contributed significantly to failures. Efforts by unions to get the farmworkers to come under the protection of the National Labor Relations Act (Wagner Act) and extend the right of workers to collective bargaining, had repeatedly failed. Ultimately, however, the NFWU, and in the early 1960s AWOC, provided the organizing foundation upon which the present-day United Farm Workers was built.

NATIONAL FARM WORKER ASSOCIATION   In 1962, Cesar Chavez embarked upon his historical and difficult journey of forming the National Farm Workers Association (NFWA), precursor to the present United Farm Workers (UFW).[239] Between 1962 and 1965, Chavez and two other close associates, Dolores Huerta and Gil Padilla, using a *mutualista* model, built the infrastructure that led to the UFW.[240] For Chavez and his fledgling NFWA, these three years were the calm before the storm. Thus, by 1965, the stage was set for the rise of a new labor struggle to organize farmworkers.

Ballot Box Politics: The Struggle for Empowerment Begins

While ballot box politics has deep roots in the evolution of the Mexicano political experience in the United States, it was during these postwar years (1946–1965) that it began to take off in states other than Nuevo México. What occurred was a political awakening among some Mexicanos for engaging in electoral politics. This push for supporting candidates could be ascribed to the ethos fostered by the MAG. Most old and new organizations encouraged their members to become involved in politics. Yet organizing efforts had to overcome a myriad of obstacles that impeded political participation, for example, poll tax, literacy tests, white primaries, gerrymandering, at-large elections, and physical coercion. In comparison to previous epochs, Mexicanos were more educated, more middle class, and more politicized. The electoral agenda became a growing concern in their struggle to enfranchise their communities. While electoral politics still remained essentially a middle-class phenomenon, working-class Mexicanos became increasingly involved in organized voter registration, political education, and get-out-the-vote drives. Also contributing to the political awakening was the emergence of buffer-style political leaders driven by the quest for power and representation.

California: The Rebirth of Ballot Box Politics

After World War II, California and most of Aztlán experienced a rebirth of ballot box politics. Imbued with rising expectations and hope for a better future, some Mexicano veterans refused to accept the impoverished and segregated status of their barrios and *colonias*. They had experienced integration in the military, seen new lands, gotten an education, and upon their return, benefited from the G.I. Bill, which allowed them to go to school and buy a home outside the barrios. Inspired by the emerging Mexican American Generation ethos, they became involved in building organizations, taking on issues, and running and supporting candidates for local public office. Hence, in spite of the barrios' internal colonial status, these Mexicanos challenged its external administration.

In 1946, the Unity Leagues became an organizational template for ballot box politics. Their buffer-oriented political agenda included voter registration, education, get-out-the-vote drives, and support of candidates. That year they successfully elected Andrew Morales to the Chino city council and ran Herman Moraga for the city council in Ontario. Although Moraga lost, he garnered some nine hundred votes. The results of these unprecedented elections sent a very powerful message to all concerned: the seeds of Mexicano self-determination had been planted.[241] One year later in Chino, Alicia Cortez ran unsuccessfully for the Chino School Board, and in 1948, in an attempt to elect a second Mexicano to the Chino City Council, Samuel Morales ran. Although he managed to garner only 401 votes, he lost by 156 votes.[242] His defeat came as a result of the Unity Leagues' failure to get out the vote effectively. The white candidates simply had better organization and were successful in splitting the Mexicano vote.[243]

The Unity Leagues' political renaissance ended abruptly in 1948. The unprecedented periods of ballot box and organizational activism did not end, but dramatically diminished. The leagues had been an organizational experiment that gave rise to the CSO that same year. With the defeat of Samuel Calderon in the Chino City Council race in 1948 and the increased infighting, the Unity Leagues disbanded and many of their members joined the CSO and other organizations. The league's main leader, Ignacio Lopez, continued to be active politically and occasionally supported the Mexicano candidates that ran locally. As Mario Garcia has documented, Lopez was hypercritical of the lack of political acumen of Mexicano politicians. In particular, he criticized Morales for allegedly being "lazy," "incompetent," and "ineffective." Lopez went so far as to accuse Morales of being a "traitor" to Mexicanos for voting against federal support for low-cost housing.[244] In the end, Morales was reelected in 1950, but lost reelection four years later. During the 1950s, some ballot box activity continued within the area. Two Mexicanos, Manuel Gonzales and Jess Carlos, angered by the lack of representation in the city's barrios, ran at large for the Riverside City Council, but unsuccessfully.[245]

Such leaders as Ignacio Lopez, Eduardo Quevedo, and Bert Corona, to name a few, can be categorized as the political "movers and shakers" or architects of California Mexicano ballot box politics. However, of all of them, it was Edward Roybal who became California's main Mexicano politician. Born in Nuevo México on February 10, 1916, in Albuquerque, he grew up in Boyle Heights in East Los Angeles and graduated from Roosevelt High School. After working for the Civilian Conservation Corps, he attended the University of California, Los Angeles, where he majored in accounting. After graduation, Roybal worked for Twentieth Century studios, subsequently became a health administrator, and during World War II served in the army, then after discharge returned to health administration.[246]

Politically, Roybal's first attempt to election to the Los Angeles city council in 1947 ended in defeat. Although he received four thousand votes, he placed third, losing by a mere 370 votes. Roybal's candidacy served to encourage other

Mexicanos to run for public office. Although unsuccessful, Richard Ibañez ran for Superior Court judge in 1948 and garnered some 171,000 votes. John Chavez unsuccessfully ran for the Fifty-first Assembly District twice in 1948 and again in 1950. But in 1949, due to a massive voter registration drive by the CSO, Roybal was able to orchestrate an unprecedented campaign, defeating Parley Christianson by a vote of 20,581 to 12,015.[247] He served in the city council for thirteen years and fought for antidiscrimination measures, increased public housing, and against rabid anticommunism and police brutality.[248] In 1957, the city of Los Angeles wanted to remove a barrio, Chavez Ravine, and build the new Dodger Stadium. Roybal was alone in protesting the forcible eviction of Mexicano families. He opposed the redevelopment plans for the Bunker Hills area, which negatively impacted senior citizens and Mexicano families. At the time, Roybal had little support in the city council since most members were pro-growth at the expense of minority neighborhoods.[249]

While still in the city council in 1954, Roybal ran unsuccessfully for lieutenant governor. He was strongly supported by the California Democratic Council, a volunteer network of Democrats that in 1954 had some forty thousand members. Kenneth Burt writes, "In the November election, all but one Democrat lost. Roybal, however, received more votes than the party's gubernatorial candidate. The lone victor was incumbent Attorney General Edmund G. Pat Brown."[250] He received only token support from the Democratic Party. Most of the funding came from the Mexicano community statewide.[251] In 1958, Roybal considered making another run for lieutenant governor, but decided against it due to lack of support from the Democratic Party leadership. Instead, he ran for Los Angeles County supervisor, and although he won on the first ballot, he lost after three recounts. "At one point," according to Acuña, "they misplaced the ballots and then found them again. Ernest Debs, the elite's puppet won."[252] The defeat of Henry "Hank" Lopez, a Harvard-trained attorney, in 1958 for secretary of state persuaded Roybal to lay the groundwork for the creation of MAPA. With the exception of Lopez's loss, the 1958 gubernatorial election proved to be one of the most impressive electoral victories for Democrats since 1889. Democrats won control of the state legislature and the congressional delegation, and won all but the state treasurer position in which Lopez was narrowly defeated. With strong support from MAPA, Roybal was elected in 1962 to the Thirteenth Congressional District, which was only 9 percent Mexicano. This meant that he represented a multiethnic constituency, including blacks and Jews.[253] Roybal was the pacesetter who represented the political apogee of the epoch. That same year, John Moreno and Phil Soto were elected to the California State Assembly. The former lost his allegedly "safe" seat due to infighting and a well-publicized drink-ing problem, while the latter was reelected for one more term.[254]

At the local level of electoral politics in California, Mexicanos did not experi-ence another cycle of ballot box activism until the 1960s. With the birth of MAPA, interest in local politics increased. In Riverside in 1961, John Sotelo became the first Mexicano elected to the city council, while Augustine "Teen" Flores was defeated for a second seat. As councilman of the Second Ward, Sotelo served until 1972. When interviewed, Sotelo described how his unprecedented political victory was not well received by some of the white councilmen. He said one councilman for over two years deliberately mispronounced his last name, called him "Suntello."[255] Meanwhile, in Los Angeles increasing factionalism doomed MAPA's efforts to elect a Mexicano to fill Congressman Roybal's former Los Angeles City Council seat.[256] By the end of 1963, some fifteen Mexicanos served on California's city councils.[257] As 1965 came to a close, with Roybal in Congress and MAPA's leadership held by Quevedo and Corona, the Mexicano electoral agenda prioritized empowerment.

The Rise of Ballot Box in Tejas

After World War II, Mexicanos in Tejas, as in California, experienced their own political awakening. One can argue that the political climate in Tejas was more oppressive and less hospitable than it was in California. Racial discrimination and segregation was the result of the Mexicano's internal colonial subordinated status. The gringo "Remember the Alamo" syndrome continued to impede Mexicano ballot box politics, yet some Mexicanos sought to circumvent the obstacles, for example, poll taxes, literacy tests, and white primaries. At the forefront of the Mexicano political struggle for representation was Democrat Henry B. González, who became the counterpart in Tejas to Roybal in California. González's political career paralleled to some degree that of Roybal.

González was born in 1916 in Tejas to Mexicano parents who were middle class and were refugees from México's violent revolution. While in México, his father, Leonidas González, was mayor of Mapimi, Durango. After the family immigrated to San Antonio, Tejas, his father became the managing editor of San Antonio's major Spanish-language newspaper, *La Prensa*, in 1913. Henry Gonzá-lez attended the University of Texas at Austin and received his law degree from Saint Mary's University Law School in San Antonio. In 1943, he began an exten-sive career in the social service sector as a juvenile probation officer. After that he joined the U.S. Army and served in an intelligence unit. Following the war, Gon-zález returned to work as a juvenile probation officer. In 1947, he was hired as executive secretary of the newly formed Pan-American Progressive Association (PAPA). After resigning from PAPA in 1948, González set up a translation business and got a part-time job working as the educational director for the International Ladies Garment Workers Union in San Antonio.

During the next two years, González was involved in local politics and built up an impressive network of individuals and organizations. In 1950, he ran unsuccessfully for the Tejas State House of Representatives. Even though he had secured support from LULAC's founder, attorney Alonso Perales, he ran against a conservative and made it to the runoff, but lost by a two thousand-vote margin. From 1950 to 1953, he worked for the San Antonio Housing Commission developing low-cost housing.[258] His political career took off in 1953, when he got elected to the San Antonio City Council. He ran for the position on a nine-member candidate slate called the "San Antonians." Although he was the only Mexicano on the slate, his opposition was another Mexicano, George De La Garza, an automobile salesperson. Gonzáles won by a large margin along with other "San Antonians." Because of his major contribution to the slate, he was designated mayor pro tem under Mayor Jack White. González developed a reputation as being an assertive hard-working semiliberal and semiconservative politician committed to the defense of civil liberties, desegregation of parks, and lower water rates. In 1956, González resigned his seat on the city council and made political history by being elected to the Tejas State Senate, the first Mexicano to serve since statehood. He developed a reputation as a fighter for civil rights, exemplified by his participation, along with state senator Abrahm Kazen, in a thirty-six-hour filibuster against a segregationist bill that gave him national visibility on the floor of the Senate.

González once again made history in 1958. He became the first Mexicano to run for governor of Tejas in the Democratic primary, challenging the powerful incumbent Democrat, Price Daniel. Although González was defeated, he received a commendable 19 percent of the vote statewide, finishing second in a field of three candidates. In 1960, he was reelected to the State Senate and participated in a key leadership role in the Viva Kennedy Clubs in Tejas. With the strong support of the Kennedy administration, in 1961 he ran for and was elected to a congressional seat from Bexar County. González's election paved the way for the election of another Mexicano to Congress in 1964. From the Rio Grande area of South Tejas, Eligio "Kika" de la Garza gave Tejas two Mexicanos in the U.S. Congress. However, by 1965 González was the most influential buffer-oriented Mexicano politician in Tejas. As a result of their election, Mexicanos nationwide including Roybal from California had a total of only three congressmen by 1965.

There were few Mexicanos elected to the Tejas state legislature. In 1950 there was not one Mexicano in the state legislature. By 1960, however, the number had increased significantly to seven, but in 1965, the number decreased to six.[259] At the local level, there were only twelve incumbent mayors and twenty-eight county commissioners who were Mexicanos.[260] Of special significance was the election in 1956 of Albert Peña, Jr., who became a champion of civil rights as commissioner of Bexar County. During this time, electoral politics in Tejas took a backseat to pressure group politics, especially in dealing with issues of discrimination and segregation. Overall, but especially in South Tejas, Mexicanos were still relatively disenfranchised and had little or no representation on numerous school boards, city councils, and county commissions. This was an internal colony reality, particularly in south Tejas: many times whites in the minority controlled the governance process of local government.

In El Paso, Tejas, Raymond Telles, a decorated air force lieutenant colonel during the Korean Conflict, was elected as the city's first Mexicano mayor in 1957.[261] Overcoming great odds, particularly deep-seated white racism, Telles was the first Mexicano in the twentieth century to be elected mayor in a large urban U.S. city. Strongly supported by LULAC and other groups, his victory was a result of a massive grassroots campaign that strategically de-emphasized his Mexicano ethnicity. In spite of the vitriolic attacks by whites and his conservative politics, Telles won the election, garnering 90 percent of the eligible Mexicano vote.[262] The election results shattered the myth that Mexicanos were apolitical and apathetic. On the contrary, two years later, he won reelection without a serious challenge.[263] Telles as a buffer *politico* did not effectuate major political reforms during his two terms; rather he followed a moderate course that emphasized honesty and efficiency in governance.[264] For many Mexicanos throughout Aztlán, he became a symbol of an emerging political awakening. After campaigning for Democrat John F. Kennedy, in 1961 Telles was appointed ambassador to Costa Rica. Some of his close Mexicano supporters were displeased with his decision. They had hoped that he would instead run for Congress.[265]

The PASO Revolt in Crystal City, Tejas, also served as a catalyst for Mexicanos to become more engaged in local ballot box politics.[266] After a tumultuous two years of infighting and wrangling with the local white elites, PASO's Los Cinco lost control of the city council to a white-controlled political coalition of both whites and Mexicanos. The struggle for political representation at the local level was still at an embryonic stage in 1965. Juan Gómez-Quiñones states, "Mexicanos only held 31 of the state's 3,300 elective posts and of the 11,800 appointments only 5 were Mexicanos."[267] However, the Cristal Revolt of 1963 and the election of two Mexicanos to the U.S. Congress signaled the beginning of political activism both within ballot box and organizational arenas.

Nuevo México: Locus of Political Development

In Nuevo México, Mexicanos continued to wield significant political clout. Throughout most of the epoch, as in California and Tejas, one man, Dennis Chavez, was the dominant Mexicano political *patron*. Born in Nuevo México in 1888, Chavez was a grade school dropout. Because he was voracious reader, he was able to educate himself. At the age of thirty-two, he earned a law degree by going to night school and in 1920 set up his own law practice in Albuquerque. Ten years later, he was elected to Congress and in 1935 was appointed to the U.S. Senate upon the death of Senator Bronson Cutting, and was elected the following year.[268] He was reelected to five terms and served in the U.S. Senate from 1935 until his death in 1962. Gómez-Quiñones notes, "Arguably, Chavez was the most influential federal official until the late twentieth century." He was instrumental in the establishment of the Fair Employment Practices Committee and passage of the National Labor Relations Act, and was a national advocate for Mexicanos.[269] He had a liberal voting record that included condemning Senator Joseph McCarthy and exerted his political influence in support of both LULAC and AGIF's organizing efforts.[270]

In foreign affairs, he was an advocate of stronger relations between México and the United States. Mexicanos in Nuevo México also continued to be elected to statewide offices, the state legislature, and Congress. Joseph Montoya served in the state Senate from 1941 to 1946. Between 1946 and 1951, he also served two consecutive terms as lieutenant governor. Because of a two-term consecutive limitation, between 1953 and 1954, Montoya served one more term as a state senator. In 1954, he was once again elected lieutenant governor, in 1957 was elected to Congress, and in 1964 to the U.S. Senate. This made Nuevo México the only state in the country with a Mexicano senator.

In 1948, Ralph Gallegos ran unsuccessfully for the Democratic gubernatorial nomination. Even though influential Mexicano Democrats supported him, Manuel Lujan, who had won the Republican nomination for governor, lost to a white Democrat in the 1948 elections. In 1950, the brother of Senator Chavez, U.S. District Court judge David Chavez, lost in a bitter campaign for governor.

While no Mexicano was ever elected governor, three Mexicanos served as lieutenant governors during the years from 1940 to 1956. These included Montoya, who has already been discussed, and Tibo J. Chavez, from 1951 to 1954. Between, 1940 to 1960, over one hundred Mexicanos served in the State Senate and State House of which some two-thirds were Democrats.[271] In 1950, Nuevo México had a total of twenty state legislators and by 1965 the number had increased to twenty-two Mexicanos.[272] Some served as Speakers of the House and Senate leaders. All reflected a moderate political orientation, although their perspectives ranged from liberal Democrat to conservative Republican. Some ran as progressive third-party candidates; none were elected.[273] A cardinal reason for Nuevo México's substantial number of elected Mexicano officials was its large Mexicano population base and population concentrations. However, due to an influx of whites by 1960 the Mexicano population experienced a decrease to approximately only 30 percent.

Ballot Box Politics in Other States
During this epoch, Mexicanos in Arizona and Colorado were also politically active. Both states lacked large Mexicano population concentrations; consequently, few Mexicanos were elected to public office. Neither state was acknowledged to be politically liberal or progressive. On the contrary, their political cultures tended to be rather conservative, especially in Arizona. This meant Mexicanos were subject to discriminatory practices. In Colorado, Mexicanos were particularly active in ballot box politics in the Denver and Pueblo areas. These two areas had the largest concentration of Mexicanos. Rodolfo "Corky" Gonzales was heavily involved in Democratic Party politics during the late 1950s and early 1960s. In 1960 he was the state coordinator of the Viva Kennedy Campaign.[274] In 1964 he ran unsuccessfully for the state's House of Representatives. He was disqualified on the grounds that he was ineligible to run for the seat due to residency requirements. Soon thereafter, he became an activist leader within Los Voluntarios, a local community action group.[275] Thus, throughout much of the epoch, ballot box politics for Mexicanos in Colorado was slow in developing. This is illustrated by the fact that Colorado in 1950 had no Mexicano state legislators, but by 1965 had just one.[276]

In Arizona in particular, the political status of Mexicanos was that of a colonized community. Arizona also had two major Mexicano population pockets: Tucson and Phoenix. Historically the Tucson region had experienced the most ballot box activity by Mexicanos. Tucson had a rich tradition of Mexicano elite political participation and of having some representation at the local and even state levels. Yet its stifling conservative political culture was not conducive to the Mexicano's political development. Tucson politics essentially involved the Mexicano political and economic elites and not the impoverished masses. Yet in 1962 the newly formed American Coordinating Council on Political Education (ACCPE), was successful in organizing the state's first Mexicano political takeover by electing five Mexicanos to the seven-member city council in Miami, Arizona. Their victory gave Mexicanos in and out of Arizona a rising expectation that finally Mexicanos were politically gaining momentum. Overall, Arizona's Mexicano political representation by the end of 1965 had improved and was better than that of Colorado. Whereas Arizona had no Mexicano state legislators in 1950; by 1960 it had four; and in 1965 the number increased to six.[277]

Thus, greater progress was realized during this epoch; it set the political stage for the next more assertive period—the epoch of the politics of militant protest.

Notes

1. Manuel P. Servín, *The Mexican Americans: An Awakening Minority* (Beverly Hills, Calif.: Glencoe Press, 1970), 99.

2. David G. Gutiérrez, *Walls and Mirrors: Mexican Americans, Mexican Immigrants, and the Politics of Ethnicity* (Berkeley: University of California Press, 1995), 141.

3. Matt S. Meier and Feliciano Rivera, *Mexican Americans, Mexican Americans: From Conquistadors to Chicanos* (New York: Hill & Wang, 1993), 251.

4. Rodolfo Acuña, *Occupied America: A History of Chicanos*, 4th ed. (New York: Addison Wesley, 2000), 275.

5. Emilio Zamora, "The Failed Promise of Wartime Opportunity for Mexicans in the Texas Oil Industry," *Southwestern Historical Quarterly* Vol. 95 (January 1992): 323–50.

6. Richard Griswold Del Castillo and Arnold De León, *North to Aztlán: A History of Mexican Americans in the United States* (New York: Twayne Publishers, 1996), 91.

7. Acuña, *Occupied America*, 4th ed., 91.

8. Meier and Rivera, *Mexican Americans, Mexican Americans*, 168.

9. Meier and Rivera, *Mexican Americans, Mexican Americans*, 167–68.

10. Meier and Rivera, *Mexican Americans, American Mexicans*, 169.

11. Leo Grebler, Joan Moore, and Ralph Guzman, *The Mexican-American People: The Nation's Second Largest Minority* (New York: Free Press, 1970), 201.

12. Meier and Rivera, *Mexican Americans, American Mexicans*, 252.

13. Grebler, Moore, and Guzman, *The Mexican-American People*, 201.

14. Acuña, *Occupied America*, 4th ed., 297.

15. Mario T. Garcia, *Mexican Americans* (New Haven, Conn.: Yale University Press, 1989), 210.

16. Carlos G. Vélez-Ibáñez, *Border Visions: Mexican Cultures of the Southwest United States* (Tucson: University of Arizona Press, 1996), 203.

17. For a much more detailed background and history on each of the six Medal of Honor recipients see Raul Morin, *Among the Valiant: Mexican-Americans in WW II and Korea* (Los Angeles: Borden Publishing Co., 1963), 259–76.

18. Will be further examined in the section of this chapter on organizational development and politics. For a thorough examination of this organization's involvement against the Korean Conflict see Garcia, *Mexican Americans*, 208–11.

19. John Chala Elac, *The Employment of Mexican Workers in U.S. Agriculture, 1900–1960, A Binational Economic Analysis* (Los Angeles: University of California, May 1961), 43.

20. Oscar J. Martinez, *Mexican-Origin People in the United States: A Topical History* (Tucson: University of Arizona Press, 2001), 34.

21. Report of the President's Commission on Migratory Labor, "Migratory Labor in American Agriculture," 1951, 38–40.

22. Meier and Rivera, *Mexican Americans, American Mexicans*, 175–76.

23. Anne Lawrence, "The Formation of Labor Market Boundaries: A Comparative Analysis of the Bracero Program in Agriculture and the Railroad Industry in the Southwest," unpublished paper. Cited in Mario Barrera, *Race and Class in the Southwest: A Theory of Inequality* (Notre Dame, Ind.: University of Notre Dame Press, 1979), 117.

24. Meier and Rivera, *Mexican Americans, American Mexicans*, 175–76.

25. Nelson Gage Copp, *"Wetbacks" and Braceros: Mexican Migrant Laborers and American Immigration Policy, 1930–1960* (San Francisco: R&E Research Associates, 1971), 21.

26. Acuña, *Occupied America*, 4th ed., 286–87.

27. Acuña, *Occupied America*, 4th ed., 286–87.

28. Meier and Rivera, *Mexican Americans, American Mexicans*, 178–79.

29. Kitty Calavita, *Inside the State: The Bracero Program, Immigration, and the I.N.S.* (New York: Routledge, 1992), 25.

30. Acuña, *Occupied America*, 287–88.

31. Julian Samora, "Mexican Immigration," in *Mexican Americans Tomorrow: Educational and Economic Perspectives*, ed. Gus Taylor (Albuquerque: University of New México Press, 1975), 71.

32. Richard B. Craig, *The Bracero Program: Interest Groups and Foreign Policy* (Austin: University of Texas Press, 1974), 68–69.

33. Juan Ramon Garcia, *Operation Wetback: The Mass Deportation of Mexican Undocumented Workers in 1954* (Westport, Conn.: Greenwood, 1980), 70.

34. Calavita, *Inside the State*, 25, 27.

35. Meier and Rivera, *Mexican Americans, American Mexicans*, 179.

36. Meier and Rivera, *Mexican Americans, American Mexicans*, 181.

37. Copp, *"Wetbacks" and Braceros*, 30.

38. Copp, *"Wetbacks" and Braceros*, 30.

39. Craig, *The Bracero Program*, 71.

40. Copp, *"Wetbacks" and Braceros*, 30.

41. Gonzales, *Mexicanos*, 172.

42. Meier and Rivera, *Mexican Americans, American Mexicans*, 183.

43. Samora, "Mexican Immigration," 72.

44. Gonzales, *Mexicanos*, 173.

45. Subsequently in this chapter, a much more in-depth examination on the anti-migrant position taken by both organizations is made. Suffice it to say that some of these more assimilationist-oriented groups perceived *braceros* and undocumented workers as impeding their integration into the system.

46. Ernesto Galarza, *Farm Workers and Agri-business in California, 1947–1960* (Notre Dame, Ind.: University of Notre Dame Press, 1977), 204.

47. Martinez, *Mexican-Origin People in the United States*, 34.

48. Gonzales, *Mexicanos*, 175.

49. Meier and Rivera, *Mexican Americans, American Mexicans*, 184.

50. Del Castillo and De León, *North to Aztlán*, 108.

51. Garcia, *Operation Wetback*, 198.

52. Arthur Corwin, "Causes of Mexican Emigration to the United States," *Perspectives in American History*, 1973, 627.

53. Barrera, *Race and Class in the Southwest*, 122.

54. Leobardo F. Estrada, F. Chris Garcia, Reynaldo Flores Macias, and Lionel Maldonado, "Chicanos in the United States: A History of Exploitation and Resistance," in *Latinos and the Political System*, ed. F. Chris Garcia (Notre Dame, Ind.: University of Notre Dame Press, 1988), 48.

55. For a brief analysis on the forces impelling the influx of Mexicano undocumented workers into the United States see Julian Samora, *Los Mojados: The Wetback Story* (Notre Dame, Ind.: University of Notre Dame Press, 1971), 1–12.

56. Acuña, *Occupied America*, 4th ed., 303.

57. Meier and Rivera, *Mexican American, American Mexican*, 187.

58. Meier and Rivera, *Mexican American, American Mexican*, 186.

59. John Chavez, *The Lost Land: The Chicano Image in the Southwest* (Albuquerque: University of New México Press, 1984), 125.

60. Estrada et al., "Chicanos in the United States," 48.

61. Interestingly, Samora and other scholars as well as politicians and organizational leaders in the Mexicano community unfortunately described undocumented workers using the parlance in vogue used by nativists at the time. Samora, *Los Mojados*, 9.

62. Julian Samora and Patricia Vandel Simon, *A History of the Mexican American People* (Notre Dame, Ind.: University of Notre Dame Press, 1977), 143

63. While *wetback* denotes an undocumented worker that got wet crossing into the United States, *alambre* means "wire" in English. Both *wetback* and *alambre* in most cases conjured up negative connotations. Persons or groups that were supportive of Mexicanos that allegedly were illegally in the United States preferred not to use either of the two terms. For an elaboration on their usage see Samora, *Los Mojados*, 6–11.

64. Meier and Rivera, *Mexican Americans, American Mexicans*, 187.

65. Samora and Simon, *A History of the Mexican American People*, 187.

66. Joan W. Moore with Alfredo Cuéllar, *Mexican Americans* (Englewood Cliffs, N.J.: Prentice Hall, 1970), 43.

67. Acuña, *Occupied America*, 4th ed., 304.

68. Acuña, *Occupied America*, 4th ed., 304.

69. Samora, "Mexican Immigration," 71.

70. Craig, *The Bracero Program*, 125.

71. Cited in Samora, "Mexican Immigration," 70.

72. Acuña, *Occupied America*, 4th ed., 300.

73. Garcia, *Operation Wetback*, 231.

74. Acuña, *Occupied America*, 4th ed., 301.

75. Gutiérrez, *Walls and Mirrors*, 161

76. For a brief examination of the impact of the McCarran-Walter Act on Mexicanos in the United States see Gutiérrez, *Walls and Mirrors*, 172–78; and Acuña, *Occupied America*, 4th ed., 300–3.

77. Gutiérrez, *Walls and Mirrors*, 172–78.

78. Acuña, *Occupied America*, 4th ed., 301.

79. Acuña, *Occupied America*, 4th ed., 301.

80. For an extensive case study on Operation Wetback see Garcia, *Operation Wetback*.

81. Cited in Calavita, *Inside the State*, 47.

82. *New York Times*, service broadcast, May 9, 1953, quoted in John Myers, *The Border Wardens* (Englewood Cliffs, N.J.: Prentice Hall, 1971), 79–80.

83. American G.I. Forum of Texas and Texas State Federation of Labor (AFL), *What Price Wetbacks*, Austin, Texas, 1954.

84. Gutiérrez, *Walls and Mirrors*, 142–43.

85. *Reorganization of the Immigration and Naturalization Service*, Hearings before the Subcommittee on Legal and Monetary Affairs of the Committee on Government Operations, House, 84th Congress, first session, March 9 and 17, 1955, p. 3.

86. Acuña, *Occupied America*, 4th ed., 304.

87. Acuña, *Occupied America*, 4th ed., 304.

88. Meier and Rivera, *Mexican Americans, American Mexicans*, 189.

89. Moore and Cuellar, *Mexican Americans*, 43.

90. Moore and Cuellar, *Mexican Americans*, 43.

91. Samora, *Wetbacks*, 46.

92. Moore and Cuellar, *Mexican Americans*, 43.

93. Cited in Grebler, Moore, and Guzman, *The Mexican-American People*, 68.

94. Garcia, *Operation Wetback*, 235.

95. Garcia, *Operation Wetback*, 522–23.

96. Del Castillo and De León, *North to Aztlán*, 114.

97. Grebler, Moore, and Guzman, *The Mexican-American People*, 67–69.

98. Moore and Cuellar, *Mexican Americans*, 57.

99. Grebler, Moore, and Guzman, *The Mexican-American People*, 126.

100. Moore and Cuellar, *Mexican Americans*, 57.

101. Grebler, Moore, and Guzman, *The Mexican-American People*, 106.

102. Grebler, Moore, and Guzman, *The Mexican-American People*, 106.

103. Cited in Moore and Cuellar, *Mexican Americans*, 29.

104. Juan Gómez-Quiñones, *Chicano Politics: Reality & Promise, 1940–1990* (Albuquerque: University of New México Press, 1990), 41.

105. Meier and Rivera, *Mexican Americans, American Mexicans*, 252.

106. For a brief examination of the urbanization trend that developed during this epoch see Samora and Simon, *A History of the Mexican American People*, 153–54, 156–58; and Gonzales, *Mexicanos*, 165–70.

107. Del Castillo and De León, *North to Aztlán*, 109.

108. Moore and Cuellar, *Mexican Americans*, 60.

109. Frank G. Mittelbach and Grace Marshall, *The Burden of Poverty*, Advanced Report 5 (Los Angeles: University of California, Mexican American Study Project, 1966), 5.

110. Moore and Cuellar, *Mexican Americans*, 71.

111. For two excellent works by Oscar Lewis see *Pedro Martinez* (New York: Vintage, 1964) and *The Children of Sanchez* (New York: Random House, 1961).

112. Moore and Cuellar, *Mexican Americans*, 60–62.

113. Most of these figures are from Leo Grebler, *The Schooling Gap: Signs of Progress*, Advanced Report 7 (Los Angeles: University of California, Mexican American Study Project, 1967).

114. Grebler, *The Schooling Gap*, 13.

115. For a case study on the manifold aspects of segregation that examines the adherence to the politics of community control in Crystal City (Cristal), Texas, see my book *The Cristal Experiment: A Chicano Struggle for Community Control* (Madison: University of Wisconsin Press, 1998), chapter 1.

116. Frantz Fanon writes that inherent to colonialism is the omnipresence of violence among the colonized. He postulates that for the colonized "violence is a cleansing force. It frees the native from his inferiority complex and from his despair and inaction; it makes him fearless and restores his self-respect" (Frantz Fanon, *The Wretched of the Earth* [New York: Grove Press, 1968], 94).

117. Mittelbach and Marshall, *The Burden of Poverty*.

118. For a thorough examination of these aspects of the Mexicano condition of that time, see A. Taher Moustafa and Gertrude Weiss, *Health Status and Practices of Mexican Americans*, Advanced Report 11 (Los Angeles: University of California, Mexican American Study Project, 1968).

119. See Lucian W. Pye, "Political Science and the Crisis of Authoritarianism," *American Political Science Review* Vol. 84, No. 1 (March 1990): 3–19.

120. Wayne A. Cornelius, *Mexican Politics in Transition: The Breakdown of a One-Party Dominant Regime* (La Jolla, Calif.: Center for U.S.-Mexican Studies, UCSD, 1996), 26.

121. For further information and a much more comprehensive examination on the subject of the Mexican American Generation see Garcia, *Mexican Americans*, chapter 1.

122. Carlos Muñoz, Jr., *Youth, Identity, Power: The Chicano Movement* (New York: Verso, 1989), 49.

123. Garcia, *Mexican Americans*, 297.

124. Ellwyn R. Stoddard, *Mexican Americans* (New York: Random House, 1973), 185.

125. Ignacio Garcia, *Chicanismo: The Forging of a Militant Ethos* (Tucson: University of Arizona, 1997), 9.

126. Mario Barrera, *Beyond Aztlán: Ethnic Autonomy in Comparative Perspective* (New York: Praeger, 1988), 27.

127. Gonzales, *Mexicanos*, 187–89.

128. Meier and Rivera, *Mexican Americans, American Mexicans*, 252

129. Del Castillo and De León, *North to Aztlán*, 116.

130. Miguel Tirado, "Mexican American Community Political Organization: The Key to Chicano Political Power," *Aztlán: Chicano Journal of the Social Science and Arts* Vol. I., No. 1 (Spring 1970).

131. For a case study on this influential *mutualista* organization see Jose Hernandez, *Mutual Aid for Survival: The Case of the Mexican American* (Malabar, Fla.: Robert E. Krieger Publishing Co., 1983), chapter VII.

132. Kay Lysen Briegal, *Alianza Hispano-Americana, 1894–1965: A Mexican American Fraternal Insurance Society*, PhD dissertation, University of Southern California, 1974, 154.

133. Briegal, *Alianza Hispano-Americana, 1894–1965*, 153–57.

134. Hernandez, *Mutual Aid for Society*, 49.

135. Briegal, *Alianza Hispano-Americana, 1894–1965*, 176–80.

136. Briegal, *Alianza Hispano-Americana, 1894–1965*, 51.

137. Hernandez, *Mutual Aid for Survival*, 56.

138. For details on the various aspects of its decline see Briegal, *Alianza Hispano-Americana, 1894–1965*, chapter 7; and Hernandez, *Mutual Aid for Survival*, 57–59.

139. Nicolás C. Vaca, *The Presumed Alliance: The Unspoken Conflict between Latinos and Blacks and What It Means for America* (New York: Rayo, 2004), 80–82.

140. Joan Moore and Harry Pachon, *Hispanics in the United States* (Englewood Cliffs, N.J.: Prentice Hall, 1985), 177–78.

141. Acuña, *Occupied America*, 4th ed., 279.

142. Benjamin Marquez, *LULAC: The Evolution of a Mexican American Political Organization* (Austin: University of Texas Press, 1993), 43.

143. Garcia, *Mexican Americans*, 56.

144. Cited in Gonzales, *Mexicanos*, 181.

145. Acuña, *Occupied America*, 4th ed., 279.

146. Garcia, *Mexican Americans*, 57–58.

147. Acuña, *Occupied America: A History of Chicanos*, 5th ed. (New York: Pearson and Longman, 2002), 262

148. Acuña, *Occupied America*, 5th ed., 59–60.

149. Meier and Rivera, *Mexican Americans, American Mexicans*, 202.

150. Gómez-Quiñones, *Chicano Politics*, 63.

151. Gutiérrez, *Walls and Mirrors*, 143.

152. Armando Navarro, *Mexican American Youth Organization: Avant-Garde of the Chicano Movement in Texas* (Austin: University of Texas Press, 1995), 50.

153. Gómez-Quiñones, *Chicano Politics*, 53.

154. Acuña, *Occupied America*, 4th ed., 315.

155. Cited in Gutiérrez, *Walls and Mirrors*, 168, 169.

156. Gutiérrez, *Walls and Mirrors*, 169.

157. Tirado, "Mexican American Community Political Organization," 63–64.

158. Gutiérrez, *Walls and Mirrors*, 169.

159. Gómez-Quiñones, *Chicano Politics*, 54–55.

160. Gómez-Quiñones, *Chicano Politics*, 53.

161. For an in-depth case study on the history and development of the American G.I. Forum see Henry A. J. Ramos, *The American G.I. Forum: In Pursuit of the Dream, 1948–1983* (Houston, Tex.: Arte Público Press, 1998). Also, for an excellent biography of Dr. Hector García and his involvement with the AGIF see the recent study by Ignacio Garcia, *Hector P. García: In Relentless Pursuit of Justice* (Houston, Tex.: Arte Público Press, 2003).

162. Barrera, *Beyond Aztlán*, 28.

163. For an examination of all the aims and objectives see Ramos, *The American G.I. Forum*, 5–6.

164. Tirado, "Mexican American Community Political Organization," 65.

165. Acuña, *Occupied America*, 280.

166. Tirado, "Mexican American Community Political Organization," 65.

167. Acuña, *Occupied America*, 4th ed., 280.

168. Gómez-Quiñones, *Chicano Politics*, 61.

169. Ramos, *The American G.I. Forum*, 6, 28.

170. Gonzales, *Mexicanos*, 184.

171. Acuña, *Occupied America*, 4th ed., 280–81.

172. Gutiérrez, *Walls and Mirrors*, 155.

173. Gómez-Quiñones, *Chicano Politics*, 61.

174. Gómez-Quiñones, *Chicano Politics*, 61.

175. Acuña, *Occupied America*, 322.

176. Briegal, *Alianza Hispano-Americana, 1894–1965*, 173

177. Acuña, *Occupied America*, 316.

178. Tirado, "Mexican American Political Community Organization," 69.

179. Tirado, "Mexican American Political Community Organization," 69.

180. Tirado, "Mexican American Political Community Organization," 69.

181. Tirado, "Mexican American Political Community Organization," 61.

182. Garcia, *Mexican Americans*, 101.

183. Garcia, *Mexican Americans*, 101.

184. Acuña, *Occupied America*, 4th ed., 314.

185. Garcia, *Mexican Americans*, 100.

186. Acuña, *Occupied America*, 4th ed., 314.

187. Garcia, *Mexican Americans*, 100.

188. Gómez-Quiñones, *Chicano Politics*, 52.

189. For a case study of the history and political development of MAPA see Kenneth Burt, *The History of MAPA and Chicano Politics in California* (Sacramento, Calif.: Mexican American Political Association, 1982), 4.

190. Burt, *The History of MAPA and Chicano Politics in California*, 4.

191. Richard Santillan, *The Politics of Cultural Nationalism: El Partido de la Raza Unida in Southern California, 1968–1978*, PhD dissertation, Claremont Graduate School, 1978, 33.

192. Mario Garcia, *Memories of Chicano History: The Life and Narrative of Bert Corona* (Berkeley: University of California Press, 1994), 197.

193. Gómez-Quiñones, *Chicano Politics*, 67.

194. Kay Briegal, "The Development of Mexican American Organizations," in *The Mexican Americans: An Awakening Minority*, ed. Manuel P. Servín (Beverly Hills, Calif.: Glencoe Press, 1970), 174.

195. Maurilio Vigil, *Chicano Politics* (Washington, D.C.: University Press of America, 1977), 202.

196. Burt, *The History of MAPA and Chicano Politics in California*, 5.

197. Burt, *The History of MAPA and Chicano Politics in California*, 5.

198. Briegal, "The Development of Mexican American Organizations," 175.

199. Garcia, *Memories of Chicano History*, 210.

200. Burt, *The History of MAPA and Chicano Politics in California*, 10.

201. Burt, *The History of MAPA and Chicano Politics in California*, 207.

202. Gómez-Quiñones, *Chicano Politics*, 68.

203. Ignacio Garcia, *Viva Kennedy: Mexican Americans in Search of Camelot* (College Station: Texas A&M Press, 2000), 47–48.

204. Garcia, *Viva Kennedy*, 54.

205. Garcia, *Viva Kennedy*, 88.

206. Mark R. Levy and Michael Kramer, *The Ethnic Factor: How America's Minorities Decide Elections* (New York: Simon & Schuster, 1972), 77–78.

207. David Montejano, *Anglos and Mexicans in the Making of Texas, 1836–1986* (Austin: University of Texas Press, 1987), 282.

208. For an excellent analysis on this, see Garcia, *Viva Kennedy*, chapter 5.

209. While the Civil Rights Act of 1964 mandated nondiscrimination in employment and in the use of public facilities and accommodations, the Voting Rights Act of 1965 eliminated barriers to political participation, such as literacy tests.

210. For a comprehensive and incisive biography on Dr. Hector García see Ignacio Garcia, *Hector P. García: In Relentless Pursuit of Justice* (Houston, Tex.: Arte Público Press, 2003).

211. Garcia, *Viva Kennedy*, 124.

212. For an examination of the various ethnic identification terms used by Mexicanos see Fernando Peñalosa, "Toward an Operational Definition of the Mexican American," *Aztlán* I (Spring 1970): I–12.

213. Paul Sheldon, "Mexican American Formal Organizations," in *Mexican Americans in the United States*, ed. John Burma (Cambridge, Mass.: Schenkman Publishing Company, Inc., 1970), 271.

214. For an examination of PASO's political development in Texas, especially PASO's role during the 1962 gubernatorial election, see Garcia, *Viva Kennedy*, chapter 6.

215. For a rather complete examination of PASO's unprecedented victory in Cristal, Texas, see my book *The Cristal Experiment*, chapter 1.

216. Briegal, "The Development of Mexican American Organizations," 176.

217. Robert A. Calvert and Arnoldo De León, *The History of Texas* (Arlington Heights, Ill.: Harlan Davidson, Inc., 1990), 391.

218. Matt S. Meier and Margo Gutiérrez, *Encyclopedia of the Mexican American Civil Rights Movement* (Westport, Conn.: Greenwood, 2000), 9–10.

219. Meier and Gutiérrez, *Encyclopedia of the Mexican American Civil Rights Movement*, 9–10.

220. Armando Navarro, "The Evolution of Chicano Politics," *Aztlán: Journal of the Social Sciences and the Arts* (Spring/Fall 1974): 57–82.

221. Martinez, *Mexican-Origin People in the United States*, 173.

222. Meier and Rivera, *Mexican Americans, American Mexicans*, 208–9.

223. Acuña, *Occupied America*, 4th ed., 321.

224. Meier and Rivera, *Mexican Americans, American Mexicans*, 204.

225. Acuña, *Occupied America*, 4th ed., 321.

226. Del Castillo and De León, *North to Aztlán*, 114.

227. Acuña, *Occupied America*, 322.

228. Meier and Gutiérrez, *Encyclopedia of the Mexican American Civil Rights Movement*, 17.

229. Meier and Rivera, *Mexican Americans, American Mexicans*, 204.

230. Del Castillo and De León, *North to Aztlán*, 114.

231. Gómez-Quiñones, *Chicano Politics*, 50.

232. Gómez-Quiñones, *Chicano Politics*, 51.

233. Albert Camarillo, *Chicanos in California: A History of Mexican Americans in California* (San Francisco, Calif.: Boyd & Fraser Publishing Co., 1984), 89.

234. Acuña, *Occupied America*, 4th ed., 290.

235. Del Castillo and De León, *North to Aztlán*, 117.

236. Acuña, *Occupied America*, 4th ed., 291.

237. Acuña, *Occupied America*, 4th ed., 291.

238. Acuña, *Occupied America*, 4th ed., 291.

239. In the next chapter, a broader examination of both the AWOC and the UFW is presented.

240. For a historical overview of the United Farm Workers as a union see Richard Del Castillo and Richard A. Garcia, *Cesar Chavez: A Triumph of Spirit* (Norman: University of Oklahoma Press, 1995).

241. Cited in Garcia, *Mexican Americans*, 103.

242. Garcia, *Mexican Americans*, 103–4.

243. Garcia, *Mexican Americans*, 104.

244. Garcia, *Mexican Americans*, 105.

245. Interview, Johnny Sotelo (former Riverside City councilman), February 25, 2003.

246. Meier and Gutiérrez, *Encyclopedia of the Mexican American Civil Rights Movement*, 205.

247. Cited in Santillan, *The Politics of Cultural Nationalism*, 18.

248. Del Castillo and De León, *North to Aztlán*, 113.

249. Acuña, *Occupied America*, 4th ed., 315.

250. Burt, *Mexican American Political Association*, 3.

251. Garcia, *Memories of Chicano History*, 195.

252. Acuña, *Occupied America*, 316.

253. Gómez-Quiñones, *Chicano Politics*, 73.

254. Briegel, "The Development of Mexican Organizations," 175.

255. Interview, Sotelo.

256. Briegal, "The Development of Mexican American Organizations," 175.

257. Briegal, "The Development of Mexican American Organizations," 8.

258. For more biographical information on Congressman Gonzales see Gomez-Quiñonez, *Chicano Politics*, 56–59; and Meier and Gutiérrez, *Encyclopedia of the Mexican American Civil Rights Movement*, 96–97.

259. Moore and Pachon, *Hispanics in the United States*, 185.

260. Martinez, *Mexican-Origin People in the United States*, 172.

261. For a biography on the former El Paso, Tejas, mayor see Mario Garcia, *The Making of a Mexican American Mayor: Raymond L. Telles of El Paso* (El Paso: Texas Western Press, University of El Paso, 1998); also see Garcia, *Mexican Americans*, 113–41.

262. Garcia, *Mexican Americans*, 113.

263. Arnoldo De León, *Mexican Americans in Texas: A Brief History* (Arlington Heights, Ill: Harlan Davidson, Inc., 1993), 113.

264. Martinez, *Mexican-Origin People in the United States*, 172.

265. Garcia, *Mexican Americans*, 141.

266. For a thorough examination of the PASO Revolt see my book *The Cristal Experiment*, chapter 1.

267. Gómez-Quiñones, *Chicano Politics*, 73.

268. For more biographical information on Senator Chavez see Meier and Gutiérrez, *Encyclopedia of the Mexican American Civil Rights Movement*, 41.

269. Gómez-Quiñones, *Chicano Politics*, 45–46.

270. Acuña, *Occupied America*, 308.

271. Acuña, *Occupied America*, 47–48.

272. Cited in Moore and Pachon, *Hispanics in the United States*, 185.

273. Gómez-Quiñones, *Chicano Politics*, 48.

274. Navarro, *Mexican American Youth Organization*, 37.

275. For a much more detailed examination of Gonzales's politics see Armando Navarro, *La Raza Unida Party: A Chicano Challenge to the U.S. Two-Party Dictatorship* (Philadelphia: Temple University Press, 2000), 81.

276. Moore and Pachon, *Hispanics in the United States*, 185.

277. Moore and Pachon, *Hispanics in the United States*, 185.

Epoch of Militant Protest Politics (1966–1974)　　5

ROM 1966 to 1974, Mexicanos in occupied Aztlán experienced the most dynamic transformation with the epoch of militant protest politics. The tumultuous and at times turbulent epoch rejected the politics of social action and replaced it with cultural nationalism, which was impelled by militant protest politics. Adaptation and accommodation-oriented politics and the ethos of the Mexican American Generation were discarded. Instead, many Mexicanos, especially the youth, refused to play the role of buffer and opted for the assertive social change-oriented political role of advocate transformers. Never before in the Mexicano political experience of occupied Aztlán had Mexicanos experienced the scope of change, leadership formation, organizational development, political mobilizations, and people's participation. Although initially they embraced some aspects of the Mexican American generation, by late 1968 a dialectical change occurred. Aztlán experienced the rise of a new dynamic political generation—that of the "Chicano Generation"—that was driven by the quasi-ideology of Chicanismo. During this epoch, an unprecedented militant spirit of protest, change, and cultural nationalism pervaded Aztlán and the country's barrios and *colonias*, which gave rise to the "Chicano experience."

Historical Antagonisms Impacting the Experience

The Etiology of the Chicano Movement

The Mexicano political experience throughout occupied Aztlán was dramatically altered during this epoch due to the rise of the Chicano Movement (hereafter Movimiento will be used interchangeably). The use of the dialectical method is important to the transition that occurred from social action to protest politics. No previous epoch had ever produced such a dynamic social movement.[1] The Chicano Movement was a heterogeneous political reform movement comprised of "multiple" leaders, organizations, competing ideologies, and protest mobilization strategies and tactics. While some organizations within its ranks perceived themselves as revolutionary, ultimately its modus operandi proved to be essentially reformist in orientation. As a social movement, it was equipped with all the requisite ingredients.[2] One, it was conceived in a political climate that was ridden by discontent, frustration, unrealized expectations—in short, relative deprivation.[3] Two, it had multiple primary and secondary leaders. Three, it incorporated numerous diverse organizations. Four, although it did not have a clear ideology, it was impelled by Chicanismo, a quasi-ideology. Five, it adhered to a strategy and tactics predicated on unconventional militant protest direct action. And six, on numerous occasions, it demonstrated a power capability to mobilize the masses.

The Chicano Movement was a product of the dialectical historical forces or antagonisms that pervaded the country and much of the world at the time. It was characterized by a more defiant mode of "militant protest politics." To James Q. Wilson, protest in the context of powerless groups, namely blacks, relies on the use of mass action and negative inducements as a way of enhancing their bargaining posture in the pursuit of change.[4] Michael Lipsky defines protest "as a mode of political action oriented toward objection to one or more policies or conditions, characterized by showmanship or display of an unconventional nature, and undertaken to obtain rewards from political and economic systems, while working within the system."[5] Unconventional denotes the use of marches, civil disobedience, sit-ins, school walkouts, picketing, rallies, riots, and even the use of violence. "The emergence of a protest movement," according to Frances Fox Piven and Richard A. Cloward, "entails a transformation both of consciousness and of behavior."[6] The rise of the Movimiento epitomized the use of militant protest, and as a social protest movement it engendered a new consciousness that set it apart from previous struggles of resistance.

During the epoch of militant protest, the previous mode of social action politics based on accommodation and adaptation was categorically repudiated and replaced by militant protest. The Movimiento's eight years were unparalleled in the degree of activism, struggles for change, leadership, and organizational formation. Aztlán's barrios and *colonias* experienced a new sense of cultural nationalist consciousness fostered by an abundance of dynamic leaders and protest organizations, which was illustrated by an unprecedented level of participation by the people in innumerable protest demonstrations and mobilizations. Thus, the scope of change effectuated during what I call the Chicano experience, was an intrinsic aspect of the Mexicano political experience.

Mexicano scholars in the United States have divergent views of the epoch that produced the Chicano Movement. Historian Rodolfo Acuña propounds the view that the Movimiento was merely another phase in the struggle for Chicano liberation from racism and liberal capitalist exploitation. On the other hand, political scientist Carlos Muñoz argues that its student movement component particularly "signaled a departure from the struggles of the past because of its youthful nature, its ideological tendencies, and its search for identity."[7] Another political scientist, Mario Barrera, acknowledges the important legacy of Chicano political activism, and accentuates the role of Chicano youth. He also stresses the importance of external conditions or forces as catalysts in the Movimiento.[8] Historian Juan Gómez-Quiñones argues that it was a struggle for self-identification and a quest for a historical past.[9] "The Chicano Movement," according to historian Manuel G. Gonzales, "consisted of hundreds of organizations focusing on a variety of issues."[10] Historian Ignacio Garcia defines the Movimiento in the following manner:

> The Chicano Movement was not simply a search for identity; or an outburst of collective anxiety. Rather, it was a full-fledged transformation of the way Mexican Americans thought, played politics, promoted their culture. Chicanos embarked on a struggle to make fundamental changes, because only fundamental changes could make them active participants in their lives.

As a political scientist, however, I see the Movimiento as a heterogeneous collection of leaders and organizations committed to fundamental social change. They were driven by a mode of protest politics and inspired by a cultural renaissance of Chicanismo.

Most political movements are products of a multiplicity of factors, and the Movimiento was no exception. Out of the vortex of discontent, frustration, and rising expectations, several exogenous (external) and endogenous (internal) antagonisms gave rise to La Causa (The Cause) within the Movimiento. The following chart identifies the salient exogenous and endogenous antagonisms that gave rise to the Movimiento.[11]

Exogenous Antagonisms

The above exogenous (external) antagonisms induced a climate of change that proved propitious for the emergence of the Movimiento. Without their presence, its internal momentum would not have sufficed to foster its rise. It was their combined effect that produced a pervasive climate of protest that radicalized the country's politics. No previous political epoch in this country had produced the combination of social movements that so effectively challenged the policies, beliefs, and even the structures of the existing liberal capitalist social order. There

Chart 5.1   Salient Antagonisms That Gave Rise to the Movimiento

Exogenous	Endogenous
Civil Rights Movement	History of Mexicano Resistance
New Left	Change in Socioeconomic Status
War on Poverty	Demographic Growth
Vietnam Antiwar Movement	Tijerina and the Alianza
Black Power Movement	Chavez and the UFW
Foreign Social Movements	Gonzales and the Crusade

was discontent and frustration among the ethnic groups in the United States that induced the rise of the politics of militant protest and massive mobilization. Thus, without the presence of the Civil Rights Movement, the New Left, Vietnam antiwar, Black Power,[12] and foreign movements as well Johnson's War on Poverty programs, the Movimiento would have not emerged.

The Civil Rights Movement was the cardinal endogenous antagonism that helped produce the period of protest.[13] The Supreme Court's *Brown v. Board of Education* that ended de jure segregation (1954), the Rosa Parks bus incident (1955), the successful Montgomery bus boycott (1955–1956), and the rise to leadership of Reverend Martin Luther King, Jr., acted as antagonisms that gave rise to the Civil Rights Movement. The direct action tactics brought the civil rights struggle out of the courts and into the streets.[14] From 1956 to 1965, the Civil Rights Movement raised expectations among blacks. The newly formed Southern Christian Leadership Conference (SCLC), Student Nonviolent Coordinating Committee (SNCC), and Congress on Racial Equality (CORE) relied on unconventional protest tactics, for example, demonstrations, civil disobedience, marches, and sit-ins, against pernicious de facto segregation and Jim Crow laws. The effectiveness of such protest pressure facilitated a climate of change and resulted in the passage of the Civil Rights Act in 1964 and Voting Rights Act in 1965.

The presence of the New Left was a second exogenous antagonism that contributed to the Movimiento's rise.[15] As a social movement, the New Left emerged by the late 1950s; it helped energize the Civil Rights Movement and was energized by it. By 1965, the New Left also impacted the rise of the Vietnam Antiwar Movement. Ideologically, the New Left was comprised of mostly young white college radicals like Tom Hayden, who rejected orthodox Marxism, but was hypercritical of liberal capitalism. The Students for a Democratic Society (SDS) promulgated its radical manifesto, the "Port Huron Statement," in 1962 as well and had a progressive agenda of participatory democracy. They called for major social change within the country's political, economic, and social order.[16]

President Lyndon B. Johnson's War on Poverty programs also influenced the Movimiento's rise. After the assassination of President John F. Kennedy in 1963, the Johnson administration contributed to the radicalization of U.S. politics with its War on Poverty programs. Predicated on the notion of "maximum feasible participation," they sought to involve the country's poor in the struggle to eradicate poverty and build a "Great Society." From 1965 to 1968, other federally funded programs, such as VISTA (Volunteers in Service to America), further contributed to the county's change in vision by politicizing many of the poor, including Mexicanos. The passage of the latter legislation served to heighten expectations among the increasingly frustrated and disenchanted blacks and Mexicanos. Their discontent stemmed from the slowness and limited scope of changes enacted.[17]

By 1965, the Vietnam Antiwar Movement[18] led the growing contagion of protest and mobilization across the country. The winds of protest grew stronger in 1964 when the UC Berkeley Free Speech Movement began. Student activism was already on the rise in many university and college campuses and was mobilized in 1965 as a result of the U.S. military involvement in Vietnam. The Gulf of Tonkin incident, in which U.S. naval vessels allegedly came under attack by North Vietnamese vessels, resulted in the U.S. bombing of North Vietnam and a commitment of U.S. ground troops. Antiwar demonstrations brought out thousands of protestors against U.S. involvement in the Vietnam War. By 1966, the country's universities and colleges became hotbeds of militant protest. For the duration of the war movement, the print and electronic media showed graphic color portrayals of the destructiveness of the war. The plethora of protests against the war served to nurture and sustain the country's intensifying climate of change.

The emergence of the Black Power Movement by 1966 was another exogenous factor in the rise of the Movimiento.[19] With the passage of the Civil Rights Act and Voting Rights Act, the Civil Rights Movement entered into a decline. Some black activists became increasingly hypercritical of the movement since little economic or political change had improved in the impoverished and powerless ghettos. A sense of acute frustration and discontent led some activists to rebuke Dr. Martin Luther King, Jr.'s, philosophy of nonviolence and integration. Influenced by the charismatic leadership of Malcolm X, who was assassinated in 1965, new leaders emerged, such as Rap Brown, Stokely Carmichael, Huey Newton, and Eldridge Cleaver. They propounded a black nationalist ideology, largely predicated on the notion of "Black Power" and community control of the ghetto's political and economic structures. These ideas radicalized the Student Nonviolent Coordinating Committee (SNCC) and the formation of the Black Panther Party by 1966, which espoused armed self-defense and revolution via class struggle, were indicative of the epoch's growing political radicalization. With Reverend Martin Luther King's assassination in 1968, the Civil Rights Movement spiraled downward and gave the emerging Black Power Movement impetus. Its strong cultural nationalist posture and militant actions during the late 1960s influenced the nascent Movimiento.

Lastly, the presence of numerous foreign movements—from student to revolutionary—also acted as an exogenous antagonism for change. Throughout much of the world numerous social movements emerged, particularly by the second half of the 1960s. The Cuban Revolution and various revolutionary movements in Latin America, Africa, and Vietnam increased the consciousness of emerging activists who could see the similarity of these struggles to that of the internal colonial status of Chicanos in the United States. The revolutionary leadership and exploits of Che Guevara, Fidel Castro, Mao Tse-tung, Vladimir Lenin, Leon Trotsky, and others made them icons of various revolutionary movements both outside the United States and within as well. Protest movements against liberal capitalist regimes were commonplace, especially in Europe and Latin America. In particular, the student protest in México in 1968 against the Olympics held in México City led to the slaughter of over 500 students by the Mexican Army. In the words of Juan Gómez-Quiñones, "Importantly the sixties were a time of discontent and conflict in México, a time of militant organizing by progressives, labor, intellectuals and students who challenged the dominant ideology and institutions."[20]

Endogenous Antagonisms

The rise of the Movimiento was also induced by a combination of endogenous antagonisms. The Mexicano's history of resistance and struggle was one such factor. As described earlier, the Mexicano experience was driven by a vibrant history of resistance against oppressive and exploitive conditions, first in México and later in the United States. The various epochs examined in this work clearly illustrate a dialectical process that fostered major changes in Mexicano politics in the United States. With each passing decade, Mexicanos not only continued to resist their oppression, but new leaders forged new organizations and strategies in the pursuit of change. By the 1960s, with the country entangled in the imbroglio of protest and mass mobilizations, some Mexicanos, especially the youth, became increasingly radicalized in their politics and more determined to resist their second-class citizenship. Gains had been made during the previous epoch of social action, especially against discrimination and segregation through the dynamism of the Civil Rights Movement. The result was that the barriers of racism and prejudice had not been fully removed, only lessened. Some Mexicanos were not satisfied; they became increasingly impatient and sought change. This was a result of relative deprivation,[21] in a country in which expectations were never met; this in turn fostered growing discontent. For years depicted as the "Forgotten Americans," Mexicanos became more assertive in rebuking such characterizations in 1966.[22]

A slight improvement in the socioeconomic status of Mexicanos served only to raise expectations. By the mid-1960s, they faced a paradox: on the one hand, some socioeconomic improvement; on the other, continued poverty and social problems due to internal colonialism. Ever since World War II, a small but increasing number of Mexicanos had achieved middle-class status. With more Mexicanos given access to better paying jobs, such as in factories, a middle class emerged. Like its black counterpart, they were also impelled by rising expectations. According to 1960 U.S. Census data, Spanish-surnamed professionals comprised 4.6 percent, managers and proprietors 4.9 percent, clerical workers 5.5 percent, craftsmen 18.2 percent, and operatives 25.4 percent. Yet in spite of such socioeconomic progress, in the words of Moore and Cuellar, "Mexicans [held] the poorer jobs inside most job classifications."[23]

The socioeconomic reality was that many Mexicanos lived under the specter of an impoverished internal colonial status. By the mid-1960s, their level of socioeconomic progress was more illusionary than substantive. Except for the relatively small indigenous population, no other ethnic or racial population in the Southwest was as severely economically pinched as were Mexicanos. They earned only $.47 per person for every dollar of white income earned per person. Moreover, the median income of all Mexicano males in the Southwest in 1959 was $2,768. This was only 57 percent of the median earned by white males in the same area. Thirty-five percent lived below the poverty line of $3,000 annual income.[24] They held poorer jobs paying less money, and most urban Mexicano males were employed as semiskilled and laborers.[25]

By the late 1960s, the median income for Mexicano males over the age of sixteen was $4,839. In Tejas, Mexicanos earned only 60 percent of median income made by whites; while in California and Arizona they earned 75 percent. Twenty-four percent of all Mexicanos fell below the poverty line (the average poverty threshold for a non-farm family of four was $3,743 in 1969), which represented an improvement over the 1960 figure of 35 percent. Once again, Tejas had the highest percentage of families living in poverty. In occupational distribution, Mexicanos within the white-collar category made a slight improvement: from 19.1 percent in 1960 to 21.6 percent in 1970. Yet within the blue-collar category they slightly declined from 80.9 in 1960 to 78.4 in 1970; most remained in what economists called the "secondary labor market," an economic symptom of internal colonialism.

Internal colonialism also had a negative impact on the Mexicano's low levels of education. The crisis in education was evident in 1960: Mexicanos attained a median of 7.1 years of education compared with 12.1 for whites and 9.0 for nonwhites. Despite this, some progress was made since the 1950 census. The median years of education completed in 1950 were 5.4; by 1960, it increased to 7.1. The incidence of functional illiteracy (equivalent to zero to four years of elementary education) was seven times that of the whites and nearly twice that of nonwhites as a whole. Also, only 5.6 percent of Mexicanos had attended college, compared to four times as many whites and twice as many nonwhites.[26]

By 1970 the median level of education increased from 7.1 to 9 years, compared to whites with more than 12 years. Schooling was highest in California with a median of 9.7 years and lowest in Tejas with 6.7 years. Although more Mexicanos graduated from high school and college in comparison to 1960, their numbers were still very low in comparison to whites and blacks. Eighty-six percent of whites graduated from high school and 23.5 percent from college; 66.8 percent of blacks graduated from high school and 8.3 from college. The figures for Mexicanos were much lower: only 60.3 percent graduated from high school and 5.4 percent from college. Educational levels of attainment were correlated with segregation of the many colonized barrio schools.[27] Further contributing to the crisis, Mexicano children also had high push-out and functional illiteracy rates.

Overall, from a socioeconomic perspective, the barrios in both the urban and rural areas were becoming cauldrons of discontent. By the mid-1960s, most barrios were plagued by abject poverty, unemployment, prejudice and racism, inferior education that produced high push-out rates and few college graduates, gang violence, crime, drugs, alcoholism, dilapidated housing, lack of health care, and political and economic powerlessness. Increasingly cognizant of their plight, some Mexicanos were inspired by the gains made by blacks in the Civil Rights Movement and became more vociferous in their demands for their own social change. They became resolute in demanding redress from governmental structures.

As an antagonism, the rapidly growing Mexicano population in the United States created another impetus for change. According to the U.S. 1960 Census, the Mexicano population rapidly increased by 51 percent, against 37 percent for whites and 49 percent for nonwhites. At the national level, Mexicanos numbered some 3,842,000. Within Aztlán's five southwestern states, Mexicanos comprised

12 percent of the total population of 28 million. Eighty-seven percent of the total U.S. Mexicano population resided within Aztlán. In addition, most Mexicanos lived in California and Tejas with populations of a little over 1.4 million each. These two states accounted for 82 percent of Aztlán's total population. The three remaining states of Nuevo México, Arizona, and Colorado contained only 18 percent.[28] Another important aspect of this demographic profile was that by 1960 urbanization had increased to where four-fifths of Mexicanos living in the Southwest lived in cities and towns. One-third of all Mexicanos lived in colonized barrios of the following four cities: Los Angeles, San Antonio, San Francisco, and El Paso.[29] The Los Angeles metropolitan area, however, had the greatest concentration, with slightly more Mexicanos than the combined populations of Colorado, Arizona, and Nuevo México.

During the next ten years, the Mexicano population continued its rapid growth. With the termination of the Bracero Program in 1964, the migrant exodus from México into the United States once again accelerated. This was attributable to two factors: the continued influx of documented and undocumented immigration and high birthrates. In 1966 the number of Mexicano legal immigrants was 45,163 and by 1973 increased to 70,141.[30] This was in great part due to the passage of the Immigration and Nationality Act, which eliminated national-origin quotas. According to Rodolfo Acuña, "the law was revolutionary because it changed its policy of admitting immigrants by family preferences instead of by national origins which preserved the Nordic heritage of the United States and restricted the immigration of those of less favorable ethnic and racial origins."[31] As amended, it stipulated a ceiling of 120,000 persons per year from the Western Hemisphere and put a cap of 40,000 from any one country. Immediate relatives of U.S. citizens, such as parents, spouses, and children, could also be admitted without limit. Its passage invigorated the flow undocumented migrants into the United States, which significantly contributed to the Mexicano population growth. In explaining the significance of this legislation, David E. Lorey writes, "Coming as it did at the end of the Bracero Program, this reform (and further modifications of the law in 1976) converted the status of a large portion of the long-established Mexican migrant flow from legal to illegal."[32]

This was evident with the deportation to México of some 89,751 in 1966 and 201,638 in 1969.[33] By 1973 an astronomical increase in undocumented workers occurred, 480,588; the estimate of the actual number was somewhere between 600,000 and one million. About one-third of the apprehensions were of repeaters, meaning those who were apprehended at least once previously. México's perennial poverty coupled with its rapid economic development, which had the effect of displacing many rural workers, provided the key to continued exodus.

For México's government, both legal and illegal immigration continued to act as a stabilizing force or safety valve.

The second contributing factor to the Mexicano population growth was their high birthrates. In fact, Mexicanos had higher birthrates than all other ethnic/racial groups.[34] Mexicanos also had the largest families in the country. The average family size in 1970 was 3.6 persons; for Mexicanos it was 4.5 and for blacks, 4.1 persons. Not only did Mexicanos have larger families, they also had a younger population: their median age was 20.2 years. It was nine years lower than that of the U.S. population as a whole and 2.5 lower than that of nonwhites. In addition, 46 percent of the population was below the age of eighteen, a contrast to 33 percent of the rest of the country's population.[35]

The Mexicano population dramatically increased. Because of the use of different criteria to count Mexicanos during the 1970 U.S. Census, it is difficult to state an actual count. One such estimate of persons who identified as being of Mexicano origin was 4,532,000, which by 1973 increased to between six and seven million.[36] Even by the most conservative figures, Mexicanos were the fastest growing segment in the Southwest. In a single decade they increased by some 32 percent. They comprised 15 percent of the five-state Southwest's thirty-six million inhabitants. Some 90 percent lived in the Southwest, while 50 percent alone lived in California as compared to 36 percent in Tejas. This meant that no more than 10 percent of the Mexicano population lived outside Aztlán. The three remaining southwestern states of Nuevo México, Arizona, and Colorado held only 16 percent. While nationally only 15 percent of Mexicanos lived in rural areas, in California 90 percent were urban based.[37]

The allegedly "invisible" Mexicano community became increasingly visible. The rise of Reies Lopez Tijerina and his Alianza Federal de Mercedes in Nuevo México, Cesar Chavez's United Farm Workers (UFW) in California, and Rodolfo "Corky" Gonzales's Crusade for Justice in Colorado also acted synergistically on this era of protest.[38] Their militancy of action became evident in 1965 and 1966. Tijerina's Alianza in 1966 began its shift from a conventional pressure strategy to one of unconventional protest with a march from Albuquerque to Santa Fe, Nuevo México's capital. The march produced no positive results on the issue of land grants. Tijerina, increasingly exasperated, that same year upped the militant ante with the Alianza's occupation of the echo amphitheater in Kit Carson National Park, which led to his arrest.

After three years of building the foundation for the present UFW, in 1965 Chavez initiated La Huelga (the Delano Strike) against recalcitrant grape growers in California. In 1966 farmworkers marched from Delano to the state's capital, Sacramento, where El Plan de Delano was promulgated. At that time also Gonzales was director of a War on Poverty program in Denver, and along with other Mexicano leaders participated in a walkout on March 28, 1966, at a meeting held in Albuquerque by the Equal Employment Opportunity Commission. That same year, his evolving militancy became evident with his resignation as poverty agency director and his formation of the Crusade for Justice.

Increasingly, activists rejected the social action politics and buffer role of the Mexican American Generation and by 1966 adhered to the much more assertive mode of protest politics of the emergent Chicano Generation.

The Chicano Generation: Adherents of Chicanismo

From a political generational perspective, the once dominant Mexican American Generation (MAG) and growing Mexicano generation (MG) were overwhelmed by the rise of the Chicano Generation (CG). From 1966 to 1974, the Mexicano political experience was pervaded by three concurrent political generations, which illustrated the heterogeneity of the Mexicano community. While the MG did not play a major role in forging the epoch's militant protest politics, it continued to grow due to the migrant exodus. Like the previous MG, the MG of this epoch was nurtured by México's evolving semiauthoritarian political culture, which had evolved into a parochial/subject political culture, one that was less authoritarian and a little bit more democratic.

As to the MAG, politically it played second fiddle to the CG. This meant its liberal capitalist pro-system assimilationist ethos was unequivocally rejected by scores of activist leaders, organizers, and organizations who embraced the Chicanismo of the CG. While those individuals and organizations that adhered to the MAG continued to be politically active throughout the epoch their leadership role became ostensibly secondary. They continued to practice their "mainstream" politics of adaptation and political integration. In short, they were overshadowed by the ubiquity of the militant protest politics of the Chicano Movement that pervaded Aztlán among other parts of the country where Mexicanos resided. It is important to note, however, that the CG was a dialectical progression of the MAG, meaning upon the achievement, contributions, and struggles made by the MAG a new synthesis occurred—the rise of the CG. Mario Garcia further elucidates on the MAG's contribution to CG:

> The Generation, despite the efforts of some scholars to isolate it from history, built on both the successes and failures of the Mexican American Generation. . . . The Mexican American Generation laid the foundation for the new era of politics of rising expectations. That foundation would help create a leading vanguard of the Chicano Movement of the 1960s

and 1970s: the Chicano student movement. . . . [T]he Chicano Generation moved to rectify the failures of the past and to break through the
ideological handicaps of the Mexican American Generation.[39]

Thus, the rise of the CG symbolized a departure from the system maintenance
approach of the MAG. Chicanismo consequently became the basis for what some
Chicano scholars such as Mario T. Garcia, Carlos Muñoz, Ignacio Garcia, among
others, have alluded to as the CG.[40] It is important to note, however, that during
the Movimiento's incipient years (1966–1968), most activists did not call themselves *Chicanos*. Instead, most embraced the thinking of the MAG and identified
themselves as *Mexican Americans*. The term had come into vogue as a self-identifying
term during the late 1950s and 1960s. Influenced in part by the Black Power
Movement's accentuation on nationalism, Mexicano activists from 1967 to 1969
underwent a cultural renaissance and transformation that produced a new group
identity and consciousness, which rejected the "want to be white" and buffer leadership and organizational political roles.

The emergence of the student and youth movements increasingly radicalized
the barrios' and *colonias'* political climate. By 1968 *Mexican American* began to give
way to *Chicano* as a self-identifying term. The transition was completed in 1969
with the Chicano Youth Liberation Conference held in Denver, Colorado, which
adopted El Plan Espiritual de Aztlán, which accentuated Chicanismo as defined
by the goals of "cultural nationalism" and "self-determination." Some fifteen hundred activists attended the conference, and the plan became the most important
cultural nationalist manifesto that inspired Chicanismo and the struggle for an
independent Aztlán. It became the cornerstone of the Chicano generation ethos.[41]
Hence, the idea of building a Chicano nation was grounded on El Plan Espirtitual
de Aztlán, which represented an act of symbolic defiance rather than a formal
declaration of independence.[42] A month later, Chicano activists met at the UC
Santa Barbara conference and produced El Plan de Santa Barbara, which called for
a plan of action for Chicanos in higher education and the formation of MEChA
(Movimiento Estudiantil Chicano de Aztlán). Like its predecessor, it too was also
strongly influenced by Chicanismo. Thus, *Chicano* by 1969 became the locus of
the new militancy and cultural renaissance, and name of the new social movement,
El Movimiento Chicano.

From a political cultural perspective, the Movimiento was a product of the
CG Chicanismo-inspired ethos. Among activists, especially the youth, *Chicano* by
late 1968 replaced *Mexican American* for it symbolized the emergence of a "cultural
renaissance" and "cultural rebirth." Initially, the usage of *Chicano* was problematic
for some since no one definitively knew or even today knows its true origin.[43]

Mario Suarez, a writer from Arizona, published an article entitled "El Hoyo," in the *Arizona Quarterly* in 1947 and described the inhabitants of a barrio in Tucson as "Chicanos" who "raised hell" during the weekend. Suarez did not explain its genesis, but wrote that "the term *Chicano* is a short way of saying *Mexicano.*"[44] Yet it is important to note that Manuel Gamio used the term *Chicano* in the 1920s. Ernesto Galarza, in his book *Barrio Boy*, described the Mexicano residents of Sacramento, California, in 1913 as Chicanos.

Hence, in its most basic form *Chicano* denoted a Mexicano born in the United States. Speaking from my own personal experience, for many of us who were raised in a barrio at least up to the mid-1960s, *Chicano* was synonymous with *Mexicano*. It was the truncated or abbreviated version of *Mexicano*. To some, however, especially older adults from within and outside the barrios, the term conjured up pejorative connotations of lower-class and rustic ruffian youth, *pachucos* or what Marx called the *lumponproletariat*. Yet for many of the youth from both the barrios and universities and colleges, the term *Chicano* accentuated a rediscovery of their *orgullo* (pride), an emphasis on self-determination, and self-assertion based upon a new sense of cultural identity. It connoted a sense of self-identification by those who espoused a "cultural rebirth" and challenged the Mexicano's subordinated status in the United States In brief, *Chicano* denoted a person and group committed to a "reattachment" to their cultural Mexicano roots not only within Aztlán, but with the motherland of México itself. To many *Chicano* was a powerful symbolic code.[45] And in the words of Juan Gómez-Quiñones, "Chicano was the term and litmus test for a political frame of mind."[46] In particular, youth gave it a connotation of unprecedented rebelliousness, cultural pride, and activism.

Hence, from the term *Chicano* developed the basis of Chicanismo. Its usage was also given impetus in 1967 by Rodolfo "Corky" Gonzales's epic poem, "Yo Soy Joaquin" (I Am Joaquin). His poem illustrates powerful language and symbolic images from the Chicano's historical struggle and alienation from gringo society: "I am Joaquin, Lost in a world of confusion, Caught up in the whirl of a Gringo society, confused by the rules, scorned by attitudes, suppressed by manipulation, and destroyed by modern society." For Gonzales this was "a journey back through history, a painful re-evaluation, a wandering search for my people's and, most of all, for my own identity."[47] The poem contributed to the Chicano's quest for self-definition and a positive identity. To Meier and Rivera, "like the Movement, the poem had different meanings for different people." They wrote:

> It cut across the boundaries of class, place of origin, gender, and generation. It visualized [Chicanos] unified by common experiences and by pride

in their heritage and culture. Generally, it was indifferent to assimilation and acculturation. It argued that Chicanos had the right to cultural auton-omy and self-determination. It regarded [Chicanos] as cut off from their roots and dehumanized as they were transformed by their employment into an economic commodity. It agonized over identification and felt it was necessary to develop a true Chicano identity, culture, and history.[48]

According to Carlos Muñoz, "The most significant aspect of 'I Am Joaquin' was that it captured both the agony and jubilation permeating the identity crisis faced by Mexican American youth in the process of assimilation."[49]

A myriad of explanations and definitions exist on Chicanismo, which suggests a lack of consensus exists as to its meaning. According to Rafaela G. Castro, Chicanismo emphasized ethnic, cultural, and linguistic pride, and a belief in polit-ical self-determination: it called for reclaiming of the territory lost by México after the United States War against México, 1846–1848.[50] To Juan Gomez-Quiñonez, "The emphasis on *Chicanismo* was upon community autonomy, individ-ual self-worth, cultural pride, and political and economic equity."[51] Another scholar, John Garcia, wrote, "*Chicanismo* embodies the persistence of group iden-tity that contained cultural values, symbols, and practices which result in group pride and political mobilization."[52] In explaining Chicanismo, Ignacio Garcia states:

> The Movement was driven by profound political and cultural ideas of being Chicano. By popularizing these elements through rhetoric and debate, Chicano activists developed a cultural-political taxonomy that explained their activism. This taxonomy differed from those of the past, which were either pro-America or pro-México. This new identification was pro-barrio and incorporated Americanism with the barrio's Mexican-ism. The negative aspects of the American experience combined with his-torical nostalgia of México to create a cultural milieu conducive to being Chicano.[53]

Chicanismo was a product of a growing militancy among Chicano activists, who produced their own myths inherent to a new ethos. With its ethno-nationalism, Chicanismo categorically rejected the MAG's notion of Mexicanos in the United States being part of the "melting pot," meaning assimilation and integration. F. Arturo Rosales further explains:

> All in all, tension and resentment were on the rise. Their increasing ghet-toization made Chicanos feel betrayed by the American Dream. The opti-mism that in the U.S. anything was possible proclaimed so often by the

Mexican American generation, came into question. This generation had chased an all-American status, but the real white society, it seemed, had left them behind in the barrios, perceiving them as "Mexicans."[54]

Mario T. Garcia explains, that "the Chicano Generation was a product of its historical time."[55] Activists adopted the term *Chicano* as an act of defiance and to redefine themselves by criteria of their own choosing.[56] Infused with an emerging nationalist spirit of a changing ethos, Chicanos categorically rebuked the usage of such characterizations of being Spanish, Americans of Mexican or Spanish extraction, Mexican Americans, or Hispanic or Latin. This was indicative of an identity problem that continued through the Chicano experience. What to call ourselves? became a perennial question of debate among Chicano activists.

Chicanismo was not an ideology, since it did not possess a comprehensive set of beliefs, ideas, and justification that clearly delineated a vision or direction and a strategy. Yet, it had the semblance of one. As a quasi-ideology, it embraced an admixture of cultural nationalism impelled by notions of both cultural pluralism and separatism. The former denoted a form of acculturation, meaning a process of cultural borrowing between diverse peoples resulting in a new cultural pattern or the notion of the salad bowl, the latter was based on the notion of building a Chicano nation, Aztlán. Beyond denoting the mythical homeland of the Aztecs,[57] *Aztlán* became synonymous with the Southwest. The historical antecedent for separatism had its roots in Tejas in 1915 with the insurgent "Plan de San Diego of 1915," which was squelched by the Texas Rangers and U.S. Army. A major intellectual flaw of Chicanismo was that it did not delineate in lucid language the goals of the Movimiento. If the goal was Aztlán, it was never effectively addressed as how it was going to be achieved; nor did it explain the nature of political, economic, or social system that would ensue as an alternative to liberal capitalism. Without the various aspects that make up an ideology, Chicanismo was much more of a political cultural concept.

At the core of Chicanismo was cultural nationalism, predicated on feelings of cultural pride derived from their Mexicano ethnicity, culture, heritage, and language. The concept of nationalism[58] at the most general level represents an awareness of belonging to a national entity (potential or actual) and a desire to maintain and perpetuate the identity, integrity, prosperity, and power of that nation or social group.[59] A nation can be defined as a relatively large group based upon ethnicity or race that shares a common culture, language, heritage, and geographical space. Chicanos integrated these concepts into their own essence of cultural nationalism. This was evident with the Chicanismo emphasis on cultural consciousness and identification with the pertinent Mexicano historical and political experiences in the United States. According to Harry Pachon, "*Chicanismo* saw Chicanos as basically a conquered people—a people who were stripped of their land, their history, and their culture as a result of Anglo exploitation." Chicanismo was also a political and economic response to the Mexicano's exploited and impoverished history.[60] As a cultural response, Chicanismo claimed that Chicanos had been robbed of their heritage by an intolerant white-dominated ethnocentric society and culture based on Eurocentric racist values.

Indicative of its cultural nationalist perspective, some Chicanos identified as La Raza de Bronce and adhered to their own *mestizaje* mythology. Chicanismo postulated that Chicanos were a proud mestizo (hybrid) race with a heritage of indigenous and Spanish roots.[61] While many Chicanos embraced a new identity, some were inspired by the writings of México's great philosopher Jose Vasconcelos, who postulated that the mestizo—a hybrid of Spanish and indigenous—constituted the greatness of a fifth race, La Raza Cosmica (The Cosmic Race). Some activists, especially those who had visions of an Aztlán stretching from the U.S. Southwest to Tierra de Fuego in South America, identified themselves not only as Chicano, but also of belonging to La Raza (The People). This concept fostered a sense of a common identity or belonging to the whole of the mestizo peoples of Latin America. They broadened the nationalist symbolism to be inclusive of revolutionary leaders such as Che Guevara and Fidel Castro, among others. As a result of Chicanismo, those individuals and organizations that adhered to buffer and "want to be white" political roles were denigrated as *vendidos* (sellouts) or "coconuts" (white inside and brown outside). They were viewed as not being in touch with the oppressive colonial realities of the barrios and *colonias*.

Chicanismo's critical view of U.S. white culture is captured in the words of freelance writer Armando B. Rendon, who wrote in his epic book *Chicano Manifesto*, "[U.S.] culture is not worth copying: it is destructive of personal dignity; it is callous, vindictive, arrogant, militaristic, self-deceiving, and greedy . . . it is a cultural cesspool and a social and spiritual vacuum for the Chicano . . . the corollary follows—that to be non-Anglo is to be inferior; to speak other than English is be inferior; to be brown or black or yellow is to be inferior."[62] Chicanismo emphatically rejected the notion that Chicanos were inferior, and accentuated the greatness of the Mexicano's past.

In their quest for identity, Chicanos learned that their historical roots were rich, unique, and significant. When indigenous civilizations in Mesoamerica were building pyramids, temples, aqueducts, and elaborate cities and studying the planets, whites in Europe were still living in caves and were wandering hunters. Moreover, Chicanos also discovered Aztlán's historically rich past. Insurgent leaders like Murrieta, Vasquez, and Cortina, among others, became symbols of Chicano resistance to the occupation of Aztlán. Political scientist John A. Garcia writes, "One of the objectives of the *Movimiento* was to liberate Mexican-origin people from a sense of cultural inferiority."[63] Chicanismo fostered a sense of rediscovery, a cultural renaissance impelled by the richness of the Mexicano's culture, history, language, and symbolism both within the context of Aztlán and México itself. Chicanismo for the young people was driven by a rejection of traditional notions of Americanization and assimilation, seen as nothing more than attempts by gringos to maintain their hegemony over Chicanos by destroying their culture.[64]

Chicanismo also denoted a revitalized sense of group solidarity. As a new ethos, it fostered a new sense of community of "We" rather than the "I." It acted as a catalyst for unity of action, and an unprecedented spirit of activism and militancy. According to Meier and Rivera, "It cut across the boundaries of class, place of origin, gender, and generation."[65] Chicanismo conjured up notions not only of pride or *orgullo*, but of *carnalismo* (brotherhood), *comunidad* (community), and *familia* (family). It also engendered a sense of a new belonging and *espíritu* (spirit) based on love, passion, and respect for what was Mexicano. F. Arturo Rosales writes, "It is no small wonder that an impassioned searching for roots—in *lo Mexicano*—dominated the beginning of the Chicano Movement."[66]

Chicanismo was also actuated by new nationalist symbols. Nationalist cries of "Chicano Power," "Brown Power," and "Viva La Causa," permeated the lexicon and rhetoric of activists. Identification with México's historical Mexicano experience became an integral aspect of Chicanismo as illustrated by the incorporation in marches and mobilizations of México's flag and its colors of red, white, and green; La Virgen de Guadalupe; and symbols and leaders of México's Revolution, for example, Emiliano Zapata, Pancho Villa, and Ricardo Flores Magón. México's revolutionary *corrido* music, art, and literature were rediscovered and used to reconnect to the greatness of México's indigenous civilizations—the Olmecas, Mayas, Toltecs, and Aztecs. The history of México was studied and incorporated into the Movimiento's eclectic symbolism. David G. Gutiérrez writes, "Young activists presented a quasi-nationalist vision of the Chicano people which extolled a pre-Columbian, native ancestry while diminishing or even rejecting their connection with American culture and society."[67]

By the late 1960s, Chicanismo had radicalized the Movimiento. It became increasingly critical of liberal capitalism and embraced a social agenda that had components of reform and separatism to proletarian revolution. According to Juan Gómez-Quiñones, "*Chicanismo* emerged as a challenge to the dominant institutions, assumptions, feeling of cultural rebirth, and equal opportunity." It cut across class, regional, and generational lines—a testimony to the reality that most Mexicanos had experienced some form of discrimination in their lives.[68] By the

early 1970s, some activists were inspired by the ideological promises of the Marxist class struggle, that is, of a classless society; their idea of a modified Chicanismo
became an amalgam of nationalism and Marxism. Yet other alleged Marxist activists repudiated Chicanismo for creating a "false consciousness" and its cultural
nationalist proclivities. They were hypercritical of those Chicano activists who
identified themselves as cultural nationalists or still adhered to buffer or "want to
be white" roles. Those integrationist Chicanos were perceived as misguided
reformers who were part of the inherent contradictions of the Movimiento. Chicano Marxists pursued a rigid sectarian Marxist class struggle approach that called
for a proletarian revolution. As a result, Chicanismo came under increasing attack
and scrutiny from Marxists from 1970 through 1974.

Not all who espoused Chicanismo were ultranationalist separatist proponents
or advocates of Marxism. Some activists adhered to a cultural pluralist perspective. Their perspective on Chicanismo was predicated on reform and acculturation. In essence, they sought to effect "micro" changes within the liberal capitalist
social order and embraced a more militant buffer role. They sought to remove
the inequities and exclusionary practices by working within rather than outside
the prescribed rules of the political process. Essentially, they were militant inte-
grationists who culturally wanted to be Chicano, but espoused the need for
change by integration into the system. With the decline of the Chicano Movement by 1974 cultural pluralists were by far the most numerous.

The CG, from a political generational perspective, was a product of decades
of struggles for change. It was a product primarily of the youth who rebelled
against the accommodation of the MAG and the political alienation that characterized the MG. It produced a political transient subculture that was highly participant in nature characterized by its own high-level cognitive, adaptive, and
evaluative political orientations.

The Chicano Generation's Cultural Renaissance

Integral to the Chicano cultural rebirth was its intellectual renaissance. It was
during this epoch of protest that an unprecedented number of Chicano intellectuals were produced. Through their literature, poetry, and scholarship, they made
major contributions to the emergence of the Movimiento.[69] No previous epoch
had produced a like number of distinguished intellectuals and scholars. They created an "explosion of literature that added new dynamic to letters," and which
drew on the literary tradition of México and Aztlán.[70] The power of the printed
word became a weapon in the arsenal for change, and encouraged the pursuit of
new knowledge and a cultural revival. Through their works and their pedagogy,

they contributed to the emergence of a new Chicano ethos that rejected the MAG's integrationism. The search for identity permeated the literary arena. Scores of Chicano novelists and poets, who wrote in English—but also sometimes in both English and Spanish or *calo*—contributed to the intellectual renaissance. Notable novelists of this epoch included José Antonio Villareal, Rudolfo Anaya, Oscar Zeta Acosta, Tomás Rivera, Ron Arias, Rolando Hinojosa-Smith, Miguel Méndez, and Alejandro Morales.[71]

Chicano poets used the power of the verse to dissect and examine the historical, political, cultural, and spiritual roots of the "experience." *Movimiento* poets were not only critical of "*Gringolandia*" (the United States), but their verses were often personal emotion-laden epitaphs about gringo society. Other times, they embellished their verses with calls for action, for social change, and for Chicano nationalism. Rudolfo "Corky" Gonzales's epic poem "Yo Soy Joaquin" as previously mentioned was first published in 1967, and represented the rise of Chicanismo for the CG. In its powerful opening words, Gonzales alludes to the Chicano's alienation from the gringo-dominated society: "I am Joaquin lost in a world of confusion, caught up in a whirl of a gringo society . . . destroyed by modern society."[72] Other Movimiento poets, such as Alberto Urista (Alurista), Abelardo Delgado, Richard Sanchez, Tino Villanueva, and Sergio Elizondo, were the pacesetters who contributed to the cultural renaissance.[73] In particular, Alurista's Plan Espiritual de Aztlán was Chicanismo's manifesto.

Chicano scholars ignited the CG's intellectual renaissance. It was during this epoch that the number of Chicanos in the academy increased significantly. For some, the pursuit of knowledge was a potent weapon in the struggle for social change. Because of pressure exerted by activists, coupled with affirmative action, numerous universities opened their doors to Chicanos and recruited them into their graduate programs. Financial assistance, for example, Equal Opportunity Program fellowships and scholarships, were made available to working-class Chicanos, which allowed them to go on to graduate school. Some foundations, such as the Ford Foundation, provided generous graduate fellowships.[74]

This epoch produced a new "intelligentsia" that became an integral part of the CG. Chicano scholars produced a new body of literature that sought to remedy the lack of materials on the Chicano experience. One such scholar was anthropologist Octavio Romano, who as early as 1967 published his writings in his journal *El Grito: A Journal of Contemporary Mexican American Thought* out of Berkeley, Quinto Sol Publications. It made a significant contribution to the rise of the Chicano Generation. He criticized much of the scholarship done on Mexicanos by social scientists. He categorized them as being "an ahistoric people." His writings cast the Mexicanos in the United States as activist participants in their history, and while he used the term *Mexican American*, he saw them as immersed in the process of self-identification.[75]

Historian Rodolfo Acuña was another pacesetter of the Chicano Generation, who in 1972 published his classic, *Occupied America: The Chicano's Struggle toward Liberation*. In this landmark historical work, Acuña argued "that Chicanos are a colonized people in the United States." From his perspective, "the conquest of the southwest created a colonial situation in the traditional sense—with the Mexican land and population being controlled by an imperialistic United States." For Acuña, the Chicano experience was one of internal colonialism. For many activists, his work not only became the standard text for Chicano Studies, but the bible of "El Movimiento." He was a new breed of Chicano intellectual who was Marxist in thought and was committed to the people's liberation from liberal capitalism. In 1969, in California he founded one of the first and best Chicano Studies departments in the country, at what today is California State University at Northridge.

During the epoch of protest, a number of other Chicano scholars contributed to the CG's new ethos. Through their research they helped Chicanos rediscover their identity, history, and heritage. Some were critical of the status quo and took a more cultural pluralist posture; others, influenced by a Marxist class analysis, rebuked liberal capitalism and focused their analysis on the Chicano's oppression and exploitation, and on the myriad of social problems affecting them.[76] The cultural renaissance also manifested in a number of Movimiento-oriented journals. By 1970 Chicano scholars had developed three journals: *El Grito*, edited by Octavio Romano and Nick Vaca; *Aztlán: International Journal of Chicano Studies and Research*, under the guidance of then graduate student historian Juan Gómez-Quiñonez; and the *Journal of Mexican American History*, edited by Jesus Chavarria. Of the three, *Aztlán* became the most movement-oriented. These three journals along and a few others that were irregularly published, such as *Campo Libre, Caracol, Chismearte, La Cucaracha, Con Safos, De Colores*, and *Tejidos*,[77] contributed to the CG's intellectual renaissance. They provided readers with access to the ideas of emerging Chicano writers and a venue in which to publish their works. A number of Chicano publishing houses and publishers such as Quinto Sol Publications, La Causa Publications, Trucha Publications, and Arte Público Press were but a few that contributed to the Chicano literary explosion.

Moreover, countless Movimiento newspapers contributed to the literary contagion of the CG. Cognizant of their integral importance to revolutionary struggles, activists used them for communication, propaganda, agitation, recruiting, and organizing, and as mediums of intellectual discourse and debate.[78] Organizations of all kinds—both in the communities and universities—used their newspapers as vehicles of "conscientization" and for purposes of organizing. Chicano newspapers carried articles on a diversity of topics, which included Chicano history, politics, literature, poetry, current events, and editorials, and a dose of cultural nationalist and Marxist polemics. As purveyors of La Causa, they acted as a passionate voice for the interests of the oppressed and powerless in the barrios and *colonias*. They attacked and criticized the police, educational systems, politicians, government agencies, *tio tacos* (Mexican American sellouts) "coconuts" (Mexicanos who are brown outside and white inside), and U.S. foreign policy— particularly as it related to Latin America and the war in Vietnam.

One of the first Movimiento newspapers to appear was *La Raza*,[79] in 1967. *La Raza* openly publicized that it was a barrio newspaper committed to defending the rights of the community. By the early 1970s, it adopted a magazine format, which became a template for many of the other Movimiento-oriented publications. According to Acuña, "Its photos and articles [were] a social commentary on the struggle of the Chicano to achieve social, political, and economic self-determination." He explains that without its reporting, much of the Chicano's history of the time would have been lost, ignored by the establishment press.[80] Its initial editor was Cuban-born Movimiento activist Elizar Risco. When Risco left, Joe Razo, who was assisted by Raul Ruiz, became its new editor. During the National Chicano Moratorium antiwar march of August 29, 1970, both Razo and Ruiz took numerous photographs of the riot that were used later in the inquest involving the killing of journalist Ruben Salazar.[81] Ruiz became its editor by the early 1970s and made it one of the most influential Movimiento magazines. Its articles were ideologically cultural nationalist, third world-oriented, and antiliberal capitalist with socialist underpinnings. With Ruiz's rise as one of the main Raza Unida Party leaders in California, from 1971 to beyond 1974, *La Raza* remained a powerful voice in the struggle to form the *partido*.

The Crusade for Justice in 1967 published its own newspaper, *El Gallo*, out of Denver, Colorado. Throughout the late 1960s and well into the 1970s, *El Gallo* became the Crusade's official propaganda and information outlet. In 1968 in Nuevo México, Enriqueta Longeaux and Betita Martinez published *El Grito del Norte*, a newspaper that declared its intent of promoting the "course of justice of the poor people . . . and [to] conserve the cultural heritage of La Raza."[82] Indicative of the rising Chicanismo, that same year Longeaux y Vásquez wrote,

> The *raza* in the southwest . . . wants our history back . . . our cities, our mountains, and rivers were explored and settled by Indians and Spaniards, not pilgrim's wagon masters. The first cattle raisers, cowboys and farmers were *raza*. We weren't waiting here to be saved by the great white fathers.[83]

Most of the major Movimiento organizations had their own newspapers. Gonzales's *El Gallo*; Chavez's United Farm Workers had *El Malcriado*; José Angel Gutiérrez's Raza Unida Party in Cristal, Tejas, had *La Verdad*; and the Brown Berets had *Regeneración*. *El Gallo del Norte*, which tended to focus its coverage on Reyes Tijerina's Alianza. In Tejas, the Mexican American Youth Organization (MAYO) had four active newspapers by 1969: *El Deguello*, out of San Antonio; *Hoy*, published in the Rio Grande Valley; *El Azteca*, out of Kingsville; and *La Revolución*, from Uvalde.[84] The Chicano press explosion became evident in the scores of other organizational, community, and university newspapers that surfaced: *El Machete, El Chicano, Bronze, La Voz Mexicana, La Verdad, El Tecolote, Carta Editorial, El Papel, Basta Ya, Inside Eastside, Adelante, Inferno, Tucha,* and *Que Tal*. Chicano prison inmates (*pintos*) as well had their own newspapers, for example, *El Chino, La Voz del Chicano,* and *Aztlán*. Many of these newspapers were members of the Chicano Press Association, which was a network of community newspapers dedicated to promoting unity among Chicanos in their pursuit for self-determination.[85]

Along with the newspapers, posters, buttons, and bumper stickers were also used by activists as indicators of their commitment to Chicanismo and La Causa. Influenced by México's own indigenous and revolutionary experiences, Chicano activists incorporated Emiliano Zapata, Pancho Villa, and Ricardo Flores Magón, among others in the pantheon of posters. The cries for "Chicano Power," "Brown Is Beautiful," "Aztlán Love It or Leave It," among others, were recurring themes.

Teatros (theater groups) and films also contributed to the CG's cultural renaissance. With the start of the National Farm Worker Association's (NFWA) Delano Strike in 1965, playwright Luis Valdez formed El Teatro Campesino, which became the Movimiento's pacesetting and premiere *teatro*.[86] During this epoch, a proliferation of *teatros* occurred in both the universities and communities.[87] Although their skits and plays often relied on humor, they acted as vehicles of "politicization" and "conscientization," which sought to induce activism. An important aspect of *teatros* was their use of Mexicano legends, symbols, and music, particularly the use of *corridos*.[88] They mixed English with Spanish (Spanglish) and addressed a myriad of issues related to cultural identity, class, racism, and to the system itself. Their critiques of U.S. society were also embellished by an aura of Chicanismo and cries for militant action. In describing their vital role to the Movimiento, Ignacio Garcia writes, "The *teatros* provided a simple message: Chicanos and their culture were under attack; they had to resist by knowing their history and maintaining their culture and they had to root out the *vendidos* among them."[89]

The contagion of *teatros* affected the growth of Chicano filmmaking. For years Chicanos had been depicted in films in negative stereotypes and derogatory images; emerging Chicano filmmakers fostered new positive images by using historical and cultural themes derived from the Chicano experience. The films that were produced, largely low-budget documentaries, became powerful mediums of politicization and resocialization to the CG. Luis Valdez in 1969 took Gonzales's "Yo Soy Joaquin" epic poem and turned it into an inspirational documentary film. Its historical photomontage images were set to music, with the poem's verses passionately read by Valdez. By 1971, David Garcia and Montezuma Esperza did *Requiem-29*, a documentary on the National Chicano Moratorium's August 29 antiwar march in Los Angeles and the coroner's inquest into the death of Ruben Salazar. That same year, Jesús Salvador Treviño did *América Tropical*, a film about the political controversy surrounding México's famous painter David Alfaro Siquerios's mural in Los Angeles. A year later, Treviño did *Yo Soy Chicano*, a film on the history of the Chicano experience, with an emphasis on the Movimiento and its leaders.[90] In 1973 Ricardo Soto's *A La Brava* focused on the experience of the *pintos* at Soledad prison. And by 1974, José Luis Ruiz's *The Unwanted* examined the exploitation of the undocumented immigrant in the United States.[91]

Equally important to the creation of the Movimiento's mythology were the artists. Driven by the spirit of Chicanismo and influenced by México's muralists Diego Rivera, David Alfaro Siquieros, and José Clemente Orozco, the new Chicano muralists used the brush and bright colors as aesthetic weapons to foster their own art renaissance and did much to enhance Chicanismo. Their art was eclectic, a metamorphosis of both México's and the Mexicano's historical and cultural experiences. Chicano artists painted picturesque murals on community centers, sides of buildings, schools, bridges, freeway overpasses, and canvas. A fusion of themes and icons involved symbolism from México's preconquest, postconquest, struggles for independence, and the Mexican Revolution linked with that of the Chicano experience and proliferated throughout many of the country's barrios. Among the artists who were the pacesetters of the Chicano artistic renaissance were José Montoya and Estéban Villa, who formed the Chicano Royal Air Force (a collective of Chicano artists) in Sacramento, California, during the late 1960s; Judy Baca from Los Angeles; and Manuel Martinez of Denver. Numerous other Chicano/a muralists formed art groups and centers, for example, Mujeres Muralistas, Los Four, ASCO, Mechicano Art Center, and Chicano Park in Barrio Logan, San Diego, California.[92]

Likewise contributing to the Movimiento's cultural nationalism were music and dance. México's music, especially *corridos de la Revolución*, were modified to fit the Chicano experience and created a musical renaissance. Music became a powerful organizing tool in reaching and politicizing the masses of the barrios. The guitar became an indispensable instrument that was present in numerous protest events, such as rallies, marches, and *teatro* performances. Chavez's UFW, as well as other organizations, contributed to the protest music, especially with modified *corridos*, as an integral part of this organizing techniques. "Yo Soy Chicano" became one such modified *corrido* and "De Colores" was used as a unity song. Mexicano singer composer Juan Alejandro wrote, sang, and recorded a number of protest numbers on his album, *Corridos Sin Fronteras*. Daniel Valdez's album *Mestizo* accentuated the farmworker's struggle, particularly the classic piece, "Brown Eyed Children of the Sun." Tex-Mex music with a Movimiento slant was popular in some areas. In Tejas, Little Joe and La Familia popularized *Las Nubes* in 1973, which to some became the Chicano national anthem. The cultural renaissance was especially evident in the numerous *ballet folkloricos* (folk dance groups) formed in communities, schools, and universities. These activities were symbolic of México's cultural influence on the Chicano's quest for cultural identity. Thus, the epoch of protest produced a Movimiento that fostered a CG that was politically savvy and a powerful cultural renaissance.

Salient Events of the Epoch of Militant Protest

Between 1966 and 1974, innumerable issues colored the political landscape of Movimiento protests and politics. Issues became a major source for energizing the Movimiento's militant protest politics. Education, land grant, and labor issues drove its incipient four years. However, by 1969 and early 1970s, with the rise of the Raza Unida Party, a shift occurred to electoral politics. The scope of this work prohibits examining all the issues that surfaced during this turbulent epoch. However, there were several salient events that occurred, which I feel contributed significantly to the nurturing and growth of the Movimiento and the Chicano experience. Thus, broken down on a per year basis, the following were the issues selected.

The Year 1966: The Rise of the Movimiento

Nineteen sixty-six was a pivotal year for it was at this time that both the rise of the Movimiento occurred and the Mexicano political experience was temporarily transformed into the Chicano political experience. A major event that contributed to this was the Albuquerque Employment Opportunity Commission (EEOC) walkouts. In March some fifty Mexican American leaders walked out of an EEOC meeting held in Albuquerque, Nuevo México, over charges of discriminatory employment practices. According to Kay Briegel, "When the leaders arrived, they found only one commissioner present and none of their previous complaints had been acknowledged; so they walked out."[93] This event signaled that leaders representing organizations such as LULAC, the G.I. Forum, MAPA, and PASSO, among others, were becoming more assertive in defending the interests of Mexicanos vis-à-vis employment within federal antipoverty programs.

As a result of the EEOC Chicano walkout, which became known as the "guarache out,"[94] an ad hoc group of Mexican Americans was formed to pressure the Johnson administration. A press conference was held and the leadership of the ad hoc group made a number of demands. Specifically, they demanded a meeting with President Lyndon B. Johnson, the appointment of a Chicano to the EEOC, policy-level staff positions in federal and state civil rights agencies, and participation in the 1968 White House Conference on Civil Rights. They threatened to initiate demonstrations and marches at a national level if their demands were not met.[95] The neo-militancy alarmed some Mexican American conservatives, as F. Arturo Rosales describes: "most Mexican American conservatives saw their dignity disparaged by these tactics and their positions endangered." He goes on to explain that "for younger, less-compromised Chicanos, however, and for some from the Mexican American Generation, this paved the way to using confrontation. Now there was no turning back."[96] To Bert Corona, the Albuquerque walkout was significant in that it signaled the beginning of a new militancy among Mexicanos who called themselves Mexican Americans, both young and old.[97]

Right after the EEOC walkout another important event contributed to the rise of the Movimiento—Cesar Chavez's march to Sacramento. In mid-March of that year, Chavez and his fledgling National Farm Workers Association (NFWA) began a historic twenty-five-day march from Delano to California's state capital, Sacramento. Reminiscent of the great civil rights marches of the early 1960s, the 250-mile march to Sacramento was organized with the intent of bringing national media attention to the NFWA's nationwide Delano grape strike. The cardinal strategic intent was to garner general public support. Chavez, however, sought to use the march to Sacramento not only to dramatize the inequities suffered by *compesinos* (farmworkers), but to present their grievances to Democratic governor Pat Brown. He also used it as an organizing tool to inspire farmworkers to join the emerging union. On March 17, as a Lenten sacrifice, Chavez and sixty-six *compesinos*—without a parade permit—started the march to Sacramento.

The twenty-five-day march was billed as a *peregrinacion* (pilgrimage) to Sacramento with all the trappings of religious and nationalist symbolism. The theme was clear, "Penitence, Pilgrimage, and Revolution," and Our Lady of Guadalupe, México's patron saint was selected as its symbol.[98] A sense of Mexicano revolutionary zeal was also incorporated in the writing and distribution of El Plan de Delano. Written by Luis Valdez, it was reminiscent of Emiliano Zapata's Plan de Ayala, which was promulgated during México's Revolution of 1910 and called for agrarian reform. In very powerful poetic language, it was more of a manifesto of the farmworkers' aims and aspirations.[99] The *peregrinacion* fostered an unprecedented mobilization. On a daily basis, rallies were held in the evenings at the various farmworker communities along the way. The Teatro Compesino performed skits and playlets; the Plan de Delano was read; *corridos* (ballads), such as "Nosotros Venceremos" (the Spanish version of "We Shall Overcome"), were sung; and speeches made.

By the time the march reached Sacramento twenty-five days later, it became a national media event. In part it achieved the goal of negotiating two contracts between the union and Schenley Industries and the huge Di Giorgio Corporation. They were signed just days prior to entering Sacramento on Easter Sunday. By the time the *peregrinacion* reached Sacramento on Easter Sunday, its ranks had swelled to hundreds. Tony Castro writes, "at the very front of it, alongside the union's own brilliant pennant and Mexican and U.S. flags, there waved a banner depicting Our Lady of Guadalupe together with a large cross and the Star of David."[100] By the time it reached its destination, the state capitol building, its ranks grew to some ten thousand triumphant supporters. They gathered in front of the steps of the state capitol building and held a three-hour victory rally. Democrat governor Brown chose to be in Palm Springs with Frank Sinatra rather than in Sacramento to greet Chavez and the *peregrinacion*.[101] Thus, the march was unprecedented not only for the farmworkers, but for Chicanos in general in that a victory had been scored for both.

Meanwhile, in Tejas under the direction of Antonio Orendain, the fledgling NFWA expanded its farmworker organizing efforts.[102] That same year, Chicano farmworkers initiated a "wildcat" melon strike in Starr County, Tejas, against eight growers. The strike was broken up by Texas Rangers and imported Mexicano labor.[103] As it had been done earlier by Chavez in California, Tejas farmworkers also organized a march from the Rio Grande Valley to Austin, the state's capital, to dramatize their plight. The march covered some 490 miles and took sixty-five days to complete. During the march Governor John Connolly, accompanied by other state officials, met with representatives of the farmworkers at New Braunfels and told them that he would not call a special session or approve or address a Labor Day rally dedicated to the strikers.[104] Undeterred, thousands of marchers arrived at the capitol building where a call was made to Governor John Connelly to help them enact a minimum wage law. In the words of Richard Del Castillo and Arnoldo De León, it acted "as a stimulus for political activity in Tejas years later. It was the beginning of the [Movimiento] in that state."[105]

The rise of the Movimiento also became evident in Nuevo México that summer, with Reies Tijerina's Alianza's growing militancy.[106] After three years of conventional pressure politics that produced little or no results, Tijerina's Alianza began to shift its strategy to one of increasing unconventional protest in 1966. Up to this time, Tijerina still preached nonviolence and the need to work within the system.[107] He called for the establishment of a government commission to study the land grant issue. Borrowing from Chavez's organizing tactical repertoire, the Alianza organized a three-day march from Albuquerque to Santa Fe, Nuevo México's state capital, a distance of some sixty-six miles over the Fourth of July weekend.[108] The Aliancista contingent of some 330 persons sought an audience with then-governor Jack Campbell to solicit his support for a congressional bill to investigate their land grant grievances. Tijerina's accommodating posture was evident in his recorded comments made to the governor: "We do not demand anything. We just want a full investigation."[109] While the governor agreed to look into the matter, the Alianza's land grant issue became more politicized with the release of a damaging report on the matter. It claimed that the heir's claims to the land grants were invalid and that there were outside influences manipulating them. Although nothing concrete was accomplished, it signaled a major shift in the Alianza's strategy and in the mind-set of its members. In the words of Frances Swadesh, their direct action "affirmed their identity as members of La Raza" and gave them "pride and tranquil self-confidence."[110]

The Alianza's occupation of the Kit Carson National Forest campgrounds, the Echo Amphitheater, also served to give impetus to the emerging Movimiento. The park had been an original Spanish land grant called the San Joaquín del Río de Chama and was occupied by a large contingent of Aliancistas, on October 15, 1966. For that weekend, relatively unmolested, they demonstrated their adherence to a new form of protest politics. Further demonstrating the Alianza's new militant spirit was Tijerina's symbolic formation of the new Republic of San Joaquín del Río de Chama. A governing board (ayuntamiento) headed by a mayor was elected and a people's militia formed. Letters were sent to the surrounding residents asking them to recognize the newly formed government as well as to the federal government, particularly to the Department of Agriculture, demanding that they vacate these lands.[111] Symbolically, the occupation served not only to demonstrate the Mexicano heirs' claims to the parklands, but strategically publicized an emerging secessionist movement. These actions enhanced Tijerina's rise to leadership and illustrated the Alianza's growing militancy and adherence to protest tactics.

On October 22, a confrontation ensued between armed Aliancistas and forest rangers. An Alianza contingent comprised of some 150 cars and vans drove into the park and participated in the second takeover.[112] Refusing to leave or pay the fees, the Aliancistas instead arrested two rangers and seized their trucks and radios. The rangers were subjected to a mock trial, found guilty of trespassing and being a public nuisance, were given suspended sentences, and released along with their trucks and radios.[113] The whole episode ended with the arrest of Tijerina, his brother Cristóbal, and three others on charges of conspiring to prevent forest rangers from conducting their duties. This was the crucial event in which Tijerina's Aliancistas categorically shed their accommodation politic posture for one that was confrontational protest-oriented. In other words, his role shifted from a buffer to an advocate transformer. In explaining the significance of the event, Tijerina said, "the community won in the eyes of the world. Moreover, the people of the land began to lose the terror they had for the Anglo over the past 120 years."[114]

On the negative side, the event signaled a major media offensive directed at both Tijerina and the Alianza. Traditionalist prosystem buffers and "want to be white" Hispanos, like U.S. senator Joseph Montoya, among others, sought to discredit Tijerina publicly. Some state authorities alleged that Tijerina was a communist with connections to Cuba's president Fidel Castro. Senator Montoya lashed out against Tijerina and said, "The last thing the Spanish-speaking need is agitation, rabble-rousing, or creation of false hopes." He further categorized Tijerina as an "outsider who sparked violence and set-back racial relations and was an enemy of the United States." According to Acuña, "A federal court then demanded that Tijerina hand over a list of *Alianza* members; Tijerina refused and circumvented the order by resigning as president of the association and reorganized it as *La Confederacion de Pueblos Libres.*"[115] Yet for Tijerina, the events of 1966 and the extensive media coverage served to catapult him into an advocate transformer role as an emerging major leader of the Movimiento.

The Year 1967: The Movimiento Grows

THE RISE OF TIJERNA AS A MOVIMIENTO LEADER   The Movimiento's emergence became increasingly apparent following a number of events in 1967. Once again, Tijerina and the Alianza demonstrated their confrontational posture with the unprecedented Tierra Amarilla Courthouse raid. Prior to the raid, tensions had intensified with governmental authorities and white ranchers. They feared the possibility of guerrilla warfare breaking out in northern Nuevo México. Not since Las Gorras Blancas and La Mano Negra during the late nineteenth century had they faced such a potentially ominous threat.[116] Tijerina's announcement on May 17 of the Alianza's planned occupation of the San Joaquín del Río de Chama land grant served to further exacerbate an already precarious situation. He exhorted the Aliancistas to meet in June at the village of Coyete, located within the contested San Joaquin land grant, to formulate the plans.[117] Authorities led by Tierra Amarrilla district attorney Alfonso Sanchez sought to prevent the meeting from taking place using extralegal methods, such as declaring the meeting illegal, placing roadblocks, and arresting some Aliancistas.

On June 5, twenty armed Aliancistas, believing their constitutional rights had been violated, attempted to make a citizen's arrest of district attorney Sanchez. In the notorious raid that captured national to international media attention, they entered the jail and were met with resistance. Two law enforcement officers were wounded: Nick Saiz, a state policeman, was wounded critically in the chest, and Eligio Salazar, a deputy sheriff, received a superficial wound to the head.[118] When the Aliancistas failed to find Sanchez, they headed for the mountains near Canjilón with two hostages, Associated Press reporter Larry Calloway and deputy sheriff Pete Jaramillo. Calloway was able to escape, and Jaramillo was later released.

What ensued was an unprecedented manhunt of Tijerina and the Aliancistas who had participated in the raid. In the capacity of acting governor, Lieutenant Governor E. Lee Francis mobilized a National Guard force of some 450 men. The force was equipped with several trucks, jeeps, tanks, and helicopters under the command of General John Pershing Jolly. A total force of some two thousand National Guard troops, who were mostly Mexicanos, armed state police, and other law enforcement agencies, entered the pristine Sangre de Cristo Mountains in pursuit of Tijerina and the Aliancista fugitives. Tony Castro explains the initial public's reaction: "panic and confusion swept through the state as rumors began circulating that Cuban guerrillas were leading *Alianza* raiders on an indiscriminate rampage against Anglos."[119] Meanwhile, some fifty Aliancistas, including old men, women, and children, were apprehended and held for hours without food, shelter, or water in an attempt to lure Tijerina and the Aliancista fugitives.[120] U.S. forces were engaged in Vietnam fighting a war, but within the borders of the United States, the media depicted the manhunt as an insurgency that was more comical than substantive. Considering Lieutenant Governor Francis's action an "overreaction," upon his quick return to Nuevo México, Republican governor David Cargo demobilized the National Guard on the grounds that it had only succeeded in terrorizing innocent people. The imbroglio ended peacefully with the Aliancistas' voluntary surrender after Governor Cargo ensured their safety. Rosales describes the surrender: "The fugitive leaders turned themselves in individually. . . . Tijerina was picked up at a roadblock."[121]

As a result of the Tierra Amarrilla Courthouse raid, the Alianza became entangled in legal proceedings. Tijerina was charged with fifty-four criminal counts, including kidnapping and armed assault. The others were charged with attempted murder, kidnapping, and unlawful assault on a jail. In the end, the charges against the twenty Aliancistas were dismissed. Tijerina alone went to trial. He dismissed his attorneys and eloquently defended himself. After a very spirited defense, assisted by two court-appointed lawyers, Tijerina was acquitted of all charges stemming from the Tierra Amarrilla Courthouse raid.[122] By this time, Tijerina's stature as a Movimiento leader had grown, and many Chicanos increasingly revered him, especially youth, as a sort of revolutionary icon who was audacious and fearless.

LA RAZA UNIDA CONFERENCE   During that summer of 1967, those Mexican American leaders who had participated in the 1966 EEOC walkout in Albuquerque secured a victory. For the first time, a U.S. president was pressured into positively responding to demands voiced by Mexicano leaders. President Johnson met in Washington, D.C., with five leaders representing the G.I. Forum, LULAC, MAPA, and PASSO.[123] As a result, President Johnson named Vicente Ximenes to head the EEOC's newly formed Inter-Agency Cabinet Committee on Mexican American Affairs in June 1967. Although essentially symbolic, its purpose was to coordinate a number of federal programs that affected Mexican Americans. More changes ensued, such as the appointment of more Mexicanos to important positions in the War on Poverty programs, the EEOC, and within the departments of Education, Labor, and Justice.[124] The success of these efforts suggested a change in Chicano strategies and tactics: from accommodation to a more militant posture.

Yet the euphoria of this victory proved to be transitory. In October 1967 in El Paso, Tejas, the Raza Unida Conference was convened in response to President Johnson's Inter-Agency Hearings on the Spanish-Speaking. The initial hearings were held at the University of Texas, El Paso campus to coincide with President Johnson's signing of the Chamizal Treaty with México's president Diaz Ordaz. This was not the meeting that the Ad Hoc Committee of Mexican American leaders had wanted, but they agreed to participate and use it as a way to further their grievances. Yet emerging activist leaders and organizations were excluded from participating. As a result, one week prior to the hearings being held, Tijerina held a conference in Albuquerque, Nuevo México, that attracted many young activists and groups such as MAYO from Tejas,[125] and from throughout the Southwest. A consensus was reached to hold a parallel conference to the White House hearings.

During the hearings, Chicano leaders were disenchanted that their concerns were not being addressed, and a protest and walkout was staged. When Vice President Hubert Humphrey addressed the hearings, angry Mexican American protestors that include both participants to the hearings and activists who were not participants picketed his appearance.[126] Billed as the Raza Unida Conference, the protestors met at a church hall in El Segundo, one of El Paso's poorest barrios. Several long-time Mexican American leaders, such as Ernesto Galarza and Bert Corona, joined Tijerina and Gonzales and numerous other activists in bringing national attention to the Mexicano community's manifold grievances. The protestors accused the "old guard" MAG leaders, who did not support the conference, of not representing the grassroots community. The old guard in turn accused the protestors of merely being interested in their own advancement.[127]

The conference's theme "La Raza Unida" was popularized by the activists. According to Rosales, "At that meeting, José Angel Gutiérrez from Tejas asserted that *La Raza* was the best term to identify Mexican American people—the usage of Chicano was not yet that widespread."[128] In explaining its significance to the Movimiento, Armando Rendon wrote, "After El Paso, a new phase of organization and aggressiveness developed that Chicanos had not known before. From La Raza Unida Conference there developed lines of communication between . . . groups all over the country; increased group awareness and a sense of national purpose touched everyone present."[129] Tijerina's leadership role in the conference contributed to his growing image as the leader of the emerging Movimiento, especially among the youth, who were inspired by his powerful oratory and bold actions.

By the end of 1967, these events and others as well, such as the emergence of the student and youth organizations, especially UMAS (United Mexican American Students) and the formation of the Brown Berets in California and MAYO (Mexican American Youth Organization) in Tejas, gave the nascent Movimiento a dynamism that escalated even more in 1968.

The Year 1968: The Movimiento Expands

THE POOR PEOPLE'S MARCH ON WASHINGTON   During this tumultuous year of relentless anti-Vietnam War and Black Power protests, Mexican Americans were not exempt. During 1968, both Tijerina and Gonzales participated in the Poor People's Campaign to Washington, D.C., during the months of May and June. A total of some five Mexican Americans from throughout the Southwest participated in what was for them a historically unprecedented campaign. Originally, the Southern Christian Leadership Conference's Reverend Martin Luther King made the call for the campaign. However, with King's assassination, the Poor People's Campaign's leadership fell to Reverend Abernathy. In explaining its purpose, Ernesto Vigil writes, "The Campaign's strategy was to make demands on the federal government on poor people's behalf and to bring Washington to a stand still by militant civil disobedience if the government did not respond."[130] While most campaign participants settled in the temporary quarters of "Resurrection City," the two-month ordeal produced difficulties.

The campaign became plagued with internal schisms. Differences soon arose between the Mexican American and black leadership over their input in the campaign's overall agenda. Concomitantly, fractures occurred between Tijerina and Gonzales over strategy. According to Vigil, "Gonzales's opinion, as well as the Crusade's was that Tijerina style was marked (or marred) by personal flamboyance at the expense of sound organizing." Throughout the campaign, unity of action was impeded by their growing differences. As a result, both Mexican American leaders used the high media profile of the campaign to enhance their individual leadership clout.

"King Tiger" Tijerina continued to roar and was recognized by Abernathy and the media as the leader of what he labeled as the Indo-Hispano contingent. His roar, however, was heard primarily when he was promoting his land grants issue. He threatened to pull out of the contingent if they were not given a larger leadership role, a slight that he interpreted as an insult. Tijerina in his autobiography alludes to a conversation he had with Reverend King over the conditions under which Indo-Hispanos would participate. He writes, "We do not want scraps nor charity. We want justice. We want the government of the United States to swear by the Treaty of Guadalupe Hidalgo. We want the return of the land stolen from our populations. We want our culture respected, and we want the foreign, compulsory education removed."[131] While in Washington, D.C., Tijerina also met on several occasions with governmental officials, including Secretary of State Dean Rusk, and presented them with his interpretation of the Treaty of Guadalupe Hidalgo, as it related to the land grant guarantees. With his flare for media hype, Tijerina announced to the press his intention to conduct a citizen's arrest of Chief Justice Earl Warren for committing crimes against the people. On May 29, Tijerina led a number of Chicano, Native Americans, and blacks in an attempt to symbolically take over the Supreme Court. Although the judges refused to see them, twenty delegates met with John Davis, the law clerk, and Tijerina publicized the brief encounter as a triumph, as a "defeat and humiliation" for the White House and Supreme Court.

For Gonzales, the Poor People's Campaign became a platform for national prominence within the Movimiento's leadership ranks. Initially, he held a secondary leadership role to Tijernia, but by the end of the campaign this changed. During those two months, Gonzales exerted his own leadership by refusing to settle his contingent in Resurrection City; instead they were housed at Hawthorn School. Gonzales criticized what he alleged was bad management of Resurrection

City. This issue strained the relationship between Abernathy and Gonzales. During the course of their stay, Gonzales promulgated his El Plan del Barrio. As a reform-oriented plan, it called for the following measures: "for housing that would meet the cultural needs; for schooling, basically in Spanish; for barrio businesses that would be owned within the community; and for reforms in land holding; with the restitution of lands."[132] Although Gonzales was increasingly critical of liberal capitalism, he had yet to advocate openly for separatism. However, the plan was interlaced with statements of self-determination and community control. His politics at this time can be described as being "militant reformist" in nature. Yet the scope of the changes he proposed were beyond anything previous civil rights leaders had presented.[133]

The Poor People's Campaign ended in late June 1968 in a state of disarray and failure. From a public policy perspective, it produced nothing substantive. Yet for both Tijerina and Gonzales, it paid dividends. Both of their leadership statures were enhanced nationally. Gonzales in particular had been successful in networking with numerous non-Chicano activists groups and leaders. He also became very much in demand on the speaking circuit, especially by universities.[134] Thus, even with no tangible policy impact, the campaign served to enhance the Movimiento's growing militancy.

THE EAST LOS ANGELES BLOWOUTS OF 1968   During this time, Mexican American students also initiated the historical "East L.A. Blowouts," a result of the student/youth movement that had emerged by 1967. Contributing to the Movimiento's rise were two student organizations, UMAS (United Mexican American Students) and the Brown Berets. They played a crucial organizing role in the East L.A. Blowouts. Working in collaboration with a number of high school students, these two groups prepared the strategy for the walkouts. Their agenda was to effect major educational change. On March 1, 1968, some four hundred students walked out of Wilson High School in East Los Angeles over the alleged cancellation of a play. In an orchestrated action, on March 3, two thousand students walked out at Abraham Lincoln High, along with teacher Sal Castro, carrying placards and chanting "Chicano Power," "Viva La Raza," "Viva La Revolucion."[135] The emerging cultural spirit of Chicanismo was evident. By that afternoon, the contagion had spread to Roosevelt, Garfield, and Belmont high schools. Waiting for the high school students as they walked out were members from UMAS and the Brown Berets. In support of the walkouts of the five high schools—all of which were heavily Mexicano in student population— the Mexicano community formed the Educational Issues Coordinating Committee (EICC).

For several weeks, the EICC held numerous community meetings as a follow-up on the students' demands.[136] The walkouts polarized the community; not all Mexicanos were supportive. Some perceived the student actions as too radical and counterproductive. During its one and a half week duration, according to most estimates, some ten thousand students participated in the walkout effectively paralyzing the Los Angeles school system, the largest in the country. Moreover, the walkouts got massive media coverage, locally and nationally. One reporter from the *Los Angeles Times* interpreted the walkout as "The Birth of Brown Power."[137] Angered by what students perceived to be racist educational policies and practices, they issued a core set of demands including the hiring of more Chicano teachers and administrators, bilingual-bicultural education, and classes in Chicano history and culture.[138]

As a consequence of the walkouts, a group of the protest leaders that became known as the "L.A. 13" were arrested and charged with a felony, conspiracy to disturb the peace.[139] Most of them were members of UMAS and the Brown Berets. After two years of appeals, the charges against them were found to be unconstitutional. The indictment exemplified the severe reaction by Los Angeles law enforcement agencies, which had reacted to the walkouts as if they had been an insurrection. With their batons the police had harassed and beat up protesting students. They had in particular focused on the Brown Berets, who provided security; this brought protests from the community. Teacher Sal Castro, one of the L.A. 13, became a target of persecution by school officials. Suspended from Lincoln High School, he was subjected to numerous arbitrary administrative transfers. In September of 1968, several thousand demonstrators organized by the EICC protested and marched in front of Lincoln High School, demanding Castro's reinstatement.[140] That October, thirty-five persons, mostly students, were arrested at the Los Angeles City Board of Education building for holding a "sit-in" protesting Castro's suspension from the classroom. After considerable community pressure, he was subsequently reinstated.[141]

As an organizing event, the East L.A. Blowouts were a success. Even though none of the student demands were initially met, they mobilized thousands of people who had never before participated in such a militant protest action. They started a contagion that spread into the rest of the Southwest, engendering a spirit of student unrest. Gómez-Quiñones notes that they "marked a dramatic leap in the consciousness of Mexican students and the development of new organizational forms." Student organizations such as UMAS, MAYO, and others initiated numerous school walkouts across Aztlán over the next three years and became a major part of the Movimiento's agenda.

OTHER ACTIVITIES/EVENTS   Meanwhile, during 1968, other events and issues also contributed to the rise of the Movimiento. The UFW accelerated its grape boycott. In order to avert a trend of growing violence, Chavez held a fast that brought him and the UFW international attention and support. Concomitantly, that year witnessed the formation of several regional organizations: the Southwest Council of La Raza, MALDEF (Mexican American Legal Defense and Education Fund), and CASA-HGT (Centro de Acción Social Autonoma-Hermandad General de Trabajadores). The growing activism of the Movimiento was energized by the emergence of the student/youth movement, which itself gained momentum, especially with the expansion of UMAS and the Brown Berets throughout Aztlán.[142]

The Year 1969: El Movimiento Driven by Chicanismo

THE NATIONAL CHICANO YOUTH LIBERATION CONFERENCE   In 1969 the Movimiento's activism continued to accelerate in intensity. It was the year that the spirit of Chicanismo and the CG was defined and took root. After nearly three years, the evolving cultural renaissance flourished and the usage of *Mexican American* was replaced with the term *Chicano*. The one event that crystallized these changes was the Crusade for Justice's First Annual Chicano Youth Liberation Conference. Held during the week of Palm Sunday (March 27–31) in Denver, Colorado, at the Crusade's headquarters office complex, this conference drew some two thousand activists, from Aztlán mostly. The cardinal purpose of the conference was to provide direction and cohesion to a Movimiento that was becoming disjoined and fragmented, and at the regional level needed direction. At best it was a potpourri of numerous local and area youth groups and leaders that lacked a cohesive network. In spite of these difficulties, Gonzales succeeded in gathering together a large number of students, barrio youth (former gang members), *pintos* (ex-convicts), and a few intellectuals, such as the poet Alberto Urista (Alurista), from throughout Aztlán.

The Chicano Youth Liberation Conference became the most important conference held during the epoch of protest.[143] With some one hundred groups represented and fifteen hundred activists in attendance, the conference became a cultural revival where the spirit of Chicano nationalism imbued the discussions and debates. The culmination of the conference was the drafting of El Plan Espiritual de Aztlán, a manifesto that embodied the spirit, virtues, and cultural nationalism, in short, of Chicanismo. The inspiration of a young Chicano writer and poet, Alurista, the plan asserted:

In the spirit of a new people that is conscious not only of its proud historical heritage, but also of brutal "Gringo" invasion of our territories: We, the Chicano inhabitants and civilizers of the northern land of Aztlán, from whence came our forefathers, reclaiming the land of their birth and consecrating the determination of our people of the sun, declare our power, our responsibility, and our inevitable destiny.

We are free and sovereign to determine those tasks which are justly called for by our house, our land, the sweat of our brows and by our hearts. Aztlán belongs to those who plant the seeds, water the fields, and gather the crops, and not to the foreign Europeans. We do not recognize capricious frontiers on the Bronze Continent.

Brotherhood unites and love for our brothers makes us a people whose time has come and who struggle against the foreign "Gabacho," who exploits our riches and destroys our culture. With our heart in our hands and our hands in the soil, We declare the Independence of our Meztizo Nation. We are a Bronze People with a Bronze Culture. Before the world, before all of North America, before all our brothers in the Bronze Continent, We are a Nation, We are a Union of free pueblos, we are Aztlán.[144]

Strategically it introduced the concept of Aztlán into the lexicon of the Movimiento, which denoted a step toward self-determination. The plan's adherence to both cultural nationalism and the idea of Aztlán became evident in that it proclaimed, "Por La Raza todo, Fuera de La Raza nada." Its wording, as Vigil notes, "demonstrates ethnic pride in its consciousness of a proud historical heritage."[145] The approbation of El Plan Espiritual de Aztlán signaled a change in the politics of the Movimiento, the infusion of Chicanismo.

The impact of the Chicano Youth Liberation Conference on the Movimiento was profound. For Gonzales, the conference served to further his quest to become the leader of the Movimiento. While El Plan Espiritual de Aztlán was a powerful manifesto on cultural nationalism, it lacked detail or specifics on how to create Aztlán. As a manifesto, it was so nebulous that it raised issues related to gender, class, and the indigenous people of the Southwest, and was unclear about what geographically constituted Aztlán. Nevertheless, its impact was significant and served to energize various aspects of the Movimiento's politics. As a result, *Chicano* came into vogue and increasingly *Mexican American* was regarded as passé in the lexicon of most activists.

EL PLAN DE SANTA BARBARA   A second event held that year, in fact one month after the historic Chicano Youth Liberation Conference, was the Santa Barbara Conference. It produced the second most important Movimiento document: El Plan de Santa Barbara. Chicano activists in California, inspired by the growing spirit of Chicanismo and the solidarity that ensued from the Denver conference, held a conference in April in Santa Barbara, which dealt with issues pertinent to Chicanos in higher education.[146] According to Mario Barrera, "The conference and the resulting plan were in many ways an attempt to elaborate on the themes and goals raised at the Denver Youth Conference and in the *Plan Espiritual de Aztlán.*"[147] The conference was organized by the Coordinating Council on Higher Education and comprised students, faculty, and staff from various universities and colleges. Three of the several conference organizers included poet Alberto Urista, nationalist spiritual architect of El Plan Espiritual de Aztlán; Juan Gómez-Quiñones, and Montezuma Esparza.[148] The results of the conference proved to be historically significant. A master plan of action for Chicanos in higher education was developed. It sought to foster a more unified pedagogical philosophy and curriculum for Chicano Studies programs; to ensure that Chicanos had greater access to California's universities and colleges; and to unite politically and organizationally through local programs and student organizations in California and ultimately the country.[149] The rationale of El Plan de Santa Barbara was that the country's institutions of higher learning were controlled by and served the interests of rich and powerful white elites. From a strategic perspective, El Plan de Santa Barbara provided the basis for a comprehensive plan of action for Chicanos in higher education. Reiterating the nationalist spirit of El Plan Espiritual de Aztlán and its tenets of Chicanismo it read:

For the Chicano the present is a time of renaissance, of *renacimiento*. Our people and communities . . . are expressing a new consciousness and a new resolve. As a result, the self-determination of our community is now the only acceptable mandate for social and political action; it is the essence of the Chicano commitment. . . . *Chicanismo* simply embodies an ancient truth: that man is never closer to his true self as when he is close to his community. . . . *Chicanismo* draws its faith and strength from two main sources: from the just struggle of our people and from an objective analysis of our community's strategic needs. We recognize that without a strategic use of education, an education that places value on what we value, we will not realize our destiny. Chicanos recognize the central importance of institutions of higher learning to modern progress, in this case, to the development of our community.[150]

Toward the end of the preamble, expressing its cultural nationalist proclivity, El Plan de Santa Barbara postulates that the destiny of the Chicano will be fulfilled: "To that end, we pledge our efforts and take as our credo what Jose Vasconcelos once said at a time of crisis and hope: 'At this moment we do not come to work for the university, but to demand the university work for our people.'"[151]

Despite some of its ambiguities, El Plan de Santa Barbara called for political action in the context of "political consciousness, political mobilization, and tactics" against all those institutions that affected Chicanos, especially the university. Furthermore, in order to carry out its call for action, a new "student organization of organizations" was formed, Movimiento Estudiantil Chicano de Aztlán (MEChA—Chicano Student Movement of Aztlán). As a result, it was agreed that all Movimiento-oriented student organizations would close ranks and become MEChA.

The Santa Barbara conference positively impacted the Movimiento in several ways. One, Chicanismo as an ethos was solidified as illustrated by the fact that *Chicano* was in and *Mexican American* was out. Two, the Chicano agenda in higher education became a top priority, and subsequently witnessed the expansion of Chicano Studies programs; hiring of Chicano faculty, administrators, and staff; and creation of various student programs. And three, a new student organization, MEChA, was adopted and formed with a commitment to Chicanismo and the building of Aztlán.

OTHER ACTIVITIES/EVENTS   A myriad of other events and issues fed the Movimiento's growing militancy. Driven by the pursuit for educational change, from Tejas to Colorado to California, various student/youth organizations initiated school walkouts, marches, boycotts, picketing, sit-ins, and other forms of unconventional protest. MAYO in Tejas was embroiled in numerous school walkouts and held a massive march in Del Rio where it was under attack for its alleged control of Vista Minority Mobilization Programs. MAYO's leaders promulgated the Del Rio Manifesto, but in the end, MAYO lost its access to these programs that were subsequently terminated.[152] In California as well as in other states, student organizations pushed for the establishment of Chicano Studies programs at the university and college levels.[153] During the spring of 1969 an incident occurred at the Biltmore Hotel in Los Angeles at a Nueva Vista Education Conference, sponsored by the California Department of Education. Chicano activists disrupted a speech given by then-governor Ronald Reagan and a fire was set. Thirteen activists were arrested and seven were charged on various counts of conspiracy and arson.[154]

That same year the UFW expanded its boycott both nationally and internationally. Tijerina was jailed in New México for burning a sign. In Cucamonga, California, the West End MAPA chapter under my leadership orchestrated the first political takeover of a local school board district, that is, the Cucamonga

School District, in Aztlán. Community control was actualized, and as a result major educational reforms were initiated that included an unprecedented bilingual and bicultural program.[155] Católicos Por La Raza in Los Angeles, California, for the first time challenged the hierarchy of the Catholic Church during a Christmas Eve church service. The demonstration lead to the jailing of protesters concerned with the needs of Mexicano Catholics.[156] The newly formed Chicano Moratorium Committee organized by the Brown Berets held their first demonstration in Los Angeles, California, against the Vietnam War on December 20, 1969, which was attended by some two thousand people.[157]

The Year 1970: Chicano Resistance to the Vietnam War Grows

NATIONAL CHICANO MORATORIUM   The year 1970 became the apogee of the Movimiento. On August 29, Chicanos in Los Angeles, California, held the largest antiwar demonstration and march in the history of the Movimiento. The National Chicano Moratorium Committee organized the antiwar protest. On the issue of the Vietnam War, Chicanos were at the back of the bus. The roots of the protest against the war go back to the Movimiento's beginnings in 1966. Various individuals took strong positions against the war, such as Rodolfo "Corky" Gonzales, but it was not until late 1969 that it became a priority. Previously, the high number of Mexicano families with sons in the military coupled with conservative pro-war sentiments among many Mexicanos impeded mobilizations against it. This changed, however, as a result of the release of UCLA professor Ralph Guzman's ominous report that year, which concluded that between January 1961 and February 1967, although the total Mexicano population in Aztlán was no more than between 10 to 12 percent, Mexicanos comprised 19.4 percent of the casualties killed in Vietnam. Furthermore, Guzman reported that from December 1967 to March 1969, Mexicanos from Aztlán comprised 19 percent of the casualties. Mexicanos from Tejas alone sustained 25.2 percent of the state's casualties.[158] For Mexicanos, the Vietnam War, like World War II and the Korean Conflict, were part of a paradox—while dying and killing for the United States abroad their experience at home was one of oppression, exploitation, and racism.

The first major Chicano demonstration and march against the war was held in December 1969 in Los Angeles, California, at Obregon Park. Organized by the newly formed Chicano Moratorium Committee of the Brown Berets, the unprecedented antiwar mobilization drew a modest two thousand people. Two months later, now under the joint leadership of antiwar activist Rosalio Muñoz and Brown Beret leader David Sanchez, the Chicano Moratorium Committee held its second mass demonstration in February 1970 and drew some five thousand protestors.[159] Chicano protest against the war received additional impetus at the Chicano Youth Liberation Conference held in March, where it was decided that a number of local and national moratoriums would be held.

The Chicano Moratorium Committee, now designated the National Chicano Moratorium Committee, on August 29th convened the largest ever Chicano march and demonstration in East Los Angeles against the Vietnam War. Twenty-five thousand activists from throughout the country marched through the streets of East Los Angeles with chants and placards denouncing the war, "Raza Si, Guerra No," "Aztlán: Love or Leave It." Innumerable Mexican flags colored the numerous march formations. The spirit and symbolism of Chicanismo permeated the unprecedented Chicano event. The march concluded at Laguna Park where a rally took place. Entertainment featured *conjuntos* that blared out *corridos*, poetry reading, and *ballet folkoricos*. During the course of the rally, an incident occurred at a liquor store that quickly spread into a riot. In a military formation and using tear gas, some five hundred policemen conducted a sweep of Laguna Park, beating Chicanos indiscriminately, young and old, including women, as they cleared the park.[160]

The riot quickly engulfed parts of East Los Angeles, especially along the Whittier Boulevard corridor, where protestors torched several white-owned businesses. David Sanchez writes, "The police had provoked the community into starting a riot." In the end, the riot produced violence, destruction of property, and death. Forty law enforcement officers were injured, and some twenty-five police cars were destroyed in the melee. Three Chicanos were killed, including journalist and television KMEX reporter Ruben Salazar, scores were injured, and some four hundred arrested.[161] A high velocity tear gas projectile was fired into the Silver Dollar Bar by a sheriff's deputy, which struck Salazar in the head, killing him instantly. Salazar's death ignited charges of police overreaction and abuse. In September a coroner's inquest was held and failed to produce an indictment against the sheriff's deputy. For the next few months, several marches occurred in Los Angeles and throughout the Southwest, but the focus had shifted from the war to police brutality and abuse. With the August 29 march and rally, the Chicano antiwar struggle reached an early apex and faded quickly after 1970.

OTHER ACTIVITIES/EVENTS   Two other very important events contributed to making 1970 the year of the Movimiento's zenith. After five long arduous years of struggle, Chavez's UFW scored major victories by concluding several contracts.[162] Equally important, as will be examined later, was the emergence of the Raza Unida Party (RUP) in Tejas and Colorado almost simultaneously. By the end of year, RUP organizing efforts spread to California and gave the Movimiento a "Chicano Power" political focus.

The Year 1971: The Decline of Movimiento Begins

LA MARCHA DE LA RECONQUISTA   During 1971, a decrease in the number of mass mobilizations signaled the Movimiento's decline. One such major event was La Marcha de La Reconquista (The March of the Reconquest). On the morning of May 5, 1971, the Brown Berets initiated a march that began in Calexico and several weeks later concluded in Sacramento, California. La Marcha was organized to present the Chicano community's grievances, but more specifically, for the Brown Berets to reinvigorate themselves as an organization and the Movimiento as a whole. For the next three months, Brown Berets and other activists journeyed through, stopped, camped, and held rallies in numerous *colonias* and barrios along the route. *Movimiento*-oriented groups supplied the marchers with food, water, and supplies. La Marcha concluded in Sacramento with a rally in front of the capitol building, where the marchers raised the Mexican flag. For the next five days, the Brown Berets protested, expounding on a reformist agenda that did not emphasize their earlier separatist posture. Instead the Berets focused on reform-oriented issues, such as farmworker rights, education, welfare rights, prison reform, and police brutality.[163]

Unlike Chavez's march to Sacramento in 1966, La Marcha did not attract thousands of people or much media attention, nor did it succeed in injecting the Brown Berets or the Movimiento in general with a renewed activism. This was in great part due to a radical image that was attacked by the white media and even by moderate to conservative Mexican American organizations. Thus, the failure of the Brown Berets to secure massive support from the Chicano community was symptomatic of the Movimiento's gradual decline.

OTHER ACTIVITIES/EVENTS   Other events during 1971 impacted the politics of the Movimiento. The release of Reies Lopez Tijerina from the federal penitentiary, after two years of incarceration, transformed him into a "demilitarized" leader with limited influence within the politics of the Movimiento. The expansion of RUP throughout Aztlán signaled the Movimiento's new political agenda. The Farah strike that year became a two-year labor struggle that involved some four thousand striking women in Tejas and Nuevo México.[164] In Ontario, California, the emergent RUP scored a major educational victory by organizing the second successful school walkout in the Movimiento's history.[165] The UFW's organizing confrontations with the Teamsters accelerated; the lettuce boycott continued; and the UFW moved its headquarters from Delano to its new location at La Paz near Bakersfield.

The Year 1972: Apogee of Chicano Political Empowerment

LA RAZA UNIDA PARTY CONVENTION IN EL PASO, TEJAS   During 1972, the Movimiento was driven by the Raza Unida Party's (RUP) political agenda, which reached its apogee that year. The one event that overshadowed all others that year was RUP's national convention held in September in El Paso, Tejas. After two years of building el partido, both Gutiérrez and Gonzales, who saw themselves as competitors for RUP's national leadership, and Reies Tijerina agreed to hold a national RUP convention that year.[166] Gonzales and Gutiérrez both saw the convention as an opportunity to advance their particular leadership interests, namely to capture RUP's national leadership. Specifically, Gonzales saw an opportunity perhaps to be nominated for president for the ensuing November presidential elections.[167] As for Tijerina's convention role, both Gutiérrez and Gonzales saw it as being symbolic and a tribute of respect to the fallen leader. By mutual agreement, Gutiérrez accepted the leadership task of organizing the historic convention.[168]

On September 1–5, Labor Day weekend, some three thousand delegates and activists from eighteen states gathered at the Liberty Hall Coliseum in El Paso, Tejas, to formulate national directives and strategies for the fledgling RUP. An aura of excitement and of history in the making permeated the convention proceedings. The convention was politically unprecedented: never before had so many Mexicanos gathered to determine their own political agenda, particularly that of building their own partido. From the onset to the end of the convention, activists and delegates became embroiled in the power struggle between the two RUP caudillos. Subsequently, this produced an internecine "politic of self-destruction" that contributed to RUP's rapid decline. Even prior to the convention, conflict surfaced between the two leaders over who was to speak at the convention. Gutiérrez had invited speakers, such as Cesar Chavez, Ralph Abernathy, Coretta King, Bishop Patricio Flores, and even Democrat presidential candidate George McGovern to address the convention, but Gonzales opposed them. In order to mitigate the escalating conflict, both Gutiérrez and Gonzales agreed to have Raul Ruiz, RUP leader for Los Angeles, chair the convention.

Even with Ruiz as chair the conflict between the two camps continued. The crux of the conflict was over two salient issues: Of the two caudillos, which one was going to be RUP's national leader? and What was to be RUP's ideological orientation as a partido? After a contentious campaign, Gutiérrez prevailed over

Gonzales by a delegate vote of 256-1/6 to 170-5/6, with one abstention and fourteen no votes. On the ideological issue, Gutiérrez was the "pragmatist political mechanic," who propounded a reform-oriented political strategy of extracting concessions by working within the existing electoral system. He won support over Gonzales, the perceived "nationalist ideologue," whose separatist politics were based on building RUP into a vanguard revolutionary *partido*. El Congreso (RUP's national steering committee) was approved and Gutiérrez was elected as its chairperson. After the convention, the internecine power struggle between the two *caudillos* became exacerbated. On the positive side, the El Paso Convention symbolized the zenith of RUP's development. Yet on the negative side, it ushered in a "politic of self-destruction," which significantly contributed to RUP's subsequent decline.[169]

TIJERINA'S NATIONAL CONGRESS FOR LAND AND CULTURAL REFORM   The second defining event for the Movimiento in 1972 was Tijerina's National Congress for Land and Cultural Reform held in Albuquerque, Nuevo México, on October 21–22.[170] Attended by some two thousand Movimiento and mainstream activists, Tijerina sought to use the congress to reestablish himself as a major leader of the Movimiento as well as to promote his new mainstream and prosystem image. Under the banner of "brotherhood awareness," the national conference's theme was "Unity, Before Ideas, Leaders, or Organizations." A number of mainstream Democrat political and business figures were invited to speak and participate. This drew a firestorm of protest from many of the pro-RUP activists in attendance, who were reminded by El Grito Del Norte that Tijerina had also invited two individuals allegedly associated with the Central Intelligence Agency. The admixture of RUP activists and establishment types aligned with the Democrat Party produced an explosion of discord.

The two-day congress was riddled with conflict and chaos. An issue that fostered immediate contention was a resolution presented by RUP activists loyal to Gonzales. They proposed that RUP be recognized as the official political arm of the Movimiento.[171] Tijerina refused to support or even discuss the measure. He vehemently attacked the activists and angrily walked out of his own *congreso*. Gutiérrez sought to mollify the RUP activists and Tijerina by arguing that Tijerina had the right to set the agenda since it was his *congreso*, but was unsuccessful. A related incident occurred between the Brown Berets and Alianza members further exacerbating the existing conflict. Tensions also arose over the absence of both Cesar Chavez and Rodolfo "Corky" Gonzales, who had been invited to speak. Prior to the congress, Gonzales had sent Tijerina a letter in which he was critical of his having invited Democrats:

In the past years, I have dissociated myself from these people who confuse and mislead the gullible members of our *Raza*. I can no longer bargain with despotic government representatives. . . . I want no part of alignment with political prostitutes. . . . I have no intention of creating reaction for the profitable benefit of professional program managers.[172]

The polarized *congreso* concluded with RUP activists taking control. Nuevo México RUP state chairperson Juan Jose Peña chaired the conference, and a number of resolutions were passed. Of particular importance was the unanimous vote given to the *partido*. Gonzales's supporters scored a three-way victory. First, they obviated Tijerina's quest to assert himself as the Movimiento's *lider maximo* (maximum leader). Second, Gonzales supporters prevailed in controlling the conference agenda and precluded the formation of a coalition of politicians and bureaucrats. And third, Gonzales's supporters demonstrated to Gutiérrez that the battle over control of RUP had just begun. This became evident at the first *congreso* meeting held in Albuquerque in November of that year, which also ended in conflict. Thus, as 1972 came to a close, Tijerina's conflict-ridden *congreso* was indicative of the decline of the Movimiento and the RUP.

OTHER ACTIVITIES/EVENTS   Other events marked the Movimiento's decline. In Tejas the RUP ran several candidates unsuccessfully for state offices, including Ramsey Muñiz for governor. In California, under the leadership of David Sanchez, the Brown Berets orchestrated their disastrous "invasion" of Catalina Island. Later that year, Prime Minister David Sanchez officially disbanded the Brown Berets because of internal schisms. The UFW challenged the passage of a farm labor law in Arizona that outlawed the boycott and in 1972 initiated a campaign to recall Governor Jack Williams, which set off another Chavez fast. It lasted twenty-four days, and resulted in Chavez being hospitalized. That same year the UFW led a successful campaign in California that led to the defeat of a similar initiative, Proposition 22.[173]

The Years 1973 and 1974: The Decline of the Movimiento
During the next two years (1973–1974), Chicanos continued to organize, protest, and mobilize on a variety of issues, but the dynamism and participation that characterized the movement during the earlier years diminished significantly. All of the Movimiento organizations and leaders were not able to turn the tide. Not one was on the offensive. Rather, all were on the defensive debilitated by internal strife. There were leadership and ideological power struggles, growing apathy, co-

opting of leaders, burnout, police infiltration, and a number of other internal problems. During these two years, RUP was plagued by the internecine politics of self-destruction that by 1974 moved it into decline.[174]

Moreover, protest organizations such as Gonzales's Crusade for Justice were under siege by law enforcement agencies.[175] In 1973 Luis Martinez, a Crusade leader, was killed by Denver police and others were wounded, including one dozen officers, in a violent gun battle.[176] Although some remnants of the Brown Berets existed, they lacked a membership base, organization, and leadership. Tijerina's stature by this time had diminished as well, as did the Alianza's. Chavez's UFW was the exception; it continued its struggle, but failed to recapture its earlier successes. Student organizations such as MEChA also experienced a decline due to internal ideological schisms, growing student emphasis on vocational and cultural activities, and increasing apathy and complacency. By 1974, the universities were no longer hotbeds of Chicano student militant action.[177] Also, contributing to the demise of the Movimiento was the decline of the external protest movements that had created the epoch of protest. Thus, without their presence, the Movimiento was too fratricidal to persevere and prevail.

Chicano Ballot Box Politics: The Pursuit for Chicano Power

Mexicano ballot box politics under the rubric of Chicano politics intensified during the epoch of protest. Although protest politics had used unconventional methods, Mexicanos who identified with either the Chicano Generation or Mexican American Generation were engaging in the system of ballot box politics. In fact, Mexicano political representation at both the local and state level increased significantly. By and large, this was the result of the presence of a larger, more educated, and growing middle class; of a more politically educated community; and of organizational political work done by groups such as MAPA in California, PASO in Tejas, and the ACCPE in Arizona. Changes produced during the 1960s within the political system also fostered greater voter participation among both Mexicanos and blacks. A major legislative victory of the Civil Rights Movement was the passage of the Voting Rights Act of 1965. Although directed at the black community to promote their enfranchisement, Mexicanos also benefited since the use of the literacy test was eliminated. For years, it had limited the political participation of both blacks and Mexicanos because the test was so difficult that few would pass it.

Because of the Voting Rights Act of 1965, both the at-large system of elections in favor of single-member district elections and the redistricting process through use of gerrymandering were challenged in the 1970s by means of lawsuits in the courts. Also, in 1966, the U.S. Supreme Court ruled that the poll tax was unconstitutional, which meant people no longer had to pay a tax in order to register and vote. Eliminating both the literacy requirement and poll tax enfranchised scores of new Mexicano voters. Labor unions and other liberal groups also contributed by organizing massive voter registration drives that targeted Mexicanos. The presence of the Movimiento with its emphasis on "Chicano Power," translated into the engagement of Chicanos in ballot box politics. The formation of the Southwest Voter Registration and Educational Project (SVREP) in 1974 illustrated the growing importance Mexicanos attached to voting, elections, and in general to political participation. Increasingly, however, especially by the early 1970s, the epoch experienced the continued rise of buffer politicians and organizations.

During the epoch of protest, the political clout of the Mexicano community increased. In the presidential elections of 1968 and 1972, both Democrats and Republicans began to see the Mexicano vote as a "swing vote," meaning it could determine the outcome of the election. This became evident during the 1968 presidential campaign when Democratic presidential aspirants such as Robert Kennedy and Hubert Humphrey seriously courted the Mexicano vote. Prior to his assassination in 1968 Kennedy had leaned heavily on MAPA, the UFW, and on Chicano students for his primary victory in California. At the victory party in Los Angeles, Kennedy's speech started off by publicly thanking Cesar Chavez, Dolores Huerta, and Bert Corona. Many experts credited Kennedy's victory in California to the Mexicano vote. Victorious in the California primary, Kennedy received between 80 and 89 percent of the Mexicano vote.[178] Kennedy's assassination had a disheartening effect on the Mexican American political leadership.

The organizing momentum of the Kennedy campaign failed to transfer to the Humphrey campaign. MAPA, in an unprecedented move at their endorsing convention, voted to remain neutral in the race between Democrat Humphrey and Republican Richard Nixon. After the convention, past MAPA president Corona and newly elected MAPA president Abe Tapia were openly courted by Humphrey: Tapia then endorsed Humphrey in the name of MAPA. As a result, MAPA chapters became divided over the alleged Tapia endorsement, and some refused to support Humphrey. On the positive side of the presidential election, Alex Garcia was elected to the California Assembly.[179] In Tejas Humphrey carried the state by a mere 39,000 votes, thanks to a strong Mexicano voter turnout. Humphrey received an impressive 92 percent of the Mexicano vote. Even though Nixon won the election, Humphrey received 87 percent of the Mexicano vote, while Nixon only managed to garner 10 percent.[180] Overall, Mexicano voter turnout in 1968 was lower than that of 1964 and 1960 elections, indicating a growing disenchantment with the Democratic Party.[181] It decreased by as much as one-third in some precincts in Arizona and Colorado. In California, even though Humphrey got six out of every seven votes cast by Mexicanos, the turnout was lower by one-sixth in comparison to the 1960 presidential election level.[182]

In preparation for the 1972 presidential elections, a major Latino conference was held in October 1971 in Arlington, Virginia. Sponsors of the conference included Mexican American congressman Edward Roybal (D), Congressman Manuel Lujan (R), U.S. senator Joseph Montoya (D), and Puerto Rican congressman Herman Badillo (D). Attended by some eleven hundred people, the conference agenda focused on the need to build a national political organization with muscle and to developing a strategy for Latinos to impact some eighty congressional races. Because of this agenda, two prominent Mexican American congressmen, Henry B. Gonzalez (D) and Eligio de la Garza (D), disagreed with its focus and did not attend. A fifty-three-member committee was formed as a result of the conference, comprised of Mexican Americans, Puerto Ricans, and Cubans, and several resolutions were passed.[183]

During the 1972 presidential election, the Mexicano vote was split. Democrats had lost some support from Mexicanos, particularly in Tejas with the emergence of RUP. By 1972, with RUP as the political vanguard of the Movimiento, Chicano activists were not as willing to support Democrats as they had in 1968. MAPA stayed politically neutral by making no endorsement, and the UFW endorsed Democrat George McGovern for the presidency.[184] The result was a landslide victory for Nixon. McGovern garnered 80 percent of the Mexicano vote to Nixon's 20 percent. Even though Mexicanos voted two to one for the Democratic Party, Nixon did better than any other previous Republican presidential candidate, except in 1960 when he received 25 percent. Nixon carried Nuevo México by some ten thousand votes, which suggested that Mexicanos were the "swing vote" with Nixon receiving three out of every seven votes. In California, Nixon more than doubled the percentage: from the previous 12 percent in 1968 to 26 percent in 1972. Nixon received 20 percent of the Mexicano vote, which amounted to an increase of 14 percent from 1968. RUP in Tejas had offered to support McGovern, if he supported RUP's statewide candidates; but McGovern refused to do so.[185]

In the House of Representatives and U.S. Senate, Mexicanos had little political representation. By the end of 1974, there were four congressmen: Edward Roybal (D-California), Henry B. Gonzalez (D-Tejas), Eligio de la Garza (D-Tejas), and Manuel Lujan, Jr. (R-Nuevo México). With the exception of Republican Lujan, some 85 percent of Mexicanos supported Democratic congressional candidates. In the U.S. Senate, Joseph Montoya from Nuevo México won reelection in 1970 by some sixteen thousand votes and received 77 percent of the Mexicano vote.[186]

At the state level, Mexicano political representation increased slightly. In Nuevo México, in 1968, two Mexicanos ran unsuccessfully for governor: Wilfredo Sedillo under the aegis of Tijerina's People's Constitutional Party, and Democrat Fabian Chavez, Jr., and Republican David Cargo won by three thousand votes as the Mexicano vote had split: 67 percent for Chavez, 33 percent for Cargo, and less than 1 percent for Maestas.[187] Two years later in California, the Peace and Freedom Party unsuccessfully ran Ricardo Romo for governor; he received slightly less than 2 percent of the Mexicano vote. Democrat Jesse Unruh received five out of the six votes cast in Mexicano precincts, whereas Republican Ronald Reagan got 17 percent.[188] It was not until 1974, however, that significant progress was made for statewide offices. That year both Democrat Raul Castro of Arizona and Democrat Jerry Apodaca of Nuevo México were elected governors of their respective states. In 1970, Castro had run unsuccessfully for governor and lost the election by a mere seven thousand votes. Despite his conservative politics, he garnered 90 percent of the Mexicano vote; in 1974, he ran again, and this time he won. In Nuevo México, Apodaca was in a hotly contested race but scored a major victory in his bid for the governorship. Democrat Roberto Mondragon served from 1972 to 1974 as Nuevo México's lieutenant governor.

The number of Mexicanos elected to both the assembly and state senate increased significantly. Table 5.1 provides a breakdown as of 1973 of Mexicano representation in state legislatures.

With the emergence of the RUP in 1970, electoral activity with an activist twist increased, particularly in Colorado, Tejas, and California.[189] As a force for social change, RUP repudiated the "system politics" played by buffers and especially "want to be whites." Impelled by the quest for Chicano power, RUP embodied the idea of creating a viable alternative to the country's two-party dicta-

Table 5.1   Mexicano State Representation (1973)

State	Total Number of Legislators	Number of Mexicano Legislators	Mexicano Percent of Total Legislators	Mexicano Percent of Total Population
Arizona	90	11	11.1	18.8
California	118	5	4.2	15.5
Colorado	100	4	4.0	13.0
Nuevo México	112	32	34.0	40.1
Tejas	181	10	5.5	18.4

Source: F. Chris Garcia and Rudolph O. de la Garza, *The Chicano Political Experience: Three Perspectives* (North Scituate, Mass.: Duxbury Press, 1977), 107.

torship by running its own candidates. RUP in Colorado ran an independent slate of candidates for state and federal office in 1970. Alberto Gurrule, who ran for governor, and George Garcia, who ran for lieutenant governor, each received 1.8 percent (12,296 votes) of the vote. Sal Carpio, who ran for a congressional seat in Denver, received a mere 5,257 votes, 3.2 percent of the total. Another congressional candidate, Martin Serna, received 1,739 votes, 1.3 percent of the total. RUP also unsuccessfully fielded candidates for state treasurer, University of Colorado regent, and other state and local offices. Marcella Trujillo, who ran for the regent's position, got the largest number of votes, 221,644, of any RUP candidate. In the ensuing 1972 and 1974 state elections, RUP ran candidates unsuccessfully for various federal, state, and local offices. With the Crusade for Justice under a state of siege by law enforcement agencies, RUP's electoral agenda lost support and the number of RUP candidates diminished.[190]

RUP in Tejas became an official party in 1972 via a petition drive that secured over twenty-three thousand signatures. That year it ran a number of candidates for state and local offices, and again in 1974. In 1972, former MAYO leader Ramsey Muñiz ran unsuccessfully for governor, receiving 219,127 votes or 6.4 percent. Alma Canales as a candidate for lieutenant governor in 1972 received 131,627 votes; state treasurer candidate Ruben Solis, Jr., garnered 123,135 votes; and railroad commissioner candidate Fred Garza got 159,623 votes. Flores Amaya, who ran for the U.S. Senate, received a mere 64,819 votes. A total of forty-nine candidates ran for state, federal, and local races and went down in disastrous defeat. In 1974, RUP ran only two candidates for statewide office: Ramsey Muñiz for governor and Fred Garza for railroad commissioner. Some sixteen candidates were fielded for state legislative seats and thirty-five for local offices. Muñiz received fewer votes than in 1972: he got 5.6 percent or 190,000 votes. RUP's few victories came at the local level where, for example, RUP leader José Angel Gutiérrez was elected county judge; RUP also had a majority on the Zavala County Board of Commissioners. Between 1970 and 1974, RUP also maintained community control of Crystal City's school board and city council.[191] By 1974, however, RUP's electoral victories in Tejas diminished.

In California, RUP was not on the ballot so its candidates as in Colorado ran as independents. At the state level, Raul Ruiz, editor of *La Raza* magazine, in the Los Angeles area ran against Democrat Richard Alatorre and Republican Bill Brophy for the Forty-eighth Assembly seat in 1971. Ruiz acted as a "spoiler" in that he was able to secure 7.9 percent or 2,778 votes, denying Alatorre a victory. Ruiz again ran in 1972, this time for the Fortieth Assembly District seat held by incumbent Democrat Alex Garcia. In a hard-fought campaign, even though Ruiz lost, he secured 5,130 votes or 13 percent of the total. In the San Fernando area, Guadalupe Rameriz ran unsuccessfully for the Forty-first Assembly District. In 1973 in the San Fernando area, Andres Torres ran for the State Senate and received 2,636 votes or 3.2 percent of the total. At the local level, RUP organizing committees ran candidates for local offices, for example, city council or school board, in communities such as National City, Coachella, Cucamonga, La Puente, Los Angeles, and San Fernando. Only in Cucamonga and Ontario did RUP score victories. In Cucamonga, RUP maintained control of the school board and kept on electing Chicanos up to 1974. In Ontario, RUP scored an unprecedented victory with the election of Gustavo Ramos to the Ontario City Council in April 1972.[192] He became the first Mexicano ever elected to that body.

One of the major RUP electoral efforts in California occurred in 1974 with the incorporation of East Los Angeles as a city. Raul Ruiz ran for mayor along with a slate of RUP city council candidates. They ran an aggressive grassroots campaign against Mexican American candidates with strong linkages to the Democratic Party. By 1974, Mexicanos constituted some 90 percent of the proposed city's population. That November voters defeated the measure: the yes vote on incorporation received 5,256 votes or 42 percent of the total vote and the no vote got 58 percent or 7,197 votes. Ruiz won the mayor's race and was the top vote-getter with 2,240 votes. The other four RUP candidates placed seventh through fourteenth, with vote totals ranging from 1,557 to 1,239. Throughout the campaign the conservative forces against incorporation alleged that if the measure passed the result would be higher taxes. They also depicted RUP's candidates as radicals. The measure lost because of heavy negative coverage, RUP's lack of adequate resources, and more importantly, schisms within the pro-incorporation forces.[193]

As early as 1972, RUP in Nuevo México made its political debut when the San Miguel RUP chapter ran candidates for county clerk and probate judge and three candidates for county commissioner. Running for the latter positions were Juan Jose Peña, Manuel Archuleta, and Pedro Rodriguez. The two former candidates were certified; the latter three ran as write-in candidate. With essentially no resources, little organization, and slight manpower, and categorized by the media as part of a radical fringe *partido*, the two certified candidates got two hundred votes, while the three RUP write-in candidates received only sixty votes. Again in 1973, the San Miguel chapter ran two candidates for the school board. This time the two RUP candidates received 25 and 26 percent, respectively. In 1974, again, RUP in San Miguel County ran a slate of candidates for the city council, mayor, and city police magistrate. Heading the slate was Peña, who ran for mayor, and with three slates of candidates running, RUP received 10 percent of the votes cast. The RUP slate acted as a spoiler; their votes allowed the white slate to win. Thus, up to 1974, RUP's electoral efforts were minimal and directed at the local level by one RUP chapter only.[194]

In Arizona and the Midwest RUP candidates ran unsuccessfully for local and state office. In Tucson, Arizona, in 1971 Salomon Baldenegro ran for the city council and was defeated by a Democratic Mexican American. Yet of the total 68,405 votes cast, he was able to garner 5,862. Raul Grijalva in 1972 ran for school board in Tucson and was also defeated. The last electoral effort occurred in 1973 in South Tucson. RUP fielded two candidates against the Democratic Party machine. The machine-backed candidates won easily. In the Midwest, RUP lacked major population concentration and bases, and ran few candidates. Perhaps the most significant occurred in 1973 when Angel Moreno ran unsuccessfully as an independent under the guise of RUP for Seventh Congressional seat in Illinois.[195]

With a few notable exceptions in California, RUP's electoral successes occurred only in Tejas. In most cases, RUP lacked finances and organization, had a strategy that was heavily cultural nationalist, struggled to build a sufficient base of volunteers, faced a hostile media, and lacked a concentrated population base. RUP candidates ended up running symbolic electoral organizing campaigns. For some, such as in Colorado, Nuevo México, and even California, the paramount RUP objective was to use the campaigns to organize and politicize communities. However, by 1974 the Movimiento was plagued by internal schisms and in a state of disarray. It faced a rapidly changing political climate that was much more conservative, and as a result RUP's forays into the electoral arena lessened considerably, a manifestation of RUP's own decline.

With the emergence of RUP, a political renaissance occurred in the electoral arena, and Mexicanos made ballot box politics an organizing priority. Ideas of community control, empowerment, and self-determination became powerful forces that ignited interest in electoral politics. With more Mexicanos elected to public office and greater participation by the people in the political process, the Movimiento contributed substantially to the overall political development of the Mexicano community in the United States. By 1974, especially in California, the Democratic Party began to respond to RUP's challenge by redistricting, and creating opportunities for a few more buffer and "want to be white" types to get elected to the State Assembly and Senate.

Yet in 1974 numerous obstacles still existed to Mexicano electoral efforts, such as low socioeconomic status, low levels of education, increasing undocumented population, the people's ties to México, low number of people registered to vote, lack of political organization, and a declining leadership. In a critical assessment of Chicano voters, Levy and Kramer write:

Chicano voters seem to lack the political acuity, which marks the Southern Black voter. Years of political neglect have made the Chicano voter apathetic. Even when a Chicano politician stands on the verge of a political triumph, Chicano voter response is often lackadaisical. Further, Chicano voters are generally disinterested in attempts to create third party movements. . . . Chicano voters appear little interested in ideology. They are, almost without exception, straight Democratic Party voters.[196]

By the end of 1974, the Mexicano vote in the United States was far from being a significant voting bloc. A growing specter of apathy, complacency, and alienation was returning to Aztlán's colonized barrios and *colonias*. The demise of the Movimiento contributed significantly to the aforementioned.

Chicano International Politics: A Nexus with México

During the epoch of protest, Chicanos ventured into the waters of international politics. In particular, Chicano activists sought to develop a new political relation with México.[197] This was the result of Chicano nationalist activists who sought stronger and more formal political, cultural, social, and economic nexus with México, perceived as the motherland. Leading this unprecedented effort was national RUP leader José Angel Gutiérrez. From the beginning of RUP's political takeover of Crystal City (Cristal), Tejas, in 1970 and its "Cristal Experiment," which embodied a number of major local reforms made by RUP, that ensued, Gutiérrez was cognizant of the overall importance of having linkages with México, specifically the Mexican government. This was facilitated by the extensive media coverage that RUP and the "Cristal Experiment" received in México. Mexican newspaper reporters were inquisitive about the extensive changes being enacted and to a degree romanticized the nationalist politics of RUP and its leadership. In particular, Gutiérrez from the onset saw this as an opportunity to secure financial support and technical assistance from the Mexican government for Cristal's numerous socioeconomic projects. On the political side of the equation, Gutiérrez sought to make RUP "the" political force representing the interests of the millions of Mexicanos in the United States.

What ensued was unprecedented in the context of what I call the "politics of *acercamiento*." Chicano activists sought to create a rapprochement with México, one based on the need for a closer collaborative relationship similar to that enjoyed by the Jewish community in the United States and Israel. Assisting in the collaboration was sociologist, Jorge Bustamante, who had strong personal ties to Mexican president Echevarria. The first official meeting of RUP leaders and President

Echevarria occurred in 1972 at a meeting held in San Antonio, Tejas, while Echevarria was on a U.S. visit. Various issues of common interest were discussed, but at the crux of the discussion was RUP's request to the Mexican government for support of its educational projects and economic development in Cristal. The RUP delegation presented Echevarria with a painting of México's revolutionary leader Emiliano Zapata done by an artist from Cristal. Echevarria reciprocated by agreeing to donate to the Cristal library some two thousand books related to various aspects of the Mexicano experience. That same year, as part of the agreement concluded, President Echevarria sent Pedro De Koster, director of industry, to Cristal to ascertain what kind of technical assistance the Mexican government could provide in the development of new industries. This largely ceremonial event fostered during the proceeding years an unprecedented political relationship between México's government and Chicano RUP activists.

The reaction of some gringos (white racists) to RUP's politics of *acercamiento* with México was one that bordered on treason and subversion. Some perceived the whole matter as a concerted effort by México and Chicano activists to create "La Reconquista" (the Reconquest) of Aztlán, which had been lost by México to the United States as a result of the imperialist U.S. War on México. They alleged that México was violating the sovereignty of the United States by meddling in the country's domestic politics by assisting its conationals in becoming more political, assertive, and militant.

However, some progressive Chicano activists also became critical of Gutiérrez's *acercamiento* politics. To them Echevarria's regime was a corrupt and oppressive one-party dictatorship. In spite of the criticism and numerous attacks and threats, during the next two years, Gutiérrez and other RUP leaders from Tejas met periodically in México with President Echevarria and other government officials in México City. Thus, the actions taken by RUP's leadership in Tejas became a template for a new international Chicano politic.

Chicano Organizations: Vehicles of Protest and Change

The epoch of protest produced the fourth organizational renaissance in the history of the Mexicano political experience. None of the previous periods experienced the rise of so many advocate transformer-oriented organizations. They included numerous types of protest-oriented interest groups, for example, ad hoc groups, coalitions, and unions that were in one way or another committed to effectuating change, empowering the people, and improving the people's quality of life.[198] Others were more radical in that they sought to free La Raza from their exploitation and oppression. They propounded either a separatist nation-building agenda or a Marxist socialist transformation of the liberal capitalist social order via a revolutionary struggle. Chicano activists of all ideologies realized and practiced the Saul Alinsky maxim that the most powerful weapon in the arsenal of any oppressed group is organization.[199] *Compesinos* (farmworkers), workers, students, intellectuals, and activist politicians armed themselves for political battle using the power of organization. Their formation was influenced by a multiplicity of factors: years of previous organizational struggles, increased educational opportunities, presence of a larger middle class, experience with military service, and better job opportunities. A plethora of new leaders and organizers forged new organizations that embraced the CG and repudiated the MAG. Yet paradoxically, the previous epoch's politics of social action impelled by the MAG provided the template for the new epoch's organizational and political development. The organizations active during the epoch of protest were of several ideal types. The following provides a compendium examination of the diverse types of organizations that were active during the epoch of militant protest.

Mutual Aid Societies

Mutual aid societies (*mutualistas*) remained active during the epoch of militant protest and continued to play essentially a buffer role. At no point, however, did they become major entities influential in the course of organizational politics. Traditional mutual benefit organizations, for example, such as La Sociedad Progrecista Mexicana in California, continued to function as self-help voluntary entities. They continued to provide death insurance benefits and cultural and social activities, and drew new membership from the influx of Mexicano migrants. Conservative and apolitical in their posture, some did on occasions become engaged in the militant events, issues, or mobilizations that from time to time pervaded the barrios. La Alianza Hispana Americana, the oldest combination of mutual benefit and interest group became moribund by the late 1960s. Its demise was due to internal dissension, declining membership, and fiscal mismanagement. By the end of the decade it went into receivership and never recovered.[200]

Traditional Interest Groups

The epoch of protest was not a propitious time for these traditional interest groups. Those such as LULAC, AGIF, the CSO, MAPA, and PASSO remained active and engaged in the politics of the MAG. In spite of their unpopularity with most Chicano activists, who perceived them as anachronisms, these organizations continued to adhere to either their buffer or "want to be white" organizational roles. With the exception of MAPA, none of them really ever became a vital part of the Movimiento. In most cases, they opposed its form of militant identity politics, spirit of protest, and adherence to Chicanismo. Most Chicano activists described the Mexican American interest groups as anachronistic, out of touch with the realities of the impoverished barrios, and not part of the solution, but rather part of the problem.

The traditional interest groups essentially rejected Chicanismo. They ardently espoused the political beliefs of the MAG's emphasis on assimilation and integration. The term *Chicano* was rejected in favor of the more palatable *Mexican American* and the idea of Aztlán was perceived as unrealistic, absurd, and even treasonous. The notion of a Chicano nation was repugnant and violated their sense of patriotism and allegiance to the United States. Moreover, because of their low levels of membership, they felt threatened by the new Chicano protest organizations, which seemed to emerge almost overnight with mass followings. The media and government officials had also turned their attention to these new protest organizations. Nevertheless, the traditional MAG-oriented organizations continued to resist and struggle for change using via the conventional politics of adaptation.

LEAGUE OF UNITED LATIN AMERICAN CITIZENS (LULAC)   As an interest group, LULAC went through some difficult times reflected in their loss of membership. Because of its extremely conservative image and prosystem reputation, LULAC in particular suffered a myriad of attacks from activists, who perceived it as a "want to be white" organization. Some activists alleged that LULAC's advocacy focus was extremely limited to fighting discrimination, which mostly benefited the small Mexican American middle class at the expense of the poor. Its middle-class constituency was perceived as complacent, opportunistic, and indifferent to the plight of poor barrio residents. A common perception among some activists was that LULAC was essentially a middle-class "social club" that was beholden to the white establishment and was more preoccupied with scholarships, fiestas, and conferences than with major social change. Relegated to a defensive posture, throughout the years of the Movimiento, in the words of Benjamin Marquez, "LULAC fought a decade-long battle with these organizations for leadership within the community."[201] LULAC audaciously attacked those Chicano organizations and leaders that were deemed militant, radical, or communist and antithetical to LULAC's goal of social assimilation.

In brief, LULAC maintained a political posture that the country's safety required mutual cooperation between all ethnic and racial groups[202] and that this had to be done by working within the institutionalized processes and structures of government. Overall, its social action agenda focused on educational, housing, and employment issues and programs. Founded jointly by LULAC and AGIF,

Service, Employment, and Redevelopment (SER) provided job training and placement assistance to low-income Chicanos and remained a LULAC priority. Thus, LULAC's ability to weather the militant nationalist storm of Chicanismo was in part due to its success securing federal funding for its social service programs.[203]

THE AMERICAN G.I. FORUM (AGIF)   Because of its more moderate buffer political posture, AGIF was generally less critical of the Movimiento's militancy than was LULAC. Meier and Rivera write, "Both organizations provided a vehicle for Mexican Americans who wanted to contribute to the community within a clearly defined middle-class framework."[204] This was essentially AGIF's posture during the epoch of protest, and like LULAC it too weathered a membership decline. A key problem was that returning Chicano Vietnam veterans did not join AGIF in large numbers. Unlike LULAC's, however, AGIF's moderate leadership was more flexible in adapting to the Movimiento's militant protest politics. In 1965, for example, the AGIF was instrumental in pushing the Johnson administration to establish the Inter-Agency Committee on Mexican American Affairs as well as in organizing the 1967 national El Paso conference on Mexican Americans.[205] However, while it did not formally support the militant protest action of many of the Movimiento, some of its membership did. Depending on the issue, it was not uncommon to see AGIF members wearing their caps in solidarity with Chicano protestors.

Like LULAC, AGIF was never a part of the organizational leadership of the Movimiento. This was ascribable to its orientation and to the fact that it was a major recipient of funding from federal government agencies. Both LULAC and AGIF, among others, benefited from the militancy produced by the Movimiento's militant protest politics.[206] Due to their moderate and pro-system orientation they were palatable to governmental agencies and needed to be buttressed. A primary preoccupation for AGIF during these tumultuous years was its involvement with job training through Service, Employment, and Redevelopment (SER), which had been funded by the federal government in the amount of $5 million in 1965.[207] AGIF more than LULAC was responsible for the dramatic expansion of SER, with offices established by 1968 in El Paso, Texas, and in California, San Jose, Santa Clara, Santa Ana, and San Diego. Corporate funding sources were solicited and an advisory committee was formed called "National Amigos de SER."

One major AGIF event that contributed to the Movimiento was the Coors boycott. In the arena of corporate responsibility, the AGIF was ahead of all other organizations, particularly when it came to the issue of hiring practices. The

AGIF led a nationwide boycott from 1969 to 1979 against the Adolph Coors Company of Golden, Colorado, one of the country's main beer producers. Numerous groups, from conservative LULAC to the militant Crusade for Justice and many others within the Movimiento supported the national action to where "Boycott Coors" became an intrinsic part of La Causa's lexicon. As a result of the boycott, Coors hired more Chicanos—from 47 Chicano employees in 1967 to 116 by 1969.[208] During the early 1970s, AGIF maintained a rather low profile when it came to the Movimiento, but continued its visible involvement in the social service and employment arenas.

THE COMMUNITY SERVICE ORGANIZATION (CSO)   In California, like LULAC and AGIF, the CSO also did not play a significant organizational role in the Movimiento. Less conservative than LULAC and AGIF during this epoch of protest, the CSO continued to adhere to its buffer role, but did not prevent its decline. The once vibrant Alinsky-oriented grassroots organization evolved into a social service provider by the 1960s. David Gomez notes, "CSO has largely been a middle-class operation whose conventional working-within-the-system approach is now outdated and unattractive to younger Chicanos. Its membership rolls have dwindled, Alinsky's Industrial Areas Foundation withdrew support, and many important members . . . left for other organizations."[209] Tony Rios, leader and overseer, kept the CSO alive as a Los Angeles-based social service organization that maintained a number of federally funded programs. It persevered during the tempestuous epoch of protest by staying engaged in mutual aid-type activities and social programs. It dealt with consumer education and youth, and in most cases was dependent on federal funding. On some occasions, such as the National Chicano Moratorium march and rally of August 29, the CSO supported the Movimiento. By the end of 1974, the CSO was a social service provider that had largely lost its dynamic advocacy role.

Political Pressure Organizations

MEXICAN AMERICAN POLITICAL ASSOCIATION (MAPA)   Under the leadership of Ed Quevedo, Bert Corona, and Abe Tapia, MAPA contributed significantly to the rise of the Movimiento in California. From 1966 to 1970, MAPA's leadership at the state regional and local levels took on more assertive and in some cases militant political roles. MAPA's buffer politics was replaced by a more militant, nationalist, and advocate transformer social change role. From the beginning of the Movimiento, MAPA supported Tijerina's land grant struggle, Chavez's Delano grape boycott, the Raza Unida Conference of 1967, and the

National Chicano Moratorium march and rally of August 29.[210] Also, under my leadership, the Cucamonga/Upland MAPA chapter made history by orchestrating the first political takeover of a school district in Aztlán in Cucamonga, which resulted in the implementation of major educational changes, such as bilingual/bicultural education.[211] Under the state leadership of Abe Tapia (1968–1971), MAPA contributed to the Movimiento's growing militancy and adherence to Chicanismo in California.

However, MAPA's alignment with the Movimiento fostered internal schisms. In protest, many of the more moderate to conservative MAPA chapters and members who had pursued the politics of the MAG dropped out. Further conflict ensued over the rise of the Raza Unida Party (RUP) and efforts by Tapia and Corona to support its formation and their adherence to militant protest politics. In reference to the latter, in 1971 Tapia led some two hundred demonstrators to protest the Democratic Party's failure to create a fair redistricting process for Chicanos.[212] On the former, under my leadership, the West End (formerly the Cucamonga/Upland) MAPA chapter became the organizing catalyst for RUP's formation in San Bernardino/Riverside counties in October 1970. After holding a number of regional conferences, the first major statewide RUP organizing conference was sponsored by the West End MAPA chapter in April 1971. A RUP state conference was held at Chaffey College, located in what today is Ranch Cucamonga. Attended by some six hundred activists, the strategy to form and structure RUP statewide as well as its ideology became the locus of debate that at the time turned acrimonious. MAPA's leaders, Tapia and particularly Corona, took on prominent organizing roles in advocating for RUP's formation. Other MAPA chapters also supported the RUP organizing effort, such as the National City MAPA chapter under the leadership of Herman Baca. In 1972, Baca played a significant leadership role in pushing the RUP agenda at the National Political Caucus held in San Jose, which further divided MAPA over its support for RUP.[213] The apogee of MAPA's militancy was reached in October 1972. At their national endorsement convention held in Los Angeles, a "no endorsement" vote demonstrated the failure of both Republican president Nixon and Democrat George McGovern to garner the required 60 percent of the delegate vote. This was the result of successful lobbying efforts of Mapista (MAPA members) delegates committed to RUP.[214] MAPA's militancy, however, waned by 1972 with the election of Armando Rodriguez as state chair. For the next two years, without the progressive state leadership of Corona or Tapia and others such as Baca in San Diego and me in San Bernardino/Riverside counties, MAPA regressed to a more moderate accommodation political posture reminiscent of the MAG.

While MAPA's influence grew during the early years of the Movimiento, this was not true for all Mexican American interest groups.[215] The rise of the Movimiento in 1966 contributed to the decline of some political pressure interest groups. While the ACCPE's decline in Arizona was rapid and occurred during the early 1960s, PASO's in Tejas was gradual and the group experienced its demise during this epoch.

POLITICAL ASSOCIATION OF SPANISH-SPEAKING ORGANIZATIONS (PASSO)   In reference to PASSO, Arnoldo De León explains, "By the late 1960s, however, PASSO yielded to the more militant strain of the Movement as its middle-class philosophy acted to put a distance between itself and a community that was becoming more receptive to militant politics. Thus, it lost the chance to lead an important movement which in some ways it had set forth."[216] In 1966, however, PASSO played a major role in an uncharacteristically militant manner with the farmworker struggle in Starr County, which led to the historic 490-mile march to Austin.[217] Although the march served to catalyze a new militancy that would last until 1974, little historical record remains of PASSO's subsequent activities. Plagued by internal schisms, loss of membership and chapters, and a changing political climate, PASSO was not a major player in Tejas electoral politics in its few remaining years. Instead, it resorted to a more moderate buffer political role. Indicative of its waning influence was the absorption of PASSO's college/university student chapters by MAYO during the late 1960s. With the emergence of RUP in 1970, PASSO in Tejas became politically a nonplayer.

Protest Organizations

The epoch's dominant form of social action was its protest organizations. They were interest groups that sought to influence public policy, but differed from previous forms examined. Because of their adherence to Chicanismo, a social change agenda, and militant politics, in short an advocate transformer role, they formed the organizational avant-garde of the Movimiento. Their mode of pressure politics was much more militant and predicated on the use of unconventional protest methods.[218] Traditional interest group conventional methods of lobbying and writing letters to the editor were rejected as anachronistic and ineffective. The new spirit of militant protest action was characterized by the use of confrontational methods and mobilization, such as marches, picketing, sit-ins, and boycotts. A salient characteristic of protest organizations was that they usually produced strong charismatic leaders who were strong proponents of the CG. They repudiated unequivocally rejected the accommodation politics of the MAG. Impelled by "el espiritu de Chicanismo," in most cases, they were critical of liberal capitalism and buffer and "want to be white" groups. Protest organizations became an endogenous antagonism that gave rise to the Movimiento and nurtured its development.

LA ALIANZA FEDERAL DE MERCEDES (THE FEDERAL ALLIANCE OF LAND GRANTS, HEREAFTER LA ALIANZA)   As a protest organization, La Alianza was formed in Nuevo México in 1963.[219] However, by 1967 for political reasons, it was renamed La Alianza Federal de Pueblos Libres (Federal Alliance of Free Towns). La Alianza's immediate predecessor was the Abiquiu Corporation, which had addressed the issue of the land grants. Originally, La Alianza was a rather traditional nonpartisan-oriented interest group committed to "the perpetual pro-tection of all the heirs as stated in Article V of its national constitution."[220] La Alianza was the product of its charismatic leader, Reies Lopez Tijerina, who became its national president. Its organizing agenda focused on those who were the original heirs of land grants in Nuevo México and had lost them in spite of their rights covered by the Treaty of Guadalupe Hidalgo. Not since the formation of Las Gorras Blancas and La Mano Negra had such a leader and protest organi-zation focused their political agenda on the return of millions of acres to their Mexicano heirs. Gómez-Quiñones writes, "The Alianza was part of the heritage of efforts to reclaim or to retain the land and/or maintain water rights."[221] After years of study, Tijerina argued for reclamation of the lost lands based on two major documents: The Treaty of Guadalupe Hidalgo and the Recopilación de Leyes de las Indias, a seventeenth-century document that had been the legal framework for the Spanish land grants.[222] Maciel and Peña explain, "The *Alianza* contended that the United States government had violated in spirit and practice Articles 8 and 9 of the Treaty."[223]

Although the Alianza's primary focus was on the land grant issue, language and culture were also important. Tijerina's emphasis on the "Indo-Hispano" con-tributed to the rise of Chicanismo. An emerging sense of cultural nationalism led La Alianza to make Spanish its official language.[224] Ideologically, La Alianza was critical of some aspects of liberal capitalism, but it did not offer an alternative. While initially reformist, by the late 1960s, it had evolved into a militant reform-ist group that toyed with secessionism. The Alianza, based in Albuquerque, at first adopted a conventional interest group approach based on accommodation. Tijerina relied on legal avenues for redress, and for the most part sought to regain the lost land grants through litigation. Manuel G. Gonzales explains that Tijeri-na's "research into the land grants took him to the archives of Spain and México, where he gathered materials to sustain his claims. He got nowhere; the U.S. courts refused to hear the case."[225] By 1966, the Alianza's membership soared to some twenty thousand, which included students from its youth affiliate, the Caballeros de las Indias.[226]

Frustrated and impatient, Tijerina reoriented the Alianza and adopted a protest strategy in 1966. The transition began that year with the Alianza's march to Santa Fe, followed by the occupation of the Echo Amphitheater at Kit Carson National Park. By 1967, Tijerina's Alianza received international media notoriety with its armed Tierra Amarrilla Courthouse raid, further enhancing Tijerina's radical image. The involvement of Tijerina and the Alianza in the Poor People's Campaign in 1968 served to increase the notoriety of the leader and organization among Movimiento activists. With the intent of advancing the land grant struggle, that same year, members of the Alianza formed their own third party, the People's Constitutional Party. Candidates ran unsuccessfully on an essentially populist platform. The culmination of the Alianza's attempts to renew its vitality occurred on June 5, 1969, with the ill-fated attempt to reoccupy Kit Carson National Park, which lead to Tijerina's arrest. He was charged with aiding and abetting the destruction of U.S. Forest Service property and of assaulting and threatening a federal agent.[227]

For the Alianza, 1969 was the beginning of the end. On October 13, the Supreme Court refused to hear Tijerina's appeal on the pending amphitheater case. As a result, from 1969 to 1971, he was incarcerated at the federal prison hospital in Springfield, Missouri. Tijerina's imprisonment proved disastrous for the Alianza. Without his charismatic leadership, it entered a rapid decline. Internal factionalism, continued harassment by law enforcement agencies, declining membership, lack of resources, and a low media profile all fed its decline. Released from the penitentiary in 1971, Tijerina was placed on parole for five years and prohibited from holding any leadership position within the Alianza.

Equally devastating for the Alianza was Tijerina's apparent change of attitude. El Tigre had been defanged. His parole status prohibited him from becoming engaged in protest politics. Instead, he readjusted his politics and developed a new ethos predicated on "brotherhood awareness." To some activists his behavior was eccentric. They alleged that while in prison he had been subjected to some form of behavioral modification.[228] Although not a leader of the RUP, Tijerina in September 1972 participated in RUP's national convention in El Paso, Tejas. In November 1972, both the Alianza and Tijerina sought unsuccessfully to reassert themselves at their last major Movimiento event, the National Congress for Land and Cultural Reform, which was previously examined. After this disastrous event, the Alianza and its leader were inconsequential to Movimiento politics.

The contributions of Tijerina and the Alianza to the Movimiento were many.

In their advocate transformer role, few leaders and organizations could equal the dynamism and inspiration they created within the Movimiento. As a leader he inspired both young and old to believe in La Causa, to become engaged and to be a part of the CG. His electrifying oratory and audacious actions inspired Chicano activists to break with the politics of the MAG. The Alianza with its mass base of thousands of grassroots members demonstrated that the rural and urban poor Mexicano of Nuevo México could get organized. Lastly, the absence of Tijerina and the Alianza's militant spirit during the early 1970s contributed to the Movimiento's decline.

CRUSADE FOR JUSTICE   A second organization that played an advocate transformer role and became the avant-garde of the Movimiento was the Crusade for Justice (hereafter referred to as CJ or the Crusade).[229] The Crusade evolved out of the ashes of Los Voluntarios (the Volunteers), an informal pressure group formed in 1963 by Gonzales to deal with a variety of local issues, particularly police brutality, affecting Denver's barrios. By 1966, Los Voluntarios became more assertive in its politics. When Gonzales resigned in protest as director of the local Denver antipoverty agency, his organization picketed the *Rocky Mountain News* because of its negative coverage of his resignation. By this time, Gonzales felt that the War on Poverty programs sought to pacify the poor rather than ameliorate the quality of their lives. Both sides, but especially Denver's mayor, made vitriolic attacks. Gonzales was upset at the way he was criticized and escalated the level of militant action by holding a major rally at Denver's Civic Center that drew some twelve hundred people. For Gonzales, the ordeal moved him and Los Voluntarios to embrace a more militant posture. It was at this rally that Chicano history was made. In addressing the crowd, Gonzales said, "This meeting is only the spark of a crusade for justice we are going to carry into every city in Colorado."[230] This statement carried the name of the new grassroots protest organization. By November 1966, Gonzales took the name "Crusade for Justice" and gave it to his new civil rights organization.

From the onset, the Crusade was an extension of its charismatic *jefe* or *caudillo*. As Corky Gonzales became more militant so did the organization. Gonzales never sought to transform the CJ into a statewide or national organization with chapters. He chose to keep the organization local with numerous linkages to other organizations and networks. Initially, the CJ was comprised of some thirty working-class families, headed by an executive board, whose civil rights organizing agenda included issues of education, police brutality, and cultural programs.[231] Its small membership base was limited to Denver and consisted primarily of barrio youth, students, *pintos* (former convicts), and some adults from Denver's various barrios. Like the Brown Berets, the CJ gave young Chicano rebels without a cause, a *causa*. According to Ignacio Garcia, "Gonzales sought an organization that extolled the virtues of the '*comunidad*' by sponsoring theater productions, cultural dances, and fiestas to foster unity, as well as political discussions that promoted a self-help approach to solving problems."[232] His emerging cultural nationalism became evident with the publication of Gonzales's epic poem, "Yo Soy Joaquin."

From 1966 to 1968, the Crusade went through a progressive radicalization. Supportive of Tijerina and the Alianza, Gonzales attended the Alianza's annual convention in 1966. Later in 1967, when the Alianza became embroiled in the Tierra Amarrilla Courthouse raid, Gonzales responded by staging a large rally for the Alianza and made a national call for solidarity. Two days later, he led a CJ caravan into Nuevo México's Tierra Amarrilla in support of the Alianza and provided assistance during Tijerina's brief incarceration.

In that same year, Gonzales also became a vocal critic of the Vietnam War. While few if any Mexican American organizations at the time protested against the Vietnam War, the CJ did. In August of that year, the CJ participated in an antiwar march and rally with other antiwar groups in Denver. The CJ took on a rather New Left perspective in its opposition to an unjust and imperialist war of aggression against the struggling people of Vietnam. That year, Gonzales ended his affiliation with the Democratic Party, which he considered to be out of touch with the needs of the poor, particularly Chicanos. In a scathing letter of resignation sent to Democratic Party chairman Dayle R. Tooley, Gonzales wrote, "I can only visualize your goal as complete emasculation of manhood, sterilization of human dignity, and that you not only consciously but purposely are creating a world of lackeys, political boot-lickers, and prostitutes."[233] Gonzales's leadership in La Raza Unida Conference at El Paso, Tejas, in 1967 served to enhance the CJ's growing reputation as well as that of its leader Gonzales, who by this time was very much in demand in the speaker circuit.

In 1968, Gonzales and the CJ participated in the Poor People's Campaign. It was at this time and place that he promulgated his Plan del Barrio. That year, the CJ purchased the Calvary Baptist Church, located in downtown Denver, for some $76,000. The church complex became the CJ's multipurpose headquarters. That summer, a freedom school was established in the complex where young people were taught about Chicanismo. Weekly "fisherman's meetings," as they were described, were held every Wednesday evening. Directed at barrio residents, they were used to raise the people's level of political consciousness, proselytize, and organize them. During the next few years, La Escuela Tlatelolco was established as an alternative school, social services were provided, a library established, and cultural activities held. All activities of the CJ were largely financed by donations from its members and ongoing fund-raising efforts.[234]

The rising tide of radical protest and mobilizations against the war permeating the entire country fueled the Crusade's growing radicalization. In 1969, 1970, and 1971, the CJ sponsored three National Chicano Youth Liberation Conferences. In particular, at the 1969 Youth Conference, the CJ drafted El Plan Espiritual de Aztlán, and completed its transition from a cultural pluralist to separatist ultranationalist and protest pressure organization. In between organizing these conferences, the CJ also addressed issues related to education and police brutality and held several protest marches, rallies, and pickets. Ideologically, by this time, the CJ was a zealous proponent of building a Chicano homeland, Aztlán. Gonzales viewed Chicano nationalism as the "common denominator" in the struggle to unify the oppressed colonized Chicano masses. The CJ's ideology was antithetical to liberal capitalism and was an amalgam of ultranationalism and socialism. Based on Gonzales's pronouncements, *El Gallo's* editorials and articles, organizing activities and alliances, the CJ increasingly adhered to a third world perspective.

Moreover, by the early 1970s, the CJ became the organizing force behind efforts to form RUP in Colorado, Aztlán, and the Midwest.[235] From 1971 to 1974, the CJ came under a state of siege by law enforcement agencies. Confrontations with the police became commonplace, and by 1973 a major altercation with the police occurred when an explosion partially destroyed two apartment units adjacent to CJ headquarters. The incident produced casualties: CJ leader Luis "Junior" Martinez was killed by police; three others were wounded; four policemen were also wounded; and thirty-six barrio youth were arrested in the melee.[236] Plagued by these pressures and engaged in an ongoing power struggle with Gutiérrez over control of RUP, the CJ declined in influence by the early 1970s. Thus, although it still held third world–oriented conferences and its leadership spoke out on a variety of social issues, by 1974 the CJ's clout as a protest organization was waning.

Student/Youth Advocacy Organizations

Student and youth advocacy organizations were protest groups that became an integral part of the Movimiento. Many endogenous and exogenous social factors previously examined contributed to the rise of the Chicano student/youth movement, which became ancillary to the Movimiento. Throughout Aztlán at numerous universities and colleges, Mexican American students formed student organizations and at the same time youth groups in the barrios took on protest agendas. They became indispensable to the emergence of the Movimiento. From

1967 to 1974, many barrio youth also became imbued with a spirit of Chicanismo. They were restless and motivated by rising expectations, and became eager to effect change. Of all the sectors of the Mexicano community, it was the Chicano youth that energized and kept the Movimiento invigorated. Initially small in number, they became increasingly critical of the traditional MAG-oriented groups, like LULAC, AGIF, the CSO, and even MAPA and PASSO and their politics of adaptation.

Student/barrio youth organizations were influenced essentially by Tijerina's Alianza, Gonzales's Crusade for Justice, and Chavez's UFW. Their main agenda, however, was to effectuate educational change, especially at the high school and college levels. They contributed significantly to the CG's cultural renaissance. Initially, they advocated the establishment of Mexican American courses. But by 1968, they began to push for Mexican American Studies programs; hiring of Mexican American teachers/professors, administrators, and staff; student recruitment and retention programs; financial aid; and even bilingual and bicultural education. During the incipient years of the Movimiento (1966–1968), Mexicano youth identified with the term *Mexican American*, but as previously mentioned, by 1969, the transition to a Chicano identity occurred. Of the numerous student/youth organizations that emerged, the following four played a critical role in the Movimiento: MAYO, UMAS, the Brown Berets, and MEChA. With the exception of UMAS, they pursued an advocate transformer role.

MEXICAN AMERICAN YOUTH ORGANIZATION (MAYO)   In March 1967 in San Antonio, Tejas, five Mexicano undergraduate and graduate students from Saint Mary's University founded MAYO.[237] The five young organizational architects, who later became known as Los Cinco—José Angel Gutiérrez, Mario Campean, William "Willie" Velasquez, Juan Patlan, and Ignacio Perez—forged a protest student/barrio-based organization that was unique. Prior to officially launching MAYO, they meticulously studied various movements and leaders and even visited some of them. They conducted study sessions on community organizing, parliamentary procedures, and history; and they took inventory of Tejas's power structure. They opted for a structure that included chapters and a state steering committee with an annual planning conference. As an advocate transformer, MAYO became an organization of organizers with the capacity to act statewide as a rapid deployment mobilization force.[238]

Launched in 1967, with its strong militant, cultural nationalist, and social change agenda, MAYO became the avant-garde of the Movimiento in Tejas. Even though they opted for the usage of *Mexican American*, MAYO was a fervent proponent of cultural nationalism grounded on Méxicanismo. MAYO activists had a strong attachment to México, to its history, culture, heritage, and use of Spanish. Unlike other student and barrio-based organizations of the time, most MAYO members were bilingual and articulate in both English and Spanish. As it evolved, its *Méxicanismo* became synonymous with *Chicanismo* and *Chicano* and the terms were used interchangeably. Ideologically, MAYO combined cultural nationalism with a strong antisystem approach as manifested by its four newspapers: *El Deguello* from San Antonio; *Hoy*, published in the Rio Grande Valley; *El Azteca* out of Kingsville; and *La Revolución*, from Uvalde.[239] Increasingly, with its adherence to cultural nationalism, it rejected the politics of the MAG to where it even became critical of liberal capitalism. The lexicon of its leadership was often colored by references to socialist ideas and the self-determination politics of an independent Aztlán.

During its short five years of longevity, MAYO became the most hated Movimiento organization in Tejas, both by gringos and even some Mexicano politicians and organizations that identified with the MAG. MAYO considered other organizations such as LULAC, AGIF, and PASSO as ineffective, detached from the issues and realities of the barrios, and not representative of the La Raza's interests. To MAYO's leadership, these organizations were part of the problem and not part of the solution. Both white and some Mexican American politicians, such as Congressman Henry B. Gonzalez, who was tied into the Tejas white power structure, vehemently attacked MAYO for its confrontational protests and its assertive leadership, especially that of José Angel Gutiérrez, who was accused of being "racist," radical, and even a communist. A master at manipulating the media, Gutiérrez added to MAYO's radical image by his militant rhetoric and acrimonious attacks. The most notorious of these was his "Kill the Gringo" speech made at a press conference in 1969, where he warned gringos that unless social change came to Mexicanos in Tejas, it might be necessary to use violence and eliminate some gringos by killing them. It was with MAYO that Gutiérrez garnered a reputation that helped elevate him to become one of the four major leaders—or as described by Meier and Rivera—one of the "four horseman"[240] of the Movimiento.

From 1967 to 1972, MAYO was relentless in its Movimiento crusade to bring about major social change, particularly in the areas of education and political empowerment.[241] No other student or barrio-based protest organization matched its credentials for advocacy and direct action. In the area of educational change, MAYO initiated some thirty-nine high school walkouts in 1968–1969. Edcouch-Elsa (1968), Kingsville (1969), and Crystal City (1969–1970) are three that received the most media attention. In all of its school walkouts, MAYO propounded an educational agenda that called for Mexican American courses, bilingual/bicultural education, and the hiring of Mexican American Chicano teachers, among other reforms.[242] Strategically, MAYO utilized the resources of other organizations: beginning with the Mexican American Unity Council (MAUC), which it formed in San Antonio; the newly formed Mexican American Legal Defense and Education Fund (MALDEF); and Vista Minority Mobilization Program, especially in the Del Rio area of Tejas. With MAYO leaders on the payrolls of these organizations, it was better able to carry out its varied nationalist agenda.[243]

MAYO's greatest impact was in the political arena. In Tejas it became the precursor to RUP. In 1969, MAYO ventured into the electoral waters in San Antonio by running a slate of candidates for the city council and mayor. Although the slate lost, it was the testing ground for MAYO's "community control" politics. This was embodied in its Winter Garden Project, which called for community control of the local governments of La Salle, Dimmit, Zavala, and Hidalgo counties in south Tejas. Implemented by Gutiérrez, this action set for the successful Cristal School walkout in December 1969 and for the emergence of RUP as a third party in Tejas that next year. In April 1970, Gutiérrez epitomized his role of an advocate transformer with his successful and unprecedented orchestration of RUP's political takeover of Crystal City's (Cristal's) school board and city council and other local seat victories in Cotulla and Carrizo Springs. Interpreted as a political rebellion by the white press, these electoral victories shocked the gringo and Mexican American power structure and created a prairie fire of enthusiasm and hope among activists throughout Aztlán and beyond. With RUP's emergence, MAYO became the primary force behind its formation for the next two years, and by 1972 it was absorbed by RUP. The organizing success of RUP turned out to be the demise of MAYO.[244]

UNITED MEXICAN AMERICAN STUDENTS (UMAS)   A few months after MAYO was organized in Tejas, UMAS in California emerged out of the student organizing experience. In January 1967, a dozen students from East Los Angeles College formed the first student organization, the Mexican American Student Association (MASA). From its inception, MASA's two cardinal goals were education and community involvement. However, due to high student membership turnover and ideological reasons, MASA faded quickly. At a conference, held later in May, the idea of students getting organized gained momentum.[245] A small number of students from UCLA and other Los Angeles area colleges and universities met that summer of 1967 and agreed to form UMAS. A constitution was drafted and accepted and by September, seven chapters were formed, officers elected, and the first UMAS chair elected, Alberto Juarez.

By 1968, UMAS formed a central (regional) steering committee and was successful in establishing chapters in colleges and universities located in San Diego, Riverside, San Bernardino, and Santa Barbara in southern California.[246] Like its predecessor MASA, it was concerned with educational and community issues. While some chapters focused their energies on support of the UFW's Delano grape strike, others became involved in community issues. Even though there was a growing sense of Chicanismo, most UMAS chapters in its incipient stage by and large mirrored the politics of the Mexican American generation.[247] They became increasingly activist in their politics after several Movimiento leaders spoke at their campuses, such as Tijerina, Chavez, and Gonzales. Their agendas and messages sparked a high degree of politicization and *consciencia*, which raised the level of militant protest and Chicanismo within its membership ranks. Hence, by 1968, UMAS's members were ideologically heterogeneous. Within its ranks were cultural nationalists, who personified the emerging ethos of the CG; moderates, who identified more with the MAG and cultural integration; and a small number of radical leftists who advocated class struggle.[248] Yet the MAG's thrust on assimilation was by 1968 rejected in favor of cultural nationalism and their main agenda remained educational change.

UMAS's high point of notoriety came in 1968 with its involvement in the East L.A. Blowouts, which ultimately involved some ten thousand high school students from five high schools. Although most of the demands were not met, the blowouts served to increase membership in UMAS to where new chapters were established in other southwest and midwest universities. UMAS in California held a number of organizing regional and state conferences in 1968, with issues and speakers that indicated a growing radicalization. That year, UMAS scored a major victory by playing a cardinal role in the establishment of the first Chicano Studies program at what today is called California State University at Los Angeles. By 1969, however, the intensity of Chicanismo had grown, and UMAS was supplanted by a new organization.

MOVIMIENTO ESTUDIANTIL CHICANO DE AZTLÁN (MEChA)   With the drafting of El Plan de Santa Barbara, UMAS was replaced by a new and much more cultural nationalist student group, MEChA.[249] Its emergence in 1969 was illustrative of the militant and nationalist evolution of the Movimiento. In the words of Gómez-Quiñones, "The new name signified the commitment to confront social inequities and to reject assimilation into the dominant society, commitments to be fulfilled through student militant activities both on campus and in the community."[250] Its acronym, MEChA in Spanish denoted "match"; it was to ignite the spark for a student movement inspired by and committed to the ideas of El Plan Espiritual de Aztlán and El Plan de Santa Barbara. Driven by the spirit of Chicanismo and the role of an advocate transformer, MEChA became the vanguard student organization of the Movimiento for building Aztlán.

Organizationally, MEChA was intended to consolidate the Chicano student movement organizations. UMAS, MAYO, and all others were to convert to MEChA chapters. While many of them did, such as the UMAS chapters, others such as MAYO did not. The reasons were essentially based on student parochial attitudes, turf issues, conflicting political agendas, cultural conflicts, and so on. Equally important, MEChA's primary role was to be the driving organizing force behind the implementation of El Plan de Santa Barbara. This meant building Chicano studies programs and Chicano power-based student organization with strong linkages to the barrios of Aztlán. In describing MEChA's strategy with the community, Carlos Muñoz writes, MEChA "was to establish itself as both a legitimate community organization and a student group. Legitimacy in the community would in turn depend on a successful effort to form alliances with professionals, workers, and street youth in the surrounding Mexican American communities of each local campus."[251]

By the early 1970s, MEChA became the dominant student Movimiento protest organization. During these years, however, it gradually became less militant in its actions. Increasingly, MEChA was plagued with schisms, precipitated by ideological conflicts between cultural nationalists and Marxists and differences within the leadership. According to Albert Carrillo, "Almost immediately . . . students began quarreling among themselves over tactics and strategy.[252] Students began to form career-oriented groups, for example, Chicanos and the law, medicine, while others became increasingly apolitical by focusing on cultural events. Some Chicanas gradually became engaged in various feminist agendas. A growing sense of apathy and complacency began to set in on many campuses, indicative of a changing ethos among students. At the macro level of the Movimiento, there was the power struggle between Gonzales and Gutiérrez; the decline of Tijerina's leadership; and a militant de-escalation that also contributed to MEChA's declining influence.

BARRIO-BASED YOUTH PROTEST ORGANIZATIONS   While student organizations were a powerful driving force in the Movimiento so were barrio-based youth groups that were paramilitary and self-defense-oriented. To some extent, the Black Power Nationalist Movement, represented by the Black Panther Party, influenced them. They mimicked the symbolism, rhetoric, style of military dress, and even their strategies of self-defense.[253] Their politics and orientation meant they assumed an advocate transformer role. However, it is important to note that they were not carbon copies of Black Power organizations. Each developed its own nationalist personality based on the cultural and political experiences and on needs of the Chicano community. As early as 1966, in response to a Puerto Rican riot, Chicano *veteranos* (barrio veterans) and youth in Chicago formed the Latin American Defense Organization (LADO). Led by Obed Gomez, the organization sought to physically protect the Chicano community from attacks by any other ethnic or racial community.[254] In San Antonio, Tejas Beto Martinez, a former *pinto* (ex-convict) who had the title of minister of war in LADO, formed the Mexican American Nationalist Organization (MANO). As a paramilitary self-defense force, MANO was deeply nationalist and separatist. As a clandestine group they believed that all whites should be driven out of the Southwest. However, much of its focus was on curbing police brutality in the barrios of San Antonio.[255] Another paramilitary group was the Black Berets, formed in 1969 in Albuquerque, Nuevo México. Like the Brown Berets, the Black Berets also espoused a separatist nationalist posture. With their motto of "Serve, Educate, and Defend," they adhered to a Twelve-Point Program based on principles of self-determination, self-defense, and Chicanismo.[256]

THE BROWN BERETS (BB OR BERETS)   Of all the barrio-based youth groups, the BB became the most influential of the Movimiento organizations.[257] Its genesis occurred in 1967 in East Los Angeles, California, with a group known as Young Citizens for Community Action (YCCA). Led by David Sanchez, a teenager, who, according to Acuña, was "from an upper-lower class family," in a matter of a few months the YCCA evolved from a local community service organization into a quasi-patrol group that took a defensive posture regarding the police in the barrios. Later that year, in an attempt to raise resources and provide a place of recreation for barrio youth, the YCCA opened up a coffee shop in East Los Angeles called La Piranya.[258] Influenced and inspired by the emergent Movimiento, by late 1967, the YCCA went through a name change to Young Chicanos for Community Action. In December 1967, Sanchez and other leaders such as Carlos Montez and Ralph Rameriz, dropped the former name and adopted "Brown Berets" as the name for their new organization.[259] With the name change other changes ensued: a higher level of militancy, adherence to Chicanismo, and a paramilitary posture became evident. With the transition, the Berets assumed a role of an advocate transformer. They wore brown berets, which contained an insignia of crossed rifles and a cross, khaki military uniforms, and army boots, and they openly espoused the use of armed self-defense.[260] Beret chapters trained in guerrilla warfare and use of weapons, drilled regularly, and marched in military formation. Military and political titles were used to identify the BB's leadership: prime minister, ministers of defense, justice, information, and discipline.[261] With Sanchez as its prime minister, the Berets' radical nationalism increased with its overt separatist agenda of building a Chicano nation, Aztlán.

The Berets' ardent separatism was evident in its use of the Mexican flag. Article XIV of their constitution was entitled, "We Declare a Nation," and read: "We the Chicano people of the southwest, hereby declare ourselves to be a nation, and a nation that has been the subject of a profit-making invasion. We are a nation within a land that has been temporarily occupied."[262] The Berets was the first protest organization to espouse the separatist notion of Chicano nation building. With its loosely decentralized structure of chapters, it engaged in served events and issues that accelerated its development. Between 1968 and 1972, BB chapters were formed in numerous rural and urban barrios and *colonias* throughout the Southwest and even in the Midwest. The Berets' membership ranks were comprised of mostly hardcore barrio youth and adults, many of them former gang members. They took rebellious youth and adults, from ages fourteen to thirty-five,[263] who had no cause and gave them one. For a few years at least, gang activity in the barrios subsided significantly. The Berets were the "shock troops" of the Movimiento and such was the perception held by local law enforcement agencies including the FBI's COINTELPRO; consequently, it became a prime target of their infiltration and harassment.

From their inception in 1967 to its decline in 1972, the Berets were involved in numerous marches, mobilizations, and other direct actions. One of its most visible actions was the East L.A. Blowouts. Along with UMAS, BB members acted as the security force for the thousands of protesting students. Its vital leadership role was evident in the indictment of Sanchez along with twelve others, who became known as the "L.A.13." In 1969 and 1970, the Berets participated in the Crusade for Justice's two Chicano Youth Liberation Conferences. In 1969, they became involved in the "Biltmore Hotel Incident." Then governor Ronald Reagan was speaking at an event at the hotel when several fires broke out; he was interrupted several times with the Chicano clap and shouts of "Viva la Raza" by Chicanos in the audience. Of those six ultimately arrested, known as the "Biltmore Six," two were BBs.

By late 1969, the Berets joined the antiwar protest by holding two marches and rallies. Sanchez, joined by Rosalio Munoz, in 1970 formed the National Chicano Moratorium Committee. On August 29, they staged the largest Chicano antiwar march and rally involving some thirty thousand people in Los Angeles. In many areas of the Southwest, the Berets supported and assisted as well in the organizing of RUP throughout the early 1970s. In 1971 in an unsuccessful attempt to rekindle the vigor of the Movimiento, La Marcha de La Reconquista was organized by the Berets in California. In 1972 in another desperate attempt to reignite some fire into the Movimiento, the Berets symbolically invaded the Catalina Islands off the southern California coast. It produced some media hype but no concrete victory or results. By then the Berets were under a state of siege by law enforcement agencies and plagued by growing schisms and internal conflict. At a press conference Sanchez officially disbanded the Berets later that year. A few of the Beret chapters continued to function after 1972, but as a protest organization, they were not able to successfully regroup.

OTHER NOTABLE MOVIMIENTO ORGANIZATIONS   Numerous other Movimiento-oriented groups emerged in the late 1960s. Within the Catholic Church, Chicano activists in Los Angeles formed a protest group called Catolicos Por La Raza in 1969, which assailed the Church hierarchy for neglecting the needs of their Chicano parishioners. The emerging academic community of Chicano scholars and graduate students formed the National Association of Chicano Social Scientists (NACSS) at a meeting attended by thirty-six Chicano intellectuals at New México Highlands University in 1973. Conceived as the intellectual arm of the Movimiento's struggle for social change, the NACCS's primary role was to be the avant-garde of intellectual change, scholarship committed to liberation, and consciousness building pedagogy. During its first annual conference in 1974 held at the University of California, Irvine a number of panels related to the Movimiento were held, including one on RUP, in which I participated.[264]

At a time when protest organizations were starting to decline a new one emerged—the Ad Hoc Committee on Chicano Rights (CCR). Organized and led by Herman Baca of National City, California, it developed out of the ranks of MAPA in San Diego and became the driving force behind RUP for the area. As an advocate transformer, the CCR was effective in taking on a number of community issues, for example, police brutality, education, immigration.

Labor Unions: The Rise of the UFW

UNITED FARM WORKERS (UFW)   The farmworker's struggle to unionize became an integral part of the Movimiento. Efforts to change the plight of the *compesino* were begun in 1962 with the formation of the Farm Worker Association (FWA). In 1964 a name change occurred, to the National Farm Workers Association (NFWA). Its organizing architect was Cesar Chavez, former CSO state director, who was assisted by two loyal organizers, Dolores Huerta and Gil Padilla. In 1962 Chavez resigned from the CSO due to the board of director's failure to support his proposal to organize farmworkers. He moved his family to

Delano, where he started to organize.[265] After months of intensive organizing—holding numerous house and community meetings throughout the area—Chavez held a conference in September in Fresno. Attended by some 150 delegates, the conference gave rise to the FWA. The delegates chose their flag, an eagle on a black and red background; elected temporary officers; agreed to lobby for a minimum wage covering farmworkers; adopted Viva La Causa as its motto; and voted that each member should pay membership dues of $3.25 per month.[266]

From 1962 to 1967, the NFWA was not a labor union as such; it was still a buffer-oriented association. Chavez intended to eventually convert the NFWA into a full-fledged union, but during the interim, used a *mutualista* approach to provide a multiplicity of services to farmworkers in the Delano area of California. These services included life insurance, a gasoline station, a grocery store, a drugstore cooperative, and a medical clinic. By 1965, the NFWA's membership ranks had increased to some seventeen hundred; it had established its own newspaper, *El Malcriado*; and under the direction of Luis Valdez it had formed El Teatro Compesino. Of great assistance to Chavez and the NFWA in their organizing was the termination of the Bracero Program in 1964 and by 1965, the country's tumultuous political climate. In 1965, the fledgling Agricultural Workers Organizing Committee (AWOC), led by Filipino labor leader Larry Itlong, requested the assistance of Chavez and the NFWA in a grape strike it had initiated in September. The strike sought to gain higher pay and recognition of the AWOC.[267] On September 16, Mexican Independence Day, the NFWA decided to support the AWOC request. As a result, the Delano strike or La Causa began, and Chavez and the NFWA increasingly assumed an advocate transformer role. Within no time, Chavez emerged as the strike's leader. He espoused nonviolence in the tradition of Gandhi and Martin Luther King and proved his adroitness in successfully manipulating political symbols and in his sense of timing. During the ensuing months, Chavez demonstrated his organizing acumen, pragmatism, and adroitness by garnering a broad base of support and adopted an assertive buffer role; Mexican organizations such as MAPA gave the NFWA their support as well as numerous non-Mexican organizations and leaders from the civil rights, New Left, and antiwar movements. Unions, churches, and key Democrat politicians also supported Chavez and his fledgling NFWA/AWOC alliance.

By early 1966, the strike went national and received wide media exposure. That year's march to Sacramento was a major success for both Chavez as a leader and the NFWA as an emerging union. The NFWA/AWOC Alliance produced El Plan de Delano, negotiated the first contract between the union and the Schenley Corporation, and brought some ten thousand protestors to the front of the capitol building in Sacramento. Di Giorgio Corporation became the next target of the boycott. During 1967, under the aegis of the AFL-CIO, the NFWA strengthened its position, merged with AWOC, and became known as the United Farm Workers Organizing Committee (UFWOC, later the United Farm Workers of America).[268]

The ready-formed UFWOC mounted an international boycott of grapes and initiated farmworker organizing efforts in Texas and the Midwest. In April 1967, the UFWOC signed union contracts with the Di Giorgio Fruit Corporation. They further intensified their efforts by making Guiamarra Corporation the next big target. In 1968, violence threatening to plague the grape boycott against Guiamarra, Chavez called for a "fast" that lasted twenty-one days; he was visited by presidential candidate U.S. senator Robert Kennedy and became a national media event. In 1969, the Guiamarra grape boycott was expanded to include all California grape growers, and the national grape boycott intensified to where it became internationalized. After nearly five years of struggle, on July 29, 1970, in Delano, Chavez's UFWOC scored a series of unprecedented victories: some twenty-nine growers including Guiamarra concluded contracts. The victory meant that 85 percent of California's growers were under a union contract[269]—a fete never again replicated by the UFW.

The UFWOC in California next targeted lettuce growers and became embroiled in a relentless power struggle with the competing Teamsters Union, which produced few UFWOC victories. As a result of the lettuce strike, in December 1970, Chavez was jailed in Monterey, California, for not complying with a picketing injunction.[270] In Arizona, in October 1971, the UFWOC in an effort to defeat a farm labor law that outlawed the boycott and limited strikes mounted an unsuccessful recall effort against Governor Jack Williams. In order to dramatize the ongoing struggle in Arizona, in April 1972, Chavez held another fast that lasted twenty-four days. In November 1972 in California, Republicans, under the guise of Proposition 22, sought to pass a similar piece of legislation. Although it specifically outlawed the use of the secondary boycott, it was ably defeated by the UFW (by this time it was no longer an organizing committee; it was a full-fledged union designated UFW). During the next two years, the UFW's ongoing conflict with the Teamsters escalated to violence, especially in the Coachella area of California. The UFW initiated another national boycott, this time directed at Gallo products.[271] That year, after much pressure, the Teamsters agreed to give up their campaign to organize farmworkers.[272]

At the close of 1974, unlike other Movimiento organizations, the UFW was stable and holding, continuing its struggle, and not in a decline mode. Chavez and the UFW's La Causa were a powerful catalytic force in the development of the Movimiento. Interestingly, however, Chavez never claimed to be a leader of it, although it can be argued that at times he demonstrated definite cultural nationalist proclivities. He described himself foremost as a "labor" organizer who represented a union rather than a leader of the Movimento. Yet of all the leaders of the Movimiento, he became the most acclaimed, visible, and supported across the board.[273]

While the UFW was the locus of Chicano farmworker organizing efforts, other labor struggles were also part of the Movimiento epoch. One such struggle was the "Farah strike," which involved some four thousand mostly Mexicana workers from El Paso, San Antonio, Victoria, and Las Cruces, Nuevo México, who struck the Farah clothing company for intolerable working conditions and harassment of workers at its various plants. In July of 1972, the Amalgamated Clothing Workers Union of America (ACWUA) promulgated a national boycott of Farah garment products that lasted some two years. As historian Rodolfo Acuña explains, "the backbone of the strike were women, who went on speaking tours, creating their own group called *Unidad Para Siempre*, Unity Forever." In 1974 the Farah strike that took a great toll on the striking workers ended and a contract with the ACWUA was signed. However, as Acuña points out the harassment of union activists continued well into 1976 when Farah began to move its operations into México.[274]

A Chicano Third Party: La Raza Unida Party

THE RISE OF LA RAZA UNIDA PARTY (RUP)   The emergence of RUP in 1970 became "politically" the year's most important event.[275] After some 122 years of electoral dependency on the Democrat and Republican Parties, in 1970 Chicano activists repudiated the country's two-party dictatorship system and opted to form their own political party. Alienated from the do-nothing politics of both Democrats and Republicans, activists sought to create their own *partido* in their struggle to empower the barrios of Aztlán. For purposes of analysis, it is important to recognize that political parties organizationally differ from interest or protest groups. Briefly, the former seeks control of governmental structures and policies, whereas the latter in most cases merely seek to influence policy. Anthony Downs defines a political party as a "team of men [and women] seeking to control the governing apparatus by gaining office in a duly constituted election."[276] Whereas Dan Nimmo and Thomas D. Ungs focus on what a party does: it is "a coalition of fairly stable, enduring, and frequently conflicting interests, organized to mobilize support in competitive elections in order to control public policy."[277] In short, political parties run candidates to win control of the aspects of the superstructure, in particular public policy.

The rise of RUP in 1970 was tantamount to a political rebellion directed at the country's two-party dictatorship. Many activists perceived both major parties as being insensitive, unresponsive, and unrepresentative of the Mexicano's needs and interests. At the core of activist rationale for establishing RUP were the words of Rodolfo "Corky" Gonzales, who said, "The truth is that both parties, the elite Republicans and the party of promises, the Democrats, operate for their own selfish interests. They are both ruled and controlled by money and racism." And Gonzales concluded, "The two party system is one animal with two heads eating out of the same trough." Never in the history of the Mexicano political experience had Mexicanos ever opted to form their own ethnic-based third party. Only twice did Mexicanos play a crucial political role in the formation of a third party, once during the 1890s in Nuevo México with the formation of El Partido del Pueblo Unido (The United People's Party), and again in 1968, with Tijerina's People's Constitutional Party.[278]

As a third party, RUP emerged in early 1970 both in Tejas and Colorado in the role of an advocate transformer. It was a product of the leadership and organizational experiences of Gutiérrez and MAYO in Tejas and the Gonzales and Crusade for Justice in Colorado. In particular, organizationally both became precursors to RUP's formation. In Tejas, with the success of the Cristal school walkouts, Gutiérrez in January officially announced the intent to form RUP. In March, at the conclusion of the second Chicano Youth Liberation Conference, Gonzales likewise made a national call for RUP's formation. With the unprecedented electoral city council and school board victories orchestrated by Gutiérrez in Zavala, Dimmit, and La Salle counties, the political template for the rise of RUP was created. RUP's community control of Cristal's city council and school board fostered a "peaceful revolution."[279] With the cry for "Chicano Power" actualized, the political, educational, socioeconomic, and cultural changes that ensued until 1975 were dramatic and unprecedented. Cristal became the "political mecca and capital" of the Movimiento. As a result of RUP's formation, Gutiérrez was catapulted into major leadership status within the pantheon of Movimiento's leadership, joining Tijerina, Chavez, and Gonzales.

Efforts to organize RUP quickly spread like a prairie fire throughout the Southwest. From California to Tejas and the Midwest, activists shifted their agenda from educational change to political empowerment. Starting in late 1970 and well into 1971, numerous RUP state, regional, and local conferences and meetings were held and organizing committees formed. Although unsuccessful, RUP in Colorado in 1970 ran a number of candidates as independents for several state offices on a cultural nationalist platform. While efforts in California were begun in 1971 to get RUP on the ballot, in Tejas RUP did get on the ballot that year via a difficult statewide petition drive that produced some twenty-three thousand signatures. That next year, numerous RUP candidates ran unsuccessfully for local to state office, including Ramsey Muñiz for governor. By September 1972 in El Paso, Tejas, the first and last RUP national convention was held and drew some three thousand activists from some eighteen states. The power struggle between the clashing titans, Gutiérrez and Gonzales, came to a crescendo with the former winning the *partido's* chairmanship. Never before had so many Chicanos politically gathered to develop their own political agenda. The convention became the apogee of RUP's development, and the start of its decline began.

After the convention, RUP was plagued by an intensifying power struggle between the two intransigent *caudillos* for control of the Congreso (RUP's National Steering Committee). Further exacerbating the aforementioned were increasing ideological conflicts within its ranks and leadership. Both Gutiérrez and Gonzales were ideologically hypercritical of liberal capitalism and both were ardent proponents of Chicanismo. Yet there were differences: Gonzales propounded a rather vanguard *partido* position and was committed to the separatist politics of nation building, while Gutiérrez advocated a rather pragmatic approach predicated on effectuating change by working within the existing political system that accentuated an electoral "balance of power" strategy. The ideological struggles were further compounded by clashes between cultural nationalists and Marxists of sorts. Thus, by 1974, RUP's organizing efforts throughout the country declined to where only in South Tejas at the local level did it win a number of local offices.

Formation of New Interest Groups: Vehicles of the Mexican American Generation

Integral to the epoch of protest's organizational renaissance was the formation of several new conventional interest groups. Even though they were spawned under a political climate of militancy, protest, and massive mobilizations, because of their buffer roles, they eschewed the politics of the CG and identified more with the integrationist ethos and politics of the MAG. This was reflective of the Movimiento's heterogeneity in which there was a great diversity of views and perspectives as to what constituted La Causa. According to Oscar Martinez, "Former activists who successfully made the transition from fighting the system from outside to working to change it from within founded or staffed many of these groups."[280] Thus, while not considered avant-garde Movimiento organizations; yet in their own way, they too contributed to its sustenance.

RISE OF NEW ORGANIZATIONS   Three such new buffer interest groups that in the subsequent epoch became major advocacy organizations were the National Council of La Raza (NCLR), the Mexican American Legal Defense and Education Fund (MALDEF), and the Southwest Voter Registration Education Project (SVREP). All three were in great part products of funding secured from the Ford Foundation.[281] The NCLR was originally named the Southwest Council of La Raza. It was founded in Phoenix in 1968 and in 1972 was renamed the National Council of La Raza, and its general purpose was to promote community and economic development. More specifically, its primary function was to provide assistance to community service organizations in proposal writing, leadership training, funding allocation, and so on.[282]

MALDEF was founded in Tejas in 1968, as a result of a $2.2 million grant from the Ford Foundation. It was patterned after the Legal Defense fund of the National Association for the Advancement of Colored People (NAACP).[283] Ford Foundation monies via the Southwest Council of La Raza were used to jumpstart MALDEF's operations. For the first five years, Pete Tijerina was MALDEF's executive director, followed by Mario Obledo and by 1973 Vilma Martinez. Essentially, it functioned more as a legal aid society rather than a full-fledged legal advocate pressure group. Yet between 1968 and 1969, MALDEF handled some two hundred cases and complaints. In 1970 MALDEF attorneys launched a number of lawsuits that challenged the vestiges of segregation and discrimination. Perhaps the most important of these was *Cisneros v. Corpus Christi Independent School District.*

As will be further examined in chapter 8, former MAYO leader Willie Velasquez formed the Southwest Voter Registration and Education Project (SVREP) in 1974. Its primary mission was to enhance voter participation of Mexicanos by organizing voter registration drives throughout Aztlán.

The Movimiento's decline became evident with the formation of several other types of organizations. During the early 1970s, several "professional"-oriented organizations were formed that represented the economic interests of the middle class. They advocated a more gradualist and reform-oriented nonconfrontational approach that meant that the ethos of the MAG was not moribund. One such organization formed in 1973 was the Incorporated Mexican American Government Employees (IMAGE). It lobbied the federal, state, and local levels of government for equal employment opportunities and counterdiscrimination not only against Mexican Americans, but also for Latinos in general.[284] Several "economic development" oriented organizations also got a jumpstart during the early 1970s. One of the most successful was The East Los Angeles Community Union (TELACU), established in 1970. For the next four years, TELACU, beyond its development projects, became a major political player in East Los Angeles politics. Also, during the early 1970s, "religious-based" organizations, such as Padres Asociados para Derechos Religiosos, Educativos, y Sociales (PADRES), comprised of Chicano Catholic priests, were formed. It sought to foster change within the structures of the Catholic Church. A counterpart for nuns and Catholic laywomen was Las Hermanas (The Sisters) founded in 1970 in Tejas. In San Antonio, Tejas, in 1974, supported by several Catholic parishes and assisted by Saul Alinsky's Industrial Areas Foundation, an advocacy grassroots organization, Communities Organized for Public Service (COPS), was formed and developed into a powerful organization.[285]

Chicana Organizations and Activism

MEXICANAS: VICTIMS OF MACHISMO   Throughout the "Mexicano political experience of occupied Aztlán," Mexicanas have been long victimized and subjected to machismo and sexism. Subjected to a patriarchal Mexicano culture, *las mujeres* within the context of the Movimiento, with few exceptions, did not reach the level of leadership prominence of *los hombres*. By and large, *la mujer* was relegated to a secondary leadership role. The one major exception was Dolores Huerta, who was a cofounder of the UFW. From the onset of La Causa, she played an indispensable leadership role as organizer, negotiator, and lobbyist. Yet most Movimiento organizations including those that were student- and barrio youth-based were male dominated. One of the first major regional debates on the role of *la mujer* in the Movimiento occurred in 1969 at the Crusade for Justice's Chicano Youth Liberation Conference. Chicanas supported Chicanismo; however, they spoke out and sought inclusion and did not adopt an antimale attitude.[286] By the late 1960s in Los Angeles, Chicanas began to move on their own organizationally. One such example was Alicia Escalante, who formed the East Los Angeles Welfare Rights Organization.

CHICANA ORGANIZATIONS FORMED   By the early 1970s, Chicanas assumed greater leadership roles and became more assertive, vocal, and visible and in the process formed their own organizations.[287] In October of 1970, Francisca Flores and Ramona Morin in Los Angeles spearheaded the formation of La Comisión Femenil Mexicana Nacional.[288] These two Chicana leaders played a pivotal role in organizing the first national Chicana conference, Mujeres Por La Raza, held in 1971 in Houston, Tejas. Attended by some six hundred women throughout Aztlán and Midwest, the conference was a reaction to the exclusionary male leadership practices of most Movimiento organizations. In November

1972, Chicanas participated in a third world women's conference in San Anselmo, California, where the agenda focused on defining third world and third world concerns.[289]

By this time, participating in the conference were Chicanas who fell into two conflicting gender camps: the "loyalist" verses the emerging "feminist."[290] Debates occurred between the "loyalists," who were critical of their leadership exclusion, but because of their Chicanismo inclinations prioritized continued support for the Movimiento, and the nascent "feminists," who argued that the main enemy was sexism and traditional macho attitudes. After a very spirited debate, with only half of the conference participants voting, several resolutions were passed that reflected their concerns. The resolutions focused on issues related to sexual equality, free legal abortions, and birth control; encouragement of higher education for all women; changes in traditional roles to recognize women as breadwinners; and a denouncement of the Catholic Church's opposition to feminist ideas. From 1972 through 1974, several other conferences were held that focused on various issues related to women exercising an equal leadership role. As a result, it was during this time that the emerging Chicana feminist struggle was given impetus and assumed an increasingly advocate transformer role.

Chicanas particularly took on a greater leadership role in the formation of RUP in Tejas. A number of them were elected to the school board, city council, and county commissioner positions in Tejas; while others ran unsuccessfully for statewide office. Virginia Muzquiz, Luz Gutierrez, Viviana Santiago, Martha Cotera, Evy Chapa, and many more played key leadership roles within the *partido*. They were instrumental in forming the Federacion de Mujeres de La Raza Unida, which sought to represent the interests of *mujeres* within RUP. However, Tejas was the exception: RUP's organizing efforts throughout the rest of the Southwest and Midwest was basically male-dominated. In California, in order to leverage their influence, RUP Chicanas formed the Mujeres Pro-Raza Unida. Martha Cotera by 1973 became a staunch feminist and in 1973 helped form the Texas Women's Political Caucus. Meanwhile in California, in academia regarding the issue of Chicana feminism and Chicano Studies at the forefront of that struggle was Anna Nieta-Gomez, Gracia Molina de Pick, and Corina Sanchez.[291] Thus, while still in its infancy during the early 1970s, the Chicana feminist struggle weathered well the decline of the Movimiento, which had given it political life.

Sectarian Marxist Organizations: Rise of the Chicano Left

Several ideological sectarian Marxist organizations during the epoch colored the Movimiento's panorama. While ideologically Marxist and advocate transformers in their role, they were strategically diverse sectarian third parties, such as the Communist Party U.S.A., Socialist Worker's Party, Progressive Labor Party, Communist Revolutionary Party, October League, Communist Labor Party, and Democratic Workers Party, among others. Some through their front organizations sought to penetrate and infiltrate the ranks of Chicano organizations. They participated in numerous Chicano-organized protest mobilizations, issues, and conferences. Their cardinal intent was to proselytize Chicanos into the class struggle against liberal capitalism. They stressed themes of class inequality, inequality between men and women, and inequality between rich and poor regardless of ethnicity or race.[292] They were antithetical alternatives to buffer and "want to be white"-oriented entities. By the early 1970s, Marxist-oriented organizational activity within the Chicano community increased. In particular, the Socialist Worker's Party's youth arm, the Young Socialist Alliance (YSA), was active in the formation of RUP. Through its newspaper, *The Militant*, numerous issues impacting Chicano communities were addressed. Ideological conflicts likewise began to develop among several Movimiento organizations, especially those within student sector and later within RUP.

CHICANO LIBERATION FRONT   At the extreme end of the advocate transformer role was the Chicano Liberation Front (CLF). Formed in 1970, the CLF was a clandestine terrorist group, which demanded the removal of police and other "outside exploiters" from East Los Angeles. When its demands were not met a series of bombings occurred in the East Los Angeles area. The CLF's targets were mostly banks, such as the Bank of America, Safeway Markets, and schools. In a taped message to the *Los Angeles Free Press*, the CLF accepted full responsibility for some twenty-eight bombings that occurred between March 1970 and July 18, 1971.[293] The communiqué also said the following:

We would not jeopardize the life of any person. We would look around our community and find it occupied by murdering, racist police, lying politicians and greedy businessman. Most of our acts are against these invaders. Some so-called radicals and revolutionaries say that our tactics are wrong. Our answer is that desperate situations call for desperate measures.[294]

THE RISE OF CASA-HGT (CENTRO DE ACCIÓN SOCIAL AUTÓNOMA-HERMANDAD GENERAL DE TRABAJADORES   During the course of the Movimiento, in response to the intensification of the migrant exodus, immigration as an issue began to take on a greater importance. The formation of CASA-HGT is intertwined with that of its precursor, La Hermandad Mexicana Nacional (The Mexican National Brotherhood or HMN). Initially formed in 1951 in San Diego, California, the HMN had been led by Phil and Albert Usquiano, two trade union leaders. Corona explains that it was organized in response to efforts by the INS after World War II to cancel the work visas of many Mexicanos who worked in San Diego but lived in Tijuana. However, after a few years of activity, it became dormant until its reactivation by progressive activist/organizer Bert Corona, who, assisted by Soledad "Chole" Alatorre, Juan Mariscal, and Estella Garcia, among others, reconstituted the HMN in late 1968.²⁹⁵ With its reemergence, the HMN's cardinal mission during the ensuing years was to assist and protect specifically the constitutional rights of Mexicano working-class undocumented workers, so an office was opened up in Los Angeles.²⁹⁶ In explaining the HMN's incipient organizing activities, Gómez-Quiñones writes, "When it began an organization, [it] was devoted to modest services for undocumented persons and built a membership determined by the payment of a small fee in return for a card."²⁹⁷ From the onset, the HMN opened an office in Los Angeles and provided undocumented workers assistance and protection from increasing Border Patrol and INS deportation pressures.

By the early 1970s with its self-help *mutualista* orientation, the HMN expanded its organizing activities of undocumented workers by forming CASA (Centro de Acción Social Autónoma) in various communities. While the HMN was the advocacy arm, CASA was established to be the immigration service arm. As a result, an amalgamation occurred that fostered a name change: CASA-HGT (Centro de Acción Autonoma-Hermandad General de Trabajadores). Rodolfo Acuña writes that during these years of transition "CASA in reality set the progressive template for the protection of the foreign born."²⁹⁸ By 1972, although CASA's structure was decentralized, its membership had grown to some five thousand paid members. Through its newspaper, *Sin Fronteras*, CASA linked the struggle of Mexicano workers both to México and the United States.²⁹⁹ Corona up to about 1974 served as CASA-HGT's executive director, and Alatorre was his indispensable labor organizer. When interviewed by historian Mario Garcia, Corona explained the relationship between the two organizations.

The HMNs remained as broad immigrant organizations that continued to build political community among immigrants, but the specific services were directed out of CASAs. Both HMNs and the CASAs had their own separate boards. . . . In some communities where CASAs were not formed, HMNs provided the various services. There were linkages, but it represented an effort to systemize our large operations. . . . While the HMNs were composed predominantly of recent immigrants, including many of the staff volunteers, the CASAs—especially their staffs—were composed of young Chicano professionals, social workers, priests, nuns, and students.[300]

However, by 1973, CASA-HGT, which included professionals, students, and workers who had participated in Casa Carnalismo, the Committee to Free Los Tres, and the Comite Estudiantil del Pueblo lead by barrio attorney Antonio Rodriguez, took on a Marxist-Leninist sectarian posture.[301] As will be examined more comprehensively in chapter 8, by 1974 CASA entered in words of Mario Barrera into "a more ideological and more radical phase."[302] What ensued was a power struggle that Corona lost by the end of 1974. Thus, as the epoch of protest came to a close, CASA-HGT had positioned itself as a major organizational player in what was left of the arena of Movimiento politics.

THE AUGUST TWENTY-NINTH MOVEMENT (ATM)   At the close of 1974, the former RUP Labor Committee that operated out of Los Angeles established the ATM.[303] As a Marxist-Leninist sectarian organization, ideologically the ATM embraced a Maoist perspective, which put it on a collision course with other sectarian groups, such as the Trotskyite Socialist Workers Party that had been actively involved in organizing Chicanos and the Stalinist CASA-HGT. The ATM sought to challenge the contention that Chicanos and Mexicanos constituted a single nation.[304] As will be examined in chapter 8, the result was that for the next three years, a sectarian ideological war was waged between these three groups over which group was going to be the vanguard for the Chicano struggle for liberation.

Thus, with the end of the Movimiento in 1974 a new era emerged, one appropriately called the epoch of the Viva Yo Hispanic Generation.

Notes

1. The question of what theoretically constitutes a social movement is a major focus of my next book, tentatively entitled *What Needs to Be Done? The Building of a New Movement.* However, for purposes of giving further depth to this work's analysis it is important to define what a social movement is. For John Wilson, author of *Introduction to Social Movements* (New York: Basic, 1973), a social movement is "a conscious, collective, organized attempt to bring about or resist large-scale change in the social order by noninstitutionalized means." James L. Wood and Maurice Jackson, who wrote *Social Movements: Development, Participation, and Dynamics* (Belmont, Calif.: Wadsworth, 1982), define a social movement

"as unconventional groups that have varying degrees of formal organization and that attempt to produce or prevent radical or reform type of change."

2. For a further examination of this author's social movement paradigm see my book *La Raza Unida Party: A Chicano Challenge to the U.S. Two-Party Dictatorship* (Philadelphia: Temple University Press, 2000). As previously alluded to this analysis is comprehensively dealt with in my sixth book, *What Needs to Be Done? The Building of a New Movement*, which I am currently working on. From my perspective, a social movement, particularly a "reform or revolutionary" political movement, is a form of collective action, which promotes either "progressive" or "regressive" change. It is conceived in the midst of a climate of change permeated by growing discontent, frustration, and rising expectations and is impelled by the presence of multiple leaders, informal and formal organizations, an ideology or set of ideas, and a strategy and tactics, and is sustained by a power capability.

3. "Relative Deprivation is defined as a perceived discrepancy between men's value expectations and their value capabilities. Value expectations are the goods and conditions of life to which people believe they are rightfully entitled. Value capabilities are the goods and conditions they think they are capable of attaining or maintaining given the social means available to them. Societal conditions that increase the average level of intensity of expectations without increasing capabilities increase the intensity of discontent" (see Ted Robert Gurr, *Why Men Rebel* [Princeton, N.J.: Princeton University Press, 1970], 13).

4. For a thorough examination of this argument on protest see James Q. Wilson, "The Strategy of Protest: Problems of Negro Civic Action," *Journal of Conflict Resolution* V (September 1961): 291–303.

5. Michael Lipsky, *Protest in City Politics: Rent Strikes, Housing and the Power of the Poor* (Chicago: Rand McNally, 1970), 1–6. Lipsky qualifies the use of "protest" by explaining that the strategic goal of the powerless in protest activity is to activate "third parties," meaning the activation of other groups into the political arena in support of the powerless.

6. Frances Fox Piven and Richard A. Cloward, *Poor People's Movements: Why They Succeed, How They Fail* (New York: Vintage, 1979), 3–4.

7. Carlos Muñoz, *Youth, Identity, and Power: The Chicano Movement* (New York: Verso, 1989), 7.

8. Mario Barrera, *Beyond Aztlán: Ethnic Autonomy in Comparative Perspective* (New York: Praeger, 1988), 44.

9. Juan Gómez-Quiñones, *Chicano Politics: Reality and Promise* (Albuquerque: University of New México Press, 1990), 101.

10. Manuel G. Gonzales, *Mexicanos: A History of Mexicans in the United States* (Bloomington: Indiana University Press, 1999.

11. I make the argument that the Chicano Movement was a product of several exogenous and endogenous antagonisms in my first book, entitled *Mexican American Youth Organization: Avant-Garde of the Chicano Movement* (Austin: University of Texas Press, 1995), 1–8. For a more current examination see my journal article "The Post Mortem Politics of the Chicano Movement: 1975–1996," *Perspectives in Mexican American Studies* (Tucson: Mexican American Studies & Research Center, the University of Arizona) Vol. 6 (1997): 52–79.

12. For a major work that encompasses an examination of all the preceding movements including the indigenous struggles of the 1960s see Terry H. Anderson, *The Movement and the Sixties: Protest in America from Greensboro to Wounded Knee* (New York: Oxford University Press, 1995).

13. For an excellent case study on the history of the Civil Rights Movement see Robert Weisbrot, *Freedom Bound: A History of America's Civil Rights Movement* (New York: Penguin, 1991). See also Piven and Cloward, *Poor People's Movement*, chapter 4; Fred Powledge, *Free at Last? The Civil Rights Movement and the People Who Made It* (New York: Harper Perennial, 1992).

14. Jerome Skolnick, *The Politics of Protest* (National Commission on the Causes and Prevention of Violence, 1969), 100–101.

15. For a comprehensive appraisal on the historical aspects of the New Left see the following works: Ayn Rand, *The New Left: The Anti-Industrial Revolution* (New York: Signet, 1971); Edward J. Bacciocco, Jr., *The New Left in America: Reform to Revolution, 1956–1970* (Stanford, Calif.: Hoover Institution Press, 1974); Matthew F. Stolz, *Politics of the New Left* (Beverly Hills, Calif.: Glencoe Press, 1971); John P. Diggins, *The American Left in the Twentieth Century* (New York: Harcourt Brace Jovanovich, 1973); Dave Dellinger, *More Power, Than We Know: The People's Movement Toward Democracy* (Garden City, N.Y.: Anchor Press, 1975).

16. For a comprehensive case study on the SDS's history see Kirkpatrick Sale, *SDS* (New York: Random House, 1973).

17. Marguerite V. Marin, *Social Protest in an Urban Barrio: A Study of the Chicano Movement, 1966–1974* (Lanham, Md.: University Press of America, 1991), 41.

18. For a major work that incorporates the politics of the civil rights, New Left, Vietnam antiwar, and Black Power movements and indigenous struggles see Anderson, *The Movement and the Sixties.*

19. For an examination specifically of the Black Power Movement see Malcolm X, *The Autobiography of Malcolm X* (New York: Grove Press, Inc., 1964); Stokely Carmichael and Charles V. Hamilton, *Black Power: The Politics of Liberation in America* (New York: Random House, 1967); and Floyd B. Barbour, *The Black Power Revolt* (Boston: Porter Sergeant, Inc., 1968).

20. Juan Gómez-Quiñones, *Mexican Students Por La Raza: The Chicano Student Movement in Southern California, 1967–1977* (Santa Barbara, Calif.: Editorial La Causa, 1978), 12.

21. In its most basic definition, relative deprivation denotes the gap between what people get and what they think they should get. More elaborately, it is "a perceived discrepancy between men's value expectations and their value capabilities. Value expectations are the goods and conditions of life to which people believe they are rightfully entitled. Value capabilities are the goods and conditions they think they are capable of attaining and maintaining" (see Gurr, *Why Men Rebel*, 13).

22. See Julian Samora, ed., *La Raza: Forgotten Americans* (Notre Dame, Ind.: University of Notre Dame Press, 1966).

23. Joan Moore and Alfredo Cuellar, *Mexican Americans* (Englewood Cliffs, N.J.: Prentice Hall, 1970), 61.

24. For an excellent socioeconomic profile of Mexicanos in the Southwest see Leo Grebler, Joan W. Moore, and Ralph Guzman, *The Mexican American People: The Nation's Second Largest Minority* (New York: Free Press, 1970), 13–23.

25. Moore and Cuellar, *Mexican Americans*, 1st ed., 61.

26. Moore and Cuellar, *Mexican Americans*, 1st ed., 65.

27. Moore and Cuellar, *Mexican Americans*, 1st ed., 66–72.

28. Moore and Cuellar, *Mexican Americans*, 1st ed., 66–72. For a thorough examination of the Mexicano demographic profile for 1960 refer to pages 14–18.

29. Cited Gonzales, *Mexicanos*, 192.

30. See table of immigration into the United States from México from 1910 to 1973 in Leo Grebler, *Mexican Immigration to the United States: The Record and Its Implications*, Advance Report 2 (University of California, Los Angeles: Mexican American Study Project, 1966), 106. Years from 1965 to 1973 as supplements are based upon annual reports of the U.S. Immigration and Naturalization Service and its predecessor agencies. Cited in Joan Moore and Harry Pachon, *Hispanics in the United States* (Englewood Cliffs, N.J.: Prentice Hall, 1985), 41.

31. Rodolfo Acuña, *Occupied America: A History of Chicanos*, 4th ed. (New York: Addison Wesley, 2000), 348–49.

32. David E. Lorey, *The U.S.-Mexican Border in the Twentieth Century* (Wilmington, Del.: Scholarly Resources, Inc., 1999), 163.

33. Julian Samora, *Los Mojados: The Wetback Story* (Notre Dame, Ind.: University of Notre Dame Press, 1971), 46.

34. Benjamin S. Bradshaw and Frank D. Dean, "Trends in the Fertility of Mexican Americans: 1950–1970," *Social Science Quarterly* 53 (March 1973): 688–96.

35. Joan W. Moore and Harry Pachon, *Mexican Americans*, 2nd ed. (Englewood Cliffs, N.J.: Prentice Hall, 1976), 60.

36. U.S. Department of Commerce, Bureau of the Census, "Persons of Spanish Origin in the United States: March 1973," *Current Population Reports*, Series P-20, no. 259, January 1974.

37. U.S. Department of Commerce, Bureau of the Census, "Persons of Spanish Origin in the United States: March 1973," *Current Population Reports*, Series P-20, no. 259, January 1974, 54–58.

38. For a historical overview of the significance of these three leaders and their organizations see my book *Mexican American Youth Organization*, 23–44.

39. Mario Garcia, *Mexican Americans: Leadership, Ideology, & Identity* (New Haven, Conn.: Yale University Press, 1989), 299.

40. For an extensive examination of the Chicano Generation, see Ignacio Garcia, *Chicanismo: The Forging of a Militant Ethos among Mexican Americans* (Tucson: University of Arizona Press, 1997); and Muñoz, *Youth, Identity, and Power*.

41. Matt S. Meier and Feliciano Rivera, *Mexican Americans, Mexican Americans: From Conquistadors to Chicanos* (New York: Hill & Wang, 1993), 215.

42. David G. Gutiérrez, *Walls and Mirrors: Mexican Americans, Mexican Immigrants, and the Politics of Ethnicity* (Berkeley: University of California Press, 1995), 185.

43. For years the word *Chicano* has been a subject of controversy and debate as to its origin, meaning, and contribution. Briefly, as explained in the introduction, from my perspective it is synonymous with *Mexicano*; the cardinal difference is that *Chicano* denotes a Mexicano born in the United States. *Chicano* is the masculine form and *Chicana* is the feminine. There are, however, several theories as to its origin, but none are conclusive. One theory gives *Chicano* an indigenous base, allegedly derived from Nahuatl origin suggesting *Mexicas* who pronounced the *x* as "shi," so they were called *Meshicas*. The result was that with time, the word *Mexicano* became *Meshicano*. Eventually, the first syllable was dropped and the "shi" was replaced by the hard "ch." A second theory was that the word came from the Mexican city of Chihuahua, and that the *chi* from the name was added to the *cano* of *Mexicano*, and this gave birth to *Chicano*. A third theory is based on the notion that as whites migrated into the Southwest they called Mexicanos *chico*, equivalent to the designation of "boy," as blacks were called in the South, and that with time "ano" was added to *chico*. A fourth theory asserts that it was conventionally formed by suffixing "ano" to *chico* (a young boy) as one would form, for example, *Mexicano* from *México*. Some also speculate that *Chicano* is related to the Spanish word *chicazo*, meaning a poorly educated young man who aimlessly, as a vagabond, roams the streets. The fact is that no one really knows it true genesis. However, the usage of *Chicano* has been commonplace in many of Aztlán's barrios and *colonias* since the early 1900s. Also, it is important to note that historically as a term it has a pejorative connotation to some because it was used to describe and often adhered to by lower-class rambunctious barrio youth. See Edward Simmen, "Chicano: Origin and Meaning," in *Pain & Promise: The Chicano Today: Vivid Accounts of the Reawakening of a Proud and Oppressed People* (New York: New American Library, 1972), 53–56; and Rafaela G. Castro, *Chicano Folklore: A Guide to the Folktales, Traditions, Rituals, and Religious Practices of Mexican Americans* (New York: Oxford University Press, 2001), 46–47.

44. Simmen, "Chicano: Origin and Meaning," 53–56.

45. Simmen, "Chicano: Origin and Meaning," 53–56.

46. Gómez-Quiñones, *Chicano Politics*, 104.

47. Cited in Muñoz, *Youth, Identity, Power*, 61.

48. Meier and Rivera, *Mexican Americans, American Mexicans*, 218–19.

49. Muñoz, *Youth, Identity, Power*, 61.

50. Rafaela G. Castro, *Chicano Folklore* (New York: Oxford University Press, 2001), 46.

51. Gómez-Quiñones, *Chicano Politics*, 189.

52. John A. Garcia, "The Chicano Movement: Its Legacy for Politics and Policy," in *Chicanas/Chicanos at the Crossroads*, ed. David R. Maceio and Isidro D. Ortiz (Tucson: University of Arizona Press, 1996), 85.

53. For an extensive examination of Chicanismo, see Garcia, *Chicanismo*, 8.

54. F. Arturo Rosales, *Chicano! The History of the Mexican American Civil Rights Movement* (Houston, Tex.: Arte Público Press, 1997), 174–75.

55. Garcia, *Mexican Americans*, 300.

56. Gutiérrez, *Walls and Mirrors*, 184.

57. The origin of *Aztlán* like *Chicano* is problematic. However, it is important to note that according to Aztec legend Aztlán is the place from which the Mexica or Aztecs originated geographically. The exact location of their origin is open to speculation, but some allege it was somewhere within Arizona or Utah. Legend has it that Mexica migrated south around the eleventh century guided by the vision given to them by their god Huitzilopochtli, who advised them to migrate south until they came to an eagle perched on a cactus, devouring a snake. This occurred around 1325, and as a result they found a new home and built the great city of Tenochtitlan. See Castro, *Chicano Folklore*, 13–14. More specifically, *Aztlán*, in the ancient Nahuatl language meant "the lands of the north." In the contemporary context, it means all the lands lost by México to the United States in 1848 as a result of U.S. imperialism, which today is considered the Southwest.

58. For general works on nationalism see Ronald Beiner, *Theorizing Nationalism* (New York: State University of New York Press, 1999); and John Hutchinson and Anthony D. Smith, *Nationalism* (New York: Oxford University Press, 1994).

59. For an extensive overview on the concept of nationalism and nation building see Reo Christenson et al., *Ideologies and Modern Politics*, 2nd ed. (New York: Dodd, Mead & Co., 1975), 23–45.

60. Moore and Pachon, *Hispanics in the United States*, 182.

61. Castro, *Chicano Folklore*, 46.

62. Armando B. Rendon, *Chicano Manifesto: The History and Aspirations of the Second Largest Minority in the United States* (New York: Collier Books, 1971), 178–79.

63. Garcia, "The Chicano Movement," 84.

64. Gutiérrez, *Walls and Mirrors*, 185.

65. Meier and Rivera, *Mexican Americans, American Mexicans*, 219.

66. Rosales, *Chicano!*, 175.

67. Gutiérrez, *Walls and Mirrors*, 185.

68. Gómez-Quiñones, *Chicano Politics*, 104.

69. For excellent compendiums of the literary explosion that permeated the Chicano Generation during the epoch of protest (1966–1974) see Garcia, *Chicanismo*, chapter 2; Meier and Rivera, *Mexican Americans, American Mexicans*, 235–41; and Richard Griswold Del Castillo and Arnold De León, *North to Aztlán: A History of Mexican Americans in the United States* (New York: Twayne Publishers, 1996), 144–46.

70. For an excellent overview of the significance of the contributions to the Chicano intellectual renaissance made by literary and scholarly figures of the Chicano Movement see Del Castillo and De Leon, *North to Aztlán*, 144–46.

71. Based on their order of listing, some of their major works written within the period of the Chicano movement include José Antonio Villareal, *Pocho* (New York: Anchor Books, 1989); Rudolfo Anaya, *Bless Me, Ultima* (Albuquerque: University of New México Press, 1972); Oscar Zeta Acosta, *The Autobiography of a Brown Buffalo* (1972) and *Revolt of a Cockroach People* (San Francisco: Straight Arrow Books, 1973); and Tomás Rivera, *And the Earth Did Not Part (Y No Se Lo Trajó la Tierra)* (Berkeley, Calif.: Editorial Justa Publications, 1976).

72. For a complete version of this epic poem and other writings see Rodolfo "Corky" Gonzales, "Yo Soy Joaquin," in *Message to Aztlán: Selected Writings [of] Rodolfo "Corky" Gonzales*, ed. Antonio Esquibel (Houston, Tex.: Arte Público Press, 2001), 16–29.

73. *Message to Aztlán*, 16–29.

74. I was a recipient of a Ford Fellowship, which allowed me to obtain a PhD in political science at the University of California, Riverside. It is important to note that in 1974, four other Chicanos obtained their PhDs in political science, a record no other university in the country has been able to replicate. Beside myself, the four included Ada Sosa-Riddel, Gilbert Gutierrez, Arturo Martinez, and Cesar Sereseres.

75. Two of his most important writings that impacted the rise of the Chicano Generation were "The Anthropology and Sociology of the Mexican American: The Distortion of Mexican American History, *El Grito* Vol. 2 (1968): 13–14; and "The Historical and Intellectual Presence of Mexican Americans," *El Grito* Vol. I, No. I (Fall 1967): 32–46.

76. Some of these pacesetter scholars included Ralph Guzman, Ernesto Galarza, Julian Samora, Juan Gómez-Quiñones, Matt S. Meier, Feliciano Rivera, Manuel Rameriz, Manuel Servín, Julian Nava, Carlos Cortéz, Renato Rosado, Wayne Moaquin, Rudolfo Anaya, Gilberto Lopéz y Rivas, Carlos Muñoz, Mario Barrera, Carlos Ornelas, José Angel Gutiérrez, and Richard Santillan. The writings of journalist scholars such as Enriqueta Longeaux y Vásquez and Elizabeth "Betita" Martinez, Armando Rendon, and Tony Castro also contributed significantly to the Chicano Generation's intellectual renaissance. A number of non-Chicano scholars, such as Carey McWilliams, Stan Steiner, Joan Moore, Leo Grebler, Leonard Pitt, Joan London, Henry Anderson, Patricia Bell Blawis, Richard Gardner, Peter Nabokov, Edward Simmen, David J. Weber, and John Staples Shockley were also major contributors.

77. Matt S. Meier and Feliciano Rivera, *The Chicanos: A History of Mexican Americans* (New York, Hill & Wang, 1972), 253–54.

78. Navarro, *Mexican American Youth Organization*, 112–15.

79. *La Raza* as a concept literally means "the people or race." It was very much used by cultural nationalists as a way to denote *el meztizage* as accentuated by Jose Vasconcelos's work, *La Raza Cosmica*.

80. Acuña, *Occupied México*, 228.

81. Acuña, *Occupied México*, 228. For an examination on the crucial role *La Raza* played in the documentation of Ruben Salazar's death at the National Chicano Moratorium and particularly its subsequent role at his inquest, see pp. 261–63.

82. Cited in Garcia, *Chicanismo*, 58.

83. Enriqueta Longeaux y Vásquez, "Nuestros lectores," *El Grito del Norte*, September 15, 1968, 2.

84. Navarro, *Mexican American Youth Organization*, 113.

85. Navarro, *Mexican American Youth Organization*, 72–73.

86. For more information on the Teatro Compesino see Roy Eric Xavier, "Luis Valdez and El Teatro Compesino," in *Chicano Politics and Society in the Twentieth Century*, ed. David Montejano (Austin: University of Texas Press, 1999), 175–200.

87. The names of other important *teatros* included El Teatro de la Esperanza (Theater of Hope), El Teatro de la Gente (Theater of the People), Teatro de la Causa de los Pobres (Theater of the Poor People's Cause), El Teatro Mestizo (Mestizo Theater), and Teatro Alma Latina (The Latin Soul Theater). These *teatros* in 1971 came together and formed an association called Teatro Nacional Aztlán (TENAZ). Subsequently, TENAZ sponsored an international *teatro* festival (see Del Castillo and De León, *North to Aztlán*, 141.)

88. Del Castillo and De León, *North to Aztlán*, 141.

89. Garcia, *Chicanismo*, 55.

90. For an informative account of the history to the filming of these two films see his book *Eyewitness: A Filmmaker's Memoir of the Chicano Movement* (Houston, Tex.: Arte Público Press, 2001), 225–58.

91. Del Castillo and De León, *North to Aztlán*, 142–43.

92. Meier and Rivera, *Mexican Americans, American Mexicans*, 242–43.

93. Kaye Briegel, "The Development of Chicano Organizations," in *The Mexican Americans: An Awakening Minority*, ed. Manuel Servín (Beverly Hills, Calif.: Glencoe Press, 1970), 176–77.

94. Gómez-Quiñones, *Chicano Politics*, 108.

95. Rosales, *Chicano!*, 166.

96. Rosales, *Chicano!*, 166.

97. Mario T. Garcia, *Memories of Chicano History: The Life and Narrative of Bert Corona* (Berkeley: University of California Press, 1994), 225.

98. Jan Young, *The Migrant Workers and Cesar Chavez* (New York: Julian Messner, 1974), 120.

99. Joan London and Henry Anderson, *So Shall Ye Reap* (New York: Thomas Y. Crowell Co., 1970), 154.

100. Tony Castro, *Chicano Power: The Emergence of Mexican America* (New York: Saturday Review Press, 1974), 87.

101. Richard Del Castillo and Richard A. Garcia, *Cesar Chavez: A Triumph of Spirit* (Norman: University of Oklahoma Press, 1995), 53.

102. Arnoldo De León, *Mexican Americans in Texas: A Brief History* (Arlington Heights, Ill.: Harlan Davidson, Inc., 1993), 134.

103. David Montejano, *Anglos and Mexicans in the Making of Texas, 1936–1986* (Austin: University of Texas Press, 1987), 284.

104. Robert A. Calvert and Arnoldo De León, *The History of Texas* (Arlington Heights Ill.: Harlan Davidson, Inc., 1990), 392.

105. Del Castillo and De León, *North to Aztlán*, 128.

106. For an excellent autobiographical historical examination of Tijerina and the Alianza see Reies López Tijerina, *They Called Me "King Tiger": My Struggle for Land and Our Rights*, translated and edited by José Angel Gutiérrez (Houston, Tex.: Arte Público Press, 2000).

107. Rosales, *Chicano!*, 159.

108. Tijerina, *They Called Me "King Tiger,"* 63.

109. Cited in Rosales, *Chicano!*

110. Frances L. Swadesh, "The Alianza Movement: Catalyst for Social Change in New México," in *Chicano! The Beginnings of Bronze Power*, ed. Renato Rosaldo, Gustav L. Seligmann, and Robert A Calvert (New York: Morrow, 1974), 27–37.

111. Tijerina, *They Called Me "King Tiger,"* 67.

112. Tijerina, *They Called Me "King Tiger,"* 67.

113. David Maciel and Juan José Peña, "La Reconquista: The Chicano Movement in New México," in *The Contested Homeland: A Chicano History of New México*, ed. Erlinda Gonzales-Berry and David Maciel (Albuquerque: University of New México Press, 2000), 275.

114. Tijerina, *They Called Me "King Tiger,"* 68.

115. Acuña, *Occupied America*, 1st ed., 238.

116. Navarro, *Mexican American Youth Organization*, 25.

117. Rosales, *Chicano!*, 162.

118. Rosales, *Chicano!*, 162–63.

119. Castro, *Chicano Power*, 122.

120. Maciel and Peña, "La Reconquista," 276.

121. Rosales, *Chicano!*, 165.

122. Rosales, *Chicano!*, 276–77.

123. Henry A. J. Ramos, *The American G.I. Forum: In Pursuit of the Dream, 1948–1983* (Houston, Tex.: Arte Público Press, 1998), 100.

124. Garcia, *Memories of Chicano History*, 220.

125. For a more detailed examination of MAYO's role at La Raza Unida Conference see my book *Mexican American Youth Organization*, 151–52.

126. Navarro, *Mexican American Youth Organization*, 235.

127. Rosales, *Chicano!*, 167.

128. Rosales, *Chicano!*, 178.

129. Rendon, *Chicano Manifesto*, 134.

130. Ernesto B. Vigil, *The Crusade for Justice: Chicano Militancy and the Government's War on Dissent* (Madison: University of Wisconsin Press, 1999), 55.

131. For an account by Tijerina of his participation in the Poor People's Campaign see: Tijerina, *They Call Me "King Tiger,"* 103–16.

132. Gómez-Quiñones, *Chicano Politics*, 114.

133. Garcia, *Chicanismo*, 93.

134. Garcia, *Chicanismo*, 93.

135. For a much more comprehensive examination as to the various historical aspects of E.L.A. Blowouts see Muñoz, *Youth, Identity, Power*, 64–72.

136. Acuña, *Occupied America*, 4th ed., 362–63.

137. Rosales, *Chicano!*, 185.

138. Gómez-Quiñones, *Mexican Students Por La Raza*, 31.

139. David Sanchez, *Expedition through Aztlán* (La Puente, Calif.: Perspectiva Publications, 1978), 2.

140. Acuña, *Occupied America*, 4th ed., 163.

141. Sanchez, *Expedition through Aztlán*, 3.

142. For a comprehensive analysis on the youth student movement see my book *Mexican American Youth Organization*.

143. For a historical overview of the conference and its impact on the Chicano movement see Garcia, *Chicanismo: The Forging of a Militant Ethos among Mexican Americans*, 93–95; Vigil, *The Crusade for Justice*, 97–100; and Navarro, *Mexican American Youth Organization*, 40–41.

144. Cited in Luis Valdez and Stan Steiner, ed., *Aztlán: An Anthology of Mexican American Literature* (New York: Vintage, 1972), 402–3.

145. Vigil, *Crusade for Justice*, 98.

146. For a more comprehensive examination of the Santa Barbara conference see Navarro, *Mexican American Youth Organization*, 68–70; and Muñoz, *Youth, Identity, Power*, 89–90.

147. Barrera, *Beyond Aztlán*, 41–44.

148. Meier and Rivera, *Mexican Americans, Americans Mexicans*, 222.

149. Meier and Rivera, *Mexican Americans, Americans Mexicans*, 222; and Gomez-Quiñonez, *Chicano Politics*, 73.

150. For a complete examination of the text of the El Plan de Santa Barbara, see Muñoz, *Youth, Identity, Power*, 191–202.

151. For a complete examination of the text of the El Plan de Santa Barbara, see Muñoz, *Youth, Identity, Power*, 191–202.

152. For a more thorough examination of MAYO's organized Del Rio March see my works *Mexican American Youth Organization*, 99–101, 160–68, 253–56; and *La Raza Unida Party*, 26–27.

153. For an examination of these and other events that occurred throughout 1969 see my book *Mexican American Youth Organization*.

154. Acuña, *Occupied America*, 1st ed., 267. According to Acuña, after two years of appeals, the seven were finally tried. The defense argued that the fire had been provoked by an undercover agent, Fernando Samaya. The jury evidently agreed with the defense, since all but two of the defendants was acquitted; they were unable to reach a verdict on the remaining two.

155. For a thorough analysis and examination on this unprecedented takeover and what became known as the "Cucamonga Experiment" see my book *La Raza Unida Party*, chapter 5.

156. Meier and Rivera, *Mexican Americans, Mexican Americans*, 227.

157. Acuña, *Occupied America*, 4th ed., 377.

158. Acuña, *Occupied America*, 4th ed., 377.

159. Sanchez, *Expedition through Aztlán*, 3–4.

160. I was there as one of the organizers of a large contingent of 250 from Riverside/San Bernardino counties and participated along with numerous others from our contingent with efforts to assist fleeing people on exiting Laguna Park as the police conducted their military sweep.

161. Gómez-Quiñones, *Chicano Politics*, 127.

162. Del Castillo and De León, *Cesar Chavez*, 94.

163. For a much more comprehensive examination of the events related to La March de la Reconquista see Sanchez, *Expedition through Aztlán*, 15–54. For an abbreviated account see Navarro, *Mexican American Youth Organization*, 65.

164. For a further examination of the particulars of the Farah Strike see Acuña, *Occupied America*, 4th ed., 401.

165. For an examination of the "Ontario School Walkouts" see my book *La Raza Unida Party*, chapter 5.

166. For an extensive examination of the historic El Paso, Tejas, RUP convention, see my book *La Raza Unida Party*, 236–43; José Angel Gutiérrez, *The Making of a Chicano Militant: Lessons from Cristal* (Madison: University of Wisconsin Press, 1998), 224–31; and Rosales, *Chicano!*, 238–42.

167. Rosales, *Chicano!*

168. Gutiérrez, *The Making of a Chicano Militant*, 223–24.

169. Navarro, *La Raza Unida Party*, 236–43.

170. For a further examination of this important conference see my book *La Raza Unida Party*, 243–44; and Maciel and Peña, "La Reconquista," 278–79.

171. Maciel and Peña, "La Reconquista," 278–79.

172. Richard Garcia, "New México Meeting Backs Raza Unida," *The Militant*, November 17, 1972.

173. Del Castillo and De León, *Cesar Chavez*, 121.

174. Navarro, *La Raza Unida Party*, chapter 11.

175. For a comprehensive examination of this issue see Vigil, *The Crusade for Justice*.

176. Vigil, *The Crusade for Justice*, 209–13.

177. For a further examination of the decline of student organizations see Muñoz, *Youth, Identity, Power*, 84–97.

178. Richard Santillan, *The Politics of Cultural Nationalism: El Partido de la Raza Unida in Southern California, 1969–1978*, PhD dissertation, Claremont Graduate School, 1978, 44–45.

179. Kenneth Burt, The History of MAPA and Chicano Politics in California (Sacramento, Calif.: Mexican American Political Association), 15.

180. Mark R. Levy and Michael S. Kramer, *The Ethnic Factor: How America's Minorities Decide Elections* (New York: Simon & Schuster, 1973), 79.

181. Santillan, *The Politics of Cultural Nationalism*, 45.

182. F. Chris Garcia and Rudolph O. de la Garza, *The Chicano Political Experience: Three Perspectives* (North Scituate, Mass.: Duxbury Press, 1977), 102.

183. Santillan, *The Politics of Cultural Nationalism*, 46–47.

184. Santillan, *The Politics of Cultural Nationalism*, 49.

185. Garcia and de La Garza, *The Chicano Political Experience*, 103.

186. Garcia and de La Garza, *The Chicano Political Experience*, 104.

187. Levy and Kramer, *The Ethnic Factor*, 81.

188. Levy and Kramer, *The Ethnic Factor*, 82–83.

189. For a comprehensive examination of the various RUP electoral activities throughout the Southwest and Midwest see my book, *La Raza Unida Party*.

190. Navarro, *La Raza Unida Party*, chapter 4.

191. Navarro, *La Raza Unida Party*, chapters 1, 2, and 3.

192. Navarro, *La Raza Unida Party*, chapters 5, 6, and 7.

193. Navarro, *La Raza Unida Party*, chapter 7, 163–66.

194. Navarro, *La Raza Unida Party*, chapter 9.

195. Navarro, *La Raza Unida Party*, chapter 10.

196. Levy and Kramer, *The Ethnic Factor*, 85.

197. This section is merely an overview of a section on RUP's international politics from my book *La Raza Unida Party*, chapter 11.

198. John A. Garcia, "The Chicano Movement: Its Legacy for Politics and Policy," 83–107.

199. For a comprehensive exposure to the ideas and principles of organizing developed by Alinsky see his works *Revelle for Radicals* (New York: Vintage, 1969) and *Rules for Radicals: A Pragmatic Primer for Realistic Radicals* (New York: Vintage, 1971).

200. Meier and Rivera, *Mexican Americans, American Mexicans*, 199.

201. Benjamin Marquez, *LULAC: The Evolution of a Mexican American Political Organization* (Austin: University of Texas Press, 1993), 66.

202. Marquez, *LULAC*, 67.

203. Marquez, *LULAC*, 73.

204. Meier and Rivera, *Mexican Americans, American Mexicans*, 206.

205. Gómez-Quiñones, *Chicano Politics*, 61.

206. For an extensive examination of the AGIF's social service activities during the epoch of protest see Ramos, *The American G.I. Forum*, 109–21.

207. Gómez-Quiñones, *Chicano Politics*, 61.

208. Ramos, *The American G.I. Forum*, 11–116.

209. David F. Gomez, *Somos Chicanos: Strangers in Our Own Land* (Boston: Beacon, 1973), 96.

210. Garcia, *Memories of Chicano History*, 245–85.

211. For an extensive examination on what became known as the "Cucamonga Experiment" see my book *La Raza Unida Party*, 108–33.

212. Kenneth Burt, *The History of MAPA and Chicano Politics in California* (Sacramento, Calif.: MAPA, 1982), 17.

213. For further information on the politics of this important event see my book *La Raza Unida Party*, 232–33.

214. Burt, *The History of MAPA and Chicano Politics in California*, 19.

215. Navarro, *La Raza Unida Party*, 204.

216. Cited in De León, *Mexican Americans in Texas*, 126.

217. Roberto A. Calvert and Arnold De León, *The History of Texas*, 391–92.

218. For an excellent analysis on the use of protest as a resource for change see Michael Lipsky, "Protest as a Resource," *American Political Science Review* Vol. 62 (December 1968): 1144–58.

219. For an examination of the development of the Tijerina's Alianza see Patricia Blawis Bell, *Tijerina and the Land Grants: Mexican American in Struggle for Their Heritage* (New York: International Publishers, 1971); Michael Jenkinson, *Tijerina* (Albuquerque: Paisano Press, 1968); Rosales, *Chicano!*, chapter 9; Navarro, *Mexican American Youth Organization*, 23–28; Gómez-Quiñones, *Chicano Politics*, 115–18 and 142–44.

220. *Constitucion Nacional de La Alianza Federal de Mercedes* (National Constitution of the Federal alliance of Land Grants). Approved September 21, 1963, Albuquerque, Nuevo México.

221. Gómez-Quiñones, *Chicano Politics*, 115.

222. Del Castillo and De León, *North to Aztlán*, 129–30.

223. Maciel and Peña, "La Reconquista," 274.

224. Maciel and Peña, "La Reconquista," 274.

225. Gonzales, *Mexicanos*, 203.

226. Maciel and Peña, "La Reconquista," 273.

227. For a historical overview of the Alianza's various events of the late 1960s see my book *Mexican American Youth Organization*, 23–28.

228. Navarro, *Mexican American Youth Organization*, 27–28.

229. For a further and more extensive examination of the Crusade for Justice see Vigil, *The Crusade for Justice*; Castro, *Chicano Power*, 129–47; Elizabeth Sutherland Martínez and Enriqueta Longeaux y Vásquez, *Viva la Raza! The Struggle of the Mexican-American People* (Garden City, N.Y.: Doubleday, 1974), 229–63; Navarro, *Mexican American Youth Organization*, 36–44; Navarro, *La Raza Unida Party*, 80–107.

230. For a major historical account of the history, politics, and particularly of the infiltration of law enforcement agencies into the Crusade see Vigil, *Crusade for Justice*.

231. Gómez-Quiñones, *Chicano Politics*, 113.

232. Garcia, *Chicanismo*, 34.

233. Excerpt is taken from my book *Mexican American Youth Organization*, 37.

234. Navarro, *La Raza Unida Party*, 87.

235. Navarro, *La Raza Unida Party*, 80–133.

236. Navarro, *La Raza Unida Party*, 99.

237. For an extensive and very comprehensive examination of MAYO's history and development see my books *Mexican American Youth Organization*; *La Raza Unida Party*, chapter 1; and *The Cristal Experiment*, 55–72. This abbreviated section on MAYO is taken from the preceding three works. However, there are two other excellent books that examine MAYO's development: Ignacio M. Garcia, *United We Win: The Rise and Fall of La Raza Unida Party* (Tucson, Ariz.: Mexican American Studies & Research Center, 1989), 15–36; and José Angel Gutiérrez, *The Making of Chicano Militant: Lessons from Cristal* (Madison: University of Wisconsin Press, 1998), chapter 6.

238. Navarro, *Mexican American Youth Organization*, chapter 3.

239. Cited in Navarro, *Mexican American Youth Organization*, 113.

240. Meier and Rivera, *Chicanos*, chapter 15.

241. For a comprehensive examination of MAYO's development, particularly its rise

and demise see my book *Mexican American Youth Organization*. In addition, however, the following works also present an excellent analysis on MAYO's history: Garcia, *United We Win*, 15–36; and Gutiérrez, *The Making of Chicano Militant*, chapter 6.

242. Navarro, *Mexican American Youth Organization*, chapter 4.

243. Navarro, *Mexican American Youth Organization*, chapter 5.

244. Navarro, *Mexican American Youth Organization*, chapter 6.

245. For an excellent examination of the emergence of the student movement and its myriad of organizations, see Juan Gómez-Quiñones, *Mexican Students Por La Raza*.

246. For a brief case study on the development of UMAS see also Navarro, *Mexican American Youth Organization*, 56–60.

247. Muñoz, *Youth, Identity, Power*, 59.

248. Navarro, *Mexican American Youth Organization*, 57.

249. For a comprehensive examination on the history of El Plan de Santa Barbara and on MEChA's development as a student organization see: Muñoz, *Youth, Identity, Power*, 75–98.

250. Gómez-Quiñones, *Chicano Politics*, 119.

251. Muñoz, *Youth, Identity, Power*, 81.

252. Albert Carrillo, *Chicanos in California: A History of Mexican Americans in California* (San Francisco: Boyd & Fraser Publishing Co., 1984), 100.

253. For a more comprehensive analysis see my book *Mexican American Youth Organization*, 60–61.

254. Ellwyn R. Stoddard, *Mexican Americans* (New York: Random House, 1973), 215.

255. Castro, *Chicano Power*, 315.

256. For an examination of the Black Berets in more detail see "Black Beret Organization," in *La Causa Politica: A Chicano Politics Reader*, ed. Chris Garcia (Notre Dame, Ind.: University of Notre Dame Press, 1974), 405–8.

257. For a comprehensive study of the rise and decline of the Brown Berets see Sanchez, *Expedition through Aztlán*.

258. Acuña, *Occupied America*, 2nd ed., 359.

259. Julian Samora and Patricia Vandel Simon, *A History of the Mexican American People* (Notre Dame, Ind.: University of Notre Dame Press, 1977), 197.

260. For a detailed autobiographical account by David Sanchez of the Brown Berets' rise and decline see his book *Expedition through Aztlán*.

261. Maurilio Vigil, *Chicano Politics* (Washington, D.C.: University Press of America, 1977), 175.

262. Sanchez, *Expedition through Aztlán*, 206.

263. Vigil, *Chicano Politics*, 175.

264. For an analysis on the development of NACSS, which by 1976 became NACS (National Association of Chicano Studies) see Muñoz, *Youth, Identity, Power*, 149–56.

265. For an excellent historical overview of the development of the UFW see Rosales, *Chicano!*, 130–51.

266. Jacques Levy, *Cesar Chavez: Autobiography of La Causa* (New York: Norton, 1975), 175.

267. Gonzales, *Mexicanos*, 198.

268. Camarillo, *Chicanos in California*, 91.

269. Del Castillo and Garcia, *Cesar Chavez*, 184.

270. Rosales, *Chicano!*, 148.

271. Rosales, *Chicano!*, 149.

272. Del Castillo and Garcia, *Cesar Chavez*, 126.

273. Acuña, *Occupied America*, 3rd ed., 326.

274. Acuña, *Occupied America*, 4th ed., 401.

275. For a major examination on the political history of RUP's rise and fall as a third party see my book *La Raza Unida Party*. In addition, also see Garcia, *United We Win*; Rosales, *Chicano!*; and Richard Santillan, *La Raza Unida Party* (Los Angeles: Tlaquila Publications, 1973).

276. Anthony Downs, *An Economic Theory of Democracy* (New York: Oxford University Press, 1957), 25.

277. Dan Nimo and Thomas D. Ungs, *American Political Patterns*, 3rd ed. (Boston: Little, Brown, 1973), 275.

278. For a further examination of these two political parties see my book *La Raza Unida Party*, chapter 8.

279. For a comprehensive case study on the various aspects of RUP's "Peaceful Revolution in Cristal," see Navarro, *The Cristal Experiment*.

280. Oscar Martinez, *Mexican-Origin People in the United States* (Tucson: University of Arizona Press, 2001), 178.

281. Del Castillo and De Léon, *North to Aztlán*, 135.

282. Navarro, *La Raza Unida Party*, 207.

283. Navarro, *La Raza Unida Party*, 207.

284. Cited in Gómez-Quiñones, *Chicano Politics*, 176.

285. Meier and Rivera, *Mexican Americans, American Mexicans*, 226–27.

286. Meier and Rivera, *Mexican Americans, American Mexicans*, 330.

287. For an excellent work on the numerous contributions and important roles women have played in politics and organizations in Chicana history see Vickie Ruiz, *From Out of the Shadows: Mexican American Women in the Twentieth Century* (Oxford: Oxford University Press, 1998); Cynthia E. Orozco, "Beyond Machismo—La Familia, and Ladies Auxiliaries: A Historiography of Mexican Origin Women's Participation in Voluntary Associations and Politics in the United States, 1870–1990," *Perspectives* Vol. 5 (1995); and Antonia Castañeda, "Women of Color and the Rewriting of Western History: The Discourse, Politics, and Decolonization of History," *Pacific Historical Review* Vol. 61, No. 4 (1992).

288. Gonzales, *Mexicanos*, 217.

289. Martínez and Longeaux y Vásquez, *Viva la Raza!*, 332.

290. Anna Nieta Gomez, "La Femenista," *Encuentro Femenil* Vol. 1 (1974): 34–47.

291. Gonzales, *Mexicanos*, 218.

292. Barrera, *Beyond Aztlán*, 47.

293. Cited in Santillan, *The Politics of Cultural Nationalism*, 95.

294. Santillan, *The Politics of Cultural Nationalism*, 95.

295. Garcia, *Memories of Chicano History*, 291.

296. Acuña, *Occupied America*, 4th ed., 349–50, 403–5.

297. Gómez-Quiñones, *Chicano Politics*, 151.

298. Gómez-Quiñones, *Chicano Politics*, 349–50.

299. Jesús Salvador Treviño, *Eyewitness: A Filmmaker's Memoir of the Chicano Movement* (Houston, Tex.: Arte Público Press, 2001), 341.

300. Garcia, *Memories of Chicano History*, 297.

301. CASA as an organization will be dealt with more extensively in the next chapter. For a brief overview of CASA see Acuña, *Occupied America*, 403–4; Camarillo, *Chicanos in California*, 97–98; Barrera, *Beyond Aztlán*, 46–52.

302. Barrera, *Beyond Aztlán*, 46–52.

303. For more information on RUP's Labor Committee see my book *La Raza Unida Party*, 150–53.

304. Ernesto Chavez, *Mi Raza Primero: Nationalism, Identity, and Insurgency in the Chicano Movement in Los Angeles, 1966–1978* (Los Angeles: University of California Press, 2002), 109.

Epoch of the Viva Yo Hispanic Generation (1975–1999)   6

A DIALECTICAL CHANGE occurred in 1975 within the politics of the Mexicano experience in occupied Aztlán. The turbulent epoch of militant protest was replaced with the neoconservative epoch of the Viva Yo Hispanic Generation. Throughout the next twenty-four years, the winds of militant protest and mass mobilization became increasingly quiescent. The various social movements that gave rise to the epoch of militant protest had declined. As noted in the previous chapter, the Chicano Movement declined by 1974. Mexicanos as a whole were not exempt from the ubiquitous trend toward neoconservatism. The epoch produced major changes that impacted the Mexicano's political experience. Unfortunately, however, these changes exacerbated the socioeconomic problems in the barrios and *colonias* of occupied Aztlán.

The Etiology of the Decline of the *Movimiento*

Exogenous Antagonisms

After nine years of dynamic militant protest, the Movimiento became moribund.[1] The myriad of endogenous and exogenous antagonisms, that is, changes, that gave it political life also became the antagonisms that created its decline. On the exogenous side of the political equation, all of the social movements that had an impact on the Movimiento became defunct by 1974.[2] This was true of the Civil Rights Movement, which reached its apogee in 1965 with the passage of the Voting Rights Act. Although Reverend Jesse Jackson and others continued to be active, after the assassination of Reverend Martin Luther King, Jr., in 1968, the movement had all but disappeared by 1975.[3] Black politics concomitantly took on a more moderate to liberal political accommodation posture. Blacks likewise were not immune to the political impact of the country's political turn to the right. As the "mother" of the diverse social movements that rose during the epoch, its ostensible absence created a change vacuum in the country's politics.

The New Left as a social movement had been impacted first by the Civil Rights Movement and second became absorbed by the militant protest politics of the Vietnam Antiwar Movement. With U.S. direct military involvement in the Vietnam War ending in 1973 coupled with the victory of communist North Vietnam over the U.S.-backed South Vietnamese government by 1974, both the New Left and the powerful Vietnam Antiwar Movement came to an end. The numerous antiwar coalitions that had mobilized hundreds of thousands of protestors all but disappeared and Students for a Democratic Society with its progressive participatory agenda was absent from the country's university and college campuses. The Black Power Movement also became extinct by the early 1970s due to internecine power struggles, ideological cleavages, subversion, infiltration, incarceration, and murder of its leadership by law enforcement agencies. With the demise of the Student Nonviolent Coordinating Committee and the Black Panther Party, as well, the calls for black liberation had all but disappeared.

In spite of the continued cold war, by 1974 few foreign movements served to energize the declining activist sectors of the country. The War on Poverty programs had been substantially curtailed by the Republican Nixon and Ford administrations.[4] With the election of Richard Nixon in 1968, the idea that the federal government had the power and economic capacity to eradicate poverty in the United States was replaced by a neoconservatism that was antithetical to welfare capitalism and sought a return to laissez faire capitalism. In short, the exogenous social movements that gave birth to the unprecedented epoch of militant protest became casualties of a growing conservative political climate.

Another exogenous factor that contributed significantly to the demise of the above movements was law enforcement's use of espionage, infiltration, subversion, and judicial litigation against its organizations and leaders. From the police to the FBI's COINTELPRO,[5] law enforcement agencies sought and in most cases succeeded in destabilizing and neutralizing their effectiveness. The Chicano Movement was not exempt from law enforcement and COINTELPRO destabilization efforts. According to Ignacio Garcia, "The onslaught was constant and intense. People lost jobs, were arrested, suffered economic hardships, and became socially marginalized in their community because of their activism. The constant pressure also led to internal conflicts."[6] During the Movimiento's nine-year longevity, organization after organization, leader after leader, activist after activist were subjected to what Ernesto Vigil describes as "the government's Gatekeeper dissent," including Gonzalez's Crusade for Justice, Tijerina's Alianza Federal de Mercedes, Gutiérrez's Raza Unida Party, and Sanchez's Brown Berets.[7] These synergetic protest movements and the War on Poverty programs were the target of law enforcement destabilization efforts, which ultimately contributed to the demise of the Chicano Movement.[8]

Endogenous Antagonisms

Several endogenous antagonisms also contributed to the Movimiento's demise. Although some leaders and protest organizations continued their activism well into the early 1980s, the dynamism that had energized the Movimiento now lacked the intensity and nationalist fervor. In great part, the Chicano leaders and organizations that had been the catalysts in its rise were politically passé. Tijerina was no longer a major force and his Alianza Federal de Mercedes by the mid-1970s had become defunct. While the farmworker struggle continued, Chavez's leadership as well as that of the UFW entered into decline. Rodolfo "Corky" Gonzales's Crusade for Justice was also a victim of a siege by law enforcement agencies. The Brown Berets were officially disbanded in 1972 due to internal power struggles. Likewise, José Angel Gutiérrez's efforts to consolidate the Raza Unida Party by 1974 had failed. The student sector of the Movimiento was fractured by ideological schisms and apathy.

The pervasiveness of the internecine politics of self-destruction that permeated the Movimiento contributed significantly to its decline. By the early 1970s, it was acutely plagued by nefarious power struggles and ideological cleavages that depleted its activist ranks. Power struggles were often fueled by the prevalence of personalism or better yet *caudillismo* and *caciquismo*. Even though the Movimiento never developed a clear ideology of its own, some activists battled each other to give it one—from cultural nationalism to variegated forms of Marxism. Too often activists misdirected their frustration and anger against each other instead of the system. In the end, this gave some credence to the gringo's stereotypical image of the "Mexican Crab Syndrome."[9]

By 1975 the country's barrios and *colonias* were plagued by a growing apathy, complacency, and alienation. The activism that had permeated many of them became increasingly nonexistent. Juan Gómez-Quiñones, explains, "The intensity of the decade had exhausted some activists, and some activism itself had become a consciously delimited activity."[10] This change in the political climate was evident as the mode of Mexicano politics in the United States shifted from one of militant protest to a neo-accommodation and adaptation. This prosystem perspective was part of the rise of the new Hispanic Generation.

Era of Conflicting of Political Generations

The Post-Movimiento Era: The Liberal Capitalist "I" Ethos

For Mexicanos in the United States, a new political era began to take form, significantly reshaping their ethos as a people. The change in the country was toward a more conservative, materialist, and "I"-oriented ethos. It categorically rejected militancy, protest, and nationalist and Marxist ideas or politics. With its emphasis on individualism, preservation of the status quo, and political accommodation, the post-movimiento era adhered to the basic tenets of the liberal capitalist system. Without the energizing presence and direct action politics of the epoch of militant protest, there was little to thwart the ubiquitous socialization forces of liberal capitalism. The fall of the Soviet Union in 1991 marked the end of Marxism as a viable ideological alternative, and liberal capitalism became global in scope. The country's politics without the presence of a significant liberal or progressive wing in either political party, especially the Democrats, moved politically to the right of center.

The resurgence of the Right can be traced to the 1964 Goldwater presidential candidacy and the Nixon and Ford administrations' conservative politics. The Democratic Jimmy Carter, Republican Ronald Reagan and George Bush, and Democratic Bill Clinton administrations all contributed to the country's heightening neoconservative political culture. Mario Garcia further elucidates: "Rigid conservativism and political reaction, as epitomized by the Reagan-Bush administrations and a cautious Democratic Party, have more forcefully opposed the legitimate demands of racial minorities such as Mexican Americans."[11] None of these administrations prioritized the expansion of civil rights, promotion of social justice, and eradication of poverty. Instead, Democrats and Republicans, particularly the Reagan and Bush administrations, sought to unfetter the federal government and economy from what they called the tentacles of Big Government. Their domestic and international policies sought to expand the wealth and power of the country's military-industrial complex. During this epoch liberal capitalism's earlier experiments with Democrat Franklin D. Roosevelt's "New Deal," John Fitzgerald Kennedy's "New Frontier," and Lyndon B. Johnson's "Great Society" were rejected in favor of a return to a more laissez-faire capitalist form.

Big Government with its adherence to Keynesian economics and a liberal agenda were under severe attack by moderate to conservative politicians. The attacks were intensified during the Reagan administration, which ardently followed its own "supply-side economics," also called "voodoo economics," or "trickle down" economics by its detractors. Supply-side economics was predicated on tax cuts for the rich and deregulation, which resulted in a reduction in federal government expenditures to the poor and put an end to the welfare state. Reaganomics took the political creed of life, liberty, and the pursuit of property, and translated it to mean unbridled wealth and greed for the rich. Individualism, relentless competition, and materialism pervaded the county's political climate and culture. The emphasis on the accumulation and concentration of wealth by the few at the expense of the many, especially of the middle class, the poor, and minorities, was a persistent theme in subsequent Republican and Democratic administrations. According to Kevin Phillips, "The top 10 percent of households . . . controlled approximately 68 percent. Accumulation and concentration would be simultaneous hallmarks of the 1980s." In fact, he writes, "the 1980s were the third such capitalist and conservative heyday over the last century or so." For the rich it was the "best of times" and for the poor, the "worst of times."[12]

During the next decade, Democrat Bill Clinton's administration repudiated the old Roosevelt/Kennedy/Johnson liberal agenda, in favor of a much more conservative posture. He steered a "Center Right" course for his administration, which became known as the "New Democrats." While the Clinton administration moved the country's economy to an impression of prosperity, its policies on the domestic scene were at times more Republican than Democratic in substance. One only has to look at the administration's positions on welfare reform, militarization of the U.S./México border, immigration, weakening of affirmative action, and civil rights to see that the liberal agenda was virtually nonexistent. The country's political culture by the late 1990s had become much more conservative. The monopoly of power exercised by the ruling plutocratic two-party dictatorship continued unabated.[13]

In the international arena, with the decline of the Soviet Union and its bloc, the Clinton administration sought to buttress its hegemony over the world with its pursuit of neo-imperialism, the realization of a new "Pax Americana." Without the Soviet threat, the United States became the world's most formidable existent economic and military empire. In the words of Michael Parenti, "under neo-imperialism, the flag stays home, while the dollar goes everywhere—frequently assisted by the sword."[14] The United States assumed the sole superpower status and the sun never set on its imperial empire, built on the globalization of capital. With its omnipresent military might, the United States by the end of the twentieth century was "the" feared and indomitable protector of global capitalism.

As a result, especially during the late 1970s and 1980s, the country's Left became increasingly ineffective and divided. Torn apart by schisms, lacking a common strategy and leadership, it was not able to adjust to the post-antiwar conservative period that ensued. The collapse of the Soviet Union in 1991, in the words of Roger Burbach, "rendered the left and progressives largely progressive."[15] The few that remained sounded more like liberals than progressives. Russell Jacoby in his book *The End of Utopia*, alludes to this detrimental trend:

> Almost everywhere the left contracts, not simply politically but perhaps more decisively, intellectually. To avoid contemplating the defeat and its implications, the left now largely speaks the language of liberalism—the

idiom of pluralism and rights. At the same time, liberals, divested of a left
wing, suffer from waning determination and imagination.[16]

Others became proponents of "postmodernist politics," which were largely anti-
ideological, cultural-oriented, and based on single issues of identity, race, gender,
and religion. By the end of the epoch, however, antiglobalization struggles began
to increase and challenge U.S. world hegemony both domestically and internationally.

The Rise of the Viva Yo Hispanic Generation

The Mexicano in the United States was not exempt from the dramatic changes
that occurred in the country's political climate. In fact, as the country moved
ideologically to the right of the ideological spectrum, so did Mexicanos and Latinos in general. Mario Garcia called this the "post–Chicano Movement" era or
the "Hispanic Generation."[17] Another historian, Ignacio Garcia, called the era
the "Mexican American/Hispanic Generation."[18] And political scientist Carlos
Muñoz also recognized the generational transition from Chicano to Hispanic.
This epoch produced a new political generation, the "Viva Yo Hispanic Generation" (hereafter identified as the Hispanic Generation—HG). Its emergence fostered the existence of conflicting multipolitical generations imbued with divergent
political subcultures. With the decline of the Chicano Movement, the Chicano
Generation (CG) lost its dominant role. However, during the early years of the
epoch, the Mexican American Generation (MAG) experienced a brief resurgence,
while the existent Mexicano Generation (MG) supported by a dramatic increase
in the migrant exodus became the "Neo-Mex Generation (NMG)."

From 1975 to 1999, the Mexicano political experience from a political cultural perspective was driven by the hegemony of the HG over the other political
generations. The pervasiveness of the HG's system maintenance ethos dramatically changed the mode of Mexicano politics in Aztlán. The rise of the politics
of the HG fostered the decline of the militant protest politics of the CG. A
cardinal difference between the HG and CG was that the former repudiated the
latter's cultural nationalist ethos. While vestiges of the CG continued to exist
until the end of this epoch, the ethos of the HG became the most prevalent
among both Mexicanos and Latinos in general. This became evident in the
epoch's lexicon, which among Mexicanos experienced a transition from the usage
of *Chicano* to *Hispanic*. Increasingly, after 1974, the usage of *Chicano* and its quasi-
ideological counterpart *Chicanismo* came under cultural scrutiny. In writing about
where all the nationalists have gone, Martín Sánchez Jankowski explains, "As the

1960s and 70s passed, less and less was heard from those who identified themselves as nationalists, and by the late 1980s, there appeared to be virtually no one who supported nationalist politics."[19]

Yet vestiges of the CG's Chicanismo continued to exist even though its zealous adherents were in the minority. A few activists, academicians, and some students and barrio youth continued to identify with the legacy of the Movimiento. Between 1976 and well into the 1990s, Chicanismo with its nationalist underpinnings became dichotomized into two schools of thought: the ultranationalist, and the cultural pluralist.[20] The former were the few advocate transformers, who adhered to either the politics of self-determination or nation building. The latter were those whose nationalism was lukewarm, largely based on preserving language, customs, music, food, and politically were generally prosystem.

Instead of Chicano, terms such as *Hispanic, Latino, Mexican American,* and *Mexicano,* in that order, were used as identifying terms, particularly by the middle class. Within Aztlán's barrios and *colonias,* while some identified themselves as Hispanic, Latino, or Mexican American, *Mexicano* and *Chicano* were generally the terms of preference. As Peter Skerry explains, twenty years later Mexicanos were still caught up in "the Battle of the Name." He described them quite appropriately as the "Ambivalent Minority," who disagreed about "whether they were an ethnic or a minority group."[21] Throughout the epoch's years no unanimity was reached as to what Mexicanos born in the United States should call themselves. Endless identity debates were commonplace, especially at student youth conferences and meetings. In general, Mexicanos continued to be caught up in an intricate web of cultural confusion, ambivalence, and identity conflict. The words of Rodolfo "Corky" Gonzales's epic poem "Yo Soy Joaquin" applied more than ever. Joaquin, who symbolized the Mexicano was still "lost in a world of confusion, caught up in a whirl of a gringo society," "confused by the rules," and had yet to "choose" what to call himself or herself.

The so-called Mexicano identity crisis became evident in the results of various studies. In a national survey conducted in 1976, 50.7 percent of Mexicanos identified themselves as "Mexican American" and "Mexican" was selected by 20.1 percent. In addition, some variant of "Spanish" was chosen by 20.7 percent; only 4.4 percent chose "Mexicano," and 4.0 percent chose "Chicano."[22] During the summer of 1983 the *Los Angeles Times* published an article on ethnic labeling. It found that "generally, the native born preferred Mexican-American followed by Latino. The term Hispanic was third in preference. Mexican immigrants favored the term Mexicano followed by Latino. While a plurality could agree on Latino, only a small minority (4 percent) acknowledged the term Chicano fit them."[23] As the survey pointed out, *Chicano* had nearly become an anachronism. Still, some young people and a few activists used *Chicano*. *Mexican American* was more popular especially among older and mainstream-oriented Mexicanos.

Yet during the early 1970s the use of *Hispanic* was encouraged by federal governmental agencies. As early as 1973, the Task Force on Racial/Ethnic Categories recommended it to the Department of Health, Education, and Welfare.[24] More so by 1978, in preparation for the 1980 U.S. Census, the Carter administration via the Office of Management and Budget adopted it as a generic term to count those of Latin American/Spanish heritage. They perceived *Hispanic* to be a non-threatening term that avoided negative stereotyping and could be attached to national-origin labels. By the 1980s, the use of *Hispanic* became commonplace in governmental documents and use by the media.[25] Roberto M. De Anda explains, "For Mexican Americans it meant subsuming their Chicano ideology for the label 'Hispanic,' which gained its importance and strength from being a national rather than original descriptive term."[26] Juan Gómez-Quiñones further adds, "It quickly became the preferred term by bureaucrats, academics, businesses, and media."[27] Few cared that *Hispanic* connoted more of a cultural lineage to Spain rather than México. It remained controversial, but in the county's growing conservative climate, some Mexicano and non-Mexicano scholars alike adopted the use of Hispanic.[28] According to José Cuello, "it is used by HUPPIES, Hispanic Upwardly-mobile Professionals, who want to integrate themselves into the mainstream of and corporate cultures."[29] As the epoch progressed, increasingly some Mexicanos, Puerto Ricans, and Cubans, among others, preferred the use of *Hispanic* as a term of self-identity.

This was not the case, however, with every Mexicano. Why? Because *Hispanic* essentially denotes all peoples in the United States whose cultural identity is based in the experiences of both Latin America and Spain. In explaining the opposition to *Hispanic*, Jorge J. E. Garcia writes, "They will have nothing to do with a term which they believe primarily designates a former oppressor and whose cloud still hangs over those whose ancestors it once dominated."[30] Arnoldo Carlos Vento is critical of the term "because it obviates the Native American or indigenous side of the Mestizo culture."[31] Hispanic comes from the Latin term *Hispania*, which was used by the Romans to allude to the Iberian Peninsula.[32] In the true sense of the meaning, *Hispanic* accentuated the direct cultural, heritage, and language linkages to Spain and occasionally Portugal. Historically, *Hispanic* was also associated with the centuries-old use of *Hispano*, which was used particularly by those who assert their Iberian cultural roots and rejected those with México, especially its indigenous experience. To some Mexicanos who identified as Hispanos, namely from Nuevo México, *Mexicano* was a pejorative term that conjured up feelings of inferiority.

In another context, Peter Skerry defines *Hispanic* as "a generic term viewed by many Mexican Americans as an ill-conceived label concocted by federal bureaucrats, but also used freely by barrio political entrepreneurs when it suits their purposes."[33] In particular during the 1980s, Rodolfo Acuña explains, "Chicano leaders attempted to create a Hispanic identity in order to create a voting bloc."[34] Even corporations were cognizant of the fact that the increasing numbers meant a growing economic marketing power and proclaimed the 1980s as the "Decade of the Hispanic." Rosales writes,

> In the 1980s, the word Hispanic came into use as a self-identifier. Soon Chicanos formulated a fanciful conspiracy theory that asserted the term was coined either by Nixon, the Carter or the Reagan administration, and was foisted on Mexican Americans as a nondescript word, which stripped them of their particular ethnic identity. . . . The term put Chicanos in an ethnic category with other Latinos to which they did not belong and diluted their power as the largest Latino group. . . . Mexican Americans who use the word Hispanic are accused of pathologically denying their Mexican-Indian background.[35]

During the epoch, through the combined power of the federal government and corporate America and their pervasive influence over the "mental" means of production, that is, the printed and electronic media, the term *Hispanic* was imposed. The broad use of *Hispanic* did not originate from Mexicanos themselves; rather it came foremost from "Eurocentric"-oriented government and corporations. Combined they contributed significantly to shaping the ethos of the HG, an ethos of domination and occupation.

Throughout much of the epoch, however, the HG was politically the dominant political generation. From a political cultural perspective, its "ethos" embraced the ideological beliefs, values, and symbols of liberal capitalism. The emphasis was on the "I" rather than the "we," and it embraced the Horatio Alger "bootstrap" argument that anyone can make it or be successful providing they are competitive, hardworking, and willing to sacrifice. Moreover, it adhered to a rather middle-class to higher-class bias toward free enterprise, consumerism, materialism, individualism, and pursuit of unbridled wealth. "What's in it for me" was a pervasive attitude, thus getting involved in activities that produced no material reward nor enhanced a person's mobility was rejected. Making money and gaining material reward combined was the major driving force. Consequently, materialism superseded values of community and magnanimity. Education was not perceived as a vehicle for ameliorating community problems or changing society, but for individual financial mobility.

Proponents of the HG embraced either a buffer or "want to be white" political role. The call for "Chicano power" was replaced with the more palatable term *Hispanic empowerment*. Chicanismo's emphasis on cultural nationalism, self-determination, and Chicano power were refuted and perceived as politically dangerous, and anachronistic. Instead, they identified with a "pan-Hispanic" macro approach, which sought to combine and unify those whose heritage had roots in Latin America and Spain. A sense of creating a collective consciousness under the rubric of *Hispanic* was sought. Politically, the HG was moderate to conservative and ostensibly system maintenance or status quo-oriented. Attitudes of "rocking the boat," militancy, protest, polarization, conflict, cultural nationalism, and socialism were categorically rejected. Instead, they adhered to the political beliefs inherent to liberalism[36] and espoused a "mainstream" posture predicated on adaptation, accommodation, and integration politics. Those of the HG identified with conventional interest group politics that did not threaten the system, but rather reinforced it.

Alluding to their moderate to conservative political posture, Ignacio Garcia notes, "They do not speak openly about Anglo-American racism and are less likely to promote themselves as a 'Chicano' candidate to the general populace." Yet in spite of its strong system maintenance orientation, a strong dosage of identity politics permeated it. Mario Garcia describes the impact of the "Hispanic Generation" on Mexicano politics in the United States, he notes:

Harder political times in turn have weakened Mexican American leadership and its resolve to wage concerted campaigns for equal rights, equal rewards, and ethnic integrity. While some pockets of progressive Mexican American leadership remain, primarily in the labor movement and university campuses, Mexican American Leadership on the whole has seemed more disposed to conform to the conservative temper of the time. Mexican American leaders, besides pursing a reduced agenda on the civil rights front, have allowed government and the mass media to define them as "Hispanics" and thus obliterate or disguise the historically based effort by Mexican Americans at self-definition. These displays of powerlessness have instead helped to create a nebulous and weak "Hispanic Generation."[37]

Garcia posited the argument that the HG adopted some of the Mexican American Generation's tenets, such as those of integration, adaptation, and accommodation. It rejected, however, most aspects of what Ignacio Garcia called the "liberal agenda."

Few Mexicanos who identified with the HG had any or wanted any direct linkages to the colonized impoverished and segregated barrios and *colonias*. Most divorced themselves from these colonized realities and sought refuge in suburbia. The suburb was perceived as the barrios' antithesis and escape into a middle-class lifestyle. They craved a more secure environment, the white picket fence, soccer and Pop Warner football youth activities, excellent schools, nice parks, shopping centers, and numerous adult recreational outlets, such as weekend golf and jogging. Paradoxically, however, many of the social problems, especially drugs and even gang violence, endemic to the barrios followed these Hispanics into their suburbs sanctuary. Some had evolved from the "UFW generation of protest" to the "Want to be BMW generation of the status quo." In actuality, however, few could afford the purchase of a BMW and settled for Hondas and Toyotas.

The HG was at times anti-migrant or anti-immigrant, due to either their cultural pluralist or assimilationist inclinations, which de-emphasized or rejected their Mexicanidad. Some perceived migrants as detrimental to Hispanic progress. At times they concurred with white nativists, who polemically argued that migrants should be deported since they were in the country illegally, were a burden to taxpayers, were taking jobs away from U.S. workers, and thus were a detriment to the country's welfare and progress. As a result, the HG further exacerbated existent intra-ethnic schisms, which served to further divide Mexicanos as a community. The preceding became evident during the 1990s when some Mexicanos in California supported several nativist-oriented propositions, 187, 209, and 227, which are examined subsequently. The result was a lack of unified action on a variety of political and social justice issues.

The HG like the MAG embraced the country's dominant political culture. With its middle- and upper-class "I," materialist, and assimilation-driven ethos, it's cognitive, evaluative, and affective political orientations surpassed those of the MAG, CG, or MG.

The Neo-Mexicano (Mex) Generation

With the influx of migrants from México and their rapidly increasing demographic numbers, a major rekindling of the "Mexicano Generation" occurred. With the migration of millions of Mexicanos via legal and undocumented migration during the epoch, especially during the 1990s, the Mexicano Generation was revitalized and became the "Neo-Mex Generation (NMG)." Its revitalization and growth signaled a challenge, particularly to those who identified with the HG or MAG. To those of the CG it was a welcome development since it meant a strengthening of their Mexicanidad. By the latter years of the epoch, many Chicano activists and intellectuals used *Chicano* and *Mexicano* interchangeably, suggesting a "cultural metamorphosis" was in progress. Like their predecessors, most of the newly arrived Mexicano migrants were committed to the preservation of their culture, heritage, and retention of their Spanish language. They still exhibited a passionate affinity to nationalism and a high degree of group consciousness. Their political culture was deeply imbedded with those values, beliefs, norms, and symbols endemic to México's political experience and semiauthoritarian political system. Most migrants still adhered to México's largely subject-parochial political culture that was supported by a culture of poverty, which meant that many had negative perspectives on civic participation and voting.

This identification with México also became apparent during the 1990s with the rise of the Mexica Movement (pronounced Meh-shee-kah in the Nahuatl language). Their ethos was direct repudiation of the HG and MAG as well as some aspects of the CG. *Hispanic* and *Latino* were considered "racist genocidal terms," anti-Mexicano, anti-Chicano, anti-Central American, and anti-indigenous. Hispanic meant *Spaniard*, and *Latino* referred to the colonialist people of Europe who invaded "Anahuac" (the region that includes México, Central America, and the western part of the United States—Aztlán).[38] They had a profound commitment to the *indigenismo* experience that lasted some four thousand years. The Mexica Movement was an ardent form of indigenous nationalism that rejected European, including U.S., culture and civilization. They rejected both the Spanish and English languages and identified with the Nahuatl language, which united them. The following illustrates the historical aspect of their ethos taken from one of their documents:

> Our beginnings as a civilized people began before Rome or Athens was even started, or before any part of Europe was civilized!!! We had created and developed magnificence in art and architecture. We had made discoveries in mathematics, engineering, astronomy, and medicine. We were the first people in the history of humanity to have a mandatory education for males and females, of all classes. We had developed universities (in many ways superior to those in Europe), libraries, the world's most accurate calendar, and one of the great theologies and bodies of literature of the world. We had created our own world of brilliant accomplishments and genius. All this greatness of our people came to an end with the European invasion of our lands. All of this great past has been kept silent to protect the guilty—the Europeans who destroyed it.[39]

They believed that all people who are Mexica must become cognizant of their history of enslavement, knowledgeable of their indigenous identity and true heritage. They rejected the mestizo identity of the Mexicano experience because from their cultural perspective, it simply meant "mixed" in the colonial Spanish language.[40] Concomitantly the use of *raza* was also rejected, as a pejorative term that negated the indigenous culture of the Anahuac. These views clashed with the Chicano's adoption of the hybrid concepts of mestizo and *raza*.

The Rise of the Latino Generation

The HG, by the 1990s, was challenged by the rise of still another political generation, the Latino Generation (LG), which had its genesis as a pan-ethnic term during the 1980s.[41] The term describes subgroups from over twenty countries whose own cultural and historical experiences are deeply rooted in the Latin American. *Latino* and *Hispanic* were increasingly used interchangeably. Political scientist John Garcia in his work *Latino Politics in America* used both terms interchangeably, although his primary preference as a "pan-ethnic" term was *Latino*, while he recognized the extensive use of *Hispanic* by the mass media, public officials, and the general public.[42] There were differences, however, between the two terms. Among most Mexicanos in the United States, particularly those in the West and Midwest, *Latino* as a broad multi-subgroup unifying umbrella term became more palatable and popular than *Hispanic*. This was because the use of *Hispanic* provoked debates from some, who saw it not only as an inaccurate term, but one that conjured up negative cultural and political connotations for reasons previously explained. While the former was assimilation-oriented the latter was much more cultural pluralist. Being Latino allowed national-origin groups to retain an attachment to their own ethnicity while concomitantly allowing them to embrace a more encompassing multi-subgroup group (pan-ethnic) identity.

Some proponents of the LG argued that it was politically less conservative, or system-oriented than Hispanic. While still purveyors of liberal capitalism, the LG were more moderate, tolerant, and open to progressive ideas than those of the HG. According to Ilan Stavens, *Latino* is the "choice of liberals," while *Hispanic* is "preferred by conservatives."[43] *Latino* is a politically charged term that denotes a more assertive liberal posture, which embraces the cultural experiences of all the divergent peoples of Latin America, including *mestizage* and *indigenismo*. It could be argued that politically, in comparison to the HG, the LG was less sectarian and more eclectic in their politics. The issue of Fidel Castro and Cuba, for example, for most of the HG was a negative; conversely, for most of the LG, it was really not an issue. Like those of the HG, from a political cultural perspective, most adhered to a buffer role because of its largely middle-class base.

Hence, by the late 1990s, the usage of *Hispanic* as an umbrella term was increasingly rejected and *Latino* was becoming the term of preference, especially among Mexicanos, as an all-encompassing umbrella term. One can postulate that this was the result of the incipience of a LG, which began to challenge the ethos of the HG. Yet according to historian Rodolfo Acuña, while there was pressure for Mexicanos to shift from *Chicano* to *Latino*, it was still met with resistance. He explains that the "quest for an identity was made more complex with the arrival of over a million war refugees from Central America."[44] Thus Mexicanos identified with a term that represented them as well as the peoples, whose roots were in the Latin American experience, and by the end of the 1990s, increasingly chose to be identified as Latinos rather than Hispanic.

By the end of the twentieth century, the Mexicano political experience was beset with competing political generations, which precluded unity of action. While the HG's ethos was still the most prevalent, it came increasingly challenged by the NMG and LG. As Mexicanos entered the new millennium, they had yet to resolve their political identity problems.

The Hispanic Cultural Renaissance

The intellectual, literary, and arts renaissance engendered by the CG evolved into a hybrid form. The numerous literary works and art produced generally lacked the cultural nationalist focus of the CG. Some were influenced by the MAG or HG or particularly postmodernism. With the demise of the Movimiento, Chicano scholars were susceptible to the influences of the HG. Nevertheless, numerous works, especially in the humanities and literary areas, still dealt with the Movimiento. Historian Juan Gómez-Quiñones writes that these years were a time of "cultural and artistic flowering."[45] While the CG's literary awakening continued well into the 1980s, it gradually withered. It was kept alive by the works of several Chicano scholars in the humanities and social sciences, such as Rodolfo Acuña, Juan Gómez-Quiñones, Mario Barrera, Carlos Muñoz, and a host of other "post–Chicano Generation" scholars.[46] Acuña's four editions of *Occupied America* continued to be the "historical bible" of the overall Mexicano experience of "occupied America." Other scholars played a vital role in keeping the legacy of the Movimiento alive in the midst of a conservative quagmire of Hispanicism. By the late 1990s, a brief resurgence of the Chicano intellectual renaissance occurred, which produced a rekindling of interest in the Movimiento's history and politics, and on the legacy of this dynamic generation.[47] The short story and longer fiction were favorite Chicano literary genre as illustrated by the works of Francisco Jiménez, Sabine Ulibarrí, Ron Arias, Estela Portillo Trambly, Miguel Méndez, Rosaura Sánchez, and Sergio Elizondo, among others.

While Chicano authors continued to publish, numerous other authors surfaced, such as Ron Arias, Nash Candelaria, Arturo Islas, Victor Villaseñore, and Rudolfo Anaya who reflected the influence of the HG.[48] Even though there were several works of high literary quality produced, many of them lacked the Chicano Generation's ethos. Charles M. Tatum writes,

> By the mid-1970s much of the political activism, excitement, and commitment to radical change had dissipated as leaders and their followers turned to trying to effect change by reforming the two party system and established social institutions. This is not to say that the poets and other writers did not remain committed to their ideals and to expressing these ideals through their literary works, but the public forum that had been available to them on college campuses, at festivals, and at demonstrations and rallies no longer existed.[49]

The overall political climate of the HG stultified Chicano literature and research. After 1975 it did not produce a wealth of best-sellers or a poet laureate. Major publishing houses on the East Coast remained impervious to the literary merits of Mexicanos. One such example was Victor Villaseñor, author of the nonfiction work *Rain of Gold*. This story of his family's migration from México to California and the trials and tribulations encountered ran into problems with New York publishers because of the book's title and family history. Angry over the proposed changes, he had his book published in 1991 by the independent Arte Público Press, a Chicano publishing company in Houston.[50]

Among scholars, by the late 1990s ideological and intellectual debates were rare. The result was a pervading sense of "mainstream" conformity. Few Mexicano scholars produced cutting-edge works that were critical of liberal capitalism or social change or were public policy-oriented. Hence, the Mexicano academy in the United States was plagued by intellectual stagnation, especially when it came to theoretical and applied research. Most think tanks that addressed policy issues did so without proposing major reforms of the social order. By the 1990s, most academic conferences that adhered to a HG perspective did not deal with controversial themes. They were largely professional and mainstream-oriented. Intellectually, this epoch produced no Plan Espiritual de Aztlán or Plan de Santa Barbara. As a result, too many of the conferences held were thus for "party time," job-hunting, or simply to reconnect with friends and not for meaningful intellectual debate. What intellectual discourse did occur was largely devoid of any discussions or insight on the decolonization of the barrios and *colonias* or creating change within the liberal capitalist system.

Proponents of the HG sought an end to the debate on ideology. In great part this was induced by the dramatic fall of the Soviet Union in the early 1990s. Afterward, the Chicano Left in the academy all but disappeared and those that remained kept a rather low profile. Others went through a self-imposed ideological catharsis seeking to remove traces of their leftist inclinations. Attempts to consolidate the remnants of the Chicano Left failed. Some on the Left joined the ranks of those interested in the growing postmodern paradigm. On the cultural nationalist side extremely few scholars espoused the notion of nation building—the recreation of Aztlán. This separatist agenda was relegated to a few Chicano community and student activists, as was the case with the diminishing number of avowed Marxists. Ultranationalists, who were also decreasing in number, were in a quandary about how to achieve their seemingly insuperable goal of creating Aztlán within the heart and soul of the liberal capitalist empire. Thus, by the turn of the century, the reality was that few Mexicano scholars through their research or leadership were agents of change. Far too many rode the fast train of mainstream mobility, prosperity, and job security and at best acted as buffers.

The result was an intellectual paralysis. No consensus of thought or creativity of ideas sought to answer the question, "What Needs to Be Done?" Intellectually, the Mexicano political experience was at a critical juncture and quandary as to its future direction. Few Mexicano scholars across the disciplines were willing to intellectually challenge the hegemony of liberal capitalism. Internal colonialism, nationalism, and Marxism were criticized and considered by many as anachronisms in a changing world of globalization. Some turned to mainstream scholarship, which from a social change perspective had little impact on the colonized impoverished conditions of the barrios or *colonias* of Aztlán. Others were more interested in becoming "scholar-entrepreneurs," who spent most of their academic time in the pursuit of foundation and governmental research grants. Scholarship became increasingly equated with entrepreneurship, a business for making money and positioning oneself for promotion and mobility.

The irony is that most academic studies did address social issues, but the conclusions were micro- rather than macro-oriented. They seldom offered policy solutions or prescriptions for change, even when conclusions were controversial. In most cases, the studies were unremarkable exercises of scholarship that had little or no impact on the community or society, and ultimately ended in some library or bookshelves. Other studies made advances in the area of political participation and political reform demonstrating how so-called Hispanics were struggling for empowerment, such as getting more Latinos elected to public office, registered to vote, and actually voting. The premise of the research was complete integration into the country's plutocratic system of accommodation politics.

From a political cultural perspective, some scholars rejected the use of the terms *Chicano* or *Mexicano* and the ethos of the CG or NMG; instead, they opted for the HG ethos or the emergent LG.

During this epoch, many Mexicano and Latino intellectuals rejected the notion of being activist scholars in the tradition of Antonio Gramsci's "organic intellectual."[51] Few scholars propounded the virtues of conducting applied research, formulating theories, or constructing paradigms to effect major social change. Even fewer were engaged in any form of praxis; consequently, too many remained aloof, indifferent, and disconnected from the ominous realities of the country's barrios and *colonias*. The few that were active often were criticized severely by their peers for not being "scholarly oriented." These events created a major leadership problem, because as the literature on social movements clearly points out a prerequisite to any successful reform or revolutionary movement is the active participation of the intelligentsia. Without their participation, few movements will either rise or succeed.[52]

Postmodernism's Impact on the Hispanic Generation

The existent dissatisfaction with Chicanismo among some scholars and students was evident in their affinity for postmodernism.[53] The concept of postmodernism is problematic because it has numerous connotations that relate to a style of architecture, to art that breaks with modernity, and to a rejection of modernist culture and theories.[54] Ramon Gutiérrez explains that "postmodernism is a term that means different things in different disciplines. A postmodern culture is one in which a formerly unified subject is split into constituent parts, in which a single homogeneous style is superseded by a number of heterogeneous fashions."[55] With its intellectual roots in Europe, it developed after World War II as a reaction to the end of modernity, originating in literary studies. Those who propound postmodernism are characterized by their belief in the twin failures of science and reason as a means for explaining and understanding the world.[56] Postmodernists dispute the predictability of rationally derived propositions based upon "totalizing" theories, such as Marxism, utilitarianism, and Freudianism. Steven M. Buechler described postmodernism as being predicated "on other logics of action (based in politics, ideology, and culture) and other sources of identity (such as ethnicity, gender, and sexuality) as the sources for collective action."[57]

To Roger Burbach, postmodernism, besides being largely cultural, is "linked to mass consumerism, the rise of the information and the media ages, the constant sense of change and impermanence, and in its extreme form, the breakdown of the barriers between reality, fiction, appearance and imagination."[58] Within the academy, postmodernism has stirred up controversy and debate. Some scholars argue that earlier theories of change are more germane. Others, in the words of Roberta Gardner, assert that the world is "at the brink of a new age, an epoch that is dramatically different and modern; this new era will force western social scientists to give up their Enlightenment faith in scientific inquiry and the possibility of historical progress."[59]

Postmodernists mobilized on cultural and symbolic issues that were linked to identity rather than economic grievances, which characterized working-class movements. They adhered to postmaterialist values that focused much more on the individual and an autonomous lifestyle rather than collective class interests. Instead of an emphasis on wealth and material well-being, they supported cultural and quality of life issues. Politically, they tended to be pragmatic, middle class-based, and sought institutional reforms rather than violent revolutionary change. Organizationally, their emphasis was on decentralized advocacy groups that are antihierarchical, egalitarian. They supported participatory democracy and were advocates of "contentious politics" (use of unconventional protest strategies and tactics).[60]

An explanation of postmodernism is important because of its impact on the Mexicano political experience's intellectual discourse. By the 1980s several Mexicano and Latino scholars rejected the CG and according to Ramon Gutiérrez "embraced postmodernism as an analytic mode."[61] Intellectual clashes occurred between those who still supported the ethos of the CG and postmodernists. Adherents to a postmodern ethos rejected class and nationalism as common motivators for collective action. This was particularly evident with the emergence of the feminist struggle among some Mexicanas during the 1970s. Emerging feminists perceived the Movimiento as patriarchal, sexist, and homophobic; yet, as traditional Mexicano values slowly broke down, Chicanas had more opportunities to excel in their scholarship and mobility—no longer was *Chicano* an all-inclusive term. Instead what occurred was the separation of genders: Chicana and Chicano.

For the postmodern converts, one perspective on the Movimiento from a feminist view was Berta Ornelas's *Come Down from the Mound*, published in 1975. It was a novel that examined the struggle of love and politics within the context of the Movimiento. One year later, Isabella Rios wrote the novel *Victim*, which was the first attempt to examine the psychological dimensions of Chicanas.

After the 1980s, Mexicana scholars produced a proliferation of literature that was autobiographical and influenced by the postmodern thought.[62] During the next twenty plus years, feminism evolved to challenge some of the values, beliefs, and assumptions of the Chicano Generation. Much of the focus of Mexicana scholars and activists centered on gender and sexuality and not on building a socialist society in Aztlán or fostering collective change. Few adherents of post-modernism adhered to a social change agenda that was based on the collective improvement of the community. There was no direct interaction with the barrio's masses or with their issues. Ironically, some postmodernists made it a point to make vehement attacks on scholars and activists who still identified with the Chicano Generation. Those who spoke out against their emphasis on issues of sexuality and gender were categorized as sexist and homophobic. Nevertheless, in the academy during the 1980s and 1990s postmodernist thought was influential. When it came to literature, poetry, and art, postmodern scholars were a power to be reckoned with. For CG proponents to challenge this school of thought was considered not being "politically correct."

Mexicanas or Chicanas, in general made significant scholarly contributions. In citing the influence of postmodernism on Mexicana feminism, Rodolfo Acuña explains that the theme of identity was a focus of feminists; Alicia Gasper de Alba, Emma Pérez, Cherrie Moraga, Gloria Anzaldúa, and Ana Castillo are but a few who struggled for acceptance by the Chicano community.[63] Mexicanas, Ana Castillo, Sandra Cisneros, and Denise Chavez were three of the most prolific novelists.[64] During this epoch, *la mujer* contributed significantly to the Mexicano literary renaissance and rivaled *los hombres* (the men), particularly in producing novels.

Mexicana intellectuals significantly increased their numbers by the 1990s to where they outnumbered *los hombres*. This was attributable to the fact that more *mujeres* (women) were graduating from college than *hombres*. A study conducted in 1991 by the American Council on Education concluded that Latinas earned 20,455 baccalaureates compared to 16,157 for Latinos. The transition was so significant that by the mid-1990s there were more Latinas in the universities than there were Latinos.[65]

Richard Rodriguez's anti-CG works exemplified the impact of postmodernism on Mexicano literary efforts. He rejected categorically the ethos of Chicanismo and embraced the ethos of the HG. Influenced by a combination of conservative and postmodern thought, Rodriguez was a prolific writer and perhaps the most prominent and controversial literary Mexicano figure of the epoch. Among his various works, the best-selling and most controversial was his autobiography *Hunger of Memory* (Boston, Mass.: D. R. Godine, 1982). In this work, caught in his own identity crisis, he zealously embraces the cultural values and ethos of the white at the expense of his Mexicano ethnicity. He stresses the importance of speaking English rather than Spanish, opposes bilingual education and affirmative action, and is critical of ethnic identity politics. Because of his anti-Chicano perspective, he was the target of severe criticism by other more moderate and progressive Mexicano scholars.

Sharing Rodriguez's assimilationist and conservative views was Linda Chavez. During the 1980s, as a Republican conservative, she headed the "English Only" effort. She argued that Latinos should assimilate in order to invalidate criticism of their patriotism and to prevent the country's "Quebecization."[66] In her book *Out of the Barrio: Toward a New Politics of Hispanic Assimilation* (New York: Basic, 1991) she explored a new theory of assimilation arguing that Latinos, including Mexicanos, just as previous white ethnic immigrants, should, and in fact were integrating. Along with Rodriguez, Chavez represented a strong current of conservativism that ran through the heterogeneous HG.

Other literary trends could be observed, especially in poetry and arts. After the demise of the Movimiento in 1974, CG poets Ricardo Sanchez, Abelardo Delgado, Alurista, and others continued to produce Movimiento-oriented poetry, but at a diminishing pace. One prolific poet was Gary Soto, whose individual vision transcended Chicanismo and the Movimiento. His poetry and short stories had personal themes that used evocative language. Also, the influence of postmodern feminism was evident in the works of such poets as Bernice Zamora, Alma Villanueva, Lorna Dee Cervantez, Gloria Anzaldúa, Cherrie Moraga, and others.

The Renaissance in Theater, Filmmaking, Art, and Music

Mexicanos in theater altered their cultural revolutionary emphasis and became an amalgam of the MAG and HG. Recognized as the father of Chicano theater, playwright Luis Valdez later in the 1970s began his transition into mainstream acceptability. This was illustrated by his 1978 play, *Zoot Suit*, which in 1981 was produced as a film and in 1986 as a play, *I Don't Have to Show You No Stinking Badges*. By the 1990s, his Teatro Compesino productions turned to themes that focused on women.[67] Manuel G. Gonzales notes, "Through the years, Valdez has gradually moved away from political satire to embrace more mystical and universal themes."[68] Carlos Morton likewise accented themes of sexuality in most of his dramatic works, which won him the Hispanic Playwrights Festival Award and the New York Shakespeare Festival Award. Other playwrights who made significant contributions included Ruben Sierra, Fausto Avedaño, and Estella Portillo Trambely. Literary critique and historian Nicolás Kanellos aptly summarized the state of Chicano theater in the 1980s: "The days of teatro as an arm of revolutionary nationalism are over. The revolutionary aims of the movement have resulted in modest reforms and certain accommodations." He points out that Luis Valdez was a member on the California Arts Council and that others were members of local arts agencies and boards throughout the Southwest. Others were in academe, scholars, and editors of books and journals on Chicano literature and theater.[69]

The cultural renaissance in filmmaking continued well into the new epoch without many of the earlier themes of the CG. With an expanding Latino demographic presence the demand for filmmaking and television program access increased. This was true in spite of the overt discriminatory, exclusionary, and stereotyping practices directed against Mexicanos and Latinos in general. Historically, it was commonplace for Mexicanos to be cast in negative or demeaning roles, such as criminals, drug addicts, prostitutes, or rapists. *Los Angeles Times* reporter Steven D. Stark noted, "In the warped world according to the entertainment industry, Mexicans and Mexican Americans have always made great bandits, terrific gardeners, and outstanding businessmen—as long as the business is drugs."[70] A 1991 study of TV content concluded that Latinos were the country's most stereotyped group. They comprised only 2 percent of all TV roles and were four times as likely as whites to portray unskilled workers. In addition, between 1975 and 1991 an astounding 22 percent of Latino characters on fictional TV had committed a crime.[71] A study conducted by the Tomás Rivera Policy Institute in 1998 reported that nonwhites need not apply for other roles. Latinos comprised only 4 percent of the Screen Actors Guild and received only 3.5 percent of the guild roles; they accounted for only 2 percent of the membership of the Writers Guild of America. By 1999, guild figures showed a significant decline in membership to 3.5 percent for actors and 2.3 percent for directors. Latinos made up a mere 1.3 percent of the writers of prime-time television and held an insignificant 1.9 percent of the executive positions at major studios and television networks.[72]

In 1979 the film *Boulevard Nights* was released and was significant for its all-Latino cast and its focus on gang life in the barrios. However, a number of independent Mexicano film producers, such as Montezuma Esparza, Jesús Treviño, Richard Cheech Marín, Gregory Nava, Luis Valdez, and Paul Espinosa all made significant film contributions: *The Ballad of Gregorio Cortez* by Esparza; *Seguín* by Treviño (1982); *El Norte* (1983) by Gregory Nava; *Born in East L.A.* (1987) written and directed by Marín; *La Bamba* (1987) by Valdez; and the *Earth Did Not Part* (1992) by Espinosa. Esparza in 1988 coproduced with Robert Redford *The Milagro Beanfield War*, which depicted life in a small Nuevo Mexicano town and its struggle to preserve its old ways in the face of white cultural intrusion. And the film *Stand and Deliver* (1988), directed by Ramon Menéndez and featuring actor Edward James Olmos,[73] portrayed the life of East Los Angeles math teacher Jaime Escalante. The film earned Olmos an Academy Award nomination for his performance.

The number of Latino films did not appreciably increase by the 1990s. In 1992 Olmos's *American Me* was a film that presented Chicanos in prison life in a very controversial manner. *Mi Familia* (My Family) was a film cowritten and directed in 1995 by Nava and had a strong performance by actor Jimmy Smits. That same year Tomás Rivera's classic award-winning short novel *Y no se lo tragó la Tierra* was made into a film produced by Pete Espinosa, and directed and written by Severo Pérez. In 1997 Gregory Nava and Montezuma Esparza produced and directed *Selena*, a biography of Tex-Mex singing star Selena Quintanilla Pérez, who was tragically killed at the age of twenty by her business manger. Jose Valenzuela in late 1999 produced the film *Lluminarias*, for less than $1 million, but failed to get the support and promotion of Hollywood. In response, Valenzuela said, "We're still in the days of the teatro." These works contributed to what Gonzales described as "Hispanic Hollywood."[74] Despite the increasing numbers of Latinos, access to the film and television industry was still problematic in 1999.

The film documentaries continued, but with less frequency on Chicano themes or topics. Filmmakers such as Sylvia Morales, Paul Espinoza, Jesús Salvador Treviño, and Montezuma Esparza were at the forefront in keeping the spirit of the Chicano Generation alive with their numerous documentaries.[75] During the late 1990s Treviño was busy directing various Hollywood television dramas, such as *NYPD Blue*, *Star Trek Voyager*, and *Resurrection Blvd.*, among others.

As was the trend with literary works so it was with art and music. Chicano artists continued to proliferate, but their art, especially their murals, lost much of their militant nationalist thrust. Increasingly, their art became more private than public and focused more on commercial success. As a result, mural art declined as the major form of Chicano artistic expression. Without the presence of a Movimiento, artistic expressions multiplied, especially those of postmodernism. Some of the most prominent artists of the epoch were John Valdez, Luis Jimenez, Carmen Lomas Garza, and Carlos Almarez, whose works graduated from the streets to the salons.[76]

Mexicano music also reflected the influences of the HG, and underwent a metamorphosis of sorts. Rancheras, musica Norteña, boleros, rumbas, cumbias, cha cha, merengue, and Tex-Mex continued to be part of the Mexicano musical repertoire. In particular, however, a renaissance of mariachi music occurred and the number of mariachis and *ballet folkoricos* proliferated. Mexicano singers Vicente Fernandez, his son Alejandro, Antonio Aguilar, Marco Antonio Solis, Juan Gabriel, and *conjuntos* like Los Tijeres del Norte could be heard across the airwaves in numerous barrios throughout the country. Numerous *conjuntos* and orchestras continued to make Tex-Mex music popular. Other non-Mexicano musical forms emerged as well as "banda" music, rooted in the brass tradition of central México, and salsa, from the Caribbean and South America, were popular. There were a number of Mexicano and Latino artists who crossed over and adopted white musical forms: Freddy Fender, western; Carlos Santana, a mix of salsa with rock; Los Lobos, who combined rock and Norteño music; and Selena, who did Tex-Mex and pop. Hip-hop/R&B were also popular, especially among the barrio youth. In Tejas many young Chicanos abandoned Tex-Mex and switched to bilingual hip-hop.[77] Also, by the late 1990s, Latino pop artists from a variety of Latin American countries became part of the heterogeneous musical tastes of Mexicanos. Non-Mexicano crossover artists included Enrique Iglesias, Ricky Martin, Jennifer Lopez, and Marc Anthony, among others. They contributed to shaping the country's pop culture and "Latino craze."

The above artists' cultural impact was such that some described it as being part of "Generation ñ," referring to young Latinos who were bilingual and bicultural. Increasingly, they rejected assimilation and rejected being called Hispanics. They found a new pride in being Latino, Mexicano, or Chicano. In a special *Newsweek* poll, Latinos over thirty-five were most likely to identity themselves as American; conversely, those under thirty-five were more likely to identify themselves as Latino or Hispanic. Where previous generations crossed geographic boundaries, the young people of Generation ñ crossed cultural ones.[78] Their lexicon at times was one that combined English and Spanish, better known as "Spanglish."

By the turn of the century, the HG was challenged by the rise of the LG and the NMG. Both rejected assimilation and adhered to a form of cultural pluralism. Their emergence was the result of changing Mexicano and Latino demographics. With a constant influx of hundreds of thousands of legal and undocumented migrants huge concentrations formed in both rural and urban areas. These new migrants were nationalistic, especially Mexicanos. They were not interested in assimilation or of severing their cultural, political, or economic ties with México or their respective Latin American countries. Living in segregated barrios and even suburbs, many saw no urgent need to learn English at the expense of losing their Spanish language and opted for bilingualism and biculturalism.

Due to the proliferation of Latino television and radio stations, newspapers, and magazines, more Mexicanos and Latinos sought to retain their ethnic culture and use of the Spanish language. These mediums of communication significantly contributed to the rise and growth of both the LG and NMGs. The growth of Spanish-language radio stations was phenomenal. In 1980 there were only sixty-seven Spanish-language radio stations in the United States; by the end of the 1990s the number increased to 559.[79] The same applied to television with the growth of two powerful nationwide networks, Univision and Telemundo. Scores of Spanish-language television stations operated in most major Latino markets with programming originating mostly from México and Venezuela. They acted as powerful and effective socializing agents for both the NMG and LG. Univision attracted some 90 percent of all Spanish-language TV viewers and Telemundo only a mere 8 percent.

By 1999, Univision was the country's fifth largest broadcast network. It owned twenty-six television stations, had thirty-two affiliates, and owned a cable network and an Internet portal. Telemundo owned ten TV stations in cities such as Los Angeles. It had affiliates in most other markets and had a cable network as well.[80] Affiliated with Univision, Entravision was formed in 1996 under the corporate leadership of Walter Ulloa, and by the turn of the century it operated some twenty-two television stations, owned and operated fifty-seven radio stations and some forty-seven affiliates, and owned a newspaper and 11,000 billboards in Los Angeles and New York.[81]

Since 1990 the number of Latino-oriented publications grew some 69 percent, nationally from 742 to 1,256 of which 84 percent were in Spanish. Los Angeles County alone boasted some 135 Latino publications, which included *La Opinion*, a Latino daily owned by the *Los Angeles Times*, with the largest circulation in the country. About 120 publications, which comprised a tenth of the national total, were members of the National Association of Hispanic Publications founded by Kirk Whisler in 1982 and in 1999 headed by Andres Tobar. Combined they represented 7.5 million in circulation, about a quarter of the total of the country's Latino publications. Increasingly, corporations were spending millions on Latino advertising. Some $572 million in ad revenues was recorded by Latino publications in 1998 alone.[82]

Thus, the aforementioned literary, cultural, and media changes that occurred were a result of the demographic inspired changes of the "re-Mexicanización of Aztlán, and the "Latinoización of the United States."

The Latino Population Explosion: A Changing Demographic/Socioeconomic Profile

It was during the epoch of the HG that the Latino population experienced unprecedented growth. So significant was the impact of the changing demographics that the "re-Mexicanización" of Aztlán was dramatically accelerated, as the "Latinoización" of the United States was nationally. Within those southwest states located in Aztlán, the Mexicano population increased and by the end of the twentieth century constituted the region's largest ethnic minority. In addition, at the national level, by the end of the decade of the 1990s, Latinos were on the verge of becoming the country's largest ethnic minority, displacing African Americans. It also meant that the Latino diaspora had reached every state in the country. In the ensuing pages, the Latino demographic profiles of the 1980 and 1990 Census are examined.

The 1980 U.S. Census

The 1980 Census revealed that the country's Latino population experienced substantial growth. In conducting the census the U.S. Bureau of the Census used *Hispanic* as its designated term to count Latinos and disseminate its census results.[83] Based upon a method of self-identification, it allowed persons of Spanish surname to use a number of identifiers, which included Mexican American, Mexicano, Chicano, Puerto Rican, Cuban, Central and South American, and other Spanish origin. On the question of race, Hispanics were asked by the U.S. Census to identify themselves by race, either black or white, a full 40 percent of Hispanics chose "other." There were some 3,113,867 people who chose to classify themselves as other Hispanics rather than as of Mexican, Puerto Rican, or Cuban origin. Of these, 8 percent resided in Colorado and Nuevo México.[84] *Hispanic* was used to identify the second largest national minority group, rather than a mere regional group.

According to the U.S. Census, the Hispanic population in 1980 was estimated at 14.6 million, which translated to about 6.5 percent of the country's total population of 226,545,805. Latinos were the fastest growing ethnic group in the country, experiencing an increase of 61 percent between 1970 and 1980. This was compared to a mere increase of 8 percent for whites. Blacks, who formed the largest nonwhite population, numbered some 27 million, or almost 12 percent. By 1983, the country's Latino population increased to an estimated 16.9 million. Of the preceding total almost 60 percent or 8.7 million were Mexicanos, 15 percent or 2 million were Puerto Rican, and about 5 percent were of Cuban origin; of the remainder, 3 million said they were from Spain or other countries in Latin America.[85] Specifically, this translated to a whopping 93 percent increase, whereas Puerto Ricans increased by 41 percent and Cubans by 47 percent.[86]

Other aspects of the national Latino demographic profile revealed some interesting facts. First, it was estimated by the U.S. Census that during the 1980s the Hispanic population was undercounted by some three million. Second, the national Latino demographic profile was highly urbanized, which meant that compared to 74 percent of the total U.S. population, some 87 percent of Latinos lived in metropolitan areas.[87] Third, one of the most remarkable results was the Latino population's comparatively low median age. Hispanics were twenty-two compared to thirty for the total U.S. population. Next to Puerto Ricans, Mexicanos had the lowest median age, twenty-one years.[88] Lastly, next to immigration, high birthrates also contributed significantly to the Latino population growth. In 1980 the Latino birthrate was 23.5 live births per 1,000 population compared to 14.2 for whites and 22.9 for blacks. Of all the Latino subgroups, Mexicanos had 26.6 live births.[89]

Throughout Aztlán, Latinos were the largest ethnic minority. Mexicanos overwhelmingly constituted the largest Latino subgroup, which contributed to the re-Mexicanización of Aztlán. This became particularly evident in the significant Mexicano population growth that occurred within Aztlán's numerous cities, barrios, and *colonias*. By region, the heaviest Mexicano population concentration was in Aztlán (the five southwestern states of California, Tejas, Nuevo México, Arizona, and Colorado). Mexicanos numbered some 7,227,339, compared to the total regional population of 44,808,166. In the Midwest, they numbered some 820,218, compared to 344,305 in the South and 87,776 in the Northeast.[90] The percentage distribution was 82.7 percent for the Southwest, 9.4 percent for the Midwest, 3.0 percent for West, and 1.0 percent for the Northeast.[91] Most Puertorriqueños were concentrated in New York, while Cubanos were heavily located in La Florida, but during the 1980s the pattern began to change.

The Latino population was concentrated primarily in ten states. The largest Latino population was in California (4,544,331), followed by Tejas (2,985,824), New York (1,659,000), La Florida (858, 000), Illinois (636,000), New Jersey (492,000), Nuevo México (477,000), Arizona (441,000), Colorado (340,000), and Michigan (162,000).[92] California and Tejas had not only the highest level of Latinos in the country but of Mexicanos. Half of the Latino population lived in these two states, which were predominantly Mexicano. A noticeable population shift was occurring from Tejas and Arizona to first California and later to the Midwest. This is illustrated by the fact that in 1980 Illinois had more Mexicanos than did the traditional states of Arizona, Nuevo México, and Colorado.[93]

The 1990 U.S. Census

The results of the 1990 Census continued the trend toward "Latinoización" of the United States. As a whole, the U.S. Census again designated the Latino population as the fastest growing ethnic minority and it continued to be the second largest minority group in the country. According to U.S. Census figures, the Hispanic population grew to some 22.35 million, a 53 percent increase between 1980 and 1990—five times as fast as the total population and eight times as fast as the non-Hispanic population. The Latino population increased to some 9 percent of the total U.S. population, which numbered some 248,709,873.[94] This meant that one in eleven people were Latino. In comparison blacks numbered 29.99 million, Asian/Pacific 7.2 million, and Native Americans 1.9 million. By 1995, however, the U.S. Census reported that the Latino population had increased to some twenty-seven million, a nearly five million increase in just five years. Two years later, the Latino population increased by two million to twenty-nine million and comprised 11 percent of the total population. Whereas the Latino population from 1990 to 1996 grew by 27 percent, the non-Latino population increased by a mere 9 percent.[95]

Of the several Latino subgroups, between 1980 and 1990, Mexicanos increased by nearly 4.8 million. Approximately 84 percent of the growth occurred in Aztlán as a region. Also, Mexicanos accounted for only a mere 5.4 percent of the country's total population, which translated to 13.5 million in 1990.[96] In comparison to the other subgroups, Mexicanos comprised 62.6 percent of the total Latino population, Central and South Americans 13.8 percent, Puerto Ricans 11.1 percent, Cubans 4.6 percent, and other Latinos 7.6 percent.[97] The percentage of Mexicanos by 1995 increased to some 64 percent of the Latino population.[98]

The Latino demographic profile of the 1990 census experienced some dramatic changes. First, the great majority of Hispanics continued to live in urban areas, 91.8 percent compared to 72.8 percent for non-Hispanics. Specifically, the percentage for Mexicanos was 90.5 percent, compared to 95.2 percent for Puerto Ricans, 95.7 percent for Cubans, 97.0 percent for Central and South Americans. Second, Latinos again proved to be younger than other U.S. residents as of 1991, with a median age of 26.2 compared to 33.8 for non-Hispanics. Of all the Hispanic subgroups, Mexicanos were the youngest with a median age of 24.3 years, compared to 26.7 for Puerto Ricans, 27.9 for Central and South American, and 39.3 for Cubans.[99]

At the state level, changes were more evident, particularly among Mexicanos. According to the U.S. Census, over half of the Latino population lived in California (34 percent) and Tejas (18 percent). Moreover, 85 percent lived in these two states plus New York (10 percent), La Florida (7 percent), Illinois (4 percent), New Jersey (3 percent), Arizona (3 percent), Nuevo México (3 percent), and Colorado (2 percent).[100] The actual Mexicano population on a state basis was as follows: California 6,118,996; Tejas 3,890,820; Illinois 623,688: Arizona 616,195; Nuevo México 328,836; Colorado 282,478; La Florida 161,499; Washington 155,864; Michigan 138,312; and New York 93,244.[101]

The "re-Mexicanización of Aztlán" accelerated significantly by 1990. According to the U.S. Census, Mexicanos resided in every state including the District of Colombia. Mexicanos became a nationally based ethnic group, but their greatest concentration was in Aztlán. The total Mexicano regional population reached some 11,237,325 persons,[102] and one out of five residents was Mexicano. The so-called cactus curtain (Cortina de Nopal) that separated the two countries continued to move ever northward and, one could argue, was becoming nonexistent.

Numerous cities also experienced a dramatic growth in their Mexicano population. The ten cities with the largest Mexicano population included Los Angeles (936,507); San Antonio (478,409); Houston (358,503); Chicago (352,560); El Paso (338,844); San Diego (194,400); Dallas (185,096); Phoenix (176,139); San Jose (173,803); and Santa Ana (173,776). In addition, a host of smaller communities, especially in South Tejas, had concentrations of over 85 percent— from Soccoro, Texas, with 93 percent to California's Calexico, with 92.9 percent.[103] In California, the city of Los Angeles was 40 percent Latino and East Los Angeles was 95 percent. Other municipalities were even higher: Maywood, 93 percent; Huntington Park, 92 percent; Bell Gardens, 88 percent; Irwindale, 86 percent; and San Fernando, 83 percent. Numerous other cities experienced huge increases: in Orange County, Anaheim's growth was 122 percent and Santa Ana's was 111 percent. The city of Long Beach doubled its mostly Mexicano population to 101,419.[104]

During this epoch, the migrant exodus continued. Latinos constituted the earliest and the most recent immigrants to the United States. As a result of push factors, such as increasing poverty, internal political conflicts, and insurgencies, hundreds of thousands of immigrants came from México, Central America, Cuba, and other countries of Latin America and contributed to the "re-browning" of the country. In particular, this meant that the exodus from México to Aztlán accelerated during these years. From 1950 through 1990, some two million Mexicanos immigrated to the United States, more than the total of newcomers from any other country in the world.[105] Between 1961 and 1990, 18 percent of all legal immigration came from México, 30 percent from Latin America, 31 percent from Asia, and 18 percent from Europe. By 1996, the Latino population increased by a rate of 900,000 a year, a net immigration of 350,000.[106] Three years later, it increased to some 31.5 million.[107]

Between 1981 and 1996, some 3.3 million Mexicans entered the United States legally.[108] By the late 1990s, legal immigration into the United States totaled some eight hundred thousand. By 1998, the figure for México increased to 20 percent.[109] In particular, the Mexicano population increased dramatically in the border states of California, Arizona, Nuevo México, and Tejas. According to David E. Lorey, "By 1990, the border's Mexican-origin population was 16.8% of the total population in Arizona, 20.6% in California, 21.7% in Nuevo México, and 22.9% in Tejas." He goes on to cite that "in 1990, 14.2% of Arizonans, 20% of Californians, 22.1% of Texans, and 27.9% of New Mexicans spoke Spanish at home."[110] During the 1967–1997 fiscal years the Immigration and Naturalization Service (INS) accepted some eight hundred thousand as documented immigrants. The 1990s set a record for legal immigration. The country's immigrant population constituted about one in ten U.S. residents, the highest percentage since 1930. Of any country in the world, México had, by far, the largest percentage of 18 percent.[111]

The re-Mexicanización of Aztlán was also fueled by undocumented migration. Despite more stringent enforcement of immigration laws and the militarization of the border, for example, Operation Gatekeeper, by the mid-1990s the influx of undocumented migration continued unabated. Indicative of this was the number of Mexicanos who were apprehended without papers: 989,000 in 1979; 831,000 in 1989; and 1.6 million in 1996.[112] In 1996 the INS estimated that out of a total of five million the number of undocumented Mexicanos was 2.7 million.[113] By fiscal year 1999 the figures for those undocumented migrants arrested across the Southwest topped 1.5 million, slightly more than in 1998 and 20 percent higher than during the first year of Operation Gatekeeper.[114] The INS reported in 1999 that the undocumented population living in the United States had reached some 5.5 million, a figure that was increasing annually by 275,000. The overwhelming majority of them were from México, Central America, and Latin America. About 40 percent of the country's undocumented population resided in California.[115] With an increased budget of $3.9 billion, the INS added some sixteen hundred additional Border Patrol agents and immigration inspectors for the militarization of the U.S./México border.[116]

Beyond the exodus from México and Latin America, high birthrates further increased both the Latinoizacíon of the United States and the re-Mexicanización of Aztlán. Even without immigration, the Mexicano population would have increased, due to having the highest birthrates among the country's several ethnic groups. Birthrates touch upon various aspects of the family structure and roles of women. Another indicator of high birthrates among Hispanics was family size. Latinos in 1980 contained one more person than did the average white family. Mexicano families were the largest with 4.07, followed by Puerto Ricans with 3.67, Cubans with 3.58 persons, and then others of Spanish origin with 3.37.[117] Ten years later, the Bureau of the Census once again reported that birthrates for the overall population in 1990 showed a birthrate of 67.0 per one thousand women aged fifteen through forty-four. More specifically, the birthrate for white women was 65.2, for black women 74.8, for Asian/Pacific Islander 58.1, and for

Hispanic women 93.2.[118] A pattern became apparent: when women increased their levels of education and economic standing, their birthrates declined.

A reverse white exodus also contributed to an increase in the Latino's population density, especially in California. In 1995 the U.S. Census reported on out-of-state migration over the past four years. The state had a net migration outflow of 138,000 in 1990 to 2001, for a 0.5 percent decline. That rate nearly tripled in 1995 by a loss of 426,000, representing a 1.4 percent decline. The Los Angeles-Anaheim-Riverside metropolitan area, in particular, showed the highest decline: for every person who came to the region, three left, resulting in a net loss of 351,000 people.[119] Throughout most of the 1990s the majority of the out-of-state migration consisted of whites and some blacks.

The Latino Socioeconomic Profile

The Latino socioeconomic status during this epoch was mixed. Charles Dickens's description in the *Tale of Two Cities* was applicable to the Latino experience: "The best of times, the worst of times." This paradox was evident: the Latino upper and middle classes grew and their incomes overall increased. However, so did Latino poverty and social problems of the colonized barrios and *colonias* throughout Aztlán. Increasingly, the Latino community became more stratified, and Mexicanos were no exception. The class distinctions became more apparent and acute. The fruits of liberal capitalist prosperity reached primarily the small Latino[120] upper and growing middle class that had primarily internalized the ethos of the HG.

The Best of Times Scenario

On the positive side, the Latino demographic explosion continued to enhance the growing awareness of the importance of the Latino communities. This occurred especially among *politicos*, bureaucrats, corporate executives, media, and nativists as well. In particular, the media did numerous reports and stories on the "re-browning of the United States." It became a well-recognized fact that by the late 1990s Latinos would soon constitute the country's largest ethnic minority. The Latino population explosion also created more negative media attention, which induced a resurgent nativist response. One can argue that during this epoch certain socioeconomic changes did occur that could be interpreted as being positive. By 1998 Latino purchasing power, for example, mushroomed to some $370 billion, greater than that of many emerging nations in the Pacific Rim and Latin America.[121] Between 1987 and 1997, the number of Latino business increased 232 percent, outpacing other groups. By 1999, the number of Latino-owned businesses had increased dramatically to some 1. 4 million. In southern California alone there were some 307,000 Latino-owned businesses. Business organizations flourished, such as the U.S. Hispanic Chamber of Commerce and Latino Business Association in Los Angeles.[122]

During this epoch, the Latino middle and upper class increased significantly. Affluent Latinos, those with annual incomes of more than $50,000, grew from 191,000 in 1972 to 638,000, an increase of 224 percent. The proportion of Latino households living in affluence increased from 7 percent of all households in 1972 to 11 percent in 1988, surpassing the proportion of middle-class blacks, which was at 10 percent.[123] By 1997 some 193,000 Latino households had incomes of over $100,000. In 1998 the Latino median income increased to some $28,300; even though it still lagged behind the national average of $38,885.[124] Harry Pachon, president of the Tomás Rivera Policy Institute, stated in 1997, "More Latinos in the middle class. That's the great untold story of the Latino community. We are everywhere."[125] Other indicators of this "best of times" scenario included increased occupational mobility, more Latinos living in suburbia, more Latinos graduating from high school and college, and political representation increasing. Yet for most Mexicanos who resided in the country's colonized barrios and *colonias* it was still the "worst of times."

The Worst of Times Scenario

Most Mexicanos throughout the epoch were still living in a colonized reality. This was particularly evident in the areas of income and occupational mobility. Latino income in 1980 increased over the 1970 figures, but was still below that of whites and other groups. The median income for Hispanic families was reported at $14,700, below the national median of $19,900 for non-Latino families. Latina heads of household faced a worse situation. By 1975, Mexicana households earned 30 percent less while Puerto Rican households earned 29 percent less than white households. As a whole, however, Latinos earned only about three-fourths as much as whites, and Mexicanos earned only 72 percent as much as non-Latinos. During the recession of the early 1980s, Latino median income dropped by 6.8 percent, whereas for whites the decline was only 1.7 percent.[126]

The disparity of income between the various ethnic/racial groups continued. Data from the 1990 Current Population Survey indicated that in 1989, white median family income was $35,975, the Latino median was $23,446, and the black median was $20,209. A major income discrepancy existed: Latino median income was 65.2 percent of white family income, down from 65.3 percent in 1985, 67.2 percent in 1980, 66.9 percent in 1975, and 69.2 percent in 1973.

The acuteness of this income disparity was even more evident among Latinas, particularly Mexicanas. The median annual income of working Latinas in 1990 was $10,099, compared to $12,436 for non-Latinas, with Mexicanas earning the least of all the Latina subgroups, $9,286. Latino workers faced the same gross income disparity: they earned a median of $14,141 compared to $22,207 for non-Hispanic men. Again, among all Latino subgroups, Mexicanos earned less, $12,894.[127] By 1997, the median household income rose for every other ethnic and racial group except for Latinos; it dropped 5.15 percent.[128] In 1998, for example, Latinos in California accounted for 28 percent of the labor force but earned only 19 percent of its aggregate income compared to whites, who were 53 percent of the state's workers, but earned 62 percent of its income.[129] By the end of the twentieth century, the income gap between Latinos and whites was not narrowing, but widening.

Over this period's twenty-four years, Latinos experienced a slight improvement in socioeconomic status, but overall the results were not positive. Latinos, both men and women, along with blacks, were underrepresented in the better-paid occupations, including executive and professional positions. In the executive, administrative, and managerial positions of employed males, Latinos comprised a mere 5.7 percent, while blacks and whites made up 4.7 percent and 12.4 percent, respectively. In the professions, Latinos comprised 4.6 percent, blacks 4.9 percent, and whites 10.6 percent. For Latinas the situation was no better: they made up 4.4 percent of the executive, administrative, and managerial positions, compared to 7.5 percent for white women and 4.2 percent for black women. In the professional specialties, Latinas comprised 6.9 percent, black women 10.6 percent, and white women 14 percent. Many more Latinos were overrepresented in the unskilled or semiskilled labor category. Specifically, in the factories, Latinos comprised about a third of all males and a fifth of all female semiskilled workers.[130]

During the 1990s, Latinos in general were the most employed in low-paying jobs. According the National Council of La Raza's Demographic Overview report in 1991, just 11.4 percent of Latino males, compared to 27.6 percent of non-Latino males, were employed in managerial and professional jobs. In addition, 26.2 percent of Latino women, compared to 17 percent of non-Latino women, held service jobs; and 14 percent of Latinas compared to 7.6 percent of non-Latino women had jobs as operators, fabricators, and laborers.[131] By the mid-1990s, Latino men were more likely to be in the labor force than non-Latinos, 78 percent to 73 percent.[132] This occupational job crisis was exacerbated by the fact that Latinos suffered from higher than usual unemployment rates. The non-Latino rate peaked at 7.5 percent in 1992 and then started down, while Latino unemployment, 11.3 percent in 1992, continued to climb to 11.9 percent in 1993.[133] The differential between Latinos and non-Latinos fluctuated between 2 percent and 4 percent.

The third contributor to the Mexicano/Latino's worst of times was the education crisis. No people can expect to progress if they do not have access to a quality education, and Latinos were no exception. While some progress was made during this epoch it was extremely limited. The acuteness of the educational crisis faced by Hispanics during the early 1980s is examined by Moore and Pachon, who explain:

> Hispanic dropout rates are nearly double those of blacks and Anglos between the ages of 14 and 25 years of age. Stated another way, for every 100 Hispanic children who enter kindergarten, only 55 graduate from high school, 25 enter college, and 7 complete college. Only 4 will enter graduate school and 2 will finish.[134]

During the 1980s, the country's public schools changed demographically. In the last twenty years, white children's numbers fell 16 percent, blacks' increased by 5 percent, and Latinos' grew by some 103 percent.[135] Latinos, however, made few educational strides. They still lagged behind most other non-Latino groups. Their high school completion rates for ages eighteen to twenty-four dropped from 62.8 percent in 1985 to 56 percent in 1989.[136] Taken from the U.S. Census, the following profile exemplifies the preceding statement. Twelve percent of Latinos twenty-five years and over had less than a fifth grade education. Thirty-six percent of those with a fifth to twelfth grade education did not possess a high school diploma. Only 27 percent had a high school education without any college, and 27 percent had some college but did not have a degree. Latino students had the highest concentration in the community colleges, 56 percent compared to whites' 36 percent and 42 percent for blacks.[137] Only 4 percent had an associate of arts degree and 6 percent had a bachelor's degree, while only 2 percent had a master's degree and 1 percent had professional or doctoral degrees. Of the preceding 1 percent, 0.8 had a professional degree and 0.2 had PhDs.[138]

The devastating Latino educational crisis continued to pervade the 1990s. In 1992, 17.3 percent of Latinos were eligible for admission into the California State University system, compared to 18.6 percent for blacks, 38.2 percent for whites, and 61.5 percent for Asian Americans.[139] Another indicator was the continued high "push-out rates" among Latinos. In 1995, only about 53 percent of Latinos completed high school compared to 83 percent for non-Latinos. The failures of the county's educational systems to provide Latinos with a marketable education by the late 1990s resulted in a widening gap in graduation rates from both high school and college. Latinos had the highest high school dropout rates of any other ethnic/racial group in the country.[140]

Significantly, the crisis faced by most Latinos was further exacerbated by institutional racism at the primary and secondary levels of education. There was a dramatic increase in the segregation of the barrio schools; cutbacks on bilingual education (Proposition 227 in California passed in 1998 to end bilingual education); inadequate facilities, books, and equipment; lack of qualified, competent, and committed teachers; discriminatory testing methods; insufficient numbers of Latino, particularly Mexicano, teachers, principals, superintendents, and administrators; outdated curricula and diminishing bilingual/bicultural programs; and the prevalence of crime, drugs, and gang violence in the schools. In California, as I will subsequently examine, the passage of nativist-inspired propositions 187, 209, and 227 had disastrous educational implications for Latinos.

At the level of higher education, the situation was more severe. Few Mexicanos graduated from four-year colleges and universities; even fewer from graduate and professional schools. Chicano Studies programs and department came under attack; and the numbers of Mexicanos in administration, for example, college presidents, chancellors, vice presidents, and deans, were extremely low. The passage of Proposition 209 in California, which brought an end to affirmative action in higher education, led to a decrease in the small number of Latinos who graduated from college. In comparison to other ethnic/racial groups, few Latinos received either masters or PhD degrees. According to *The Chronicle of Higher Education*, Latinos in 1999 received about 2 percent of the total PhDs granted. This shortage of Latinos with graduate degrees was indicative of the deliberate lack of access to graduate education, and reflected in the small percentages of Latinos attending the country's graduate schools. At the University of California, Riverside in 1999 only 5.6 percent of the total number of graduate students was Latino.

This deleterious pattern was commonplace throughout the country. It was apparent that the country's white-dominated higher educational systems were not interested in educating the mass of Latinos, particularly Mexicanos in Aztlán. At the turn of the century, at all levels of education, the racist effects of colonialism continued. In particular, Mexicanos were increasingly being relegated to a de facto "apartheid" status.

Another indicator of the worst of times scenario was poverty. Poverty rates among Latinos increased throughout much of the epoch. According to the U.S. Census, in 1972, Latinos accounted for 22.8 percent of those in poverty.[141] In 1979, the figure decreased slightly to 21.8 percent, but by 1982 increased dramatically to 29.9 percent. Women-headed households were the most affected. The 1982 figures showed that some 53 percent of Mexicana and Puerto Rican women head of households were poor. This meant that Mexicano families were two and a half times more likely to live in poverty than were white families.[142] The national poverty rate for non-Latinos in 1987 was 9.7 percent; however, for Latinos in California it was 36 percent.[143]

The Latino poverty rate during the 1990s remained higher than for most non-Latinos. In 1991, for example, Latinos were more likely than non-Latino white persons to be living in poverty, 28.7 percent compared to 9.4 percent. In addition, while Latinos represented some 9 percent of the country's total population, they represented about 17.8 percent or about twice that percentage of all persons living in poverty. The specter of poverty was especially evident with children under eighteen years of age. In 1991, about 40.4 percent of Latino children lived in poverty. While Latino children represented some 11.6 percent of all children in the United States, they comprised 21.5 percent of all children living in poverty.[144] In 1993, 29 percent of Latinos lived below the poverty line and were three times as likely to live in poverty as non-Latino whites.[145] By 1995, 30 percent of all Latinos were considered poor, meaning they earned less than $15,569 for a family of four. That was almost three times the percentage for whites living in poverty. Of those with incomes of less than $7,500 or less for a family of four, 24 percent were Latinos.[146] The impact of poverty was also evident in the purchase of a home. Home ownership for all people in 1997 reached a record of 65.7 percent. More specifically, however, the rate for whites was 72 percent, while for Latinos and blacks it was just 45 percent.[147]

The National Council of La Raza's "State of Hispanic America 1991" report was bleak. It concluded that the nation's Latino population faced the greater educational, health, and employment problems than those of the rest of the population. Raul Yzaguirre, president of the NCLR, commented that by virtually every measurable standard, Hispanics were a severely disadvantaged population.[148] Arturo Vargas, who headed the National Association of Latino Elected officials (NALEO), said this in reference to the status of Latinos: "It is the American nightmare, not the American dream."[149]

Epoch's Salient Issues and Events

During this epoch, Mexicano efforts for social change were not part of a social movement. Rather the issues and events that did occur were sporadic and not driven by charismatic leaders, mass organizations, a well-defined plan of action or ideology, or a strategy predicated on militant protest. Most of the issues dealt with were crisis orientated. Although from time to time, some events or issues had a semblance of a social change agenda, in most situations the political actions taken by Mexicanos lacked consistency and were essentially more reactionary in nature. In the previous chapter, some of the most salient political events were examined on a year-to-year basis. Every year from 1966 to 1974, there were activities that were often inspired by or were products of deliberate planning and strategically implemented a number of change agendas within the context of the Movimiento. During this following epoch, however, this was not the case. These "worst of times" produced a nativist state of siege directed primarily at Mexicanos as illustrated in their immigrant bashing and racist impelled Propositions 187, 209, and 227.

Immigration: The Wedge Issue

Immigration continued to be a priority because of increasing nativist attacks. From 1975 to 1999, especially for Mexicanos, immigration became the wedge issue of the epoch. This was due to the continuing exodus of migrants both legal and undocumented from México and Central America into the United States. Millions fled from poverty and deprivation in search of a better way of life. The reinvigorated migrant exodus was the product of a combination of "push" and "pull" factors. A new flood of immigrants came from Central America, the Caribbean, and South America. The most salient push factors were first, chronic poverty; second, especially in the case of Central Americans, political repression and political instability; and third, family reunification. The paramount pull factor was the United States' insatiable appetite for cheap labor.

For México the cardinal push factor was chronic poverty, not political repression. With a burgeoning population, the Mexican economy throughout the epoch was incapable of producing a sufficient number of jobs for its people. The Mexican Revolution of 1910 had effected a massive transformation of the social order, but poverty permeated the whole of México's economy. In fact, the migrant exodus was driven by the desperation, discontent, and intolerable socioeconomic conditions that resulted from chronic poverty. Neither México's adherence to a mixed economy or a free market economy by the 1990s had succeeded in extricating it from its third world status or halted the exodus of "economic refugees" into the United States. Héctor Aguilar Camín and Lorenzo Meyer argue that the 1980s was plagued by an economic crisis that produced "severe features of inequality." They explain,

> A total of 22.3 million Mexicans—46 of every 100—lacked the minimal standards of welfare in nutrition, education, heath, and employment. In

contrast, only 14.8 million Mexicans—30 of every 100—showed levels of marginalization. . . . 35 of every 100 families had incomes below the minimum wage (scarcely above $100 per month) and 19 million persons were undernourished—13 million of them in rural areas.[150]

Research conducted in 1987 pointed out that the number of poor had increased from 40 percent of the population to nearly 60 percent. With this increase, the 1980s produced an acceleration of the migrant exodus into the United States.

Starting in the late 1980s and throughout the 1990s, México's economy evolved from a mixed economy to a free market economy that continued to produce acute poverty and growing class antagonisms. In particular during the 1990s, the socioeconomic situation for most Mexicanos deteriorated. Inflation had long been an acute economic problem and worsened during the early part of the decade. The ongoing economic crisis was further aggravated in 1994 with the collapse of the peso, which threatened México with bankruptcy and precipitated the infamous "crash of 1995." With the devaluation of the peso, one million jobs were lost, the costs of consumer loans dramatically increased, and inflation soared to a horrendous 52 percent.[151] The free market economic policies of presidents Carlos Salinas de Gortari and Ernesto Zedillo only served to further exacerbate the people's economic plight. President Zedillo in 1995 negotiated a bailout of $20 billion from the United States and an additional $28 billion from international sources.[152]

Contributing to México's ongoing economic crisis was high unemployment and underemployment, particularly in the rural areas. In 1995 México's unemployment rate reached some 23 percent, and experts concluded that without the "safety valve" of immigration the rate would have been around 35 percent.[153] In 1997 it was reported that in the rural areas of México and among the indigenous populations twenty-four million lived in "extreme poverty." Only 20 percent earned more than the minimum wage, which at 23 pesos was equivalent to three U.S. dollars.[154] The *campesino's* acute marginalization was evident in the high number of unemployed, which in 1997 totaled some thirteen million.[155] No appreciable progress had been made by 1999: 20 percent of the workforce made the minimum wage of 34.50 pesos or $3.63 dollars.[156]

México's disparity of wealth further intensified with the signing of the North American Free Trade Agreement (NAFTA), which went into effect on January 1, 1994, the day the Zapatista insurgency struck in the state of Chiapas. Under the web of globalization of capital, México's economy became further dependent on the United States and was unable to produce enough jobs to accommodate its growing population. The *maquiladoras*, a product of the Border Industrialization

Program started in 1965, were evidence of crass economic exploitation. They consisted of hundreds of assembly plants operated chiefly by U.S., Japanese, and Korean transnational corporations along the U.S./México border. While they created some employment, they paid their workers subsistence wages.[157]

By 1997 the Zedillo administration succeeded in arresting high inflation to a level of 17 percent and moved the economy toward a positive growth rate of 8.8 percent, but two years later, 40 percent of all Mexicanos still lived in dire poverty. At the turn of the century, in spite of the militarization of the U.S./México border and restrictionist U.S. immigration policies, the migrant exodus continued to fuel the reoccupation of Aztlán.

Thus, at the turn of the century, México's biggest export into the United States continued to be its people. Both legal and undocumented immigration served as a safety valve, which reduced the domestic pressures on México. This allowed the social order to maintain a semblance of stability. One can postulate that without the migrant exodus, México would again have been swept by the turbulent winds of social revolution.

Throughout the epoch, the migrant exodus fostered a resurgence of nativism. Even prior to 1975, in 1971, Operation Clean Sweep INS apprehended some 348,178 undocumented workers. The next year the number increased to 430,213, and in 1973 to 609,573. Paradoxically, as the sweeps were conducted, the United States also proposed the reintroduction of a Bracero Program, which would have involved annually importing some three hundred thousand Mexicano *braceros*. The primary reason it was not enacted was the breaking off of negotiations by México's Echevarria administration. Moreover, as early as 1971 in California, nativists succeeded in passing the Dixon Arnett Act, which fined employers who hired undocumented workers; it was later declared unconstitutional. At the federal level, in 1972, Congressman Peter Rodino (D) from New Jersey introduced legislation that made it a felony to knowingly employ undocumented workers with penalties that ranged from warnings to jail terms for repeated offenders. Senator Edward Kennedy also introduced a similar bill, which included amnesty for those undocumented workers who had been in the country for at least three years, but it was killed in committee.[158] With the end to the war in Vietnam in 1973, the following recession served to fan the fires of nativism even further.

For the next three years, the media with its acrimonious reports nurtured an anti-immigrant hysteria. The resurgent nativism depicted the migrant exodus as an "invasion" of the United States from México. Undocumented workers were often cast as criminals who caused poverty and social problems and took jobs from U.S. workers. By 1976, the political climate was such that Congressman

Joshua Eilberg (D) of Pennsylvania successfully introduced legislation (the Western Hemisphere Act) that extended the preference system and lowered the number of legal immigrants entering the United States from any one Latin American country from 40,000 to 20,000. This was particularly a slap at México, the only Latin American country to send 40,000 annually to the United States. A backlog of 173,000 visa requests from México existed in 1980, which served to further encourage undocumented immigration.[159]

The nativist hysteria was fueled as well by exorbitant INS estimates of the number of undocumented workers. The estimate in 1975 was between four and twelve million, mostly Mexicanos. A year later the estimate was modified to six to eight million; and by 1978, the new INS commissioner, Leonel Castillo, projected a figure of three to six million.[160] These figures fueled the increasingly right-wing activists and politicians who pandered to the fears of the public and intimated that the security of the country was threatened.

As early as 1975, reacting to the influx of immigrants, some U.S. policy makers raised issues of national security. As early as 1975, Arthur Corwin sent a letter to Secretary of State Henry Kissinger in which he demanded that action be taken to halt the incessant migration from Latin America. He argued that the United States was becoming a "welfare reservation" and if it continued the Southwest would become a "Quebec." In addition, he requested that the president militarize and seal the border and that Congress appropriate $1 billion for the INS so that fifty thousand border patrolman could be hired and an electrified fence be built. Although the Ford administration did not heed Corwin's recommendations, nevertheless, it was indicative of the growing vitriolic nativism directed at Mexicanos.

Once again in 1978, the specter of nativism was evident when CIA director William Colby depicted the migrant exodus as the single most serious threat to the security of the United States. He went so far as to equate the influx of Mexicano migrants into the country as a greater threat than that of the Soviet Union. He warned about the possibilities of a Quebecois-like separatist movement emanating from within the Southwest. Senator Alan Simpson echoed Colby's call by alleging that the exodus threatened the country's national unity and stability. Arthur F. Corwin again that year, in an essay cowritten with John M. McCain, reminded the country that undocumented immigration was aiding the militancy of the so-called Chicano. The two authors made the following argument: "Chicano nationalism, sprouting in barrios across the country [United States], and reinforced by mass immigration, works for the political re-conquest of the Southwest by the Mexican race, that is, la raza, and the spiritual restoration of the mythical Aztlán, or the original homeland of the Aztecs."[161]

By 1978 the pressure on Congress to do something about the immigration crisis increased to where a sixteen-member Select Committee on Immigration and Refugee Policy was formed, headed by Reverend Theodore Hesburgh, president of Notre Dame University. After three years of intensive research and numerous hearings, a report was concluded and released in 1981. Some of the more important recommendations included employer sanctions, an amnesty or legalization program, and expansion of the U.S. Border Patrol. By the turn of the decade, nativists continued to voice warnings of the pending "balkanization" of the United States, and the Select Committee's report provided the justification for more stringent immigration laws and more rigid border enforcement. Two years later, the Simpson-Mazzoli legislation was proposed.[162]

The Mexicano Activist Response

In response to the aforementioned nativist attacks, Chicano activists during the 1970s gradually became engaged with the issue of immigration. As early as 1968, Bert Corona was a visionary in realizing that immigration was going to be the new battleground. At the forefront during these years was Corona's CASA-HGT (Centro de Acción Social Autónoma-Hermandad General de Trabajadores, or Center for Autonomous Social Action-General Brotherhood of Workers). However, by the late 1970s the organizational leadership on immigration in California shifted briefly to the Committee on Chicano Rights (CCR), organized by Chicano Movement activist Herman Baca, to be examined extensively in the next chapter. During those early years, it became engaged in a number of immigration-related issues. One such major mobilization occurred against San Diego County sheriff John Duffy, who had issued a referendum calling for taxicab drivers to report alleged "illegals." According to Herman Baca,

> From 1970 to 1976, the issue of immigration grew from an anthill to a Mount Everest issue. The Committee on Chicano Rights, as an advocacy group, became increasingly involved in immigration related issues. This was because of our proximity to the U.S./México border. The issue of immigration itself caused a lot of fear among our people. We saw the undocumented as part of our Chicano community problem. For us, the San Diego border area was the Vietnam of the Southwest.[163]

Yet during the early 1970s, few other Movimiento-oriented organizations had prioritized the issue of immigration. Most activists were wrapped up in building the Raza Unida Party (RUP) or with education, police brutality, and farmworker issues. Resistance against the resurgent nativism did occur. Chicano activists, such as Bert Corona, Herman Baca, and others, effectively opposed both the Dixon-

Arnett bill and at the federal level the Rodino and Kennedy bills, which died in committee. With the decline of the Movimiento activists grappled for a new cause; the issue of immigration got on their radar screen of priorities by 1976.

The National Chicano Forum was held in May 1976 in Salt Lake City, Utah, under my leadership and that of poet Abelardo Delgado; some six hundred activists met. Although the agenda focused on ways of reviving the Chicano Movement, dialogue also occurred on the issue of immigration. However, no major plan of action came out of the forum. It was not until 1977 that mobilization on the evolving immigration crisis began.[164] The precipitating organizing event, under my leadership, was a summit meeting held on May 5 in Ontario, California, attended by some forty-five activist leaders and scholars from throughout Aztlán. A consensus was reached in response to the increasing deportations and opposition to the proposed immigration policy of the Carter administration. A few days after the summit, RUP leader José Angel Gutiérrez was asked to make a "call for action" at a conference called by RUP leaders in Tejas. On May 23 he sent letter to numerous activists throughout the country.[165] In part the letter read: "The Carter Administration is designing a new immigration policy. We are the main targets. The phobia mongers insist our people, because of our numbers, birthrate, geographic spread and undocumented status threaten the very underpinnings of this society."[166]

As a result of the call for action two immigration-related events were held during the latter part of 1977: the National Chicano and Latino Immigration Conference and a mobilization march along the California San Ysidro/Tijuana border. The former was hosted by RUP in Tejas on October 28–30 at the Tropicana Hotel in San Antonio. Some fifteen hundred activists from throughout the country attended the largest conference ever held on immigration. The agenda was to formulate a strategic response to the Carter administration's immigration plan, which included employer sanctions, more stringent border enforcement giving the U.S. Border Patrol expanded police powers, and amnesty to undocumented workers already residents of the United States.[167] In the midst of the debate, however, the participants representing organizations from divergent ideological persuasions came into conflict.

The conflict emanated from the participation of the Socialist Workers Party (SWP) that was at odds with the Maoist August Twenty-ninth Movement (ATM), the Marxist-Leninist CASA, and other Chicano cultural nationalists who were aligned with Gutiérrez's arch rival, Rodolfo "Corky" Gonzales. Opposition to the Left-supported resolutions was further heightened by such HG organizations as LULAC, MALDEF, the National Council of La Raza, and the American G. I. Forum.[168] Despite the outbursts and schisms, a ten-point plan calling for unconditional amnesty of all undocumented workers was endorsed and a call for nationwide protests to take place was made.[169]

At the same time as the National Conference was held, Chicano activists led by Herman Baca and his CCR organized a mobilization march along the San Ysidro/Tijuana U.S./México border. Two factors contributed to the march: a boycott of the National Chicano and Latino Conference and the visit of Ku Klux Klan (KKK) leader David Duke to the San Ysidro/Tijuana border. The CCR was supported by numerous other Chicano activists and leaders, including Rodolfo "Corky" Gonzales, Bert Corona, Abe Tapia, Raul Ruiz, and myself, among others, in promulgating a call for a boycott of the San Antonio conference due to the SWP's participation. Baca released an open declaration condemning the SWP "for not respecting the right of Chicanos to pursue their own struggle for self-determination." Also, a few weeks prior to the march, KKK leader David Duke toured the San Ysidro/Tijuana border with the collaboration of the U.S. Border Patrol. Organized as a media event, it sought to dramatize the so-called invasion of the United States by undocumented workers. Some four thousand infuriated Chicano activists participated in the border mobilization march. It stretched for a few miles along the border in protest against the KKK and specifically against the Carter administration's immigration proposals.

Both the National Conference and the march sparked a contagion of increased activism. For the next year or so, activists from California, from various organizations, such as the CCR; CASA; the National Institute for Community Development (NICD), which I organized and founded; RUP; and others forged an immigration advocacy coalition. Several meetings were held throughout southern California, but by 1979 without resources each group resorted to its own programs. In some instances, however, they briefly coalesced on immigration-related issues. Specifically, from 1977 to 1981, the CCR held three more marches along the San Ysidro/Tijuana border. In 1981 it protested the proposed Simpson-Mazzoli legislation and held its last major mobilization march. When interviewed Baca explained why he decided against holding such a march again: "When we were marching along the border I saw and heard some Border Patrolman mocking the march. It was then that I decided to never return or repeat such a march in a non-violent fashion."[170]

From 1977 to 1992 the NICD, its sister grassroots-based organization, el Congreso para Pueblos Unidos (the Congress for United Communities) and by 1983 the Institute for Social Justice (ISJ), which I also organized, directed numerous direct action mobilizations in southern California.[171] In one particular case, the U.S. Border Patrol in 1977 had gone into Our Lady of Guadalupe Catholic Church in Ontario and apprehended several undocumented workers. Press conferences, letters of protest, meetings with Border Patrol officials, and finally a meeting with INS commissioner Leonel Castillo ended the Border Patrol's "gestapo-like raids," at least for a time, in San Bernardino/Riverside counties. During the ensuing years, numerous mobilizations on immigration occurred.

While a few of the remaining activists during the late 1970s responded to the growing nativist attacks, the media and government officials pandered to the fears of the people by arguing that so-called illegal immigration was out of control. As a result of the increased pressure, Congress in 1978 created a sixteen-person Select Commission on Immigration and Refugees. After conducting considerable research and holding hearings in some dozen cities, in March of 1981, it released its findings in a final report, which essentially purported some of the major planks of the Carter Plan, for example, employer sanctions, expanded U.S. Border Patrol, and an amnesty or a legalization program.[172] When the report was released the Bureau of the Census claimed that there were between 3.5 million and 6 million undocumented immigrants. The commission was under the misconception that these measures would curb the influx of undocumented immigrants into the country and failed to acknowledge the real culprit—liberal capitalism.

During the early part of the 1980s, the issue of immigration continued to elicit a nefarious nativist response. This xenophobic atmosphere throughout the country made the undocumented worker the "scapegoat" for many of the country's socioeconomic ills. There was a growing paranoia of an alleged "invasion" of undocumented immigrants into the United States. In 1983 alone, the number of undocumented immigrants arrested and deported dramatically increased to some 1,250,000. Republican president Ronald Reagan further added to the nativist alarm by stating in 1984, "We have lost control of our borders."[173] The political reality was that both Democrats and Republicans collaborated in pushing for federal legislation to deal with what was perceived to be a growing crisis.

Nativist politicians used the commission's recommendations in 1982 to draft the Simpson-Mazzoli immigration reform legislation, which became a locus of debate for the next two years. Essentially a takeoff on the Carter Plan employer sanctions, expansion of the U.S. Border Patrol, and an amnesty or legalization program it also included an absolute annual limit on immigration, including first-preference immigrants. The debates over the proposed legislation were exacerbated when some nativists also proposed a national identity card and a *bracero*-like guest worker program (the H-2 program) that provided for the importation of seasonal workers from México and the Caribbean in case of a labor shortage. Republican senator S. I. Hayakawa also sought unsuccessfully to attach an "English as the official language" provision.[174] A number of non-Mexicanos, that is, civil libertarian, human rights, and church groups categorically opposed it, especially the employer sanctions and the guest worker aspects of the legislation.

With few exceptions, most Mexicano activists and organizations strongly opposed it. La Hermandad Nacional Mexicana, the CCR, LULAC, MALDEF, the National Council of La Raza, the CPU, MAPA, and other organizations across the country strongly lobbied against various aspects of its provisions. In opposition to Simpson-Mazzoli, KMEX television station general manager Danny Villanueva and MALDEF general counsel Vilma Martinez held three summit meetings in 1984 in Washington, D.C.; Denver, Colorado; and Los Angeles, California. The focus of the three summits was to formulate a strategy to defeat the Simpson-Mazzoli legislation. At the Los Angeles summit, attended by such leaders as Henry Cisneros, Tony Bonilla, Mario Obledo, and some thirty others including myself, a strategy was agreed upon, which included picketing the Democratic Convention and a heavy lobbying campaign specifically directed at Democratic presidential candidate Walter Mondale to get him to oppose the legislation, which he did.[175]

Yet, some activist organizations did support some of the anti-immigrant provisions. Initially, the American G.I. Forum supported restricted immigration and increased support for the U.S. Border Patrol. Later, it changed its posture and supported the amnesty provision. Cesar Chavez's UFW at the onset also supported Simpson-Mazzoli, but due to increased pressure from other Mexicano organizations, activists, and leaders, it modified its support for immigration restrictions. Also in support of the measure was the Congressional Hispanic Caucus. Ultimately the effectiveness of the combined pressures by both non-Mexicano and Mexicano organizations succeeded in 1984 in preventing its passage.

After two years of additional debate, in November 1986, a compromise measure, the Immigration and Control Act (IRCA-Simpson-Rodino Act), was passed by Congress and signed by President Reagan. IRCA sought to control the influx of undocumented immigration in four ways: through the use of employer sanctions, which entailed the use of fines and even incarceration; via amnesty and eligibility of citizenship of undocumented immigrants who had lived continuously in the United States since January 1, 1982; through a Special Agricultural Worker program, for those who had worked a minimum of ninety days in the United States in agriculture between May 1985 and May 1986;[176] and through strengthening of the U.S. Border Patrol. IRCA also had provisions to safeguard and investigate any violations of law particularly against the rights of Mexicanos and Central Americans.[177]

Whereas the opposition to Simpson-Mazzoli by Mexicanos in 1984 was well organized, strong, and effective, the opposition to IRCA in 1986 was divided and ineffective. The offer of amnesty defused the efforts of those activists who opposed it, such as Herman Baca's CCR whereas some long-time activists, such as Bert Corona's La Hermandad Mexican, among others, strongly supported its passage. With the passage of IRCA, numerous former advocates of immigration made their transition to the service program arena. With the federal government's allocation of some $1 billion to IRCA's amnesty component, for four years, agencies solicited grants to provide classes in English, U.S. history, and government, mandatory for amnesty applicants. These federal funds created an effective form of co-optation, which diminished the community's capacity to advocate for their rights. Some 2.96 million had applied for amnesty by January 1989 of which some 70 percent were Mexicanos.[178]

IRCA, however, did not stop the migrant exodus. The reality was that IRCA only temporarily slowed it down. By the late 1980s, the migrant exodus resumed with greater intensity. As early as 1987 the numbers of undocumented migrants continued to increase and by 1988 they were up to pre-IRCA levels. By 1991 the U.S. Border Patrol apprehended some 1.13 million, and this figure increased in 1992 to 1.5 million.[179]

The continued migrant influx increased the level of nativism directed against them. Nativist politicians continued their migrant bashing attacks and continued to make immigration a wedge issue. Dallas mayor pro tem Jim Hart in 1986 warned voters that undocumented immigrants had no "moral values" and alleged that they were destroying Dallas neighborhoods and presented a security threat to the city. That same year in California an "English Only" initiative passed overwhelmingly, and by the mid-1990s, seventeen states had approved similar legislation.[180] California Republican congressman Elton Gallegly unsuccessfully proposed a constitutional amendment that would have denied citizenship to U.S.-born children of undocumented immigrants. Democrats as well got caught up in the nativist fervor. California congressman Anthony Bielson, considered a progressive Democrat, supported the nativist amendment.[181] Colorado governor Richard Lamn's controversial book *The Immigration Time Bomb* portrayed particularly Mexicano migrants as a threat to the country's economy and "way of life." KKK leader David Metzger's *White Aryan Resistance* directed its xenophobic efforts against migrants in California. These and other nativists argued that migrants were responsible for soaring crime rates, unemployment, displacement of the U.S. workers, rising welfare costs, and moral decay.[182]

The result was that much of the 1990s produced a crescendo of nativist attacks on Mexicanos. In fact, it was during this decade that in California migrants politically came under attack by nativist-inspired initiatives and policies. At the federal level, a number of policy actions designed to curb illegal immigration were initiated. Both the Bush and subsequently Clinton administrations pushed for the militarization of the U.S./México border. This was done in the context of an economic recession, a growing perception of socioeconomic insecurity and on images of an existent U.S./México border crisis that was out of control.[183] As early as 1990, the first Bush administration approved the building of an eleven-mile-long fence along the San Ysidro/Tijuana border area as part of its Operation Gatekeeper. Two years later, the Clinton administration installed floodlights along a thirteen-mile stretch. Attorney General Janet Reno also approved accelerated raids and blockades of the San Diego and El Paso border areas. In nationalizing such actions, Democratic president Bill Clinton stated, "In this decade, [immigration] will be the single most difficult problem we face together."

The Militarization of the U.S./México Border
With the nativist hysteria increasing manipulated by the media, efforts to militarize the border increased by 1993. In Tejas, Silvestre Reyes, the U.S. Border Patrol chief of the El Paso sector, arbitrarily launched "Operation Blockade," subsequently renamed "Hold-the-Line." In a well-publicized show of force, Reyes deployed four hundred agents and their vehicles along the twenty-mile stretch marking the El Paso/Ciudad Juarez border and inspections at official ports of entry were intensified. The strategy represented a major shift. Instead of the U.S. Border Patrol waiting to apprehend undocumented migrants after they crossed into the United States, the intent was to stop them before they crossed. With a dramatic decrease in apprehensions, INS border chief Gustavo De La Viña and the heads of San Diego County and city police departments called for increased federal funding for border enforcement. Governor Pete Wilson joined the political bandwagon and called for the implementation of a similar operation along the Tijuana/San Ysidro border area.[184]

The Clinton administration initiated its war against illegal immigration in 1994 by militarizing the 1,900-mile-long U.S./México border. Pressured by the nativist politicians of California, it buckled under the pressure and instituted the heinous and racist "Operation Gatekeeper." Similar to the "Hold the Line" Operation in El Paso, Tejas, its geographical focus was the San Ysidro/Tijuana border, which became ground zero in Clinton's anti-immigrant war.[185] Joseph Nevens further explains, "Opportunistic politicians and nativist organizations presented the 'illegal' immigrant not only as a lawbreaker, but more importantly, as a threat to national sovereignty and the American social and economic fabric. Such imagery is rooted in the history of largely race-based anti-immigrant sentiment in California and, more generally, the United States."[186]

Funded for $300 million, Operation Gatekeeper was designed to fortify and seal the U.S/México border between Tijuana and San Ysidro, California. Based upon a "prevention through deterrence" approach, it entailed the construction of a Berlin-type of iron curtain, deployment of more U.S. Border patrolmen, placement of electronic monitoring equipment, utilization of helicopters and ultimately aircraft for surveillance, and use of the U.S. military and National Guard troops in a supportive role in border enforcement. The use of military personnel was justified under the federal government's so-called War on Drugs. In explaining its impact Wayne Cornelius writes, "Gatekeeper has sought to force crossings into the much less hospitable, mountainous terrain in the eastern portion of San Diego County and into the desert of neighboring Imperial County." Furthermore, it theorized that preventing the entry of the undocumented migrants would deter them from leaving their place of origin, and that those who did reach the border and failed to cross would become so discouraged that they would return home.[187]

Between 1994 and 1999, the Clinton administration expedited the militarization of the U.S./México border by implementing two other similar operations.[188] Right after Operation Gatekeeper was instituted, "Operation Safeguard" was launched in Nogales, Arizona. Two years later in the southern part of the Tejas U.S./México border "Operation Rio Grande" was implemented. The Clinton administration also increased the size of the U.S. Border Patrol by 45 percent between 1993 and 1996, and Attorney General Janet Reno was appointed the "Border Czar" of all enforcement efforts. In September 1996, President Clinton signed the Illegal Immigration Reform and Immigration Act that nearly doubled the U.S. Border Patrol; by the year 2001 the patrol would increase from 5,175 to nearly 10,000. The new legislation also called for more stringent enforcement measures such as the building of a triple iron fence along the fourteen-mile Tijuana/San Ysidro border. The penalties for undocumented smuggling were also increased.[189] Even legal immigration came under heavy scrutiny. The INS in 1998 reported that legal immigration dropped to 637,000, its lowest level in a decade. It reflected a 17 percent drop from 1997 and a 28 percent drop from the year before.[190]

The results of the militarization efforts proved ineffective in curbing the migrant exodus. Although illegal entry was more dangerous and difficult, no evidence existed that supported the overall effectiveness of enforcement despite an INS budget that by 1999 had swelled to $3.9 billion. The number of total border apprehensions increased from 1,212,886 in 1993 to 1,368,707 in 1997, an increase of 12 percent. By the end of the 1998 fiscal year, the total number increased to 1,527,000. It was estimated that in 1999 there were some 5.5 million undocumented migrants, a figure that increased annually by at least 275,000.[191]

While proponents of Operation Gatekeeper claimed success in apprehensions along their particular border sectors, the fact was that the migrant exodus moved east to other areas of the U.S./México border. Migrants shifted to the east, toward dangerous snake and scorpion-infested desert areas of the Arizona and California border. In the Nogales/Douglas sector of Arizona, the entry of some four hundred thousand was reported, while in California's San Ysidro/Tijuana sector the number dramatically decreased to less than two hundred thousand. Moreover, in California's Imperial County sector some ninety-five deaths were recorded in 1998, more than in any other border region of the country. However, by August 1999, the number of dead was at sixty-four. Yet previously, in 1995 only six had perished, twelve in 1996, and thirty-nine in 1997. The deaths were due to dehydration in the oppressive summer heat, canal drowning, crime-related incidents, and other accidents.[192]

The militarization of the border by the late 1990s became a powder keg, fueled by the growing violence perpetrated against undocumented migrants. Increasing numbers became victims of numerous crimes, that is, robbery, rape, assault, and murder, along the various border sectors. Some migrants became victims of the U.S. Border Patrol and U.S. military personnel. There were a number of Border Patrol shootings of migrants from Tejas to California. Even the military was not exempt from such incidents. One such incident occurred in 1997, when a U.S. Marine, a Mexicano enlisted man, shot and killed eighteen-year-old Ezequiel Hernandez, who allegedly was mistaken for a drug trafficker while tending his family's goat herd.[193] After an inquiry, the marine, a Mexicano, was exonerated.

By the end of 1999, migrants also faced persecution and violence by armed white vigilante ranchers, specifically on the Arizona and Tejas side of the border. With the migrants perceived as "invaders," they became increasingly engaged in a well-publicized campaign to apprehend and detain them as they crossed their properties, and deliver them to the U.S. Border Patrol.[194] In some cases, the xenophobic ranchers resorted to the use of violence; some undocumented migrants were beaten, shot, and wounded. By the turn of the century, a climate of warfare permeated much of the U.S./México border.

While the Clinton administration pushed for the militarization of the border in California, nativist forces accelerated their political offensive against immigrants in general. Their emergence was quite evident as early as 1986 with their success of Proposition 63, "the English Only Initiative," which passed by a three to one margin, making English the official language in California. By the early 1990s, California was caught up in a devastating recession. Latinos' unprecedented population growth served to enhance nativist fears of "La Reconquista of Aztlán." Nativist forces led by Republican governor Pete Wilson and a number of right-wing organizations, for example, Voices of Citizens Together and Federation for American Immigration Reform accelerated their "migrant bashing" campaign from 1993 to 1998. During the ensuing years, they were successful in pushing through three racist-inspired propositions.

California's Nativist Propositions: 187, 209, and 227

PROPOSITION 187   By 1994 the nativists blamed the state's socioeconomic ills on scapegoat migrants, especially those from México. Using a highly vitriolic rhetoric, they alleged that a Mexican invasion of the Southwest was in progress. Manipulating the fears of the largely white conservative electorate, nativist forces were successful in placing the draconian SOS (Save Our State) Initiative on the 1994 ballot, otherwise known as Proposition 187. In the midst of a gubernatorial election, Governor Pete Wilson endorsed and used it effectively to politically pander to the growing racial fears of the white electorate. As a result, Latinos, but Mexicanos in particular, came under siege by nativist forces. Proposition 187 proponents proclaimed that "we" must be "saved" from "illegal aliens" and their "invasion." The punitive effects of Proposition 187 were twofold: it sought to deny public education (from primary to postsecondary levels) to children of migrant parents, regardless if they were U.S. citizens, and it sought to deny social services, and health care, with the exception of emergency services, to undocumented migrants. The measure also sought to have local law enforcement agencies report and turn in to the INS suspected undocumented migrants and expedite the deportation of migrant criminals.[195]

The racist political climate was such that even Democrats added to it. California U.S. senatorial candidate Dianne Feinstein ran an ad in which she claimed that some three thousand so-called illegals crossed the border each night. Although most Democrats opposed Proposition 187, their opposition was lukewarm. The fact was the great majority of the electorate supported it, and this included some Latinos. In September, a *Los Angeles Times* poll showed that 52 percent of Latinos supported it. In spite of the opposition, in November, Proposition 187 passed with 59 percent of the votes cast. Two out of three whites (67 percent) voted for it, while nearly half of both African Americans and Asian American voters supported it; and only 23 percent of Latinos voted for it.[196] The passage of Proposition 187 sent a powerful nativist symbolic message: white voters expressed their concern and anger if not their racism on the related issues of immigration and the growing Latino population. The passage of Proposition 187 increased a nativist discrimination against Latino migrants across the country.

Proposition 187 was quickly challenged in the courts by MALDEF. In 1995, a federal judge struck down the provision of the law that denied public services to undocumented migrants. Also, in 1996 nativists failed in their attempts to put on the ballot another initiative called "Save Our State," which sought to deny citizenship to children born in the United States of undocumented migrant parents. After years of political and legal pressure, newly elected Democratic governor Gray Davis in 1999 abandoned any further court proceedings on the contested proposition. The only provision that was maintained was the one that pertained to penalties for the production and use of fraudulent immigration documents.[197] According to Oscar Martinez, "The burial of Proposition 187 marked one of the most significant political victories ever achieved by Latinos/as in the Golden state."

PROPOSITION 209   The second nativist issue that impacted the Mexicano political experience during this epoch was the attack on affirmative action. While nativists continued their siege on the immigration issue, by 1995 and well into 1996, they also directed their political guns at affirmative action. Now the population under siege was California's "people of color." After nearly thirty years of promoting the principle of "equal opportunity" in employment and contract compliance, affirmative action programs[198] came under attack in California again from ultra-right-wing nativist forces, which sought its termination. For years challenges to affirmative action had been commonplace and had intensified, particularly since the infamous U.S. Supreme Court decision of 1978, of *Regents of the University of California v. Bakke*. In a five to four decision, based upon the 1964 Civil Rights Act, the U.S. Supreme Court ruled that "race" could not be used as the sole criterion for admission; consequently, it struck down alleged quotas or "preferential admissions." However, it did allow race to be taken into consideration as one of the several "plus" factors designed to enhance the diversity of a school's student body.[199] During the ensuing post-*Bakke* years, affirmative action came under increasing scrutiny and attacks by white conservatives.

During the 1990s, affirmative action became a political wedge issue. In college admissions, the post-*Bakke* years showed some improvement for people of color, but improvements were erratic. According to Susan Welch and John Gruhl, "The number of minorities in medical and law schools showed little increase during the decade from 1976 to 1986." They explain that it was "less than 0.5 percent in the case of black medical, nearly 1 percent for Hispanics, and close to 3 percent for both in law schools." Yet between 1987 and 1994, black and Latino college enrollments increased. For Latinos, overall college enrollments increased by over 50 percent, as did the number of bachelor's degrees awarded. Increases in master's degrees occurred as well, and the number of PhDs granted increased by some 30 percent. In professional schools the number of Latinos and blacks increased by some 50 and 40 percent, respectively. While not a panacea, affirmative action programs did make a difference in admissions.[200]

With nativist forces in California savoring their victory with Proposition 187 they next turned to attacks on affirmative action programs. Just as with Proposition 187, which had been in great part driven by white fears about the state's rapidly growing minority population, nativists also played their race and ethnic cards. The vitriolic assaults on affirmative action reached an apogee in 1996 with a new initiative on the California ballot, Proposition 209, designated the "California Civil Rights Initiative (CCRI)." The University of California Regents in 1995, supported by Governor Wilson, an ex-officio member, voted to prohibit affirmative action preferences in admissions, employment, and contracts.[201] That same year, two white scholars, Glynn Custard and Thomas Wood, wrote the CCRI and successfully got it on the ballot as an initiative. The racist initiative defined affirmative action as "preferential treatment" in employment and contract compliance, which was forbidden on the basis of race, sex, ethnicity, or national origin.[202]

Anti-affirmative action zealots alleged that affirmative action discriminated against whites who were better qualified, and that it was unconstitutional as it applied to California's public institutions.

At the helm of the nativist leadership was UC regent Ward Connerly, who was black and was supported by the California Association of Scholars, Republicans, Governor Pete Wilson, Voices of Citizens Together (VCT), and others. Again, with President Clinton running for reelection, Democrats failed to mount an effective counteroffensive because of their fear of alienating white voters. Only toward the end of the campaign did the Democratic Party take a more active stance against the measure.[203] While the electorate voted 54 percent in favor to 46 percent against the measure, Latinos voted three to one against it.[204]

PROPOSITION 227   Nativist groups and politicians in 1998 continued their relentless siege and again demonstrated their power within the electoral arena. Proposition 227, insidiously called the "English for the Children" initiative, qualified in December 1997 for the ensuing June ballot.[205] Its paramount goal was to dismantle bilingual education programs in public schools. Specifically, Proposition 227 called for students with limited English skills to receive a year of intensive English instruction or "immersion" and then be moved to regular English classes. Few exceptions would be allowed, and educators who violated its provisions could be sued. In addition, it would take effect two months after its passage.[206] It was estimated that out of the 1.4 million students in California who needed help learning English, 80 percent were Latino.[207]

For Mexicanos in particular, bilingual education coupled with its bicultural component was the product of the activism of the Movimiento. Impelled by Chicanismo, activists sought to create a Mexicano that was truly bilingual and bicultural. Yet by the 1990s, the bicultural component had long been dropped, and bilingual education evolved to where it was merely a transition vehicle from Spanish into English. To nativists bilingual education presented a serious threat to their "English Only" cultural hegemony. Hence, Proposition 227, like the two previous racist propositions, was a reaction by nativists to the escalating "rebrowning of California." Even at the federal level, nativist politicians such as Republican house speaker Newt Gingrich, who had presidential aspirations, launched a withering attack on bilingual education in January as part of a seventeen-state tour. In one of his many pronouncements on the issue, Gingrich stated, "The fact is English is the common commercial language of America" and argued for "English immersion."[208]

At the helm of the antibilingual education nativist leadership was Silicone Valley millionaire Ron Unz, who paradoxically had opposed Proposition 187. Nativist governor Pete Wilson, Los Angeles mayor Richard Riordan, and other Republicans openly supported the passage of Proposition 227. Even though Republicans had almost unanimously supported Propositions 187 and 209, some were cognizant of the growing Latino electoral strength, and a few Republican politicians chose not to support 227. One such Republican politician was candidate for attorney general Dan Lungren. Again as was the case with two previous propositions, Democrats did little to help defeat the measure. The Clinton administration, after much internal debate, did not openly oppose Proposition 227 until late April.[209] Democrats in California, including Latino legislators, vacillated on the issue, but finally a few weeks prior to the election went against it. The nativist-inspired electorate approved Proposition 227 by a landslide 61 percent. Whites overwhelmingly supported it, while Latinos opposed it by a two to one margin: 63 percent voted against it and 37 percent voted in favor, which was still a significant share.[210]

Latino Resistance to Nativist Propositions

The resistance from Latinos and Mexicanos to the nativist siege was slow in coming. During the early years of the 1990s, few advocacy groups were functional, and those few neither had the desire or capacity to mount an effective countermobilization. A cardinal reason was that too many former immigrant advocacy groups had become social service providers. With millions of dollars for natural-ization programs from the federal government, few were willing to jeopardize their funding. This dependency on federal funding discouraged them from reas-serting their role as advocates for undocumented migrants. A second reason was that few were willing to speak out, and most did not have an organized power base. As will be explained in the next chapter, the nativist siege caught the Mexi-cano community in its weakest stage of organization and leadership. The counter-attacks against the nativist attacks were largely ineffectual and defensive. But in late 1993, with the introduction of Proposition 187, Mexicanos and Latinos began to heighten their involvement.

On January 6, 7, and 8, 1994, a National Summit Conference on Immigra-tion was held at the University of California, Riverside, by the newly formed Ernesto Galarza Public Think Tank on Public Policy (EGTTPP) of which I was founder and director. Held at Riverside's Raincross Square Convention Center, some 450 scholars, leaders, politicians, activists, and others gathered to address nativist immigrant bashing at both the state and national levels. The summit received state, national, and international media coverage. Numerous speakers addressed the summit in a number of panels held on aspects of the immigration crisis. Former Nuevo México governor Toney Anaya gave the summit keynote address, reminding participants of the many positive contributions immigrants had made to the country and to their communities. He also emphasized that Latinos should use their numbers and purchasing influence to exert their political power on the matter. Former Raza Unida Party leader José Angel Gutiérrez took issue with Governor Wilson's proposal to deny citizenship to children born to undocumented residents in the United States, despite its being a constitutional right.

In reference to the immigration debate, California state senator Richard Polanco warned summit participants that it was "going to get ugly this year. There's been a lot of political posturing, and it's hardening and polarizing our communities." And in my address, I reminded them that in order to counter the nativist siege Latinos needed to "mobilize and get reorganized," that only through the formation of "grassroots coalitions" committed to "mobilizations of direct and electoral action" was there a chance of defeating Proposition 187.[211] The culmination of the three-day summit was "El Plan de Riverside."[212]

Later at a press conference and rally held at Olvera Street in Los Angeles in February, in the presence of scores of Mexicano activists and organizational representatives, "El Plan de Riverside" was formally unveiled. It was released simultaneously at other similar events in California, Tejas, Nuevo México, and Illinois. At a press conference in Los Angeles, the participants called for a mobilization against the nativist "immigrant bashing" forces. The main message conveyed was that if Mexicanos and Latinos did not respond and get organized, the anti-immigrant hysteria would worsen. The sixteen-page plan of action called on Latino lawmakers and advocacy groups to launch a concerted election year lobbying, an education and media campaign against nativist "xenophobic attacks." The plan was critical of the militarization of the U.S./México border and attacked both Democratic California U.S. senators Dianne Feinstein and Barbara Boxer for their stand on activating the California National Guard to assist the U.S. Border Patrol in controlling undocumented immigration at the border. The summit contributed to mobilizing Latinos against Proposition 187.[213]

In California, the racism of Proposition 187 engendered an unprecedented number of Latino mobilizations for the November elections. Endorsed by the summit, La Coordinadora, a coalition of organizations under the direction of One Stop Immigration, a local immigration service/advocacy agency from Los Angeles, in February held a march in Los Angeles that drew some six thousand. On May 28, La Coordinadora again held a second march and rally in Los Angeles; this time it drew some eighteen thousand protestors. During September and October in protest against Proposition 187, thousands of high school students in various parts of the state initiated spontaneous one-day walkouts waving Mexicano flags. Acuña cites that in the San Fernando Valley alone some ten thousand students walked out from thirty-nine schools.[214]

On October 16 in Los Angeles, downtown at City Hall, La Coordinadora made history by holding the largest march and demonstration ever in the history of the Mexicano political experience. Estimates of the size of the crowd ranged from seventy-five thousand to one hundred thousand. Many of the marchers carried placards, banners, and Mexican flags and displayed an ardent nationalist fervor. Some Latino moderate *politicos* and organizations voiced their concern that such a display of Mexicano nationalism served to alienate and anger white voters. Undeterred, several other anti-187 marches and demonstrations were organized throughout the state by a number of organizations and coalitions. In response, in November, on election eve, a concert was held at East Los Angeles City College, attended by some ten thousand "U.S. flag waving people" protesting Proposition 187.[215] In spite of the numerous mobilizations, Proposition 187 passed overwhelmingly. Its passage fostered an unprecedented contagion of nativist efforts in various parts of the country. In Arizona and other states during the remaining years of the decade, other nativist propositions were initiated.

With the passage of Proposition 187, immigration continued to be the wedge issue among many activists. On January 13 and 14, 1995, the EGTTPP held at the University of California, Riverside, its second national summit conference entitled "The Immigration Crisis, Proposition 187: A Post Election Policy Analysis on Its Implications." Some five hundred activists, academicians, leaders, politicians, and community leaders met to decide what needed to be done to counteract the passage of Proposition 187. The second summit took on the spirit of a Movimiento revival since several former activist leaders such as Reies Lopez Tijerina, José Angel Gutiérrez, Herman Baca, and numerous others, spoke and addressed the summit. As with the first, the second EGTTPP summit received wide media national and international coverage. At the summit I presented a plan of action entitled "Post 187 Strategy for Mobilization," which called for the formation of a National Latino United Front, and a combination of direct action and electoral mobilizations, including a national march on Washington, D.C.; a resource development fund; a revitalization of the student organizations; and securing international linkages and support.[216]

Not long after Proposition 187's passage, a number of lawsuits were filed by MALDEF to stop its implementation. For the next five years, it remained caught up in legal challenges. It was not until 1999 when newly elected Democratic governor Gray Davis effectively killed the implementation of Proposition 187 after years of legal wrangling. Davis agreed not to appeal an earlier court ruling that held that the initiative was unconstitutional, which precluded lawyers on both sides from taking it to the U.S. Supreme Court. The nativists reacted to Davis's decision with anger. President of the nativist Voices of Citizens Together said, "Davis sold his soul for the Hispanic vote, and now he is paying for it."[217]

During 1996, the nativists continued their anti-immigrant crusade. While their main focus in California shifted to pushing the anti-affirmative action initiative, their attacks on immigrants in general continued. At the national level, inspired by the passage of Proposition 187, Congress raised the nativist banner and passed new legislation that restricted immigration and reduced benefits for immigrants. One such piece of legislation was the Immigration and Financial Responsibility Act of 1996. It significantly expanded the INS's enforcement capacity, increased penalties for smugglers and those who produced fraudulent papers, stipulated immediate deportation of migrants with criminal records, and granted states the authority to deny services and benefits to undocumented migrants. Specifically, under the new law, migrants' access to the courts was limited and their rights to judicial review were restricted.[218] A second law was the Personal Responsibility and Work Opportunity Reconciliation Act, which incorporated new restrictions on health, social security, and welfare entitlements formerly extended to legal immigrants.[219] Up for reelection that year, President Clinton acted out of political expediency and signed the restrictionist immigration legislation. In desperation, his Republican rival, Senator Robert Dole, adopted a pro-nativist posture on the issue of immigration.

In California, Governor Pete Wilson continued his "immigrant bashing" offensive with his attempts to cut off food stamps to some four hundred thousand legal immigrants and prenatal care to undocumented migrants.[220] Indicative of the violence suffered by some migrants, a beating incident occurred in April 1996 that was recorded on the television cameras of a news helicopter: Riverside County sheriffs viciously pounded with their batons two migrants while others ran for cover following a dramatic chase on a Los Angeles freeway. One of the officers was fired and the other was suspended.[221]

Meanwhile, the anti-immigrant climate continued and so did the migrant exodus. A small number of pro-immigrant groups and activists focused their limited resources on lobbying for a new amnesty program. During the Republican National Convention held in San Diego, California, a coalition of organizations and individuals that I had organized in 1988, under the aegis of IMPACTO 2000, held a rally and march on August 10 at the San Ysidro/Tijuana border area to protest to the Republican nativist anti-immigrant politics. With nearly one thousand protestors in attendance, the rally held at the San Geronimo Ranch featured numerous speakers and protest music. The nearly five-mile-long march traveled along the "iron curtain" portion of the border and culminated with a short rally at Border Field Park.[222] The protests at the border were part of the dozens of demonstrations held in downtown San Diego by numerous protest groups, including nativists such as Voices of Citizens Together. A second "Marcha de la Reconquista" organized by MEChA students from San Diego had started weeks before in Sacramento, traveled to San Diego, and culminated with a protest demonstration. The San Diego Federation, an umbrella social service-type organization, also held a daylong National Latino Leadership Summit to denounce the "politics of scapegoating" and to foster a voter mobilization for November.[223]

The transient activism that had surfaced in 1996 culminated in October with the first Latino National March on Washington, D.C. Under the organizing auspices of La Coordinadora, the march was in support of immigrant rights. With crowd estimates ranging from twenty-five thousand to fifty thousand, Latinos from throughout the country gathered for a one-day show of Latino power.[224]

During the ensuing years, Latino advocacy efforts were largely defensive rather than offensive in nature. La Coordinadora continued to build up its national immigration network and lobbied for unconditional amnesty. In advancing its *politica sin fronteras* (politics without borders), in February 1997 it was successful in negotiating with México's leading political parties the "Pacto de

Californias," which focused on improving protection for the human and labor rights of immigrants in the United States.[225] In March 1997, under my leadership, IMPACTO 2000 made a call for action against Voices of Citizen Together, which had held a large demonstration in support of the U.S. Border Patrol and Operation Gatekeeper at Howard Lane Park in San Diego. With some two hundred people in attendance, a picket was set up and a press conference held. The two adversarial groups exchange taunts and racial epithets while separated by a police barrier and uniformed police.[226] Roberto Martinez from the American Friends Committee in San Diego recorded the innumerable abuses of migrants at the hands of the U.S. Border Patrol.

The political response of Latinos in California to CCRI was at best lackadaisical. While MALDEF and a few other organizations spoke out against the measure, no groundswell occurred to mobilize against it, unlike with Proposition 187. "Unfortunately," explains Acuña, "the Latino community did not organize marches of any magnitude against Proposition 209."[227] While some events, such as rallies, colloquia, and conferences were held at universities, no major student mobilizations occurred. As usual, most Latino politicians procrastinated and failed to exercise their leadership on the issue.

With the passage of Proposition 209, California continued to be a pacesetter for the exportation of nativist propositions and legislation. By 1998 a version of Proposition 209 was passed in the state of Washington. In Tejas, the U.S. Court of Appeals for the Fifth Circuit stunned the country with its "Hopwood decision." They held that the affirmative action plan devised by the University of Texas School of Law could not be constitutionally justified as a remedy for past educational discrimination by the school or by the state of Tejas itself as a justification of diversity. In other words, the Hopwood decision dismissed the role of race as a diversifying characteristic in law school admissions.[228] By the late 1990s, the nativist contagion against affirmative action had spread: the University of Michigan had two lawsuits pending vis-à-vis its affirmative action programs, the University of Washington had a similar suit dealing with affirmative action, and Ward Connerly sought to get an anti-affirmative action initiative on the ballot in Florida. In December 1999, with the support of Republican governor Jeb Bush, Florida's Board of Regents put an end to affirmative action in the state's ten public universities. The Bush plan prohibited the use of race in admissions in state universities, but guaranteed admission to the top one-fifth of graduates of every high school.[229]

The ill effects of Proposition 209 and the Hopwood decision continued to negatively impact Latino student enrollments. From 1996 to 1999, the number of Latino, black, and Native American students decreased dramatically. Within

California's UC system, figures indicated a drop of underrepresented minorities from 17.5 percent of the freshman fall class in 1997 to 15.6 percent of the fall class of 1998. The detrimental effects of Proposition 209 were more evident at UC Berkeley and UCLA. The former during the fall of 1998 accepted 66 percent fewer blacks and nearly 53 percent fewer Latinos, while the latter admitted 43 percent fewer blacks and 33 percent fewer Latinos.[230] According to a report released by the Tomás Rivera Policy Institute in November 1999, acceptance rates for the school year at UC campuses were down for Latinos. The study concluded that the elimination of race and ethnicity as considerations for admissions caused an increase of 39 percent in the rejection of Latino freshman applications.[231] Latino enrollment at UC Berkeley by 1999 had fallen by some 34 percent during the past two years, and was down 57 percent for blacks.[232] According to Jorge Chapa, "For Chicanos, the most underrepresented Latinos, fall enrollments fell from 385 in 1997 to 219 in 1999."[233]

In response to the Hopwood decision, the Tejas state legislature in 1997 passed new legislation, "The Top 10 Percent Plan." It required all Tejas public universities to automatically admit high school students who graduate in the top 10 percent of their class. In 1998, in response to the draconian impact of Proposition 209 on admissions, the UC regents adopted the so-called Top 4 Percent Plan, which made eligible the top 4 percent of graduates from each California high school for admittance into the UC system.[234] That same year, Democratic governor Gray Davis vetoed a bill for outreach programs for the recruitment of minorities and women and supported former governor Wilson's executive order of cutting off information gathering on contracts with minorities and women. Thus, the nativist crusade, not satisfied with their attacks on immigration and affirmative action, next targeted bilingual education.

Latino resistance to Proposition 227 was nothing to applaud about; it was mediocre at best. Assembly Speaker Antonio Villaraigosa, state senator Richard Polanco, and Congressman Estaban Torres, among a few others, waited until just a few weeks prior to the June election to come out strong in opposition to the measure. None of the so-called national Latino organizations did much organizing against the measure; most provided largely symbolic opposition. MALDEF was the exception in that it provided the most visible and vociferous opposition. There were other non-Latino organizations, such as the American Civil Liberties Union (ACLU) and California Teachers Association (CTA) that ardently opposed it. Latinos by and large failed to galvanize a sufficient critical electoral mass to defeat the measure.[235] The impact of the HG, particularly from those who propounded assimilation, became evident in the divided stance on the issue. In April of 1998, just two months prior to the primary election, a *Los Angeles Times* poll taken revealed that some 50 percent of Latino voters supported it and 32 percent opposed it.[236] Even hero teacher Jaime Escalante, who achieved national fame for his ability to produce top Latino students in math and was depicted in the film *Stand and Deliver*, supported the anti-bilingual initiative.[237]

Prior to the June election, only a few coalitions resisted the measure; press conferences, demonstrations, and conferences were held denouncing the measure. Although Mexicano and Latino activism against Proposition 227 did surface, again it occurred too late to make a difference. Overall, it was too little too late: they were poorly organized and failed to foster massive direct action or an electoral mobilization. In June, in Los Angeles just before the election, some five hundred students, mostly from Belmont High School walked out of class for a day to protest what they perceived to be a racist initiative. The walkout was ostensibly spontaneous; it lacked planning, organization, and its impact ostensibly was symbolic. A few students were arrested, but the walkouts failed to create other walkouts or mobilizations.[238]

With the approval of Proposition 227 by the electorate, a number of civil rights organizations led largely by MALDEF and ACLU days after the election initiated a legal challenge to block its implementation. The suit alleged that the initiative was unconstitutional and violated federal laws guaranteeing equal access to education.[239] California State Board of Education officials announced that requests for exemptions from the law would be denied.[240] That July, a federal judge refused to halt its implementation, which cleared the way for its enactment. Some school districts sought to maintain a semblance of bilingual education via the use of waivers. As law, it provided for the use of a waiver, providing parents requested to keep their children in bilingual classes, if the student already knew English, was at least ten years old, and had special physical, emotional, psychological, and educational needs. By September, some thirty-seven school districts requested waivers, and by October the state Board of Education "OK'd" their use.[241] For the next two years, various school districts were successful in circumventing its egregious provisions.

Thus, during this nativist-plagued epoch, the struggles of resistance and change continued via a diminishing number of organizations that waged a largely defensive political war against the nativist state of siege and politicians within the ballot box arena.

Notes

1. The essence of the arguments made in this section of the chapter is derived from an article I wrote and published in 1997: "The Post Mortem Politics of the Chicano

Movement: 1975–1996," *Perspectives in Mexican American Studies,* Mexican American Studies & Research Center, University of Arizona, Tucson, Vol. 6, 1997.

2. For an excellent study of the histories of the various social movements of the 1960s see Terry Anderson, *The Movement and the Sixties: Protest in America from Greensboro to Wounded Knee* (New York: Oxford University Press, 1995).

3. See Robert Weisbrot, *Freedom Bound: A History of America's Civil Rights Movement* (New York: Plume, 1999).

4. For a critique of the War on Poverty programs see Daniel P. Moynihan, *Maximum Feasible Misunderstanding* (New York: Free Press).

5. COINTELPRO translates to Counterintelligence Program, which was under the auspices of the FBI's Domestic Intelligence Division (Division 5). It used a number of nefarious and illegal methods, such as wiretapping, infiltration, burglaries, espionage, and blackmail, against groups and leaders perceived as a domestic threat to the security of the United States.

6. Ignacio Garcia, *Chicanismo: The Forging of a Militant Ethos among Mexican Americans* (Tucson: University of Arizona Press, 1997), 142–43.

7. For an excellent case study on the Crusade for Justice and on the "government's Gatekeeper dissent" on it as an organization and its leader, Gonzales, see Ernesto B. Vigil, *The Crusade for Justice: Chicano Militancy and the Government's War on Dissent* (Madison: University of Wisconsin Press, 1999).

8. I make this same argument in my third book: *La Raza Unida Party: A Chicano Challenge to the U.S. Two-Party Dictatorship* (Philadelphia: Temple University Press, 2000), 59–60.

9. The essence of the "Mexican Crab Syndrome" is based on the racist tale that two whites while after fishing successfully for crabs and having buckets full of them on a hot Texas sunny day became thirsty and decided to go for some beers. Yet during the course of making the decision, one of the white fishermen asks the other, "what do we do with all the buckets of crabs we caught today?" The other responded, "we do not have to worry about them: they are Mexican crabs; they are not going anywhere. They pull each other down."

10. Juan Gómez-Quiñones, *Chicano Politics: Reality of Promise, 1940–1990* (Albuquerque: University of New México Press, 1990), 184.

11. Mario Garcia, *Mexican Americans* (New Haven, Conn.: Yale University Press, 1989), 301.

12. Kevin Phillips, *The Politics of Rich and Poor: Wealth and the American Electorate in the Reagan Aftermath* (New York: Harper Perennial, 1990), ix–xiii, chapter 1.

13. For an extensive examination on this thesis that the United States is governed by a "two-party" dictatorship that serves the interests of plutocratic elites see my book *La Raza Unida Party: A Chicano Challenge to the U.S. Two-Party Dictatorship* (Philadelphia: Temple University Press, 2000), chapter 1.

14. For a further provocative and insightful analysis on this argument on neo-imperialism see Michael Parenti, *Against Empire* (San Francisco: City Lights Books, 1995),

15. In developing his analysis, he defines "imperialism" as the "process whereby the dominant politico-economic interests of one nation expropriate for their own enrichment the land, labor, raw materials, and markets of another people (p. 1).

15. Roger Burbach, *Globalization and Post-Modern Politics: From Zapatistas to High Tech Robber Barons* (London: Pluto Press, 2001), 82.

16. Russell Jacoby, *The End of Utopia: Politics and Culture in an Age of Apathy* (New York: Basic, 1999), 7.

17. Garcia, *Mexican Americans*, 301.

18. Garcia, *Chicanismo*, 143.

19. Martín Sánchez Jankowski, "Where Have All the Nationalists Gone? Change and Persistence in Radical Political Attitudes among Chicanos, 1976–1986," in *Chicano Politics and Society in the Late Twentieth Century*, ed. David Montejano (Austin: University of Texas Press, 1999), 201.

20. Jankowski, "Where Have All the Nationalists Gone?" 201. This nationalist dichotomy derived from the analysis of Jankowski in said work.

21. Peter Skerry, *Mexican Americans: The Ambivalent Minority* (New York: Free Press, 1993), 25.

22. John A. Garcia, "Yo Soy Mexicano: Self-Identity and Sociodemographic Correlates," *Social Science Quarterly* Vol. 62 (1981): 88–98.

23. Richard Griswold Del Castillo and Arnoldo De León, *North to Aztlán: A History of Mexican Americans in the United States* (New York: Twayne Publishers, 1997), 148.

24. For an excellent examination and definition of the various terminology used to describe those peoples of Latin American and Spanish descent see Jose Cuello, "Latinos and Hispanics: A Primer on Terminology," Wayne State University, unpublished paper, December 2, 1996.

25. Ilan Stavens, *The Hispanic Condition: The Power of a People* (New York: HarperCollins, 1995), 25.

26. Roberto M. De Anda, *Chicanas and Chicanos in Contemporary Society* (Boston: Allyn and Bacon, 1996), 198.

27. Gómez-Quiñones, *Chicano Politics*, 185.

28. Although there were others, the following are two examples: Joan Moore and Harry Pachon, *Hispanics in the United States* (Englewood Cliffs, N.J.: Prentice Hall, 1985); and Maurilio E. Vigil, *Hispanics in American Politics* (Lanham, Md.: University Press of America, 1987).

29. Cuello, "Latinos and Hispanics."

30. Jorge J. E. Garcia, *Hispanic/Latino Identity: A Philosophical Perspective* (Malden, Mass.: Blackwell, 2000), 17.

31. For an extensive examination in differentiating between the various terms used see Arnoldo Carlos Vento, *Mestizo: The History, Culture, and Politics of the Mexican and the Chicano* (Lanham, Md.: University Press of America, 1998), chapter 7.

32. For an extensive examination of the origins of the term *Hispanic* see Garcia, *Hispanic/Latino Identity*, chapter 1.

33. Skerry, *Mexican Americans*, 25.

34. Rodolfo Acuña, *Occupied America: A History of Chicanos*, 4th ed. (New York: Addison Wesley, 2000), 462.

35. F. Arturo Rosales, *Chicano! The History of the Mexican American Civil Rights Movement* (Houston, Tex.: Arte Público Press, 1997), 262.

36. Navarro, *La Raza Unida Party*, 11.

37. Garcia, *Mexican Americans*, 301.

38. Quote is cited from Internet website www.mexicamovement.org/timexihcah/intromain.htm#glossary.

39. Quote is cited from Internet website www.mexicamovement.org/timexihcah/intromain.htm#glossary.

40. Quote is cited from Internet website www.mexicamovement.org/timexihcah/intromain.htm#glossary.

41. "Pan-ethnicity" denotes "a sense of group affinity and identification that transcends one's own national-origin affinity group. A pan-ethnic identity does not necessarily replace national-origin affinity, but it includes a broader configuration in defining the group. Latino or Hispanic include several national origins." Cited in John A. Garcia, *Latino Politics in America: Community, Culture, and Interests* (Lanham, Md.: Rowman & Littlefield, 2003), 15.

42. For an extensive examination of the usage of these two terms see Garcia, *Latino Politics in America*, 16–30.

43. Stavens, *The Hispanic Condition*, 23–24.

44. Acuña, *Occupied America*, 4th ed., 462.

45. Gómez-Quiñones, *Chicano Politics*, 189.

46. The list of the post–Chicano Generation scholars who in their research dealt with the Movimiento or some aspect of it included: Richard Griswold Del Castillo, Arnoldo De Léon, Rudolph O. de la Garza, F. Chris Garcia, Ignacio Garcia, Juan Garcia, Mario Garcia, Manuel Gonzales, David G. Gutiérrez, José Angel Gutiérrez, David Maciel, David Montejano, Alfredo Mirandé, Armando Navarro, F. Arturo Rosales, Richard Santillan, Roberto E. Villarreal, Ernesto Vigil, and Maurillio E. Vigil, among others.

47. During the late 1980s and 1990s, examples of the aforementioned included Carlos Muñoz's *Youth, Identity, and Power: The Chicano Movement* (New York: Verso, 1989); Ignacio Garcia's two works, *United We Win: The Rise and Fall of La Raza Unida Party* (Tucson, Ariz.: Mexican American Studies & Research Center, 1989) and *Chicanismo* (1997); F. Arturo Rosales's *Chicano!* (1997); José Angel Gutiérrez's *The Making of Chicano Militant: Lessons from Cristal* (Madison: University of Wisconsin Press, 1998); Vigil's *The Crusade for Justice*; and my three works among a few others. These works were written in a conservative climate that was antithetical to radical analysis, especially those that were hypercritical of liberal capitalism.

48. Some of these works included Ron Arias's social commentary *The Road to Tamasunchale* (Albuquerque, N.M.: Pajarito Publications, 1978); Nash Candelaria's *Memories of Alhambra* (Palo Alto, Calif.: Cibola Press, 1977); Arturo Islas's semiautobiographical nov-

els, *The Rain God: A Desert Tale* (Palo Alto, Calif.: Alexandrian Press, 1984) and *Migrant Souls* (New York: Morrow, 1990); Victor Villaseñor's *Rain of Gold* (Houston, Tex.: Arte Público Press, 1991); and Rudolfo Anaya's three mystery novels, *Zia Summer* (New York: Warner, 1995), *Rio Grande Fall* (New York: Warner, 1996), and *Shaman Winter* (New York: Warner, 1999).

49. Written for classroom use, an excellent examination of the various aspects of what the author calls "Chicano popular culture" is Charles M. Tatum, *Chicano Popular Culture: Que Hable el Pueblo* (Tucson: University of Arizona, 2001).

50. Del Castillo and De Léon, *North to Aztlán*, 167

51. Antonio Gramsci was a stellar Marxist scholar/activist, who epitomized the idea that intellectuals should apply their intellect by way of the praxis of working-class struggles.

52. I make this argument in my concurrent work entitled, *What Needs to Be Done? The Building of a New Movement*, scheduled to be completed by late 2006.

53. For an excellent introduction to postmodernism see Frederick Jameson, *Postmodernism or the Cultural Logic of Late Capitalism* (Durham, N.C.: Duke University Press, 1991).

54. Marcy Darnovsky, Barbara Epstein, and Richard Flacks, ed., *Cultural Politics and Social Movements* (Philadelphia: Temple University Press, 1995), 13.

55. Ramon Gutiérrez, "Chicano History: Paradigm Shifts and Shifting Boundaries," in *Voices of a New Chicana/o History*, ed. Refugio I. Rochín and Dennis N. Valdés (East Lansing: Michigan State University Press, 2000), 103.

56. Iain McLean and Alistair McMillian, *Oxford Concise Dictionary of Politics* (New York: Oxford University Press, 2003), 429.

57. Steven M. Buechler, *Social Movements in Advanced Capitalism: The Political Economy and Cultural Construction of Social Activism* (New York: Oxford Press, 2000), 46.

58. Roger Burbach, *Globalization and Postmodern Politics: From Zapatistas to High Tech Robber Barons* (London: Pluto Press, 2001), 69.

59. Roberta Garner, *Contemporary Movements and Ideologies* (New York: McGraw-Hill, 1996), 377.

60. Armando Navarro, *What Needs to Be Done? The Building of a New Movement*, unpublished book manuscript, chapter 1, 44–45.

61. Gutiérrez, "Chicano History," 104.

62. Griswold Del Castillo and De Léon, *North to Aztlán*, 146.

63. Acuña, *Occupied America*, 4th ed., 448.

64. Initially a poet, Castillo produced two major works that won her acclaim, *The Mixquiahuala Letters* (Binghamton, N.Y.: Bilingual Press/Editorial Bilingue, 1986) and *So Far from God* (New York: Norton, 1993), winner of a Carl Sandburg Award. Sandra Cisneros's *The House on Mango Street* (Houston, Tex.: Arte Público Press, 1983), *Women Hollering Creek, and Other Stories* (New York: Random House, 1991), *My Wicked, Wicked Ways* (New York: Turtle Bay Books, 1992), and numerous poems and essays have been recognized for their exceptional scholarly value. Chavez, a playwright, poet, and short story writer produced two major novels, *The Last of the Menu Girls* (Houston: Arte Público Press, 1986)

and *Face of an Angel* (New York: Farrar, Straus & Giroux, 1994), and like Castillo and Cisneros, was recognized and won a number of literary prizes and recognition. See Del Castillo and De León, *North to Aztlán*, 161.

65. Del Castillo and De León, *North to Aztlán*, 245.

66. Del Castillo and De León, *North to Aztlán*, 161.

67. Matt S. Meier and Feliciano Rivera, *Mexican Americans, Mexican Americans: From Conquistadors to Chicanos* (New York: Hill & Wang, 1993), 238.

68. Gonzales, *Mexicanos*, 252.

69. Cited in Del Castillo and De León, *North to Aztlán*, 167.

70. Steven D. Stark, "Nativism on Film: A World of Bandits and Crooks," *Los Angeles Times*, November 14, 1993.

71. Stark, "Nativism on Film."

72. Tatum, *Chicano Popular Culture*, 81–82.

73. Olmos became one of the leading Mexicano actors of the epoch. He played a major role as the *pachuco* in *Zoot Suit* in 1978 and supporting roles in *Wolfen* (1981) and *Blade Runner* (1982). He played leading roles in film *Ballad of Gregorio Cortez* (1982), television program *Miami Vice* (1984), film *Stand and Deliver* (1987), and in the 1990s did numerous other films and television appearances. By the late 1980s he ventured out and established his own production company. See Del Castillo and De León, *North to Aztlán*, 166.

74. Gonzales, *Mexicanos*, 254–55. References to above film works cited also from Meier and Rivera, *Mexican Americans, American Mexicans*, 238–39.

75. These included Morales's *Chicana*; Espinoza's *Trail North* (1983); Espinoza and Isaac Artenstein's *Ballad of an Unsung Hero* (1984) and Break *of Dawn* (1988); Marilyn Mulford's *Chicano Park* (1989); Susana Ortiz's *The Art of Resistance* (1994); Ray Telles and Rick Tejada Flores's *The Fight in the Fields: Cesar Chavez and the Farmworkers' Struggle* (1996); and Ulla Nilsen and Selene Jaramillo's *Voices in the Fields* (1997). In particular Treviño's documentary *Yo Soy* (1985) and his PBS four-part documentaries series *Chicano! The History of the Mexican American Civil Rights Movement* (1999) kept the legacy of the Movimiento alive.

76. Del Castillo and De León, *North to Aztlán*, 169.

77. Diane Solis, "Young Latinos, with the Aid of a Dallas-Based Company, Are Abandoning Tejano and Switching the Dial to Hip-Hop," *La Voz* [newspaper], May 10, 2001.

78. John Leland and Veronica Chambers, "Generation ñ," *Newsweek*, July 12, 1999, 53.

79. Hector Tobar, "Heartland Tuning in to Spanish," *Los Angeles Times*, June 23, 2001.

80. Frank Del Olmo, "English Isn't a Second Language on TV," *Los Angeles Times*, January 20, 2002.

81. Lee Romney, "Entravision Launches 2 Spanish TV stations," *Los Angeles Times*, March 30, 2001.

82. Lee Romney, "Publications for Latinos Booming in L.A.," *Los Angeles Times*, March 6, 1999.

83. Even though the Bureau of the U.S. Census and other governmental entities as well corporations used *Hispanic* to describe those persons whose ethnic and cultural roots and linkages were with México, Latin America, and Spain, in this chapter in its place I use *Latino*, which I feel is more appropriate as an umbrella term. Only when the analysis warrants will *Hispanic* be used.

84. Moore and Pachon, *Hispanics in the United States*, 51–52.

85. Moore and Pachon, *Hispanics in the United States*, 51–52.

86. Moore and Pachon, *Hispanics in the United States*, 56.

87. Moore and Pachon, *Hispanics in the United States*, 52–58.

88. Moore and Pachon, *Hispanics in the United States*, 62.

89. Moore and Pachon, *Hispanics in the United States*, 53.

90. Rogelio Saenz and Clyde S. Greenless, "The Demography of Chicanos," in *Chicanas and Chicanos in Contemporary Society*, ed. Roberto M. De Anda (Boston: Allyn and Bacon, 1995), 9–23.

91. U.S. Bureau of the Census, General Population Characteristics.

92. Cited in Vigil, *Hispanics in American Politics*, 5.

93. Moore and Pachon, *Hispanics in the United States*, 56.

94. Saenz and Greenless, "The Demography of Chicanos," 13.

95. Juan Andrade and Andrew Hernandez, *The Almanac of Latino Politics 2000* (Chicago, Ill.: United States Hispanic Leadership Institute, 1999), 1.

96. Andrade and Andrew Hernandez, *The Almanac of Latino Politics 2000*, 9.

97. National Council of La Raza (NCLR), "State of Hispanic America 1991: An Overview," Washington, D.C., August 2001.

98. Randolph E. Schmidt, "Hispanics Get New Census Profile," *The Press Enterprise*, July 27, 1995.

99. NCLR, "State of Hispanic America," August 2001.

100. NCLR, "State of Hispanic America," August 2001.

101. Saenz and Greenless, "The Demography of Chicanos," 14.

102. For a national breakdown of the total Mexicano population on a state basis, see U.S. Bureau of the Census, *1990 Census of Population and Housing Summary Tape 1C*.

103. Saenz and Greenless, "The Demography of Chicanos," 16–17.

104. Frank Sotomayor, "State Shows 69.2% Rise in Latino Population," *Los Angeles Times*, March 28, 1991.

105. Leonard Dinnerstein, Roger L. Nichols, and David M. Reimers, *Natives and Strangers: Blacks, Indians, and Immigrants in America*, 2nd ed. (New York: Oxford University Press, 1990), 270.

106. Robert A. Rosenblatt, "Latinos, Asians, to Lead Rise in U.S. Population," *Los Angeles Times*, March 14, 1996.

107. Armando Acuña, "Think Tanks, Researchers No Longer Ignore Latinos," *Los Angeles Times*, November 12, 1999.

108. Cited in Oscar Martinez, *Mexican-Origin People in the United States: A Topical History* (Tucson: University of Arizona, 2000), 39.

109. Arturo González, *Mexican Americans & the U.S. Economy: Quest for Buenos Días* (Tucson: University of Arizona Press, 2002), 25.

110. David E. Lorey, *The U.S.-México Border in the Twentieth Century* (Wilmington, Del.: Scholarly Resources, Inc., 1999), 135.

111. Patrick J. McDonnell, "1990s on Track to Set a Record for Immigration," *Los Angeles Times*, January 24, 1999.

112. Martinez, *Mexican-Origin People in the United States*, 39.

113. Gonzalez, *Mexican Americans & the U.S. Economy*, 28.

114. Ken Ellingwood, "Data on Border Arrests Raise Gatekeeper Debate," *Los Angeles Times*, October 1, 1999.

115. McDonnell, "1990s on Track to Set a Record for Immigration."

116. Sue Schultz, "INS to Add 1,600 Agents, Inspectors," *The Press Enterprise*, February 18, 1999.

117. Moore and Pachon, *Hispanics in the United States*, 53, 64.

118. NCLR, "State of Hispanic America 1991," Washington, D.C., 1991.

119. Colleen Kruger, "California's Residents Are Now Outwardly Mobile," *Los Angeles Times*, October 11, 1995.

120. The term *Latino* will be used throughout this socioeconomic analysis. I do not agree with usage of *Hispanic*; consequently, *Hispanic* is used only when it is absolutely necessary to make a point.

121. Kevin Baxter, "Univision Means Success in Any Language," *Los Angeles Times*, April 13, 1999.

122. Lee Romney, "Latinos' Old Guard Passing the Torch," *Los Angeles Times*, September 15, 1999.

123. Del Castillo and De León, *North to Aztlán*, 152.

124. Lee Romney, "Tapping into Latino Wealth," *Los Angeles Times*, October 26, 1999.

125. George Ramos, "Latino Middle Class Growing in Suburbia," *Los Angeles Times*, November 30, 1997.

126. Moore and Pachon, *Hispanics in the United States*, 69–70.

127. NCLR "State of Hispanic America in 1991: An Overview."

128. Carey Goldberg, "U.S. Hispanics Struggling Hardest to Make Ends Meet," *The Press Enterprise*, January 30, 1997.

129. Nancy Cleeland, "Latinos' Economic Gap Persists over Time," *Los Angeles Times*, August 19, 1999.

130. Moore and Pachon, *Hispanics in the United States*, 71–72.

131. NCLR, "State of Hispanic America 1991: An Overview."

132. Schmidt, "Hispanics Get New Census Profile."

133. Schmidt, "Hispanics Get New Census Profile."

134. Moore and Pachon, *Hispanics in the United States*, 68.

135. Manuel J. Justiz, Reginald Wilson, and Lars G. Björk, ed., *Minorities in Education* (Phoenix, Ariz.: Oryx Press, 1994), 5.

136. Justiz, Wilson, and Björk, ed., *Minorities in Education*, 6.

137. Justiz, Wilson, and Björk, ed., *Minorities in Education*, 7.

138. U.S. Department of Commerce, "The Hispanic Population in the United States," 1 and 4.

139. Ann Bancroft, "Study: White Men Still Lead in Workforce," *Daily Bulletin*, March 28, 1995.

140. Goldberg, "U.S. Hispanics Struggling Hardest to Make Ends Meet."

141. Poverty was defined in 1980 as a male-headed non-farm family with two children whose household income fell under $8,418.

142. Moore and Pachon, *Hispanics in the United States*, 79–80.

143. Aida Hurtado et al., *Redefining California: Latino Social Engagement in a Multicultural Society* (Los Angeles: UCLA Chicano Studies Research Center, 1992), 50.

144. U.S. Department of Commerce, "The Hispanic Population in the United States: March 1992," Bureau of the Census, Current Population Reports, July 1993, p. 9.

145. Associated Press, "Census Bureau report says," *The Press Enterprise*, August 23, 1993.

146. Goldberg, "U.S. Hispanics Struggling Hardest to Make Ends Meet."

147. Paul Shepard, "Race Factor Falls in Housing," *The Press Enterprise*, April 22, 1998.

148. Michael Doyle, "Latinos Being Passed over, Report Says," *The Sun*, February 7, 1992.

149. Goldberg, "U.S. Hispanics Struggling Hardest to Make Ends Meet."

150. Héctor Aguilar Camín and Lorenzo Meyer, *In the Shadow of the Mexican Revolution: Contemporary Mexican History, 1910–1989* (Austin: University of Texas Press, 1993), 227–28.

151. Chris Kraul, "México Says Economy Grew 8.8% in Quarter," *Los Angeles Times*, August 19, 1997.

152. Mark Freeman, "México Uses $4 Billion from U.S. Bailout to Pay Investors," *Los Angeles Times*, April 5, 1995.

153. Maria del PilarMarrero, "Califica de 'Bomba' la Ley de Inmigracion," *La Opinion*, April 23, 1997.

154. Francisco Robles, "Cerca de 24 Milliones de Mexicanos se Encuentran en Pobreza Extrema," *La Opinion*, January 16, 1997.

155. Francisco Robles, "13 Milliones sin Trabajo en Campo Mexicano," *La Opinion*, March 26, 1997.

156. Associated Press, "México Workers' Patience Wears Thin," *The Press Enterprise*, January 2, 2000.

157. For an examination of the *maquiladora* program see Lorey, *The U.S.-Mexican Border in the Twentieth Century*, chapter 5.

158. For an excellent historical overview on the immigration issue see Acuña, *Occupied America*, 4th ed., 402–7.

159. Meier and Rivera, *Mexican Americans, American Mexicans*, 285.

160. Meier and Rivera, *Mexican Americans, American Mexicans*, 266.

161. Arthur F. Corwin and John M. McCain, "Wetbackism since 1954," in *Immi-*

grants—*and Immigrants: Perspectives on Mexican Labor Migration to the United States*, ed., Arthur F. Corwin (Westport, Conn.: Greenwood, 1978), 73.

162. Meier and Rivera, *Mexican Americans, American Mexicans*, 266.

163. Interview, Herman Baca, May 10, 2002.

164. For a more extensive examination on the National Chicano Forum see my book *La Raza Unida Party*, 249.

165. Navarro, *La Raza Unida Party*, 249.

166. Gutiérrez's letter was published in its entirety in *The Militant*, "A Call for Action," June 10, 1977.

167. Del Castillo and De León, *North to Aztlán*, 162.

168. Del Castillo and De León, *North to Aztlán*, 135.

169. Navarro, *La Raza Unida Party*, 251–52.

170. Navarro, *La Raza Unida Party*, 251–52.

171. In the subsequent chapter in the section dealing with organizational development a more extensive examination of these organizations is provided.

172. Meier and Rivera, *Mexican Americans, American Mexicans*, 266.

173. Maldwyn Allen Jones, *American Immigration* (Chicago, Ill.: The University of Chicago Press, 1992), 287.

174. Del Castillo and De León, *North to Aztlán*, 162.

175. As executive director of the ISJ, I was both a participant and observer of the leadership summit on Simpson-Mazzoli held in Los Angeles. Under the organizational leadership of the Congreso para Pueblos Unidos, I organized various direct action activities and events against the passage of Simpson-Mazzoli.

176. Gonzales, *Mexicanos*, 230.

177. Del Castillo and De León, *North to Aztlán*, 163.

178. Acuña, *Occupied America*, 4th ed., 424.

179. Meier and Rivera, *Mexican Americans, American Mexicans*, 268–69.

180. Joe R. Feagin, "Old Poison in New Bottles: The Deep Roots of Modern Nativism," in *Immigrants Out! The New Nativism and the Anti-Immigrant Impulse in the United States*, ed. Juan F. Parea (New York: New York University Press, 1997), 35.

181. Acuña, *Occupied America*, 4th ed., 425.

182. Del Castillo and De León, *North to Aztlán*, 163.

183. For a comprehensive examination of Operation Gatekeeper see Joseph Nevins, *Operation Gatekeeper: The Rise of the "Illegal Alien" and the Making of the U.S.-México Boundary* (New York: Routledge, 2002), 11.

184. Nevins, *Operation Gatekeeper*, 90.

185. Nevins, *Operation Gatekeeper*, 11.

186. Nevins, *Operation Gatekeeper*, 11.

187. Wayne A. Cornelius, "The Structural Embeddedness of Demand for Mexican Immigrant Labor: New Evidence from California," in *Crossings: Mexican Immigration in Interdisciplinary Perspectives*, Marcelo M. Suárez-Orosco (Cambridge, Mass.: Harvard University Press, 1998), 129.

188. For an interesting and in-depth analysis on the military aspects of the various border operations see José Palafox, "Militarizing the Border," *CAQ* No. 56 (Spring 1996).

189. Peter Andreas, "The U.S. Immigration Control Offensive: Constructing an Image of Order on the Southwest Border," in Suárez-Orosco, *Crossings*, 345.

190. The Associated Press, "Legal Immigration Rate Drops to Its Level in a Decade," *The Press Enterprise*, August 12, 1999.

191. Sue Schultz, "INS to Add 1,600 Agents, Inspectors," *The Press Enterprise*, February 18, 1999; Elsie Ackerman, "Finally, an Effective Fence," *U.S. News & World Report*, October 19, 1998; Ken Ellingwood, "Data on Border Arrests Raise Gatekeeper Debate," *Los Angeles Times*, October 1, 1999; and Michelle Mittlestadt, "INS Deports Record Number of Illegal Immigrants," *The Press Enterprise*, November 13, 1999.

192. Leticia Garcia-Irigoyen, "Aumenta Cifra de Muertes en la Frontera," *La Opinion*, August 5, 1999; Mark Henry, "Death Looms for Unwary Bent on Crossing Border," *The Press Enterprise*, March 29, 1999.

193. *La Resistencia*, Summer Border Project Newsletter #1, June 30, 1997.

194. Esther Schrader, "INS Defends Ranchers in Detaining of Migrants," *Los Angeles Times*, May 19, 2000.

195. For an abbreviated analysis on Proposition 187 see Kevin Johnson, "The New Nativism: Something Old, Something New, Something Blue," in *Immigrants Out!*, 177–180; Acuña, *Occupied America*, 4th ed., 452–53; Marcelo M. Suárez-Orozco, ed., *Crossings: Mexican Immigration in Interdisciplinary Perspectives* (Cambridge, Mass.: Harvard University, David Rockefeller Center for Latin American Studies, 1998), 97–98; Nevins, *Operation Gatekeeper*, 91–92.

196. Leo Chavez, "Immigration Reform and Nativism: The Nationalist Response to the Transnationalist Challenge," in *Immigrants Out!*, 63.

197. Martinez, *Mexican-Origin People in the United States*, 43–44.

198. As a result of the great pressures produced by the Civil Rights Movement on the issue of putting an end to discrimination in the job place affirmative action programs were born. They were a product of several executive orders, legislation, and government regulations. John Kennedy's Executive Orders 10925 and 11114 prohibited discrimination on the basis of race, national origin, or religion and required affirmative action to ensure nondiscrimination by government contractors. The Johnson administration passed successfully its Civil Rights Act of 1964, which under Title VII empowered courts to order firms guilty of discrimination to take "affirmative action" in order to ensure "equal opportunity." In 1965, President Johnson signed Executive Order 11246, which rebuttressed President Kennedy's earlier executive orders. Paradoxically, it was Republican president Richard Nixon who was initially responsible for introducing quotas as illustrated by his adoption during the early 1970s of the "Philadelphia Plan," which called for the direct imposition of hiring goals in the construction trade. For a comprehensive examination on the history and politics of affirmative action programs as they apply to various ethnic groups see John David Skrentny, ed., *Color Lines: Affirmative Action, Immigra-*

tion, and Civil Rights Options for America (Chicago: University of Chicago Press, 2001); and Carol M. Swain, "Affirmative Action: Legislative History, Judicial Interpretations, Public Consensus," in *America Becoming: Racial Trends and Consequences*, Vol. 1, ed. Neil J. Smelser, Julian Wilson, and Faith Mitchell (Washington, D.C.: National Academy Press, 2001), 318–47.

199. Swain, "Affirmative Action," 328.

200. For an excellent examination of the effects of the *Bakke* decision on affirmative action programs see Susan Welch and John Gruhl, *Affirmative Action and Minority Enrollments in Medical and Law Schools* (Ann Arbor: University of Michigan Press, 1998), 107–44.

201. Skrentny, *Color Lines*, 53.

202. For an excellent overview on the issue of Proposition 209 see Acuña, *Occupied America*, 4th ed., 453–54.

203. Skrentny, *Color Lines*, 53.

204. Skrentny, *Color Lines*, 53.

205. Nick Anderson and Peter M. Warren, "Bid to Cut Bilingual Classes Qualifies for June '98 Ballot," *Los Angeles Times*, December 24, 1997.

206. Nick Anderson, "Debate Loud as Vote Nears on Bilingual Ban," *Los Angeles Times*, March 23, 1998.

207. Stewart M. Powell and Eun Lee Koh, "Clinton to Fight Bilingual Ban," *The Press Enterprise*, April 28, 1998.

208. Cragg Hines, "Gingrich Wants End to Bilingual Education," *The Press Enterprise*, January 6, 1998.

209. Jonathan Peterson, "White House to Announce Opposition to Prop. 227," *Los Angeles Times*, April 27, 1998.

210. Acuña, *Occupied America*, 4th ed., 455.

211. Frank Trejo, "Hispanic Officials, Organizers Meet to Fight Anti-immigrant Views," *The Dallas Morning News*, January 9, 1994; *Associated Press*, "Hispanics Condemn Political Attacks," January 9, 1994; Mark Bryant, "Conference Puts out Call for Latino Power," *The Press Enterprise*, January 9, 1994; Jeff Dillon, "Latinos See Unity as Key to Future," *Desert Sun*, January 9, 1994.

212. Armando Navarro, proceedings entitled "The Immigration Crisis: Latino Public Policy Response," Ernesto Galarza Think Tank on Public Policy, University of California, Riverside, January 6, 7, and 8, 1994.

213. *Los Angeles Times*, "Plan Unveiled to Counter Anti-Immigrant Sentiment," February 12, 1994; Rosalva Hernandez, "Hispanics Offer Own Immigration Reform," *Orange County Register*, February 12, 1994; George Ronney, "Anti-Immigrant Fervor Targeted by Latino Activists," *The Press Enterprise*, February 12, 1994; Teresa Jimenez, "Latinos Call for Immigrant Rights," *The Sun*, February 12, 1994; *La Opinion*, "Líderes Latinos Lanzan el 'Plan Riverside' para Proteger a los Inmigrantes," February 12, 1994.

214. Acuña, *Occupied America*, 4th ed., 453.

215. I along with numerous other people from throughout San Bernardino/Riverside counties participated in the said three marches. Hence this brief account is based upon

my involvement as a participant-observer. It is important to state that I, among others, intervened in the various school walkouts from the perspective of ensuring the safety and security of the students. In October, in San Bernardino, an anti-Proposition 187 coalition of which I assisted in its formation, held a march and rally, which was attended by some one thousand people.

216. Armando Navarro, "A Post 187 Strategy for Mobilization," Ernesto Galarza Public Policy and Humanities Research Institute, January 13 and 14, 1995, located in my archives.

217. Patrick J. McDonnell, "Davis Won't Appeal Prop. 187 Ruling, Ending Court Battles," *Los Angeles Times*, July 29, 1999.

218. Ben J. Seely, "That Was No Reform: It's a Sellout of Our Border," *Los Angeles Times*, October 30, 1996.

219. Martinez, *Mexican-Origin People in the United States*, 44.

220. *Los Angeles Times*, "Let Washington Pick up the Check," December 3, 1996.

221. Martinez, *Mexican-Origin People in the United States*, 44; and David Ogul, "1 Deputy Fired, 1 Suspended," *The Press Enterprise*, June 12, 1996.

222. IMPACTO 2000 Press Release, "National Mobilization for a Rally and March along the U.S./México Border in Protest of the Republican Convention," July 26, 1996.

223. Invitation letter, Chicano Federation of San Diego County, July 27, 1996.

224. I was a participant of the march along with several people from San Bernardino/ Riverside counties.

225. Document, "Puntos De Acuerdo De La Segunda Reunion De Los Signatarios Del Pacto De Californias," February 11, 1997. Navarro archives.

226. Adriana Chavira, "Latinos Plan Counter-Rally near the Border," *Daily Bulletin*, March 2, 1997; Frank Kilmko, "Taunts Traded at Rally Marking Construction of New Border Fence," *The San Diego Union-Tribune*, March 23, 1997.

227. Acuña, *Occupied America*, 4th ed., 454.

228. W. Robert Gray, *The Four Faces of Affirmative Action: Fundamental Answers and Actions* (Westport, Conn.: Greenwood, 2001), I, 44.

229. The Associated Press, "Anti-Affirmative Action Crusade Goes to Florida," *The Press Enterprise*, March 15, 1999; Rich Bragg, "Connerly Fights in Florida," *New York Times*, June 7, 1999; Associated Press, "Fla. Regents Endorse Plan to End Affirmative Action," *Los Angeles Times*, November 20, 1999.

230. M. S. Enkoji, "UC Admission Plan Called 'Radical Change,'" *The Press Enterprise*, May 6, 1998.

231. Cited in article by Oswaldo Zavala, "Study: Acceptance Rates at UC Campuses Down for Hispanics," *Hispanic Link Weekly Report* Vol. 17, No. 48 (December 6, 1999).

232. Adam Cohen, "When the Field Is Level," *Time*, July 5, 1999.

233. Jorge Chapa, "Affirmative Action, X Percent Plans, and Latino Access to Higher Education in the Twenty-first Century," in *Latinos: Remaking America*, ed. Marcelo M. Suárez-Orozco and Mariela M. Páez (Berkeley: University of California Press, 2002), 375–88.

234. Kenneth R. Wiess, "The Top 4% Solution," *Los Angeles Times*, March 31, 1999.

235. Mary Ballesteros-Coronel and Lillian de la Torres-Jimenez, "Demandarán si la 227es Aprobada," *La Opinión*, May 30, 1998.

236. Cathleen Decker, "Bilingual Education Ban Widely Supported," *Los Angeles Times*, April 13, 1998.

237. Roberto Rodriguez and Patrisia Gonzales, "A Bifurcated Approach to Bilingual Education," *Los Angeles Times*, December 14, 1997.

238. Mary Ballesteros-Coronel, "Protestan contra la 227," *La Opinion*, June 12, 1998.

239. Nick Anderson and Louis Sahagun, "Judge Refuses to Stand in Way of Prop. 227," *Los Angeles Times*, July 16, 1998.

240. Richard Lee Colvin and Dough Smith, "Prop. 227 Foes Vow to Block It Despite Wide Vote Margin," *Los Angeles Times*, June 4, 1998.

241. *The Press Enterprise*, "Prop. 227 Waiver for Schools Urged," September 11, 1998; and The Associated Press, "New Bilingual Education Rules Ok'd," *The Press Enterprise*, October 9, 1998.

Epoch of Hispanic Generation Politics (1975–1999)

D RIVEN BY Mexicano and Latino demographic growth, the Movimiento's cry for Chicano power was replaced with a call for "Hispanic or Latino empowerment." During the epoch of Hispanic Generation politics, from local to federal levels of government, Mexicano and Latino political representation increased significantly. "Brown ballot box" politics was driven by new registered voters and naturalized citizens. No previous epoch experienced the dramatic increases that this one did. The mode of Mexicano politics, however, dramatically shifted from the Chicano Generation's (CG) militant and unconventional protest to mainstream conventional accommodation politics predicated largely on the ethos of the Hispanic Generation (HG). New organizations committed to the HG also emerged, adherents of the CG declined, and the number of Neo-Mex Generation (NMG) organizations increased. A few sectarian Left organizations also formed that adhered to an advocate transformer role. As for the barrios and *colonias* of Aztlán, they remained largely unorganized and were still "colonized" and "occupied."

Hispanic Ballot Box Politics

Struggles for Political Empowerment

With the decline of the Movimiento, the epoch's mode of politics was predicated largely on the ethos of the HG. From 1975 to 1999, *Mexicano* or *Chicano* politics was largely replaced with the rubric of *Latino* or *Hispanic* politics. Even the usage of *Mexican American* to describe politics was no longer in vogue. The emphasis was no longer on direct action protest politics, but instead on a mainstream type of politics based on a resurgent mode of accommodation, adaptation, and integration. From an internal colonial perspective, it was a politic controlled by politicians and organizations that functioned as buffers and "want to be whites." While a few activists, organizations, and scholars still antithetical to the country's liberal capitalist plutocratic politics remained active, most Mexicanos, particularly those active in ballot box politics, strongly supported the new mode of HG politics. The epoch produced largely "system maintenance" politicians who came with few or no ideas as to how to reform or change the Mexicano's oppressive colonial reality. In most cases, they embodied the essence of the HG's Viva Yo ethos, which accentuated the "I" rather than the "we." Thus, in this epoch of Hispanic empowerment politics, it was the *politico*, not the activist who became the locus of political leadership.

Latino Voter Registration and Voting (1970s–1990s)

During this epoch, Mexicano electoral representation significantly increased. The increases were attributable to both the Mexicano/Latino population's rapid growth and the dramatic increases in the number registered to vote. The Southwest Voter Registration Education Project (SVREP) more than doubled Mexicano voter registration in Tejas, from 488,200 in 1976 to over a million in 1990. In California, voter registration went from 715,000 in 1976 to 1,218,000 in 1990. Nationwide, it went from 2,000,000 in 1976[1] to 3,091,000 in 1982 to 4,442,000 in 1990, an increase of some 43.7 percent in eight years.[2] Significant increases occurred during the 1990s—from 5.5 million in 1994 to 6.8 million in 1998.[3] Latinos experienced the fastest growth among all ethnic groups when it came to voter registration. From 1976 to 1996, Latinos increased their voter registration by 164 percent compared to 21 percent for the rest of the country,[4] whereas the number of non-Latino voters decreased from 82.2 million in 1994 to 79.0 million in 1998.[5]

At the national level, the Latino vote during the 1990s was concentrated in nine states: Arizona, California, Colorado, La Florida, Illinois, New Jersey, New York, Nuevo México, and Tejas. Latinos represented 11 percent of the U.S. population, and by 1998 some ten million were eligible to vote.[6] California and Tejas had the greatest number of Latinos registered to vote. The latter experienced increases from 1,384,000 in 1992 to 1,748,700 in 1998, while the former went from 1,203,000 in 1992 to 1,608,800 in 1998. Of the remaining three southwestern states Nuevo México experienced increases from 172,000 in 1992 to 210,000 in 1998; Colorado in 1992 numbered some 136,000 and by 1998 dropped to 103,800; and Arizona in 1992 had some 156,000 and by 1998 also decreased to 120,300.[7]

The rise in the number of Latinos registered to vote contributed to increases in the number of Mexicano and Latinos that cast their votes in presidential elections. Table 7.1 provides the total number of Latino votes cast in presidential elections from 1976 to 1996.

Table 7.1   Latino Votes Cast in Presidential Elections (1976–1996)

Year	Total Number of Votes Cast	% of U.S. Total Votes Cast
1976	2,098,000	2.4
1980	2,453,000	2.6
1984	3,092,000	3.4
1988	3,710,000	3.6
1992	4,238,000	3.7
1996	4,928,000	4.7

Source: U.S. Bureau of the Census. Current Population Surveys on Registration and Voting 1976–1996.

As the above figures indicate, in every presidential election between 1976 and 1996 a steady increase occurred in the total number of Latinos voting in presidential elections. From presidential election to presidential election, a differential increase varied from 500 to 600 thousand.

Yet the number of Latino votes cast in "nonpresidential" election years was smaller than the votes cast in presidential elections. Table 7.2 illustrates this argument.

As the above figures indicate, Latinos voted in less numbers during nonpresidential elections. This is not a unique voting characteristic of Latinos, since it is indicative of the country's voting pattern as a whole.

Latino Politics in Presidential Elections, 1976–1996

From the 1976 to 1996 presidential elections, Latinos did not become a "swing vote" or "balance of power" as a voting bloc. Yet in several states, particularly by the 1990s, Latinos had the potential to become the "swing vote." At the federal level, according to Acuña, "Eight states with 187 electoral votes housed 83 percent of the nation's Latino population: Arizona, 8; California, 54; Colorado, 8;

Table 7.2   Latino Votes Cast in "Nonpresidential" Election Years (1974–1994)

Year	Total Number of Votes Cast	% of U.S. Total Votes Cast
1974	1,397,000	2.2
1978	1,593,000	2.3
1982	2,217,000	2.8
1986	2,866,000	3.6
1990	2,894,000	3.5
1994	3,522,000	4.1

Source: U.S. Bureau of the Census. Current Population Surveys on Registration and Voting 1974–1994.

Florida, 25; Illinois, 22; Nuevo México, 5; New York, 33; Tejas, 32."[8] Of these, particularly Mexicanos were sufficiently numerous enough in six of the eight states to be considered to have a "swing vote" status.

As to political affiliation, since Roosevelt's New Deal, the great majority of Mexicanos consistently voted Democrat. This was principally ascribable to the socialized perception fostered during the Depression held by many Mexicanos, who perceived the Democrat Party as the "party of the poor," and the Republican Party as the "party of the rich." Most failed to recognize that both major political parties represented powerful liberal capitalist plutocratic interests.[9] By the 1980s, however, the effects of the HG began to alter this. In 1980, 67 percent of Latinos were registered as Democrats, 15 percent as Republicans, and 18 percent as Independents. Eight years later, Democratic Party affiliation decreased to 64 percent, whereas Republican affiliation increased to 16 percent, and Independent as an identification grew to 20 percent.[10] During the 1976, 1980, 1984, and 1988 presidential elections, Mexicanos voted solidly Democrat. Jimmy Carter (1976/ 1980), Walter Mondale (1984), and Michael Dukakis (1988) all received over 60 percent of the Mexicano vote.

Influenced by the Latino community's growing population base and increased political representation, Republicans during the 1980s accelerated their efforts to go after the so-called Hispanic vote. In 1976 Democrat Jimmy Carter received 81 percent of the Latino vote, but by the 1980 presidential election, Republican Ronald Reagan garnered 37 percent of the Hispanic vote.[11] During the 1984 presidential elections, Hispanic Republicans formed the "Viva 84" drive under the auspices of the newly formed National Hispanic Assembly. In response, Hispanic Democrats organized "Hispanic Force 84," under the leadership of Governor Toney Anaya, Mayor Henry Cisneros, and a few others.

In 1984 and again in 1988 some Latinos also became engaged in Reverend Jesse Jackson's "Rainbow Coalition" unsuccessful bid for the Democratic presidential nomination. In both the 1984 and 1988 presidential elections, Democrats won the Latino vote, but the size of the margin became the subject of debate. For instance, according to NBC News, in 1984 nationwide Mondale won 68 percent of the Hispanic vote and Reagan got 32 percent. CBS News, on the contrary, had Mondale winning over Reagan 61 percent to 37 percent, respectively. And ABC News reported that Mondale won 56 percent and Reagan 44 percent of the Hispanic vote.[12] The final percentage of Latinos who voted for Reagan was 34 percent, while Mondale received 66 percent.[13] During the 1988 presidential elections, a *New York Times*/CBS News Poll reported that Democrat Michael Dukakis garnered 69 percent of the Hispanic vote, while another exit poll conducted by Cable News/*Los Angeles Times* indicated that only 61 percent of Hispanics voted for Dukakis and 38 percent went to Republican George Bush.[14] In the end, Bush received 30 percent and Dukakis got 70 percent of the Latino vote.[15] What the results of the two presidential elections suggested was that the Latino vote was becoming increasingly up for grabs: less Democrat and gradually more Republican.

The presidential elections held during the 1990s followed similar patterns, except for a lull at the beginning of the decade. In the 1992 presidential election, Democrat Bill Clinton defeated Republican George Bush with strong support from Latinos. He garnered 61 percent of the Latino vote, while Bush received 25 percent.[16] While the general population voter turnout was 65.5 percent, for Latinos it was only 48.3 percent. A so-called Latino gap of 14.4 percent separated Latinos from the rest of the general population. The increasing number of noncitizens continued to be a political obstacle. In 1994, 43.8 percent of the Latino adult population were non-United States citizens, compared to 7.8 percent of the country's general population. Regardless, for the 1996 presidential election, Latino voter participation increased, giving Democrat incumbent Bill Clinton a victory over his Republican rival Robert Dole. Clinton received 72 percent of the Latino vote, while Dole garnered only 21 percent.[17] Journalist Lou Canon was so impressed with the Latino voter turnout that he concluded, "The Latino giant sleeps no more."[18]

According to the NALEO 2000 *Latino Election Handbook*, the Latino share of the national electorate increased in 1996 and again in 1998 from 4.69 percent to 4.90 percent. While the number of Latino voters grew from 3.5 million in 1994 to 4.1 million in 1998, the number of non-Latino voters decreased from 82.2 million in 1994 to 79.0 million in 1998. Voter participation of Latinos and non-Latinos began to parallel, in 1998 32.8 percent—or less than one out of three Latino citizens—voted. The gap between Latino and non-Latino voter turnout also changed, from 15.2 percent in 1994 to 13.4 percent in 1998. Latino naturalized citizens, percentage-wise voted in higher numbers than native-born Latinos: 37 percent of naturalized Latinos voted in comparison to 31 percent of the native-born Latinos.[19] For Latino naturalized citizens, the nativist politics that emanated out of California were a cardinal factor for the increase. Whereas naturalized citizens were more motivated to vote out of fear for the perceived threat to their interests, native-born Latinos seemed to be less passionate or concerned.

Latino Politics at the Federal Level, 1976–1989

At the federal level, by the late 1970s there was not one Latino in the U.S. Senate. Joseph Montoya, Democrat from Nuevo México, defeated in 1976, was the last

Latino to serve as a U.S. senator. In the House of Representatives, Latinos constituted a mere 2.3 percent of the membership, while they comprised 8 percent
of the country's total population.[20] During the 1970s the number of Mexicano
congresspersons did not increase. In 1976 there were four congressmen: Henry
B. Gonzalez, Democrat, Tejas; E. Kika de la Garza, Democrat, Tejas; Edward
Roybal, Democrat, California; and Manuel Lujan, Republican, Nuevo México.
In 1970, Puertorriqueño Herman Badillo, Democrat from New York, was elected
to Congress. Badillo was later replaced by Robert Garcia, who was also a Democrat and Puertorriqueño.[21] Consequently, during the decade, the total number of
Latinos in Congress was five.

Of the four Mexicano congresspersons, Gonzales and Roybal were the most
influential. Gonzales by 1975 was chairman of the House Committee on Banking,
Finance, and Urban Affairs, while Roybal was chair of the Committee on Aging
and in the 1980s served on the powerful Appropriations Committee. Both Gonzalez and Roybal were traditional liberal New Deal Democrats, who were strong
supporters of social and economic legislation while being strong on defense and
more conservative. De la Garza served as chairman of the House Agricultural
Committee. Ultraconservative Lujan enjoyed some popularity within the emergent Hispanic Republicans and party officials.[22] In 1982, three more Mexicanos
were elected to Congress: Esteban Torres and Mathew "Marty" Martinez, both
from California, and Bill Richardson from Nuevo México, all of which were
Democrats. By 1984 the number of Latino congressmen increased to eleven. By
the close of the 1980s, the Cuban community of Miami, Florida, elected Republican Ileana Ros-Lehtinen to Congress,[23] making the total of Latinos serving in
Congress ten. In 1986 one of Colorado's most successful politicians, Polly Baca
Barragan, who served in the House and State Senate, was defeated in her bid for
Congress. By 1988, Mexicanos had seven congressmen: three from California,
three from Tejas, and one from Nuevo México,[24] all of which played a buffer
role.

From the late 1970s to the 1980s, the number of Mexicano presidential federal appointments increased. In 1976, after receiving some 81 percent of the
Mexicano vote, Democratic president Jimmy Carter reciprocated by making more
federal appointments than any previous administration. He appointed some two
hundred, which included Dr. Julian Nava as ambassador to México; Raul Castro,
ambassador to Argentina; Mari-Luci Jaramillo, ambassador to Honduras; and Dr.
Ralph Guzman to the State Department.[25] Carter's successor, Republican president Ronald Reagan during the 1980s appointed a lesser number of Mexicanos.
This was illustrated by the fact that Carter's percentage of appointments to the

Federal District courts was higher, 6.9 compared to Reagan's 4.8 percent. To the Court of Appeals, Carter's percentage was 3.6 versus Reagan's 1.3 percent.[26]

Those Mexicanos that Reagan did appoint reflected his ultraconservative policies. Nestor D. Sanchez, who had retired from the Central Intelligence Agency in 1981, was appointed deputy assistant secretary of defense for inter-American affairs. He became Reagan's chief architect—a cold war hawk on national security issues involving Central America. Linda Chavez, appointed to the staff of the U.S. Civil Rights Commission, is described by Rodolfo Acuña as one of "Reagan's hatchet wielders of the commission." Chavez openly displayed her virulent antipathy for affirmative action and the rights of undocumented immigrants. Cathi Villapando was appointed special assistant to the president. Like Chavez, she was a zealous advocate for Reagan's ultraconservative policies.[27] With only a few months left in his administration, Reagan in 1988 appointed Mexicano Dr. Lauro Cavazos as secretary of education. The federal appointments made by the Carter and Reagan administrations were not commensurate with the country's Latino population, nor did they represent the interests of the poor Mexicano.

State and Local Latino Politics, 1974–1988

During the 1970s and 1980s, Mexicano political representation increased at both the state and local levels. In 1974 Democrat Jerry Apodaca of Nuevo México and Democrat Raul Castro of Arizona were elected governors of their respective states. Apodaca became the first Mexicano governor to be elected in Nuevo México in some fifty years.[28] Eight years later, Toney Anaya was elected governor of Nuevo México and served as the epoch's last Mexicano to do so. In La Florida, voters during the late 1980s elected Republican Bob Martinez, who became the state's first Latino governor of Cuban ancestry.[29] None of the Mexicanos elected governors were proponents or products of the CG activism. Apodaca was politically a moderate, Castro a conservative, and Anaya a liberal. As exponents of the HG, with the exception of Anaya, neither Apodaca nor Castro did much in the way to politically uplift the Mexicano's quality of life or advocate for their interests in their respective states. Former governor Apodaca in 1986 became the national president of the newly formed Hispanic Association on Corporate Responsibility (HAMAS).[30] As explained by Rodolfo Acuña, "Arizona Governor Raul Castro . . . spent most of his time supporting the state's right to work law and placating Arizona's conservatives." In 1977, he resigned under a cloud of suspicion yet was appointed by the Carter administration as ambassador to Argentina.[31] Anaya, however, particularly after his tenure as governor, embraced at times a strong liberal advocacy leadership role, dealing with a number of domestic and foreign policy issues. While serving as governor, he spoke out on U.S. intervention in Nicaragua and on the racist apartheid politics of the South African government.[32]

In California, former state secretary of welfare and health Mario Obledo ran unsuccessfully for governor in 1982. His main competitor for the Democrat Party nomination was Los Angeles mayor Bill Bradley. In examining the primary election results, Thomas Weyr writes, "It proved to be an embarrassment. Obledo could not muster much Hispanic support. Instead of a million votes and a $500,000 campaign chest, he raised $150,000 and won 3 percent of the ballots cast." He further concluded, "The outcome embarrassed Hispanics and turned many off voting. The conclusions from the debacle, however, were the same as in other gubernatorial races—Hispanics votes count."[33]

During the 1980s, only a handful of Mexicanos served in other statewide offices. Nuevo México had the largest number of state elected officials. Elected in 1982 along with Anaya were Clara Padilla Jones, secretary of state; Albert Romero, state auditor; Jim Baca, state land commissioner; and Eric Serna, corporation commissioner.[34] In California, Governor Jerry Brown in 1982 appointed Cruz Reynoso to the State Supreme Court.[35] Two years later in Tejas, another Mexicano, Raúl González, made political history by becoming the first to be elected associate justice of the Tejas Supreme Court by popular vote.[36] Reynoso suffered the wrath of powerful nativist forces. Because of his alleged liberal tendencies, he became the target of white corporate interests and conservatives. In 1986, he became a political casualty of a successful conservative nativist offensive that removed three Supreme Court Justices, Reynoso, Rose Bird, and Joseph Grodin. The nativists also succeeded with Proposition 63, the "English Is the Official Language" initiative,[37] which pandered to the non-Latino communities' "cultural fears" that California was becoming too "Latinoized" and "re-Mexicanized."

At the state legislature level during the late 1970s and 1980s, Mexicanos did not make significant gains. A net increase of only two occurred during the decade. In 1974, of the five southwest states, Nuevo México had the largest number with thirty-three, followed respectively by Tejas with fifteen, Arizona with eleven, California with eight, and Colorado with six. During the 1980s, Nuevo México had the highest number with twelve of forty-two members in the State Senate and twenty-two of seventy members in the State House of Representatives. The Senate majority leader was Senator Michael Alarid, and in the House of Representatives Ray Sanchez was the Speaker of the House. Arizona had the second highest proportion of Mexicanos in its legislature: six of thirty state senators and six out sixty state representatives. Tejas had four Mexicano state senators out of thirty-one and twenty in the 150-member State House. California had only three state senators in the forty-member Senate and four out of eighty in the State Assembly. Of particular significance was the election in 1982 of the first Mexicana, Gloria Molina, to the California Assembly. Colorado had two Mexicanos in the thirty-member State Senate and five in the sixty-five-member House of Representatives.[38] As a whole, few Mexicano legislators were vocal on the myriad of issues that specifically impacted Mexicanos, such as bilingual education and the farm-worker.

The most significant Mexicano and Latino electoral gains occurred at the local level. In 1986 there were 304 county officials, 1,048 municipal officials, and 530 court and law enforcement agents of Mexicano descent. There were also some 183 Latino mayors.[39] In great part this was a result of the enforcement of the Voting Rights Act, particularly its 1975 and 1982 amendments, which cleared the way for enhancing political participation via several lawsuits initiated by both SVREP and the Mexican American Legal Defense and Education Fund (MALDEF) on redistricting, at-large elections, and annexation. As to the amendments, according to Rodney E. Hero, they "brought a number of electoral processes at local government level under scrutiny, requiring local governments to undertake special efforts, such as the provision bilingual ballots, to assure the protection of 'language minorities.'"[40] Court suits also removed various barriers denying Latinos political participation and representation. One such case was the *Watsonville v. Gomez* decision of 1986, which allowed for the creation of single-member districts in Watsonville, California. As a result of this decision, numerous other cities shifted from at-large to single-member districts, which resulted in an increase in Latino representation.

Hispanic Generation politics at the local level was given impetus with the election of Henry Cisneros to the San Antonio city council in 1975 and as mayor in 1981. In 1977, Ray Salazar, a less well-known political figure, was elected mayor of El Paso, Tejas, and served a two-year term; and Federico Peña was elected mayor of Denver in 1982. As mayors of large cities, all three were cross-over politicians favored by powerful white economic interests, not dependent on their Mexicano power base. In the case of Cisneros, Acuña writes, "The Cisneros victory inspired more Chicano political participation and two years later [1977] Chicanos and Blacks took over the San Antonio City Council." With Mexicanos comprising only 18 percent of Denver's population, Peña became Denver's first Mexicano mayor by playing down his ethnicity. During the course of the campaign, he said, "I am not a Hispanic candidate. I just happen to be Hispanic."[41] Cisneros did the same by not promoting either his ethnicity or the special interests of the Mexicano community.[42]

In Tejas because of the Raza Unida Party (RUP) in the 1970s and voter registration efforts by SVREP and MALDEF's legal suits in the 1980s scores of Mexicanos were elected to local offices. A number of small communities in South Tejas, such as Crystal City, Cotulla, and Carrizo Springs, had Mexicano majorities in both the city council and school board. By the time Cisneros was elected mayor in 1981, San Antonio was a showcase with a majority of five Mexicanos and one black on the city council. This was the result of pressure exerted by the Justice Department in 1977 for San Antonio to adopt single-member districts. At the county level, the number of county commissioners and judges in Tejas increased from 72 in 1973 to 105 in 1984.

In 1987 in its annual report the National Association of Latino Elected and Appointed Officials (NALEO) reported that Latino representation had doubled since 1980, increasing to some 3,317 throughout the country. The four southwest border states of California, Arizona, Nuevo México, and Tejas had the largest concentrations of Latino elected officials, with emerging concentrations in La Florida, New York, and other Midwest states.[43] This occurred even though scores of Latinos, especially Mexicanos, were not eligible to vote due to their undocumented status. The increase in the number of Latino elected officials was due to voter registration drives, lawsuits, improved organization, greater political experience, coalition building, and an increase in the availability of financial resources.

Ideologically, in most cases, throughout the alleged "Decade of the Hispanic," Mexicano *politicos* espoused a rather liberal to conservative political posture with most as centrists that embraced a pro-system liberal capitalist position. At the partisan level of politics, Latino *politicos* who identified as Democrats in most cases ostensibly played buffer political roles, whereas most Latino Republicans gravitated toward a "want to be white" roles. Most were part of what historian Rodolfo Acuña described as the "age of brokers." In Los Angeles both former assemblyperson Richard Alatorre and former assemblyperson Gloria Molina were elected to the Los Angeles City Council. Alatorre was elected in 1985 became the second Mexicano during the twentieth century to serve on the city council. Molina, in a direct challenge to Alatorre's power group, in 1987 became the first Mexicana to be elected to the Los Angeles City Council.[44] With her victory, she too joined the ranks of competing Mexicano elite power brokers. Increasingly, Los Angles Mexicano politics became a game of competing cliques of buffer-type broker elites. Their individual interests prevailed over those of the community, which were secondary.

As Mexicano political representation increased so did the power struggles and schisms among them. Multiple centers of power and influence developed to the point that *politicos* battled each other over who was the most powerful or influential political leader, or better yet "broker" for the Latino community. Some *politicos* could not resist the vices of power. "In California," according to Meier and Rivera, "State Senator Joseph Montoya was indicted on twelve counts for selling his votes and federal District Judge Robert Aguilar was indicted on charges of trying to influence two judges in criminal cases."[45] In Tejas, the golden boy of Hispanic politics Mayor Henry Cisneros resigned after his extramarital affair became a public scandal.

Although Latinos experienced some impressive political gains, several demographic-related factors reduced their electoral efficacy. A cardinal impediment was the high number of Latinos who were undocumented. Some 37 percent of all Latinos were noncitizens, consequently ineligible to vote, and one-third of Latinos were too young to vote.[46] Further impediments included low levels of education, high poverty rates, lack of organizing leadership, disorganization, inadequate financial resources, voter dilution due to unfair redistricting, and gerrymandering. Voter alienation and apathy, especially among Mexicanos, were other impediments that in great part was ascribable the apolitical omnipresence of the Neo-Méx Generation and their colonized status.

Mexicano/Latino Politics in the 1990s

Mexicano/Latino ballot box politics experienced its greatest "empowerment surge" during the 1990s. The increases were due to major increases in the Latino population; voter registration, education, and get-out-the-vote drives; and in California, nativist propositions, such as 187, 209, and 227, that instilled fear and anger among the growing Latino electorate. A contributing factor, however, was the number of Latinos who became naturalized citizens during the 1990s. Since 1991, some 1.1 million Latinos were naturalized as U.S. citizens with another 4 million in the pipeline for the year 2000.[47] In 1996 alone some 250,000 Latinos became citizens and voted in record numbers. According to the NALEO 2000 Report, "The registration and turnout rates of Latino naturalized citizens were higher than those of the Latino native-born. In 1998 this pattern remained the same for the turnout rate of naturalized citizens: 37 percent of naturalized citizens voted as compared to 31 percent of native-born Latinos."[48] Nativist governor Pete Wilson's anti-immigrant politics coupled with racist initiatives fostered a persuasive incentive for Latinos to become naturalized citizens, register to vote, and actually vote. Paradoxically, racist Republican politicians and policies became the catalytic stimulus for Latinos to organize politically.

At the federal level, the 1990s produced major advances in both Mexicano and Latino representation. While still no Latino served as a U.S. senator, the number of congresspersons increased. By 1998, the number of Latino representatives in Congress increased to eighteen: eleven alone were from Tejas and California. More specifically, six were from Tejas, five from California, and one from Arizona. As to their ethnicity, twelve were Mexicanos, three Cubanos, and four Puertorriqueños.[49] As to presidential appointments, the Republican Bush administration (1988–1992) like the Democratic Clinton administration (1992–2000) appointed very few Latinos to cabinet positions. President Bush Sr. appointed former Nuevo México congressman Manuel Lujan as secretary of the interior. Clinton did better with the appointments of former San Antonio mayor Henry Cisneros as secretary of housing and urban development, former Denver mayor Federico Peña as the secretary of energy and secretary of transportation, and former Nuevo México congressman Bill Richardson as ambassador to the United Nations and secretary of energy.[50] In 1998 President Clinton appointed Louis Caldera as the country's first Mexicano secretary of the army.

At the state level of electoral politics, both Mexicanos and Latinos made substantial political strides. Table 7.3 illustrates the increases in the number of Latinos elected to the state legislatures of Aztlán's five major states from 1990 to 1998.

Table 7.3's figures illustrate how California underwent the most dramatic increase during the decade, from seven in 1990 to eighteen in 1998. Colorado regained in 1998 the eight held in 1992, since in 1996 it had gone down to six. Nuevo México continued to have the highest number in the State Senate and House, but since 1992 with a high of forty-five experienced a loss of six by 1998. Arizona actually declined in its level of Latino representation, from eleven in 1990 to nine in 1998. Tejas experienced significant growth, increasing from twenty-five in 1990 to thirty-six in 1998. In the other states of Aztlán not listed in the above table, Latino representation was relatively low. Utah in 1998 had one state representative and one state senator, whereas Nevada had one state senator and two state representatives. Outside of Aztlán, other states also made elec-

Table 7.3   Number of Latinos Elected to Aztlán's Five State Legislatures from 1990 to 1998

	1990	1992	1994	1996	1998
Arizona	11	11	10	6	9
California	7	12	14	14	18
Colorado	10	8	7	6	8
Nuevo México	40	45	42	41	39
Tejas	25	32	33	35	36

Source: NALEO 1990, 1992, 1994, 1996, and 1998 "National Directory of Latino Elected Officials."

toral gains in the state legislatures. In 1998 Illinois had four Latino state representatives and two state senators; New York, eight state representatives and four state senators; La Florida, eleven state representatives and three state senators; and New Jersey, four state representatives and no state senators.[51]

During the 1990s only a minimal number of Mexicanos served in state executive positions. Cruz Bustamante in 1996 was one of the few exceptions. He was elected as the first Speaker of the California State Assembly, and two years later, he was elected lieutenant governor. His election was extraordinary since he was the first Mexicano elected lieutenant governor since Republican Romualdo Pacheco in 1871. Also that year, in California, became the second Mexicano to be elected Speaker of the Assembly. In Tejas, Raúl A. Gonzalez held a seat on the State Supreme Court from 1984 to 1997, Dan Morales held the post of Tejas attorney general from 1990 to 1998,[52] and in 1998 Tony Garza served as railroad commissioner. With a total of five, Nuevo México in 1998 continued to have the largest number of state executives: Jerome D. Block, corporation commissioner; Eric P. Serna, corporation commissioner; Stephanie V. Gonzales, secretary of state; Michael A. Montoya, state treasurer; and Robert E. Vigil, state auditor.[53]

Again, the most impressive Latino electoral strides made during this decade were at the local level. By 1998 the total number of Latino elected officials increased to 4,985. Tejas had the largest number of Mexicano elected officials, some 1,749 of which 1,706 were local elected officials.[54] Particularly significant was that Tejas had the largest number of Mexicano or Latino local officials: county, 213; municipal, 531; and school board, 590.[55] Particularly, throughout South Tejas, Mexicanos continued to exercise "majority control" of various local counties, municipalities, and school boards; such was the case in San Antonio, where a Mexicano majority served on the city council. Ironically, however, in Crystal City, a small city of some ten thousand, where Mexicanos comprised over 90 percent of the population and which was the birthplace of the Raza Unida Party in Tejas, whites constituted a majority on the city council. Of the five serving on the council, only two were Mexicano. Powerful white economic interests, divisions within the Mexicano community, and a stultifying political apathy contributed to this paradox. Yet the city's school board was totally controlled by Mexicanos. Despite Mexicanos constituting majority populations in several South Tejas counties, few were controlled by Mexicano county officials. Five exceptions included Zavala, Dimmit, Alton, Zapata, and Duval. Even where Mexicano political representation existed, the people's quality of life in most cases did not improve, symptomatic of the effects of colonialism.

California in 1998 had the second largest number, with a total of 789 elected officials of which 766 were elected at the local level. At the county level, throughout the state there were a total of twenty-three Latino county officials. San Joaquin County with three Latino county supervisors had the most, followed by Kern and Merced counties, each with two. Even Imperial County where Mexicanos constituted approximately 68 percent of the population only had two county supervisors and a county recorder.[56] In Los Angeles County, Gloria Molina's supervisorial district, one of five, had some 1.9 million people and a board member oversaw a $13 billion budget.[57] Latinos at the county level suffered their highest level of underrepresentation. In great part this was ascribable to the exorbitant amount of resources required to challenge the hegemony of the entrenched white power elites.

At the municipal and school board levels, Mexicano representation in California increased. In Los Angeles County, especially in the San Gabriel Valley, Mexicano representation increased at the city council level. The city of Los Angeles had three Mexicanos on the city council: Mike Hernandez, Nick Pacheco, and Alex Padilla. Large cities such as Fresno, San Jose, and San Bernardino each had at least three Mexicanos serving on their city council. San Jose had a Mexicano mayor, Ron Gonzales, as did San Bernardino, Judith Valles. As for the city of Salinas, a major city in California, Mexicanos comprised a majority on the city council and the mayor, Ana Caballero, was Mexicana. There were other municipalities where Mexicanos constituted majorities, such as Coachella, Hawaiian Gardens, Irwindale, Maywood, Norwalk, Orange Cove, Parlier, Pico Rivera, and San Fernando, some of which had Mexicano mayors. A similar trend existed at the school board level. Again, Salinas became the political showcase with a Mexicano majority of four on the board. Mendota, Calexico, Little Lake City, Oxnard, and National City school districts, among a few others, also had Mexicano majorities on the school board. Illogically, Los Angeles only had one Mexicana school board member, Victoria Castro.[58]

Throughout Aztlán and the rest of the country, local Latino representation also increased. Nuevo México had a total of 602 Latino elected officials; 558 were elected at the local level. Of Arizona's 273 Latino elected officials, 263 were local. And in Colorado, of 159 Latino elected officials, 151 were local as well. Nevada had a total of five elected officials; only two were local. And Utah only had a total of two elected officials, one in the State Senate and one in the State House, but none at the local level. Significant local representation also existed in states outside of Aztlán, such as Illinois, New York, La Florida, and New Jersey, among others.[59]

The Rise of Chicana/Latina Politics

For generations Mexicano ballot box politics was "male" dominated. Mexicana "underrepresentation" was attributable to vestiges of patriarchal values that permeated the Mexicano's "divergent generations" and a political system that discouraged their direct political involvement. In spite of sexism that pervaded it, the Movimiento experienced challenges to the male-dominated culture by some Mexicano activists exhorting attitudinal changes of inclusion and participation. This change was further buttressed by Latina activism. In 1977, President Carter appointed Mari-Luci Jaramillo ambassador to Honduras. The political push for Latinas to be elected to political office accelerated during the 1980s. Urged not to run in 1982, Gloria Molina ran successfully against Richard Polanco, who was the favorite of the Mexicano "Good Ole Boy" network. She became an advocate of women and community-related issues and proved to be a shrewd and savvy politician. Other Latinas began to run, and consequently, according to Del Castillo and De León, "A higher proportion of Latinas won election (18 percent), compared with women in the general population (12 percent)."[60]

Women by 1990 comprised 40 percent of the total number of Latinos elected and appointed to municipalities throughout Aztlán. Three prominent Latinas, in this case Mexicanas, who served in the city councils of large cities were Gloria Molina, Los Angeles; Maria Berriozabal, San Antonio; and Debbie Ortega, Denver.[61] Molina in 1991 became the first Latina to be elected to the Los Angeles County Board of Supervisors. By 1993, nonetheless, of 193 Latino mayors in the country only twenty-two were Latinas, which included six in Tejas and two in California. Furthermore, as cited by Oscar Martinez:

> Between 1984 and 1993, Latinas nationwide experienced a 179 percent growth in the numbers of offices won at the polls. In Arizona, Latinas made up 27 percent of all Hispanic elected officials in 1993, 29 percent in California, 19 percent in Colorado, 22 percent in New México, and 20 percent in Texas. . . . In Illinois as a whole in 1993 Latinas made up a whopping 65 percent of all Hispanic elected officials.[62]

By the late 1990s, the number of Latinas elected varied from state to state. However, it was during this decade that Latina political representation increased substantially at all levels. At the federal level, specifically the Congress, by 1998 of the eighteen congresspersons, four were Latinas (two were Mexicanas, one Puertorriqueña, and one Cubana). Two were from California, one from New York, and one from La Florida. But it was at the state level where Latinas showed significant numbers. By January 1998, the five southwestern states of Aztlán had experienced increases in Latina elected officials. Of 789 elected Latino officials in California, 262 were female: 1 in the State Senate and 7 in the Assembly; 5 county officials; 148 on school boards; and 82 at the municipal level. In Arizona, a total of 273,103 were women: 3 served in the State House, none in the State Senate, 5 as county officials, 47 on school boards, and 37 municipal. Of Nuevo México's 602 Latino elected officials, 132 were female: 2 served at the state executive level, Patricia Madrid as attorney general and Rebecca Vigil-Giron as secretary of state. In addition, 5 served as state senators, 4 as state representatives, 38 as county officials, 29 as school board members, and 37 at the municipal level. Colorado with 159 Latino elected officials had 46 females, 3 that served as state representatives, none in the State Senate, 7 as county officials, 13 on school boards; and 23 as municipal officials. As for Tejas with a whopping total of 1,749 elected officials, 381 were Mexicanas: 1 state senator and 9 state representatives, 72 county officials, 140 school board officials, and 101 city officials. A similar pattern existed in several other states.[63]

Thus, politically, Latinas by the close of the century were on the offensive, shattering male hegemony of ballot box politics and assuming major leadership roles. The "macho politics" of the past was being replaced by a new co-gender politics predicated on equity and equal access.

Chicano International Politics: Acercamiento with México and Cuba

At the international level, the politics of *acercamiento* that grew out of the activism of the epoch of protest continued. Some Mexicano activists and politicians adhered to the idea of fostering a viable nexus or relationship with México, Cuba, and Central America. In particular, activists wanted to secure support for their domestic struggle and agenda in the United States, while others endeavored to promote formal linkages via cultural, educational, and economic programs and activities. Numerous delegations traveled primarily to México, Cuba, and Central America to meet with the respective countries' high government officials, at times the president himself; academicians; labor, party, and church officials; and student leaders. In some instances, they met with guerilla insurgency leaders. The linkages that did develop produced in some cases academic and cultural exchanges, economic networking, and political interaction on a number of issues and concerns.

As previously examined, the "politics of *acercamiento*" originated during the latter years of the epoch of protest. From 1972 to 1978, José Angel Gutiérrez was the "Chicano connection" to México's governing PRI (Institutional Revolutionary Party) leadership. Numerous RUP delegations traveled periodically to México to meet with presidents Luis Echevarría (1970–1976) and José López Portillo (1976–1982) as well as other high government and PRI officials. During these same years, Gutiérrez, Juan Jose Peña, and Xenaro Ayala, among other RUP leaders, developed a working relationship with the PST (the Workers Socialist Party) that continued until 1980.[64]

In 1975 Gutiérrez expanded his *acercamiento* politics to include Cuba. He led a sixteen-person RUP delegation on a ten-day trip and met with various Cuban government officials on various aspects of the Cuban Revolution. Inspired by the accomplishments of the Cuban Revolution upon his return to the United States, Gutiérrez created an embarrassing situation over his controversial comments that RUP was going to create "many little Cubas in South Texas." That same year RUP leader Fred Aguilar among others traveled to the People's Republic of China. In 1978 some RUP activists from Nuevo México traveled to Nicaragua and became engaged in support of the revolutionary armed struggle of the Sandinistas. In 1980 a nine-person RUP delegation traveled to Lebanon and met with Yasir Arafat and other PLO (Palestinian Liberation Organization) officials.[65]

By the end of Portillos's six-year presidential term in 1982, RUP leaders and Chicano activists had been replaced with the Latino leadership of moderate HG-oriented organizations. During the early 1980s, some bilateral interaction occurred with the Congressional Hispanic Caucus, MALDEF, National Council of La Raza (NCLR), and League of United Latin American Citizens (LULAC).[66] By 1985 some Chicano activists, including myself, were hypercritical of U.S. foreign policy vis-à-vis Latin America, particularly as it affected Cuba and Central America. As a result, occasionally, Latinos organized protests or held colloquia against U.S. interventionist policies in El Salvador, Nicaragua, Honduras, and Guatemala.

San Antonio mayor Henry Cisneros in 1983 was appointed by President Reagan to the National Bipartisan Commission on U.S. Policy in Central America. Named the "Kissinger Commission," it made policy recommendations that in essence justified the military interventionist policies of the Reagan administration in Central America. Antonio Gonzales explains Cisneros's involvement: "On one hand, his participation in the Kissinger Commission legitimized Chicano involvement in foreign policy matters at the national leadership level. On the other hand, Cisneros's substantive positions, though dissenting from right wing majority, embraced the practice of U.S. military intervention, negated self-determination, and ignored the root causes of the region's revolutions: poverty and repression."[67]

Some Chicano activists, especially students, became hypercritical of Cisneros's involvement with the said commission. Yet those who adhered to the HG's politics applauded Cisneros for his involvement. Mario Obledo in 1984, as national president of LULAC promulgated the Latin American Project designed to foster debate and discussion on U.S. foreign policy in Latin America. That year Obledo led a LULAC delegation to México, Cuba, and Nicaragua. While debates were held at LULAC's national conventions on issues related to Latin America, LULAC's Latin American Project was purely an academic exercise.[68] LULAC as well as other HG-oriented organizations chose not to criticize U.S. interventionist policies in Central America. In fact in 1985, Nuevo México congressman Bill Richardson as chair of the Congressional Hispanic Caucus supported reinstating aid to the Contras in Nicaragua, which was prohibited by the Boland Amendment.[69]

A second major wave of *acercamiento* politics occurred during the years 1985 to 1990. This time the leadership came from the activist sector. In 1985 as executive director of the Institute for Social Justice (ISJ), a community organizing institute that dealt with a variety of domestic and international issues, in collaboration with other groups, I organized and headed a peace delegation that traveled to México, Honduras, El Salvador, Nicaragua, and Cuba, which met with government officials in each of the respective countries as well as government opposition leaders. The delegation's primordial objective was to push for peace initiatives, specifically México's Contadora's Peace Initiative. The delegation traveled to Honduras and met with the country's leading political parties' leadership; to El Salvador into guerrilla-held territory and met with the FMLN's (Farabundo Marti National Liberation Front) top leadership; to Nicaragua, where it met with Daniel Ortega and other Sandinista leaders; and to Cuba, where it was received by President Fidel Castro himself, and met with Cuban government officials. A fact-finding report, which was hypercritical of Reagan's interventionist policies, was submitted to the appropriate U.S. congressional committees.

The ISJ also carried out its own form of *acercamiento* politics with México. In 1987 an eleven-person delegation comprised of various organizational representatives traveled to México City and met with several secretaries of President Miguel de La Madrid's administration. The intent was to address issues of mutual concern, especially education, immigration, and business. Equally important, however, was the strengthening of political and cultural bonds between Chicanos/ Mexicanos in the United States and México. In 1988 the ISJ augmented its *acercamiento* politics with the formation of a national coalition called IMPACTO 88. Meetings were organized in Tijuana and Mexicali with México's three major presidential candidates: Carlos Salinas de Gortari (PRI) and Cuauhtémoc Cárdenas (Corriente Democratica) in Tijuana; and Manuel Clouthier (PAN) in Mexicali. The meetings, especially the one with Gortari, received international media coverage. For the next two years, IMPACTO 88, which in 1989 became IMPACTO 2000, was the Mexicano political connection in the United States to México's political leadership, and numerous meetings were held on educational, cultural, economic, and immigration-related issues.[70]

During the decade of the 1990s the politics of *acercamiento* changed with the approval of the North American Free Trade Agreement (NAFTA) and the Chiapas insurgency. By the early 1990s, the Gortari administration moved to secure support from as many Latino organizations and leaders as possible for its campaign for the approval of NAFTA. Once some of the IMPACTO leadership voiced their opposition to NAFTA, Gortari's operatives expeditiously dropped IMPACTO as the contact. Instead support shifted to the leadership of the United Farm Workers (UFW), MALDEF, LULAC, NCLR, SVREP, and the Hispanic Chamber of Commerce, among others. For the next few years, it was the leadership of these organizations and Latino politicians that were the interpreters of the "politics of *acercamiento*." Under Gortari and subsequently under the administration of Ernesto Zedillo several Latino leaders were recipients of various accolades. Regardless of who was the connection to México, the fact was that Mexicanos in the United States were increasingly becoming, especially politically and economically, a priority for the Mexican government.

During the latter part of the 1990s the struggling activist sector again assumed a leadership role in *acercamiento* politics. From 1995 to 1999, a number of Mexicano groups, such as La Coordinadora, an immigration network of several organizations and leaders from throughout the country, became major political conduits to México's political parties, especially the PRD (Democratic Revolutionary Party). However, the leadership of the national alphabet of Latino or Hispanic organizations and politicians continued to massage the so-called international connection with México. But it was the plethora of emergent clubs and organizations comprised of Mexicanos from México with deep roots in their respective states that by the late 1990s, as will be examined subsequently in this chapter, assumed the primary organizational leadership role.

The Zapatista insurgency in Chiapas in 1994 garnered support among some Mexicano activists and fostered activism on its behalf. In 1998 Maria Anna Gonzales from the University of California, Riverside, Ernesto Galarza Public Policy Center (EGPPC), which I founded, and I organized a small peace delegation that traveled to Chiapas to meet with Zapatista officials and supporters. In 1999, under my leadership and with support of Gonzales and EGPPC, a sixty-member delegation traveled to Cuba that included several prominent Chicano scholars and activists to participate in a three-day conference that was held at the University of Havana on the Chicano Political Experience and the Cuban Revolutionary Experience. During the one-week stay, the delegation met with several high-ranking Cuban government officials, such as Ricardo Alarcon, Cuba's president of the National Assembly. A number of possible projects were discussed with Cuban officials, particularly in education, that would be mutually beneficial. By the end of the decade, both "Latino ballot box politics" and "*acercamiento* politics" with México and Cuba had intensified.

Mexicano/Latino Organizations

Vehicles of Resistance and Change

Organizational development during the epoch of the HG continued to play a significant role within the context of the Mexicano political experience. Unlike the previous epoch of militant protest, this epoch did not produce a renaissance of protest or ideologically based organizations. Instead it experienced the demise of several Movimiento organizations and ushered in a number HG-oriented organizations that adhered to a buffer pro-system and liberal capitalist orientation. These included local, state, and national organizations of various forms of which some were business and professional associations and media coalitions. Some traditional organizations that were products of the MAG adapted rather expediently and expeditiously to the emergent HG politics. New forms of community grassroots or mass-based advocacy organizations also decorated the political organizational landscape of occupied Aztlán. One could argue that Mexicanos and Latinos did not suffer from a lack of organization, but on the contrary, suffered from an abundance of organization. However, few were in "practice" advocacy change-oriented and those that were lacked an effective power capability, and the scope of reform change sought was limited. On a negative note, of the few that were advocacy oriented, Roger E. Hernandez writes, increasingly, some were "marked by infighting and special interest brokering."[71]

At the close of 1999, at a national level, none of the organizations possessed a "fear factor capability" predicated on a power capability. They suffered from what can be described as the "Rodney Dangerfield Syndrome," which meant they got little or "no respect" from either the white political and economic establishment or the Mexicano/Latino communities due to their inability to exercise actual power over the public policy processes. The epoch's political culture based upon the HG's ethos accentuated buffer political roles of "organizational adaptation" and a "mainstream orientation." Few organizations were driven by a vision predicated on reforming or transforming the liberal capitalist system or on the building of a "Chicano" nation. Political scientist Mario Barrera explains, "While the rhetoric of some of these groups obscured their true nature, in essence they represented continuity with their liberal reformism that has dominated Chicano politics since the time of the New Deal."[72] Using a cursory case study format, the salient organizations that impacted the Mexicano political experience are briefly examined.

Protest Organizations: Their Demise and Decline

One salient aspect of the HG was the demise and decline of numerous Movimiento protest organizations. The end of the Movimiento in 1974 signaled the end of protest organizations, such as the Alianza Federal de Mercedes, Brown and Black Berets, Mexican American Youth Organization (MAYO), United Mexican American Students (UMAS), and scores of others that became moribund by 1975. Their decline was also a result of chronic infighting resulting from power struggles and ideological differences, burnout of activist leaders and followers, and a changing political culture that by 1974 repudiated the ethos of the CG. Thus, during this epoch, protest organizations became increasingly unpopular and scarce, and the few that did survive by 1999 were barely functional.

Crusade for Justice (CJ)

From 1975 until its demise in 1982, the CJ was constantly under a state of siege by law enforcement agencies. It concurrently faced a precarious existence due to a myriad of political and financial problems.[73] The country's rapidly changing conservative political climate, especially in Colorado, the home base of reactionary tycoon Joseph Coors, also contributed to its decline. With no Movimiento to buttress its nationalist agenda, the CJ became increasingly isolated and was relegated to a "survival defensive posture." Indicative of the hard times the CJ faced, in 1975 Gonzales was arrested on charges of "interference" in the investigation of "Gary Garrison," who faced arson and bombing charges. Although the charges were dropped, the incident reflected the volatile relationship between the CJ and police. Gonzales filed but lost a lawsuit for $1,100,000 for eleven claims of false arrests, false imprisonment, deprivation of rights, and conspiracy.

The CJ also came under increasing pressure and scrutiny by law enforcement agencies, including the FBI. No other Movimiento organization came under as much law enforcement scrutiny, surveillance, infiltration, and attack as did the CJ.[74] This was in part due to its close political working relationship in 1975 with the Puertorriqueña separatist FALN (Fuerzas Armadas de Liberacion Nacional or Armed Forces of National Liberation). For the next two years, the FBI sought to implicate CJ members as terrorists, alleging that they had purchased dynamite. In January 1976 Juan Haro, vice chairperson of the CJ, was convicted on charges of violating federal firearm laws, specifically, possession of hand grenades, and was sentenced to six years in prison. The CJ countered by alleging that Haro was innocent and had been framed by an undercover agent. At about the same time, the Denver police alleged that Gonzales plotted to assassinate Denver's chief of police, which Gonzales denied unequivocally. In another incident that same year, this time with the FBI, the CJ and the American Indian Movement (AIM) in June 1976 were both implicated in a memorandum entitled "Kill a Cop Day" that read, "The objectives of the groups are disturbance and terrorism. They are reported to have plans to kill a cop each day in each state." Both the CJ and AIM denounced the allegations, which had fostered wide media attention and an alert of law enforcement agencies in several states, including the Texas National Guard. The CJ and AIM under scrutiny by COINTELPRO were categorized as terrorist organizations.[75]

The effects of the siege on the CJ impacted its delivery of services and programs, especially La Escuela Tlatelolco, which in 1975 lost several of its foundation grants, causing serious financial hardships to the fledgling school. Adding to the school's problems was that parents, concerned and afraid over the escalating violence directed at the CJ by the police, pulled their children out of the school. From 1971 to 1975, the school graduated some fifty-one students, eight who later obtained bachelor's degrees. Between 1975 and 1979 only twenty-one students graduated. Starting in 1976, the CJ moved aggressively to create a number of nonprofit organizations that included child care, youth boxing, cultural programs, legal defense, and media, but none were successful in garnering the requisite resources to keep the CJ's operation financially solvent. Indicative of its rapid decline was the CJ's cancellation in 1979 of its weekly barrio "Fishermen's meetings." Divisions with local HG organizations also became exacerbated over a number of issues.

Adding to the CJ's political situation was its conflict with another Movimiento organization, Centro de Acción Social Autónoma (Center for Autonomous Social Action or CASA). At the core of the heated political battle were political turf and finances. A political confrontation occurred when CASA called for a national meeting in Greenly, Colorado, in November 1975, which was facilitated by RUP and CJ leader José Calderon. With some fifty CASA leaders in attendance, the CJ's leadership responded by making physical threats. A bomb was found in a car parked outside the meeting place. As a result of the political polarization, José Calderon resigned from both organizations.[76]

The siege the CJ was under among other problems compelled it to shut down its RUP organizing efforts in 1976. That year the CJ became engaged in yet another bellicose-like political controversy, this time with the Socialist Workers Party (SWP).[77] An altercation between SWP organizers and CJ leaders occurred at CJ's headquarters. The incident became an issue of heated discussion and debate among those few remaining activists around the country.[78] Because of increasing conflicts with the SWP and CASA, the CJ did not attend the National Chicano Forum in Salt Lake City, Utah, and in 1977 the National Immigration Conference in San Antonio, Tejas, facilitated by Tejas's RUP.[79]

The CJ's decline accelerated during its last five years of existence. Law enforcement agencies and the FBI continued their harassment and targeting of the organization and its leadership. Counter lawsuits involving Gonzales and police continued to be commonplace as well as press conferences conducted by the CJ denouncing the police. Despite the debilitating pressures, the CJ continued to hold meetings and conferences, and participated as well in direct actions. But as the CJ's decline accelerated so did the interest in the CJ. According to Ernesto Vigil, who was one of the CJ's top leaders and author of a study on it, "The Crusade functioned, but its activities, constituency, and effectiveness greatly declined." He explains that by the late 1970s few new members joined the organization, and in the four and a half years that followed, "the Crusade was unable to grapple effectively with the changing political environment and its loss of human and material resources—ceased to be a powerful organization."[80]

The CJ's struggle for change and Aztlán were replaced with the perennial struggle of paying the bills—utilities, telephone, and staff. The CJ's official newspaper, *El Gallo*, was published on a regular basis only until 1980. The Gonzales family, however, sporadically published it until 1985. With the closure of the CJ's complex in 1982 came an end to the CJ, one of the most influential Movimiento protest organizations and that of its leader, Gonzales. La Escuela was relocated to Servicios de La Raza, a North Denver social service agency where Gonzales's daughter was employed. In 1987 Gonzales suffered a major stroke while driving his vehicle; he lost control of his car, causing him to crash into a building. He suffered serious head injuries that kept him hospitalized for weeks. As a result of his injuries he was disabled, which impeded him from becoming engaged in advocacy issues. Periodically, however, during the late 1990s, he did travel to political events for special appearances. The CJ existed through the 1990s, at least on paper, as a nonprofit corporation with limited membership and a board composed mostly, if not entirely, of his family members.[81] The Gonzales efforts focused entirely on La Escuela Tlatelolco, which in 1999 remained functional. Thus, the demise of the CJ left an organizational void that has yet to be filled. Without a doubt, the CJ and Gonzales left a legacy unequaled in the Chicano struggle for self-determination and left a historical imprint that will remain in the annals of the struggles of the Mexicano experience in the United States.

Movimiento Estudiantil Chicano de Aztlán (MEChA)

Of the Movimiento student organizations that existed during the epoch, MEChA continued to be the largest and the most dominant. Especially throughout Aztlán, it was the only one that had direct links to the politics of protest of the late 1960s.[82] After the demise of the Movimiento in 1974, the student activist sector was plagued by even worse internecine conflicts, stultifying apathy, complacency, and a growing moderation in its politics. Even prior to 1974, according to Manuel Gonzales, MEChA "went into a serious tailspin between 1971 and 1973, from which it never completely recovered."[83] Beyond the growing negative conservative political effects of the HG, MEChA was not immune to the "politics of self-destruction"—from the external and internal ideological struggles between cultural nationalists and Marxists to RUP's leadership power struggles. Issues of class verses ethnicity and whether to support Gonzales or Gutiérrez for RUP's leadership fostered polarizing schisms that debilitated MEChA's role as a change agent. Between 1975 and 1976, some MEChA chapters, especially in California, also became embroiled in the ideological war between Marxist-Leninist CASA and the Maoist August Twenty-ninth Movement (ATM).

During the 1970s, some students became turned off by MEChA's infighting and confrontational student politics. According to Muñoz, "Most Chicano students no longer perceived MEChA as a viable organization for meeting their academic and social needs."[84] Instead many students opted for a career orientation that emphasized individual advancement. Ad hoc groups that eventually became full-fledged organizations focused on medicine, law, teaching, business, and engineering, and not student activism or politics. While some students still culturally adhered to a cultural nationalist perspective, most gradually became consumed by the ethos of the HG. Taking courses or majoring in Chicano Studies lost its appeal, indicating the growing "Hispanicization" of the student sector.

Without the presence of a Movimiento, MEChA's politics of protest and nation building (Aztlán) during the 1980s underwent a change. Its nationalist separatist posture was gradually replaced with a much more reformed, moderate, and adaptation mode of politics. Only a thin veneer of Chicanismo was maintained, while it adhered increasingly to mainstream reform politics predicated on liberal capitalism. Some Mechistas (MEChA members) during the 1984 and 1988 presidential elections supported Reverend Jesse Jackson's bid for the Democratic Party's presidential nomination. Increasingly, while some chapters maintained a high profile of activism, others resembled "culture clubs," meaning they generally avoided direct action and were consumed with holding cultural and social events, such as Cinco de Mayo, Mexican Independence (16th of September), and Dia de la Raza (October 12) celebrations, speaker's forums, symposia, dances, and local student conferences.

MEChA's annual national and state conferences continued to debate the virtues of nationalism verses Marxism. One such occasion was when nationalist and Marxist zealots, specifically La Liga and the Maoist League Revolutionary Struggle (LRS), squared off at the seventh annual National Chicano Student Conference held at UC Berkeley during the spring 1986. The conference produced further divisions based upon the debates and conflict over the rise of feminism within MEChA's ranks. According to a writer who chose the pseudonym "Cielito Lindo," some Chicanas became hypercritical of the Chicano Generation. They alleged that *machismo* and the patriarchic aspects of Mexicano culture, nationalism, and the Chicano male were responsible for their plight. In the ensuing years, Mechistas became divided over cultural nationalism versus postmodern feminism.[85] Also, endless debates occurred in conferences over issues related to El Plan Espiritual de Aztlán or El Plan de Santa Barbara.

MEChA during the 1990s suffered from serious structural problems. At both the national and state levels it did not have an effective coordinating structure. MEChA's basic structural unit was the local chapter, which was autonomous. Chapters within a given area or region formed a "central" or regional confederation comprised of several college and university chapters that met periodically. At the *centrales* meetings, members discussed and acted on issues collectively. The various *centrales* convened at statewide meetings as well as at an annual conference to discuss issues, conduct planning, and act on priorities.[86] Yet it had no mechanism to implement the myriad of resolutions passed at its annual state or national conferences. Also, due to limited funding, MEChA was dependent on university or college administrative funds and on fund-raising events, which impeded its advocacy ability to address campus and community problems. In California, according to Roberto Tijerina, who was MEChA chair at UCR in 1996, stated that MEChA statewide or nationally for the aforementioned reasons "was basically a joke."[87]

Throughout much of the 1990s, much of the student sector continued to be apolitical. MEChA chapters, however, at times occasionally came alive politically and engaged in university and community-related issues. In particular, in California, during the struggles against Propositions 187, 209, and 227 some MEChA chapters in coalition with other groups became revitalized and initiated direct actions, for example, marches, rallies, speak-outs, and in voter mobilization efforts, such as voter registration, political education, and get-out-the vote drives. However, some of the student mobilizations, especially against Proposition 187, were not conducted by college or university students but rather by high school students. It was at the high school level that MEChA chapters among other students organizations engaged in a transient manner in militant protest action against Proposition 187 via spontaneous school walkouts, which appeared at times anarchistic, lacking in organization and strategy. Their actions were criticized by both the press and some HG groups and politicians, especially for their use of México's rather than the U.S. flag as well as their use of nationalist rhetoric and symbolism. Many of the protesting students came from the political cultural ranks of the NMG, since their parents were either documented or undocumented migrants.

During the rest of the decade, some MEChA chapters periodically adopted a militant protest mode. MEChA chapters at the University of California, Los Angeles (UCLA); University of California, Riverside (UCR); and University of California, Berkeley (UC Berkeley), among a few others, were particularly active. On several occasions they organized hunger strikes, sit-ins, marches, and pickets on issues related to the establishment of Chicano studies departments, retention of Chicano faculty, and in support of affirmative action. However, after the crisis or issue subsided, so did much of their activism, which resulted in most cases to a return to general apathy or "symbolic cultural activism." While some student activism occurred in other states, such as in Tejas, especially on the issue of affirmative action, it was in California, however, where MEChA was most active.

By the late 1990s, conflicts intensified between MEChA and other student organizations on university campuses. In some campuses, MEChA became engaged in internecine conflicts, particularly with emergent Hispanic/Latino fraternities and sororities (both products of the HG). Integral to the conflict was a class factor as well as major differences over ideology, issues, personalities, and lastly, turf. Unlike in the 1970s and 1980s, by the 1990s, Mexicano students entering the universities increasingly came from the ranks of the middle to upper-middle class. Consequently, many adhered to the ethos of their parents, which increasingly were grounded essentially on the values, beliefs, and morals of the HG.

MEChA also faced internal challenges and schisms over the growing presence of "postmodern feminism." On this issue, a former MEChA leader using the pseudonym Cielito Lindo provocatively argues, "In a ten year span 1990 through 2000, Lesbian (Chicana) Feminists infiltrated MEChA's at many universities." The author alleged that they used "Chicana feminism as a catapult into MEChA for their own agenda." Moreover, that due to opposition from nationalists, they failed in their efforts to rename MEChA to the Movimiento Estudiantil Chicana/o de Aztlán.[88] Regardless of the issue, women during the late 1990s took up in greater numbers the mantle of MEChA's leadership. They significantly contributed to positive efforts that obviated MEChA's decline. Thus, during the late

1990s, some MEChA chapters shifted their locus ideologically from cultural nationalism to a more postmodern perspective that emphasized gender, culture, and group identity issues.

The "Mexica Nation" also gained access into the ranks of MEChA, which added to existent schisms. Organizers for the Mexica Nation asked Mechistas to make a three-year agreement that entailed a zealous adherence to *indigenismo*. They were required to learn *danza* (dance), the ritual of the sweat lodges, and about the old indigenous cultural ways and return to them, and accept their opposition to modern Western liberal capitalist-oriented cultures. On many campuses, some Mechistas answered the call and joined the Mexica Nation. With a declining membership base and other organizational pressures, MEChA statewide and certain *centrales* purged themselves of members of the Mexica Nation. By the turn of the century, MEChA was in a critical juncture due to its diminishing loss of Movimiento purpose, mission, and activism.

Committee on Chicano Rights (CCR)

The National City-based cultural nationalist protest organization out of California with its roots in the early 1970s was formed in 1975 and incorporated in 1977. The CCR was a product of various other organizational efforts, which included the Mexican American Political Association (MAPA) and Raza Unida Party organized by its founder and leader Herman Baca. What made the CCR different from the other groups was that its paramount focus was on "Chicano Rights." The CCR was created as the result of an incident involving the police shooting of a young Puerto Rican in National City in 1975. Baca's CCR alleged police brutality, and a number of community direct action mobilizations and an unsuccessful recall of the city council were initiated. From 1975 to 1981, the CCR was at the avant-garde of the pro-immigrant struggle in California. It organized several large protest marches along the U.S./México border at San Ysidro and dealt with a number of local rights issues. In 1981, CCR's leadership met with government officials in México and the United States to address various aspects of the immigration issue.[89] That same year some of its cadre leadership and membership left over differences of ideological direction and formed the Union del Barrio, which is subsequently examined in this chapter.

During the Simpson-Mazzoli (1982–1984) Immigration Reform and Control Act (IRCA, 1986) legislative battles, the CCR spoke out and advocated against its passage. After 1987 the CCR entered into a gradual decline mode. When interviewed in 2002 and asked why the CCR began to decline, Baca's response was terse: "What was left of the *conciencia* of the Chicano Movement was dead." Imbued with frustration, Baca explained that the CCR as a volunteer organization did not have the resources to compete with other federally funded immigration and service agencies. He said, "We couldn't compete with the "poverty pimps and their agencies, who had joined forces with the 'Gestapo' [U.S. Border Patrol] to implement IRCA in 1987."[90] Via Baca's leadership, the CCR continued to openly admonish and criticize vociferously those leaders and organizations that played either buffer or "want to be white" political roles.

During the 1990s, faced by personal economic hardships, Baca was not able to maintain a consistent CCR organizing effort. Instead, Baca resorted to periodically making pronouncements on a variety of issues, and in general the CCR's actions lessened to a trickle by the late 1990s. Although, however, the CCR on a few occasions still addressed some issues, such as when white nativists patrolled San Diego's airport with the intent of apprehending undocumented workers. Baca's major vehicle of protest became not the CCR, but some of the media that still sought his views on a number of issues.

By the late 1990s, the CCR's status was tenuous if not precarious. Frustrated by what he perceived was a multiplicity of contradictions inherent in the HG's politics and lacking a formal structure, sufficient resources, and a community base of support, Baca was not deterred, however, from periodically espousing his nationalist politics and views on issues impacting Mexicanos.

Mexicanos and the Labor Struggle

The UFW Struggle for Survival

The UFW entered the new epoch in 1975 with some encouraging momentum. During the early 1970s, the UFW had been plagued by jurisdictional disputes with its archrival Teamsters Union, a declining membership, and alleged administrative weaknesses, which became public. Although weakened, the UFW continued to wage its lettuce and grape and Gallo boycotts. A modified compromise version of Assemblyman Richard Alatorre's legislation, the Agricultural Labor Relations Act (ALRA) was introduced in 1974 and approved in 1975 by the legislature. With its passage and approval by newly elected Democratic governor Jerry Brown, the UFW experienced a transient rebound that was illustrated by an increase in its membership to some forty-five thousand. The ALRA gave the UFW what it wanted: secret-ballot elections administered and certified by an Agricultural Labor Relations Board (ALRB), voting rights for migrant seasonal workers, and control over the timing of elections.[91] With its enactment in 1975 the UFW won half of the 406 elections.[92]

The UFW's political triumph turned sour when the ALRB ran out of money in 1976. In response to the ALRB's financial crisis, the UFW gathered some seven hundred thousand signatures and was successful in placing on the ballot Proposition 14, which granted the ALRB sufficient funding and allowed free access to union organizers. The Republicans, powerful growers, oil, and business interests, pumped in some 1.8 million dollars for a massive media blitz campaign in order to defeat the initiative, which lost by a two-to-one margin.[93] The loss of Proposition 14 did irreparable damage to the UFW. During the ensuing years, the California state legislature emasculated the ALRB by failing to provide it with adequate funding for the ALRA's enforcement. Meanwhile, the Reagan administration's appointment of conservative John R. Norton as U.S. deputy secretary of agriculture, who sought to weaken the UFW, further exacerbated the ALRB's problems.[94] On the defensive and weakened, the UFW in 1978 "called off" its boycott of grapes, lettuce, and Gallo wine. By the late 1970s, its membership again declined, this time to some twenty-one thousand.[95]

At both the national and state levels, with Republicans in power, the UFW during the 1980s faced insurmountable political forces. In California, Governor Deukmejian, in the words of historian Acuña, "torpedoed the Agricultural Labor Relations Board (ALRB) by appointing David Stirling, a grower hatchet man, general counsel to the board." Under Stirling only 10 percent of the cases reached the ALRB, compared to 35 percent during the Brown administration.[96] The situation worsened for the UFW with Governor Deukmejian's conservative anti-UFW appointments to the ALRB. After ten years, the ALRB in 1984 had not made one single award for a labor violation of the ALRA.[97] Governor Deukmajian cut the ALRB's budget by one-third to where in 1986 the ALRB became inoperative.[98]

Recognizing the failure of its legislative lobbying approach, the UFW during the early 1980s again reverted to the use of the boycott. This time, however, it utilized modern techniques, meaning the use of computers, mailing lists, a printing press, and TV spots, yet did not foster the needed UFW resurgence. This became evident in 1984 when it experienced a decrease in the number of contracts. In 1984, only fifteen of the seventy grape growers were under UFW contract in the Delano area. Its membership decreased to only twelve thousand active members and it initiated fewer strikes. A debilitated UFW lessened its focus on field organizing and prioritized efforts against pesticides and on the development of migrant social programs. The UFW also became active in immigration-related issues, however, at times much to the dismay of Chicano activists. During the debate on Simpson-Mazzoli (1984) and the IRCA (1986), the UFW took a strong stance in support of employer sanctions and more stringent border enforcement.[99]

In 1986, Chavez kicked off what was billed by the UFW as its "Wrath of Grapes" campaign to draw public attention to the pesticide poisoning of grape workers and their children. Chavez in 1988 relied on the use of the fast to bring a greater attention and awareness to the issue. He fasted for thirty-six days in Delano to protest the use of pesticides. Initially it went unnoticed, but with the visit and support of Rev. Jesse Jackson, actors Martin Sheen and Robert Blake, and members of Robert Kennedy's family, the fast got national media notoriety. For a short period of time, the UFW's posture and that of its leader were rekindled. By the late 1980s, while the UFW called for continued support for its grape boycott, in reality its organizational posture was that of a public interest group rather than that of a union.

During the 1990s, the Republican complicity with growers and other powerful business interests continued under the leadership of President George Bush and California governor Pete Wilson. A number of internal problems further compounded the UFW's organizing efforts: firings, resignations of top officials, allegations of heavy-handed tactics and undemocratic behavior, loss of contracts, costly court battles with growers, and questions over finances.[100] Intentionally, the UFW's adversaries and a hostile media made many of these issues public as a way of further diminishing its image and credibility.

A dramatic tragedy hit the UFW in 1993 with the death of its charismatic and inspirational leader, Cesar Chavez. He died in his sleep from exhaustion, pushing himself to the limits while on an organizing trip to Arizona. Chavez's death fostered a national mobilization of some forty thousand leaders, notables, and supporters from all over the country who came and marched at his funeral in Delano. He was buried in La Paz, the UFW's California headquarters, near a bed of roses in front of his former office. Chavez's son-in-law Arturo Rodriguez was selected as the new UFW president. In 1994, in a White House ceremony, President Clinton acknowledged Chavez's leadership contributions and presented Cesar's widow Helen Chavez with the "Medal of Freedom" award. Clinton praised Chavez for having "faced formidable, often violent opposition, with dignity and nonviolence."[101]

In an effort to rekindle the UFW's spirit of struggle, Arturo Rodriguez in 1994 headed a replay of Chavez's historic 343-mile-long Delano march of 1966. At California's state capitol with some seventeen thousand supporters present, Rodriguez pledged to rebuild the struggling union by returning to field organizing.[102] By 1999, the UFW had won eighteen union elections and signed twenty-four new or first-time agreements with growers.[103] The agreements were with rose, mushroom, strawberry, wine grape, and lettuce and vegetable growers in California, La Florida, and Washington. On a positive note, the UFW's membership increased from twenty thousand in 1993 to some twenty-six thousand in 1999,[104] and its radio stations and service centers continued to grow. Yet the UFW struggled, for it lacked the level of power and influence it once had in 1970.

Other Union Activity

During the epoch, inspired by the UFW's organizing efforts other unions were formed. In 1967, Jesus Salas in Wisconsin organized an independent farmworkers union called Obreros Unidos (United Workers), but because of financial difficulties and its loss of support from the AFL-CIO it became moribund by 1970. That same year in Michigan migrant workers, protesting their low wages and poor working conditions, took part in a seventy-mile "March of Migrants" from Saginaw to Lansing. In Ohio, migrant workers formed the Farm Labor Organizing Committee (FLOC) and in 1968 organized protests and demanded better wages and enforcement of health and housing codes. That year FLOC signed some twenty-two contracts in Ohio and Indiana with several food processors. These and other farmworker organizing efforts continued in other parts of both Aztlán and the Midwest.[105] During the early 1970s in Cristal, Tejas, integral to the Raza Unida Party's "peaceful revolution" was the formation of a union, Obreros Unidos Independientes (Independent United Workers), which successfully wrestled power from the Teamsters at the local Del Monte plant.[106]

At the national level, in 1972 twenty-five founding members met in Albuquerque, Nuevo México, and formed and incorporated the progressive Labor Council for Latin American Advancement (LCLAA), which sought for Latinos to have a voice within the powerful American Federation of Labor-Congress of Industrial Organizations (AFL-CIO). The LCLAA's emergence was a product of over two years of organizing chiefly done by Albert Hernandez, who along with a few other labor activists formed in California the Los Angeles Political Education Council, which included representation from several unions. Its cardinal objective was to work on political campaigns to elect Mexicanos and Latinos to public office. With the support of the AFL-CIO, the decision was made in 1972 to form a national entity that could lobby within the AFL-CIO for advancing Latino working-class interests. As stated in its constitution, "LCLAA works with Latino union members to Advocate for the rights of all Latino workers and their families at all levels of the American trade union movement and the political processes."[107]

In the ensuing years, chapters were formed and a national structure created, yet politically it took a rather low profile on the issues impacting Mexicano and Latino workers and essentially adhered to Hispanic Generation politics, with much of the leadership identifying itself as "Hispanic." In addition, the LCLAA's dependence upon and affiliation with the AFL-CIO impeded its ability to address controversial issues impacting Mexicano and Latino workers.[108] However, by the latter part of the 1990s, with the discovery of labor unions of the value of organizing the burgeoning migrant workers, the LCLAA too began adopting a more assertive organizing labor agenda.

One of the most significant was that of the Texas Farm Workers Union (TFWU), led by former UFW organizer Antonio Orendain. After differences of strategy and tactics in organizing the farmworkers in Tejas, Orendain split from the UFW in 1975 and established the TFWU. After two years of organizing, Orendain in 1977 led a march of hundreds from the Rio Grande areas of South Tejas to Austin, where then governor Dolph Briscoe met them, but refused to support their demand for collective bargaining legislation. Without the base of support enjoyed by Chavez's UFW, for example, liberals, other unions, churches, the TFWU failed. With his organization withering and without much support, in 1982 Orendain stepped down as TFWU director, which meant its demise.[109]

During the 1990s, a number of new unions were formed, particularly in California, that sought to organize the large labor pool of migrant legal and undocumented workers. For decades, the "unionization of immigrant workers" had not been a priority. In fact, most unions were supportive of restrictionist immigration policies—including the UFW, AFL-CIO, and many others. It was not until the late 1980s that major unions like the AFL-CIO prioritized their organizing. Up until the 1960s, this was the shared attitude of the more traditional unions. Bert Corona, longtime activist and labor organizer, explains:

> Many of the AFL-CIO unions refused to organize undocumented workers. The few exceptions were unions such as the Teamsters, the United Auto Workers, the Longshoremen's Union, the United Electrical Workers, and the Hotel Employees and Restaurant Employees Union. But the unions in the building trades and the metal trades, as well as the big service unions, would have nothing to do with the undocumented. . . . They believed that these workers were not organizable, because the INS could come in and threaten them with deportation, and the people would run like quail.[110]

However, with the organizing success of the UFW and Hermandad Mexicana Nacional, among others, organized labor began to change. Pragmatically, "Big

Labor," driven by the objective of reversing its decline of past years by the late 1980s, understood only too well that its future was dependent on their ability to readjust to the changing labor market, especially in Aztlán. An illustration of this change was the Laborers Immigration Assistance Project, which sought to help eligible immigrants wade through the amnesty process and stimulated the AFL-CIO in 1989 to establish the California Immigrant Workers Association (CIWA). With a membership of some twelve thousand workers by 1994, it played a key role in several union organizing efforts.[111] Many Latino workers who had just become naturalized citizens responded with fervor, conviction, and courage to the cry to "organize" and "unionize." Thus, by the turn of the 1980s, especially in California, the composition of a number of unions had become mostly Mexicano and Latino based.

One such union organizing effort came about in 1989 with the election of María Elena Durazo, a former CASA (Center for Autonomous Social Action) member, who in 1987 was elected president of the HERE (Hotel Employees and Restaurant Employees) Union. Under her leadership, HERE struck the giants of the Hyatt Hotel chain using various acts of civil disobedience, which led to the arrests of several union leaders. During the early 1990s, it struck the New Otani Hotel and also pressured the Japanese American National Museum of Little Tokyo for the Tokyo-based Kajima Corporation to open up its construction bidding.[112] By 1994, HERE's membership increased to some thirteen thousand workers. During the ensuing years, it continued to accelerate its union organizing struggles for immigrant workers.

Concomitantly, in the Los Angeles area, the Service Employees Industrial Union (SEIU), Local 399, known as "Justice for Janitors," made a call to organize. Fearing the displacement of its mostly migrant workers in 1990, it launched a major organizing effort, which during the years 1990 to 1995 dramatically increased its membership. In a major *Los Angeles Times* article on the SEIU, Sonia Nazario wrote:

> Like many unions, the SEIU treated the immigrants as the enemy as they replaced previous janitors, most of them African Americans. The state of the union became grim: Los Angeles membership plunged 77% from 1983 to 1987, down to 1,500. Since then, the union has won contracts with a dozen large companies, who clean 350 buildings, boosting its Los Angeles membership to 7,000.[113]

Activist janitors hastily moved to unionize in Los Angeles County, under the guise of the "Justice for Janitors" campaign, which was described by the press as using assertive "guerrilla warfare-like tactics" that included strikes and other forms of direct action. An expression of their militancy was the 1990 clash with Los Angeles police. The clash occurred with some 150 policemen when some 400 janitors marched in protest from Beverly Hills to Century City to picket buildings where janitors had gone on strike demanding higher wages. A confrontation occurred when the police ordered the protestors to disperse. Described as one of the most violent confrontations in recent years, sixty janitors were injured and another eighty-five were brutalized or arrested.[114] In 1993, the union filed a suit and won $2.35 million for its members. In spite of its successful unionizing of janitors during the years 1987 to 1993 by the latter year the SEIU janitors still made a mere subsistence wage of $6.72 per hour and had health care, whereas nonunion janitors were paid only $5.00 per hour and had no health care.[115] The SEIU by 1995 was plagued by internal schisms that debilitated its organizing effectiveness. Charges and countercharges made by the old leadership and the new emergent leadership resulted in placing the SEIU in receivership, and Mike Garcia of San Jose was named interim head.[116]

During the 1990s numerous other unions were also formed. In 1990 and 1992, respectively, machinists at American Racing Equipment and drywall hangers in Orange County organized and staged wildcat strikes. They pressured the AFL-CIO in 1997 to put more focus on a major recruiting drive with a cardinal goal of attracting new members. In addition, some $2 million was directed specifically to organize strawberry pickers in California and tens of thousands of construction, hotel, and health care workers in Las Vegas, Nevada,[117] of which many were Latino migrants. Gardeners in 1998 also organized themselves into the Association of Latin American Gardeners in Los Angeles. The issue was not allowing them to use leaf-blowers because of the noise they made. Within the emergent Latino labor power movement, not only was the membership Latinos, but the leadership as well. For instance, Miguel Contreras headed the powerful Los Angeles County Federation of Labor, an AFL-CIO umbrella organization that represented some eight hundred thousand workers and several influential unions.[118]

Thus, while Los Angeles County could be described as the bastion of the resurgent labor movement directed at Latinos, especially migrants, similar organizing efforts also occurred in other parts of the country. The downside of this labor activism was that most contracts negotiated failed to rescue the workers from the grip of poverty since wage increases secured in many cases were no better than subsistence wages.

RUP: Chicano Third-Party Movement Declines

As a third-party movement, RUP reached its apogee in 1972 and because of a multiplicity of problems and issues declined by 1982. The detrimental effects of the "politics of self-destruction," the internal fighting, and schisms based upon the Gutiérrez/Gonzales power struggle were "the political straw that broke RUP's back." As a result RUP never became either a regional or nationwide third party. RUP's National Steering Committee, the Congreso, established in 1972, during the ensuing three years was plagued by internecine schisms and confrontations, which fostered a paralysis of growth. As the Movimiento declined throughout Aztlán and the Midwest, RUP also declined. Its structures collapsed; supporters and visibility vanished; and political activity, especially in the electoral arena, ceased.[119]

RUP's "peaceful revolution" in Crystal City, Tejas, began to "self-destruct" by 1975. Motivated by the acquisition and control of power, young RUP "turks" rebelled politically and took control of the city council and school board from Gutiérrez, who had been the "Cristal Experiment" main architect and political boss of RUP's political machine in Cristal. Perpetual conflict with the RUP bastion further impacted RUP's overall decline. This was manifested by the fact that by 1976, across Tejas RUP secured only a few local electoral victories and organizing activity declined dramatically. The impact of the "politics of self-destruction" in Zavala County was such that the Board of Commissioners of which Gutiérrez had been elected county judge in 1974 and RUP had a majority under Democrat control by 1978. Adding to RUP's decline was the arrest and federal penitentiary incarceration in 1976 of former RUP gubernatorial candidate Ramsey Muñiz on drug charges. His imprisonment caused major disillusionment within the already depleted *partido* ranks. RUP gubernatorial candidate Mario Compean in 1978 was soundly defeated and was unable to obtain the required 2 percent of the vote needed to retain RUP on the ballot as an official party. As a result, RUP was decertified, which brought closure to its existence in Tejas. In January 1981, Gutiérrez was pressured by the Democrats to resign as county judge. As a result, he and his family left Cristal and moved to the state of Oregon into what some described as "political exile."[120]

As RUP disintegrated in Tejas the same occurred throughout Aztlán and the Midwest. In Colorado, 1976 was the last year RUP would run candidates: Eddie Joseph Montour, who ran for county commissioner in the Pueblo area, and Alfredo Archer, who ran for the Third Congressional District.[121] Not having had a political victory in six years and with the CJ under an intense state of siege,

RUP in Colorado became moribund. RUP in California between 1975 and 1981 likewise experienced no major electoral activity. The exception occurred in the city of San Fernando where RUP ran candidates for the city council and governor unsuccessfully. A cardinal reason for its nonelectoral activity was that by 1976, RUP was ideologically eclectic—an admixture of separatist ultranationalism and Marxism. Increasingly, RUP in California functioned more like an "ideological interest group," concerned about ideas and issues rather than elections. While RUP's structure included a state central committee and few chapters, after 1978 most of them were in the Los Angeles area. RUP's membership base had dwindled to a small number of true believer zealots. By 1981, battered by the hegemony of the politics of the HG, RUP's small *partido* infrastructure collapsed, leaving only one chapter in San Fernando still functional. Even though statewide RUP ceased to exist, from 1981 to 1999, the San Fernando chapter continued to function as a small RUP organizing committee lead by Xenaro Ayala, an ultranationalist separatist.

In Nuevo México, RUP in 1976 ran unsuccessfully and endorsed several candidates for statewide and federal office as independents. At the federal level, RUP endorsed Socialist Workers Party (SWP) presidential candidate Peter Camejo. Out of some four hundred thousand votes cast, he received a mere 2,462. RUP's candidate for the U.S. Senate, Ernesto Borunda, garnered only 1,087 votes to Republican Harrison Schmitt's 234,681. RUP's congressional candidate Jesus Aragon, who ran against Republican incumbent Manuel Lujan, secured only 1,159 votes. RUP's candidate for state corporation commissioner, Sam Sanchez, received 3,132 votes compared to the Democratic candidate, who got 192,767.

RUP's relationship to the SWP became problematic and contributed to the growing ideological conflicts within RUP in other states. The decline of RUP became evident when in 1978 it sought to run candidates for state and federal offices, but was unsuccessful in getting them on the ballot. In Rio Arriba County under the leadership of Antonio De Vargas, RUP unsuccessfully challenged Democrat Emilio Naranjo's political machine by running candidates. From 1978 to 1981 RUP in Nuevo México functioned as it did in California, as an ideologically cadre-oriented sectarian, ultranationalist, nationalist/Marxist, separatist *partido*.

RUP's lack of victories outside of Tejas, the prevalence of internecine schisms and power struggles, and the changing political climate impacted its decline in other states. In Arizona RUP by 1975 ceased to exist. By 1974, RUP's cadre leadership of Solomon Baldenegro, Lupe Castillo, and Raul Grijalva, among others, in Tucson became disillusioned. They stopped organizing RUP and got involved with other community social service organizations and local issues. RUP in Utah lasted only until 1977. With its cultural nationalist orientation and under the leadership of Hector Rodriguez, RUP functioned ostensibly as an interest group that focused on issues. Its demise came as a result of other organizations, namely Spanish-Speaking Organization for Community Integrity and Opportunity (SOCIO), that assumed a statewide leadership role; a stultifying apathy and complacency; and the prevalence of the politics of the HG. In the Midwest, RUP after 1975 was all but nonexistent. The exception was in Wisconsin, where under the leadership of Ernesto Chacon, RUP continued to function until 1979. In Illinois, Michigan, and Nebraska, RUP politically all but disappeared prior to 1975. RUP, however, took on the appearance of social service organizations, which at times kept its identification with RUP until the late 1970s. With the resignation in 1981 of Juan Jose Peña as its national leader/organizer and a withering membership, RUP became defunct. Thus, RUP as a third-party movement ended in failure unable to overcome the ubiquitous and omnipotent power of the country's two-party dictatorship.

During the rest of the epoch, however, a facsimile of RUP was kept alive by the leadership of Xenaro Ayala in California and later in the 1990s by Enrique Cardial from Nuevo México. During these years, RUP went through a name change from RUP to Partido Nacional de La Raza Unida (PNLRU). Ideologically as an advocate transformer, it continued to adhere to an ultranationalist and separatist agenda, which adhered to "revolutionary nationalism." It repudiated the buffer and "want to be white" political roles of most existent HG *politicos* and organizations. The PNLRU's politics resembled those of CASA, which will be subsequently examined, an admixture of ultracultural nationalism and Marxist-Leninism. With its ardent antiliberal capitalist posture, ideologically, the PNLRU perceived Aztlán as being a colony of the United States. Moreover, it repudiated ballot box politics and structured itself as a "vanguard cadre" separatist *partido*—more specifically as a "Chicano Mexicano Revolutionary Nationalist Party" committed to "justice, equality, dignity, self-determination, and national liberation." PNLRU politics of self-determination sought the creation of a unified Chicano/Mexicano nation, Aztlán, and espoused a form of "Pan-Americanism" that adopted as a motto "Somos Uno Porque America Es Una," which denoted support for the "liberation of all indigenous throughout the Americas."[122]

By the late 1990s, the PNLRU was ostensibly limited to three organizing committees: one in San Fernando, California; another in Albuquerque, Nuevo México; and one in Dallas, Tejas. Hence, the PNLRU's organizing activities were largely local, limited to the areas of the preceding cities and basically devoted to local "conscious raising" and "community organizing." Its activities included working meetings; participating in conferences and direct action activities; holding its own conferences; working with youth, especially in San Fernando; and developing its literature for outreach. It coalesced with other Left sectarian groups, such as the Union del Barrio, for the purpose of addressing a myriad of issues.

The Decline and Rise of Sectarian Left Organizations

Centro de Acción Social Autónoma (CASA)

While RUP by 1976 joined the ranks of other existent "sectarian Left" groups, several others were active during the epoch of the HG. One such advocate transformer group was CASA, which continued active from 1975 to 1978. After several years of growth, a power struggle occurred in 1974 that resulted in the ouster of Bert Corona from CASA's leadership. At this juncture, Corona left CASA and merged into La Hermandad Mexicana Nacional, which had been formed in the San Diego area in 1951 to protect the rights of the foreign born.[123] The power struggle was a result of a merger that occurred within CASA precipitated by an influx of Marxist activists from the National Committee to Free Los Tres (CFLT) and Comite Esudiantil del Pueblo. Pepe Jacques, one of CASA's main leaders, when interviewed explained that CASA's merger meant it openly adhered to Marxist-Leninism and disparaged and attacked cultural nationalism as being divisive.[124] Ernesto Chavez writes, "CASA described itself as Marxist-Leninist organization, but its policies reflected the preeminence of ethnicity and cultural nationalism."[125]

CASA's paramount objective was to ultimately become a "revolutionary vanguard proletarian party" that adhered to democratic centralism, scientific socialism, and was anti-U.S. imperialist. As a Marxist-oriented change entity, it was hypercritical of buffer and "want to be white" *politicos* and organizations that from its perspective served to "prop up" the existing social order. Although CASA adhered to the principle of collective leadership, Antonio Rodriguez and his brothers became an influential leadership force. Jacques said, "Increasingly CASA took on the appearance of a political party that wanted to combine theory and revolutionary action."[126] Organizationally, CASA's new leadership also opted to transform CASA from a popular mass-based organization to one that was revolutionary cadre-based. Integral to CASA's ideological vision was the reunification of Aztlán and México under a socialist government via a strategy of class struggle. This ideological shift from Corona's less doctrinaire and pragmatic approach to a sectarian Marxist-Leninist one fostered clashes within the old guard Casistas within CASA.

Beyond its cordial relationships with CPUSA (Communist Party of the United States of America) and Partido Comunista Mexicano (Mexican Communist Party), CASA under the leadership of its "political commission" that included Antonio Rodriguez, Felipe Aguirre, and Carlos Vasquez, by 1975 established linkages to the Puerto Rican separatist groups, for example, the Puerto Rican Socialist Party. In December 1977, following an invitation by the Cuban government, CASA sent a delegation to Cuba and openly publicized its solidarity with all working-class struggles, especially those of Latinos. Other trips were made to México, where CASA announced its solidarity with México's Left. In 1977 Carlos Vasquez was sent to the World Federation of Trade Unions Conference on youth in Nicosia, Cyprus, where he promulgated CASA's solidarity with the national liberation struggles being waged in Eastern Europe.[127]

On the domestic side, under the leadership of Isabel Rodriguez Chavez and subsequently that of Carlos Vasquez, CASA strengthened its outreach and circulation of its newspaper, *Sin Fronteras* (Without Borders). CASA continued to focus on immigration-related issues, such as the defeat of the Rodino Bill and on organizing the migrant Mexicano workers into unions. It participated in numerous strikes between 1975 and 1976. During this time, it also launched a major campaign on behalf of affirmative action, especially targeting the *Bakke* decision.[128] Concomitantly, CASA expanded its number of immigration service centers in some areas like San Antonio, Tejas, called TU CASA, in Greenly, Colorado, MI CASA, and so on. A fee of $50 was charged for membership, services rendered, and a credential card. With its ability to provide immigration services coupled with that of developing its political base, CASA grew in membership, clout, and visibility. CASA's organizing and service operations became self-sustaining.[129] Yet because of CASA's radical ideological shift, some CASAs that were more immigration service-oriented by 1976 withdrew, for example, San Diego and San Jose.

In 1976 CASA leadership and activities came under increasing surveillance from both law enforcement and the FBI. From 1972 to 1976, the FBI had infiltrated CASA and gathered information on its activities and leadership. The FBI justified its action as Chavez explained on the grounds "that the organizations [CASA and the Committee to Free Los Tres] are involved in activities that could constitute violations of Title 18, U.S. Code, Section 2383 (Rebellion or Insurrection), 2284 (Seditious conspiracy), 2385 Advocating the Overthrow of the Government as well as possible violation of neutrality laws."[130] Jose "Pepe" Jacques Medina, who had been one of the major leaders of the 1968 student demonstrations in México, as one of CASA's main leaders was targeted by the FBI for deportation. On January 26, 1976, he was arrested and charged by the Immigration and Naturalization Service with illegal entry into the country. Medina requested political asylum on the grounds that if returned to México he faced possible prosecution, if not death, for his involvement in the 1968 student riots in México City. For CASA, Medina was utilized as a national organizing and conscious-raising tool. A legal defense committee was organized and supported by the CPUSA. From 1976 to 1977, he was busy on the speaking circuit visiting some fifty-two cities throughout the country. For the next seven years, Medina was in and out of court until the charges were officially dropped in 1982.[131]

CASA, from 1975 to 1977, took a rather bellicose posture toward other leftist competitors. With its dialectical materialist politics of creating and exposing what it deemed contradictions, CASA often acted as a divisive organizing force that further contributed to the destruction of what was left of the *moviemiento*. With its intransigent Marxist-Leninist posture, CASA challenged other Marxist groups, such as the Trotskyite SWP and the Maoist August Twenty-ninth Movement, as well as Chicano cultural nationalists for control of what was left of the Movimiento. At conferences and at community meetings, CASA was relentless in its push for its Marxist separatist agenda. Confrontations with competing groups became commonplace, such as at the National Chicano Forum held in 1976 in Salt Lake City and the National Immigration conference held in 1977 in San Antonio, Tejas. Yet by 1977, CASA went through its own internal chasm over questions of strategy and tactics. With a decreasing membership base of only one thousand members, disagreements among CASA's leadership developed over what should be the emphasis, trade union organizing or popular community organizing. Other related issues caused further divisions, such as the total absence of industrial workers within its membership; its leadership that was comprised mostly of professionals, student, and community activists; and CASA's role in the universities and colleges.

By late 1977, the external conflicts coupled especially with the internal conflicts signaled the end of CASA. Carlos Vasquez and Jose Calderon among others resigned from CASA that year. Particularly, the resignation of Vasquez, who was director of *Sin Fronteras* and a member of the Political Commission, and differences over strategy and tactics, allegations of nepotism, an overly bureaucratic and hierarchical structure, and its eclectic Marxist/nationalist ideology that failed to appeal to the masses in the barrios all contributed to CASA's decline by 1978. CASA's decline as explained by Carlos Vasquez was due to "fundamental weaknesses for [a] revolutionary organization among our people to fall into at this time, and more seriously not correct when the errors are pointed out."[132] According to Medina, the internal conflicts were such that CASA's Central Committee by "decree" ruled to "disestablish" or better yet dismantle itself as an organization.[133] Barrera points out that by 1978, CASA "had for all practical purposes ceased to exist."[134] Some of CASA's leadership and membership for years to come continued to be active with other local groups and issues. Thus, in the words of historian Juan Gómez-Quiñones, "Indisputably, CASA contributed to radical mobilization and discourse during the seventies, and its legacy informed the work of other organizations in the eighties."[135]

August Twenty-Ninth Movement

An ideological nemesis of CASA was the August Twenty-ninth Movement (ATM). Marxist in its revolutionary principles, but Maoist in its revolutionary strategy and tactics, the ATM also as an advocate transformer became a competitor to CASA, the SWP, and cultural nationalists as well. Like CASA, it too was critical of the existent buffer and "want to be white" system maintenance *politicos* and organizations. The ATM's historical roots stemmed to RUP's Labor Committee in Los Angeles, which had been Marxist-Leninist. With the rapid decline of RUP after 1972, the Labor Committee focused much of its organizing activities on labor issues, such as the Farah Strike, and also underwent an ideological metamorphosis, which by 1974 produced a shift in its Marxist-Leninist posture to one that was Maoist in nature. The ATM sought to create a multiethnic vanguard Communist Party committed to the "Chicano Question"—the liberation of Aztlán into a separate Chicano socialist country.[136]

Whereas CASA followed the Soviet Union Communist line, the RUP Labor Committee and subsequently the ATM pursued the teachings of Mao Tse-tung and identified with the People's Republic of China. In a pamphlet entitled *Fan the Flames* that was published in 1976, the ATM accentuated national self-determination, which meant specifically that Mexicanos in the Southwest had a right to secede from the United States and form their own socialist nation-state. CASA stressed the importance of waging a revolutionary struggle of "*sin fronteras*" for it propounded the belief that Chicanos and Mexicanos constituted a single Mexican nation.[137] Barrera writes, "While CASA ideologists attacked the concept of 'Aztlán' as divisive, the ATM elevated it to a national principle."[138] The ATM dogmatically distanced itself from CASA's ideology and strategy on the aforementioned points. Instead, the right to secede is listed as their third basic demand, entitled "Right of Political Secession (Self-Determination)." The peasant aspect to its Maoist framework vis-à-vis Chicanos was de-emphasized but qualified by arguing that most Chicanos came from both a *campesino* and a working-class historical materialist experience.

The ATM, while embracing the "Chicano Question," repudiated cultural nationalism as being too narrow and antithetical to proletarian socialist internationalism. In linking the relationship of the "multiethnic" working class in general in the United States to that of the Chicano struggle, the document read:

> It is clear that the national movement and the working class movement are already "linked"—they are linked in the sense that every blow by the Chicano people against imperialism brings the proletariat a step closer to its goal of socialist revolution. Therefore, we must **Fan the Flames** of the Chicano revolution, support it, and strive to give it the consistent and determined revolutionary leadership that it **demands** us.

For the next three years the ATM became a competitor to the SWP, CASA, and cultural nationalist groups. The ATM's fight to become the vanguard of the Chicano revolutionary struggle was relatively short. Up to 1977, the ATM was engaged in a relentless ideological war and organizational struggle against CASA, the SWP, and some MEChA chapters with cultural nationalist inclinations. By 1976 the ATM and CASA were engaged in an internecine conflict over control of Chicano student organizations, especially MEChA, and Chicano Studies programs, as was the case with California State University, Los Angeles. In describing the effects of their conflict, Carlos Muñoz explains, "At a few campuses a bitter struggle took place over control of MEChA or of the Chicano Studies program. But for the most part these organizations failed to have much impact on the majority of Mexican American students."[139] Conferences became the ideological battlefield, which produced acrimonious infighting, as was the case with the National Chicano Forum held in 1976 in Salt Lake City, Utah, and the National Chicano/Latino Conference on Immigration held in 1977 in San Antonio, Tejas. Polemical debates imbued with Marxist jargon and at times altercations only served to turn off potential converts to their causes, especially apolitical students.

As CASA in 1977 was plagued by internal ideological squabbles so was the ATM. By 1978, without much public notice, ATM leaders and members coalesced with other groups and in 1979 formed the multinational League of Revolutionary Struggle (LRS).[140] Similar in ideological focus to the ATM, the LRS was better organized and focused its organizing activities on student and labor issues. The LRS like the ATM sought to infiltrate and control MEChA chapters, particularly at its state conferences. Throughout much of the 1980s this created conflicts with the newly formed Union del Barrio, a Marxist/nationalist separatist cadre organization, over ideas as well as over political turf. According to Gómez-Quiñones, "ATM continued to prefer covert rather than overt work, infiltration rather than direct mobilization, and to conduct both a public and a closed discourse."[141] Plagued by internal schisms, a decreasing membership base, and a pervasive conservative climate, the LRS was disbanded in 1989.

Hermandad Mexicana Nacional (HMN)

Where CASA left off, the HMN picked up, meaning that from the mid-1970s through the 1990s it established in various states several immigration and social/legal services. The HMN for several years continued to play an advocate, pressure, lobbying, and advocate transformer role, but one that diminished with time. Bert Corona's quasi-ideological/pragmatic style of leadership meant that the HMN by the late 1980s took on ostensibly a buffer political role, unlike other Left sectarian groups. However, this was not the case during the late 1970s and early 1980s. During the former, it organized against the Carter Plan and in 1982 and 1984 worked for the defeat of the Simpson-Mazzoli legislation. During these years, the HMN became a strong advocate on immigrant rights. It participated with several organizations, such as MAPA, LULAC, and the NCLR, as well as with non-Latino organizations, as part of the National Coalition for Fair Immigration Laws and Practices for the defeat of the latter. In 1986 the coalition fell apart and IRCA was approved. With its approval, the HMN began to shift its organizational focus from adhering to an advocate transformer role to increasingly a buffer advocate/service provider to that of being first a service provider and then an advocate.

With the passage of IRCA, the HMN until the early 1990s was engaged in various aspects of IRCA's amnesty program, especially the legalization part. HMNs in various parts of the country provided assistance to those who qualified for amnesty, by helping them complete the language and civics requirements. The HMN also filed several suits regarding the INS refusal to accept late applications when the cause was that the INS had failed to set up a reasonable process to inform people. By 1989 HMN agencies offered English classes. That year, some forty thousand were taught, and by 1992 the number increased to a total of one hundred and sixty thousand. After that it moved into the naturalization business, and thousands went through its citizenship training. The advocacy component diminished significantly except, in the words of Corona, "to lobby more funds for these amnesty classes."[142] During 1990s, the HMN service focus was evident: it chose not to assume an avant-garde leadership role against the militarization of the border or against Proposition 187. Instead, its focus remained being a program service provider on immigration as manifested; as reported in 1996 by La Opinion, the HMN's total funding was $8.5 million, but it had spent 8.7 million.[143]

From 1996 to the turn of the century, HMN agencies in Los Angeles and Santa Anna became the locus of controversy over allegations of voter fraud and mismanagement of funds. In the 1996 election in Orange County of Democrat

Loretta Sanchez to the Forty-sixth Congressional District, a win over incumbent Republican Robert Dornan, the HMN was accused in December of registering noncitizens to vote. That year the HMN reported that it registered some 1,357 people countywide, of which nearly eight hundred voted in the November elections. The HMN's registration drive factored into the election of HMN executive director Nativo Lopez to the Santa Ana Unified School District.[144] Dornon contested the election and alleged election fraud, contending that noncitizens had illegally been registered by the HMN, voted, and consequently cost him the election. The nine-term ultraconservative incumbent lost the election to Sanchez by a mere 974 votes. Local, state, and federal officials conducted an investigation that found that 1,160 people had been registered by the HMN, of which 721 were ineligible to vote because they were not citizens and of those, 442 voted in the November 5th election.[145]

The controversy escalated to where in February 1997 the HMN was denied refunding of $2.1 million to teach English and citizenship classes. At the time an average of 2,500 people a month were taking HMN classes at some seventy sites in southern California.[146] By March 1997 similar charges of noncitizens being registered to vote by the HMN were made against its Los Angeles office. An investigation revealed that the number was much lower: only forty-six were identified as being noncitizens.[147] With the completion of the investigation in May, the HMN's funding was restored to the sum of $1 million. In the end, the HMN was clear the HMN faced another major crisis, Corona's bad health. By the turn of the century, Corona was seriously ill and required medical attention. As for the HMN, its progressive advocacy agenda by the 1990s had changed into an ostensibly status quo service provider. Thus, plagued by scandals, decreasing funding, and its leader Corona's bad health, the future of the HMN in 1999 was precariously in doubt.

Union del Barrio (UB)

The UB was formed in 1981 by a half dozen activists under the leadership of Ernesto Bustillos, Howard Holman, and a few others, most of whom were originally part of the Committee on Chicano Rights (CCR).[148] The cardinal reasons for the fracture were two: the CCR's primary focus on immigration and its reform cultural nationalist posture. They felt that in order to rebuild the Movimiento, they needed to create a new militant "multi-issue organization" that ideologically espoused an antiliberal capitalist and "separatist political agenda" thus embracing an advocate transformer role. From their perspective what was needed was a clear alternative to the status quo politics of existent buffer and "want to be white" oriented Mexicano and Hispanic organizations. Their departure was not seen as an organizational "split," but a "parting of the way."[149]

Operating out of San Diego, the UB's leftist sectarian organization orientation is evident in its "Eleven Point Program." In the introduction of its book entitled *Un Pueblo Sin Fronteras*, in lucid language the UB describes itself as eclectically ideologically being Marxist/nationalist and anticolonial/anticapitalist. It perceives Aztlán not only as an occupied but colonized territory. Since its formation, it has "based its practice and ideology on dialectical materialism, and on achieving the ultimate objective of Mexicano freedom fighters: the national liberation and revolutionary reunification of the Mexican nation." Its Mexicano ultranationalist posture became evident early on with the adoption of the "Aztec Eagle Knight" as its organizational symbol, which represents the Mexicano's indigenous reality.[150]

Throughout the 1980s the UB struggled to strengthen its organizational cadre capability and networks. Starting in 1982 in collaboration with MEChA chapters, the UB organized several "Barrio Unity conferences" and conducted meetings in various parts of the state. The focus of each conference shifted to the issues affecting the barrios. With the objective of developing the people's consciousness or *"consciencia,"* each conference was used to advance its Marxist/nationalist agenda and build up its cadre membership base. In moving its agenda, the UB networked and formed coalitions with a number of other progressive nationalist groups, such as the PNLRU led by Xenaro Ayala, several MEChA chapters, CISPES (Committee in Solidarity with the People of El Salvador), and Voz Fronteriza. In particular, by 1984, the UB forged a tentative *frente* (front) with the PNLRU. The UB also developed a collaborative relationship with the African People's Socialist Party and its leader Omali Yeshitala. By 1987, however, the UB faced some internal leadership problems. Due principally to disagreements over its ideological direction, three of its founding members, Jesse Constancio, Jeff Garcilazo, and Howard Holman, left the organization, but it weathered the schism.[151]

In 1987, the UB formed Somos Raza, a "barrio-based youth" organization committed to the national struggle for self-determination. With its formation, *Somos Raza* magazine was published with a commitment to "Mexicano power" and raising the social and cultural *consciencia* of youth.[152] That same year Centro Aztlán was established in San Diego, California, as the UB's official headquarters. As a result of a meeting hosted by MEChA from Mira Costa in 1989, the Raza Rights Coalition was formed, which included the UB and six other local organizations. The UB that same year established *La Verdad* newspaper as its official resource of information. In 1990 the UB set out to create a network of "progressive and liberation oriented Raza newspapers" and reestablished the Chicano Press Association (CPA). That same year, the UB also moved to reactivate the National Chicano Moratorium Committee (NCMC). During the month of August, under the auspices of the NCMC, a march of some three thousand persons was held in Los Angeles to commemorate August 29th.[153]

During the 1990s, the UB struggled to build up its cadre infrastructure and political base. Beyond building alliances with coalitions and groups that had compatible interests it also formed and sustained various other entities and projects that were integral to its network. Some of these groups from throughout the country included the Brown Berets de Aztlán, the PNLRU, Chicano Park Steering Committee, Chicano Studies Concilio, and several MEChAs. Even through the end of 1996, the UB's infrastructure included Somos Raza, La Verdad, the Raza Rights Coalition, the CPA, and the NCMC. During this decade, a few additional entities were added to its growing infrastructure: the Chicano Mexicano Prison Project (1993) and the Women's Commission and El Comite de Mujeres Patricia Marin (1995).[154] The UB was involved in several issue areas, such as police brutality, immigration, education, and prisons. It held and participated in several conferences and town hall meetings and became engaged in a number of direct actions that included marches, picketing, and press conferences. Some of the UB's leadership traveled to Cuba in 1999 as part of a broader-based delegation organized under my leadership.

Thus, the UB and its various affiliate entities, with their Marxist/nationalist agenda, found it difficult in the Mexicano barrios to overcome the "politics of the Hispanic Generation." Like the PNLRU, it too lacked a clear and well-defined strategy and mass base to bring about the national liberation of Aztlán.

Mutual Benefit and Old Interest Groups

Mutualistas

Especially by the latter part of the epoch, the oldest form of Mexicano organization, the *mutualistas*, were threatened with extinction.[155] For decades they were the organizational avant-garde of protection, security, and self-reliance for Mexicano migrants living in the United States. However, while several were still functional and continued to function as buffers, the country's continued socioeconomic and political changes and particularly those that occurred within the Mexicano experience threatened their existence. With the continued changes enacted by welfare capitalism via the federal government's myriad of social programs (Social Security, unemployment compensation, welfare) and improvement in the arena of civil rights the Mexicano's dependency on *mutualistas* lessened and added to those organizations' continued decline. Thus, the few *mutualistas* that did exist during this epoch, such as the Sociedad Progresista Méxican and La Sociedad Zaragoza in California, continued to provide its declining membership with death burial insurance and cultural activities.[156]

League of United Latin America Citizens (LULAC)

The increasingly growing conservative political climate and rise of the HG contributed to LULAC's revitalization. As a social action interest group, LULAC once again became one of the leading national Latino organizations that embraced the politics of adaptation. LULAC continued to focus on issues related to education and employment training, for example, Operation SER; held its annual conference; and established a nonprofit tax-exempt corporation for the purpose of securing grants and corporate contributions. In spite of the ongoing Coors boycott, the LULAC foundation in 1977 took a $50,000 contribution from the Adolph Coors Foundation to establish an operational office in Denver, Colorado.[157] LULAC also took a strong position against President Carter's immigration plan, calling it "unconscionable and objectionable" and argued that it would subject resident Mexican nationals to a "second-class citizenship" status.[158]

During the 1980s LULAC experienced a transient "golden period" of progressive activism. In essence, a shift occurred from a "want to be white" to a buffer role. This was a result of the leadership of Ruben Bonilla (1979–1981), Tony Bonilla (1981–1983), Mario Obledo (1983–1985), and its executive director Arnold Torres (1981–1985). While still committed to integration and adaptation and middle-class oriented, LULAC propounded a more assertive advocacy reformist role, which for at least the next five years or so enabled it to shed some of its conservative image. Its more activist leadership sought to transform LULAC into the most prominent and largest Hispanic "civil rights organization" in the country. In doing so, LULAC's leadership made exaggerated claims as to the size of its membership base. While in 1982 it had no more than five thousand paying members, Bonilla audaciously promulgated that LULAC had over one hundred thousand members. While it had numerous councils in several states across the country, its primary base of operation and sphere of influence remained largely Tejas.

During 1982 and 1983, LULAC took on the national television networks, ABC, CBS, and NBC, for the lack of Latinos in their programming and employment in general. A summit held in San Diego, California, organized by John Gamboa and myself on behalf of LULAC, brought some 150 Latinos who met with network officials. In 1982, Tony Bonilla announced a "full partnership" between LULAC and "Corporate America." In actuality no agreement was reached. In 1982 LULAC received for its efforts some $96,000 for its annual convention.[159] A year later, Bonilla joined Jesse Jackson's Operation PUSH's "corporate responsibility" agenda, which reached an accord with the Southland Corporation.

During the next three years, LULAC signed several accords with various corporations, especially the beer corporations, for example, Anheuser Bush and Miller. In 1984, the American G.I. Forum, National Council of La Raza, U.S. Hispanic Chamber of Commerce, Cuban National Planning Committee, and National Puerto Rican Coalition signed an accord with Coors, which officially brought closure to the boycott.[160] Initially, LULAC refused to ratify the agreement because the amount of financial contributions returned to the organizations would be predicated on the Latino community's consumption of the company's beer. However, by 1985 with election of a new and more conservative leadership, LULAC ratified the pact.[161]

From 1981 to 1984, Torres, on a myriad of issues effectively manipulated the national media on behalf of LULAC. Torres, who developed LULAC's legislative agenda in Washington, D.C., became the most visible LULAC leader, especially on immigration issues. His confrontational and assertive style of leadership got him national media exposure and notoriety, for example, on *The Phil Donahue Show* and *Firing Line* with William F. Buckley. As LULAC's chief lobbyist in Washington, D.C., Torres garnered valuable links to legislators and on several occasions gave testimony before various congressional committees.[162] Torres's leadership complemented that of Bonilla, who likewise was articulate, knowledgeable on the issues, and apt in the workings of the media. Both were hypercritical of Reagan's economic policies, especially of his federal deficit and defense build-up.

In 1984 LULAC national president Mario Obledo led a five-person delegation to Cuba and met with high-ranking Cuban government officials. That year, he took another delegation to Nicaragua, meeting with Sandinista leadership. These visits to the alleged foes of the United States infuriated the Reagan administration and fostered internal schisms within LULAC's rather conservative membership. Along with other organizations in 1982 and 1984, LULAC effectively opposed the Simpson-Mazzoli immigration reform bill. During 1984, LULAC faced serious financial problems; the year before it came close to declaring bankruptcy. Contributing to its financial crisis was its failure to effectively collect membership dues. Schisms began to develop over LULAC's mission, strategy, and positions taken by its national leadership. This fostered bickering between the councils, central office, and membership. In 1984 Torres resigned as a result of

LULAC's support of Edwin Meese to the post of U.S. attorney general and over LULAC's increasing support of the Reagan administration.[163]

Through 1985, LULAC was also engaged in protecting bilingual education from threats by the Reagan administration. SER Jobs for Progress had established a network of some ninety-six programs located in various states and had its own board, paid staff, and national office in Dallas, Texas.[164] However, with the election of Republican Oscar Moran in 1985, LULAC retrenched itself and adopted a much more conservative "want to be white" political posture. Marquez writes, "National President Moran promised to work for closer ties with the corporate sector, and halt LULAC's attacks on President Reagan."[165] Moran was reelected to three one-year terms without any major opposition to his conservative politics. LULAC during his tenure as president avoided provocative issues and developed a working relationship with both the Reagan and Bush administrations and "Corporate America." It refocused its attention on its national and state conventions, which with scores of exhibits took on more of a "carnival-like atmosphere." With its heavily middle-class orientation, "cocktail activism" became prevalent and in vogue.

However, during the late 1980s some "social action" activism did occur. In 1986 it did take on a major leadership position in defining the interests of Mexicanos regarding the Immigration Reform and Control Act of 1986. That same year in Tejas, LULAC succeeded in stopping an "English Only" resolution from coming out of committee. Again in 1987, in Tejas, LULAC filed a class action suit, *LULAC v. INS*, which forced the Immigration and Naturalization Services (INS) to process amnesty class applicants. In 1989, in another suit, *LULAC vs. Mattox*, it challenged the selection of judges in Tejas.

During the early part of the 1990s, LULAC's political posture continued to be that of a corporate-dependent civic, social, and cultural interest group that embodied the spirit of the Hispanic ethos. Marquez writes that the "LULAC of the 1990s [was] dramatically different from the small, tightly knit group of individuals that came together in 1929. Once on the cutting edge in the battle for civil rights for Mexican Americans, LULAC [had] lost its predominant position in the community."[166] Also, LULAC no longer was primarily Mexicano oriented. Influenced by the Hispanic Generation, it marketed itself as being a "Hispanic" civil rights organization.[167] Paradoxically, inherent to its "Pan-Latino" focus was its usage of *Hispanic* in its publications. LULAC's leaders also used *Hispanic* rather than *Latino* or its original term, *Latin American*, and by the mid-1990s a Nicaraguan-born Puerto Rican was elected as national president. Four years later, in another first, LULAC elected Belen Robles as its first female national president. By the end of the decade, LULAC claimed to have a membership of

110,000 and more than 600 councils serving all Hispanic nationality groups throughout the United States and Puerto Rico.[168] It maintained a staffed national office in Washington, D.C., out of which it coordinated its national organizing and lobbying efforts.

LULAC continued to address some policy issues, especially in education. In 1990, for example, it filed a suit, *LULAC v. Clements*, that challenged the allocation of funds to Texas universities.[169] It also continued to provide community service projects and programs—from job training, to health fairs, to mentoring business and housing initiatives. LULAC Educational Centers and Project SER—Jobs for Progress continued to operate and represent its growing social programmatic capability. LULAC's Corporate Alliance advisory board, comprised of some thirty major corporations, for example, AT&T, IBM, and General Motors, sought to foster stronger partnerships between corporations and the Latino community.[170] Youth leadership training programs were also added to the list of programs offered by LULAC.

By the late 1990s, while courted by the Republican Party, LULAC remained nonpartisan. Its councils conducted voter registration drives and citizenship education programs. Increasingly, LULAC in some instances came to the defense of undocumented migrants who were under attack by nativists and was hypercritical of the militarization of the U.S./México border. Ideologically, LULAC posited a "want to be white" role based upon the ethos of the HG and embraced liberal capitalism. At the close of the century, while LULAC was one of the country's leading national Hispanic organizations, it lacked the power base, resources, and the advocacy will to push for major reforms.

American G.I. Forum (AGIF)

Like LULAC, during the epoch, AGIF too experienced a resurgence of expansion and activity, especially between 1975 and the mid-1980s. During the Reagan years (1981–1988), AGIF became the Hispanic organizational connection to the Republican administration. Under the leadership of National Chairman José R. Cano, a Republican who was elected in 1980, AGIF's political posture moved to the Right, adopting a "want to be white" role. Cano and other AGIF leaders embraced Reagan's New Federalism. An exception was Dr. Hector Garcia, who in 1981 was unable to attend AGIF's national convention due to illness, in a written statement included in the convention's brochure was hypercritical of President Reagan's policies:

> I hope the organization continues to work for the poor, the uneducated, the elderly, and the suffering. During this year and other years to come,

[government] programs for the poor will be cut. I foresee more suffering, more hunger, and less education for our people. I foresee efforts to completely eliminate bilingual education. We must not permit this to happen.[171]

Cano's Republican ties gave the organization access to important leaders, including President Reagan himself. Its conventions drew numerous Republican leaders and were trumpeters for Republican Party initiatives that included program cutbacks, deregulation, increased military spending, and military intervention in Central American. In 1983 Cano secured President Reagan as the keynote speaker at its thirty-fifth Annual Convention held in El Paso, Tejas. This shift to the Right created divisions and disputes both internally and externally. Latino Democrats among others from several Latino organizations vehemently criticized Cano's Republican politics. One such incident occurred, according to Henry A. J. Ramos, when LULAC executive director Arnold Torres at a private meeting with AGIF staff "characterized Cano as a 'traitor' and a 'sellout' for having taken the positions he did."[172] AGIF embraced many of the tenets of the HG, especially its patriotic posture on defense-related issues and on the maintenance of the liberal capitalist system.

During the 1980s, AGIF collaborated with other national Latino organizations on a number of issues, especially corporate responsibility. In 1984, AGIF was one of the main groups that signed an agreement with Coors that officially brought an end to the national boycott. In 1986 AGIF also participated with other major Latino organizations such as the NCLR in the formation of HACER (Hispanic Association on Corporate Responsibility), a national alliance of Latino organizations committed to the exclusive goal of concluding corporate/Latino accords. AGIF benefited since it was able to secure grants from various corporations. AGIF also collaborated with other organizations on such issues as bilingual education, immigration, and affirmative action. AGIF's cardinal involvement, however, continued to be dealing with issues and programs related to Hispanic veterans.

After 1985, AGIF gradually began to decline in size of membership, stature, and influence. In spite of its decline mode, it secured two major victories: it lobbied to prevent the Reagan administration from dismantling bilingual education and lobbied for the appointment in 1987 of Dr. Lauro Cavazos as secretary of education. On the latter, activists argued that his appointment was blatantly used by the Reagan administration to further its conservative agenda and that of the Republican Party. For during his brief tenure as secretary of education, Cavazos alleged that Chicanos and Latinos did not value education.[173] Cavazos proved to be a major disappointment for Latinos. Because of the overt affiliation of AGIF's leadership to the Republican administrations, a lot of chapters fell apart, and consequently members quit.[174]

During the 1990s, AGIF's decline mode became more evident by its dwindling resources and decrease in membership. On the former, the funding by corporations and foundations was so scarce AGIF did not have enough money to carry out several of its programs and activities. By 1995 Project SER was also plagued by financial problems, and HACER had yet to deliver to AGIF substantial corporate funding. Outside of Project SER, the other funding received came from corporations, such as Boeing, Coors, Pacific Bell, and PG&E. Newly elected national chair Francisco F. Ivarra initiated a membership drive, which for a short time brought it back to financial solvency.[175] By the late 1990s, AGIF located its national office and small staff in Denver, Colorado, but was not fully operational due to its recurrent financial crisis.

On the latter, the financial recovery did not last long due to AGIF's failure to sign up enough new members. At the beginning of 1990, AGIF had an estimated membership of some twenty thousand in some thirty states that included the District of Colombia. In describing AGIF's impact, Meier and Rivera write, "Its heavy middle-class membership has given it a voice and influence with many government officials, particularly in recent more conservative administrations."[176] According to Mariana Tinco, California AGIF chairwoman, "It had chapters in some thirty-eight states, from Washington to New York. In California, AGIF had some twenty-five chapters from Sacramento to San Diego and a state membership of about 600."[177]

In addition to its regular chapters, AGIF had women's and youth chapters. In California, by the late 1990s, however, it had only five women's and two youth chapters. AGIF's constitution specified that female chapters had the right to elect a female state chairperson, have their own board of directors and own membership, and were allowed to have their own projects and activities. However, if a woman was a veteran she had the option of participating in either the women's or regular AGIF chapters.[178] At the national level, there were only about twenty women's chapters with a membership of some twelve hundred. Tinco ascribes the existence of women's chapters to what she described as the Mexicano patriarchic culture. She said, "Men cannot handle the fact that women can be just as competent and can lead. All we want is to walk side by side with men, no more no less."[179] Although women were eligible to be national commander, as of 1999 none had done so.

Despite its difficulties, AGIF continued to address local and national issues that impacted Hispanic veterans, especially those related to health, jobs, and discrimination. Yet it did not arouse the attention of the national media. Using an accommodation buffer approach, AGIF maintained a good working relationship with both the Bush and Clinton administrations. This became evident with AGIF's support for the Bush administration's Persian Gulf War. When questioned on this issue, Tinco answered, "[Hector] Garcia taught us to always support our country when at war." During the eight years of the Clinton administration, AGIF was in the loop of Hispanic organizations it dealt with. Thus, by the turn of the twentieth century, AGIF, plagued by a decreasing membership base and diminishing resources, was still functional but faced a questionable future.

Other Older Pressure Groups

Once the dynamic grassroots-based Community Service Organization (CSO) had been the epitome of a viable social action organization. But during this epoch, the CSO's decline culminated with its demise by the late 1990s. By the 1990s, left with a few social service chapters, as a statewide organization it lost funding and became plagued by administrative and financial controversies. Schisms within the CSO leadership led to lawsuits. By 1998 the aforementioned problems became so acute that the CSO lost its social service building in Los Angeles. In order to avoid bankruptcy, the new CSO board decided to "downsize" or better yet dismantle the CSO at the state level. The two or three remaining local CSO chapters each reincorporated as separate nonprofit entities. According to Carlos Montez, "The CSO chapter in Los Angeles incorporated as Centro CSO and adopted a grassroots organizing posture."[180]

During this epoch, there were also other older interest groups that emerged during the previous epoch that continued to be active. One such organization at the regional to national level was Incorporated Mexican American Government Employees (IMAGE). Founded in Denver, Colorado, in 1973, by 1975 it had nearly one hundred chapters, which sought to increase governmental employment opportunities for Mexicanos.[181] In California the Association of Mexican American Educators (AMAE), established in 1965[182] as an educational advocacy interest group of teachers, continued to be active. Both by the end of 1999 were in a decline mode, however, due to their inability to transcend their single-issue orientation and their failure to develop the requisite leadership, infrastructure, viable membership and funding base, and strategic action program needed to expand into viable change agents.

The Rise of Hispanic Interest Groups

National Council de La Raza

With the decline of the Movimiento and protest organizations, a number of interest groups that identified with the politics of the HG rose to prominence. One such organization was the National Council de La Raza (NCLR). By 1975, the NCLR had been functional for some seven years. With a staff of forty and a national headquarters office in Washington, D.C.,[183] it had program operations offices in Phoenix, Chicago, and Albuquerque.[184] The NCLR's growing "organizational clout" became evident as early as 1976 with its formation of the National Hispanic Leadership Conference (NHLC), which restricted membership to twenty-one Hispanic organizations. The NHLC replaced the NCLR's first effort, the Forum of National Hispanic Organizations, to unify Hispanic organizations at the national level. Its primary function was twofold: create a forum for discussion on issues and work to influence policy affecting Hispanics.[185] Although some sixty-two organizations were brought together, it lacked a focus and became increasingly unwieldy. From its incipience to 1991, the NHLC met and drafted policy papers, but as a group "it never caught fire." Former San Antonio mayor Henry Cisneros started a similar group in 1987 called the Unity Task Force of the National Hispanic Agenda, which in 1991 joined forces with the NHLC and formed and officially became the National Hispanic Leadership Agenda.[186]

By the 1980s, although never a proponent of Chicanismo, the NCLR, with its national headquarters now in Washington, D.C., assumed a buffer role. According to Christine Sierra, "Its chosen roles now would be political advocacy in Washington for Chicano causes, the monitoring of political developments in the nation's capital, and the playing of a broker, or middleman role, between Chicano organizations and national agencies."[187] Programmatically, involved in the areas of economic and community development, by the turn of the decade, it was an ardent proponent of "Brown capitalism," which meant it did not seek alternatives to liberal capitalism's deleterious and exploitive nature. Christine Sierra, who did an exhaustive examination of the NCLR, wrote that although it attempted to carry out a wide range of activities, it did not do so in a very effective manner. However, its ties to some one hundred "affiliates" remained tenuous at best.[188]

Buttressing the rise of the HG, the NCLR's leader Raul Yzaguirre proclaimed the 1980s as the "Decade of the Hispanic." It was during this decade that the NCLR's stature as an organization grew into national prominence. As an "organization of organizations," throughout the epoch the NCLR provided its affiliates with technical assistance in proposal writing, program development, and access to funding sources. It continued to carry out liaison services with federal government agencies and also provided information, data, and perspectives on public policy issues to the public via reports.[189] Also for purposes of disseminating information on its activities, it published a bimonthly magazine titled *Agenda* as well as other printed materials.[190] On an annual basis, the NCLR also held an annual conference, which by the 1990s was the largest of any Hispanic organization.

Under the able leadership of Yzaguirre, the NCLR increasingly took on an "advocacy role." With its presence in Washington, D.C., it was successful in gaining access to powerful politicians from both political parties. Yzaguirre adroitly manipulated the politics of the HG to the advantage of the NCLR. During these years, the NCLR made its transition from initially being primarily a Mexicano-based organization to one that embraced the total Hispanic ethnic spectrum. Organizationally, its member affiliates increased and embraced, along with LULAC, a number of issues, such as "corporate responsibility." As a result it played a pivotal leadership role in the signing of numerous accords. The NCLR played a major organizational role in the formation of HACER, which perhaps by design greatly benefited the NCLR, since it received numerous grants from several corporations and foundations, which contributed to its financial solvency. In the advocacy arena at the national level, the NCLR, especially after 1985, replaced LULAC as the leading Hispanic organization. Through the NCLR's monitoring of legislation, research on issues, lobbying, and public pronouncements, Yzaguirre seized the moment and spoke out on a number of policy issues as if the NCLR was "the" national Hispanic organizational leader.

By the 1990s relatively speaking, the NCLR was the most influential HG organization in the country, meaning no other could rival its budget and resources. The Ford Foundation alone, from 1968 to 1991, contributed to the NCLR a total of $9.6 million.[191] Its administrative budget in late 1990 was around $14 million, making it the largest of the existing Hispanic interest groups. By the late 1990s, the NCLR had some 230 formal affiliates, who together served 39 states, Puerto Rico, and the District of Columbia. Within its organizational network, it served more than twenty thousand groups and individuals nationwide, and reached more than three million Hispanics annually. Beyond its headquarters in Washington, D.C., the NCLR had field offices in Los Angeles, California; Phoenix, Arizona; Chicago, Illinois; San Antonio, Tejas; and San Juan, Puerto Rico, which provided services on resource development, program operations, management, and governance.[192]

The NCLR as an advocate interest group was also equipped with an applied research capability that focused on policy analysis. Numerous issues that affected

Hispanics were dealt with, such as immigration, federal appointments, education, housing, health, employment and training, and civil rights enforcement. The NCLR released reports and press releases, met with legislators and bureaucrats, lobbied, and networked with other Latino and non-Latino organizations. Strategically, however, the NCLR adhered to a buffer role of circumspection when it came to tackling issues. As a rule, circumspect it rebuked direct action protest and avoided controversial issues that could jeopardize its funding or blemish its mainstream image. It relied on a conventional accommodation approach largely based on lobbying, disseminating information, and utilizing media, and categorically rejected any use of an unconventional protest approach.

Along with the National Association for the Advancement of Colored People (NAACP) and other Latino and non-Latino organizations, the NCLR participated in negotiations with representatives of the ABC, NBC, CBS, and Fox networks on the issue of improving diversity both on-screen and behind the scenes. The NCLR later reported that the number of Latino characters on prime-time television remained dismal at a miniscule level of 1 percent.[193] In a rather bold unprecedented action, the NCLR collaborated with the National Media Latino Coalition in calling for a "Brownout Latino" to protest the lack of Latinos in the four major television networks' programming. However, without having the power capability to develop a critical mobilization mass, the media issue produced no significant results.

In the arenas of social and cultural issues, the NCLR sponsored various events. With the strong financial support of several corporations, its annual conferences drew thousands of people and attracted the participation of both Republican and Democrat power holders. The NCLR also held its annual Congressional Awards, which annually honored members of Congress for their support and commitment on policy issues critical to "Hispanic Americans."[194] By 1999, even though the NCLR was the most influential Hispanic organization in the country, it had few policy answers and lacked the commitment and power capability to effectively address the myriad of issues affecting Latinos, especially Mexicanos.

Mexican American Legal Defense and Education Fund (MALDEF)

Comparable in national stature to the NCLR was MALDEF, which continued to assume a buffer legal advocate role. During the late 1970s and early 1980s, under the able leadership of Vilma Matínez, MALDEF's legal advocacy increased, particularly in the areas of education, immigration, political representation, and citizen rights. In 1975, MALDEF created a legal intern/extern program to train and later assist prospective Mexicano attorneys in setting up their law practices. In addition, MALDEF continued to provide scholarships for Mexicanos attending law school. By 1977, immigration became one of MALDEF's main issue priorities. In October 1977, it participated in the First National Chicano/Latino Conference on Immigration and Public Policy, held in San Antonio, Tejas.[195] MALDEF collaborated with LULAC, AGIF, and the NCLR, among others, in the formation of coalitions for the defeat of Carter's immigration plan. At the same time, MALDEF's leadership made a strategic decision to be more selective with the cases MALDEF would litigate. According to Karen O'Conner and Lee Epstein, "Generally, it began to limit its participation to important test cases that were considered to have 'broad implications.' "[196]

During the 1980s, first under the brief leadership of Joaquin Avila followed by that of Antonia Hernandez, MALDEF grew in influence and stature. Believing education was the key to economic, social, and political opportunities for Latinos in the United States, MALDEF addressed a number of issues related to education, such as segregation in the schools, biased testing procedures, inequities in public school finance, and failure of school systems to address language problems.[197] After a series of test cases dealing with education, in 1982 it scored its most impressive legal victory. In what would become a landmark decision, *Plyler v. Doe*, the United States Supreme Court accepted MALDEF's legal contention that Tejas could not exclude the children of undocumented migrants from its public schools.[198] MALDEF successfully argued that refusing to allow the children of undocumented immigrants to attend school violated the equal protection clause of the Fourteenth Amendment. Maurilio Vigil explains, "The U.S. Supreme Court affirmed MALDEF's position and ordered an end to the exclusionary process."[199] This decision increased MALDEF's credentials as an effective legal advocate. The victory also provided MALDEF with the legal precedent upon which to initiate other suits, particularly those dealing with voting rights and immigration.

In another education suit, *Vasques v. San Jose Unified School District*, MALDEF in 1986 successfully charged that the San Jose School District discriminated against Latino students by means of segregation. Initially, MALDEF lost the case, but successfully appealed the ruling to the U.S. Ninth District Court of Appeals. The decision was overturned on the grounds that the district had deliberately kept Latino students segregated since 1962. MALDEF attorneys worked with school officials and developed a desegregation plan and an early childhood bilingual education program.[200]

Beyond the arena of education, MALDEF during the 1980s assumed a major organizational leadership role in the struggle against restrictionist immigration policies. In fact, Peter Skerry wrote, "It was the center of Mexican American opposition to the Simpson-Mazzoli immigration legislation and subsequent reform efforts."[201] In conjunction with other immigrant rights organizations, MALDEF carried out a concerted lobbying and educational effort against it in 1984. With the passage of the Immigration Reform Control Act (IRCA) in 1986, MALDEF initiated a program designed to educate both the employer and employee of their rights under the new law and monitored as well immigration enforcement practices and existing immigration policies.

MALDEF also prioritized Latino political empowerment. As a result it became heavily involved with the 1980 U.S. Census, which sought to ensure the accurate count of Latinos. In 1982, MALDEF filed a redistricting suit to end "gerrymandering." In California, MALDEF became a major administrative contributor and participant to a statewide Mexicano coalition, Californios for Fair Representation (CFR), of which I was its state director and organizer. Comprised of some fifty organizations, its strong direct action and lobbying efforts successfully pushed for the creation of two congressional seats that were heavily populated with Mexicanos. MALDEF in 1986 in one of its most publicized cases, *Gomez v. City of Watsonville*, argued that at-large elections denied Latinos, approximately 50 percent of the city's population, representation on the city council. On July 1988, the Ninth District Court of Appeals ruled that the at-large system of elections diluted the voting strength of Mexicanos. The court ruled that the city of Watsonville was in violation of Section II of the Voting Rights Act of 1965. As a result of this case, MALDEF won a total of five cases in Tejas, one in Nuevo México, and one in California, all of which involved challenges to the at-large voting system.[202]

MALDEF also challenged discriminatory practices in the hiring of Latinos. In Tejas in a class action suit, MALDEF successfully challenged the discriminatory hiring and promotion practices of San Antonio's largest grocery store chain, H. E. Butt Company. As a result of the settlement, the court adopted a consent decree that required annual goals for the promotion of Latinos into supervisory positions and ordered the company to establish a $250,000 scholarship fund in order to prepare Latinos for new jobs. MALDEF also collaborated as a member of HACER in numerous corporate responsibility efforts. In California, MALDEF reached a settlement on behalf of Latinos against the Ralph's supermarket chain. Ralph's agreed to hire Latinos in some 120 stores in proportion to their availability within the workforce. In another similar case, MALDEF won a settlement, which provided for a ten-year hiring promotion plan. In a case known as *Cota v. City of Tucson*, MALDEF argued that the Tucson police department relied almost exclusively on Mexicano officers to patrol and serve the Mexicano community of Tucson. Furthermore, MALDEF argued that they were worked under harsher conditions, were denied promotions and transfers, and lacked training opportunities. In response, the U.S. District Court concurred and directed the police department to take remedial action in order to correct the problems.[203]

By the 1990s, from a legal advocacy perspective, MALDEF became the most effective Hispanic organization in the country. In a suit involving its Immigrant's Rights Program, MALDEF scored a major litigation victory in 1992 with the settlement of the case *International Molder's and Allied Workers v. Nelson*. The court ruled on behalf of those Latino workers and employers whose Fourth Amendment rights had been violated by the INS during illegal search and seizures perpetrated in workplace raids. The settlement compelled the INS to stop conducting workplace raids unless they had secured a search warrant, valid extenuating circumstances, or voluntary consent. This meant that the INS could no longer conduct raids and seize individuals merely because they looked like they were undocumented workers.[204] MALDEF concurrently addressed issues of redistricting, political access, immigration, affirmative action, and bilingual education. In a political access suit, *Bonilla v. City of Chicago*, MALDEF unsuccessfully charged that the Latino vote was diluted in Chicago's 1992 city redistricting of its fifty wards.[205] Its most significant legal success of the decade, however, was its legal challenge of Proposition 187. As a result of a final settlement in the case, *Gregorio T. v. Wilson*, Democrat governor Gray Davis agreed in 1999 to strike down the section of Proposition 187 that denied education to children of undocumented parents.

Beyond its litigation efforts, MALDEF also developed a number of programs. Increasingly during the 1990s, MALDEF took on a more programmatic developmental focus and was less active in litigation matters. It continued to expand its Law School and Communications Scholarship Fund, which provided valuable financial assistance in the form of fellowships to a number of Latino law and communication students. MALDEF also developed and implemented a "Leadership Development Program" that offered leadership training classes to those interested in becoming strong advocate leaders for Latinos. Its Parent Leadership Training Program sought to get parents involved as advocates in their children's education. Another related program was its National Parent/School Partnership Program that sought to strategically provide the infrastructure for Latino parent involvement.[206] Late in 1999, MALDEF initiated "Hagase Contar!" (Make Yourself Count!), a national U.S. Census campaign designed to reduce the undercount of Latinos.

By the late 1990s, MALDEF had its national headquarters in Los Angeles and four regional offices located in San Francisco, California; San Antonio, Texas;

Chicago, Illinois; and Washington, D.C.[207] MALDEF's thirty-five-member Board of Directors included public officials, businessmen, journalists, educators, and community leaders. It had no membership base and depended on its professional staff of seventy-five employees and twenty-two attorneys to move its multifaceted advocacy agenda. Like the NCLR, MALDEF was the financial creation of the Ford Foundation. From 1968 to 1991, MALDEF received $14.2 million from the foundation.[208] Anheuser Bush Corporation was also another of its largest contributors. In 1998 MALDEF had fifty-five foundation contributors that included nearly 130 corporate contributors, such as General Motors Corporation, Hughes Aircraft, AT&T, Bank of America, and Toyota Motor Sales USA, Inc., and fourteen individual contributors.[209] MALDEF's budget for 1991–1992 was $4.9 million; by 2000 its annual operating budget was expected to increase to nearly $6 million.

Thus, in spite of its dependency on external sources for funding, throughout the decade MALDEF established an impressive record of legal advocacy on behalf of Latinos. In great part MALDEF's successful longevity has also been secure due to its powerful linkages with numerous politicians, Jewish and other non-Latino power holders. No other Latino interest group in the country could match its preeminent record of successes via the courts. Yet concerns existed over its diminished advocate role in the 1990s and its powerful corporate ties.

New Hispanic Organizations

The epoch produced a plethora of new Latino or Hispanic buffer-oriented interest groups and coalitions largely committed to the ethos and politics of the HG. The birth of many of the new organizations was based upon a professional or a one-issue focus. Some were national, while others were state or regionally based, but none reached a level of "power and change" prominence. One such new interest group was the U.S. Hispanic Chamber of Commerce (USHCC). Formed in 1979, in Nuevo México the USHCC's several local and state Hispanic chambers coalesced into a national business advocacy interest group.[210] Throughout the epoch, with its liberal capitalist business focus and some two hundred Hispanic chambers and business organizations, the USHCC became a national and international networking advocate, particularly with corporations and the U.S. government.[211] Politically, the USHCC became a breeding ground for Republican "conservative politics."

During the epoch, a second organization to emerge in prominence was the National Hispanic Leadership Agenda (NHLA). It was formed and officially incorporated in 1991 as a result of a merger between the NCLR's National Hispanic Leadership Conference and Henry Cisneros's Unity Task Force of the National Hispanic Agenda. The NHLA's advocacy policy focus was on issues predicated on consensus, such as better schools, bilingual education, and political empowerment. It avoided controversial issues for fear of breaking its fragile alliance. Essentially, it was an elitist organization comprised of politicians, community activists, businessmen, and leaders of various Hispanic national and regional organizations who adhered to different political philosophies. Without a grassroots power base, its elitism was evident in its forty-five-member board, which included five cochairs that represented the troika of the Hispanic ethnic spectrum, that is Mexicanos, Puerto Ricans, and Cubans: Henry Cisneros (Mex), MALDEF's Antonia Hernandez (Mex), the NCLR's Raul Yzaguirre (Mex), Bronx Borough president Fernando Ferrer (Puerto Rican), and Miami congresswoman Ileana Ros-Lethtinen (Cuban).[212] Throughout the 1990s, at best the NHLA was known for its powerless pronouncements on public policy issues that were noncontroversial in nature. Like other HG organizations, it lacked a power capability.

Lastly, coalition building became a popular medium for unifying various organizations with different agendas on issues of common interest. While there are far too many to list, suffice it to say coalition building was particularly commonplace, especially at the local level in dealing with a number of issues, such as immigration, education, affirmative action, and police brutality. Most of the coalitions proved to be largely transitory: once the issue was resolved or died out so did the coalition. Their demise was also a result of insufficient structure, resources, personality leader differences, and conflicting intraorganizational clashes. Participation in coalitions at times weakened organizations rather than strengthened them.

The Rise of Chicana/Latina Interest Groups

Of particular significance during this epoch was the rise of several Latina interest groups. The politics of the Movimiento that pervaded the past epoch of protest coupled with the rise of the white feminist movement acted as propelling forces for the establishment of several Chicana/Latina organizations. Although initially apprehensive of the white-led feminist movement, the pervasiveness of what they perceived as "triple victimization," meaning being victims of discrimination due to class, race, and gender, Chicana activists formed their own interest groups. During the 1970s, issues of male sexism, rape, abortion, and sterilization induced controversy and debate.[213] At times, conflict and friction ensued as a result of disagreements on these and other issues with their Chicano male counterparts. Like other existent male-dominated organizations, they too took on a buffer political role.

At the national level, women continued to play pivotal leadership and supportive roles within LULAC and AGIF. Particularly, LULAC's Mujeres en Acción had the largest membership of any of the women's organizations.[214] In 1974 the Mexican American Women's National Association (MAWNA) was formed, headed by its first president Evangeline Elizondo of Tejas, as the counterpart to the National Organization of Women (NOW). Its cardinal thrust was to advance the status of Mexicanas and achieve equality between genders in the common pursuit for their rights. Moreover, it sought to develop leadership among women in order to obtain leadership parity.[215] MAWNA's cardinal organization thrust was the empowerment of Latinas through leadership development, community service, and advocacy via a number of programs.[216] During the epoch, its advocacy activities were rather limited, since they focused on programs, publishing a newsletter, and holding an annual convention. By the 1990s, it was based out of the eastern part of the United States and in an effort to broaden its Latino ethnic base in 1998 changed its name to "MANA: A National Latina Organization."[217]

During the late 1970s, three other national women's organizations were formed: the Chicana Forum, established in 1976; the Mexican American Women's National Association, also started in 1976; and the National Network of Hispanic Women, formed in 1977. The two former advocacy organizations sought to promote the careers of their membership, while the latter was a "network" of leaders from professions, private businesses, education, and corporations who essentially did the same.[218]

At the national level, Mexicanas during the 1980s expanded their organizing activities. In 1982 women activists held several panels on women's issues at the annual National Association of Chicano Studies (NACS). In another related initiative, to strengthen Chicano Studies, women in 1983 formed Mujeres Activas en Letras y Cambio Social (MALCS). Comprised of university women and students, MALCS supported research in the field, held summer institutes to encourage intellectual advancement of gender studies, published a newsletter and a monograph series, and held conferences.[219] At a NACS conference held in 1984 at Austin, Tejas, entitled "Voces de la Mujer"[220] a Women's Caucus was established, which became the controlling power throughout the epoch. There were numerous other women's organizations that surfaced that claimed to be national in scope.[221]

At the regional and state levels, several other Mexicana/Latina organizations were also formed. According to Meier and Rivera, "To free themselves from gender-based restrictions of their culture Mexican American women developed over regional and national groups by the early eighties." The first strictly Chicana-oriented interest group, La Comisión Femenil, was formed in California in 1970.[222] Throughout the epoch, it continued to grow and was influential in the politics of the Chicano community. It produced a number of influential political leaders, such as Gloria Molina (L.A. county supervisor), Leticia Queseda (L.A. School Board), and Lucille Roybal-Allard (congresswoman). By the 1990s, while still involved in a number of women-related issues and operating a service center in Los Angeles, La Comisión Femenil's focus shifted from politics to the promotion of professionalism.[223]

As a women's political pressure HG-oriented interest group, Hispanas Organized for Political Equality (HOPE) became a competitor to La Comisión Femenil. Founded in 1989, HOPE's mission as a nonprofit, nonpartisan organization was to ensure political and economic parity of Latinas through leadership, advocacy, and education. A major architect of HOPE was founding president Maria Contreras-Sweet. HOPE's central organizing agenda has aggressively evolved around the thrust of "Latina empowerment." With funding provided mostly by the corporate sector, HOPE holds workshops, educational seminars, debates, and town hall meetings. In 1999, HOPE launched the HOPE Leadership Institute, which was an eight-month leadership training program designed to empower Latinas to create critical change in the areas of health, education, and economics. According to political scientist Ada Sosa-Riddell, "HOPE is mostly comprised of younger middle class women who as of yet have not been willing to take on the issues the way Comisión Femenil did years back."[224]

At the local grassroots level, "Mexicana empowerment" was illustrated by the formation of Mothers of East Los Angeles (MELA), a religious lay advocacy group. In 1986 a coalition of some four hundred women from two Catholic parishes in East Los Angeles formed MELA in their struggle to stop the construction of a prison in East Los Angeles. Gloria Molina provided leadership support and used the issue very effectively as a springboard for her election in 1987 to the Los Angeles City Council.[225] Facilitated by Reverend John Morretta and led by Juana Gutierrez, MELA mounted an effective mobilization that included rallies of fifteen hundred to three thousand people; picketing; lobbying of *politicos*; and support of powerful allies, for example, Archbishop Roger Mahony. After nearly seven years of incessant struggle, MELA scored a major victory with the defeat of the proposed construction site in 1992. Once the issue was won, MELA became a transitory organizational phenomenon.[226]

Thus, during this epoch, Latina organizations were formed and played a significant advocacy role. However, with the exception of MELA, in most cases, they prioritized issues that impacted their gender rather than the Latino community as a whole.

Political Pressure Organizations

Mexican American Political Organization (MAPA)

During the epoch, the oldest functional Mexicano political pressure organization in the country was MAPA. By 1975 MAPA had survived the militant protest politics of the Movimiento and shifted to a more buffer political role. Historically, it had been plagued by schisms, diversity of agendas, partisan conflicts, and a declining membership, which continued throughout the epoch. In 1975, with only thirty chapters statewide, Margaret Cruz, the first woman to lead MAPA, prioritized its rebuilding, especially the regional structures and local chapters. Along with twenty-three other Latino organizational leaders that year she attended a meeting with Republican president Gerald Ford in Washington, D.C., and represented MAPA at the United Nations-sponsored International Year of the Woman Conference held in México City.[227] Yet despite Cruz's rebuilding efforts, due to MAPA's moderate political posture some Movimiento-oriented members and Democrat liberals left the organization. The political reality was that some chapters were products of election years: elections attracted new members; new chapters were formed because of support for a candidate(s); and elections often revitalized old existing chapters. However, once the election was over so was the active participation of many of its members and chapters. Between 1975 and 1977, under the inept leadership of President Manuel Lopez, MAPA was on the verge of extinction. It had a mere twelve chapters statewide and its membership decreased to a low of four hundred;[228] several previous attempts to expand MAPA into a national bipartisan political pressure organization had failed.

Regardless of MAPA's internal problems, the media was a major asset, particularly during its state endorsing conventions. Kenneth Kurt explains why candidates solicited MAPA's endorsement:

> The candidates, though, knew how to make the endorsement work for them. They sought support not because the group could deliver a large block of votes, money, or even campaign workers. Its principle value had become its symbolic importance, potential use in the community, and the immediate news coverage that could be generated. These factors had all increased in value with the near dominance of the media.[229]

In 1976, Democrat presidential candidate Jimmy Carter addressed the MAPA convention via a telephone hookup from his home in Georgia. Throughout the remaining years of the 1970s, regional and state endorsing conventions were MAPA's mainstay of political activity.

In 1977 Eduardo Sandoval was elected MAPA state president and inherited an organization that was financially broke and declining. He sought to revitalize MAPA by establishing a more positive relation with then-California governor Jerry Brown. That year, he mobilized MAPA and came to the defense of Secretary of Health and Welfare Mario Obledo, who had been accused by *Reader's Digest* and others of having linkages to the prison-based gang the "Mexican Mafia." Sandoval succeeded in securing the support of thirty other statewide organizations and overtly defended Obledo and held a highly publicized testimonial dinner attended by some two thousand persons honoring Obledo. In 1978 at its state convention, MAPA endorsed incumbent Democrat Jerry Brown for reelection as governor. A $1,000 check was donated to the Brown campaign, and MAPA committed itself to raise an additional $30,000 from the Latino community. Sandoval had the bylaws amended so that he could run for reelection and was reelected in 1979. With a sense of invigoration, MAPA formed new chapters, revitalized existing ones, and initiated quarterly conferences that dealt with a variety of state policy issues. In dealing with Governor Brown, MAPA pushed for more appointments and was more assertive in its demands.[230]

During the early 1980s, MAPA continued to function as a volunteer organization. It had a very limited budget and resources, no staff or office, and was essentially reliant on membership dues and local fund-raisers for resources. The quarterly conferences continued under the aegis of Sandoval's leadership. In 1981 MAPA sought to be at the forefront on the issue of reapportionment. A battle over political turf erupted with a newly formed Californios for Fair Representation (CFR). MAPA lacking the resources, technical expertise, and networks of support, CFR dominated the politics of redistricting. With the election of Julio Calderon in 1982, MAPA politically moved again to the Right and embraced the Republican Party. Numerous Republican Party-based chapters were formed. By the summer of 1982, MAPA's membership increased from six hundred to some two thousand with the number of chapters doubling to forty. Efforts were also made to organize chapters in other southwestern states, and in the state of Washington.[231] In 1982 Calderon was invited to the White House by Republican president Ronald Reagan to witness the signing of the extension to the Voting Rights Act.

During the 1982 primaries, many Mapistas supported Democrat Mario Obledo's unsuccessful bid for the Democratic Party's gubernatorial nomination. Subsequently, at MAPA's endorsing convention, a political struggle occurred between those Mapistas who supported Democrat mayor Bill Bradley and those who supported Republican George Deukmejian. It was one of those rare times when MAPA reached an actual level of bipartisanship. The gubernatorial conflict spilled over into the election of MAPA state president between Fernando Chavez, son of UFW leader Cesar Chavez, and Republican Calderon. The differences escalated to where Calderon and Chavez actually got into an altercation. With scores of UFW members and supporters joining MAPA, Chavez was the victor.[232] An exodus of Mapista Republicans occurred, which decreased MAPA's membership and number of chapters. In 1984 some Mapistas became strong supporters and members of the "Rainbow Coalition" supporting Democrat Jesse Jackson's bid for the presidency. In spite of the strong effort, MAPA endorsed Democrat Walter Mondale.

In 1985 with the election of Beatriz Molina as state president, Republicans once again returned in large numbers to MAPA's membership ranks. Yet in 1986, during the state primary, MAPA endorsed Democrat Charles "Chuck" Pineda from Sacramento as its candidate for governor. In 1988 MAPA, along with numerous other organizations and individuals, participated with IMPACTO 88, a coalition committed to forging an *acercamiento* with México and fostering a Mexicano voter mobilization for the 1988 presidential elections. In an unprecedented political move, MAPA in 1988 endorsed neither presidential candidate, Republican George Bush or Democrat Michael Dukakis. At the endorsing convention in San Diego, California, Jesse Jackson received the support of the majority of MAPA delegates. Two MAPA leaders, Ben Benavidez and Jenaro Valdez, were Jackson delegates at the Democratic Party Convention in Atlanta, Georgia.[233]

In 1989, Benavidez, who was from the Fresno area, in a hard fought battle with Julio Calderon was elected MAPA state president. For the next ten years, Benavidez became the leadership power behind MAPA. With his election, MAPA throughout the 1990s took on a rather populist Chicano/Mexicano quasi-nationalist posture that was liberal capitalist in practice and partisan Democrat oriented. In 1990 Benavidez promulgated that the decade of the 1990s was to become the decade of the Mexicano/Chicano, indicating a major shift from the ethos of HG politics. Benavidez's populism was evident in the theme he embraced: "*La Lucha es la de mi pueblo*" (My struggle is the struggle of my people).[234] MAPA's organizing agenda during the decade included addressing issues of education, redistricting, police brutality, economic empowerment, immigration, and discrimination, particularly in the San Joaquin Valley.

From 1991 to 1993, MAPA waged a struggle of support for Agrupacion de Madres Activas en Educacion (Group of Active Mothers in Education) against the Dinuba School District. After a number of boycotts, marches, and walkouts in 1992 that included the arrest of four mothers and Benavidez, La Agrupacion and MAPA won concessions to increase the number of Mexicano teachers, counselors, and administrators in the schools. In addition, the four Dinuba mothers who had been arrested won a million and a half dollar lawsuit in 1993. As a consequence of a Voting Rights Act suit and the Dinuba victory some sixty-one school districts from Bakersfield to Stockton changed from at-large to single-member district elections.[235] At the height of the Dinuba organizing effort in 1992, Benavidez suffered a major stroke that required some six months of rehabilitation. Semi-recovered in 1993, he reconnected to MAPA's ongoing empowerment efforts in Dinuba. MAPA from 1992 to 1999 along with twenty-four other groups participated with the Greenlining Coalition and signed thirty-five agreements with banks and utilities, which paid off.[236] Some of MAPA's biggest corporate contributors included Wells Fargo Bank, AT&T, Home Savings, Bank of America, and Pac Bell. Profits made from MAPA's annual conventions, banquets, and membership drives helped sustain its electoral and advocacy pressure activities.

MAPA organized between 1994 and 1998 against the passage of propositions 187, 209, and 227. Benavidez's confidant Hector Brolo was elected to a two-year term in 1996 as MAPA state president. Even though MAPA had a new state president, Benavidez remained the leadership power behind MAPA. In San Bernardino and Riverside counties in 1996, Benavidez personally took charge in the formation of some twelve chapters. That same year, he along with other Mapistas participated in a protest march and rally against the militarization, for example, Operation Gatekeeper, of the U.S./México border in San Ysidro, California. That next year, Benavidez, while organizing marches in Dinuba and Delano and protesting several wrongful shootings by police, suffered his second stroke, which was almost fatal. While MAPA continued to address a number of policy issues, it concurrently held state and regional endorsing conventions. Benavidez's protégé Gloria Torres in 1999 was elected as MAPA's new state president, the third female to hold the post.[237] When interviewed, Benavidez said that in 1999, MAPA's membership was approximately fourteen hundred and that it had some seventy chapters.[238] Thus, by the turn of the century, MAPA was precariously still active as a political pressure interest group, but lacked a power capability and appeared to be in decline.

Southwest Voter Registration and Education Project (SVREP)

During the late 1970s, the fledgling SVREP focused its organizational energies on the promotion of "Mexicano political empowerment," meaning getting more Mexicanos elected to public office. From the start, SVREP's organizing activities focused on voter registration, political education, and get-out-the-vote drives. While it funded several voter registration projects throughout Aztlán, its main area of concentration and political work was Tejas. Former MAYO leader Willie Velasquez preached the gospel of political participation to Mexicanos in countless communities throughout Tejas and later Aztlán. Strongly supported by Democrats, SVREP adhered to a political buffer role as manifested by its strong support for what some scholars have called the "Liberal Agenda." Its cardinal reform purpose was not to transform the country's liberal capitalist system, but rather to make it politically more inclusive of Mexicanos and subsequently Latinos in general.

Due to increased funding and support, during the 1980s SVREP grew and expanded throughout Aztlán and even into the Midwest. Especially in the small rural communities of Tejas, the number of Mexicanos registered to vote more than doubled. A major benefactor of SVREP's voter registration efforts was Henry Cisneros, who in 1981 was elected mayor of San Antonio. The increase was truly dramatic; it went from 488,200 in 1976 to 1,034,922 in 1984, which translated to an increase in 1976 of 32 percent to 51 percent in 1984.[239] From 1975 to 1985, SVREP claimed that it had registered over half a million Mexicano voters in Aztlán and the Midwest.[240] Across the country, from 1972 to 1984, Latino voter registration increased by 27 percent.[241] As voter registration figures increased so did Mexicano political representation, which was in part induced by a number of suits filed by both MALDEF and SVREP under MALDEF's leader Joaquin Avila. The national increase in voter registration and elected Latino officials was attributable to SVREP organizing efforts.

With its successful growth and desire for further expansion, SVREP's targeted population by the 1980s was broadened to include "all" Latinos. Its operating budget in 1980 was about $1 million of which approximately half came from several foundations. Churches provided about 30 to 35 percent of its funds, and unions contributed around 2.8 percent.[242] From the onset, SVREP relied on a grassroots network of volunteers to carry out its empowerment mission. Since its formation, SVREP maintained an office in San Antonio, Tejas, and by the 1980s it established another in Los Angeles, California. Up until 1984, it had had problems in Los Angeles garnering support from both local politicians and even some activists. One problem among several was that some considered SVREP an "outsider" political organizing force. "Bruised egos" and a lack of cooperation and support from the Democrat Party establishment elites also impeded its expansion efforts into California. However, by the late 1980s, much of the opposition to SVREP diminished due to Velasquez's folksy erudite leadership.

In 1984 Velasquez established a national nonprofit, nonpartisan research institute, which was named the William C. Velasquez Institute (WCVI). Its main mission was to conduct research, particularly with election analysis, which could be useful to improving the level of political participation in Latino communities.[243] The WCVI conducted exit polls during presidential and state elections in which the polling data was made public via press releases and reports, titled "Southwest Voter Registration Notes." Other related topics dealing with political empowerment issues were covered as well. In 1988, however, tragedy hit both entities with the death of their charismatic founder, Willie Velasquez, who at the age of forty-four succumbed to cancer. Andy Hernandez replaced Velasquez as head of SVREP and was successful in continuing its dynamic growth.

Supported by foundations, corporations, and sources within the Democratic Party, SVREP continued to maintain a small staff and two offices through the 1990s. Hernandez resigned in 1994 to become the Hispanic Outreach director for the Democratic National Committee (DNC). In explaining the reason for his appointment, Geoffrey Fox stated, "The very fact that the DNC thought it needed a Hispanic outreach was largely due to the effectiveness of the SVREP in increasing the Hispanic vote."[244] In 1994 Antonio Gonzalez replaced Hernandez as president and executive director. In 1996, SVREP had an operating budget of some $3 million. During the 1996 presidential campaign, President Clinton was supportive of SVREP since even though it was officially nonpartisan, the great majority of Mexicanos registered Democrat. This helped SVREP secure financial support from other Democrats. It audaciously claimed that during the last twenty years it had registered some 2 million Latinos to vote, 4,500 leaders had been trained in civic participation, and over 1,800 projects had been initiated in the 200-targeted communities within Aztlán.[245]

SVREP during the 1990s like other Latino organizations also resorted to expensive annual conferences that catered to the middle and upper class and Latino political elites, which for barrio residents were out of reach. Its conference themes accentuated issues and projects that SVREP was involved with, such as political empowerment and even U.S. foreign policy, particularly as it impacted Latin America. Since the late 1980s, for purposes of building linkages with Latin America, especially El Salvador, Cuba, and México, SVREP sent several delegations to these countries. Domestically, during the late 1990s, it expanded its agenda to include issues of public education, immigration, health care, and election reform. Through its "National Latino Academy," SVREP provided training on the basics of grassroots organizing, mass voter registration, leadership training of community leaders and elected officials and accountability of elected officials.[246]

By the late 1990s, there was no other organization in Aztlán comparable to SVREP in its focus, purpose, and effectiveness. The work of the WCVI with its exit polls and reports provided invaluable research data and analysis on Latino electoral politics. Thus, at the close of 1999, while SVREP and the WCVI continued to expand their activities, the barrios and *colonias* remained politically largely not organized, powerless, and colonized.

Midwest Voter Registration and Education Project (MVREP)

MVREP was established in 1982 as a counterpart to SVREP in the Midwest as a result of SVREP's failure to establish a base of support in the region. In the Midwest the Latino population was less concentrated, more dispersed, and ethnically more diverse. For the next eighteen years, MVREP adopted a buffer political role by providing technical and financial support (small grants) for voter registration and political education drives throughout the various states of the Midwest. Juan Andrade, like Willie Velasquez with SVREP, was MVREP's driving organizing force. As a result of MVREP's countless voter registration drives, a more educated Latino community, and better organization, particularly in states such as Illinois, Minnesota, Kansas, and Indiana, the region experienced increases in the number of Latinos elected. In addition to proving small grants for voter registration, MVREP, according to Richard Santillan, routinely sponsored numerous state and regional conferences, which provided vital information regarding the critical essentials for organizing successful campaign efforts.[247] MVREP in collaboration with MALDEF and the Puerto Rican Legal Defense and Education Fund initiated various suits that focused on altering election systems, improving access to voter registration, and challenging local and state reapportionment plans.[248]

During the remaining 1980s and well into the 1990s MVREP experienced dramatic growth. This was due in part to the rapidly increasing Latino population throughout the Midwest and Northeast. This was illustrated by a name change it underwent in 1987, from MVREP to the Midwest-Northeast Voter Registration Education Project (MNVREP). Throughout the mid-1990s MNVREP conducted field activities in 18 states, including 535 nonpartisan voter registration campaigns, which resulted in the registration of more than one million new voters. Concomitantly, it published more than 170 studies on political behavior and demographics and sponsored 11 Hispanic Leadership Conferences. With expansion in mind, Andrade sought another name. In 1996, the MNVREP became the United States Hispanic Leadership Institute (USHLI) based on the rationale that a name change would promote the building of a new national Hispanic organization that would be active in some forty states with a capacity to conduct nonpartisan voter registration drives and leadership development programs.

USHLI's cardinal mission was "to fulfill the promises and principles of democracy by empowering minorities and similarly disenfranchised groups and by maximizing civic awareness and participation in the electoral process."[249]

Like other buffer HG-oriented groups that went through a name change, USHLI de-emphasized Mexicano and placed greater accentuation on Hispanic and other minorities. Specifically, it offered educational and leadership development programs for high school and college students, grassroots community leaders, campaign management, and candidate formation. By the end of 1999 over 120,000 Latinos had gone through its leadership development programs. Like other HG-oriented organizations, it too was dependent on corporate and foundation grants. Remarkably, in 1982 its expenditures were a mere $150,000, but by 1990 they increased to some $1 million.[250] By 1999, USHLI was in the midst of a collision course with other rivals, principally SVREP. This was evident in the areas of funding, competition over political turf, and access to the political elites of both political parties. Thus, essentially the criticisms levied against SVREP were also applicable to USHLI.

National Association of Latino Elected Officials (NALEO)

Another new Latino political pressure group formed during the epoch was NALEO. Although under the principal leadership of Congressman Edward Roybal, Congressmen Herman Badillo, and E. Kika de La Garza, Jaime Benites collaborated in the founding of NALEO in 1975. Initially, it was called the National Association of Latino Democratic Officials (NALDO), but underwent a name change to NALEO. Initially a partisan organization, NALEO became a nonpartisan, nonprofit organization devoted to in the words of Maurilio E. Vigil "to bring together Hispanic public officials in an effort to inform Hispanics on the issues affecting them and to register Hispanic voters."[251] Governed by a seven-member Board of Directors, NALEO's paramount purpose was to bring together Latino elected and appointed officials in order to forge them into a power bloc of influence for dealing with a multiplicity of public policy issues affecting the country's Latino community. NALEO, according to Juan Gómez-Quiñones, sought to provide "issue analysis and dissemination, training, information exchange, and advocacy at the national level. It also sought to increase funds for political analysis and research."[252] From its incipience, NALEO's buffer role was evident: its focus was reformist and predicated on an ardent adherence to the tenets of liberal capitalism and the politics of the HG. The usage of Latino, according to Harry Pachon, was strategically deliberate. He explains that "by using the term 'Latino' and by having both Mexican American and Puerto Rican leadership, it [was], in effect, the first coalition of Mexican Americans, Puerto Ricans, Cubans, and other Hispanics represented by elected officials."[253]

Throughout the 1980s, NALEO experienced major membership growth and program and activity expansion. According to Rodolfo Acuña, "NALEO had 2,500 members, with a potential of 5,000."[254] Moreover, NALEO's Board of Directors reflected a national cross section of Latino groups that worked together to formulate domestic and foreign policies and to share technical and leadership resources.[255] In order to better carry out its political empowerment vision through ongoing programmatic efforts, a second entity was established in 1981, the NALEO Educational Fund. Structured as a tax-exempt nonprofit corporation, its mission is to empower Latinos to participate in the political process, from citizenship training to public service. It also seeks to develop and implement programs that promote integration of Latino immigrants into American society by developing future leaders among youth, providing assistance and training to the nation's Latino elected and appointed officials, and conducting research and advocacy on issues important to the Latino population.[256] Programmatically, the NALEO Education Fund began to publish its annual report on the number of Latino elected officials at all levels of government.

The NALEO Educational Fund, with its fifteen-member Board of Directors, was comprised of representatives from both the corporate and political sectors, whereas the NALEO Board of Directors, expanded to twenty-five, was comprised of elected officials from various levels of government and representatives from the main Latino subgroups from throughout the country. The latter also served in an advisory capacity to the Board of Directors of the NALEO Educational Fund. The divergent activities and programs of both entities were administered by a main office in Los Angeles and three branch offices in Houston, New York, and Washington, D.C. NALEO principally depended on its membership dues and sponsorships, while the NALEO Educational Fund largely relied on corporate and foundation funding to carry out its programmatic objectives. Ford Motor Company, AT&T, Anheuser Bush, PG&E, Kraft, Miller Brewing, and Univision were but a few of the corporations that supported its various programs. NALEO's expenditures for the decade showed a gradual increase—from $1.2 million in 1990 to $1.6 million in 1995.[257]

Throughout the epoch, NALEO hosted annual conferences, which attracted hundreds of mostly elected officials as well as notable Democrat Party leaders. In 1999, for example, at NALEO's Sixteenth Annual Conference Vice President Gore and Energy Secretary Bill Richardson were the featured speakers. The conference themes varied as did the workshops, but all focused on some issue that either NALEO or the NALEO Educational Fund was working on. NALEO also served as an advocacy interest group and dealt with a number of issues. It issued press releases, lobbied, participated in coalitions, and used the political leverage of its elected official membership base. Since its formation, the NALEO Educational Fund focused on the development of a myriad of programs and institutes that dealt with such issues as the census, naturalization, immigration, health care, education, leadership training, campaign management and finance, redistricting, and research on empowerment and policy-related issues. By the end of the 1990s, both entities were stable and expanding due to an increased number of elected and appointed officials. Thus, by the turn of the twentieth century, both NALEOs were recognized by some as two of the most important "Hispanic" organizations in the country.

Mexican American Democrats (MAD)

By December 1975, driven by the two objectives of making the Democratic Party in Tejas more accessible to Mexicanos and to counteract the threat of the Raza Unida Party, Mexican American Democrats (MAD) was formed. In January 1976, MAD held its first state meeting and elected Democratic National Committee member Joe Bernal as its first temporary chairperson and Rick Hernandez as its executive director. MAD sought to present an alternative to RUP's nationalist politics and act as a countervailing organizing force. From the start MAD adopted a buffer political role, which was to "seek full representation of Mexican Americans at all levels and in all activities of the Democratic Party, taking appropriate public stands on issues relevant to our communities; and proposing, supporting, and when necessary, opposing legislation relevant to the Mexican American community."[258] In May of 1976, MAD opened up offices in Austin and Houston. That year it supported the presidential candidacy of Democrat Jimmy Carter. By the end of the year, it had some nine representatives on the Democratic Party State Executive Committee. President Carter in 1977 rewarded MAD for its support with the appointment of Leonel Castillo as commissioner of the Immigration and Naturalization Service and Rick Hernandez as director of operations for the Small Business Administration.[259]

In October 1977 at its state convention, MAD delegates elected permanent officers, which included State Representative Matias (Matt) García as its chair.[260] During the ensuing three years, MAD's development was gradual, but consistent. On an annual basis, it held its state convention and published a newsletter for its growing membership. It collaborated with SVREP on numerous voter registrations, political education, and get-out-the-vote drives; formed chapters; held annual conventions; and on even years endorsed candidates. In 1979 MAD opened its state headquarters in Austin and appointed Grace Garcia as its executive director.

During the 1980s, MAD gradually became politically more visible in Tejas state and local politics. The following served as its state chairperson: Marc Campos of Houston (1979–1981), Richard Moya of Austin (1981–1983), Juan Maldonado of San Juan (1983–1985), Ruben Bonilla of Corpus Christi (1985–1987), Norberto Salinas of San Antonio (1987–1989), and Nora Linares of San Antonio (1989–1991).[261] By 1980, MAD had some thirty-three chapters and six thousand paid members. In both the 1984 and 1988 presidential elections, MAD was a strong supporter of the Democratic Party's presidential candidates. In 1988, for example, MAD collaborated with twenty-nine South Tejas county judges in support of Michael Dukakis. Concomitantly, during these years, MAD pushed for the election of more Mexicanos to local, county, state, and federal positions as well as for increasing the number of Mexicanos registered to vote.

Ideologically, MAD from the start was a strong proponent of the liberal capitalist system and did not function as a major advocate for reform. MAD adhered to an accommodation approach and sought policy change, but "foremost" struggled for political access and power sharing. Specifically, it pressed for more appointments, especially to campaign staffs, and through its endorsements sought to increase the number of Mexicano elected officeholders. In 1990 some one thousand people, not all of whom were MAD members, attended its state convention. In a major electoral victory, MAD supported the election of Dan Morales in his successful bid for state attorney general.

The decade of the 1990s produced schisms within MAD. Signs of pending problems became evident in 1991 with its declining membership of 3,226 and 33 chapters. During a ten-year period, MAD suffered nearly a 50 percent reduction in its membership and a 35 percent decrease in chapters. With MAD in a decline mode, former RUP supporter Roberto Alonzo was elected state chair in 1991. His two-year term by 1993 became plagued by internecine conflicts due to power struggles. Adding to the conflict was the support given by Alonzo's supporters to former RUP leader José Angel Gutiérrez, who in 1993 ran unsuccessfully for the U.S. Senate. At MAD's state convention in September of 1993, the controversy boiled over to where Barrientos and his supporters walked out in protest. In the ensuing months, efforts were made by both sides to reconcile their differences. A temporary agreement was reached, which called for both factions to split the leadership positions, but this quickly fell apart due to a lack of a permanent consensus.

The schisms became so exacerbated that by 1997 MAD split into two competing partisan Democratic groups: MAD versus Tejano Democrats (TD). The political split occurred as a result of a major power struggle between Alonzo and Gonzalo Barrientos as to who was going to be the next state chair of MAD. Alonzo represented the more progressive Mexicano wing of Democrats, many of them whom were former RUP leaders and supporters, whereas Barrientos represented the much more traditional moderate Latino or Mexican American sector of the Democratic Party in Tejas. The Barrientos faction formally broke away from MAD and formed the TD. When interviewed on the split, Alonzo explained, "The reason for the split was that they were committed first to serving the interests of the Democratic Party, where we in MAD were committed first to defending the interests of the Mexicano community."[262]

During the late 1990s, both MAD and the TD operated within the axis of the Democratic Party in a state of seemingly perpetual competition and conflict. They both had state conventions and competed for the attention and support of Tejas's powerful Democratic Party leadership and candidates. For instance, MAD during the 1990s met with President Clinton, other administration officials, and Mexican government officials as well. Both, however, endorsed candidates; addressed legislative policy issues; and encouraged Mexicanos to run for office, register to vote, and get involved in civic affairs. In reference to membership both groups were about the same in size. Neither maintained full-time offices and staff and both were volunteer-based. MAD relied on membership and special events, for example, banquets, to raise its funding sources, whereas the TD while doing the same also received funding from business and corporate sources. At the end of 1999, both were still entangled in an acrid and relentless power struggle over which group was the true representative of Mexicano Democrats in Tejas.[263]

Other New Political Pressure Groups

Both major political parties during the epoch constructed their own buffer political pressure organizations. Most, however, were Democrat in composition and functioned within the partisan party orbit and politically were literally extensions of the Democrat or the Republican Parties to the Latino electorate. At a national level, the Democratic Party by the late 1970s formed Hispanic American Democrats (HAD), again with a mission to strengthen its hold on the Latino vote and registration. By the 1980s, plagued by internal schisms, HAD disappeared from the national orbit of the Democratic Party and was replaced by Chicano or Latino state caucuses and groups such as MAD and Tejano Democrats.

Republican Political Pressure Groups

As a counterpart to the Democrats, Republicans also developed political pressure organizations for the purpose of garnering electoral support from Latinos in general. During the 1980s, Latino Republicans formed the Republican National Hispanic Assembly (RNHA), headed by Fernando Oaxaca. It was strongly supported by Nuevo México congressman Manuel Lujan and other Republican Hispanic elites.[264] Moreover, as was the case with Democrats, Republicans also formed their own state and local party satellite organizations. In Tejas, it was called Mexican American Republicans, and in Michigan they named themselves the Hispanic Republicans of Michigan.[265] While the Democratic Party caucuses and satellite organizations ideologically were moderate to liberal, on the Republican side they were conservative and antithetical to the liberalism of Roosevelt, Kennedy, Johnson, and McGovern. Hispanic Republican political pressure groups embellished themselves as being at the avant-garde of HG politics and zealots of liberal capitalism. By the end of 1999, especially at the national level, within the umbrella of the Republican Party, the RNHA was the leading Hispanic Republican political pressure group. Limited by their numbers within the Republican Party and the absence of a power base among the Hispanic electorate, the RNHA and others were largely ineffective as political pressure groups in marketing their conservative legislative agenda; the one exception was the Cubanos in La Florida.

Congressional Hispanic Caucus (CHC)

Formed in 1976 by five Latino congressmen, the CHC's leadership was primarily provided by Democratic congressman Edward Roybal from California and Congressman Kika de La Garza from Tejas. Concerned about developing a national Latino legislative agenda, it adopted a buffer political role within the Congress. The CHC concerned itself with issues of immigration, bilingual education, police brutality, and housing, among other issues impacting Latinos.[266] The founder's cardinal goal was to work in conjunction with other groups, both inside and outside Congress, to strengthen the federal government's commitment to the Latino communities and to enhance their awareness of the workings of the country's political system.[267] The CHC's major functions were to monitor legislative, executive, and judicial actions;[268] to act as a legislative proposing mechanism; to conduct lobbying within the House of Representatives on behalf of Latinos; and to oppose legislation that was inimical to their interests. Ideologically, the CHC's political voice became one of moderation and one that propounded the virtues of liberal capitalism. Strategically and tactically it adopted a conventional approach based on lobbying and pressure. With the exception of Republican Lujan, CHC members demonstrated a high rate of Democrat congruence. Its political posture was first to advance the interests of the Democratic Party, second that of the CHC, and third of the Latino community.

From the incipience of its formation, the CHC never developed a lucid legislative agenda or vision. Rodolfo Acuña cites that the CHC during this time neither had the political muscle or ideological clarity of that of the Black Caucus.[269] In a study conducted by Rodney E. Hero that measured ideological leanings of the CHC's members during the 100th Congress, the argument was made that the "Latino members of Congress [were] on the whole more liberal than the average congressperson but less liberal than blacks." In addition, "Latino representatives' voting patterns suggest less cohesion than that among blacks."[270] In great part this was due to the CHCs membership adherence to HG politics.

In 1978 Congressmen Roybal, Kika de la Garza, and Baltazar Corrada incorporated a parallel tax-exempt 501C3 nonprofit corporation, CHC, Inc. Its primary mission was to develop educational and other programs designed to buttress the CHC's legislative agenda. From the onset, CHC, Inc., had a small budget, staff, and office located in Washington, D.C. However, due to a regulation drafted in 1981 by the House Committee on the House Administration that stipulated that all caucuses involved in fund-raising had to move this particular activity off of government premises, two major changes were made by the CHC's membership. One, it was decided that in order to maintain a legislative support organizational presence on Capitol Hill, the CHC would continue to operate independently. And two, CHC, Inc., moved to a new residence and acquired a new name, the Congressional Hispanic Caucus Institute (CHCI).[271] During the Carter administration (1977–1981), the CHC met on a regular basis with the president to discuss a number of issues, especially education and political representation, and concurrently sought to enlarge and strengthen the role of Latinos within the federal government.[272]

During the 1980s, the CHC and CHCI coordinated their efforts but operated based upon a division of labor. The CHC continued as the legislative lobbying mechanism, whereas the CHCI was programmatically education-oriented. In reference to the latter, by 1985, its Board of Directors was expanded to include influential Latinos from the private sector and community leaders who brought to the CHCI policy-related knowledge and experience at all levels of government.[273] In great part this was done with the intent of attracting more corporate and foundation funding. CHC advocacy was predicated on its adherence to a multi-issue approach in dealing with concerns of public policy issues impacting Latinos.

A related aspect of the CHC's political reality of the 1980s was its inability to wield a unified front among its congressional members. The CHC operated as a loose coalition of congresspersons who wielded individual power. Parochialism, a seniority system that produced committee and subcommittee chairmanships, and conflicting partisan and individual agendas and priorities all contributed to the CHC's inability to project a power capability. Some veteran members such as Democrats Henry B. Gonzalez and Kika de la Garza and Republican Manuel Lujan never really perceived the CHC as a strong cohesive advocacy force capable of showing national power and influence. They felt the CHC should be loosely structured, which would allow its congressional members to remain loyal foremost to their parochial interests and agendas of their home districts.[274] Illustrating the aforementioned, Maurilio E. Vigil writes, "It is clear that aside from a fairly concerted effort in opposition to the Simpson-Mazzoli Bill, the CHC has not functioned as a unified group within Congress, the inability of the Caucus to present an alternative to Simpson-Mazzoli was an embarrassing admission that they could not agree to an alternative proposal on immigration, even if they were united in their opposition to Simpson-Mazzoli."[275] Five of the eleven members openly supported its passage.[276]

Changes occurred within both the CHC and CHCI during the 1990s that gave both increased visibility and influence. In great part this was due to an increase in the number of Latino congresspersons. By 1998 there were nineteen Latinos in Congress,[277] nearly double that of the 1984 figure. Both entities in January 1993 lost their founding architect: Congressman Edward Roybal retired from Congress.[278] In spite of the increase, due to internal schisms over policies, the CHC's membership was lower. Congressman Henry B. Gonzalez from Tejas, who retired in 1992, and Congressman Matthew Martinez were not members; nor were the two Cuban Republicans from La Florida. In particular, policy differences over affirmative action, immigration, and the U.S. economic embargo on Cuba were a few of the issues that contributed to the chasms. On the latter issue, when CHC chairman Xavier Becerra from California and a few other Mexicano congressmen visited Cuba during the late 1990s they were chastised by their Cuban counterparts. Republican congressperson Henry Bonilla from Tejas, while a member of the CHC, was more emphatic about pushing the Republican Party's conservative agenda than addressing the myriad of issues related to the impoverished colonial conditions of South Tejas and beyond.

During the 1990s, the CHC continued to lack a well-defined legislative reform agenda and was still driven by individual rather than collective power agendas. Like the other national Hispanic old and new advocacy interest groups previously examined, the CHC was involved in holding "expensive" cocktail activist conferences and special events. In 1999, the CHC celebrated its twenty-second annual gala during its annual Hispanic Heritage Month activities. The event attracted the powerful elites of Washington, D.C., as well as corporate and other Latino and non-Latino organizational representatives.

Meanwhile, the CHC's sister organization, the CHCI experienced expansion with the development of many more programs, especially on education. The CHCI was heavily dependent on corporate and foundation funding sources. Programmatically, the CHCI provided scholarships to Latino students, educational programs and services that impacted some fifty thousand Latino students, newsletters and other materials exhorting students to continue their higher education and listing available financial assistance, and fellowships for college graduates and graduate students in a variety of fields, and encouraged parental involvement. The CHCI was engaged in the promotion of workforce diversity and networking, coalition building, and leadership development. Its annual gala as well as its issue conferences was utilized politically to promote its networking and coalition-building efforts. In the leadership arena, the CHCI provided a fellowship program that allowed for college graduates and graduate students to work as interns with members of the CHC. A similar internship summer program was available to undergraduate college students.[279] Thus, by 1999, the CHC in particular provided no significant leadership in addressing the multitude of policy issues and problems confronting Mexicanos and Latinos in general.

Community-Based Power Organizations

Integral to the organizational renaissance that occurred during the epoch was the emergence of "community-based power organizations (CBPO)." While this type of organization in accordance with traditional political science jargon theoretically was an "interest group," CBPOs as buffer social change entities were unique in their genesis, power base, organizing strategy and tactics, structure, and even in overall orientation. None of the other previously examined Mexicano or Latino interest groups were comparable to CBPOs. First, their uniqueness was based on the fact that they were organizing products of organizing institutes, primarily Saul Alinsky's Industrial Areas Foundation (IAF).[280] Secondly, CBPOs' power base and leadership came from the "grass roots," meaning the people of the barrios, communities, or parishes or a combination of. Third, strategically nonpartisan, CBPOs tactically combined the use of both conventional and unconventional means to advance their reform change issue agendas. Fourth, built on a mass or broad membership base, CBPOs' confederation or federation structure was buttressed by full-time organizers, office, and a financially supported budget. Lastly, ideologically, CBPOs were proponents of liberal capitalism, which meant they espoused a reform multiethnic orientation predicated upon a multi-issue change agenda.

The most impressive and effective CBPOs that emerged during the epoch were those organized by the IAF. Founded in Chicago, Illinois, in 1940, the IAF was the brainchild of one of this country's greatest and most brilliant and erudite community organizers, Saul Alinsky. The IAF grew in stature out of Alinsky's struggles of the 1930s in Chicago and other poor communities as he effectively organized numerous poor "people's organizations" in urban slum areas.[281] The Unity Leagues and the CSO were organizing projects of IAF in the late 1940s. With Alinsky's death in 1972, Edward Chambers became the new IAF national director, and an erudite lead organizer Ernie Cortes was hired. Under his leadership, numerous Mexicano barrios throughout Aztlán became the focus of CBPO formation.

Communities Organized for Public Service (COPS)

Organized in San Antonio, Tejas, in 1974, COPS from 1974 to 1999 was the flagship of the various IAF-initiated organizing projects throughout Aztlán. It was the brainchild of IAF lead organizer Ernie Cortes, who was able to coalesce into a people's organization several Catholic and a few Protestant parishes. With the support of San Antonio bishop Francis Furey, Archbishop Patricio Flores,[282] and parish priests and the active participation of thousands of lay parishioners, especially from the impoverished barrios of San Antonio, COPS was formed. At the micro level of organizational power, COPS became the most powerful CBPO in Aztlán, if not the country. This was attributable to the IAF's emphasis on the development of lay leaders and organizational power, which paid off. COPS scored a number of major victories in the areas of budget reallocation of funds to poor neighborhoods; building and restoring drainage systems; pavement of streets; construction of curbs, gutters, and sidewalks; and construction of parks and libraries across San Antonio's west and east sides. In 1989, COPS was joined in San Antonio by another IAF CBPO, the Metro Alliance, a product of a merger of the East Side Alliance and Metropolitan Congregational Alliance. Where COPS was mostly Mexicano in composition, the Metro Alliance was mostly white.[283]

Politically, COPS was effective due to its demonstrated "power capability" to mobilize a critical mass of power. Politicians and bureaucrats respected COPS due to its consistent track record of simply showing power. Its network of parishes gave COPS the ability to produce thousands of people at the voting polls, town hall meetings, or major demonstrations at city hall. Working with SVREP, COPS registered thousands of new voters who were politicized and voted. Henry Cisnero's political career as councilman and then as mayor of San Antonio in great part was made possible by the political support he received from COPS. Its endorsement of candidates was buttressed by thousands of actual votes. Indicative of its state political clout, on November 20, 1983, Governor Mark White proclaimed "COPS day in Texas."[284] From the time of its inception, COPS endured and continued to work on a number of "winnable" local issues that served to improve significantly the people's quality of life.

As a result of COPS successes, numerous similar IAF-organized CBPOs were established in cities that contained large numbers of Mexicanos and Latinos. One such CBPO was United Neighborhood Organization (UNO), established in the barrios of East Los Angeles in 1976. With Cortes again as the lead organizer, buttressed by the strong leadership of Catholic priest Luis Oliveras and others, several Catholic and protest churches coalesced and formed UNO. For several years into the 1980s, UNO, like COPS, wielded great mobilizing power and took on a number of local winnable issues, but unlike COPS it failed to become self-sufficient. Although UNO declined by the 1980s, what was left was integrated in the 1990s into a larger regional IAF Los Angeles Valley organizing effort, Valley Organized in Community Efforts (VOICE). By the end of the 1990s, in Tejas, Arizona, California, and Nuevo México, IAF had organized some seventeen CBPOs, twelve of which were in Tejas alone. California with nearly eleven million Latinos had only one VOICE.

Congreso para Pueblos Unidos

Independent of IAF, another CBPO effort was organized under my leadership in 1977 that emanated from the counties of San Bernardino and Riverside. In December 1976, I returned from Salt Lake City, Utah, after teaching political science for nearly three years at the University of Utah. Upon my return, with me came organizers Lorenzo Archuleta, Lillian Rodriguez, Roberto Cruz, and Tomas Archuleta; all but the latter I had trained at the university while I was the director of a leadership training program there. With only $500 that was raised in Utah as a startup fund and support from Proyecto Accion Social (PAS), a nonprofit social service agency under the direction of Vicente Rodriguez, in 1977 the National Institute for Community Development (NICD) was established. A hybrid organizing institute and service action provider, the NICD was incorporated, and I became its executive director. An office was established in a semi-abandoned school building in one of San Bernardino's barrios, and some funding was secured.

Based upon the Trinity Concept of Community Development (TCCD), the NICD was different from the IAF model. A major difference was that the TCCD's primary purpose was to reignite and reenergize the moribund Movimiento and to give it a unifying vision. Other differences were evident: briefly, the TCCD was predicated on the notion that social change or community development had to be "holistic," meaning it had to encompass major concurrent political, economic, and social change. In addition, the TCCD propounded that the common denominators of organizational unity combined the Movimiento's cultural nationalism with Christian socialism (theology of liberation) and Alinsky's organizing methodology based upon "self-interest." Overall, the TCCD was hypercritical of liberal capitalism and advanced the notion that the next dialectical stage of Chicano politics was to advance the eclectic vision of building a "nation-within-a-nation." It sought to become an alternative to existent buffer-oriented political and social change groups. Using a synthesis of Mormon, Black Muslim, and Palestinian models, it stressed the idea of working pragmatically within the existing order, but not losing site of the vision. Secondly, the idea was for Mexicanos and Latinos to take "control" of the political, economic, and social structures of their communities. Lastly, cognizant of the changing demographics, it acknowledged the strategic option of Aztlán.[285]

Under the NICD's organizing efforts Mexicano political history was made. In May 1977, the embryonic NICD held a Southwest summit meeting that brought together some fifty top Chicano Movement leaders and scholars. The agenda focused on the rebuilding of the Movimiento, particularly on the issue of immigration. On the latter, a consensus was reached and José Angel Gutiérrez agreed to make a call for the "National Immigration Conference" that was held later that year in San Antonio, Tejas. Also, a California-based coalition on immigration was formed that included the CCR, CASA, NICD, MEChA, RUP, and a few others: NICD took the lead organizing role.

During the late 1970s, the NICD took on a number of issues and projects. It collaborated with the Committee on Chicano Rights on the marches and mobilizations it held along the U.S./México border. Under the NICD, on October 12, 1977, "Dia de La Raza," NICD organizers and community leaders organized a march that began in San Bernardino's eastside barrio that culminated downtown with a town hall meeting attended by over one thousand Mexicanos from throughout the communities, barrios, and parishes of San Bernardino and Riverside counties. It was at the town hall meeting where I promulgated El Plan de San Bernardino, which I had drafted with some input from NICD organizers. The crux of the plan called for the revitalization of the Movimiento via adherence to several of the principals inherent to the TCCD. Ideologically, predicated on tenets of the "theology of liberation," it called for the formation of El Congreso para Pueblos Unidos (CPU), an advocacy social change and political pressure federation of parish chapters and community organizations.

From 1977 to 1980, the NICD focused on the building of the CPU and concomitantly developed social action programs that complemented the aforementioned. In 1977, the NICD in order to stop the resurgent gang violence worked with numerous gangs and formed el Concilio de Barrios Unidos (CBU— Council of United Neighborhoods). During this time, the CPU was built into a statewide political advocacy federation of some twenty-one chapters with a membership that by 1980 topped at fifteen hundred. Numerous immigration issues were successfully dealt with using direct action mobilizations. In 1978 the CPU, supported nationally by PADRES and Hermanas, mobilized and pressured the Vatican on the specific issue of the Catholic Church's need to appoint more Mexicano bishops in the United States. The issue was precipitated when auxiliary bishop Gilberto Chavez from San Diego was not appointed bishop of the newly created Dioceses of San Bernardino. Supported by Cesar Chavez and the UFW, massive marches were held in San Bernardino and Redlands, involving up to three thousand people. A national delegation of lay and religious leaders traveled to México City in 1979 with the intent to deliver a document to Pope John Paul II, which I wrote, entitled, "Declaration of a New Vision," which called upon the Vatican to institute several changes, including the designation of more Mexicano bishops in the United States and to embrace and support the basis of the theology of liberation. Meanwhile, assisted by NICD organizers, CPU chapters took on a number of local issues.

During the 1980s, the NICD continued to be the organizing backbone of the CPU. Because of the "bishop issue" and the CPU's highly political and visible controversial advocacy role, the new white bishop Phillip Stralling retaliated by discouraging parishes from participating or supporting politically the CPU or NICD financially. As a result, even though several chapters continued to operate until 1985, with the exception of the Castroville chapter led by Nick Torres, the CPU became defunct. Yet during these five years, the NICD organizers effectively dealt with education, immigration, affirmative action, police brutality, consumer affairs, and political empowerment issues. "Have injustice will travel," became the NICD's organizing motto. The NICD organized or helped facilitate the formation of several regional or state coalitions that dealt with a number of issues, of which the CPU was a participant, including People against Racism (PAR, 1981) against the KKK; Californios for Fair Representation (CFR, 1981–1982) on redistricting; Project Vote (1982) on voter registration; Operation Corporate Responsibility (OCR, 1982–1983) on corporate responsibility. In 1982 and 1984, NICD and CPU chapters organized forums and demonstrations against Simpson-Mazzoli. On numerous occasions the NICD via the CPU took on the

U.S. Border Patrol and law enforcement agencies on immigration and police brutality and held numerous state and regional unity conferences.

Because the NICD was not tax exempt, for purposes of securing funding from foundations and donations, the Institute for Social Justice (ISJ) was established as a nonprofit 501c3 tax-exempt corporation in 1983 as its replacement. After the transition to ISJ was made, the main sources of funding were CPU membership dues; fund-raising, for example, banquets and special events; local government funding of specific projects; and Project Self-Reliance, based upon monthly contributions of $25.00 by some 150 people. At the time, few groups in California had the capacity to hold banquets that drew from six hundred to eleven hundred people, at times from all over the state, and attracted the attendance of numerous state and national political leaders.

For the next seven years, with the NICD displaced by the ISJ, several organizing struggles ensued. At times using the shell of the CPU, MAPA chapters, or coalitions it formed, the ISJ addressed local, state, national, and international issues. With the imminent threat of an invasion of Nicaragua and further military intervention in El Salvador by the United States, in 1985, under the ISJ, a peace delegation headed by myself went to México, Honduras, El Salvador, Nicaragua, and Cuba and met with top government and opposition leaders. In 1987, an ISJ delegation of leaders traveled to México and met with top Mexican government officials and dialogued on improving relations between Mexicanos in the United States and México. Immigration, IRCA, affirmative action, and education issues were addressed by the ISJ via advocacy, marches, picketing, conferences, and colloquia. Also, under the shell of the CPU, political campaigns, voter registration, political education, and get-out-the-vote drives were organized.

In 1988, the ISJ organized IMPACTO 88, a year later changed to IMPACTO 2000, a national coalition of various organizations and leaders that promoted an *acercamiento* with México and fostered a voter mobilization for the 1988 presidential elections. In 1988, IMPACTO 88 under the organizing leadership of the ISJ convoked unprecedented meetings in Tijuana and Mexicali, México, with México's leading presidential candidates: the PRI's Carlos Salinas de Gortari; the PRD's Cuauhtémoc Cárdenas; and PAN's Manuel Cloutier. That same year, the ISJ received international notoriety over the "Victorville Five," in which five undocumented Mexicano migrants were violently beaten by San Bernardino County sheriffs, which was recorded on video by a neighbor. Two years later, in a major suit, the five were awarded some $600,000 by the courts. ISJ organizers continued to organize on several issues; but due to dwindling resources in 1992, I resigned as executive director and took a teaching position in Ethnic Studies at the University of California, Riverside. After another year of struggling to keep the ISJ afloat by its new executive director Maria Anna Gonzales, the ISJ's doors closed in 1993. With its closure, a major chapter in my life came to a close and up to 1999, no other entity had yet to replace it.

Rise of Mexicano-Based Organizations

The New Organizational Wave

By the mid-1990s a new organizational model surfaced—Mexicano-based organizations (MBOs). It meant organizations of sorts formed by nationals from México who resided in the United States. While some MBOs were apolitical and more *mutualista*-oriented nonprofit organizations, others were either civil rights or political pressure-oriented interest groups. Regardless of their focus of activity, one common thread was their profound sense of "nationalism" toward México. Even though they adopted essentially a buffer role, MBOs refused to sever the nexus with La Madre Patria—México. Like most *mutualistas*, MBOs also displayed a great love and passion for México and its rich culture, heritage, language, which meant that they were unequivocally against assimilation. They passionately sought to preserve their "Mexicano" culture, meaning most subscribed to the ethos of the rising "Neo-Mex Generation (NMG)." During the last six years of the 1990s MBOs proliferated. This was a result of the burgeoning Mexicano population in the United States and the escalating vitriolic nativism directed at Mexicanos. Literally an "organizational renaissance" occurred by the late 1990s among Mexicano nationals in the United States. Essentially, three ideal types of MBOs were formed, which prescribed to the NMG: civic-culture/economic (CCE), service provider, and human/civil rights. In actuality, however, some MBOs assumed multiple roles.

CCE Organizations

As a form of organization, CCEs were the most plentiful and active. Their membership came from a specific state in México. Their zealous loyalty to their state of origin combined service, culture, and some advocacy. Their ardent loyalty to their native state was manifested via remittances to relatives, establishment of community projects in their home villages or communities, and in their efforts to maintain their cultural ties with México. CCEs contributed to México's economic progress and development through their member remittances and assistance they provided their respective native states in México. CCEs were found in various parts of the country wherever there were concentrations of Mexicano nationals. One such CCE in California was La Federación de Clubes Zacatecanos del Sur de California. Comprised of several clubs, it was formed in 1998 when the visit of Zacatecas governor Ricardo Monreal made a call for its establishment.[286] Organized and led by Manuel de la Cruz by the close of 1999, it was one of the most influential and best-organized MBOs in the country.

Several Service Providers (SSP)

Essentially, this type of MBO was a product of the post-IRCA 1986 years. In almost every major urban area where Mexicanos resided, SSPs were active, providing a multiplicity of services, especially related to immigration, citizenship, health care, job discrimination, and crisis intervention. In California, there were several SSPs in the Los Angeles area: One-Stop Immigration and Education Center;[287] Comite Pro-Uno in Maywood; Libreria del Pueblo, San Bernardino; Training Occupational Development Educating Communities (TODEC), Perris. In Illinois, specifically Chicago, there was Centro Aztlán, among many others. Like many other Latino social service providers, the funding for SSPs came mostly from both state and federal sources. In most instances with some exceptions this financial dependency either obviated or impeded their capacity to advocate.

Human Civil Rights (HCR)

A number of HCR advocacy interest groups were also established. They dealt with social justice and human and civil rights issues, especially the issue of immigration. As interest groups, HCRs advocated for "amnesty programs," dual citizenship, securing the vote for Mexicanos in the United States, and political representation in México's congress. At the national level, two examples of HCRs were La Coordinadora, a national coalition of several HCRs that included unions based out of Los Angeles, California, and La Coalicion Internacional de Mexicanos en el Exterior (CIME), a binational coalition based in Chicago, Illinois, with member groups in both México and the United States.

Other HCRs were formed at the state or local levels, such as Comite Pro-Uno in Maywood, California.[288] HCRs often adhered to a multi-issue approach and relied on a combination of conventional and direct action methods. This included the use of lobbying, letter writing, press conferences, and town hall meetings and picketing, marches, boycotts, and demonstrations. Also, some HCRs such as La Coordinadora, CIME, and Comite Pro-Uno were deeply involved in establishing México's Partido de la Revolución Democratica (PRD) in the United States.[289] MBOs were active organizing the Mexicanos from México not only throughout Aztlán, but the rest of the country as well. Through the "power of organization," MBOs sought to advance their respective agendas both in México and United States.

Thus, by the turn of the twenty-first century, after nearly twenty-five years of the politics of the HG, the "Mexicano political experience of occupied Aztlán" was dialectically in transition, actuating the possible rise of yet another epoch that perhaps could alter its political mode and direction.

Notes

1. Juan Andrade and Andrew Hernandez, *The Almanac of Latino Politics 2000* (Chicago, Ill.: United States Hispanic Leadership Institute, 1999), 3.

2. The U.S. Census Bureau, "Voting and Registrations in the Elections of November 1980, 1982, 1984, 1986, 1988, 1990 Elections," cited in NALEO Report, "The Latino Vote during the Decade: 1980–1990."

3. NALEO, *2000 Latino Election Handbook*, NALEO Educational Fund, Los Angeles, California, 2000, 1.

4. Andrade and Hernandez, *The Almanac of Latino Politics 2000*, 3.

5. NALEO, *2000 Latino Election Handbook*, 1.

6. Rodolfo Acuña, *Occupied America: A History of Chicanos*, 4th ed. (New York: Addison Wesley, 2000), 450.

7. NALEO, *2000 Election Handbook*, 6–13.

8. Acuña, *Occupied America*, 4th ed., 450.

9. For an examination of this argument see my book *La Raza Unida Party: A Chicano Challenge to the U.S. Two-Party Dictatorship* (Philadelphia: Temple University Press, 2000), chapter 1.

10. NALEO, "The Latino Vote in 1992," Background paper #19, NALEO Educational Fund.

11. Cited in Andrade and Hernandez, *The Almanac of Latino Politics 2000*, 11.

12. Peter Skerry, *Mexican Americans: The Ambivalent Minority* (New York: Free Press, 1993), 308.

13. Andrade and Hernandez, *The Almanac of Latino Politics 2000*, 11–12.

14. Skerry, *Mexican Americans*, 429.

15. Andrade and Hernandez, *The Almanac of Latino Politics 2000*, 11–12.

16. Andrade and Hernandez, *The Almanac of Latino Politics 2000*, 11–12.

17. Andrade and Hernandez, *The Almanac of Latino Politics 2000*, 11–12.

18. Cited in Armando Navarro, "The Post-Mortem Politics of the Chicano Movement," *Perspectives in Mexican American Studies* 6 (1997): 72.

19. The statistics provided are taken from NALEO's *2000 Latino Election Handbook*, 1.

20. Rodney E. Haro, *Latinos and the U.S. Political System: Two-Tiered Pluralism* (Philadelphia: Temple University Press, 1992), 89.

21. Joan Moore and Harry Pachon, *Hispanics in the United States* (Englewood Cliffs, N.J.: Prentice Hall, 1985), 195.

22. Juan Gómez-Quiñones, *Chicano Politics: Reality of Promise, 1940–1990* (Albuquerque: University of New México Press, 1990), 168–69.

23. Geoffrey Fox, *Hispanic Nation: Culture, Politics, and the Constructing Identity* (Tucson: University of Arizona Press, 1996), 168.

24. Navarro, "The Post-Mortem Politics of the Chicano Movement," 58.

25. Navarro, "The Post-Mortem Politics of the Chicano Movement," 58.

26. Haro, *Latinos and the U.S. Political System*, 86.

27. Acuña, *Occupied America*, 3rd ed., 415–16.

28. Matt S. Meier and Margo Gutierrez, *Encyclopedia of the Mexican American Civil Rights Movement* (Westport, Conn.: Greenwood, 2000), 267.

29. Haro, *Latinos and the U.S. Political System*, 71.

30. Isidro D. Ortiz, "Latino Organizational Leadership Strategies in the Era of Reaganomics," in *Latinos and Political Coalitions: Political Empowerment for the 1990s*, ed. Roberto E. Villareal and Norma G. Hernandez (New York: Praeger, 1991), 87–88.

31. Acuña, *Occupied America*, 4th ed., 410.

32. Acuña, *Occupied America*, 4th ed., 444.

33. Thomas Weyr, *Hispanic U.S.A.: Breaking the Melting Pot* (New York: Harper & Row, 1988), 105.

34. Weyr, *Hispanic U.S.A.*, 86–87.

35. Acuña, *Occupied America*, 4th ed., 441.

36. Matt S. Meier and Feliciano Rivera, *Mexican Americans, Mexican Americans: From Conquistadors to Chicanos* (New York: Hill & Wang, 1993), 256.

37. Acuña, *Occupied America*, 4th ed., 441.

38. Maurilio E. Vigil, *Hispanics in American Politics: The Search for Political Power* (New York: University Press of America, 1987), 89.

39. Meier and Rivera, *Mexican Americans, American Mexicans*, 256.

40. Haro, *Latinos and the U.S. Political System*, 94.

41. Haro, *Latinos and the U.S. Political System*, 442, 445.

42. Carlos Muñoz and Charles P. Henry, "Coalition Politics in San Antonio and Denver: The Cisneros and Peña Mayoral Campaigns," in *Racial Politics in American Cities*, ed. Rufus P. Browning, Dale Rogers Marshall, and David H. Tabb (White Plains, N.Y.: Longman, 1990), 170–90.

43. Cited in Richard Griswold Del Castillo and Arnoldo De León, *North to Aztlán: A History of Mexican Americans in the United States* (New York: Twayne Publishers, 1997), 155.

44. For an excellent comparative study on Los Angeles and San Antonio local politics see Skerry, *Mexican Americans*.

45. Meier and Rivera, *Mexican Americans, American Mexicans*, 257.

46. NALEO, "The Latino Vote in 1992."

47. John Jacobs, "English and Español Take Their Turns," *The Press Enterprise*, March 7, 1998.

48. NALEO, 2000 *Latino Election Handbook*, 1.

49. NALEO, "1998 National Directory of Latino Elected Officials," NALEO Educational Fund, Los Angeles, California.

50. Martinez, *Mexican-Origin People in the United States*, 182.

51. NALEO, "1998 National Directory of Latino Elected Officials."

52. Martinez, *Mexican-Origin People in the United States*, 182.

53. NALEO, "1998 National Directory of Latino Elected Officials."

54. Local elected official category includes county, municipal, judicial/law enforcement, school board, and special district officials.

55. NALEO, *1998 Latino Election Handbook*, NALEO Educational Fund, Los Angeles, 4.

56. NALEO, "1998 National Directory of Latino Elected Officials," 16.

57. Acuña, *Occupied America*, 4th ed., 456.

58. For a complete breakdown of Latino political representation see NALEO, "1998 National Directory of Latino Elected Officials."

59. NALEO, "1998 National Directory of Latino Elected Officials."

60. Del Castillo and De León, *North to Aztlán*, 155.

61. Meier and Rivera, *Mexican Americans, American Mexicans*, 259.

62. Cited in Martinez, *Mexican-Origin People in the United States*, 181–82.

63. For a comprehensive breakdown of the number of Latinas elected to public office see NALEO, "1998 National Directory of Latino Elected Officials."

64. For a more extensive examination of RUP's politics of *acercamiento* with México, Cuba, and other countries see my book *La Raza Unida Party*, 254–60. In addition, for an examination of México's policies toward Mexicanos in the United States see Maria Rosa Garcia-Acevedo, "Return to Aztlán: México's Policies toward Chicanas/os," in *Chicanas/Chicanos at the Crossroads: Social, Economic, and Political Change*, ed. David R. Maciel and Isidro D. Ortiz (Tucson: University of Arizona Press, 1996), 130–55. For an examination of SVREP's efforts in Central America see Antonio Gonzalez, "Chicano Politics and U.S. Policy in Central America, 1979–1990," in *Chicano Politics and Society in the Late Twentieth Century*, ed. David Montejano (Austin: University of Texas Press, 1999), 154–74.

65. For a more detailed account of the aforementioned see my book *La Raza Unida Party*, 254–60.

66. Garcia-Acevedo, "Return to Aztlán," 138.

67. Gonzales, "Chicano Politics and U.S. Policy in Central America, 1979–1990," 159.

68. Gonzales, "Chicano Politics and U.S. Policy in Central America, 1979–1990," 161.

69. The Boland Amendment adopted by Congress in 1982 forbade the U.S. government from providing military equipment, training, or advice, or other forms of military support for activities designed to overthrow the government of Nicaragua or for provoking a military exchange between Nicaragua and Honduras. See Richard Alan White, *The Morass: United States Intervention in Central America* (Cambridge: Harper & Row, 1984), 54–55.

70. Much of the subsequent information is taken from my own personal archives, which are located in my home in Riverside, California.

71. Roger E. Hernandez, "Hispanic Organizations: Searching for Unity," *Hispanic*, September 1991.

72. Mario Barrera, *Beyond Aztlán: Ethnic Autonomy in Comparative Perspective* (New York: Praeger, 1988), 55.

73. Much of the narrative of this section on the CJ during the early 1970s up to 1976 was taken in a very condensed version from my book on RUP, particularly the chapter on RUP in Colorado. See *La Raza Unida Party*, chapter 4.

74. For an excellent and comprehensive study on the Crusade for Justice and its constant siege and surveillance by local and federal law enforcement agencies see Ernest Vigil, *The Crusade for Justice: Chicano Militancy and the Government's War on Dissent* (Madison: University of Wisconsin Press, 1999).

75. For an excellent detailed examination of this and other related events involving the CJ see Vigil, *Crusade for Justice*, 328–33.

76. Interview, Pepe Jacques, July 5, 2002

77. As an ardent nationalist separatist, the CJ did not care for the aggressive organizing approach of the SWP, especially since it felt the SWP was encroaching on the CJ's political turf. Nor did the CJ agree with the SWP's brand of Trotskyite Marxism.

78. Navarro, *La Raza Unida Party*, 105–6.

79. Vigil, *The Crusade for Justice*, 377.

80. Vigil, *The Crusade for Justice*, 364, 374.

81. Vigil, *The Crusade for Justice*, 364, 381.

82. Carlos Muñoz, *Youth, Identity, Power: The Chicano Movement* (New York: Verso, 1989), 183.

83. Gonzales, *Mexicanos*, 211.

84. Muñoz, *Youth, Identity, Power*, 87.

85. Cielito Lindo, "The Gay Agenda vs. MEChA," unpublished paper, March 18, 2002.

86. Interview, Roberto Tijerina, July 9, 2002.

87. Roberto Tijerina, *The MEChA Leadership Manual: History, Philosophy, and Organizational Strategy*, unpublished book manuscript submitted in 2002 for publication.

88. Cielito Lindo, "The Gay Agenda vs. MEChA," 1.

89. Interview, Herman Baca, July 10, 2002.

90. Interview, Herman Baca, July 10, 2002.

91. Richard Del Castillo and Richard A. Garcia, *Cesar Chavez: A Triumph of Spirit* (Norman: University of Oklahoma Press, 1995), 130.

92. Gonzales, *Mexicano*, 200.

93. Gonzales, *Mexicano*, 200.

94. Acuña, *Occupied America*, 4th ed., 438.

95. Meier and Gutiérrez, *Encyclopedia of the Mexican American Civil Rights Movement*, 229.

96. Acuña, *Occupied America*, 4th ed., 438.

97. Del Castillo and Garcia, *Cesar Chavez*, 135.

98. Acuña, *Occupied America*, 4th ed., 438.

99. Del Castillo and Garcia, *Cesar Chavez*, 167–69.

100. Martinez, *Mexican-Origin People in the United States*, 105.

101. www.ufw.org/ceswstory.htm

102. Fred Alvarez, "UFW Member Total Is Questioned," *Los Angeles Times*, June 10, 2002.

103. www.ufw.org/dh.htm

104. Alvarez, "UFW Member Total Is Questioned."

105. For a more detailed examination of these farmworker organizing efforts see Acuña, *Occupied America*, 4th ed., 355–56.

106. For additional information on the activities of Obreros Unidos Independientes see my book *The Cristal Experiment* (Madison: University of Wisconsin Press, 1998), 302–6, 312–13.

107. www.lclaa.org. Membership-Constitution.

108. The overview on the LCLAA is taken largely from a research paper entitled *The Roots and El Futuro of the Labor Council for Latin American Advancement*, done by Raquel España for a class, The Politics of the Chicano Movement, I taught at the University of California, Riverside, March 2004.

109. Meier and Gutiérrez, *Encyclopedia of the Mexican American Civil Rights Movement*, 171–72.

110. Garcia, *Memories of Chicano History*, 296.

111. Gregory Rodriguez, "Is L.A. the Place for a Resurgent Union Movement?" *Los Angeles Times*, February 16, 1997.

112. Acuña, *Occupied America*, 4th ed., 431–32.

113. Acuña, *Occupied America*, 4th ed., 431–32.

114. Sonia Nazario, "For This Union, It's War," *Los Angeles Times*, August 19, 1993.

115. Nazario, "For This Union It's War."

116. Acuña, *Occupied America: A History of Chicanos*, 5th ed. (New York: Pearson-Longman, 2004), 376–77.

117. Steven Greenhouse, "AFL-CIO Puts New Focus on Recruiting Drives," *The Press Enterprise*, February 17, 1997.

118. Mateagold and Nancy Cleeland, "Labor's Clout Set to Help Chose Next L.A. Mayor," *Los Angeles Times*, February 12, 2001.

119. This section on RUP in its abbreviated form is taken mainly from my two studies on the RUP: *La Raza Unida Party* and *The Cristal Experiment*. However, for another extensive examination on RUP see Ignacio Garcia, *United We Win: The Rise and Fall of La Raza Unida Party* (Tucson: Mexican American Studies & Research Center, University of Arizona, 1989).

120. Navarro, *La Raza Unida Party*, specifically chapter 3.

121. Navarro, *La Raza Unida Party*, 105.

122. larazaunida.tripod.com/program/natlib.htm

123. Acuña, *Occupied America*, 4th ed., 404.

124. Interview, Pepe Jacques Medina, July 5, 2002.

125. For an excellent book chapter on CASA see Ernesto Chavez, *Mi Raza Primero! Nationalism, Identity, and Insurgency in the Chicano Movement in Los Angeles, 1966–1978* (Berkeley: University of California Press, 2002), 98–120.

126. Interview, Medina.

127. Chavez, *Mi Raza Primero!*, 113.

128. Chavez, *Mi Raza Primero!*, 112.

129. Chavez, *Mi Raza Primero!*, 112.

130. Chavez, *Mi Raza Primero!*, 113.

131. Interview, Medina.

132. Cited in Chavez, *Mi Raza Primero!*, 115.

133. Cited in Chavez, *Mi Raza Primero!*, 115.

134. Barrera, *Beyond Aztlán*, 50.

135. Gómez-Quiñones, *Chicano Politics*, 152.

136. Gómez-Quiñones, *Chicano Politics*, 152.

137. Chavez, *Mi Raza Primero!*, 109.

138. Barrera, *Beyond Aztlán*, 51.

139. Muñoz, *Youth, Identity, Power*, 95.

140. Union del Barrio, *Un Pueblo Sin Fronteras: A History of the Union del Barrio, 15 Years of Struggle for the National Liberation of the Mexican People* (San Diego, Calif.: La Verdad Publications, 1998), 55.

141. Gómez-Quiñones, *Chicano Politics*, 152.

142. Garcia, *Memories of Chicano History*, 320.

143. Mary Ballesteros-Coronel, "Hemandad Mexicana Recibe Fondos," *La Opinion*, May 16, 1997.

144. Peter M. Warren, Nancy Cleeland, and H. G. Reza, "Noncitizens Say They Voted in Orange County," *Los Angeles Times*, December 27, 1996.

145. *The Press Enterprise*, "INS to Help 1.3 Million Voters in Orange County," March 18, 1997.

146. *The Press Enterprise*, "Immigrant Group Loses Federal Funds," February 28, 1997.

147. Efrain Hernandez, Jr., Jose Cardenas, and Susan Abram, "Latino Group Registered 46 Noncitizens to Vote," *Los Angeles Times*, June 8, 1997.

148. Interview, Herman Baca, July 10, 2002.

149. Union del Barrio, *Un Pueblo Sin Fronteras*, 5.

150. Union del Barrio, *Un Pueblo Sin Fronteras*, 5.

151. Union del Barrio, *Un Pueblo Sin Fronteras*, 59.

152. burn.ucsd.edu/~udb/history/somos/history.html

153. Union del Barrio, *Un Pueblo Sin Fronteras*, 58–59.

154. Union del Barrio, *Un Pueblo Sin Fronteras*, 55–225.

155. Interview, Miguel Flores, September 18, 2002. Mr. Flores has been involved in a leadership capacity with the Sociedad Progrecista Mexican in California. In 2002 he was its state secretary to the Supreme Committee.

156. Interview, Miguel Flores, September 18, 2002.

157. For a comprehensive examination of LULAC's activities during the 1970s and 1980s see Benjamin Marquez, *LULAC: The Evolution of a Mexican American Political Organization* (Austin: University of Texas Press, 1993), 77.

158. David G. Gutiérrez, *Walls and Mirrors: Mexican Americans, Mexican Immigrants, and the Politics of Ethnicity* (Berkeley: University of California Press, 1995), 201.

159. For an excellent article on LULAC and the other organizations involved in the promotion of corporate responsibility see Isidro D. Ortiz, "Chicana/o Organizational Politics and Strategies in the Era of Retrenchment," in *Chicanas/Chicanos at the Crossroads*, 112.

160. The accord pledged Coors to contribute between 1985 and 1990 some $350 million to the Hispanic community in the form of investments with Hispanic businesses, grants, and scholarships and the hiring and promotion of more Hispanics to its workforce.

161. Acuña, *Occupied America*, 4th ed., 409.

162. Christine Marie Sierra, "Latino Organizational Strategies on Immigration Reform: Success and Limits in Public Policymaking," in *Latinos and Political Coalitions: Political Empowerment for the 1990s*, ed. Roberto E. Villareal and Norma G. Hernandez (New York: Praeger, 1991), 65.

163. Sierra, "Latino Organizational Strategies on Immigration Reform," 92.

164. Marquez, *LULAC*, 79.

165. Marquez, *LULAC*, 93.

166. Marquez, *LULAC*, 109.

167. Geoffrey Fox, *Hispanic Nation: Culture, Politics and the Construction of Identity* (Tucson: University of Arizona Press, 1996), 173.

168. The published literature on LULAC on current LULAC status is limited and largely dated. I had to resort to the Internet via the LULAC website: wwww.lulac.org/Index.html

169. wwww.lulac.org/Historical%20Files/Resources/History.html

170. wwww.lulac.org//Programs/CorpAll.html

171. Cited in Henry A. J. Ramos, *The American G.I. Forum: In Pursuit of the Dream, 1948–1983* (Houston, Tex.: Arte Público Press, 1998), 133.

172. Ramos, *The American G.I. Forum*, 133.

173. Maciel and Ortiz, ed., *Chicanas/Chicanos at the Crossroads*, 157.

174. Interview, Mariana Tinco, June 12, 2002.

175. Interview, Tinco.

176. Meier and Rivera, *Mexican Americans, American Mexicans*, 206–7.

177. Interview, Tinco.

178. www.agifnat.org/constitution/preamble.htm

179. Interview, Tinco.

180. Interview, Carlos Montez, April 22, 2003.

181. Meier and Rivera, *Mexican Americans, American Mexicans*, 254.

182. Acuña, *Occupied America*, 4th ed., 345.

183. Henry Santiestevan, "A Perspective on Mexican American Organizations," in *Mexican American Tomorrow: Educational and Economic Perspectives*, ed. Gus Tyler (Albuquerque: University of New México Press, 1975), 200.

184. Vigil, *Hispanics in American Politics*, 119.

185. Vigil, *Hispanics in American Politics*, 119.

186. Roger E. Hernandez, "Hispanic Organizations: Searching for Unity," *Hispanic*, September 1991.

187. Cited in Barrera, *Beyond Aztlán*, 56. For a comprehensive examination of the NCLR from 1965 to 1980 see Christine Sierra, "The Political Transformation of a Minority Organization: The Council of La Raza, 1965–1980," PhD dissertation, Stanford University, 1982.

188. Barrera, *Beyond Aztlán*, 56.

189. Santiestevan, "A Perspective on Mexican American Organizations," 200.

190. Matt S. Meier and Feliciano Rivera, *Dictionary of Mexican American History* (Westport, Conn.: Greenwood, 1981), 246–47.

191. Fox, *Hispanic Nation*, 158.

192. NCLR: www.nclr.org/about/

193. NCLR: www.nclr.policy.net/coroner/

194. NCLR: www.nclr.org/special/

195. Gutiérrez, *Walls and Mirrors*, 200–1.

196. Karen O'Conner and Leo Epstein, "A Legal Voice for the Chicano Community: The Activities of the Mexican American Legal Defense and Education Fund, 1968–1982," in *Latinos and the Political System*, ed. Chris Garcia (Notre Dame, Ind.: University of Notre Dame, 1988), 268.

197. Erika Gallardo, "Mexican American Legal Defense and Education Fund: The Legal Voice for the Chicano Community," unpublished student research paper, no date available, University of California, Riverside.

198. Meier and Gutierrez, *Encyclopedia of the Mexican American Civil Rights Movement*, 147.

199. Maurilio Vigil, "The Ethnic Organization as an Instrument of Political and Social Change: MALDEF a Case Study," *Journal of Ethnic Studies* Vol. 18 (Spring 1990): 19.

200. Vigil, "The Ethnic Organization as an Instrument of Political and Social Change," 19.

201. Skerry, *Mexican Americans*, 116.

202. Skerry, *Mexican Americans*, 25.

203. Gallardo, "Mexican American Legal Defense and Education Fund," 7.

204. MALDEF Annual Report 1991–1992, 6.

205. www.maldef.org/programs.htm

206. www.maldef.org/leadership_and_development_progr.htm

207. MALDEF: www.maldef.org/Policy_Issues_Presidential.htm

208. Fox, *Hispanic Nation*, 158.

209. American Patrol: american patrol.com/MALDEF/MALDEFcontributors 97_98.html

210. Vigil, *Hispanics in American Politics*, 120.

211. www.ushcc.com/mission.htm

212. Hernandez, *Hispanic Organizations*, 22.

213. Meier and Rivera, *Mexican Americans, American Mexicans*, 230.

214. Gómez-Quiñones, *Chicano Politics*, 178.

215. Meier and Gutierrez, *Encyclopedia of the Mexican America Civil Rights Movement*, 138–39.

216. Interview, Ada Sosa-Riddell, September 23, 2002.

217. Meier and Gutierrez, *Encyclopedia of the Mexican America Civil Rights Movement*, 138–39.

218. Gómez-Quiñones, *Chicano Politics*, 176.

219. Del Castillo and De León, *North to Aztlán*, 164.

220. Del Castillo and De León, *North to Aztlán*, 164.

221. The following are but a few examples of Latina organizations with a national or regional focus: National Hispana Leadership Institute, National Latina Health Organization, National Network of Hispanic Women, Mexican American Women's National Association, and Southwest Institute for Research on Women.

222. Meier and Rivera, *Mexican Americans, American Mexicans*, 230.

223. Interview, Sosa-Riddell.

224. Interview, Sosa-Riddell.

225. Acuña, *Occupied America*, 4th ed., 445.

226. Del Castillo and De León, *North to Aztlán*, 157.

227. Kenneth Burt, *The History of MAPA and Chicano Politics in California* (Sacramento, Calif.: Mexican American Political Association, 1982), 20–21.

228. Burt, *The History of MAPA and Chicano Politics in California*, 21.

229. Burt, *The History of MAPA and Chicano Politics in California*, 21.

230. Burt, *The History of MAPA and Chicano Politics in California*, 22–23.

231. Burt, *The History of MAPA and Chicano Politics in California*, 25–27.

232. Interview, Ben Benavidez, July 2, 2002.

233. Interview, Benavidez.

234. Interview, Benavidez, July 2, 2002.

235. Pamphlet, "S. Ben Benavidez," MAPA, no date.

236. Pamphlet, "43rd Anniversary," MAPA, January 5, 2002.

237. Pamphlet, "43rd Anniversary."

238. Interview, Benavidez, July 2, 2002.

239. F. Chris Garcia, ed., *Latinos and the Political System* (Notre Dame, Ind.: University of Notre Dame Press, 1988), 501.

240. Meier and Gutiérrez, *Encyclopedia of the Mexican American Civil Rights Movement*, 218.

241. Garcia, *Latinos and the Political System*, 501.

242. Stine Santiesteven, "Willie Velasquez: Changing the Political Realities," *Hispanics and Grant Makers: A Special Report of Foundation News*, 1981, 58.

243. William C. Velasquez Institute, "WCVI.ORG," Vol. I, Issue 3 (Winter 2000).

244. Fox, *Hispanic Nation*, 164.

245. Anita Goularte, "Southwest Voter Registration and Education Project," Unpublished student paper, University of California, Riverside, Winter 1996.

246. www.carnegie.org/reporter/03/backpage/latino2.html

247. Richard Santillan, "Latino Politics in the Midwestern United States: 1915–1986," in *Latinos and the Political System*, ed. Garcia, 112.

248. John A. Garcia, "The Chicano Movement: Its Legacy for Politics and Policy," in *Chicanas/Chicanos at the Crossroads*, ed. Maciel and Ortiz, 94–95.

249. www.lib.niu.edu/ipo/ii940742.html

250. Telephone interview, Juan Andrade, USHLI president, October 17, 2002.

251. Vigil, *Hispanics in American Politics*, 119.

252. Gómez-Quiñones, *Chicano Politics*, 166.

253. Moore and Pachon, *Hispanics in the United States*, 197.

254. Acuña, *Occupied America*, 410.

255. Santillan, "Latino Political Development in the Southwest and Midwest Regions," 122–23.

256. naleogala2001.com/about.html

257. Telephone Interview, Carol Macey, senior NALEO director of finance, October 16, 2002.

258. www.tsha.utexas.edu/handbook/online/articles/view/MM/wmm2.html

259. www.tsha.utexas.edu/handbook/online/articles/view/MM/wmm2.html

260. www.tsha.utexas.edu/handbook/online/articles/view/MM/wmm2.html

261. www.tsha.utexas.edu/handbook/online/articles/view/MM/wmm2.html

262. Interview, Roberto Alonzo, July 3, 2002.

263. Interview, Alonzo.

264. Gómez-Quiñones, *Chicano Politics*, 162.

265. Vigil, *Hispanics in American Politics*, 126.

266. Meier and Rivera, *Mexican Americans, American Mexicans*, 254.

267. For a historical overview of CHC visit their website: www.chci.org/about/history.html

268. Meier and Gutiérrez, *Encyclopedia of Mexican American Rights Movement*, 63.

269. Acuña, *Occupied America*, 4th ed., 410.

270. Haro, *Latinos and the U.S. Political System*, 91.

271. www.chci.org/about/history.html

272. Meier and Gutiérrez, *Encyclopedia of the Mexican American Civil Rights Movement*, 63.

273. Meier and Gutiérrez, *Encyclopedia of the Mexican American Civil Rights Movement*, 63.

274. Meier and Gutiérrez, *Encyclopedia of the Mexican American Civil Rights Movement*, 69.

275. Vigil, *Hispanics in American Politics*, 67–68.

276. Sierra, "Latino Organizational Strategies on Immigration Reform," 75.

277. NALEO, "2000 National Directory of Latino Elected Officials," NALEO Educational Fund, Los Angeles.

278. Meier and Gutiérrez, *Encyclopedia of the Mexican American Civil Rights Movement*, 206.

279. www.chci.org/about/impact.html

280. For an excellent comprehensive examination Alinsky CBPOs see Mark R. Warren, *Dry Bones Rattling: Community Building to Revitalize Democracy* (Princeton, N.J.: Princeton University Press, 2001); and Mary Beth Rogers, *Cold Anger: A Story of Faith and Power Politics* (Denton: University of North Texas Press, 1990).

281. IAF pamphlet, "The Southwest IAF Network: 25 Years of Organizing" (Chicago: IAF, November 1999), 8.

282. Meier and Gutiérrez, *Encyclopedia of the Mexican American Civil Rights Movement,* 59.

283. IAF pamphlet, "The Southwest IAF Network," 19–21, 34.

284. Acuña, *Occupied America,* 4th ed., 442.

285. For a more extensive examination of my model, the Trinity Concept of Community Development, see my book *La Raza Unida Party,* chapter 5.

286. Jennifer Mena, "México's 2006 Race Comes to Santa Ana," *Los Angeles Times,* July 7, 2002.

287. Due to financial, administrative, and internal political difficulties, One-Stop Immigration and Education Center in Los Angeles was forced to close down its service activities. See Maria Luisa Arredando, "Motivos De La Quiebra De One Stop Immigration," *La Opinión,* March 12, 2002.

288. Interview, Felipe Aguirre, PRD California State Chair, September 18, 2002.

289. Interview, Aguirre.

Epoch of Transition (2000–2003)   8

URING THE FIRST THREE YEARS of the twenty-first century, the Mexicano experience in occupied Aztlán was at a critical juncture. Changes that occurred within the demographic, socioeconomic, political, cultural, ballot box, and organizational areas of the Mexicano experience produced a new mode of politics. Both the re-Méxicanización de Aztlán (re-Mexicanization of the Southwest) and Latinoización (Latinoization) of the United States continued at an unprecedented pace. Socioeconomically, even though Mexicanos as a people had made some progress, Aztlán's barrios and *colonias* continued to feel the deleterious effects of internal colonialism. The Viva Yo Hispanic Generation ethos was still dominant, but the Neo-Méx Generation gained influence. While Mexicano and Latino political representation increased, they failed to produce major public policy changes. The 9/11 attacks and subsequent U.S. invasion of Iraq also played a role in increasing the uncertainty of the Mexicano in occupied Aztlán.

Mexicano/Latino Demographic Profile

The 2000 U.S. Census data released in 2001 validated the argument that the United States was still experiencing a demographic transformation, namely, a "re-browning," of its population, meaning people of color showed significant population gains and the white population experienced a decrease. The country continued to experience a Latinoización and in the Southwest a re-Mexicanización de Aztlán at a phenomenal rate. During the decade of the 1990s, the Latino population growth was driven primarily by the immigration of both documented and undocumented, Latino birthrates, and by white and black flight to other states. The 2000 U.S. Census revealed that the Latino population significantly contributed to the country's growing ethnic/racial diversity. By 2003, the Mexicano/ Latino population became the largest minority population, displacing blacks. To the dismay of white nativists, the country was evolving into what could be argued as an immutable and even more pronounced multiethnic/racial, multicultural, and multilingual society.

Mexicano/Latino 2000–2003 Census

Latino National Population Increases

While the U.S. population in 2000 reached 281 million, the Latino[1] population grew to 35.3 million. This was an increase of 58 percent from 1990 to 2000, about three million more than the Census Bureau had predicted. One out of eight residents of the United States was now of Latino origin,[2] and Latinos comprised 12.5 percent of the country's population. Also in 2000 some 40 percent of the Latino population was foreign-born and some six million had immigrated into the United States between 1990 and 2000.[3] In addition, immigrants accounted for some 12 percent of the U.S. workforce, which translated to some 15.7 million.[4] It was revealing that of the almost thirty million foreign-born, some 55 percent came from Latin America.[5] While the U.S. population grew to 284.8 million by 2001, the Latino population increased to some thirty-seven million, 13 percent of the national population. This translated to a 4.7 percent increase among Latinos between April 2000 and July 2001. The preceding totals, however, did not include Puerto Rico's nearly four million inhabitants, which if added increased the total Latino population in 2001 to nearly forty-one million. Blacks experienced a slight increase of 2 percent, from 12.6 percent or 35.5 million in 2000 to 12.7 percent or 36.1 million. Asians comprised a mere 4 percent, making them the next largest minority group.[6]

The Census Bureau in June 2003 released adjusted census figures for 2000–2002. Fueled by the growing migrant exodus from México and high birthrates, the number of Latinos in the United States increased again: from 35.3 million to 38.8 million, up nearly 10 percent from the 2000 census. As a result, Latinos became officially the largest and fastest-growing minority group in the country; surpassing blacks, who numbered 36.6 million and only grew by a mere 3.1 percent.[7] Analysis of census data by the Tomás Rivera Policy Institute at the Claremont Colleges revealed that Latinos outnumbered blacks in twenty-three states. Hence, the dramatic Latino population increase altered the country's broad demographic picture by 2003: whites constituted 68 percent, Latinos 14 percent, blacks 13 percent, Asians 4 percent, and others 1 percent.[8] During the three-year period, while the country's population increased to 288.4 million, whites grew by a mere 0.7 percent, compared to 9.8 percent for Latinos. This was nearly four times the rate of the country as a whole and seven times the non-Latino rate, which meant that Latinos accounted for half (3.5 million) of the country's total population growth (6.9 million). By ancestry, the Latino population was 66 percent Mexican, 15 percent Central and South American; 9 percent Puertorriqueño; 4 percent Cubano, and 6 percent other.[9] By the end of 2003, the country's population reached 291 million; adding Puerto Rico's four million people, Latinos numbered nearly forty-three million.

An important characteristic of the Latino demographic transformation has been its youthfulness. The U.S. Census reported that while 25.7 percent of the U.S. population was under eighteen years of age, 35.0 percent of the Latino population was below the age of eighteen, compared to 23 percent of whites. While the median age for the entire population was 35.3, for Latinos it was 25.9 years. Of the various Latino subgroups, Mexicanos had the lowest median age of 24.2 years, compared to Puertorriqueños, 27.3 years; Cubanos, 40.7 years; Central Americans, 29.2 years; and South Americans, 33.1 years. Furthermore, the Census Bureau reported that by 2002 some 5 percent of Latinos were sixty-five and older, compared to 14 percent of whites.[10] In 2002, 18 percent of the country's children were Latinos, which will contribute significantly to the Latino future population growth if this trend continues.

The 2000 U.S. Census also revealed an increase among Latinos in the number of mixed-race births and marriages. The majority of mixed births occurred in California and involved Latinos. Statewide, some one in six births in 1998 were to parents of mixed race or ethnicity, up from one in seven in 1989, and the trend was accelerating. A Latino parent was involved in nearly three-fourths of the mixed-race or mixed-ethnic births in Southern California. More specifically, 24.4 percent of all mixed births in suburbs involved a white mother and Latino father; second highest was 22.9 percent, involving a Latina mother and a white father; and fourth was 4.0 percent, which involved a Latina mother and a black father.[11]

The increase in mixed births correlated with increases in mixed-race marriages. Nearly two million of the mixed-race marriages in the United States involved couples in which one partner was Mexicano or Latino. In a survey taken on the subject of mixed marriages in July 2001, 68 percent of Latinos surveyed said it made no difference whether persons marry someone from their own ethnic/racial group or from a different group.[12] By the third generation, about half of Latinos in the United States marry outside their group.[13] This suggested that Mexicanos and Latinos had become more tolerant of mixed-race/ethnic marriages, and increasingly susceptible to assimilation.

At the national level, the Mexicano population in 2000 increased by 54 percent: an increase of some 7.1 million over 1990,[14] which meant there were some 23 million Mexicanos who resided in the United States. By 2003, however, Mexican government officials estimated the figure to be twenty-five million. For the next twenty-eight years the Mexicano population in the United States will continue to grow by a minimum of 400,000 to 500,000 due to migration from México.[15] With the sole exception of the Northeast, Mexicanos constituted the largest Latino subgroup. In the West, they comprised 74 percent; Midwest, 71 percent; South, 56 percent; and Northeast 9 percent.[16]

Latino Populations Increase by State

The Latino population explosion particularly impacted Aztlán's six major states. According to the 2000 U.S. Census, the Latino population in the western states reached 15,340,503. California, with a population of 34 million, had the largest Latino population in the country: 10,966,556, comprising 32.4 percent. Tejas had an overall population of 21 million with a Latino population of 6,669,666, which translated to 32 percent. Arizona's population reached 5,130,632 and the Latino population increased to 1,295,617 or 25.2 percent. Nuevo México had a total population of 1,819,046, with a Latino population of 765,386, constituting 42.1 percent. With a state population of 1,998,256, Nevada's Latino population surged to 393,970 making them 19.7 percent. Colorado, with a population of 3,405,565, had 320,323 Latinos, which translated to a mere 17.1 percent. Utah with a total population of 2,233,169, Latinos increased their numbers to 201,559 making them 9.0 percent.

Nationwide, the 2000 Census revealed, irrefutably, the demographic reality of the *Latinoización* of the United States. From Alaska to Washington to New York and Georgia, the 2000 Census reported the impact of the "Latino Diaspora," the dispersion of Latinos throughout the country, particularly that of Mexicanos. By 2000, Latinos constituted the largest minority group in some twenty-one states.[17] States outside of Aztlán with growing Latino populations included Washington, 441,509 (7.5 percent); Oregon, 275,314 (8 percent); Illinois, 1,530,262 (12.3 percent); Michigan, 323,877 (3.3 percent); Massachusetts, 428,729 (6.8 percent); New York, 2,867,583 (15 percent); New Jersey, 1,117,191 (13.3 percent percent); and La Florida, 2,682,715 (16.8 percent).

In the southern states, historically the bastions of conservatism and segregation, Mexicanos from Aztlán and México were lured by jobs in the expanding poultry processing plants and textile mills. They migrated in large numbers to Alabama, Arkansas, Georgia, South Carolina, North Carolina, and Tennessee.[18] Indicative of the phenomenal Latino population growth was North Carolina with a 393.9 percent increase—from 76,000 in 1990 to 379,000 in 2000. Georgia's Mexicano/Latino population increased from 108,022 in 1990 to 435,227 in 2000, a 299.6 percent increase.[19] The migrants altered the demographic, cultural, and economic complexion of the South, and there were increasing tensions between the newly arrived mostly Mexicano migrants and blacks and whites.[20]

The Midwest as well was not exempt from Latinoización. Major Latino population increases occurred, especially in Iowa, Nebraska, Kansas, and Minnesota, where both legal and undocumented migrants reinvigorated the declining white populations in midwestern towns. Driven by the availability of jobs in meat processing plants, Latino migrants came in their quest of a more prosperous future.[21] As their numbers increased so did the tensions with nativist whites.

Thus, by 2003, in every state within Aztlán the Latino population increased significantly, intensifying its re-Mexicanización. In California, the Latino population increased to 34 percent or twelve million, and Mexicanos made up nearly 80 percent of the Latinos or ten million people. In Tejas, the Latino population surpassed seven million and the great overwhelming majority were Mexicanos. The Latino population, over 90 percent Mexicano, in Nuevo México reached a high of 800,000, making them nearly 45 percent of the population. Significant Latino population growth also occurred in Arizona, Nevada, Colorado, and Utah.

Latino Population Growth at the Local Levels

The "Latino population explosion" was most evident at both the county and city level. According to the 2000 U.S. Census, Latinos constituted a majority in some fifty counties, and of these, thirty-five were in the South, thirty-four in Tejas alone, and fifteen in the West. Of the latter, Nuevo México had nine counties with Mexicano majorities, and Arizona, Colorado, and California had two each. Latinos were between 25 percent and less than 50 percent of the population in some 152 counties. Los Angeles County had the largest number of Latinos in the country, numbering over 4.2 million (42 percent). With a combined population of 1,248,586 in Riverside and San Bernardino counties, Latinos respectively comprised 36.2 percent and 39.2 percent. They experienced a phenomenal growth rate of 323 percent from 1980 to 2000, making them the sixth largest Latino region in the country.[22]

The 2000 Census also revealed that Latinos were a highly urbanized population. Nearly 46.4 percent lived in a central city within a metropolitan area, while 45.1 percent lived outside of central cities but within a metropolitan area.[23] According to a July 2002 Brookings Institution report, an exodus of Latinos from the cities to the suburbs had begun: 54 percent of the nation's Latinos lived in the suburbs, which represented a 71 percent increase since 1990.[24] The urbanization and suburbanization of the Latino population was evident in their large presence in the country's large cities: Los Angeles, 1,719,073 (47 percent); Chicago, 753,644 (26 percent); Houston, 730,865 (37.4 percent); San Antonio, 671,394 (58.7 percent); El Paso, 431,875 (76.6 percent); Dallas, 422,587 (35.6

percent); Phoenix, 449,972 (34.1 percent); and San Jose, California, 269,989 (30.2 percent). People of color, essentially Latinos and blacks, became the "New Minority-Majority" in the country's top 100 cities between 1990 and 2000. Latinos and blacks were respectively 23 percent and 24 percent.[25]

Throughout the country, especially in Aztlán, there were numerous smaller cities where Mexicanos and Latinos constituted a majority. Indicative of the colonized status of the barrios, the 2000 U.S. Census revealed that in a majority of the country's cities, Latinos and Asians were the country's "most isolated" or most segregated ethnic groups.[26] Moreover, cities were becoming increasingly "re-brownized." The U.S. Census in 2003 reported that although Miami, La Florida, as a city had the highest percentage of foreign born at 61.6 percent, California dominated the nation's top ten-ranked cities: Santa Ana, 48.4 percent; Los Angeles, 41.3 percent; Anaheim, 40.3 percent; San Francisco, 36.7 percent; San Jose, 36.5 percent; Long Beach, 30.9 percent; and San Diego, 27.9 percent.[27]

Forces Fostering the Latino Population Explosion

The Latinoización of the United States and the re-Méxicanización of Aztlán were foremost the products of undocumented and legal migration. They were driven by the push factors of poverty, unemployment, subsistence wages, political repression, reunification of families, and the pull factor of the United States' insatiable hunger for cheap labor. The Census Bureau 2003 demographic report for 2000–2002 revealed that of the nearly 10 percent Latino population increase, 53 percent was attributed to undocumented migration.[28] Although estimates varied from source to source, the U.S. General Accounting Office reported in August 2001 that the number of undocumented was between five and eleven million.[29] During the 1990s, the undocumented population doubled, and close to half was from México. The Mexicano distribution of undocumented by state included 2,000,000 in California; 700,000 in Tejas; 540,000 in New York; 350,000 in La Florida; 290,000 in Illinois; 135,000 in New Jersey; and 115,000 in Arizona.[30] By 2002 the Immigration and Naturalization Service (INS) calculated that nationwide there were a total of some 8.7 million undocumented of which 3.9 million or 44 percent were from México.[31] During 2002, even though a decrease of 29 percent had occurred, the number of undocumented apprehended along the U.S./México border reached some nine hundred thousand. The amount was still high, which suggested the migrant exodus was still thriving.[32]

Legal migration also contributed to the Latino population explosion. During fiscal year October 2000 to September 2001, Mexicanos comprised almost a fifth of some 1,064,318 legal migrants that came into the United States, more precisely 206,426 or 19.4 percent. While other Latin American countries such as El Salvador had 31,272 (2.9 percent); Cuba, 27,703 (2.6 percent); Dominican Republic, 21,313 (2 percent); Nicaragua, 19,986 (1.9 percent); Colombia, 16,730 (1.6 percent); and Guatemala, 13,567 (1.3 percent). Over one-quarter of the total documented immigration or 282,957 (26.6 percent) settled in California.[33] Without a doubt, it could be argued that México's main export was human capital.

High fertility or birthrates were the second major source of Latino population growth. The nation's birthrate in 2002 dropped to its lowest level since 1909. The rate fell to 13.9 births per 1,000 women ages fifteen to forty-four, down 1 percent from 2001 and 17 percent from its most recent peak in 1990. The birthrate also fell to its lowest level on record, 43 births per 1,000 among teen women ages fifteen to nineteen.[34] Conversely, this was not the case for Latinas. Of all the country's major ethnic and racial groups, Latinas had the highest birthrates. This was revealed by the Census Bureau 2003 report that said that 47 percent of the two-year 10 percent increase was ascribable to high birthrates.[35]

In California, Latinos dominated the birth statistics. According to a study conducted by the UCLA Center for the Study of Latino Health and Culture under the direction of David Hayes-Bautista, Latinos for the first time accounted for more than 50 percent of California's births. During this quarter, there were 138,892 births in California of which 69,672 were Latino. Non-Latino whites accounted for 31.4 percent of the births for the quarter, while Asians and Pacific Islanders comprised 11.3 percent and blacks 6.1 percent. During the subsequent three months, the percentage of Latino births experienced another increase to 50.6 percent, while non-Latino whites experienced a birth decrease to 30.4 percent. Asian and Pacific Islanders' percentage increased to 11.7, and blacks maintained at 6.1 percent.

The impact of Latino high birthrates was particularly evident at the county level. Los Angeles had the highest Latino birthrate with 63 percent; Riverside, 58 percent; San Bernardino, 55 percent; Ventura, 54 percent; and Orange, 50 percent.[36] According to the U.S. Census, at the national level, among women between the ages of fifteen and nineteen per 1,000, the Latino birthrate was 93.4, compared to 81.0 for blacks and 34.0 for whites. As reported by the U.S. Census, Latinos had the largest families of any other ethnic/racial group. The average family size for Latinos was 4.27; blacks, 3.32; Native Americans, 3.70; Asians, 3.70; and whites, 2.95.[37] Thus, the 2000 Census data showed that compared to Latinos, whites as well as other ethnic/racial groups were simply not having as many babies.

The growing Latinoización of several communities continued to trigger "white flight," especially within Southern California's coastal counties.[38] The outward white migration from California to other states contributed to the re-Mexicanización of California. White flight impelled by the state's economic difficulties; declining good-paying job opportunities, especially in the aerospace industry; growing social problems; and the demographic re-browning of the state, contributed to an increase in the Latino population density and concentrations. It was particularly evident around Los Angeles and suburbs in California. During the 1990s, the white population in Los Angeles shrank from 3.6 million to 2.96 million.[39] Moreover, southern California's five counties lost a total of 840,000 people due to white flight.[40] Droves of Californians, mostly whites, left the state and sought to live their golden years in states such as Tejas, Washington, Arizona, Nevada, Oregon, or Colorado.[41] Between 1995 and 2000, almost 568,000 people migrated out of California to Nevada (199,125), Arizona (186,151), and Tejas (182,789) alone.[42] In 2001 it was reported that in 1999 alone somewhere between 80,000 and 115,000 more people left the state than came into the state. In California, by 2002 whites constituted 47 percent of the state's population, converting them into the new ethnic minority.[43] White flight also occurred in other urban and rural areas of Aztlán.

The growing Latinoización also induced "black flight," particularly in Southern California. In what had been primarily black areas, such as Watts, Compton, Inglewood, and South Central Los Angeles, Latinos now were the new majorities. As a result of these demographic shifts, antagonisms between Latinos and blacks were heightened as illustrated by increasing conflicts between black and Latino gangs in the streets, prisons, and schools, and in the program allocation of resources. Blacks were also losing political representation to Latinos, especially Mexicanos, at all levels of governance.[44] Thus, while the Latino population in 2003 continued to grow dramatically, so did their socioeconomic problems.

The Best of Times, Worst of Times

From academicians to politicians, among many others, the "best of times, worst of times" debate was rooted in the previous epoch and concerned the scope and quality of the socioeconomic progress made by Mexicanos and Latinos up to 2003. The debate was induced by class, ideological, and cultural generational differences. The "optimists" propounded a "best of times" reality; while the "pessimists" claimed a "worst of times" perspective. The former adhered to the notion that Mexicanos and Latinos were progressing; the latter claimed that it was insignificant. Those who identified with the "best of times" perspective adhered essentially to the ethos of the Hispanic Generation (HG). They were generally middle to upper class and ideologically moderate to conservative with liberal capitalist leanings. Conversely, those who took the "worst of times" perspective were generally poor to lower middle class. Their politics were liberal to progressive Left, were hypercritical of the HG, and viewed the existent social order as in need of some change.

The Best of Times Perspective

Proponents tended to be confident and optimistic about the scope of progress made during the transition by Mexicanos and Latinos in general. They were also buoyant about their future prospects for progress. According to U.S. Census, the median household income of Latinos[45] grew from $25,000 in 1995[46] to $33,447 in 2000, up 5.3 percent from $31,767 in 1999. The Latino was still considerably below the whites, whose median income was $45,904, Asian and Pacific Islanders at $55,521, and blacks at $30,439. Between 1993 and 2000, along with other ethnic/racial groups, Latinos also experienced a significant per capita income increase of 19.3 percent—from $10,317 to $12,306.[47] In May 2001, the Tomás Rivera Policy Institute (TRPI) released a report that purported great strides had been made by the growing Latino middle class. The report concluded that, fueled by the growing national economy, the number of Latino middle-class households in the United States, those with annual incomes above $40,000, increased from fewer than 1.5 million in 1979 to almost 2.7 million by 1998, an increase of about 80 percent. "Latino economic progress has been significant," said Harry Pachon, TRPI director.[48]

According to scholar Arturo González, "At the upper end of the income distribution, nearly 120,000 second and third generation families, about 5 percent, earned more than $100,000 in 1998, compared to only 52,000 first generation (2 percent) of first generation Mexican American families."[49] Another scholar, Robert R. Brischetto, notes, "Between 1979 and 1999, the Hispanic middle class grew 71.2 percent to number 9.5 million." He further explains, "Hispanic households earning between $40,000 and $140,000 annually reached 2.5 million in 1999.[50] In September 2002, *Hispanic Business* reported that on its "Rich List" there were a total of seventy-five Latino families or individuals who had a combined wealth of $11.4 billion. For instance, the Goizueta family of Atlanta, Georgia, was the richest with a worth of some $980 million alone.[51] This suggested the rise of a Latino upper class and of growing stratification and class distinctions among Latinos.

Former U.S. housing secretary Henry Cisneros was an optimist, an ardent proponent of the "best of times" perspective. In a speech he gave in Dallas in 2001 Cisneros was euphoric about Latino economic achievements. He claimed using the term *Hispanics* should make them feel good about themselves; they were revitalizing U.S. cities, buying homes, paying taxes, spicing up the country's culture, and pumping $452.4 billion in annual spending power into the U.S. economy,[52] an increase of 118 percent over 1990. By 2003, Latino purchasing power had dramatically increased to nearly $600 billion. Latinos now comprised 6.9 percent of the total U.S. purchasing power.[53] Optimists argued that the dramatic increase in Latino purchasing power demonstrated their growing economic clout, progress, and economic empowerment. They pointed out that in 2002 the number of Latino-owned businesses had increased from eighty-six thousand in 1992 to 1.56 million ten years later and was projected to grow to 1.76 million by 2005.[54] The National Council of La Raza (NCLR) in a report released in August 2001 was rather optimistic about the Latino's socioeconomic status.[55] In spite of the preceding optimistic picture, the reality was that during the transition, particularly for most Mexicanos living in Aztlán's barrios and *colonias*, progress was more illusory than factual.

The Worst of Times Perspective

During the transition, some Mexicanos and Latinos refuted the "best of times" perspective. They perceived their deteriorating socioeconomic conditions as a growing crisis. They were inclined to be cynical about the socioeconomic progress made by Mexicanos in particular and Latinos in general and were pessimistic about their future prospects. Progressive Left activists felt that the socioeconomic conditions of Aztlán's barrios and *colonias* were worsening. The election of Republican George W. Bush as president in 2000 only exacerbated the "worst of times" crises. The Democratic Clinton administration surplus by 2003 was replaced by a major deficit of some $500 billion and a worsening recession. The country's poor and middle class bore the brunt of the Bush administration's insidious tax cut policies that strongly favored the rich. Indicative of the "worst of times" crises was the high number of Mexicanos and Latinos who lived in poverty.

Paradoxically, the 2000 Census revealed that poverty in the United States, the richest liberal capitalist country of the world, had increased. Poverty was a phenomenon that affected Mexicanos and Latinos in both urban and rural areas. According to the U.S. Census, the national poverty rate rose to 11.7 percent in 2001 from 11.3 percent the previous year. This meant that some 32.9 million people lived in poverty. By the end of 2003 the figure increased to 35 million. Poverty households increased from 1.2 million in 1979 to 2.6 million households in 1998.[56] The poverty rate for Latinos in 2001 was 21.4 percent, whereas for blacks it was 22.7 percent; 10.2 percent for Asians and Pacific Islanders; and for whites, it increased from 9.5 percent to 9.9 percent. Latino poverty was expected to increase in 2002 to 23.2 percent.[57]

As poverty increased, the median household income also declined by some 2.2 percent.[58] While household income levels declined for all ethnic/racial groups, for Latinos it decreased from $34,094 to $33,565. For a family of four, 17.2 percent of all Latinos earned below $14,999, while 35.1 percent made $15,000 to $34,999; 34 percent made between $35,000 to $74,999; and 13.5 percent of all Latinos made $75,000 or more. This meant that 53.3 percent of Latino families made below $35,000; the majority thus lived in poverty or near poverty.[59] The Census Bureau reported that by 2002 among full-time, year-round workers, 26 percent of Latinos made $35,000 or more, compared with 54 percent of whites.[60] A report released in 2003 concluded that some 63 percent of Latino families with children earned insufficient income to survive economically.[61] Many Latino families like other non-Latinos were one paycheck away from being homeless. Poverty especially affected the country's growing migrant population. Some 34 percent of the Latino children below the age of eighteen were poor, and 45 percent of all immigrant families who were poor were Mexicanos.[62] Moreover, between 1979 and 1999 household income for those who were foreign born declined, and the number of low-income households more than doubled from 2.2 million to 4.9 million.[63] A study released by the Pew Hispanic Center in January 2002 concluded that the country's recession might end soon; however, the "financial problems for Latinos could stretch long after the national economy recovers."[64]

The growing crises were also evident in the Latino's extremely low level of access to health care. Of a total of 9.3 million Latino children eligible for the Children's Health Insurance Program in 2000 only 3.3 million were enrolled, while the other 6 million were not enrolled in that program or Medicaid. Only 12 percent of Latino children eligible for child-care subsidies received them.[65] Mortality rate for children remained extremely high. Another report concluded that Latino children had a disproportionate share of health ills, for example, asthma and obesity, and were not being adequately treated;[66] some suffered from malnutrition. Latinos also had the highest uninsured rates of any other ethnic/racial group. The U.S. Census reported in 2001 that the number of people uninsured in the country had increased to 41.2 million and that 33.2 percent or 12.4 million Latinos did not have medical insurance.[67] AIDS in 2002 was another growing medical problem for Latinos. Some 19 percent in the country were reported to have AIDS, compared to 26 percent for whites and 54 percent for blacks. Also, it was reported in 2000 that immigrants entering the United States suffered from high rates of tuberculosis.[68] Thus, as a result of poverty, and especially the lack of medical insurance, many Latinos went untreated. Some were compelled to travel to México's border cities in pursuit of affordable health care, drugs, and hospitalization.

Unemployment was also a major crisis for Latinos. With the exception of blacks, it was higher for Latinos than for other ethnic groups. Between 2000 and 2002, the Latino unemployment rate differential ranged 2 to 3 points from the U.S. total. In January 2001 unemployment for whites reached 4.2 percent, for Latinos 6.0 percent, and for blacks a high of 8.4 percent.[69] By May 2003, Latino unemployment reached a high of 7.5 percent, and black unemployment 10.9 percent, while white unemployment reached 5.2 percent.[70] Since the Bush administration took office in January 2001, some 2.5 million manufacturing jobs had been lost. The general unemployment rate rose to 6 percent by October 2003. Thus, from 2001 to 2003, the country's economy was in transition from factory jobs to service sector work; consequently, the result was a loss of good-paying jobs.[71]

Indicative of the ongoing "worst of times" crises was the relative absence of Latinos in the country's corporate boardrooms. In spite of various Latino organizational efforts in the arena of corporate responsibility, Latino struggles to penetrate the boardrooms of corporations produced dismal results.[72] After over thirty years of affirmative action, cultural diversity, and corporate responsibility efforts, the upper tiers of boardrooms remained the bastions of aging white males. As of November 2002 of the 11,500 Fortune 1,000 board seats, Latinos merely held 86, while women held 1,584 and blacks 388. Latino board representation suffered a dramatic drop of 9 percent, whereas the decrease for blacks was 4 percent. Hence, the corporate engines that drove liberal capitalism proved to be inaccessible to Latinos and blacks even though combined they constituted nearly 28 percent of the country's population. Efforts of Hispanic Generation leaders and organizations, such as those of President Anna Escobedo Cabral of HACR (Hispanic Association on Corporate Responsibility), failed to penetrate the allegedly collegial white males.[73] Their discriminatory message was clear: they wanted access to Mexicano and Latino cheap labor and to their purchasing power and markets, but were not willing to give them access to the reins of corporate power.

The egregious effects were also evident in the country's prison-industrial complex.[74] From 1985 to 1997, the U.S. prison population had more than doubled, from 502,376 to 1,240,962.[75] By 2002 there was a total of some 2.1 million inmates incarcerated, representing a 2.6 percent increase over 2001, and it was costing federal and state governments an estimated $40 billion per year at a time

extensive. Thus, out of the preceding events, the NAHR emerged, and I became its national coordinator.

In December 2000, the CHR held a major immigration conference in Tucson. It was attended by some six hundred activists from across the United States and México, with an agenda focused on the perils of undocumented migrants who crossed the border, ending the escalating border violence, and rolling back the militarization of the U.S./México border and on U.S. immigration policies and the manifold ill-effects of globalization. Numerous resolutions were passed, but most importantly, the attendees vowed to create an international grassroots movement to assist immigrants. During the next two years, the CHR had a visible media presence on border issues. Under the able leadership of Isabel Garcia, an attorney, the CHR denounced the Bush administration's border policies and the activities of the militias in southern Arizona. She investigated and documented human rights abuses, and participated in lobbying efforts on immigration related matters in Washington, D.C.

Because of the escalating threat to migrants from rancher vigilante and by 2002 the militia, the NAHR organized two delegations that traveled to southern Arizona in 2003: the first in July and the second in November. Comprised of some thirty persons representing various organizations in the United States and political parties in México, the first NAHR delegation traveled to Phoenix, Tucson, and Douglas in July, and met with the general consul and consuls of the three respective cities to ascertain the severity of the militia activities. The delegation also traveled into México to Sasabe, Sonora, where it met and interviewed several Mexicano migrants who were about to cross into Arizona. They were unanimous in their willingness to make the perilous journey because of their extreme poverty and the lack of jobs in México. The three main militias responded to the NAHR delegation trip to southern Arizona via the Internet and the media as if there was going to be a showdown. Although it did not materialize, several members of the delegation did attempt to locate Glenn Spencer, leader of the American Border Patrol militia, in order to confront him face to face, but he was nowhere to be found. Upon the return of the delegation to California, I prepared a second report, which was released at press conferences and sent to the appropriate U.S. and México congressional committees. The report documented both the rancher vigilante and militia activities directed against migrants; repeated the NAHR's earlier call for congressional hearings, this time to be held on both sides of the U.S./México border; and called for a stronger binational approach be taken against the growing militia threat.

In November 2003, the NAHR in conjunction with the newly formed Comision de Poblacion, Fronteras y Asuntos Migratorios held a border summit in

November 2003 in Douglas, Arizona, on the issue of the "U.S./México border crisis." The militias were branded by the NAHR's leadership as "domestic terrorists" and were the focus of the summit's agenda. This time, the scheduled activities included a meeting/reception in Cananea, Sonora, a fact-finding trip to Altar and Sasabe, and a summit in Douglas, Arizona, that culminated with visits and press conferences held at militia- and vigilante-owned ranches. Some fifty people representing a number of Mexicano organizations from the United States and ten congresspersons from México participated in the unprecedented border events. With the exception of a field representative from Congressperson Raul Grijalva's office, no Mexicano or Latino U.S. congresspersons participated. Media from México covered the delegation's activities extensively, unlike the U.S. media, and two documentaries were filmed. As was the case with the earlier July delegation, the militias stayed away but verbally retaliated in the media with a barrage of attacks against the delegation's leadership. At the end of 2003, another summit on the border crisis was being planned for the following year in Arizona.

During 2003 advocacy efforts against the militias further intensified, with two lawsuits filed in Tejas by the Mexican American Legal Defense and Education Fund (MALDEF) and the Southern Law Center against Ranch Rescue. The two lawsuits filed in U.S. District Court asked for unspecified damages on behalf of six undocumented migrants who crossed the border in March and were apprehended by Ranch Rescue vigilantes at gunpoint at a private ranch owned by Joseph Sutton. The six migrants claimed their lives were threatened and that one of them was pistol-whipped, ordered to kneel down with his fingers folded behind his back. The lawsuit accused the Ranch Rescue militia of negligence, infliction of emotional distress, false imprisonment, and assault.[135]

The Driver License Senate Bill 60 (SB60) Issue

In California from 1998 to 2003 the issue of granting driver's licenses to undocumented migrants dominated the politics of immigration. In 1998 Democratic assemblyman Gil Cedillo sponsored Assembly Bill 60 (AB60) that would issue driver's licenses to some eight hundred thousand undocumented migrants. It was not until September 2002, however, that the bill passed both the State Assembly and Senate; yet Governor Davis, who was running for reelection, was reluctant to sign it. Latino *politicos* and groups issued warnings to the governor that a veto could cost him political support from Latinos.[136] The warnings failed. In September 2002 Governor Davis vetoed the hard-fought AB60 legislation, citing national security "fears" as the basis for his veto. Assemblyman Cedillo responded to Davis's veto by saying, "It is nothing but politics and not public policy. . . .

What we see is that the governor only responds to powerful interests, and he may believe that the Latino community isn't powerful enough."[137] In response to the veto, activists held a protest rally in Los Angeles and vowed to withdraw support from Governor Davis's campaign. Juan Jose Gutierrez, coordinator of the protest and director of "Latino Movement USA," was offended by the inference that immigrants were analogous to terrorists and said, "We are sick and tired of all these comparisons that paint us as potential terrorists."[138] Pressure failed to change Governor Davis's position, and he was reelected in 2002.

Now a state senator, Gil Cedillo continued his relentless crusade against the state's immigration politics in 2003. AB60 was reintroduced by Senator Cedillo in the Senate as SB60. It allowed undocumented migrants to apply for driver's licenses via a federal individual tax identification number or other forms of identification such as a *matricula consular* (a fingerprinted photo ID card issued by México's consuls) rather than a social security number.[139] Since 1993 the California legislature imposed the legal migrant status requirement on drivers, to prevent undocumented migrants from securing government benefits through the use of driver's licenses.

With a growing support of Latino legislators and Latino organizations and activists, the legislature approved SB60 without a single Republican vote. Similar legislation had been vetoed during the two preceding years on the grounds that the bills lacked adequate security measures, but facing a recall campaign and in need of Latino electoral support Governor Davis at a rally in Los Angeles signed the measure.[140] Soon afterward, the California Republican Assembly had successfully gathered some four hundred thousand signatures in two months to put the measure on the March 2004 ballot.[141] With the success of the recall in a special election in October and election of Arnold Schwarzenegger as California's new governor, Republicans were successful in reversing SB60. Senator Rico Oiler's legislation to overturn SB60 passed by a two-thirds majority with little or no opposition from Democrats and in December was signed by the new governor. The overturning of SB60 infuriated Latino activists, and organizing efforts were begun for a one-day economic boycott.

The California One-Day Latino Boycott

A one-day economic boycott was called for on December 12 in response to the repeal of SB60, making an increase in Latino activism in 2003. Nativo Lopez, state president of the Mexican American Political Association (MAPA) and director of Hemandad Mexicana Latino Americana (HML), made a call in November for a statewide Latino economic strike in protest of efforts to repeal

SB60. The rationale behind the strike was to demonstrate the political power of California's twelve million Latinos and their commitment to SB60. The goal was to have California's economy feel the loss of Latino workers and consumers, bringing it to a grinding halt. It meant that California's millions of migrants and supporters of SB60 would be able to show their protest against the repeal of SB60 by not staying at home and refraining from going to work, shopping, buying gas, banking, visiting amusement parks, or making long-distance calls—in short, from refraining from all economic activity.[142] It was strategic to hold the boycott on December 12, the same day that Latino Catholics, especially Mexicanos, celebrated the feast of our Lady Guadalupe.

Days before the "great economic boycott," the Hispanic Round Table, a Pomona-based pro-immigrant coalition led by Jose Calderon, a Pitzer College professor, held a march that started in Pomona and concluded with a rally in Los Angeles to support resurrecting SB60. Constrained by time factors, insufficient resources, low mainstream media interest, and differences among Latino organizations and politicians over its outcomes, the unprecedented economic strike produced mixed results. On the one hand, the state did not come to a screeching halt. The *Los Angeles Times* and scores of other newspapers, television, and radio news reported that schools with large Latino student populations reported heavy absenteeism and some sporadic protests. Columnist O. Ricardo Pimentel titled his piece on the boycott, "The Boycott That Got Boycotted," suggesting it had largely failed. He wrote, "A real economic boycott would have brought the state to a grinding halt."[143] Its organizers, however, especially Lopez, felt that on the contrary the boycott had been a resounding success. They argued that it set a powerful organizing precedent for Latinos in using their economic power statewide and utilizing economic boycotts as weapons for social change.[144]

The Immigration Debate Intensifies in 2003

During the transition period, a number of related immigration issues surfaced that deserve some mention. In October 2003, nine undocumented migrants who worked as janitors at giant Wal-Mart stores were apprehended. The nine filed a lawsuit that alleged they were paid lower wages, were not paid overtime, and were offered fewer benefits because they were Mexicanos.[145] By November, the U.S. Congress considered passage of the Clear Act, which would allow local law enforcement agencies to enforce immigration laws. In October, the Alabama Department of Public Safety became the second police agency in the country authorized to enforce federal immigration laws.[146] During November, a state of war surfaced between competing coyote (migrant smugglers) gangs that left four migrants dead and twenty-four arrested in a wild shootout near Phoenix, Arizona.[147]

At the close of 2003, nativists in Arizona and California were busy again pushing their modified Proposition 187 agenda. Removing Proposition 187's unconstitutional education provision that denied children of undocumented migrant parents access to an education, nativists in Arizona were busy in late 2003 gathering signatures to put the "Protect Arizona Now" (PAN) initiative on the November 2004 ballot.[148] In California, likewise, nativists were also busy gathering signatures for an identical initiative called "Save Our State," which like PAN in Arizona was a modified version of its predecessor Proposition 187. As was the case in Arizona it sought to preclude undocumented migrants from a broad array of public services, including access to driver's licenses.[149]

Politicians in México and the United States were also active in proposing immigration reform legislation. In the U.S. Congress three bills were pending to create a guest worker program, primarily for Mexicano migrants. One proposed by an Arizona Republican would allow undocumented migrants to apply for legal status after paying a $1,500 fine. Another by Tejas Republican senator John Cornyn would grant Mexicano workers temporary guest worker visas. And in California, Congressman Howard Berman cosponsored legislation that would streamline the existent H2 program such that some five hundred thousand undocumented migrant workers from México would work in agriculture and be eligible for legal residency in exchange for continued work on U.S. farms.[150]

Meanwhile, México's Fox administration intensified its lobbying efforts for a new amnesty program. Fox understood the great contributions of Mexicanos in the U.S. to México's economy. In fact next to oil revenues, it was reported that Mexicanos sent over $1 billion per month to their families in México,[151] which meant that these remittances in 2003 totaled some $14 billion. In November, President Vicente Fox traveled to Arizona, Nuevo México, and Tejas and met with each respective governor and state officials on a number of immigration and trade-related issues, including the migrant driver's license, which he wholeheartedly supported. The Bush and Fox administrations also pledged to revive the drive for immigration reform.[152]

Thus, starting in 2002 and in particular 2003, the issue of immigration was overshadowed by the Bush administration's imperialist foreign policy, especially the U.S. War against Iraq.

The Politics of the Bush War Administration

After the contested election of Republican George W. Bush to the presidency, the government swung even more to the Right. Former Democratic vice president

Al Gore won the popular vote; Bush, however, won the presidency by way of the electoral college. The Republican-controlled U.S. Supreme Court in a decision suppressed the vote recount and gave the presidency to Bush. Amid this shift to the Right came the terrorist attack on the World Trade Center and Pentagon on September 11, 2001. With some three thousand people killed that day, the Bush administration acquired free rein to manipulate the country's politics. It was successful in pushing its domestic conservative agenda, which included deregulation, tax cuts, feeding the avarice of corporate America, and internationally, a neocolonial foreign policy. The earlier Clinton administration foreign policy was given a stronger imperialist dosage of neo-Manifest Destiny and jingoism. From September 11, 2001, forward, the Bush administration set the political stage domestically for its expansionist world agenda. It pandered to the people's growing fears and insecurities, periodically announcing that more terrorist attacks were imminent. In a Machiavellian manner, it established a "state of siege" mind-set impelled by unbridled patriotism, and jingoism, at the expense of civil liberties. The "police state" mentality led the Bush administration to establish a new Department of "Homeland Security," headed by Security Director Tom Ridge. The bureaucracy became the new arm of the evolving police state.

The Passage of the USA Patriot Act (USAPA)

The new police state mentality was given greater credence with Congress's passage of the USAPA on October 26, 2001. Without significant opposition, particularly from the inept and leaderless Democratic Party, the Bush administration successfully pushed it through Congress and provided law enforcement agencies with extraordinary new powers unchecked by judicial review.[153] This meant that law enforcement agencies and international intelligence agencies as well were given sweeping new investigatory powers, which it could be argued violated the legal spirit of the First, Fourth, Fifth, and Sixth Amendments to the U.S. Constitution. Reminiscent of George Orwell's 1984, the controversial USAPA expanded the federal government's power via law enforcement agencies to conduct secret searches, wiretaps, surveillance, and interception of communications. According to Stephan J. Schulhofer, "Prosecutors gained access to the broad search and wiretap powers of the Federal Intelligence Surveillance Act."[154] The FBI was granted new access to an individual's confidential financial and education records and authorized to track Internet usage. The U.S. attorney general could also designate domestic groups as terrorist organizations and deport noncitizens that belonged to them. In an assault on habeas corpus, the USAPA gave the federal government expanded powers to detain indefinitely any noncitizens on the basis of being a risk to national security.[155]

Post 9/11, the people of the United States experienced a drastic erosion in their traditional civil liberties and civil rights—protections guaranteed by the Bill of Rights were gutted, dissent labeled "aid to the enemy," privacy rights eroded, and people's right to information about government decisions and actions almost eliminated.[156] The horrific effects of the Bush administration's imperialist foreign policy and growing police state became evident when the United States orchestrated an invasion of Afghanistan and then later Iraq.

The Invasion of Afghanistan

The Bush administration's *Pax Americana* quest became evident with its invasion of Afghanistan late in 2001. Without a declaration of war, the United States and a few allied forces pursued their "war against terrorism" and invaded, overthrew the existent Taliban regime, and occupied Afghanistan. "Regime change" became an operative aspect of the Bush administration's expansionist foreign policy that was driven by the primordial military goal of eradicating Bin Laden's al Qaeda terrorist network. While domestically some direct action protests occurred against the U.S.-led invasion, most people in the United States applauded the military exploits of the Bush administration. Indicative of the growing police state was the U.S. treatment of over six hundred captured suspected Taliban, who were labeled "enemy combatants." They were sent to and incarcerated in Guantanamo, Cuba, in violation of the Geneva Convention on war prisoners' rights. They were denied due process of law under the constitution, specifically the right to habeas corpus.[157] Thus, the military occupation of Afghanistan served to buttress the Bush administration's avarice for empire building.

A Resurgent Nativism Flourishes

The rising police state led to a resurgence of nativism in the United States. The myriad of political events that occurred post 9/11 fueled the jingoist mind-set now directed at those of Arab descent as well as at Latino immigrants. In March 2002 hate mail suspected of carrying anthrax was sent by unknown sources to some thirty Latino attorneys from the San Francisco area and to offices of various Latino national organizations.[158] Although several Mexicano workers perished as a result of the World Trade Center September 11 attacks, this did not mitigate the increased racial profiling of both Mexicanos and Latinos by law enforcement agencies. In California and Arizona, in late 2002 nativists pushed for new anti-immigrant initiatives for 2004, based upon a revised version of Proposition 187.[159]

During 2002 with the Bush administration beating the drums of war, the country's political climate became increasingly repressive, especially against immigrants of color. Yet not everyone in the country was marching in cadence to President Bush's international and domestic policies, especially the latter. In August 2002, the U.S. Sixth Circuit Court of Appeals entered a 3 to 0 decision to uphold an earlier federal ruling that secret deportation hearings were illegal. The ruling specifically found that the blanket closure of deportation hearings for individuals targeted in the post-September 11 terrorism investigations was unconstitutional, a violation of the First Amendment. In reference to the ruling, Sixth Circuit Court judge Damon J. Keith said, "When the government begins closing doors, it selectively controls information rightfully belonging to the people. Selective information is misinformation."[160]

The Iraq War Crisis

Impelled by a neo-Manifest Destiny and empire building, the Bush administration sought to precipitate a war against Saddam Hussein's Iraq on the pretext that Iraq possessed chemical, biological, and even nuclear "weapons of mass destruction," in violation of existing United Nations resolutions. On September 20, the Bush administration enunciated to the world its infamous belligerent "Bush Doctrine" of military preemption. It proclaimed the right of the United States to launch preemptive strikes on terrorists and regimes whose weapons of mass destruction posed a threat to the United States.[161]

In an unprecedented manner, the Bush administration promulgated a "neo-Monroe Doctrine," under the aegis the "Bush Doctrine," which in its original form applied to Latin America, but now it was expanded to include the entire world. In September 2002, President Bush's preemptive doctrine presumed that the entire world was the United States' sphere of influence, a clear doctrine of U.S. hegemony. With an arrogance of power and escalating U.S. militarism, he specifically propounded that the United States would topple governments and initiate unilateral preemptive attacks, warning potential rivals from trying to equal or surpass the United States' military might.[162] In addition, he warned the countries of the world, especially those he designated as being part of the "axis of evil" (e.g., Iraq, Iran, and North Korea), of the United States' willingness to unilaterally use force and "preemptive strikes" against terrorists and those countries it perceived as threatening its national security interests. Progressive critiques of the administration interpreted what I call the "Bush War Doctrine" as a façade for U.S. world hegemony, domination, and empire building.[163] Most of the country's plutocratic leaders from within the two-party dictatorship in Congress supported, buttressed by the media that increasingly acted as "cheerleaders" and in a "propagandistic role," President Bush's imperialistic and militaristic resolution.

The few opponents, mostly activists, who opposed the bellicose Bush administration's preemptive war doctrine alleged that it was in violation of Article I, Section 8, of the U.S. Constitution, which states simply that only Congress has the power to declare war. The constitution's system of "checks and balances" and separation of powers was being unraveled. Using the trauma created by the terrorism of 9/11, President Bush or "King George," as some of his adversaries described him, and his cabal of "Chicken Hawks," that is, Secretary of Defense Donald H. Rumsfeld, Vice President Dick Cheney, Deputy Secretary of Defense Paul Wolfowitz, and others, increasingly sought to usurp the power of Congress and the judiciary.

The Bush administration's belligerent pronouncements from October to December 2002 clearly demonstrated that it had little or no respect for UN Accords and international law. While UN inspectors were sent into Iraq to search for weapons of mass destruction, the United States intensified its warlike rhetoric. President Bush himself and various leaders of his administration, particularly Secretary of Defense Rumsfeld, warned the United Nation's Security Council that the United States was prepared to initiate unilateral force against Iraq if it did not disarm voluntarily, and called for a "regime change." Implicit in their warnings was the threat that if the Security Council did not act responsibly, which meant it did not follow the dictates of the United States, then the United States reserved the right to form an "International Coalition of the Willing" and would invade Iraq. Post-9/11 U.S. foreign policy became one of exacerbating tensions with the Muslim world. The United States characterization as the "Ugly American" was intensified throughout most of the Arab world, and the United States was scorned because of its aggressive stance against Iraq, its unrelenting support for Israel, and its invasion and occupation of Afghanistan. As a result numerous demonstrations were held throughout the Muslim world denouncing the United States as an imperialist infidel and "evil empire."

In November 2002, the Bush administration's war doctrine suffered a setback in the United Nation's Security Council. After weeks of wrangling, under the threat of a veto by permanent security members France, Russia, and China, the Security Council adopted Resolution 1441, which delayed military unilateral force by the United States and Great Britain and allowed United Nations weapon inspectors to go into Iraq and commence their search for weapons of mass destruction.[164] Also in November, Congress approved legislation pushed by the Bush administration and established an anti-terror Cabinet Agency for Homeland Security. It took charge of coordinating about two dozen agencies that employed some 170,000 persons responsible to counteract terrorist threats and attacks on the United States.[165]

While United Nations weapon inspectors conducted their searches, the Bush administration accelerated its war preparations in December. The United States began sending thousands of troops into the Middle East, specifically Kuwait and Qatar. Beyond Iraq, the Bush administration was distracted by another adversary from its alleged "axis of evil"—North Korea. War with Iraq was imminent, but war with North Korea seemed also possible as it restarted its nuclear weapons program. By the end of December 2002, the Bush administration's "Chicken Hawks" were convinced that the United States was militarily capable of fighting two simultaneous wars. Such talk of war occurred when the country was in a major recession and plagued by corporate scandals. Some argued that the external threats were diversions used to distract people's attention from the country's growing economic crises.

In December in spite of antiwar demonstrations in the United States and throughout the world, the United States and Great Britain continued to warn of a possible military conflagration with Iraq, while with North Korea the United States opted for a diplomatic solution. The U.S. foreign policy double standard was explainable: Iraq had oil, militarily Iraq was weaker, and the United States and Great Britain wanted hegemony over the petroleum-rich Middle East region. On the other hand, North Korea had no oil, yet had one of the world's largest militaries. It was assumed that it had at least two nuclear weapons in its arsenal and was developing more, and lastly, it had powerful friends—China and Russia. Even the once loyal South Korea sided with North Korea in advocating for a diplomatic resolution to the growing U.S.-induced military crisis.[166]

The U.S. War on Iraq

The culmination of the Bush war doctrine was the invasion of Iraq by the United States and Great Britain in March of 2003. During the months that preceded the invasion, a rapid deployment of troops had occurred and the bellicose rhetoric of the Bush administration had intensified to where the United Nations was powerless despite supporting opposition from France, Germany, Russia, China, México, Chile, and the rest of the UN members. Without the sanction of the UN, the United States and its allies invaded Iraq in late March. The pretext or justification was that Saddam Hussein's Iraq had weapons of mass destruction that represented a serious threat to the United States and to the Middle East and that Saddam had ties to Bin Laden's al Qaeda. The so-called Iraq War was declared over in a matter of a few weeks. The Iraqi armed forces were no match for the overwhelming military power of the invading mainly U.S. and British forces. On May 1, President Bush, after landing a jet he copiloted onto an aircraft carrier, in a presumptuous but premature manner before the media declared an end to major combat in Iraq. Officially the military occupation of Iraq involved at this stage some 150,000 mostly U.S. troops.[167] In the ensuing months, President Bush attempted to mask U.S. aggression against Iraq by declaring that the U.S. mission was to propagate the spread of democracy,[168] in other words, liberal capitalism.

During the ensuing months, the Bush administration's misguided Iraq policy produced a military quagmire as a result of well-organized Iraqi insurgency. From May to December, Iraqi urban guerilla warfare intensified to where coalition forces were under attack on a daily basis. In particular, the number of both Americans and Iraqis killed and wounded increased significantly. From the start of the war on March 20 to the end of December the United States suffered a total of 482 casualties[169] and over 1,500 wounded. Some eighty-two U.S. deaths alone occurred during the month of November. They were a result of road bombings and grenade and small arms fire by Iraqi insurgents.[170] By December the insurgents had seriously impeded U.S. reconstruction efforts, further exacerbating Iraq's worn-torn economy. Also by this time, many opponents of the administration's Iraq policy echoed memories of the failings of the Vietnam War.

The quagmire was not just military but political. Opposition by Iraqis to the U.S.-imposed coalition occupation increased dramatically. Bush administration officials had claimed prior to the invasion that the Iraqi people would greet the invading U.S. armies as liberators; the opposite became the case. Instead, they were greeted as unwelcome conquerors, despised and feared by most Iraqis, especially disgruntled Muslim clerics.[171] With the country's governmental infrastructure destroyed, chaos ensued in the form of the absence of electricity, water, and health care services to many of the areas. The United States imposed a colonial administration comprised of an interim twenty-four-member Governing Council of pro-U.S. Iraqis to assist U.S. civilian administrator L. Paul Bremer, who headed the Coalition Provisional Authority in the restoration of services and governance.

The Bush administration announced no exit strategy but allowed the newly formed colonial Governing Council[172] to restore the Iraqi police, rebuild the Iraqi army, draft a constitution, and hold national elections by June 2004. Despite domestic opposition, mainly from antiwar activists, in October the U.S. Congress voted overwhelmingly to pass President Bush's request for $87 billion for Iraq and Afghanistan.[173] Increasingly frustrated by the growing insurgency, the Bush administration became desperate for support from other countries, and the United Nations. By December 2003 the United States was in a conundrum: while it wanted help in the transition it did not want to cede control or share its power.[174] Thus, at the close of 2003, from both a military and political perspective, the United States faced a relentless insurgency characterized by increasing violence, attacks, casualties, and political instability—a debacle of its own creation.

Mexicano/Latino Reaction to Bush War Policies

Throughout the country, numerous white antiwar groups began to mobilize against the Bush administration's war policies by October 2002. There were few Latino organizations, politicians, or even activists who spoke out or mobilized against an impending war. In contrast to the Vietnam War protests, most university campuses were largely plagued by a pervasive political apathy among most students and faculty. This was particularly true for Mexicano and Latino students. Student organizations, such as MEChA, failed to mobilize in large numbers. Without the threat of being drafted, most Latino students adhered to the status quo of the Hispanic Generation, which de-emphasized activism and direct action. Latino faculty and administrators likewise were conspicuous by their absence.

The people in Aztlán's colonized barrios and *colonias* lacked activist progressive leadership and organizations and were largely quiescent on the issue of a U.S. war against Iraq. The possibilities of war in Iraq or President Bush's war doctrine were not on the radar screens of most Hispanic Generation organizations and leaders. Latino and Mexicano activism against the Bush war policies never reached the level of mobilization, militancy, and activism that characterized the Chicano Movement's anti–Vietnam War protests in 1970.

However, it would be incorrect to say that there was no organized Latino opposition to the Iraq war. A few scholars in California such as Jorge Mariscal, associate professor at UC San Diego; Jose Calderon; Carlos Muñoz; and me and former Movimiento antiwar activist leaders such as Rosalio Muñoz, Carlos Montez, and Jaime Cruz, started to organize by October 2002 against a possible war with Iraq. Mariscal and Muñoz organized a petition drive against the resolution's passage, which allowed President Bush unfettered authority to wage war against Iraq, unilaterally if necessary. They and others lobbied Latino congresspersons in California not to vote in support of the Bush war resolution. In Los Angeles, by December, Cruz and the National Chicano Moratorium Committee and Montez and the CSO Center had organized some antiwar activities. Ironically, in southern California at least, much of the leadership against the anti-Bush war policies came from *veteranos* (veterans) of the Chicano Movement, who still had the commitment and passion for change and a willingness to lead and organize.

The National Alliance for Human Rights (NAHR), under my direction, held press conferences,[175] an antiwar rally/prayer service in Riverside and San Bernardino,[176] town hall meetings, and teach-ins at the University of California, Riverside where I teach. NAHR also sent a letter to CHCI chair Congressman Silvestre Reyes, and each CHCI member was exhorted not to support the Bush war resolution.[177] In an unprecedented action, among the nineteen Latino voting members in the House of Representatives, fifteen Democrats voted "no" and three Republicans voted "yes." Congressman Solomon Ortiz, Democrat from Tejas, did not vote.[178] In addition, the NAHR sent a letter and petition signed by a host of organizations and individuals to President Vicente Fox requesting that México not support the Bush war resolution in the United Nation's Security Council.[179] In spite of strong opposition by Hispanic and Black caucuses, the Congress overwhelmingly approved Bush's war resolution.

In a poll of registered voters taken late in 2002 in both California and New York 60 percent of Latinos were against an attack on Iraq by the United States, only 32 percent were in favor, and 9 percent were undecided.[180] Another poll conducted in February 2003 by the Pew Hispanic Center in Washington, D.C., found that 48 percent of the four hundred Latinos surveyed supported invading Iraq to remove Saddam Hussein from power and 43 percent were against it. Fifty-two percent of U.S.-born Latinos supported it and 39 percent were against, versus 46 percent of foreign-born Latinos who supported war and 44 percent were against. A CBS/*New York Times* poll reported that 66 percent of the overall U.S. population supported a war.[181] Most polls taken during 2002–2003 showed that the percentage of Latinos who supported a U.S. war against Iraq was relatively lower than that of the overall populace, but was still high, considering their low socioeconomic status and the myriad of social problems they faced. Latinos were pretty evenly divided on the issue of President Bush's war policies and on the war itself. Thus, they were not exempt from the jingoist war contagion that was pervading the country.

In preparation for war with Iraq, during 2002–2003 the Bush administration prioritized the recruitment of Latinos into the armed forces. Recruiters conducted intensive drives in the high schools and painted an attractive picture to graduating seniors: they would be eligible for benefits, training, and college money, and for noncitizens they would expedite citizenship while on active duty. Many Latinos, especially poor Mexicanos, when recruited into the army or marines wound up in infantry, airborne, artillery, and armor units that in times of war have the highest casualty rates. Critical of the government efforts to recruit Latinos into the armed forces, Jorge Mariscal wrote, "Like many working class youth, Latinos and Latinas who buy into the vision of military service as a shortcut to college or job training are simply looking for a way to grab a piece of the

American Dream. But the reality of the Dream continued to be relatively distant for the Chicano/Mexicano community."[182] As was the case in previous wars, in military conflict the U.S. government coveted the participation of Latinos.

In 2002 Latinos comprised nearly 10 percent of the total armed forces. According to the Defense Department nearly 130,000 Latinos were on active duty. Blacks remained the largest minority in the armed forces with 22.5 percent of the total.[183] During the previous decade, the number of Latinos in the armed forces grew by 39 percent, and by 2002 Latinos made up 13 percent of the marines; 10 percent of the navy; 9 percent of the army; 6.4 percent of the coast guard; and 5.4 percent in the air force.[184] A study conducted by the Pew Hispanic Center in February 2003 found that although Latinos and blacks comprised 32 percent of all active duty personnel, they only represented a mere 12 percent of the officer corps.[185] There were also more than 37,000 lawful permanent residents—green card holders—in the U.S. military who were not U.S. citizens; about a third came from México and the rest were mostly from Latin America.[186] By late 2003, Latino congresspersons pushed bipartisan basis legislation to give green card-holder Latino soldiers their citizenship, which would impact three thousand regular U.S. military personnel and some thirteen thousand reservist migrants.[187]

Weeks prior to the start of the United States invasion of Iraq on March 20, 2003, protests and mobilizations increased dramatically. A growing antiwar contagion spread from Washington, D.C., to San Francisco to scores of cities throughout the country. Although not in large numbers, Mexicanos throughout Aztlán participated with the largely white-organized antiwar activities.[188] Mexicano activists who had been protesting the Bush war policies accelerated their own organizing activities.

In California in February 2003, for purposes of fostering a stronger Mexicano and Latino antiwar mobilization, the NAHR held a summit in Riverside to develop a strategic plan of mobilization against the Bush administration's war policies.[189] Attended by some two hundred people representing various groups, a consensus was reached to intensify Latino antiwar protests. The major outcome was a decision to hold a major march and rally in March in Los Angeles. Organized by a coalition of mostly Mexicano groups, the march duplicated the route taken during the August 29, 1970, march through East Los Angeles and the rally as well was held at Laguna Park. Only around two thousand people attended, indicative of the pervasive apathy among Mexicanos and Latinos toward the Iraq War issue. Particularly instrumental in organizing this event and other antiwar protests in Los Angeles was the coalition "Latinos against the War" led by activist leader Carlos Montes.[190]

With the start of war in late March and in the ensuing weeks, Mexicano and Latino activists and groups throughout the country participated in antiwar activities. The movement was hampered by a stultifying apathy and pervasive complacency, and the political reality was that even when the war started and Latino war casualties were being reported, no major Latino organization mobilized against the U.S. War on Iraq. During the phase of the war itself, Latino casualties were exorbitantly high. In April the media reported that 19 percent of those killed in combat in Iraq were Latinos. By December, however, the number of Latino causalities dropped to around 10 percent. After President Bush's premature announcement of the end of the war in May, antiwar protests in general declined including among Mexicanos and Latinos. Polls taken during the late months of 2003 showed that the majority of the public—up to 60 percent—supported the Bush administration's War against Iraq and U.S. occupation of the war-torn country. Thus, during the transition, the Mexicano "war paradox" surfaced once again: while they and other poor Latinos were being recruited in large numbers into the country's armed forces to fight and die abroad, at home in the impoverished barrios and *colonias*, they and their families lived under their own "occupation."

Other Salient Latino Issues and Events

From 2000 to 2002, advocacy activism among Mexicanos and Latinos—from local to national issues—reached a low point. Mexicanos in particular were poorly organized and lacked a "fear factor" and politically were not taken seriously by those in power. Lacking the requisite power capability, organization, and leadership, Mexicanos politically continued to suffer from the "Rodney Dangerfield Syndrome" of garnering "no respect." As a result, few policy issues were effectively dealt with. However, this is not to say that activism among Mexicanos was nonexistent. In comparison to the previous three epochs, during the transition, activism was less intense and effective. Beyond the two salient issues of immigration and the Bush administration's war policies, the following three issues produced transient sparks of advocacy.

The Los Angeles Janitor Strike

During April 2000, the L.A. janitor strike made history. After three years of careful and intensive planning of a well-organized strike, they won a major three-year contract. Under the auspices of the Service Employees International Union (SEIU), janitors who averaged an hourly wage of $5.75 and had no benefits initiated a strike that lasted most of April. It was successful in engendering support and participation from a number of celebrities that included Democratic presidential candidate Al Gore, U.S. senator Edward Kennedy, Rev. Jesse Jackson, Republican L.A. mayor Richard Riordan, Cardinal Roger M. Mahony,[191] and numerous organizations and unions as well. For days, janitors, most of whom were Latino and some undocumented, and their supporters wore their signature red T-shirts and caps and struck several targeted employers. Well-orchestrated direct action protests occurred. Rallies, marches, and picketing garnered wide media coverage and extensive support and empathy throughout southern California.

After a few weeks of intensive pressure, the SEIU under the leadership of Mike Garcia succeeded in negotiating a three-year contract that was approved by the two thousand striking janitors. While not a comprehensive contract, it did, however, increase their hourly wage by 25 percent over three years. Janitors in outlying areas got a 30-cent raise the first year, while those who lived in the highly unionized downtown Century City got a 70-cent boost. Wages for all janitors increased for the next two years by 60 cents per hour. All janitors received a $500 dollar bonus, contractors agreed to absorb increases in health care, and by the end of the contract janitors were scheduled to receive five days of sick leave.[192] The janitors' strike educated the country's labor leadership on the value and importance of organizing migrant workers and assisted in energizing numerous other unionizing organizing efforts.

The Bracero "Recuperation Pay" Issue

Another major issue for Latinos was the retrieval of back wage savings that were owed by México's government to *braceros*, when they had worked as contracted guest workers in the United States. This issue emerged in March 2001 when several *braceros* met and decided to organize with the intent of recuperating past wage savings for some four hundred *braceros*. The issue has its historical roots in the Bracero Program (1942–1964), but focused specifically on the years 1942 to 1949, when the Mexican government retained some 10 percent of their wages—with the legal requirement that their saved wages would be returned to them upon their return to México. Unfortunately for the *braceros*, the Mexican government never returned their deducted savings.[193]

The organizing effort developed increasing momentum with the formation in 2002 of the Alianza Bracero Proa (ABP), a coalition of several groups from both México and the United States. Alleging some $500 million were owed to them, the ABP accelerated their binational crusade and lobbying. The ABP specifically directed its efforts at the Mexican government and Wells Fargo Bank, which had processed the transfer of saved wages to México, and enlisted general public support of both countries for their cause. In March 2001 the ABP filed a class action lawsuit in federal court on behalf of the four hundred thousand former *braceros*. Moreover, rallies, town hall meetings, press conferences, and marches were held and turned into political pressure. Several Latino organizations and *politicos* in California came out in support of the ABP. California Assembly majority leader Marcos Firebaugh introduced legislation (AB2913) that would extend the statute of limitations to December 5, 2005. By late August, the bill had cleared both the State Assembly and Senate and awaited the signature of Governor Davis.[194] That same month, Judge Charles Breyer ruled that the *braceros* were not entitled to compensation by Wells Fargo or by the governments of México and the United States and that México was immune from being sued. The ABP responded to the court's decision by calling for a boycott of Wells Fargo Bank.[195]

During 2003, much of the ABP's organizing and lobbying efforts occurred in México. Meetings with Fox administration officials and congressional leaders were held as well as marches and other direct actions. Internally, the ABP was plagued by leadership schisms and factionalism concerning its legitimate leadership. By December there were three factions within the ABP competing for the *bracero* issues leadership. One of the factions led by Ventura Gutierrez was engaged in pressuring direct actions in México against the Fox administration because of its unwillingness to address the *bracero* back pay issue.

The UFW's Struggle for Binding Arbitration

As the *bracero* issue was in high gear so were the UFW's organizing efforts for binding arbitration. The UFW in August 2002 mounted a major statewide mobilization in California. A reinvigorated UFW mounted the largest Latino mobilization of the three-year period that briefly rekindled *el espirito del* Movimiento (the spirit of the Movement). The UFW sought approval of legislation that would give more teeth to the Agricultural Labor Relations Act of 1974. Democratic state senator John Burton introduced legislation (SB1736), which authorized the Agricultural Labor Relations Board (ALRB) to impose "binding arbitration" when unions and growers reach an impasse in contract negotiations.

In August, the UFW unleashed a fury of direct action activities in support of SB1736. On August 19 some thirty legislators, mostly Latinos, held a twenty-four-hour symbolic hunger strike.[196] Daily vigils were held by the UFW at the footsteps of the capitol building in Sacramento. The UFW undertook a historical replay of the 1966 ten-day 150-mile march from Delano to Sacramento. This time, however, the march was from Merced to Sacramento. The stated purpose was to pressure Democratic governor Gray Davis into signing the controversial workers' bill. On August 25, the march of a few hundred turned into a massive march of some five thousand as it entered Sacramento led by UFW president Arturo Rodriguez and joined by UFW cofounder Dolores Huerta and numerous luminaries. The march culminated in a large rally in front of the state capitol building steps where numerous speakers added their support for the UFW and lauded the pending legislation.[197] Clearly, however, the march also reignited the Chavez spirit and reasserted the UFW into the Democratic political conscious-ness.[198]

As of September, Governor Davis was facing reelection in November 2002 and the legislation was at an impasse. In late August, state senator John Burton watered down SB1736 and, supported by the UFW, introduced a new bill, SB1756. The latter legislation eliminated binding arbitration in favor of the use of a mediator, placed limits on the number of contracts the UFW could dispute, and "sunsetted" the application of the legislation until the governor reauthorized it for up to five years.[199] By September the two bills had passed both chambers of the legislature and awaited Governor Davis's signature. Again, this put Governor Davis in a political quandary. To sign either SB1736 or SB1756 meant alienating the growers who were Davis's powerful financial backers, who had contributed nearly $2 million to his reelection war chest.[200] After weeks of relentless pressure from the UFW, for example, daily vigils at the capitol, Governor Davis signed SB1756, which was redesignated SB1156 in late September. The 3,500-member Western Growers Association reacted angrily and threatened to challenge the leg-islation on constitutional grounds. This was an impressive political victory that gave new life to the fledgling UFW.[201] These issues had an important impact on the Mexicano political experience during the transition period.

The Mexicano Political Experience in Transition

Hispanic Political Culture in Flux

The various existent political subcultures obviated the unification of Latinos and the creation of a common political agenda. Politically, however, the ethos of the Hispanic Generation (HG) was still the most pervasive among Latinos and less so among Mexicanos. Their emphasis was still on the individual, materialism, and liberal capitalism. From a class perspective, both the Mexicano and Latino lower and middle classes, especially of the nascent *ricos*, were still deeply infused with the values, beliefs, and ideals of liberal capitalism. Corporations' positive view of self-interest, greed, and profit still influenced the HG through its economic and political penetration and manipulation of the Hispanic market. It collaborated and financially supported countless events organized from local to national organizations. Both the white and Latino media reinforced the pro-system values of the Hispanic Generation and covered its leaders and organizations. Governmental structures continued to be supportive of the ethos of the HG. Likewise numerous so-called buffer and "want to be white": Mexicano and Latino organizations and politicos maintained their pro-system values. The Republican Party's inroads among Hispanics were indicative of the HG's pro-system ethos.

In spite of the dominance of the HG during the transition, the clash of Generations became more acute.[202] From an organizing perspective this became problematic because of some of the differences in their cultural values. Some Mexicanos, for example, still identified themselves as Mexican American, with the acculturated ethos of the Mexican American Generation (MAG). In decreasing numbers, some Mexicanos still identified as Chicanos and with the ethos of the Chicano Generation (CG), particularly with Chicanismo. Increasingly, however, this created a cultural synthesis and renaissance, which enhanced the continued rise of the Neo-Méx Generation (NMG).

The NMG with its ethos predicated on Mexicano nationalism gained ground. Among first-generation Mexicanos, it was the dominant political generation. As a subpolitical culture, as the Migrant Exodus from México intensified and the population swelled, so did the maintenance of the Mexicano's culture, characterized by a zealous adherence to its values, mores, customs, music, food, retention of the Spanish language, and a powerful dosage of nationalism. In most cases, they categorically rejected the ethos of the HG with its propensities for integration and assimilation into U.S. culture. Politically, however, the NMG influenced by México's semiauthoritarian parochial/subject political culture was still plagued by an estrangement or aversion to ballot box or organizational politics. While some participated in Mexican-based organizations, the overwhelming majority rejected political involvement.

Buttressed by a growing sense of "group consciousness,"[203] the NMG was nurtured by a multiplicity of factors: by a Mexicano population increase that by and large was committed to the preservation of its Méxicanidad; by a growing attitude among some Mexicanos that Aztlán was not part of a foreign country, but still a vital part of México; by increasing white nativism and racism, which in turn served to reinforce the maintenance of the Mexicano culture, heritage, and the Spanish language; by countless Spanish-speaking media outlets, for example, television, radio, newspapers, magazines, which also served to reinforce its ethos; by the establishment of a myriad of businesses, organizations, and churches that were Mexicano-based; by increased Mexican government involvement in the political, economic, and cultural affairs of Mexicanos in the United States; and by the popularity of the Mexicano culture in the United States via its food, music, liquor, and particularly its festive cultural celebrations[204] and growing literary works.

The HG was challenged by the rise of the Latino Generation (hereafter identified as the Lat-Generation or LG), which in reality was a cultural modification of the former. By the turn of the twenty-first century, the terms *Hispanic* and *Latino* were used interchangeably, but by 2003 *Latino* was more in vogue. As explained previously, the LG differed from the HG in its overall focus on Latin America rather than Spain. In the words of Jose Cuello, "'Hispanic' was rejected "as a colonial imposition by the government."[205] The HG was perceived as culturally being too Spanish-oriented and dominated by the U.S. white experience. Unlike the HG, the LG did not deny the indigenous or mestizo experiences of Latin America. In fact, it adhered to a "cultural eclecticism," a pan-Latinoism predicated on America Latina's (Latin America's) cultural and historical experiences. While it embraced acculturation and rejected assimilation, it adhered to a moderate to liberal capitalist ideology.

Mexicanos and Latinos in general were culturally changing the way the country looked, felt and thought, ate, danced, and voted.[206] Because of Latinoización—from California to New York and most states in between—the country experienced an unprecedented Latino cultural transformation. The impact was so profound that the country's once white Protestant ethos was gradually being altered, becoming increasingly "Latinoized nationally and Mexicanoized regionally." The United States by the end of 2003 was experiencing an irreversible cultural transition to a "Latin America." The transformation was evident via the socialization power of various media, particularly with the crossover music of Santana, Jennifer Lopez, Ricky Martin, Juan Gabriel, Marc Anthony, and many other artists as well as television's Billboard Latin Music Awards, Alma Awards, Latin Grammies,[207] and the successful *George Lopez Show*. Increased Latino visibility in the music, film, and television industries also reinforced identification with the Lat-Generation and enhanced group consciousness and identity.

With the constant influx of migrants more Mexicanos and Latinos sought to retain their use of the Spanish language. The U.S. Census Bureau reported in 2002 that the percentage of the country's population that spoke Spanish at home rose between 1990 and 2000. In California some 12.4 million residents said they spoke a language other than English at home, and of that total, 65 percent spoke Spanish.[208] Recent arrivals from Latin America still used "national origin" as their primary identification, for example, as the Mexicano population increased so did their sense of "group consciousness." As they became regionally more concentrated in Aztlán, so did their efforts to assert and preserve their Mexicano culture and to retain their Spanish language.

For some Mexicanos born in the United States, these competing Generational identities led to the question, "What should we call ourselves?" The identity crisis prevalent in the past epochs continued well into the transition. Most first-generation Mexicanos were proud of their Mexicandidad; this was not the case with some Mexicanos born in the United States. Yet some second- and third-generation Mexicanos refused to identify as Mexicanos and perceived it to be a pejorative term. They opted for other existent terms: *Mexican American, Latino* or *Hispanic*, or *Raza*. A similar pattern existed among other Latino subgroups who sought to maintain their own sense of identity and culture. Some, however, refused to identify either as Latinos or Hispanics, but rather chose to assert their own subgroup identity, for example, *Salvadoreño, Puertorriqueño*.

Yet some migrants, especially from México and Central America, refused to identify either with *Hispanic* or *Latino* or their respective Generations. The 2002 National Survey of Latinos released by the Pew Hispanic Center and Kaiser Family Foundation revealed this fact. According to the survey only about a fourth identified with either term. The Pew study's findings also revealed that some 57 percent of Hispanics with U.S.-born parents identified themselves as "Americans," while 54 percent of those recently arrived immigrants identified themselves with the country of origin, and about a fifth identified themselves as Americans. Also, some 89 percent believed that those who migrated into the United States needed to learn English in order to succeed. The survey also revealed that from a political perspective Latinos were a hybrid—a mixture of liberal to conservative values and beliefs. On issues of abortion and divorce, foreign-born Latinos found them less acceptable than native-born Latinos. On the issue of homosexuality, 20 percent of the former found it acceptable compared to 33 percent of the latter, 38 percent of whites, and 14 percent of blacks. The majority of foreign-born Latinos believed that children should live with their parents until they get married.[209] Yet on a number of social issues, such as discrimination, immigration, and education, foreign-born Latinos tended to be moderate to liberal in their views and politics. Hispanic journalists like Ruben Navarrette, Jr., among others, concurred with the study's findings.[210]

The clash of Generational political subcultures was particularly evident in the use of "Spanglish," a hybrid language that mixed both Spanish and English. The reality is that its usage goes back to the nineteenth century, with the arrival of whites to Aztlán. In the ensuing decades this bastardization of Spanish occurred especially among second-generation Mexicanos. Spanglish was particularly popular among young urban Mexicanos and Latinos who were U.S.-born. It was a manifestation of the Latino transformation, adherence to a form of bilingualism by second-generation young people between the ages of fourteen and twenty-eight who, according to the Pew Hispanic Center, tended to speak both Spanish and English. The usage of Spanglish became a topic of controversy, and academic investigation.[211] For U.S. business corporations, the burgeoning Latino population offered a lucrative new market for exploitation and profit. In short, because of the burgeoning Mexicano and Latino demographic and cultural transformation, it was evident in 2003 that the United States was in transition to becoming a "bilingual country," dominated by both English and Spanish.

Hispanic Ballot Box Politics

During the transition period, the ethos of the HG was dominant in the politics practiced by both Mexicanos and Latinos. Ballot box politics was still predicated on the status quo maintenance, and with few exceptions Mexicano and Latino *politicos* (politicians) adhered to "buffer" political roles. They immersed themselves in the roles of power wielders and brokers on behalf of the divergent Latino communities rather than that of agents of social change. Most *politicos* had yet to transform themselves into viable political assets for the communities they supposedly represented. Seldom did they successfully address the people's social problems. In most cases, they continued to be potential rather than an actual political asset for the community, which was particularly evident at the federal and state levels of governance.

The 2000 Presidential Election

At the national level, during the 2000 presidential election, the Latino vote was sought after by both Democrats and Republicans as well as the Green Party. The Latino vote increased to where it could become a swing vote in U.S. national politics. Some 7.7 million Mexicanos/Latinos were registered to vote, making them 5.5 percent of voters.[212] An estimated 5,934,000 Latino votes were cast in the 2000 presidential election, an increase of 1,006,000 over the 4,928,000 Latino votes cast in the 1996 presidential election. There was a 20 percent increase in Latino votes cast from 1996 to 2000; whereas, for non-Latinos the increase was a mere 5 percent.[213] Presidential candidates Democrat Al Gore and Republican George W. Bush made serious efforts to secure the Latino vote. Millions of dollars were spent by both major parties in soliciting the Mexicano/Latino vote. Television, radio, and newspaper spots and ads in Spanish were purchased; political literature was developed and distributed in both English and Spanish; endorsements were secured from Latino organizations; and both Gore and Bush made appearances in major Latino media markets, such as Los Angeles, San Antonio, Chicago, New York, and Miami. Both candidates spoke broken Spanish, which signaled the growing importance of the Mexicano/Latino electorate. Even though Green Party presidential candidate Ralph Nader did a better job in addressing the diverse issues that impacted Latinos, he lacked the financial resources and campaign infrastructure and was not able to develop an effective Latino voter mobilization.

The results of the 2000 presidential election proved to be unprecedented. While Al Gore won the popular vote, George W. Bush won the electoral college vote. Gore received 51,003,894 votes to Bush's 50,459,211 votes, and Nader garnered 2,834,410 votes. Gore thus won the popular vote by 544,683 votes. With 270 electoral votes needed, Bush won with 271 to Gore's 266. La Florida became the balance of power in deciding the 2000 presidential election: Bush beat Gore by a mere 537 votes, giving Bush La Florida's 25 electoral votes.[214] Although Democrats contested the results, the U.S. Supreme Court upheld the results of La Florida's election. George W. Bush became the country's third presidential candidate to lose the popular vote but win the presidency by a majority of the electoral votes. Moderates to progressives alleged that the Republicans stole the election by intentionally disenfranchising thousands of black voters and rigging the voting machines in La Florida. In short, they believe that the Bush presidency is illegitimate.

In spite of the controversial results, the Mexicano/Latino vote had a significant impact. Latinos overwhelmingly voted for Al Gore, giving him 62 percent of the vote, but this was well short of Bill Clinton's 72 percent in the 1996 presidential election. George W. Bush received 35 percent of the Mexicano/Latino vote, which was a significant improvement over the 1996 presidential candidate, Bob Dole, who received only 21 percent.[215] The actual percentages, however, are debated because of conflicting sources. The *Los Angeles Times* exit poll showed that 61 percent of Mexicanos/Latinos voted for Gore, 38 percent for Bush, and 1 percent for Nader.[216] According to the William C. Velasquez Institute exit polls, in California, of the 2.3 million Mexicano/Latino registered voters, 70.4 percent or 1,619,000 voted: Gore garnered 73.5 percent to Bush's 24.2 percent. In Tejas out of the 1.95 million registered, 1,002,000 voted, which translated into a 51.4 percent Mexicano/Latino voter turnout. Bush received 32.5 percent to Gore's 65.7 percent, and other 1.7 percent.[217] On a regional analysis, Bush did best in the South, where he received 48 percent of the vote. In La Florida alone, he received 49 percent of the Latino vote. Gore did best in the East, where he garnered 74 percent of their vote, while Bush secured only 22 percent. In New York State alone Gore got 80 percent of the Latino vote.[218] Exit polls by Voter News Service estimated that the Latino vote accounted for 7 percent of the total 2000 presidential vote.[219] Also on the positive side, there was a 20 percent increase in Latino votes cast from 1996 to 2000, whereas for non-Latinos the increase was a mere 5 percent.[220]

On the negative side, the 2000 presidential election results revealed that Latinos continued to have low voter turnouts. One glaring revelation: only one of every four voting-age adults in predominantly Mexicano/Latino neighborhoods voted, significantly below the national rate of 51 percent. According to an Associated Press analysis of the border states, Aztlán had poor Latino voter turnouts: California, 22 percent; Arizona, 26.6 percent; Nuevo México, 19.0 percent; and Tejas, 25.6 percent. Even those states outside Aztlán did not do well: Illinois, 19.6 percent; New York, 27.2 percent; New Jersey, 26.7 percent; and La Florida, 31.8 percent.[221] Those states heavily populated by Mexicanos, Central Americans, and Puertorriqueño had lower voter turnouts, except La Florida, which had a large Cubano population with higher levels of education and income. Latino hopes for the political future were dimmed in 2002 with the release of a study that concluded that young Latino youth between the ages of eighteen and twenty-four voted in numbers 12 percent lower than their black and white counterparts.[222]

Mexicano and Latino Political Representation at the Federal Level

During the transition, the total number of Mexicano and Latino Elected Officials (MLEOs) increased. That year the total MLEOs numbered some 5,135 and in 2001 increased to 5,205.[223] However, in 2003 the NALEO Educational Fund (NEF) reported without an explanation a major decrease to 4,624.[224] In 2003 95 percent of the nation's Latino officeholders were Democrats.[225] The NEF explained the fluctuation in the number of MLEOs due to changes in the reporting of data. Meanwhile at the federal level, there were no MLEOs in the U.S. Senate or Mexicanos or Latinos on the U.S. Supreme Court. In 2002 in Nuevo México, Mexicana Democrat Gloria Tristani, the granddaughter of legendary and long-time U.S. senator Dennis Chavez, ran for the U.S. Senate, but lost to well-financed Republican incumbent Pete Domenici.[226] In December 2003 former U.S. secretary Rosario Marin declared her candidacy as a Republican for the U.S. Senate.

Within the Bush administration there was only one Latino in a cabinet level position, Mel Martinez, who was born in Cuba and served as secretary of Housing and Urban Development (HUD). Alberto Gonzalez, a Mexicano from Tejas, was appointed by President Bush as his special legal counsel. Linda Chavez, also a Mexicana, was nominated for the cabinet position of secretary of labor but withdrew after a scandal revealed that she had employed an undocumented migrant in her household. In late 2002, President Bush's appointment of Miguel Estrada to the Appellate Court met stiff opposition from a number of organizations, including the Congressional Hispanic Caucus Institute (CHCI), the Mexican American Legal Defense and Education Fund (MALDEF), National Council of La Raza (NCLR), Latino Lawyers Association (LLA),[227] and various prominent individuals. Scholar Rodolfo Acuña wrote a scathing public letter in opposition to the Estrada nomination, which ended in failure in 2003. President Bush also appointed Mexicano Antonio (Tony) Garza from Tejas as ambassador to México. He had served in the Texas Railroad Commission, which oversaw the state's oil and gas industry.[228]

By the summer of 2003 both Democrat and Republican parties actively sought support from Mexicano/Latino voters in preparation for the 2004 presidential elections. Both parties were cognizant of their potential for becoming the swing vote in the country's next election. The Mexicano/Latino vote by 2003 numbered some eight million nationwide and was significant in states with large electoral votes like California, Tejas, New York, La Florida, Illinois, and Michigan. Concomitantly, it also had a major electoral presence in smaller states such as Nuevo México, Arizona, Nevada, Colorado, Washington, and New Jersey. Polls taken in late 2003 suggested that the Mexicano/Latino vote was up for grabs. A *New York Times*/CBS News poll released four months before the election gave President Bush a 52 percent approval rating from Mexicanos/Latinos. However, the poll indicated that only 21 percent would vote for Bush. A generic Democratic candidate would beat Bush handily 43 percent to 31 percent, and 45 percent were undecided. Most polls concluded that Mexicanos/Latinos tended to be more conservative than other ethnic/racial groups. One poll reported that they favored Democrats by a 2 to 1 margin—50 percent to 19 percent—suggesting that the Democrats came closer to representing their values and needs.[229]

Recognizing the growing power of the Latino vote, six declared Democratic presidential candidates in June 2003 attended a forum moderated by Nuevo México governor Bill Richardson at NALEO's twentieth annual conference in Phoenix. Some spoke in Spanish and promised to overhaul the country's immigration policy and enlarge economic opportunities.[230] Increasingly, white, black, and even Mexicano "want to be white" *politicos*, among others, were learning to speak some

Spanish in the hope of garnering support from the growing Latino electorate. At the national level, a PAC called Democratas Unidos (United Democrats), associated with the centrist Democratic Leadership Council, was formed to galvanize the growing Mexicano/Latino vote for 2004.[231] By December 2003, six of the twenty-member Congressional Hispanic Caucus had endorsed Vermont governor Howard Dean.[232]

The number of MLEOs in the House of Representatives increased from nineteen in 2000 to twenty-two in 2002. They comprised a mere 5.5 percent of the 435 congressional members. The three newly elected Latino congresspersons were California Democrat Linda T. Sanchez, sister of incumbent Democrat Loretta Sanchez; La Florida Republican Mario Diaz-Balart, brother of Republican incumbent Lincoln Diaz-Balart;[233] and from Arizona, one-time Raza Unida Party (RUP) leader Raul Grijalva, who had turned Democrat. If Portuguese Democrat Dennis Cardoza of California was added, the number of MLEOs in Congress would have increased to twenty-three; however, the NALEO Latino Educational Fund Directory claimed only twenty-two.[234] According to NALEO, California increased its Latino congressional delegation from six to seven; Arizona from one to two; and La Florida from two to three. Tejas remained with six; New York, two; New Jersey, one; and Illinois, one.[235]

Representation at the State Levels

At the state level, prior to the November 2002 election, not one Latino served as governor. However, in Nuevo México former Democratic secretary of energy Bill Richardson defeated Republican John Sanchez in November 2002 by garnering 56.5 to 39 percent of the vote, making him the country's only Mexicano/Latino governor. He became the first Mexicano to serve as governor since Toney Anaya held the statehouse from 1983 to 1986. Five Nuevo Mexicanos were also elected to statewide posts, which no other state in the country could match. Reelected were Attorney General Patricia Madrid and Secretary of State Rebecca Vigil-Giron. Nonincumbent winners included State Auditor Domingo Martinez, Treasurer Robert Vigil, and Public Lands Commissioner Art Trujillo.[236] In California, Governor Davis named former UFW cofounder Dolores Huerta to the University of California's Board of Regents, which oversees the eleven-campus university system, in 2003.

In Tejas, Democrat millionaire Tony Sanchez made an unsuccessful and costly bid to become the first Mexicano governor in the state's history. He was badly beaten by Republican incumbent governor Rick Perry who received 58 percent of the votes to Sanchez's 40 percent,[237] who lost by some 800,000 votes. Sanchez, a rich oil tycoon, spent a total of $87 million in his campaign, some $59 million coming from his own personal fortune. His election bid proved to be "wildly dirty" and the most expensive gubernatorial race in the country's history. His loss proved that regardless of the millions Sanchez spent, white Tejanos were not ready for a Mexicano to be governor of Tejas. In one view, the "Remember the Alamo" gringo racist syndrome still permeated Tejas politics and thwarted Latino election bids. On the positive side of the political equation, the San Antonio-based William Velasquez Institute estimated that out of a total of five million votes cast, the Mexicano vote numbered some 997,500 or 21.8 percent of the total. Some 87 percent of it went to Sanchez and 40 percent of those Latinos registered cast ballots, beating the overall average of 36.4 percent. This was a very significant increase from 1998, when only 26.7 percent of Mexicanos went to the polls.[238]

In California, Green Party gubernatorial candidate Peter Camejo received 5.3 percent of the total vote. Even though his politics and the platform of the Green Party were compatible with the concerns of poor and middle-class Latinos, such as immigration, jobs, and the environment, he lost the Latino vote by a large margin.[239] Camejo lost to incumbent Democrat Gray Davis, who won reelection with 47 percent of the vote to Republican Bill Simon's 42 percent. Interestingly, in late September, the twenty-two-member Latino Legislative Caucus was led by the protest efforts of Assemblyman Gil Cedillo to deny Davis its endorsement. This was the result of his veto of Cedillo's measure that would have allowed undocumented migrants to get their driver's licenses. By early October, however, the unity evaporated when a press conference was called by seventeen of the twenty-two caucus members; led by Senator Richard Polanco they endorsed Davis for governor.[240] According to *Los Angeles Times* exit polls, Latinos gave Davis 65 percent of their vote; Simon, 24 percent; and others (including Camejo) 11 percent.[241] Cruz Bustamante won reelection as lieutenant governor with 49.4 percent of the vote over Republican Bruce McPherson's 41.7 percent. Republican Gary Mendoza lost the race for California insurance commissioner by garnering only 41.7 percent of the vote against Democrat John Garamendi's 46.6 percent.[242]

As a result of the successful recall of Democratic governor Gray Davis by Republicans in 2003, Lt. Governor Cruz Bustamante made an unsuccessful bid for governor. He sought to become California's first Mexicano governor since 1875 when Republican Romualdo Pacheco held the governor's office for nine months.[243] From August to November, the great Latino mobilization for Bustamante never materialized. While various groups, such as the NAHR, sought to ignite it and pushed for a "no vote on the recall, a yes vote on Bustamante, and a no vote on Proposition 54," which would prohibit state and other public entities from collecting information on race, ethnicity, and national origin,[244] Mexicano and Latino voters did not vote for him in great numbers. The reasons were several, but one was a charge by conservative Republican gubernatorial candidate Tom McClintock and the media that also played the nativist "brown card," alleging that Bustamante supported the so-called separatist radical student organization MEChA, which McClintock equated to the Ku Klux Klan.[245]

More importantly, Davis and much of the state Democrat Party leadership failed to give strong support to Bustamante's gubernatorial bid. Neither Davis nor several influential Democrats, for example, Senator Feinstein or former vice president Al Gore, endorsed Bustamante. In fact, it can be argued that they and others deliberately ostracized Bustamante. He also failed to secure support of some influential Mexicano and Latino political and labor leaders, such as UFW cofounder Dolores Huerta, and others, who feared that Bustamante's gubernatorial bid would jeopardize Davis's own efforts to defeat the recall. Bustamante ran on a populist theme advocating higher taxes on corporations and more regulation of oil companies, and was critical of Wal-Mart for not providing health care to its nonunion workers,[246] but in the end the so-called Latino political giant was divided and failed to consolidate itself in support of Bustamante. Prior to the special election, a *Los Angeles Times* survey reported that 54 percent of Latino voters supported Bustamante but that 37 percent planned to vote for either Schwarzenegger or McClintock.[247]

The special recall election held on October 7 revealed that Mexicano/Latino voters did not demonstrate swing vote capability. Out of a field of some 135 candidates, Schwarzenegger was the gubernatorial victor: he garnered 49 percent of the vote to Bustamante's 31 percent and McClintock's 13 percent. The recall passed by 54 percent to 46 percent, and Proposition 54 was defeated 62 percent to 38 percent.[248] Mexicano/Latino voters proved that they were not a cohesive voting bloc. On the issue of the recall, they split almost down the middle, 54 percent against and 46 percent in support; 51 percent voted for Bustamante, 33 percent for Schwarzenegger, and 7 percent for other candidates.[249] Thus, the special recall election buttressed the notion that politically Latinos were a heterogeneous group and had yet to be a viable political power in California politics.

During this period, the number of MLEOs at the state legislative level increased. As a result of the 2002 elections, they increased to a total of 217; a decade ago they had been 147. In 2002, 158 served in the lower house and 59 in the State Senate. Moreover, of the state legislators, 184 were Democrat and 32 Republican. Since 2000, Democrats had gained six House seats and five Senate seats, while Republicans had a gain of one Assembly seat. By the end of 2003, the total number of MLEOs in the Senate and Assembly/House seats were as follows: Arizona, five state senators and ten state representatives (fifteen); California, nine state senators, eighteen state representatives (twenty-seven); Colorado, one state senator, seven state representatives (eight); Nevada, one state senator, one representative (two); Nuevo México, fifteen state senators, thirty state representatives (forty-five); and Tejas, seven state senators, thirty state representatives (thirty-seven); and Utah had only one in the State Senate.[250] Thus, overall, Nuevo México had the largest number of MLEOs with forty-five, followed by Tejas with thirty-seven and California with twenty-seven.

Throughout Aztlán, despite some increases, no dramatic MLEOs gains were made in 2002 in the region's state legislatures. Arizona gained one Latino seat in the House and none in the State Senate; while Nuevo México lost one in the House and no gain was made in the State Senate. Colorado lost one in the House, but gained one in the State Senate. California lost one in the Assembly yet gained two in the State Senate. Meanwhile, Tejas gained two in the House and none in the State Senate. Outside of Aztlán, several states, including Connecticut, Delaware, Florida, Illinois, Indiana, Kansas, Massachusetts, Michigan, Minnesota, New Hampshire, New Jersey, New York, North Carolina, Oregon, and Pennsylvania had Latinos either in the state legislature or State Senate or both.[251]

Local Representation Increases

It was at the local level of governance that the number of MLEOs increased the most. A political trend became evident by 2002, especially throughout Aztlán, in which the transfer of power at the local level from whites to Mexicanos accelerated. While at the state and federal levels there was a total of 146 Latino elected officials; at the local level the total number was 5,059. This included 403 county officials; 1,443 municipal officials; 454 judicial and law enforcement officials; 2,557 school board members; and 125 special districts officials.[252]

By 2002 several cities had Mexicano or Latino mayors and other high-ranking officeholders. Two Mexicanos in Tejas, Ed Garza in San Antonio and Ray Caballero in El Paso in 2001, were elected mayors. In a landslide victory (59 percent to 29 percent) over his opponent Tim Bannwolf, Garza was the second Mexicano in recent political history to be elected mayor of San Antonio.[253] In a nonpartisan election in El Paso, Ray Caballero defeated former mayor Larry Francis by a substantial margin of 63 percent to 37 percent. In a reelection bid in McAllen, Tejas mayor Leo Montalvo also won. Meanwhile, Martin Chavez was elected mayor of Albuquerque, Nuevo México, in a seven-candidate race, defeating incumbent mayor James Baca with a mere 30.6 percent of the total vote.

In Los Angeles, former California Speaker of the State Assembly Antonio Villaraigosa, after earlier defeating Congressman Xavier Becerra and three others for the mayoral nomination,[254] lost a hard-fought election to City Attorney James Hahn by a margin of 45.2 percent to 54.8 percent. According to Steve Lopez of the *Los Angeles Times*, even though Latinos comprised some 41 percent of the eligible voters and whites 34 percent, Latinos only accounted for 22 percent of the turnout. Southwest Voter Registration and Education Project president Antonio Gonzalez stated, "About 20.5% of all registered voters [were] Latino, and 22% of all votes cast were by Latinos."[255] Later in 2002 in Houston, the Cubano city councilman Orlando Sanchez was defeated 58 percent to 48 percent in his bid for mayor of the country's fourth largest city. In January 2002, Domingo Garcia lost his bid to become mayor of Dallas, garnering only 11.1 percent of the primary vote.[256] Rockford Delgadillo, candidate for Los Angeles city attorney, that same year beat Mike Feuer by a margin of 51.6 percent to 48.4 percent of the vote.[257] In 2003, Villaraigosa was elected to the Los Angeles City Council. These races clearly illustrate two cardinal points: one, the Mexicano and Latino's growing political clout, and two, a transfer of power from whites to Latinos had begun, especially with Mexicanos in Aztlán.

Furthermore, in a number of school districts, Mexicanos and Latinos became presidents of school boards and in several of them constituted new majorities. They were challenged by complex educational issues, which routinely produced few solutions. In many instances, those who sought to effect change found themselves under attack by conservative and nativist political forces. One such case was that of school board member Nativo Lopez in Santa Ana, California, who was successfully recalled in February 2003, due to his progressive stance on preserving bilingual education. A *Los Angeles Times* analysis concluded that even in predominantly Mexicano/Latino precincts nine in ten voters cast votes to recall Lopez. Voter turnout in those precincts ranged from 39 percent to 48 percent.[258] A few local *politicos* also became embroiled in scandals and controversies over alleged charges of corruption served to especially reinforce the stereotype among whites that Latinos were ill fit for governance. With local governments dependent on state and federal funding, city councils, school boards, and even county governments were limited in their capacity to bring about major change.[259]

Voter participation among Mexicanos/Latinos in comparison to other ethnic/racial groups remained low. By 2001, they had eclipsed blacks as the largest minority group. In eligible voter numbers, this translated to a figure of some twenty-three million Mexicanos/Latinos of voting age. A year later (2002), they only made up 5.4 percent of the electorate nationwide, compared to 80.7 percent for whites. The 2000 presidential election revealed that Mexicano/

Latino naturalized citizens voted in higher percentages than native-born voters. This trend was evident in the 1996, 1998, and 2000 elections where naturalized citizens outvoted native-born voters by six to ten percentage points. It was also evident that voter participation was higher among those who were older, better educated, and had higher incomes. For example, 60 percent of seniors voted in 2000, compared to 26 percent of young Mexicano/Latino adults. Also, 68 percent of those with a college education voted, compared to 34 percent of those with only a high school education.[260] Those with higher incomes were twice as likely to vote than those with lower incomes.

In California, the share of Mexicano/Latino voters dropped from 13 percent to 10 percent, which suggested that Democrats had failed to energize Mexicano/Latino voters.[261] Even though in California they comprised over a third of the state's population they cast a mere one-tenth of its vote, which suggested that their electoral clout lagged far behind their share of the population.[262] According to a study conducted by demographers Jack Citrin and Benjamin Highton of the Public Policy Institute of California, "Latinos participate at lower levels primarily because they are less likely to be citizens and secondarily because many of them lack the socio-economic resources that boost political interest and participation." The study further revealed that 46 percent of California Mexicanos/Latinos were not citizens. In addition, that they were on average younger, poorer, and less educated, all of which led to lower political participation.[263]

At the national level as well, a cardinal impediment to present and future Latino political empowerment was the high number of noncitizens. *The Almanac of Latino Politics 2002–2004* reported that of the estimated 15,664,000 Latinos of voting age in the 2000 presidential election, 8,440,000 or 54 percent could not participate because they were not citizens. In addition, another 5,612,000 were eligible to vote but were not registered. The number of Latino registered voters that failed to vote was 1,612,000. It is important to note that 40 percent of all Latinos of voting age were precluded from voting because they are noncitizens. In states such as North Carolina and Maryland that have a rapidly increasing Latino population, over two-thirds of the adult Latinos were noncitizens.[264] In states like California and Illinois nearly half of the Latino voting population was ineligible to vote.

In another study conducted by the UCLA Chicano Studies Research Center in December 2003, the issue of noncitizens and political participation was addressed. The study reported that noncitizens made up at least 25 percent of the populations of a minimum of eighty-five California cities. In twelve California cities that included San Joaquin (63.5 percent), Maywood (59.5 percent), Cudahy (58.9 percent), and Bell Gardens (56.5 percent) noncitizen adults comprised more than half of the population. The center concluded that by denying noncitizens the right to vote, California was creating a system of political apartheid. In order to avoid such a political reality, the center recommended amending the state constitution to permit noncitizen voting rights for local offices in cities, counties, school districts, and special districts. Knowing the pervasive nativist political climate this expectation was unrealistic.[265] Thus, the high number of Latino noncitizens served to reinforce the barrios and *colonias'* growing apartheid status.

Even though the white population in California had decreased to a new minority status, the state's electorate remained overwhelmingly white. The white vote jumped from 70 percent of the total in 2000 to 76 percent in 2002.[266] By the November 2002 elections, for every one Mexicano/Latino that voted fifteen whites voted.[267] In Tejas, however, the mostly Mexicano electorate in 2000 showed some progress. Forty percent cast ballots, which was higher than the 36.4 percent overall average. This was a major increase over their 1998 turnout of 26.7 percent.[268]

Despite low voter turnouts, efforts continued to increase the number of Mexicanos/Latinos registered to vote. By 2003, overall Latino voter registration at the national level was nearly eight million. In California in 2002, Mexicanos/Latinos registered Democrat 56 percent, Republican 24 percent, and the rest Independents and other third parties. While whites constituted a 47 percent minority of the state's population, they comprised a 71 percent majority of those registered to vote.[269] At the national level, the Annenberg Public Policy Center's National Annenberg Election Survey (NAES) of 2000 found that 46.3 percent of registered Latinos were Democrats, 21.6 percent were Republican, and 21.2 percent were Independents. However, a subsequent NAES taken in the fall of 2003 found that the Democratic Party had lost some ground with the Latino electorate. The survey revealed that just 39.8 percent of Latinos who were registered to vote identified as Democrats, nearly a seven-point decrease from 2000, while Latinos who identified themselves as Republicans increased slightly by 3.3 percentage points to 24.9 percent.[270]

In another study called the "National Survey of Latinos: The Latino Electorate," during April–June 2002 the Pew Hispanic Center concluded that overall 49 percent of Latinos polled said they were registered Democrat, 20 percent were Republican, 19 percent Independent, 7 percent other third parties, and 5 percent said "don't know." The figures dramatically changed among those who were registered to vote between the ages of eighteen and twenty-nine years old: 34 percent identified themselves as Democrat, 21 percent Republican, 26 percent Independent, 13 percent other political parties, and 6 percent commented "did not know."[271]

In short, both studies indicate that the Mexicano/Latino vote had become increasingly heterogeneous, was not a united bloc, and was up for grabs. Observing the growing fluidity of the overall Latino vote, the Republican National Committee announced its pledge in 2002 to win them and other minorities who had historically supported Democrats.[272] The newest migrants were also interested in becoming citizens. The security resulting from 9/11, for example, increased INS raids, impelled Mexicanos/Latinos who were eligible to secure their citizenship. Applications in 2000 had bottomed out at 460,000, but by 2002 their number increased to an impressive 800,000,[273] with a substantial number of them being Mexicanos/Latinos.

A national poll released in August of 2002 showed that that they gave President Bush a "whopping 68%" approval rating, a major increase over the 2001 rating of 47 percent.[274] For Democrats and progressive activists alike, this was a disappointing poll because Latinos, with the exception of Cubanos who tended to be Republican, were traditionally strong Democrats in their affiliation. The poll also reported that in 2001 in California, Latinos preferred Democrat Gore over Republican Bush by 54 percent to 28 percent. A year later, according to the poll, if the election would have been held Bush would have beaten Gore by 50 percent to 35 percent. In response to the results of the poll, Roberto de Posada, Latino Coalition president, said, "Latinos now see the Republican Party as the party of President Bush, not [California Gov.] Pete Wilson and other anti-immigrant Republican leaders." The poll also concluded that in 2002, 44 percent of Mexicanos/Latinos were inclined to vote Democrat in the congressional elections, while 32 percent leaned toward the Republicans.[275]

International Politics: The Politics of Acercamiento

While still in its incipient stage, the politics of *acercamiento* gained momentum during the transition. The two countries that received the most attention particularly by Mexicanos in the United States were México and Cuba. The connections between Mexicanos in the United States and México increased in an unprecedented fashion. One such example was the support extended by U.S. Mexicanos and others to the Zapatista struggle in Chiapas. Another was the election of President Vicente Fox in 2000, which opened the political door to *acercamiento* politics even wider. Fox's controversial stance of "open borders"; his zealous push for new amnesty and guest worker programs; and the dialogue between the two countries on a variety of bilateral issues, for example, terrorism, border security, drug interdiction, NAFTA, business, water, and the environment, drove negotiations during the next two years. In short, Mexicanos on both sides of the U.S./México border recognized that their fate and future as a people were inextricably connected.

One event that characterized the politics of *acercamiento* was the Zapatista march on México City held in March 2001. Under my leadership and that of Maria Anna Gonzales, research analyst (University of California, Riverside Ernesto Galarza Applied Research Center), a delegation of the National Alliance for Human Rights (NAHR) traveled to México City in support of the Zapatista march. The delegation rented a bus and along with thousands of others participated in the historic march into México City by the Ejercito Zapatista de Liberación Nacional (EZLN) *comandancia* (command), including Sub-Comandante Marcos. While in México City, the delegation participated in the rally of tens of thousands and met with representatives of the EZLN.[276]

During the transition, Presidents Fox and Bush met on several occasions both in the United States and México. U.S. politicians (including members of the Congressional Hispanic Caucus) traveled and met frequently with Fox and other Mexican government officials. However, the terrorist attack of 9/11 changed the bilateral political climate and by 2002 President Fox's amnesty agenda was put on hold by the Bush administration. Relations between the United States and México cooled as a result of the following issues: refusal of the Bush administration to address a new amnesty program, strained relations over the timetable for repayment of México's nearly half-trillion-gallon water debt to the United States, México's refusal to sign off on President's Bush's War Resolution to the United Nations, and increasing violence being perpetrated on Mexicano migrants crossing into Arizona by white rancher armed vigilantes and militias. During the course of the transition, the Fox administration was in near paralysis. After three years of Fox's governance, México faced an escalating domestic crisis, for example, increasing poverty and policy and legislative disarray, since control of the Mexican congress was in the hands of the opposition parties. One could argue that México by 2003 was on the verge of becoming another Colombia enveloped in armed conflict that threatened its stability.[277]

With the intent of strengthening México's network with Mexicanos in the United States, President Fox established the Office of Mexicans Abroad. He appointed as its first director former University of Texas literature professor Juan Hernandez. From 2001 to 2002, Hernandez traveled extensively throughout the United States and shuttled back and forth to México meeting with numerous groups and individuals on a variety of issues affecting Mexicanos in the United States. In another *acercamiento* political maneuver, President Fox in March 2002 established the Binational Commission on Voting Abroad. He reiterated his commitment to extend the vote to expatriates in the United States by the 2006 presidential elections.[278] But because of growing criticisms that his administration was not doing enough to assist migrants in particular, in August 2002, President Fox abolished the office that Hernandez had directed. The action was precipitated by a power struggle between Hernandez and México's foreign secretary Jorge Castañeda and other cabinet officials, and Hernandez lost. Castañeda and others alleged that Hernandez had failed to consult with them on a number of issues and programs. In place of the office, Fox created a cabinet-level agency called the National Council of Mexican Communities, temporarily headed by Fox with a function of coordinating its advocacy and assistance programs.[279] Hernandez was reassigned to the position of "coordinator of presidential records," which entailed setting up an Internet site, writing reports, and being President Fox's biographer.[280]

In September 2002, President Fox named Candido Morales, a low-profile former laborer and social worker in California, as director of the Institute for Mexicans Abroad—his new point person in the United States on migrant issues. Morales's job was twofold: one, he was expected to advocate for and provide assistance to Mexicanos living in the United States; and two, he was to harness their political and economic power to assist México in its continued development. Guiding Morales was a 120-member advisory council from various cities and regions from throughout the United States. Some activists, such as Felipe Aguirre from Maywood, California, in response to Morales's efforts commented, "He is a go-between. He is not a problem solver. I wish him well, but the whole point of this is basically to shove the problem under the rug."[281]

México's major political parties also became active in soliciting political support from potential constituents in the United States. Several business and professional interest groups forged ties with President Fox's Partido Accion Nacional (PAN—National Action Party). Others continued their ties with the Partido Revolucionario Institucional (PRI—Institutional Revolutionary Party). Progressive groups and activists from California, Illinois, Tejas, Washington, and New York, as participants of La Coordinadora, continued to strengthen their ties with the Partido de la Revolución Democratica (PRD—Democratic Revolutionary Party). *Politicos* from all three political parties made frequent visits to the United States seeking support from the twenty-five million Mexicanos who resided in the United States.

All three of México's political parties recognized the invaluable contribution Mexicanos in the United States made to México's economy. In 2001, migrants sent remittances to relatives in México totaling some $8.9 billion. That meant that $24.4 million was being sent to México on a daily basis, which was an increase of 35.3 percent from 2000. By 2003 the amount of remittances increased to almost $14 billion, becoming México's second largest source of income behind oil exports.[282] This meant that 1.2 million homes, about one in five, received remittances from relatives in the United States. The Mexican government's Population Council reported that they anticipated an increase in 2003 of 10 to 20 percent.[283] The remittances were a pivotal source of income for México's poor but expanding economy.

President Fox and leaders of México's major parties during this period spent a considerable amount of time and resources in advancing their political agendas through visits to the United States and meetings with their respective supporters. This became evident during 2000 with the PRI's unprecedented election of Eddie Varón Levy, its first *diputado* (congressperson) in México via proportional representation from the United States. By early 2001, he opened an office in Inglewood, California, and planned to open others in Chicago, New York, and Tejas.[284] In another unprecedented political move in 2003, the PRD held elections for state central committees and officers in five states to establish its organizational structures.[285] In California, a twenty-nine-member PRD Central Committee was officially sworn in by PRD officials from México City in September 2002.[286] During 2003, the PRD state chairs traveled periodically to México City to represent their respective states at PRD national meetings. Thus, increasingly, the political boundary, la Cortina de Nopal (the Cactus Curtain), separating Aztlán and México continued to disappear.

For activists and groups in the United States their *acercamiento* agenda was essentially threefold: secure the right for Mexicanos in the United States to vote in México's elections, secure representation in México's congress, and push for dual nationality. Numerous meetings were held in México City, particularly in 2002 and 2003, with several senators and deputies in which several activists including myself participated. Under the leadership of Jose Jacques Medina, Jorge Mujica, Felipe Aguirre, and others, plans were drawn up to allocate several seats for Mexicanos in the United States in México's House of Deputies and be enfranchised in the presidential elections by 2006. In 1996, México's House of Deputies had passed legislation that gave Mexicanos living abroad the right to vote, but so far had failed to create a system or mechanisms to carry it out.[287]

President Fox and *politicos* from opposition parties voiced what was tantamount to "symbolic" support on the vote issue. On several occasions, *politicos* from these *partidos* visited the United States and met with various groups on the matter.[288] Mexican officials estimated that if Mexicanos living in the United States voted, México's 2006 presidential election could draw twelve million votes from the United States, of which 3.3 million would be from people born in the United States to migrant parents. Literally, if this were to occur some 15 percent of México's electorate would live outside of México.[289] This would make them a powerful political bloc with a growing impact on México's elections.

Several groups in the United States pushed the agenda of "dual nationality." For them its cardinal objective was to foster greater political unity and solidarity between México and Mexicanos in the United States. Those who qualified were individuals whose mother or father was born in México. They were guaranteed every right of a citizen except the right to vote. México's congress approved it in 1997; it went into effect in March 1998 and was scheduled to expire on March 2003. Three groups that were active in their push for dual nationality were the National Alliance for Human Rights (NAHR) in Riverside and San Bernardino counties, Comite Pro-Uno in Los Angeles County, and the Coalicion Internacional de Mexicanos en el Exterior (CIME) in Chicago, Illinois.[290] Proponents of dual nationality perceived it as merely a transitional step to dual citizenship status, which would allow them to vote in México's presidential elections of 2006.

If Mexicanos abroad (U.S.) were given the right to vote in 2006, it was anticipated that a sixth electoral district (*sexta circumscripicion*) would be established by México's congress.[291] Presently, México is made up of five legislative districts, each comprised of several states. In turn, the additional sixth electoral district would be based upon a formula of proportional representation, "x" number of seats to congress would be allocated to each political party based upon the total number of votes each party received. In their negotiations, U.S. Mexicano groups requested that by 2006 the Sixth Electoral District be comprised of ten senators and forty deputies. México's congress in 2002 had 128 senators and 500 deputies.[292]

When negotiations stalled during the summer of 2002, in retaliation, some fifty U.S. Mexicano organizations promulgated a call for a five-day boycott of remittances sent to México.[293] In September, groups of La Coordinadora, angry at the indecisiveness on the issue of the vote by México's *politicos* and *partidos* responded by another call for a boycott. Comite Pro-Uno in the Los Angeles area, supported by several other groups, called for an escalating national boycott on selected Mexicano products sold in the United States. The first of several to be targeted was Corona beer. Their strategy sought to pressure major Mexicano corporations, so that by experiencing a loss of revenue the targeted corporations would pressure the Mexican government and *partidos* to resolve the impasse. This meant that they would allocate a specified number of congressional slots to Mexicanos in the United States prior to México's congressional elections of 2003. By midsummer of 2002, however, México's congress failed to pass the requisite legislation to grant Mexicanos the right to vote in their 2003 congressional elec-tions. In an unprecedented way, in México's history, its politics transcended the U.S./México border and became an integral part of the Mexicano political expe-rience in the United States. Some argued that the incremental political integration of México and Aztlán had already begun.

Some Mexicanos in the United States concomitantly extended the politics of *acercamiento* to Cuba. This was not an easy task as the United States imposed an economic embargo on Cuba, and the Burton Law's travel restrictions made it difficult for anyone to travel or establish the basis politically for an *acercamiento* with Cuba. Nevertheless, in 2000, 2001, 2002, and again in 2003 under my leadership, and with administrative support from Maria Anna Gonzales, three delegations of Mexicanos from the United States traveled to Cuba for a week with the intent of building an *acercamiento* on education-related matters. The first delegation was comprised of some sixty distinguished scholars, students, and community and organizational leaders. They participated in a bilateral conference with their Cubano intellectual counterparts. The three-day conference agenda was organized with the Centro de Estudios de Norte America (Center of Studies on North America) under the leadership of Jorge Hernandez and focused on both themes of the "Cubano Revolutionary Experience" and on the "Chicano Political Experience in the United States." Cuba's president of the National Assembly, Ricardo Alarcon, addressed the conference.

A second delegation went to Havana, Cuba, in June 2001, but was much smaller. Comprised of fifteen scholars and a few organizational representatives, the delegation's agenda focused on learning more about Cuba's par excellence educational system. Several on-site meetings of Cuba's educational facilities in Havana were visited: a medical school and primary, secondary, and special educa-tion schools. At each site visit, Cubano educators made presentations on various aspects of Cuba's unique educational system. Five members of the delegation also did a two-hour live television *Meet the Press* type of program, *Mesa Redonda*, on the "Chicano Experience in the United States." Present at the television studio was Cuba's president Fidel Castro. After the program he met with the delegation and invited them to attend a massive rally in Manzanillo that commemorated the return of the child Elian Gonzales to Cuba and protested the U.S./Cuban Adjustment Act. The delegation traveled on the same flight as Cuba's minister of foreign affairs Felipe Perez Roque. At the rally attended by some three hundred thousand persons, the delegation was recognized and greeted by Cuba's minister of defense Raul Castro.

During the delegation's stay in Havana, meetings were held with Cubano scholars, and a consensus was reached on a number of education projects. It was agreed that the next Chicano delegation to Cuba would work to concretize an educational *acercamiento* with the University of Havana. At the top of the list of priorities was the development of a Chicano Studies program at the University of Havana to be housed within El Centro de Estudios Sobre Estados Unidos. Other possible educational projects included a faculty exchange program, collaborative research projects, and a large international conference in Cuba on the Chicano experience in the United States.

The third Chicano delegation comprised traveled to Cuba in December 2002. The delegation of eight engaged Cubano intellectuals on a number of topics, of which the Iraq War crisis and Bush war doctrine of pre-emption received the most attention. Five of the eight delegates participated in a live *Mesa Redonda* national television program that examined the status of the Chicano in the United States. An agreement was reached to establish a Chicano Studies component at the University of Havana. To initiate the effort a class on the Chicano experience in the United States was to be offered at the University of Havana in July 2003. A five-person panel from the delegation again appeared on *Mesa Redonda*.

A fourth delegation comprised of seven scholars traveled to Havana, Cuba, in July 2003. While in Cuba, they team-taught the first Chicano Studies course offered by the University of Havana via El Centro de Estudios Sobre Los Estados Unidos. Attended by many scholars as well as students, the course covered a number of topics related to the Chicano (Mexicano) experience in the United States. Meetings were held on a number of future collaborative research efforts.

During the transition, other Mexicanos and Latinos also traveled to Cuba. SVREP was one such organization that continued to send delegations to Cuba. Various scholars from Cuba made periodic visits to the United States and gave talks at several universities on a number of aspects of Cuba's Revolution. At the NACCS Conference of 2001, several Chicano scholars joined Jorge Hernandez to talk on Cuba's Revolution. These events advanced the politics of *acercamiento* between México, Cuba, and Mexicanos and Latinos in the United States at the end of 2003.

Organizations as Vehicles of Resistance

During the transition, numerous national, state, and local organizations were active in a number of struggles. Yet paradoxically, while the Mexicano/Latino population was burgeoning, organizational political activism reached its lowest point in several decades. Organizations of sorts existed that were national, regional, or statewide, but did not possess a power capability, which meant they lacked the capacity to mobilize and create a critical mass. At the local level, a debilitating "organizational crisis" pervaded most of the Aztlán's barrios and *colonias*, characterized by the absence of strong, effective, grassroots advocacy organizations. In other words, at the core of the crisis was the acute "disorganization" of the barrios and *colonias*. Also contributing to the organizational crisis was the reality that several existent organizations were weak and precariously holding on. Hence, without the presence of strong advocacy mass-based organizations at the local to national levels equipped with the requisite power capability to effectuate massive social change, the future prospects for decolonizing the barrios and *colonias* of Aztlán looked remote.

Politically, none of the existent political Generations had succeeded in building viable strong, mass-based "advocate transformer" role-oriented organizations. The few that did exist were at the local level, for example, sectarian Left organizations, and lacked a viable power base or mass following. The ideas that "organization is power" and that "the most powerful weapon in the arsenal of the oppressed is organization" had yet to be attained. Too many of the organizations were "paper tigers" led by presumptuous leaders who in essence were "generals without armies." The irony was that the majority of those in power were cognizant about the preceding organizational realities. Hence, the bottom line was that throughout Aztlán, Mexicano organizations continued to lack a credible "fear factor" and suffered from the detrimental "Rodney Dangerfield Syndrome" of "getting little or no respect" from those in power. Thus, the "organization crisis" worsened the severity of the existent "worst of times" crises.

Mutual Benefit Organizations

MUTUALISTAS   By 2003 the oldest form of Mexicano organization, the *mutualista*, during the transition, continued in its precipitous decline throughout Aztlán. This was basically ascribable to their inability to recruit new members. Even though the Mexicano population was dramatically increasing, *mutualistas* had failed to market themselves among the old or new Mexicano migrants. In addition, their leadership was aging and not being replaced, which meant that in some instances when a leader died local *logias* (lodges) succumbed or were destabilized. Too many existent *mutualistas* were dependent for their survival on a few aging leaders. Even though some *logias* still provided death insurance and sponsored a number of social and cultural activities, they were apolitical and seldom if ever got involved in ballot box or advocacy politics.

Sociedad Progrecista Mexicana (SPM)

Like so many *mutualistas* throughout Aztlán, the SPM in California faced an uncertain future. Whereas in 1986 it had a membership base of ten thousand, by

2002 it had decreased to five thousand. The number of *logias* also declined to a mere forty, with most of them located in the San Joaquin Valley and a few in Southern California. The myriad of cultural activities once so commonplace also declined, limited to an occasional dinner or dance. Statewide, the organizations offered four $1,000 scholarships to college.[294] According to Miguel Flores, pro-secretary to the SPM's Supreme Executive Committee, "The membership is dying out and we are having a difficult time in recruiting new members. Today few people are interested in promoting brotherhood or helping others."[295] Without experiencing a major revitalization in leadership, program development, market-ing, and membership, its longevity is in doubt.

Older Interest Groups

The few remaining older interest groups formed between the 1920s and late 1940s were still active during the transition. While not as influential as in prior years, they continued to play a buffer and "want to be white" political roles and adhered to the ethos of the HG. Their loss of organizational clout was attributed to loss of membership, decreasing funding sources, lack of organizational leader-ship, and the absence of an effective advocacy performance. Their emphasis on "conference and cocktail" activism deterred them from performing viable and effective advocacy. Their middle-class based, moderate to conservative politics, coupled with their emphasis on program development, services, scholarships, and social events, did not transform them into powerful influential national organiza-tions. In fact, by 2003 some old interest groups like *mutualistas* also faced uncer-tain futures.

LEAGUE OF UNITED LATIN AMERICAN CITIZENS (LULAC)   During the transition, LULAC was still the largest and most effective of the old interest groups. With some seven hundred councils nationwide,[296] LULAC's power base in 2002 remained largely Tejas-based. Yet in states such as California, with the exception of conservative Orange County, LULAC had yet to develop a strong and viable political presence. While successful in securing funding from corpora-tions, its revenue for its Washington, D.C., office operations in 2001 was a mere $1.1 million.[297] Beyond its educational focus and education and service programs (for example, Operation SER), LULAC adopted more of a buffer than its former "want to be white" political role. This change was indicative in LULAC's more assertive posture on a number of controversial issues, such as immigration, educa-tion, affirmative action, discrimination, police brutality, and redistricting. On the issue of redistricting, in September 2002, LULAC attacked both the Democrats

and Republicans for impeding the political advancement of Latinos by gerrymandering congressional districts.[298] By the end of 2003, LULAC, with its middle-
class orientation, still had no power base in the barrios and *colonias* of Aztlán and
was still a proponent of adaptation, assimilation, and HG politics.

AMERICAN G.I. FORUM (AGIF)   During the transition AGIF still had a
regional presence (Southwest/Midwest). Plagued by a declining membership and
insufficient resources, it continued to address veteran's issues and was involved
with LULAC in SER. Because of its veteran constituency and moderate to conservative politics, AGIF had access to the Bush administration. This was illustrated by the participation of sixty AGIF members in the inauguration activities
of President George W. Bush in January 2001.[299] Overall, however, AGIF's
influence had diminished substantially since the days of its founder, Dr. Hector
Garcia. Its estimated national membership in 2002 was only six thousand members. It was plagued by a declining membership, reduction of active chapters, and
a loss of corporate support.[300] During late July 2003, AGIF had its national convention in San Antonio, Tejas, and elected as its national commander David
Rodriguez of California. Juan Jose Peña, Nuevo México AGIF state vice-
commander said the following about AGIF's status at the close of 2003: "*por horita*
G.I. Forum *es una vaca muy flaca* [for now G.I. Forum is a lean cow]."[301] In short,
AGIF was precariously holding on and was in dire need of revitalization.

Political Pressure Organizations
Political pressure organizations (PPOs) as a type of interest group were still functional at both the national and state levels. While most adhered to a "buffer"
political role, they were diversified in their functions. Some PPOs functioned in
the traditional role of interest groups seeking to influence public policy. Others
endorsed candidates; prepared election and issue reports; developed leadership
programs; and specialized in voter registration, education, and get-out-the-vote
(GOTV) drives, and so on. All were still system maintenance-oriented and
adhered to the adaptation and accommodation politics of the HG. Most stayed
clear of controversial issues and avoided confrontational politics. None had a
power base or constituency in Aztlán's colonized barrios and *colonias*. In most
cases, in practice, PPOs were little more than satellite organizations of the Democratic Party. They were dependent on corporate and foundation funding for their
survival, which constrained if not precluded them from being viable social change
advocates. At the end of 2003, none of the existent PPOs could be described as
having the power base and support among the people to effectively influence public policy or do viable electioneering.

THE MEXICAN AMERICAN POLITICAL ASSOCIATION (MAPA)   MAPA continued to play its "buffer" political role but was on the verge of imploding. It was still plagued by the "politics of self-destruction," meaning the prevalence of power struggles between competing leaders and factions. In 2002 there were two MAPAs: the old one led by Ben Benavidez and a new national MAPA headed by Steve Figueroa. Both claimed to be the legitimate MAPA, and conflicts ensued over each one's contested endorsements, such as that of Republican Bill Simon for governor. While one faction publicly endorsed Simon, the other repudiated it.[302] The same occurred with the issue over San Fernando Valley city hood: one supported it; the other publicly disavowed it. As a result of these political battles several MAPA chapters collapsed and its membership declined. In 2003 MAPA underwent a leadership change: Benavides resigned due to poor health and was replaced by Maria Martinez as state/national chair. She proved to be transitional: in August at MAPA's state convention she was replaced by Nativo Lopez, director of Hermandad Mexicana Nacional.[303] In December 2003, under the auspices of MAPA and La Hermandad Lopez initiated a one-day statewide boycott that produced questionable results. In spite of MAPA's myriad of internal problems and conventions with low attendance, it continued to draw the attention of some politicians and some media. Yet its political reality in 2003 was that without some resolution of its divisive internal problems, MAPA as a PPO was traveling on the dangerous road of becoming history.

VOTER REGISTRATION, EDUCATION, GOTV PPOs   The Southwest Voter Registration Education Project (SVREP) and its sister research institute, the William C. Velasquez Institute (WCVI), still focused on political empowerment projects and activities. As "buffer" entities both were engaged in noncontroversial nonpartisan political work. While SVREP continued to conduct voter registration, voter education, and GOTV drives, and was engaged in redistricting politics, the WCVI conducted research, held leadership training sessions, and held on an annual basis a Latino Issues Conference. Meanwhile, with its geographical focus on the Midwest, the United States Hispanic Leadership Institute (USHLI) engaged in political organizing activities similar to those of SVREP and the WCVI. While all three groups did excellent research and voter registration work, none excelled in organizing the burgeoning Mexicano/Latino electorate into a viable political force. Even though they claimed to be nonpartisan, they all enjoyed support from the Democratic Party. Ideologically, they continued to be strong adherents of HG politics and liberal capitalism.

A major criticism levied against both SVREP and USHLI was that they were too busy trying to get headlines without really building a viable grassroots system of political participation. Critics pointed out that their "hit and run" or "in and out" approach to voter registration drives created no permanent organizational power base. Once the small grants ran out, in most cases, the organizing efforts came to an abrupt halt. On the positive side, however, both USHLI and SVREP contributed significantly to increasing the number of Mexicanos and Latinos registered to vote. Both were active in the November 2000 presidential elections, in which combined they registered a total of 120,000 Latinos.[304] Both were largely dependent on foundation grant money and did not become engaged in advocacy for social change. Their accommodation approach accentuated safe and noncontroversial political activities. At the close of 2003, both were well respected by Hispanic and white political elites, but lacked a permanent power base in the colonized barrios and *colonias*.

NATIONAL ASSOCIATION OF LATINO ELECTED AND APPOINTED OFFI-CIALS (NALEO) AND EDUCATION FUND   NALEO and its sister entity the NALEO Education Fund both still adhered to the politics of the HG. With its five thousand-plus members, the NALEO Education Fund held its annual conferences, conducted research on policy issues, and prepared and distributed its directory and other publications. Under the auspices of various institutes, a number of conferences were held focusing on various issues, such as Latino literacy, teacher quality, health, and providing assistance to elected officials.[305] Because of its heavy corporate support, NALEO Educational Fund's annual budget in 2002 was $2.4 million.[306] As a "buffer" advocate group, NALEO was active in addressing a number of policy issues, such as the overhaul of U.S. immigration policies[307] and redistricting, and enjoyed powerful connections in the nation's capital, particularly within the Democratic Party. Its adherence to the politics of the HG and ideologically to liberal capitalism meant it seldom if ever ruffled the feathers of those in power. Both NALEO entities lacked an organized presence in the impoverished barrios and *colonias* of Aztlán. In 2003 as a PPO, NALEO was influential, but had yet to effectively demonstrate its capacity to organize and mobilize the Mexicano or Latino electorate either at the ballot box or in policy arenas.

POLITICAL PARTY PARTISAN PPOS   During the transition, political party partisan PPOs, such as the Mexican American Democrats (MAD) and Tejano Democrats (TD), were still active. Both still functioned essentially as "satellite partisan interest groups," representing the Democratic Party's interests in Tejas among Mexicanos. The internecine conflict of the late 1990s between MAD and the TD spilled over into the transition's three years. However, in 2002, according to MAD leader Roberto Alonzo, "The avenues of conversation and dialogue opened up."[308] In June, both groups joined ranks to effect the election of Juan Maldonado as state vice-chair of the Democratic Party. In addition, both groups supported Tony Sanchez's bid for governor. Where they politically departed company was with the candidacy of Victor Morales for the U.S. Senate: MAD unanimously supported him, while the TD was split in their support. Efforts were initiated to mitigate the conflict within the Democratic Party by designating a "Mexican American Caucus" as the political body that would speak on behalf of both groups and nonaligned Mexicano Democrats in Tejas. MAD under the leadership of Steve Salazar was active with Sanchez's gubernatorial bid; the TD led by Juan Maldonado also geared up, but found itself divided between what Alonzo described as the "Old Guard" and the "New Guard."[309] By 2003 neither had a large grassroots power base, since both were largely comprised of middle-class competing political elites.

POLITICAL PARTY CAUCUSES   In Aztlán and elsewhere, within the state Democratic Party structures, Mexicanos and Latinos both participated in political party caucuses. Such was the case in Tejas with the Mexican American Caucus and with California's Latino Caucus. Political party caucuses ostensibly played a "buffer" political role, which included endorsing candidates and drawing up the party's platform. Yet these caucuses were more symbolic than anything else. As appendages to the Democratic Party, they met only periodically and mostly at Democratic Party state conventions. Latino and Mexicano Republicans also formed their own caucuses. Party caucuses served a useful purpose for ambitious political operatives with their own personnel agendas, less so, however, as vehicles of power and change.

LEGISLATIVE CAUCUSES   Another form or type of political party caucus was the legislative caucus. As "buffers," they existed in most states with Latinos elected to their respective state legislatures. In California, during 2002–2003, the Latino Legislative Caucus, Democrat-dominated, was instrumental in pushing legislation in favor of UFW, granting driver's licenses to undocumented migrants, and lobbying UC officials to support the appointment of a Latino/a as chancellor of the University of California, Riverside. At times, however, the leadership found it difficult to maintain a unified and effective legislative effort because of conflicting member agendas. When Governor Gray Davis in October 2002 reneged on his support for the driver's license measure that allowed undocumented migrants to obtain driver's licenses, the Latino Legislative Caucus in an unprecedented action decided not to endorse Davis's reelection. Later that month, however, instead of holding steadfast, seventeen out of the twenty-two members signed a letter that endorsed Davis, which was published in *La Opinion* newspaper.[310]

Thus, by 2003 throughout Aztlán, few if any of the various political party types of caucuses were paragons of major policy reform. Most were small and did not have the power and in some cases the requisite unity to successfully challenge the white-controlled Democrat Party's legislative or gubernatorial leadership.

CONGRESSIONAL HISPANIC CAUCUS (CHC)/CONGRESSIONAL HISPANIC CAUCUS INSTITUTE (CHCI)   At the federal level, both the CHC and CHCI were still active and growing. During the transition, while the CHC played the legislative "buffer" advocacy role, the CHCI continued to focus its leadership development programs and conducting research on policy issues. Dominated exclusively by Democrats, the CHC politically followed a liberal to moderate course of action. It lacked a vision for instituting major reforms. With the exception of three of its members—Congressperson Luis V. Gutierrez, Jose E. Serrano, and Nydia Velasquez—most shied away from controversial issues affecting Latinos. Case in point was that in 2000, on the issue of Arizona rancher vigilantes, I wrote a letter to then CHCI chair, Lucille Roybal-Allard requesting the intervention of the CHCI by holding hearings on abuses of undocumented migrants by white-armed vigilante ranchers in Arizona and on the detrimental impact of the militarization of the U.S./México border.[311] In spite of national media coverage and lobbying efforts on the issue, Chair Roybal-Allard failed to respond to the request and no action was taken by the CHC on the matter. Again, in 2002 and 2003, similar efforts were made by the NAHR to have the CHC call for hearings and attend a summit in Douglas, Arizona, with their congressional counterparts from México, but to no avail. Thus, the CHC on this issue was far from being the epitome of an effective policy change agent.

Led by Tejas congressman Silvestre Reyes, the CHC in 2003 had a membership of nineteen members and a record of lackluster politics. Occasionally, however, the CHC did address some policy issues, such as immigration, for example, legalization, guest worker program, amnesty, among others, but did so without having the clout to galvanize the Democratic Party leadership in Congress behind its issues, much less the Republican nativist Bush administration. In a new initiative in May 2001, the CHC announced the formation of BOLD PAC, a political action committee, which had a mission to raise $1 million for Democrat-supported candidates in 2002 and another half million for Latino voter registration efforts.[312] To their credit in October 2002, CHC members voted overwhelmingly against the Bush war resolution. In 2003 Tejas congressman Ciro D. Rodriguez, a former Raza Unida Party activist, became the CHC's new chair.

After years of little or no leadership on domestic or international policy issues, the CHC in 2003 announced its opposition the U.S. War on Iraq, and became involved in immigration issues, demonstrating an inkling of effective national leadership.

The CHC's sister organization, the CHCI, continued to develop leadership training programs, held special events dealing with a number of policy issues and topics, and sponsored several social/political events in the country's capital. In 2002 the CHCI held its twenty-fifth Annual Gala during Hispanic Heritage Month and also held its 2002 Issues Conference,[313] which largely catered to Washington, D.C.'s affluent Latino and white power elites. With a $500 registration, it was evidently not interested in securing the participation of the middle class or the disenfranchised poor. By 2003, among those who adhered to the politics of the HG, the CHC, and CHCI indeed had national prominence. Yet, among the colonized masses of Aztlán's barrios and *colonias* neither one had a political presence or following.

Protest Organizations (PO) Continued to Decline

During the transition, POs with roots in the Movimiento were few, and those that did exist were in decline. The existent POs lacked the militant *espiritu* that characterized the previous epoch of militant protest. They shifted from an advocate transformer to a buffer role. With some rare exceptions, most POs seldom used demonstrations, marches, pickets, or other forms of unconventional direct action. Instead, they adopted more conventional means, typical of adaptation and accommodation politics. Ideologically, their commitment to Chicanismo lacked a strong nationalist posture, and the ideal of Aztlán was often absent.

COMMITTEE ON CHICANO RIGHTS (CCR)   Still led by its founder Herman Baca, the CCR remained active in the San Diego, California, area. Periodically, the CCR dealt with a number of mostly local issues without really being formally organized; however, during this epoch it did not resort to unconventional forms of protest. The CCR continued to garner the attention of San Diego's media and had some support in National City, especially when it took on issues such as education, immigration, and police community relations. In 2003 Baca worked to keep the name of the CCR alive. Its power, however, was localized and rested with its founder and head and not with the people.

BROWN BERETS DE AZTLÁN (BBA)   After years of fratricidal politics, during the transition, the BBA remained active, but ostensibly only in California. David Sanchez, founder of the original Movimiento Brown Berets, led the National

Brown Berets, formerly the Brown Berets of America; as a PO it was essentially nonactive. David Ricco, who headed the San Diego BBA chapter, was active along with others in California in the organization and reactivation of BBA chapters.[314] Occasionally, the BBA participated in events or protests organized by other groups, such as the National Chicano Moratorium Committee. Other key BBA leaders, such as Miguel Perez and Seferino Garcia, were active with other groups on a number of issues, for example, establishing Chicano Studies programs in the high schools, preventing gang violence, and by December 2002–2003 protesting the Iraq War. The BBA continued to embrace a separatist and ultranationalist perspective on the question of nation building.[315] However, its militant paramilitary posture and adherence to self-defense had all but disappeared. When interviewed, Rico said, "It is going to take time, but as Berets we are still committed to getting our land back." Overall, the BBA never achieved the level of organization, activism, and visibility as its progenitor. By 2003, with little or no infrastructure and only few chapters active, the barrios and *colonias* were not being organized into BBA chapters.[316] The country's conservative political climate coupled with the politics of the HG thwarted the BBA's reorganization efforts.

MOVIMIENTO ESTUDIANTIL CHICANO DE AZTLÁN (MEChA)   The only major PO that at times demonstrated a sense of viability was MEChA. Because of its somewhat precarious status, it was not exempt from the conservative political climate that pervaded the universities, colleges, and high schools. With the overwhelming majority of Mexicano and Latino students adherents of the HG, most lacked the requisite *consciencia* and *compromiso* to get involved. As a consequence, on most campuses student apathy was pronounced and stifled activism. Nevertheless, a few MEChA chapters were active and continued to adhere to an advocate transformer role. Some MEChA chapters were active on a number of issues, for example, affirmative action, immigration, and the Iraq War. Yet as a whole, particularly at the state or national level, MEChA had become increasingly ineffective as a PO. Some chapters were plagued by internal discord over ideology, gender, and personality and community issues. At all levels, however, it lacked an organizational focus and unified action, and had yet to define its cardinal mission or vision. Increasingly, fewer Mechistas were cognizant of or adhered to the provisions of El Plan de Santa Barbara or El Plan Espiritual de Aztlán. Some failed to understand MEChA's crucial organizational role within the context of both plans. On some college and university campuses MEChA was losing the student recruitment struggle to HG-oriented fraternities and sororities, among other entities. MEChA was in dire need of organizational revitalization and of a rediscovering its original mission and vision.

Uniones: A Resurgent Labor Power

During the transition, unions as a form of interest groups accelerated their drives to organize Mexicano and Latino workers. Active throughout Aztlán and beyond, unions experienced an increase in their membership.[317] Numerous unions competed for the lucrative Latino labor market, especially that of the migrant. For Latino workers, struggles to improve their economic quality of life, better wages, working conditions, and benefits were the stimulus for their involvement. While efforts to organize Latino workers occurred throughout the country, California was the pacesetter. In California, several local/regional unions led by Mexicanos and Latinos focused on organizing migrants and gaining political strength. Unions, however, continued to serve reform and "buffer" political roles, which did not threaten the power of corporations, and to politically align themselves with the Democratic Party.

UNION ORGANIZING ACTIVITIES   At the national level, as a trade union association, the Labor Council for Latin American Advancement (LCLAA) with its 1.4 million members in forty-three international unions still exerted influence within both advocacy and ballot box arenas.[318] LCLAA as a labor interest group in 2000 had revenues of $754,658.[319] In California, the powerful Los Angeles County Federation of Labor (LACFL), of the AFL-CIO, was a labor umbrella organization headed by President Miguel Contreras in 2001 and represented some eight hundred thousand workers.[320] In conjunction with Cardinal Roger Mahony and other groups and unions, the LACFL held mass gatherings in support of a new amnesty program. Two other unions that were active in organizing Latino migrants were the Organization of Los Angeles Workers (OLAW), a coalition of unions led by Maria Elena Duarazo, and the Service Employee International Union (SEIU), headed by Eliseo Medina. These and other unions sought to become political power brokers, especially in local and state politics.[321] While some succeeded in negotiating contracts, their victories in most cases still left workers with subsistence wage earnings and few other benefits, illustrating that too many Mexicano and Latino workers were still unable to extricate themselves from their colonized status.

During the transition, the UFW underwent revitalization and a rebuilding phase. In 2002 the UFW had a mere fifty contracts. Of the 428 elections the UFW conducted since 1975, only 158 or 37 percent resulted in contracts.[322] Its membership during the early 1970s had reached nearly 100,000; however, by 2002, it had dwindled to a low of 27,000. In efforts to revitalize the UFW, leader Arturo Rodriguez took on a more proactive organizing posture. This became evident in 2001 with UFW's success in a costly five-year campaign to unionize California's fast growing strawberry workers. In March, the UFW negotiated a contract involving some 750 workers with the Watsonville-based Coastal Berry, the world's largest strawberry grower. Under the agreement workers received a three-year contract with a 7 percent raise over three years, profit sharing bonuses, and enhanced dental and medical care benefits.[323] As previously described, the UFW launched an impressive campaign in August 2002 to strengthen the Agricultural Labor Relations Act (ALRA), including binding arbitration that culminated with a march on Sacramento. During the 2002 November state elections the UFW directed manpower and money toward the reelection of Democratic governor Gray Davis. In 2003 again the UFW supported Davis against efforts to recall him and organized against Proposition 54. By 2003 the UFW was not as influential as it had been before, but showed signs of reconstituting itself as a viable farmworker union.

Sectarian Left Organizations (SLOs): Isolated Change Vehicles

Mexicano sectarian Left organizations (SLOs) while extremely few in number and politically isolated persevered in spite of the reactionary and jingoistic political climate. SLOs constituted the few advocacy organizations that adhered to an advocate transformer role. However, even after years of organizing, they still lacked the political clout to bring about major social change within the omnipotent liberal capitalist system. In particular, the few active SLOs were unable to advance their progressive agenda in the barrios and *colonias* of Aztlán. Most Mexicanos and Latinos rejected SLO's socialist/ultranationalist ideological agenda. Regardless of their class or colonized status, indicative of the country's powerful political culture and its effective socialization agents, most Mexicanos and Latinos bought into the liberal capitalist agenda.

HERMANDAD MEXICANA NACIONAL (HMN)   As a SLO, the HMN experienced serious internal problems during much of the transition. On January 15, 2001, the HMN received a major blow with the death of its famous civil rights leader, labor organizer, and founder Bert Corona, who at the age of eighty-two died of kidney failure. Truly Corona was a major Mexicano leader of historical significance, illustrated by his seventy years of incessant activism.[324] In Corona's honor, the HMN held a "People's Memorial Service and Tribute and March" in Los Angeles on January 20. Hundreds of persons, including politicians, union leaders, activists, organization representatives, and supporters, showed up to pay their respects to one of the most important Mexicano political leaders in the United States.[325]

After Corona's death, the HMN was plagued by an internecine power struggle that threatened its existence. Two factions vied for control of the HMN: one was led by Nativo Vigil Lopez, HMN leader from Orange County; while the other faction was headed by Corona's widow, Angelina Corona. The public conflict escalated by 2002, and Lopez also became engaged in a relentless political battle concerning the HMN with SEIU leader Eliseo Medina, Juan Gutierrez, and Ben Monterroso. In an open letter, Lopez accused the SEIU's leadership of "interfering" in the HMN's internal affairs.[326] As a result of the lawsuit the two contentious HMN factions become two independent organizations. Lopez's HMN was renamed Hemandad Mexicana Latinoamericana and Angelina's HMN retained its original name. In December of 2003, under the flags of HMN Latinoamericana and MAPA, Lopez called for a one-day strike in response to the reversal of SB60, which would have given migrants access to driver's licenses. At the end of 2003, neither of the two Hermandad Mexicanas could be described as advocate transformers. They were primarily service provider agencies that occasionally advocated some change.

UNION DEL BARRIO (UB)   Other Mexicano SLOs such as the UB and its sister groups, that is, the Raza Rights Coalition (RRC) and Raza Press Association, were ideologically socialist/ultranationalistic. All three could be said to identify with an advocate transformer role. With their cadre structure, they adhered to the notion that Mexicanos in the United States were an occupied people and that Aztlán and México formed one nation.[327] As SLOs, all three groups maintained their *frente* (unified front) relationship and still focused on organization and cadre formation; publication of their newspapers; consciousness-raising conferences, marches, and other direct actions; and community issues and even ran a candidate unsuccessfully for local office in the San Diego area. In February 2002, along the U.S./México border around San Diego, California, the RRC became engaged in a fracas in which Benjamin Prado was beaten and arrested by U.S. Border patrolmen while he videotaped raids in progress. Prado alleged false arrest and filed a lawsuit against the U.S. Border Patrol in 2002 on the grounds that his constitutional rights were violated under the U.S. Constitution's Fourth Amendment.[328] The UB and its sister entities were also active in a number of issues, such as opposing the militarization of the U.S./México border, the prison industrial complex, and Bush's war policies. At the close of 2003, although the UB was active and persevering, its power base was still localized and not expanding.

THE NATIONAL CHICANO MORATORIUM COMMITTEE (NCMC)   The NCMC remained active and still adhered to an eclectic brand of socialist/

ultranationalist ideology. Its advocate transformer role was evident in a prepared statement sent to me by NCMC national coordinator Jaime Cruz; he wrote, "Our new movement must become crystal clear and convincing that *nuestra causa* and its direction will bring about Liberation and Self-Determination for our Raza."[329] The NCMC and several other SLOs participated in the 1970 August 29 National Chicano Moratorium march and rally held in Los Angeles in 2002. Initially, some internal conflicts developed over duplication of events organized by an ad hoc group called Chicano Moratorium 2002 formed by the original founder of the NCMC, Rosalio Muñoz, among others. The latter group held a number of activities including a symposium in East Los Angeles with several speakers including myself, which was attended by some eighty persons.[330] Both the march and rally drew a mere three people, a far cry from the twenty-five thousand that attended the original 1970 moratorium march and rally. As a result of negotiations, both groups decided to also hold a joint symposium that was attended by some three hundred people, which featured a number of speakers, such as renowned historian Rodolfo Acuña.[331] In 2003 it participated in numerous antiwar marches and activities in Los Angeles. As a SLO, the NCMC was cadre-structured, lacked a power base, and was oriented primarily to a one-local issue basis.

PARTIDO NACIONAL DE LA RAZA UNIDA (PNLRU)   During the transition, the PNLRU's leadership still described itself as a cadre "Chicano Mexicano Revolutionary Nationalist Party" committed to "the liberation of the Chicano Mexicano people."[332] To the PNLRU, liberation still denoted the formation of a separate Chicano/Mexicano nation, Aztlán.[333] As a SLO, it maintained its separatist socialist posture and adhered to an advocate transformer role, but in actuality, it functioned not as a political party, but as an ideological/sectarian interest group. The PNLRU relied on issues, conferences, and direct actions to "conscienticize," organize, and draw new cadre members. The PNLRU operated with only two main chapters: one in San Fernando, California, led by Xenaro Ayala, the second in Albuquerque, Nuevo México, led by Enrique Cardiel. In 2002 efforts were begun to form chapters in Tucson, Arizona, and in Tejas as well.[334]

Thus, at the closure of 2003, none of the Mexicano SLOs appeared to be growing in power or in their capacity to effectively organize the colonized barrios and *colonias*. The ubiquitous power of the liberal capitalist system was difficult to surmount or challenge.

New Hispanic Interest Groups
The newer Latino "buffer" interest groups formed during the late 1960s and 1970s remained at the avant-garde of the HG. With the exception of LULAC,

none of the organizations had the resources and stature of the two new Hispanic interest groups: the National Council of La Raza (NCLR) and the Mexican American Legal Defense and Education Fund (MALDEF). Both organizations with their ardent adherence to the politics of the HG were not perceived by the country's white power structure as serious threats. Yet of the two, the former was more system-maintenance oriented; the latter was the more effective change agent.

NATIONAL COUNCIL OF LA RAZA (NCLR)   With total revenues in 2002 of $30,400,000, the NCLR had the largest budget of any Hispanic "buffer" advocacy organization.[335] This allowed the NCLR to strengthen its professional staff, maintain its office in Washington, D.C., and build up its extensive network of member organizations. During the transition years, the NCLR effectively outdid LULAC in marketing itself as the most powerful national Hispanic organization. It held gargantuan annual conferences, and a number of special events, provided technical assistance and constituency support, conducted research, and did legislative lobbying. On the down side, the NCLR was overly circumspect in not becoming embroiled in controversial issues for fear of losing corporate and federal funding or antagonizing its political connections. Also, the NCLR's president Raul Yzaguirre in 2002 announced that he had Parkinson's disease[336] and in 2003 retired. In his farewell address, he accused President Bush and Democrats alike of not delivering the goods so to speak to Hispanics and challenged both to produce.[337] In spite of its reputation, the NCLR in 2003 lacked the ability to mobilize the barrios and *colonias* of Aztlán or Hispanics as a whole.

MEXICAN AMERICAN LEGAL DEFENSE AND EDUCATION FUND (MALDEF)   MALDEF continued to be the most effective national HG-oriented interest group. It effectively addressed a myriad of legal issues: from the 2000 U.S. Census to redistricting, voting rights/political access, education, employment, immigration, public resource equity, and access to justice. Illustrative of MALDEF's advocacy were the following three major cases. First, in November 2000, MALDEF and other organizations took to task the State of Virginia's attorney general's position that undocumented children should not be enrolled in public institutions of higher learning.[338] Second, MALDEF's redistricting suit challenged the congressional and state legislative seats adopted by California's legislature, which was rejected in June 2002 by a panel of federal judges. The suit charged that district lines drawn for the San Fernando Valley and part of San Diego reduced the ability of Latinos to be elected to office by creating districts that were not majority Latino.[339] And third, that same year, MALDEF was also active in working to defeat the secessionist efforts of the San Fernando Valley and Hollywood to break away from the city of Los Angeles. MALDEF's opposition was predicated on the argument that secession would be detrimental for Latinos and other minorities.[340] MALDEF as a legal advocate was also active in conducting research, releasing reports and papers on issues, and lobbying. Late in 2003, MALDEF's general counsel Antonia Hernandez announced she was leaving.

OTHER HISPANIC/LATINO NEW INTEREST GROUPS   A plethora of other advocacy interest groups colored the Hispanic organizational landscape, and all of them played a "buffer" political role. At the national level, there were Hispanic or Latino groups that were strong adherents of HG politics. The National Hispanic Leadership Agenda (NHLA) remained unsuccessful in its attempts to provide national organizational leadership, making innocuous pronouncements on rather low-impact issues. The U.S. Hispanic Chamber of Commerce (USHCC), with the election of President George W. Bush, was successful in courting his administration and securing some appointments. The Hispanic Association on Corporate Responsibility (HACER), with an annual budget of $742,939 in 2000, continued its organizational focus on issues related to corporate responsibility. The Hispanic Association of Colleges and Universities (HACU), with a rich budget of $9.58 million continued to secure funding for so-called Hispanic-designated universities with Latino student populations of at least 25 percent. The Hispanic Scholarship Fund (HSF) had revenues of $55.9 million in 2000 and expenditures of $13 million.

In California, during the transition, numerous new state and local Latino interest groups were active. President Bush addressed the USHCC at its annual legislative conference in March 2002. Likewise, in Los Angeles, the Latino Business Association (LBA) was also active, holding its annual Latino Business Expo, and in general pushed its pro-business agenda.[341] The Latino Issues Forum continued to be active in the broad arenas of higher education, health care, citizenship, and telecommunication issues.[342] La Raza Lawyers Association was also active in promoting Latino representation at all levels of the state judiciary.[343] California's Association of Mexican American Educators (AMAE), which in 2002 had a small membership, was not very active or visible, and essentially was in decline. At the city level as well, a number of organizations were active. In Nuevo México, the Hispanic Round Table in Albuquerque, an umbrella of forty groups, focused on a number of local and state issues, for example, discrimination, affirmative action, and others.[344]

Out of San Diego, California, the National Association for the Advancement of Hispanic People (NAAHP) was formed in 2001. Mimicking the NAACP in many ways, it sought to foster greater political and economic influence, according to its founder and president, Michael Gonzalez Angel. In reality, however, its focus was on acting as a buyer's consortium that would enable its members to secure discounts. It was supposed to also function as a clearinghouse for information on government programs that benefit Hispanics. Based upon available information, the NAAHP was far from being an advocate comparable to the NAACP.[345] Unfortunately, it appeared to be just another ephemeral attempt by individuals who adhered to the ethos of the HG: to do business and make money rather than create change.

Another new advocacy group to emerge was the National Latino Media Council (NLMC). Established in 1999 as a federation of twelve Hispanic organizations that met in Houston, Tejas, to discuss the lack of Latino access to television programming and to do away with negative media stereotypes.[346] Since its formation, under the leadership of its national chairperson former congressman Estaban Torres, the NLMC joined a multiethnic Coalition for Diversity on Television (CDT) led by the NAACP. In a protracted struggle of negotiations with executives of the four major television networks in 2000, the coalition signed memoranda of understanding with the presidents or CEOs of ABC, NBC, CBS, and Fox.[347] One of the most vociferous members of the NLMC was Alex Nogales, president of the National Hispanic Media Coalition (NHMC). In July 2002, the CDT issued report cards on all four networks that "faulted them over the lack of diversity."[348] Latino television access remained problematic, since Latino groups like the NLMC and its affiliate NHMC were essentially comprised of "generals" who had no army. They were unable to engender a critical mass to pressure the white-dominated TV networks.

The rise of the new HG interest groups with their adherence to liberal capitalism had no policy solutions to Aztlán's social problems. Their impact and presence was limited if not inconsequential at best to Aztlán's colonized barrios and *colonias*.

COALITION FORMATION   Coalition formation continued to be a popular mode of organizing, especially in dealing with issues such as immigration, the Iraq War, and police brutality. Without a permanent structure or grassroots power base, and issue oriented, their capacity to effectuate social change among Mexicanos had proven to be rather limited and in most cases transitory. One exception, however, was the rise of the National Alliance for Human Rights (NAHR) formed in 2000 as a result of a U.S./México border crisis summit held in San Ysidro, California.[349] Not a coalition per se, the NAHR, under my leadership, was a progressive network of organizations and individuals that adhered to an advocate transformer role, which advocated for human rights, social justice, and political empowerment. The NAHR was engaged in a number of issues international to local in scope—from the U.S./México border crisis to the creation of a Chicano Studies Department at California State University, San Bernardino. At the local level, the NAHR in 2002 initiated a successful mobilization for the appointment of a Latino/a chancellor at the University of California, Riverside. The NAHR brought together the power of the CHCI, the California Latino Legislative Caucus, and a host of state and national organizations that effectively lobbied the UC regents and achieved the appointment of physicist France Cordova as chancellor of the University of California, Riverside. History was made: Cordova became California's first Mexicana chancellor of a UC system university.

In May and June of 2002 the NAHR along with other Mexicano-based organizations met in México City and Los Angeles with Mexican government officials to lobby for political representation in México's congress for Mexicanos in the United States. During 2002, the NAHR organized a drive for Mexican dual nationality. In October, in response to the threat of a U.S. War against Iraq, the NAHR held direct action activities in San Bernardino and Riverside counties and in 2003 organized an antiwar summit and participated in a number of protests. In 2003, the NAHR also organized against the militias and rancher vigilantes in Douglas, Arizona. Late in 2003, it organized in support of Lt. Governor Cruz Bustamante's gubernatorial bid and against the recall and Proposition 54. By the end of 2003, as an all-volunteer network, the NAHR was doing what some existent state or national Hispanic or Mexicano organizations were not doing, which was taking on controversial issues impacting Mexicanos and Latinos.

Hispanic/Latina Women's Organizations

Hispanic/Latina interest groups during the transition were few. Like primarily male-dominated Hispanic/Latino interest groups, they too identified with the politics of the HG, adopted a buffer political role, and ideologically were liberal capitalist. At the national level, MANA—a national Latina organization—continued to hold corporate-supported regional and national conferences that focused on its Latina empowerment agenda. In September 2002, during Hispanic Heritage Month, MANA held its annual Las Primeras celebration of Latina achievement in Washington, D.C. Although it claimed to be national with some sixteen chapters scattered throughout the country, the level or scope of advocacy was rather limited to conference activism, debate on Latina issues, and symbolic visibility in Washington, D.C. When interviewed about MANA's effectiveness, political scientist Ada Sosa-Riddel said, "A major problem with MANA is that it does not have a well developed infrastructure that is effective in connecting or coordinating activities between its local chapters and the National."[350]

Hispanic/Latina organizational advocacy was more pronounced at the state level. In California, while the Comision Femenil was still in decline, HOPE (Hispanas Organized for Political Equality) with its "buffer" role grew during the transition in organizing momentum. Similar to MANA in orientation, HOPE distinguished itself by pushing its Latina political agenda. Like other Hispanic Generation-oriented groups, HOPE was largely sustained by mostly corporate funding. Its organizing activities focused on conferences and other events, which accentuated Latina leadership training and acquisition of advocacy skills. With its visibility and work in Sacramento, HOPE postulated that it had contributed to the substantial increases in Latina legislative representation in Sacramento— from one in 1990 to ten in 2003. In September 2002, HOPE hosted a reception in Riverside for the newly appointed University of California, Riverside chancellor France Cordova, attended by some two hundred people. As to its efficacy, Sosa-Riddell stated, "HOPE is comprised of mostly younger women who as of yet have not been willing to take on the public policy issues La Comision Femenil did twenty years ago."[351]

In 2003 Hispanic/Latina organizations were primarily active in the areas of professional/career mobility within the private sector. By and large, with their limited middle-class constituency, they lacked a viable power base and lacked connections to the majority of women who suffered under oppressive socioeconomic conditions of Aztlán's barrios and *colonias*.

Community-Based Power Organizations (CBPOs)

CBPOs seldom became involved with other issues outside their own organizing agenda. While oriented toward social change at the micro level, they failed to focus on issues at the macro level of society, and confrontation was precipitated by the contradictory nature of liberal capitalism. Thus, while more action-and reform-oriented than other existent Hispanic interests groups, CBPO entities continued to play a "buffer" and pro-system role, although strategically and tactically, they adhered to a more advocate transformer role.

INDUSTRIAL AREAS FOUNDATION (IAF) CBPOs   As an organizing institute, the IAF was still at the avant-garde of community-based power organizations (CBPOs) throughout Aztlán. In Southern California, the Valley Organized in Community Efforts (VOICE), under the organizing leadership of Ernie Cortez, continued to solidify its power base. In San Antonio, Tejas, COPS still exerted political power both in the electoral and issue arenas. With their multi-issue agendas in 2002, neither of these two organizational efforts nor the fifteen others scattered in Tejas, Arizona, and Nuevo México had developed plans of action that sought to reform the greater society.

Thus, by the end of 2003, like other old and new interest groups examined, CBPOs were effective instruments of change at least at the local micro level. Without a budget or full-time organizers, however, they too were vulnerable to becoming moribund.

Rise of Mexicano-Based Organizations (MBOs)

Organizationally, an important impact during the transition was the formation of MBOs. Their "organizational renaissance" had started in the previous epoch and now accelerated. As "buffers," MBOs had strong Mexicano nationalist inclinations, large and active memberships, and had become the most influential type of organization in the barrios and *colonias* of Aztlán, displacing *mutualistas*. The three ideal types of MBOs examined in the previous chapter were still active and experienced growth, but a new type emerged, political pressure organizations (PPOs).

Civic culture/economic (CCE) organizations were the largest, most plentiful, and most active. Their zealous loyalty to their state of origin continued to be manifest by remittances to relatives, in the establishment of community projects in their home villages or communities, and in their efforts to maintain their cultural ties with México and their respective states. CCE organizations were found in various parts of the country, wherever there were Mexicano nationals. La Federación de Clubes Zacatecanos del Sur de California was one of several such organizations. Under the leadership of Manuel de la Cruz, it had some fifty-five clubs that were linked to an equal number of towns in Zacatecas.[352] Through its "3 to 1" self-help program, in numerous municipalities in Zacatecas, it raised $6 million, which was matched by $12 million in government money.[353] Numerous other CCEs were also formed that represented Mexicanos from several of México's states, for example, Oaxaca, Michoacán, Jalisco, Colima, and Guerrero.[354]

Service provider (SP) agencies still provided a multiplicity of services, especially related to immigration, citizenship, health care, job discrimination, crisis intervention, and so on. From California to New York, SP agencies could be found in urban and rural areas. Generally dependent on state and federal funding sources, most SP agencies faced serious funding problems as grants became scarcer due to cutbacks. In fact, some were forced to close, as was the case with One-Stop Immigration in Los Angeles in 2002. Desperate for funding, some openly lobbied for the passage of a new amnesty program, believing new resources would be available.

Human and civil rights (H/CR) organizations remained active advocates. As traditional interest groups, they were incessant in their quest for a new amnesty program, which had been on hold since the September 11 attacks. However, in 2002 several H/CR organizations, such as La Coordinadora, La Coalicion Internacional de Mexicanos en el Exterior (CIME), Comite Pro-Uno, and others engaged in influencing public policy in México's congress. Specifically, they unsuccessfully lobbied México's congress for the right of Mexicano nationals in the United States to vote in México's elections and to be represented politically in México's congress. In 2003, with the U.S./México border crisis worsening, H/CR organizations were also active in dealing with a number of local and international issues that affected their Mexicano constituencies.

In 2002, a new type of MBO emerged out of their leadership ranks—the PPOs. One such entity was MUSA (Mexicanos in the United States of America). MUSA was headed by former CASA leaders Jose "Pepe" Medina Jacques, Felipe Aguirre, Carlos Arrango, and other progressive types like Jorge Mujica, who were deeply involved with México's PRD.[355] As a PPO, MUSA was similar to MAPA in orientation, but its constituency was Mexicano nationals and its focus was on México's electoral politics. MUSA's general strategy was to become engaged in México's politics and elections and influence public policy both in México and the United States. While most of its leadership came from the ranks of the PRD, MUSA pragmatically considered itself multipartisan, meaning it solicited membership from all of México's political parties.[356] In 2002–2003, MUSA's organizing activities primarily focused on lobbying for "the right to vote and be voted upon" in México's elections for 2003 and 2006. In August 2002, MUSA unsuccessfully called for a boycott of Corona beer, believing that it would pressure México's congress to support their political agenda.

México's political parties in their organizing efforts in the United States influenced the formation of other PP organizations in California, such as the PRD's Federacion Zacatecanos en Marcha in Los Angeles[357] and Federaciónes Mexicanas (FEDMEX). In 2003 under the aegis of the PRD, Manuel de La Cruz and Jose Jacques Medina both ran unsuccessfully for seats in México's Chamber of Deputies. If elected under proportional representation, they would have represented Mexicanos in the United States.

Overall, MBOs were not exempt from some of the same organizational problems that plagued the development of previous Mexicano organizations. This included ideological and interest schisms, power struggles, organizational rivalry, lack of an advocacy and change posture, absence of a barrio and *colonia* power base, limited financial resources, and a pervading political apathy among migrants largely rooted in their adherence to the NMG. While most MBOs operated out of Aztlán's barrios and *colonias*, they were also found throughout the country, wherever there were concentrations of Mexicanos.

Thus, by the end of 2003, the Mexicano political experience in occupied Aztlán was in transition. Its future as will be examined in the ensuing epilogue is at best problematic and uncertain.

Notes

1. *Latino* is my term of preference that incorporates Mexicanos and all others whose historical and cultural roots are deeply imbedded in the region and part of the Western Hemisphere designated by most scholars as Latin America. However, when appropriate for purposes of placing emphasis on the Mexicano, but also involve other Latinos, *Mexicano/Latino* is used.

2. NCLR, *Beyond the Census: Hispanics and an American Agenda*, August 2001.

3. Cited in James A. Forrest, "Census 2000: The Plus and Minus for Hispanics," in *Chicano Studies: Survey and Analysis*, 2nd ed., ed. Dennis J. Bixler-Márquez, Carlos Ortega, Rosalía Solórzano Torres, and Lorenzo G. La Farelle (Dubuque, Iowa: Kendall/Hunt, 2001), 101.

4. *La Voz* [newspaper], "Immigrants Account for 12 Percent of the U.S. Workforce," September 21, 2001.

5. Robin Fields, "90s Saw a Tide of New People," *Los Angeles Times*, August 6, 2001.

6. Genaro C. Armas, "Hispanics Now Outnumber Blacks in U.S.," *The Associated Press*, January 22, 2003.

7. Marilú Meza, "Aumenta Población de Latinos," *La Opinion*, June 19, 2003.

8. The aforementioned figures have been rounded up. For example, the exact Latino population percentage was 13.5 percent and that of African Americans 12.7 percent.

9. The aforementioned Census Bureau demographic data was cited in the following newspaper articles: Meza, "Aumenta Población de Latinos"; Ricardo Alonso-Zaldivar, "Latinos Now Top Minority," *Los Angeles Times*, June 19, 2003; Stephan Wall, "Latino Growth Surges in U.S.," *The Sun*, June 19, 2003; Andres Viglucci and Tim Henderson, "Hispanics Pass Blacks as Largest U.S. Minority," *The Miami Herald*, June 19, 2003.

10. Alonzo-Zaldivar, "Latinos Now Top Minority."

11. Bettina Boxall and Ray F. Herndon, "Far from Urban Gateways, Racial Lines Blur in Suburbs," *Los Angeles Times*, August 15, 2000.

12. Mónica Deady, "Hispanics in Mixed-Race Marriages Report More Acceptance," *Hispanic Link Weekly Report* Vol. 19, No. 29 (July 23, 2001).

13. Alonzo-Zaldivar, "Latinos Now Top Minority."

14. Miguel Angel Vega, "4.2 Milliones de Latinos en el Condado de LA," *La Opinion*, March 11, 2001.

15. Mark Stevenson, "Mexican Population of U.S. May Reach 18 Million by

2030," *The Press Enterprise*, December 6, 2001; and Geoffrey Mohan, "Mexican Immigration Could Boom in U.S., Report Says," *Los Angeles Times*, December 6, 2001.

16. Juan Andrade, Andrew Hernandez, and Laura Barberena-Medrano, *The Almanac of Latino Politics 2002–2004* (Chicago, Ill: United States Hispanic Leadership Institute, 2002), 10–11.

17. Andrade, Hernandez, and Barberena-Medrano, *The Almanac of Latino Politics 2002–2004*, 6.

18. U.S. Census, "Hispanic Population by Type for Regions, States, and Puerto Rico: 1990 and 2000," Table 2.

19. Francisco Y. Honorio III, "New Southern Menu: Poultry and Latinos," *Hispanic Week Link Weekly Report* Vol. 19, No. 31 (August 6, 2001).

20. For an excellent work on the growing tensions/conflicts between Latinos and blacks see Nicolás C. Vaca, *The Presumed Alliance: The Unspoken Conflict between Latinos and Blacks and What It Means for America* (New York: Rayo, 2004).

21. Stephan Simon, "Latinos Take Root in Midwest," *Los Angeles Times*, October 24, 2002.

22. Sharyn Obsatz, "Inland Area a Hub of Latino Growth," *The Press Enterprise*, July 31, 2002.

23. NCLR, *Beyond the Census*; Richard T. Cooper, "Racial Ethnic Diversity Puts New Face on Middle America," *Los Angeles Times*, March 31, 2001.

24. Joe Donatelli, "Latinos Joining White Flight," *The Press Enterprise*, November 3, 2002.

25. Brooking Center on Urban and Metropolitan Policy, cited in Andrade, Hernandez, and Barberena-Medrano, *The Almanac of Latino Politics 2002–2004*, 5.

26. Robin Fields and Ray Rendon, "Segregation of a New Sort Takes Shape," *Los Angeles Times*, July 5, 2001.

27. Jennifer Mena, "7 State Cities in Diversity Top 10," *Los Angeles Times*, September 4, 2003.

28. Internet: "Growth of U.S. Hispanics Dramatic," www.quepasa.com, June 20, 2003.

29. United States General Accounting Office, "INS Southwest Border Strategy: Resource and Impact Issues Remain after Seven Years," Report to Congressional Committees, August 2001.

30. United States General Accounting Office, "INS Southwest Border Strategy."

31. *La Opinion*, "Se Duplica la Población Indocumentada en los Años 90," January 24, 2002.

32. *The Press Enterprise*, "Fewer Border Crossers Arrested," September 17, 2002.

33. *La Opinion*, "Una Quinta Parte de los 'Legales' son Mexicano," September 5, 2002.

34. Aaron Zitner, "Nation's Birthrate Drops to Its Lowest Level Since 1909," *Los Angeles Times*, June 26, 2003.

35. Internet: "Growth of U.S. Hispanics Dramatic."

36. Lisa Richardson and Robin Fields, "Latino Majority Arrives—Among State's Babies," *Los Angeles Times*, February 6, 2003; and *The Press Enterprise*, "New Majority in Births," February 6, 2003.

37. U.S. Census Bureau, "Census 2000, Summary File I General Profile I: Persons by Race, Age, & Sex; Households and Families by Race and by Type," 2001.

38. Robin Fields, "A Deepening Diversity, but a Growing Divide," *Los Angeles Times*, March 30, 2001.

39. Donatelli, "Latinos Joining White Flight."

40. Copper, *Los Angeles Times*, March 31, 2001.

41. Justin Pritchard, "State Stays Young," *The Press Enterprise*, June 1, 2001.

42. Susannah Rosenblatt, "California Is Seen in Rearview Mirror," *Los Angeles Times*, August 6, 2003.

43. In 2001 the figure used was 49 percent as manifested by following newspaper article: *La Voz* [newspaper], "The U.S. Census Has Made It Official: Whites Are No Longer the Majority in California," June 28, 2001. However, in 2002 the figure changed to 47 percent as illustrated by the following article citation: *The Press Enterprise*, "Largest Minority Group a Heavyweight at Polls," January 10, 2001.

44. Earl Ofari Hutchinson, "Do the Math—Latinos Are Gaining Power," *Los Angeles Times*, March 15, 2001.

45. Because of the U.S. Census plentiful availability of Latino socioeconomic data *Latino* is used. Hence, for purposes of analysis while the U.S. Census data used in this section applies to Latinos in general, it is concomitantly applicable to the Mexicano. Furthermore, I would argue that while most Latino subgroups face a "worst of times" crisis in some instances it is worst for Mexicanos.

46. Cited in James A. Forrest, "Census 2000," 101.

47. U.S. Census Bureau, "Money Income in the United States: 2000," Current Population Reports.

48. *La Voz* [newspaper], "National Study Finds 80% Growth in Latino Middle-Class Over Past 20 Years," May 17, 2001.

49. Arturo Gonzáles, *Mexican Americans & the U.S. Economy: Quest for Buenos Días* (Tucson: University of Arizona Press, 2002), 82.

50. Robert R. Brischetto, "The Hispanic Middle Class Comes of Age," *Hispanic Business*, December 2001, 21.

51. Joel Russell, "The Wealthiest Hispanics," *Hispanic Business*, September 2002.

52. Ruben Navarrette, "Hispanics: The Savior of Values," *The Press Enterprise*, April 1, 2001.

53. *Hispanic Business*, "Hispantelligence Report," April 2004.

54. *Hispanic Business*, "Number of U.S. Hispanic Owned Firms, 1987–2005," May 2002.

55. NCLR, "Beyond the Census: Hispanics and an American Agenda," Washington, D.C., final edition, August 2001.

56. *La Voz* [newspaper], May 17, 2001.

57. Peterson, *Los Angeles Times*, September 25, 2002; Patricia A. Gonzales-Portillo, "Aumenta el Numero de Pobres," *La Opinion*, September 25, 2002.

58. Jonathan Peterson, "Household Income Drops, U.S. Says," *Los Angeles Times*, September 25, 2002. Officially in 2001, the federal government defined the poverty threshold for a family of four as $18,104, up from $17,603. For a family of three, the threshold was $14,228.

59. Maribel Hastings, "La Pobreza se Ensaña Niños Latinos," *La Opinion*, April, 20, 2001.

60. Alonzo-Zaldivar, "Latinos Now Top Minority."

61. Karia Wucuan, "Midad de Hogares Latinos No Tienen Ingresos Suficientes," *La Opinion*, June 4, 2003

62. González, *Mexican Americans & the U.S. Economy*, 85.

63. Brischetto, "The Hispanic Middle Class Comes of Age," 22.

64. Arlene Martinez, "Study's Projects Long Recession for Latinos," *Hispanic Link Weekly Report* Vol. 20, No. 5 (January 28, 2002).

65. *The Press Enterprise*, "Report on Kids Says Nation Can Do Better," April 19, 2001.

66. Lindsey Tanner, "Hispanic Children Face More Health Ills," *The Press Enterprise*, July 3, 2002.

67. U.S. Census, "Health Insurance Coverage: 2000," Washington, D.C., September 2001; Vicki Kemper, "Fewer Have Coverage for Health Care," *Los Angeles Times*, September 30, 2002.

68. Josefina Vidal, "Más Tuberculosis entre Inmigrantes," *La Opinion*, December 18, 2000.

69. Geralda Miller, "Minorities May Be First to Feel Pain If Recession Hits America," *The Press Enterprise*, February 23, 2001.

70. Kimberly Blanton, "Blacks Unemployment Way Up," *Arizona Daily Star*, May 24, 2003.

71. Warren Vieth, "As Factory Job Losses Rise, So Do Risks to Bush," *Los Angeles Times*, October 25, 2003.

72. For an excellent analysis on this issue see Richard L. Zweigenhaft and G. William Domhoff, *Diversity in the Power Elite: Have Women and Minorities Reached the Top?* (New Haven, Conn.: Yale University Press, 1998), 118–39.

73. Gary Strauss, "Good Old Boys' Network Still Rules Corporate Boards," *USA Today*, November 7, 2002.

74. The concept of the prison-military industrial complex came into vogue during the 1990s and was popularized by Angela Davis and a number of other scholars and activists, who use the concept in the context to describe "a set of bureaucratic, political, and economic interests that encourage increased spending on imprisonment, regardless of the actual need." See Eric Schlosser, "The Prison-Industrial Complex," *The Atlantic*, December 1998.

75. Barry Holman, "Masking the Divide: How Officially Reported Prison Statistics Distort the Racial and Ethnic Realities of Prison Growth," (Alexandra, Va.: National

Center on Institutions and Alternatives Research and Public Policy Report, May 2001), 10.

76. The Associated Press, "Inmate Population Swells," *Riverside Press Enterprise*, July 28, 2003.

77. For an excellent work on the U.S. prison system see Peter G. Herman, *The American Prison System* (New York: H.W. Wilson Co., 2001).

78. www.bop.gov/fact0598.html

79. Fox Butterfield, "Number of People in State Prisons Declines Slightly," *New York Times*, August 13, 2001.

80. projects.is.asu.edu

81. Allen J. Beck and Paige M. Harrison, "Prisoners in 2000," U.S. Department of Justice, Bureau of Justice Statistics, August 2001.

82. California Department of Corrections, "CDC Facts," Sacramento, California, Third Quarter 2002.

83. Michelle Munn, "Latino Youth Offenders Face Harsher Treatment, Study Finds," *Los Angeles Times*, July 19, 2002.

84. Janette Alison, "Prop 21 Lacks Vision and Is Not a Solution to Crime," *The Highlander*, February 8, 2000.

85. Holman, "Masking the Divide," 10.

86. Munn, "Latino Youth Offenders Face Harsher Treatment, Study Finds."

87. Joel Kotkin, "Locked Out of a House," *Los Angeles Times*, September 22, 2002.

88. Richard Fausett, "Group Sees L.A. County Latino Crisis," *Los Angeles Times*, October 31, 2003.

89. Victoria Infante, "Inmigrantes, los Mas Afectados por la Escasez de Viviendas," *La Opinion*, September 24, 2002.

90. Diane Wedner, "Many Southland Workers Fall in Gap between Income, Rents," *Los Angeles Times*, September 19, 2002.

91. For an excellent work that addresses various aspects of problems endemic to Latinos in education see Eugene E. Garcia, *Hispanic Education in the United States: Raices y Alas* (Lanham, Md.: Rowman & Littlefield, 2001).

92. Wedner, "Many Southland Workers Fall in Gap between Income, Rents."

93. Gary Orfield, "Schools More Separate: Consequences of a Decade of Resegregation," The Civil Rights Project, Harvard University, July 2001.

94. The Tomás Rivera Policy Institute, "Latinos and Information Technology: The Promise and the Challenge," prepared for the IBM Hispanic Digital Divide Task Force, February 2002.

95. Daniel Weintraub, "California Export—Anti-Bilingual Ballot Measures," *The Press Enterprise*, October 23, 2002; and Eric Hubler, "Bilingual Ban Fails," *Denver Post*, November 6, 2002.

96. Hastings, "La Pobreza se Ensaña Niños Latinos."

97. U.S. Census Bureau: USA TODAY research and analysis by Paul Overberg, James West, and Anne Carey, October 2002.

98. U.S. Bureau of the Census, Educational Attainment in the U.S., March 2000.

99. Arlene Martinez, "Barely Half of Latino High School Grads Enroll in College; Rate for Whites is 63%," *Hispanic Link Weekly Report* Vol. 20, No. 25 (June 17, 2002).

100. *The Chronicle of Higher Education*, "Almanac 2000–3," Vol. XLIX, August 30, 2002, p. 29.

101. Cited in article by Fresia Rodriguez Cadavid, "More Hispanics Reach College, Fewer Graduate," *Hispanic Link Weekly Report* Vol. 20, No. 36 (September 9, 2002).

102. U.S. Census, "Census Bureau Updates Profile of Nation's Latino Groups," Washington, D.C., March 8, 2000.

103. *The Chronicle of Higher Education*, "Almanac 2002–3," p. 29.

104. Richard Fry, "Latinos in Higher Education: Many Enroll, Too Few Graduate," *Education Daily*, September 5, 2002.

105. *The Chronicle of Higher Education*, "Almanac 2002–3," p. 29.

106. NACM Report, www.nacme.org/rsch/data/highered.html

107. *The Chronicle of Higher Education*, "Almanac 2000–3," p. 29.

108. *La Opinión*, "Encuentran subrepesentación de professors hispanos en CSU," June 27, 2003.

109. *Latino* included all various ethnic subgroups. Consequently, one can deduce that the percentage of Mexicanos was probably in the neighborhood of about 3 percent.

110. *The Chronicle of Higher Education*, "Almanac 2002–3," p. 29.

111. Document produced by California assemblypersons Manny Diaz and Marcos Firebaugh, "Equitable Admissions Policies for UC Graduate Program & Professional Schools," April 2002.

112. Michelle Locke, "SAT Essay Spurs Dispute," *The Press Enterprise*, August 11, 2002.

113. Rebecca Trounson, Stuart Silverstein, and Dough Smith, "Students Prevailed against the Odds," *Los Angeles Times*, October 24, 2003.

114. Richard Huff, "Media Groups Issue Reports on Networks, Minority Employment," *The Press Enterprise*, October 15, 2003.

115. Lynn Elbar, "Study: TV Missing Growth of Hispanics," *The Press Enterprise*, June 25, 2003; and Jorge Luis Macias, "Latinos a la Zaga en la Televisión," *La Opinion*, June 26, 2003.

116. Ricardo Alonzo-Zaldivar, "Latinos Give Bush High Job Approval Rating, Poll Shows," *Los Angeles Times*, August 12, 2002.

117. Arlene Martinez, "Poll Finds Latinos in Political Flux, Immigration, Bias Are Major Issues," *Hispanic Link Weekly Report* Vol. 20, No. 34 (August 26, 2002).

118. Lisa Richardson and Patrick McDonnell, "Immigration Crackdown Ineffective, Study Finds," *Los Angeles Times*, July 17, 2002.

119. Diana Cervantes, "Siguen Muriendo Migrantes," *La Prensa*, February, 15–21, 2002.

120. *La Opinion*, "Denuncian Record de Muertes en la Frontera," July 7, 2002.

121. Julie Watson, "Migrant Deaths Decline," *The Press Enterprise*, July 6, 2002.

122. Gregor McGavin, "Fosas Comunes Marcan La Frontera," *La Prensa*, September 26–October 2, 2003.

123. Garrison, *Los Angeles Times*, October 2, 2002.

124. Associated Press, "Border Security Hurting Tourism, Official Says," *The Press Enterprise*, December 12, 2003.

125. Ruben Navarrette, Jr., "The Border Is More a Gap Than a Line," *The Press Enterprise*, July 10, 2002.

126. *La Opinion*, "Piden Tropas en la Frontera," June 19, 2002.

127. Stephan Wall, "Agents Saturated to South Post 9/11," *The Sun*, July 29, 2002.

128. *La Opinion*, "Guardia Nacional Vigilará Frontera con México," February 24, 2002.

129. Seth Borenstein and Lenny Savino, "Goals Unclear along Border," *The Press Enterprise*, March 24, 2002.

130. Jonathan Peterson, "Noncitizens Ordered to Update Addresses," *Los Angeles Times*, July 25, 2002.

131. Overview Statement on Hoffman Decision, prepared by Libertad Civil Rights Advocates, Albuquerque, Nuevo México, received April 18, 2002.

132. Deborah Kong, "Democrats Push Plan to Legalize Immigrants," *The Press Enterprise*, August 23, 2002.

133. *The Press Enterprise*, "Police Probe Killing of 2 Migrants," October 25, 2002; Maria Luisa Arredando, "Investigan Muertes en la Frontera," *La Opinion*, October 24, 2002; and *La Opinion*, "Hispano Recluta Vigilantes," December 31, 2002.

134. Much of the information on the NAHR and its activities addressing the U.S./México border crisis around southern Arizona from 2000 to 2003 has been extrapolated from two comprehensive reports I wrote specifically focusing on the rancher vigilante and growing militia activity directed against undocumented migrants. The first report, entitled, "Report on Arizona/Sonora Border Crisis," was released to the press in July 2000 and sent to appropriate U.S. and México congressional committees for review. The second report, entitled "National Alliance for Human Rights (NAHR): Delegation Report on Southern Arizona Militia and Hate Groups," was released in June 2003 and likewise was made public and distributed to the appropriate congressional entities in both the United States and México.

135. Scott Gold, "Suit Targets U.S. Border Vigilantes," *Los Angeles Times*, June 30, 2003.

136. Frank Del Olmo, "Davis Is Caught in Jaws of Two Latino Demands," *Los Angeles Times*, September 9, 2002.

137. Nancy Vogel and Dan Marain, "No Licenses for Illegal Immigrants," *Los Angeles Times*, October 1, 2002.

138. Christina Almeida, "Protesters Condemn License Bill Veto," *The Press Enterprise*, October 2, 2002.

139. Nancy Vogel, "Assembly Votes Down License Law," *Los Angeles Times*, December 2, 2003; Abraham D. Sofar, "Licenses Cross the Line," *Los Angeles Times*, November 20,

2003; and Pilar Marrero y Jorge Luis Macias, "Senado Deroga la SB60," *La Opinion*, November 25, 2003.

140. Gregg Jones, "State Moves toward Repeal of License Law," *Los Angeles Times*, November 25, 2003.

141. Vogel, *Los Angeles Times*, December 2, 2003; Nancy Vogel, "Panel OKs Repeal of License Law," *Los Angeles Times*, November 26, 2003; and Pilar Moreno, "Estancada Final a la SB60," *La Opinion*, December 2, 2003.

142. *La Opinion*, "Sube de Tono la Pugna por las Licencias de Conducer," October 21, 2003; Victoria Infante, "Proponen Boicot por Anulación de la SB60," *La Opinion*, November 26, 2003; Sharyn Obsatz and Jim Miller, "Activists Recruit Support for Strike," *The Press Enterprise*, December 6, 2003.

143. O. Ricardo Pimentel, "The Boycott That Got Boycotted," *The Press Enterprise*, December 27, 2003.

144. Latino leadership meeting of boycott organizers attended by this author, which included Nativo Lopez, on December 16, 2003, in Los Angeles.

145. Ricardo Alonzo-Zaldivar, Abigail Goldman, and Nancy Cleeland, "Immigrant Wal-Mart Janitors Arrested," *Los Angeles Times*, October 24, 2003; and Associated Press, "Nine Illegal Immigrants Arrested in Raids Sue Wal-Mart," *Los Angeles Times*, November 10, 2003

146. Ricardo Alonzo-Zaldivar, "Police May Join Hunt for Illegal Migrants," *Los Angeles Times*, November 11, 2003.

147. Frank Del Olmo, "Stop 'Coyotes' with Border Reform," *Los Angeles Times*, November 9, 2003.

148. Tamar Jacoby, "Anti-Immigrant Fever in Arizona," *Los Angeles Times*, July 12, 2004.

149. Pilar Moreno, "Gestan Nueva Version de la Prop. 197," *La Opinion*, October 16, 2003.

150. Moreno, "Gestan Nueva Version de la Prop. 197."

151. Robert Suro, "Breadwinners Who Know No Borders," *Los Angeles Times*, November 10, 2003. Suro posits that in 2003 some $25 billion was sent home from the United States by migrants to Latin America.

152. Ricardo Alonzo-Zaldivar, "U.S. and México Pledge to Revive Immigration Drive," *Los Angeles Times*, November 13, 2003.

153. Patrick J. McDonnell, "Wave of U.S. Immigration Likely to Survive September 11," *Los Angeles Times*, January 10, 2002.

154. For a critique on "USAPA" see Stephen J. Schulhofer, "At War with Liberty: Post-9/11, Due Process and Security Have Taken a Beating," *The American Prospect*, March 2003, A5–A8.

155. Pamphlet, "What Is the U.S.A. P.A.T.R.I.O.T. ACT, and How Does It Affect Me as a Student," Campus Coalition for Independent Media, No date.

156. Charles Levendosky, "Mr. Bush Is Building an Empire," *The Press Enterprise*, December 31, 2002.

157. Richard B. Schmitt, "Patriot Act Author Has Concerns," *Los Angeles Times*, November 30, 2003.

158. Louis Sahagan, "Powder-Filled Hate Mail Sent to Latinos," *Los Angeles Times*, March 14, 2002.

159. Sharyn Obsatz, "Shelved Bills under Review," *The Press Enterprise*, March 20, 2002.

160. Henry Weinstein, "Secret U.S. Deportation Hearings Ruled Illegal," *Los Angeles Times*, August 27, 2002.

161. Edwin Chen, "Bush Describes Tough Foreign Policy Vision," *Los Angeles Times*, September 21, 2002.

162. James P. Pinkerton, "'The Bush War Doctrine' Leaps into History," *Los Angeles Times*, October 8, 2002.

163. The preceding examination of the Bush administration is but a cursory summary based upon two Bush administration reports: "Rebuilding America's Defenses" and "National Security Strategy." The Internet address to the former is cryptome.org /rad.htm, while the address for the latter is www.whitehouse.gov/nsc/nsccall.html.

164. Robert Dreyfuss, "Persian Gulf—or Tonkin Gulf?" *The American Prospect*, 10–11.

165. Vicki Kemper, "Homeland Agency Is Big at Birth," *Los Angeles Times*, November 26, 2002.

166. Anthony Kahn, "South Korea, China Pledge to Try Diplomacy with North," *Los Angeles Times*, January 3, 2003.

167. Maura Reynolds, "Bush Says Iraq Effort Progressing Steadily," *Los Angeles Times*, July 24, 2003.

168. Maura Reynolds, "Bush Says U.S. Must Spread Democracy," *Los Angeles Times*, November 7, 2003.

169. Tom Reinken, Cheryl Brownstein-Santaigo, Julie Sheer, and Ross Toro, "Iraq: A Snapshot of the Last Year," *Los Angeles Times*, March 20, 2004.

170. *Los Angeles Times*, "Resistance Building Strength, Guerrilla Leaders in Iraq Say," October 7, 2003.

171. Alissa J. Rubin, "U.S. Resistance to Direct Vote Galvanizes Iraq's Shiite Clerics," *Los Angeles Times*, December 3, 2003.

172. Richard C. Paddock and Doyle Mc Manus, "U.S. Favors Quick Transition in Iraq as Means to Stem Insurgency," *Los Angeles Times*, November 11, 2003.

173. David Firestone, "Congress OKs Rebuilding Aid," *The Press Enterprise*, October 18, 2003.

174. Maggie Farely, "U.N. Role in Iraq an Open Question for All," *Los Angeles Times*, December 31, 2003.

175. NAHR Press Advisory, "Mobilization against Bush Administration's War on Iraq," October 3, 2002, Navarro archives.

176. The following are a few of the newspaper articles on antiwar NAHR-sponsored events: Ben Schnayerson, "Group of Latinos Objects to War," *The Sun*, October 5, 2002; Roberto Hernandez, "Hispanics Protest Bush's Iraq Policy," *The Press Enterprise*, October

5, 2002; Miguel Gonzalez, "Protestan Planes Bélicos contra Irak," October 5, 2002; Kahlil Ford, "Students Demonstrate against War in Iraq," October 29, 2002.

177. NAHR Letter to CHCI chair Congressman Silvestre Reyes and all members of the CHCI, October 4, 2002, Navarro archives.

178. Arlene Martinez, "Latino House Democrats Team with Anti-War Activists Groups," *Hispanic Link Weekly Report* Vol. 20, No. 41 (October 14, 2002).

179. Letter/petition to México's president Vicente Fox, October 4, 2002, Navarro archives.

180. Pilar Moreno, "Mayoria Latina de Nueva York y California contra la Guerra," *La Opinion*, October 31, 2002.

181. Guy McCarthy and George Watson, "Among Latinos, Less Support for War," *The Press Enterprise*, February 19, 2003; Maribel Hastings, "Protestas no lo Alteran," *La Opinion*, February 19, 2003.

182. Jorge Mariscal, "The Future for Latinos in an Era of War and Occupation," unpublished paper, April 18, 2003.

183. David Seaton, Sharyn Obsatz, and Guy McCarthy, "Latino Toll Reflects Risk Duties Bring," *The Press Enterprise*, April 8, 2003.

184. Pilar Marrero, "Latinos en La Guerra," *La Opinion*, March 20, 2003.

185. Frank Del Olmo, "In War, Diversity Can Be a Lifesaver," *Los Angeles Times*, May 11, 2003.

186. Mark Krikorian, "Green Card Soldiers Don't Pass Muster," *Los Angeles Times*, May 6, 2003; Ruben Navarrette, Jr., "Viva Our 'Green Card Troops,'" *Albuquerque Journal*, April 12, 2003.

187. *La Opinion*, "Exigen Ciudadania para los Soldados Inmigrantes," November 6, 2003.

188. Some of the major white antiwar groups and coalitions included International A.N.S.W.E.R. (Act Now to Stop and End Racism), Bay Area United Against War, Not in Our Name, United for Peace and Justice, and the Vanguard Foundation, which assisted in arranging transportation for protestors.

189. NAHR Flyer, no date.

190. Jose Cardenas, "Activists See New Eastside Protest as Latest Link in a 30-Year Chain," *Los Angeles Times*, February 7, 2003.

191. Jesse J. Linares, "Huelga entra en Seguda Semena," *La Opinion*, April 11, 2002; Jack Katzanek, "Union Targets Janitors in Inland Area," *The Press Enterprise*, April 11, 2000; Miguel Angel Vega,"Gore Respalda a Huelgistas," *La Opinion*, April 17, 2000.

192. Nancy Cleeland, "L.A. Janitors OK Contract in Landmark Vote," *Los Angeles Times*, April 25, 2002.

193. Lucero Amador, "Braceros Anuncian un Boicot," *La Opinion*, August 30, 2002.

194. Victoria Keith, "Extienden Plazo para las Demandas de ex Braceros," *La Opinion*, August 21, 2002.

195. Lucero Amador, "Braceros Annuncian un Boicot," August 30, 2002.

196. Victoria Keith, "Huelga de Hambre por una Firma de Gray Davis," *La Opinion*, August 20, 2002.

197. Gregg Jones, "History Echoes as Farm Workers Rally for Bill," *Los Angeles Times*, August 26, 2002.

198. *Los Angeles Times*, "Farm Workers March to the Capitol, but Davis' Steps Will Come Later," August 26, 2002.

199. Ruben Navarrette, Jr., "With These Friends, Who Needs Enemies?," *The Press Enterprise*, September 4, 2002.

200. Navarrette, "With These Friends, Who Needs Enemies?."

201. Gregg Jones, "A Big Win for Farm Workers," *Los Angeles Times*, October 1, 2002.

202. For a work that focuses on the various aspects of the identity conflicts permeating Hispanos/Latinos see Jorge J. E. Garcia, *Hispanic/Latino Identity: A Philosophical Perspective*, (Malden, Mass.: Blackwell, 2000).

203. The concept "group consciousness" as explained by John A. Garcia "refers to the cognitive elements of group attachment; a person incorporates identity(ies) as part of his social identity, along with the evaluative assessments about the group's relative position in society. This identity represents an attachment and affinity to social groupings." See Garcia, *Latino Politics in America*, 26.

204. Fred Alvarez, "Mariachi Music Strikes Chord with Students Seeking Roots," *Los Angeles Times*, December 16, 2001.

205. Jose Cuello, "Latinos and Hispanics: A Primer on Terminology," unpublished paper, Wayne State University, revised 12/02/96.

206. Veronica Chambers, Ana Figueroa, Pat Wingert, and Julie Weingarten, "Latin U.S.A: How Young Hispanics Are Changing America, *Newsweek*, July 12, 1999.

207. *The Press Enterprise*, "Santana Smooth," February 21, 2002; Adriana Sainz, "Juan Gabriel Takes Top Honors with 4," *The Press Enterprise*, May 11, 2002; John-Thor Dahlburg, "Miami Counts Up the Losses after It Loses Latin Grammys," *Los Angeles Times*, August 22, 2001.

208. *The Press Enterprise*, "More Are Speaking Spanish at Home," May 15, 2002.

209. Associated Press, "Survey Finds Split among Latinos by Place of Birth," *The Press Enterprise*, December 18, 2002.

210. Ruben Navarrette, Jr., "Latino Immigrants Are Assimilating," *The Press Enterprise*, December 22, 2002.

211. For an excellent article that provides a compendium on the Spanglish phenomenon see Daniel Hernandez, "A Hybrid Tongue or Slanguage?" *Los Angeles Times*, December 27, 2003.

212. SVREP, "Latino Vote Reporter," Vol. V, No. 4 (Winter 2000).

213. United States Hispanic Leadership Institute, *The Almanac of Latino Politics 2002–2004* (Chicago, Ill.: United States Hispanic Leadership Institute), chapter 2.

214. Aforementioned 2000 presidential election data taken from *The World Almanac and Book of Facts 2002* (New York: World Almanac Books, 2002), 558–90.

215. For an excellent statistical analysis of the Latino vote in the 2000 presidential elections see USHLI, *The Almanac of Latino Politics 2002–2004*, chapter 4.

216. *Los Angeles Times*, "The National Electorate," November 9, 2000.

217. SVREP, *Latino Vote Reporter*, November 9, 2000.

218. USHLI, *The Almanac of Latino Politics 2002–2004*, 54.

219. David Pace, "Latino Voting: Slow Growth," *The San Bernardino County Sun*, August 26, 2001.

220. USHLI, *The Almanac of Latino Politics 2002–2004*, 24.

221. Pace, "Latino Voting: Slow Growth."

222. Jessica McKnight, "Young Latino Voting Takes a Deep Dip," *Hispanic Link Weekly Report* Vol. 20, No. 26 (July 1, 2002).

223. NALEO, "2001 National Directory of Latino Elected Officials," NALEO Educational Fund, 2001.

224. NALEO, "2003 National Directory of Latino Elected Officials," NALEO Educational Fund, 2003.

225. Mark Z. Barbak, "Latino Political Clout Has Candidates Brushing-up Their Spanish," *Los Angeles Times*, June 29, 2003.

226. "A Compendium of 2002 Latino Election Returns," *Hispanic Link* Vol. 20, No. 45 (November 11, 2002).

227. Maribel Hastings, "Candidatura de Miguel Estrada divide a latinos," *La Opinion*, September 26, 2002.

228. Patricia A. Gonzalez-Portillo, "Nuevo Embajador en México Favorece Legalizar Trabajadores," *La Opinion*, November 14, 2002.

229. O. Ricardo Pimentel, "Latino Skepticism at Bush," *The Press Enterprise*, September 13, 2003; Associated Press, "Hispanics Tilt to Democrats, Unsure of Bush," *The Press Enterprise*, August 3, 2003.

230. Barabak, "Latino Political Clout Has Candidates Brushing-up on Their Spanish."

231. Frank Del Olmo, "Finally, the Democrats Refocus on Latinos," *Los Angeles Times*, July 20, 2003.

232. Nick Anderson, "Dean Gaining Support among Latino Leaders," *Los Angeles Times*, December 12, 2003.

233. Janet Hook, "Congressional Newcomers, but Hardly Neophytes," *Los Angeles Times*, November 13, 2002.

234. NALEO, "2003 National Directory of Latino Elected Officials," vii.

235. NALEO, "2001 National Directory of Latino Elected Officials," 6–214.

236. Fresia Rodriguez Cadavid, "Richardson a Winner in New México!" *Hispanic Link Weekly Report* Vol. 20, No. 28 (November 11, 2002).

237. Cadavid, "Richardson a Winner in New México!"

238. Cadavid, "Richardson a Winner in New México!"; Ruben Navarrette, "Election Previewed Hispanic Vote Trends," *The Press Enterprise*, November 11, 2002.

239. Pilar Marrero, "Camejo: El Candidato Latino a Gobernador," *La Opinion*, August 26, 2002.

240. Gregg Jones, "Latino Leaders Urge Davis Reelection," *Los Angeles Times*, October 18, 2002.

241. *Los Angeles Times*, "Election 2002: Times Exit Poll Results," November 7, 2002.

242. "Coast to Coast 2002 Election Results," *Hispanic Link Weekly Report* Vol. 20, No. 45 (November 11, 2003).

243. Leonel Sanchez, "Bustamante's Run Excites Latinos," *The San Diego Union-Tribune*, August 25, 2003.

244. *Los Angeles Times*, "Bustamante Gets a Boost in San Bernardino," August 21, 2003; Jazmin Ortega Morales, "Group Rally Urges No on Recall Effort," *The Press Enterprise*, August 21, 2003; Stephen Wall, "Rights Group: No on Ouster," *The Sun*, August 21, 2003; Eric Hsu, "Recall Stirs Both Sides to Action," *The Bakersfield Californian*, August 23, 2003.

245. Associated Press, "Bustamante Unashamed of Link to Mecha Group," *The Press Enterprise*, September 5, 2003.

246. Mark Martin, "Populist Cruz: Bustamante Tilts Left, Runs against Big Business," *San Francisco Chronicle*, September 5, 2003.

247. Alan Zarembo, "Latino Voters Can't Be Treated as a Bloc," *Los Angeles Times*, October 1, 2003.

248. Michael Finnegan, "Voters Recall Davis; Schwarzenegger's In," *Los Angeles Times*, October 8, 2003.

249. Associated Press, "Analysis Finds Votes Missing," *The Press Enterprise*, October 19, 2003.

250. Arlene Martinez, "Hispanics Advance at State, Local Levels," *Hispanic Link Weekly Report* Vol. 20, No. 46 (November 18, 2002).

251. Martinez, "Hispanics Advance at State, Local Levels."

252. Martinez, "Hispanics Advance at State, Local Levels," vii.

253. Sherry Sylvester, "Cisneros Predicts Successful Term," *San Antonio Express-News*, May 13, 2001.

254. Pilar Marrero, "Villaraigosa y Hahn Adelante," *La Opinion*, April 11, 2001.

255. Steve Lopez, "For Shame, Non-Latino No-Shows," *Los Angeles Times*, June 11, 2001.

256. "Making The News This Week," *Hispanic Link* Vol. 20, No. 29 (July 22, 2002).

257. Pilar Marrero, "Voto Latino Record," *La Opinion*, June 6, 2001.

258. Ray F. Herndon and Jennifer Mena, "Recalled Santa Trustee Lost Even His Latino Base," *Los Angeles Times*, February 6, 2003.

259. For a comprehensive analysis on the limitations of local governments to create major change see my book *The Cristal Experiment: A Chicano Struggle for Community Control* (Madison: University of Wisconsin Press, 1998).

260. USHLI, *The Almanac of Latino Politics 2002–2004*, chapter 3.

261. *Los Angeles Times*, "Voters Spoke with Silence This Year," November 7, 2002.

262. Steve Sailer, "Paradox of the Hispanic Vote," *United Press International*, January 26, 2003.

263. Cited in Sailer, "Paradox of the Hispanic Vote."

264. USHLI, *The Almanac of Latino Politics 2002–2004*, chapter 3.

265. Michelle DeArmond, "Noncitizen Voting Unlikely to Succeed," *Los Angeles Times*, December 12, 2003; Roger Lindo, "Proponen dar Voto a los Inmigrantes," *La Opinion*, December 12, 2003.

266. Dan Waters, "Gap between Voters, Nonvoters to Persist," *The Press Enterprise*, December 31, 2002.

267. Sailer, "Paradox of the Hispanic Vote."

268. Cadavid, "Texas Turnout Jumps," *Hispanic Link Weekly Report*, November 11, 2002.

269. "Blancos: Minoría en la Poblacion, pero Mayoria entre Votantes," *La Opinion*, January 10, 2002.

270. *Hispanic Business*, "Hispantelligence Report," April 2004.

271. Pew Hispanic Center/Kaiser Family Foundation, "National Survey of Latinos: The Latino Electorate," October 2002.

272. *Los Angeles Times*, "GOP Plans to Court Minorities," January 20, 2002.

273. Jonathan Peterson, "In Tragedy, an Emotional Surge in Citizenship Hopes," *Los Angeles Times*, July 24, 2002.

274. Martinez, "Poll Finds Latinos in Political Flux, Immigration, Bias Are Major Issues."

275. The poll was conducted by McLaughlin & Associates "Opinions Latinos" and was based upon sample population of 1,000 Latino adults of whom 60 percent were registered to vote with a margin of error of plus or minus three percentage points. See Ricardo Alonzo-Salivary, "Latinos Give Bush High Job Approval Rating, Poll Shows," *Los Angeles Times*, August 12, 2002.

276. Adalberto Ruiz, "Latino Activists Prepare to Join Zapatistas in March on México City," *Hispanic Link Weekly Report* Vol. 19, No. 7 (February 12, 2001).

277. Denise Dresser, "México's Beset Fox Must Redefine 'Change,'" *Los Angeles Times*, July 3, 2002; Andres Oppenheimer, "México Suffers Political Paralysis," *Los Angeles Times*, July 24, 2002.

278. *Associated Press*, "México Pledges Vote to Citizens Living Abroad by 2006," March 14, 2002.

279. Ricardo Sandoval, "Fox Taps Ex-Farm Laborer to Tackle Migrant Issues," *The Press Enterprise*, September 20, 2002.

280. Richard Boudreaux, "Fox Will Head New Agency for México Migrants," *Los Angeles Times*, August 7, 2002.

281. Jessica Garrison, "Activist to Head Agency on Mexicans in U.S.," *Los Angeles Times*, November 25, 2002.

282. Sandra Marquez, "Money Transfers to México at Peak," *The Press Enterprise*, December 31, 2002.

283. *Los Angeles Times*, "Funds Sent Home to México Like to Rise," September 16, 2002.

284. Lucero Amador, "Diputado Mexicano abre Oficina en LA." *La Opinion*, February 22, 2001.

285. In California, Felipe Aguirre was elected PRD state chair and twenty-nine others

as well were elected, including me, to the PRD State Central Committee. PRD state chairs for the four other states included Carlos Arango, Illinois.

286. Jorge A. Arizmendi-Peñaloza, "Instalan mesa Directive del PRD," *La Prensa*, September 6–12, 2002.

287. Celeste Tarricone, "México Pledges Expatriate Voting," *The Press Enterprise*, March 15, 2002.

288. I participated with others from the PRD in the United States in negotiations with deputies and senators from the PRD, PAN, PRI, and La Convergencia during the spring months of 2002 both in México City and in Los Angeles.

289. Raul Caballero, "El Voto de Afuera," *La Opinion*, March 21, 2002.

290. Under the auspices of the National Alliance for Human Rights, which I coordinated, in concert with other groups an organizing effort to get Chicanos (Mexicanos born in the United States) to secure their dual nationality was initiated. Mexicanos who were born in México but became U.S. citizens prior to 1998 were encouraged to retrieve in reality their dual citizenship. The difference between the two was insignificant; the only major difference was that dual nationals could not yet vote in 2002 in México's elections; otherwise, dual nationals enjoyed all the rights and privileges of being a Mexicano citizen. For the Riverside and San Bernardino dual national campaign see Sharyn Pbsatz and Jazmín Ortega, "Seeking Clout South of the Border," *The Press Enterprise*, July 8, 2002.

291. For an excellent overview on the cardinal aspects of the issue of the vote to Mexicanos in the United States and abroad see Raul Caballero, "El Voto de Afuera"; and Alejandro Escalona, "Amplio Consenso para Otargar ese Dercho a los Mexicanos en el Extranjero," both articles in *Nuevo Aztlán: Cultural Review of Chicano/Latino Thought*, No. 16 (May 24–25 and 26–27).

292. Jennifer Mena, "Mexican Expatriates Want Ability to Vote, Seek Office," *Los Angeles Times*, March 21, 2002.

293. Jerry Kammer, "Mexicans Aim a Boycott at Their Homeland," *The San Diego Union-Tribune*, July 12, 2002.

294. Kammer, "Mexicans Aim a Boycott at Their Homeland."

295. Interview, Miguel Flores, September 18, 2002. Mr. Flores is a state secretary for both the SPM and Sociedad Edad de Oro.

296. LULAC Press Release, "Supreme Court's Decision Hurts Immigrant Workers—Sets Precedent for Labor Violations, LULAC Says," April 1, 2002.

297. "Revenue, Expenditures of Major U.S. Latino Organizations," *Hispanic Link Weekly Report* Vol. 19, No. 50 (December 17, 2001).

298. *La Opinion*, "LULAC: Los Dos Partidos Impiden Avance Latino," September 11, 2002.

299. Interview, Maria Tioco, June 12, 2002

300. Interview, Juan Jose Peña, September 29, 2002.

301. Interview, Peña.

302. Jorge Luis Macías, "Facciones de MAPA Retiran Apoyo a Simon," *La Opinion*, August 20, 2002.

303. *La Opinion*, "Nativo Lopez, Nuevo Presidente de MAPA," August 1, 2003.

304. Fresia Rodriguez Cadavid, "Nearly $30 Million Spent to Get Hispanics to the Polls," *Hispanic Link Weekly Report* Vol. 20, No. 48 (December 2, 2002).

305. NALEO Education Fund marketing materials, August 30, 2002.

306. NALEO Educational Fund, "The NALEO Educational Fund at a Glance," March 23, 2002.

307. NALEO Educational Fund, "Lines Drawn as White House and President Fox Negotiate on Guest Worker and Legalization Programs," *Legislative Updates*, September 2001.

308. Interview, Roberto Alonzo, September 19, 2002.

309. Interview, Alonzo.

310. Matea Gold, "Fewer Latinos Back Davis This Time," *Los Angeles Times*, October 30, 2002.

311. Letter, by Armando Navarro addressed to CHCI chair Lucille Roybal-Allard, May 30, 2000, location: Navarro Archives, Riverside.

312. Charlie Ericksen, "CHC-Backed PAC Pledges to Raise $1 Million, 'Take Back the House,'" *Hispanic Link Weekly Report* Vol. 20, No. 10 (March 4, 2002).

313. www.chci.org/events/events.html

314. Telephone interview, David Ricco, May 10, 2003.

315. Telephone interview, Miguel Perez, September 11, 2002.

316. Telephone interview, Roberto Tijerina, May 10, 2003.

317. Skye Earls, "More Latinos Join Unions, but Rate, Earning Are Low," *Hispanic Link Weekly Report* Vol. 19, No. 7 (February 12, 2001).

318. John A. Garcia, *Latino Politics in America: Community, Culture, and Interests* (Lanham, Md.: Rowman & Littlefield, 2003), 156.

319. For a revenue and expenditure overview of the major Latino national organizations see *Hispanic Link Weekly Report*, December 17, 2001.

320. Matea Gold and Nancy Cleeland, "Labor's Clout Set to Help Choose Next L.A. Mayor," *Los Angeles Times*, February 12, 2001.

321. Gold and Cleeland, "Labor's Clout Set to Help Choose Next L.A. Mayor."

322. Carl Ingram and Dan Morain, "Farm Labor Bill Gets Legislature's OK," *Los Angeles Times*, August 9, 2002.

323. Nancy Cleeland, "As It Struggles to Rebuild Itself, UFW Lauds a New Strawberry Pact," *Los Angeles Times*, March 8, 2001; *The Press Enterprise*, "UFW Signs First Contract with a Strawberry Grower," March 9, 2001.

324. Hilda Marrella Delgado, "Bert Corona deja Huella Imborrable," *La Opinion*, January 17, 2001

325. *Los Angeles Times*, "Celebrating Activist's Life," January 21, 2001.

326. HMN, "Open Letter to SEIU Members from Hermandad Mexicana Nacional," no date.

327. Interview, Jose Moreno, RRC member, September 12, 2002.

328. Norma de La Vega, "Demandan a Agente de la Patrulla Fronteriza," *La Opinion*, September 20, 2002.

329. Jaime Cruz written statement on NCMC, "You Cannot Have Resistance from a Distance: The Future of the Chicano Movement," sent to Armando Navarro, dated July 22, 2002.

330. The panel of speakers included prominent historian Mario T. Garcia, Professor Raul Ruiz, Professor Jorge Mariscal, filmmaker Jesús Treviño, activist scholar Ernesto Vigil, scholar Armando Morales, and me.

331. Telephone conversation on the matter with Professor Rodolfo Acuña and Roberto Tijerina, September 10 and 11, respectively.

332. For more information on the current activities and status of PNLRU see Internet website: larazaunida.tripod.com/program/intro.htm

333. Interview, Xenaro Ayala, former RUP national chairman, February 16, 2003.

334. Interview, Ayala.

335. NCLR, "Proposed Budget for Fiscal Year 2002: Presentation to the Board of Directors," October 12, 2001.

336. Arlene Martinez, "Yzaguirre Diagnosed with Parkinson's, Will Continue Daily Duties with NCLR," *Hispanic Link Weekly Report* Vol. 19, No. 48 (December 3, 2001).

337. Jorge Luis Macías, "Yzaguirre: Bush Decepcionóa los Latinos," *La Opinion*, July 21, 2003.

338. MALDEF, News press website, November 13, 2002, December 5, 2002.

339. David Rosenzweig and Michael Finnegan, "Latino Voter Lawsuit Rejected," *Los Angeles Times*, June 13, 2002.

340. Jorge Luis Macías, "MALDEF Rechaza Secession," *La Opinion*, August 24, 2002.

341. Andrea Siedsma, "LBA Event Draws a Crowd," *Hispanic Business*, November 2000.

342. www.lif.org/about.html

343. Rich Laezman, "Striving for 'Critical Mass,'" *Hispanic Business*, October 2001.

344. Interview, Juan Jose Peña, AGIF Nuevo México state vice-commander, September 30, 2002.

345. "New Group Seeks Greater Hispanic Influence," *Hispanic Business*, July/August 2001.

346. "National Hispanic Media Coalition: President Alex Nogales Explains the Hispanicization of Network TV," *Latino Leaders*, March 31, 2001.

347. Tim Dougherty, "Taking It Up a Notch," *Hispanic Business*, July/August 2000.

348. Greg Braxton, "Coalition Faults Networks over Lack of Diversity," *Los Angeles Times*, July 18, 2002.

349. The innumerable sources pertinent to the NAHR's diverse advocacy activities are in my personal archives.

350. Interview, Ada Riddel-Sosa, September 23, 2002.

351. Interview, Riddel-Sosa.

352. Jennifer Mena, "México's 2006 Race Comes to Santa Ana," *Los Angeles Times*, July 7, 2002.

353. Mena, "México's 2006 Race Comes to Santa Ana."

354. Stephan Wall, "Home Town Heroes Give Aid, Comfort," *The Sun*, July 7, 2002.
355. Wall, "Home Town Heroes Give Aid, Comfort."
356. Interview, Jacques, July 5, 2002.
357. Interview, Aguirre, September 18, 2002.

Epilogue
Conclusions and Prospects for Change in the Twenty-first Century

Transition to External Colonialism

AFTER 155 YEARS OF OCCUPATION, Aztlán's barrios and *colonias* still today exist under the deleterious effects of internal colonialism. In the preceding chapters, I have documented the egregious effects it has wrought on the Mexicano political experience in Aztlán. While some progress has been made since 1848, Aztlán's barrios and *colonias* in 2003 were still impoverished and plagued by social problems. Today the specter of internal colonialism is rapidly evolving into an external form. Moreover, Aztlán as a region increasingly resembles a colonized "third world" "nation-within-a-nation." Mexicanos today can be equated to be the "Palestinians" of the United States, a "people without a country."

As the Palestinians in Israel have no nation-state of their own and are a colonized and occupied people, so are Mexicanos in Aztlán. And like the Palestinians, Mexicanos will soon constitute a new majority. Historically, they have been victims of marginalization by both México and the United States. For generations México neglected its people north of the U.S./México border. They have been treated with disdain, as "foreigners," and in some cases as "traitors" for leaving México and settling in the United States. Furthermore, they have also been stereotyped as being anglicized, assimilated, and of having "no loyalty" to the motherland, México. Pejorative terms such as *pochos* (Mexicanos who have become Anglicized) or *vendidos* (sellouts) were and continue to be used by some today in México to describe Mexicanos in the United States.

In the past, when the government of México has sought to assist its people in the United States, it has been circumspect, as is the case today with President Vicente Fox, who is not willing to "ruffle the political feathers" of its superpower northern neighbor. Moreover, México's ruling government and *partidos* (political parties) have refused to grant Mexicanos in the United States the right to suffrage and political representation in México's congress. México's recent rediscovery of its people's importance in the United States is in great part due to the billions of dollars in remittances sent annually, which have greatly helped sustain México's precarious economy. Thus, although the relationship has begun to improve, by and large, México's government today still treats Mexicanos in the United States as "strangers," subject to expedient and symbolic manipulation.

Likewise the United States' oppression of Mexicanos is a matter of historical fact. As this work has amply documented, since 1848 Mexicanos have been subject to white racism and an insidious colonial occupation characterized by exploitation and subordination. The historical scars of colonization are evident in the myriad of social problems that permeate today Aztlán's barrios and *colonias*. For decades, the white majority has had arguably a love-hate relationship with Mexicanos—they have tolerated them at best. White business interests economically love to have access to exploit Mexicano cheap labor. Culturally, many whites love certain aspects of the Mexicano culture such as the food, tacos, enchiladas, burritos, music, and even celebrate Mexicano holidays, for example, Cinco de Mayo. Historically, however, some whites have had a pronounced hatred of Mexicanos. Imbued with a deep sense of ethnocentrism they have perceived them to be inferior as a people. This hate is clearly prevalent among nativist whites today, who feel threatened culturally, economically, and politically by the burgeoning Mexicano population. Thus, today as Mexicanos in the United States enter the twenty-first century, the phrase in Spanish, *ni aquí, ni allá* (neither here nor there) is quite apropos to describing their precarious status and relationship to both México and the United States.

Future Demographic Prospects: La Re-Conquista de Aztlán?

The United States in the twenty-first century has become irreversibly a multicultural, multiracial, and multiethnic society. White hegemony, particularly in Aztlán, within a few decades will diminish. This means the "white racial dictatorship" that has controlled and governed this region is destined to change. If present demographic trends continue, as a result of the re-Mexicanización de Aztlán and Latinoización of the United States, the United States will be a bifurcated white and Latino bilingual and bicultural country. The number of "push" and "pull" factors that have impelled the migrant exodus into the United States will intensify. Why? The answer lies in the very nature of the United States' liberal capitalist economy, which as a pull factor is dependent upon and driven by an insatiable appetite for cheap exploitable labor. The preceding coupled with México's and Latin America's powerful push factors of increasing poverty, misery, political repression, and rising expectations will continue to nurture the incessant Latino demographic transformation.

México's detrimental entanglement with the North American Free Trade Agreement (NAFTA) and President Fox's anachronistic economic policies have helped fuel the incessant influx of migrants into the United States. If México's economic situation does not dramatically improve, that is, if it does not generate sufficient good-paying jobs and mitigate its poverty, México's largest export into the United States will continue to be its desperate and impoverished masses. México's socioeconomic crisis is so severe that it is at the brink of becoming another Colombia, a powder keg of insurgent political and economic instability, which will significantly increase the magnitude of the exodus.

Neither the militarization operations along the U.S./México border, such as Operation Gatekeeper, nor the passage of more restrictionist immigration policies will halt the migrant exodus or in short, the reoccupation of Aztlán by Mexicanos. The migrant's desperation coupled with their resolve to ameliorate their dire socioeconomic conditions will not deter them from making their perilous exodus north to the United States. In addition, for some migrants, their journey into the region of Aztlán is not considered as traveling to a foreign country; instead they consider it to be an extension of México. Many believe that Aztlán was once an integral part of México, therefore they figure that they should not be considered alien to it. With cities named Los Angeles, San Diego, Sacramento, San Francisco, Santa Fe, Tucson, San Antonio, is it a wonder they feel culturally at home. Many feel that they are simply reclaiming what was once theirs and forcibly taken by U.S. imperialist aggression.

The truth of the matter is that if nativists truly want to stop what they perceive as an invasion of their country they need to realize that the real culprit contributing to the migrant exodus is liberal capitalism. Their vociferous criticisms, immigrant bashing, and scapegoating of migrants are misdirected. Instead, at the crux of the so-called immigration crisis is the voracious and exploitative nature of the forces of capital globalization. The solution rests in understanding that the various push and pull factors driving the migrant exodus are manifestations of the inherent contradictions of liberal capitalism. The solution is clear: change the socioeconomic conditions engendering the migrant exodus.

The Alternative Is a Continuation of the Incessant Migrant Exodus

With México and Latin America as a whole (e.g., Argentina, Colombia, Venezuela, Peru, Bolivia) entering perhaps a more volatile epoch of political and socioeconomic instability and possible social upheaval, the Mexicano/Latino diaspora into the United States will continue to vitalize and nurture the re-Mexicanización de Aztlán and the Latinoización of the United States. The preceding demographic reality was buttressed by the Bureau of the Census's 2003 adjusted census report which reported that 53 percent of the 10 percent population increase by Latinos between 2000 and 2002 was due to immigration. While the United States spends some $3 billion a year on its militarization of the U.S./México border and arrests about one million every year,[1] a minimum of 400,000 undocumented Mexicanos successfully migrate to the United States annually, and over 200,000 arrive via legal immigration. The migrant exodus is unstoppable, understanding the forces impelling it. Historically it has created its own flow, and politically it is difficult if not impossible to halt. Thus, based upon present trends and previous migration history, the migrant exodus will continue to be persistent and intensify as a result of an aggravation of existent push and pull factors.

Moreover, high birthrates will continue to push and energize the Latino's demographic transformation. The cultural rise of the Neo-Mex Generation and the migrant's mostly Roman Catholic religious upbringing are and will continue to produce higher Mexicano birthrates. It is interesting to note that nativist commentator Patrick Buchanan argues that worldwide the white population—from the United States to Europe—is decreasing dramatically because of their low birthrates. Present demographic trends also suggest that in the future birthrates for whites and other ethnic/racial groups will be much lower than that of Latinos. This was clearly evident in 2003 in California where slightly over 50 percent of the babies born were Latino, and nationally nearly 18 percent of the country's youth were Latino. In the twenty-first century an aging white population and a youthful Latino population will also impact the Latino's overall greater population growth.

If present trends persist, in the ensuing years, white and black flight will also continue to contribute to the re-Mexicanización de Aztlán. As the Mexicano and Latino populations increase in the twenty-first century, existing barrios will grow and new ones will spring up. Suburbs, once perceived the havens for middle-class whites, blacks, Asian/Pacifics, and some Hispanics, in the future will constitute new segregated Mexicano/Latino urban barrios. For a number of reasons, which includes racism, this *barrioización* of Aztlán will influence non-Latinos to move out in greater numbers from their respective neighborhoods, cities, and even states. The barrios and *colonias'* impoverishment and myriad of social problems, and the growing nativist racism directed at Mexicanos and Latinos, will contribute to white and black flight, especially in California. Similar scenarios could very well occur in southern Arizona, much of central and southern Nuevo México, south and central Tejas, and the Las Vegas area of Nevada, among other parts of Aztlán and the country.

According to the U.S. Bureau of the Census demographic projections, by 2050 Latinos will comprise some 25 percent or 100 million of the country's projected total population. Whites are expected to decrease, varying by source to about 49 percent, relegating them to a national minority status. "People of color" will become the country's new ethnic/racial majority. Jeffrey Passel, a demographer at the Urban Institute, a public policy center in Washington, interprets the 2003 Census Bureau adjusted report and predicts that Latinos by 2020 could reach some sixty million. He explains, "If current trends continue as far as immigration and birth rates, Hispanics could account for 15.5% of the population in 2010 and 18% in 2020."[2]

Realistically, the preceding projections are too conservative. If current Latino population growth rates continue people of color could very well constitute the New Majority not by 2050 but by 2040. During the past decades, Latino population growth rate in percentages was 61 percent in 1980, 53 percent in 1990, and 58 percent in 2000. Using a lower 50 percent average growth rate per decade, the Latino population could very well increase to 52.5 million by 2010, 78.8 million by 2020, and 118 million by 2030. If México's projected population for 2030 of some 130 million is added, this means that the total Mexicano population in Norte America (North America, which includes México, Canada, and the United States) could reach over 200 million. Moreover, by 2050 the country's projected Latino population could very well reach not 25 percent but 35 percent and by the incipient years of the twenty-second century 50 percent. The preceding Latino demographic scenario is based on an intensification of both the migrant exodus and high Latino birthrates and continued low birth and immigration rates among whites as well as among other non-Latino ethnic/racial groups.

The preceding demographic forecast could produce at the national level a myriad of other implications. One is that by 2010 the United States will surpass Spain's population and become the second largest Spanish-speaking country in the world, second only to México. Two, by no later than 2030 Mexicanos in the United States will constitute at least 80 percent of the total Latino population. Three, by the latter part of the twenty-first century, the Latino population in the United States could well equal or surpass that of México's, making the United

States the largest Spanish-speaking country of the world. Four, the migrant exodus could continue to create a México/Latino diaspora, and throughout the country—from the state of Washington to New York to La Florida—small and large internal colonies (barrios) will proliferate within and outside of Aztlán. Five, the Latino demographic transformation will have major economic, cultural, and social policy ramifications, especially on the country's race/ethnic relations. Six, politically a shift in political power from whites to Latinos will increasingly occur, especially throughout Aztlán. Seven, the Latino population increase juxtaposed to the white decrease will mean that the growing white senior citizen population will become increasingly dependent on younger Latinos through their tax dollars for the maintenance of Social Security as well as other governmental federal and state programs.

Moreover, if the present demographic trends continue by 2050 Mexicanos will constitute Aztlán's new majority. This means that in states like Nuevo México Mexicanos will surpass 50 percent of the state population by the year 2010, if not sooner. Mexicanos and Latinos in California and Tejas will conservatively comprise at least 43 percent and 38 percent respectively of the state's populations by 2025. Another assessment suggests that by 2030 or soon thereafter, Mexicanos and Latinos in both states will reach the 50 percent mark. If the current population trends hold up, Latinos in both Arizona and Nevada could very well constitute 50 percent of the population by the year 2040 or soon after. Also, the Mexicano/Latino population in Utah and Colorado by 2040 could surpass 35 percent. As a result of migrant exodus, there has been a rise in the number of "transborder" communities. Furthermore, the concept and political boundaries of Aztlán will have to be redefined. Why? One, the re-Mexicanización of Aztlán has and will continue to blur the present U.S./México border. Two, geographically, numerous other parts of the country outside of Aztlán will also have large demographic pockets of both Mexicanos and Latinos.

Because of these major demographic shifts, metaphorically, the "cactus curtain" (La Cortina de Nopal), the border that separates México from the United States, is undergoing a major redefinition, moving hundreds of miles northward. The re-Mexicanización de Aztlán is transforming Aztlán into "nation-within-a-nation" with its own distinct cultural, linguistic, and religious cultural underpinnings. This suggests an unequivocal repudiation of the so-called American Creed as defined by Samuel Huntington.

Moreover, without any orchestration from México or from activist insurgents, México is gradually peacefully "reoccupying" Aztlán—the territories it lost in 1848 as a result of the U.S. War on México. For some Mexicano activists, the Treaty of Guadalupe Hidalgo signed under U.S. military duress in 1848 was not meant to be permanent. Instead, the $15 million paid to México by the United States was merely a payment for a lease that expires in 2048. Thus, it can be argued that Mexicanos today are in the midst of remaking history, "reoccupying and reclaiming" their conquered lands—Aztlán.

The Worst of Times Crises: Socioeconomic Issues to Intensify

The United States in a State of Decline

If the country's present socioeconomic trends continue, the crises affecting Mexicanos and most Latinos in the United States will worsen. In the ensuing years, specifically the numerous social problems previously examined in chapter 8 will intensify. The contradictions of liberal capitalism will create a deterioration of the country's "quality of life," will be more acute especially for people of color. From a policy perspective, no indicator exists today that the social conditions which propel the "worst of times" crises such as racism, poverty, unemployment, access to health care, affordable housing, quality and accessible education, crime, gang violence, drugs, increasing racial/ethnic/class conflicts, among others, will be resolved or at a minimum mitigated.

Until now, the preoccupation of both the Democrat and Republican parties has been to maintain the hegemony of liberal capitalism. Neither party has had the will, courage, or conviction to prioritize major socioeconomic change. Not since the Johnson administration's "War on Poverty" has there been a modicum of progressive domestic reforms. The country's present war economy is characterized by burgeoning military budgets ($380 billion in 2003) and expenditures of nearly $120 billion on the U.S. War on Iraq have failed miserably to address the country's worsening domestic socioeconomic agenda. The ramifications of such policies could domestically prove to be troublesome. Already the country's impoverished urban areas are powder kegs of discontent and alienation, susceptible to violent eruptions. The inherent costs of maintaining the U.S. colonial empire militarily is already impacting negatively the country's lack of a viable change domestic agenda. This suggests that in the future, as the rich become richer, the poor poorer, and the middle class decrease, the country will increasingly socioeconomically resemble a third world country. If the decline of the United States is to be averted its liberal capitalist system is in need of major change. As previously stated, it must become more egalitarian and socially democratic, politically and economically. This suggests that an equitable distribution of the country's wealth must occur if an apocalyptic scenario of decline is to be averted.

Further contributing to the decline of the United States are the plutocratic corporate interests that dominate the country's political superstructure. In general, politicians, two-party leaders, government bureaucrats, judges, and even union leaders, are ideologically controlled by their allegiance to liberal capitalism. Elections, especially at the federal and state levels, have become rituals of legitimizing the plutocratic elite's power. At all levels of the political system, the lubricant that drives the engine of politics is money. Their money and control of the media creates the illusion that the people's vote still matters and that the system is democratic. The political reality is, however, corporate-dominated power elite govern the country via an entrenched two-party dictatorship and a plethora of special interests, which control the country's politics. As corporations, their loyalty is not to this country that has made them prosperous but to the almighty god of profit. Rich and powerful multinational corporations and their globalization of capital move the country's domestic and foreign policy agendas. The impact of their corporate avarice is clearly manifested in the country's outsourcing of U.S. jobs to third world countries. Who suffers from the globalization of capital? Workers in the United States, who are losing their jobs permanently, and foreign workers in underdeveloped countries and those who are forced to work for meager subsistence wages.

The decline of the United States is also evident today in the country's political transformation from a representative democracy to an increasingly fascist plutocracy. Justified under the Bush administration's war against terrorism, the preceding is illustrated by the passage of the Patriot Act, which is seriously eroding the people's civil liberties. Under the specter of 9/11, the very nature of this country's republican form of government is threatened. In short, the country's constitution and its so-called liberal democratic institutions are under a "state of siege," violated and altered by a plutocratic Bush administration that increasingly resembles a fascist dictatorship. Ironically, in Nazi Germany during the 1930s, the people themselves supported the rise of Hitler's Third Reich. Today some people in the United States because of fear and insecurities are falling prey to supporting what can be argued is the Bush administration's graduated "coup d'etat" justified under the guise of "national security." This is a clear signal that U.S. society is moving toward George Orwell's *1984*.

Also affecting the potential decline of the United States is the rise of the People's Republic of China and the United States of Europe (the European Economic Community) to super power status. These two power blocs will rival, if not surpass, the hegemony of the United States on various fronts—from economic to military. Russia will more than likely once again rise, especially militarily, to a quasi-super power status. Other countries such as India, Brazil, Japan, Israel, and Iran will reach major regional power status.

The present U.S. War on Iraq has opened up a Pandora's box of frightening foreign policy implications for the present and future. With its neo-Manifest Destiny jingoist belief that the United States must propagate the gospel of democracy to the Middle East and the world, the truth of the matter is that the primary U.S. motivation is empire building, which translates to control of oil and markets—world hegemony. Its expansionist foreign policy threatens world peace and has damaged for years to come the image of the United States. In the eyes of many the United States has become the epitome of the evil empire.

The election of a Democrat to the White House in 2004 could possibly squelch the threat to this country's liberal democratic form of government and thwart its decline. However, if future U.S. presidents continue to adhere to the Bush administration's present militaristic, neo-Manifest Destiny, and imperialistic-driven foreign policy, the country itself and the peace of the world will continue to be in jeopardy. Recurring wars could escalate into a resurgent arms race, increased world terrorism, and ultimately a horrific nuclear Armageddon. The avarice of liberal capitalism if left unchecked will continue to create ecological disasters that could threaten the existence of life on the planet.

The aforementioned analysis suggests that Mexicanos and Latinos must become increasingly cognitive of what the future holds for the United States. Politically and otherwise, as a people, this will require them to develop the sophistication to plan for the future based on changing circumstances.

The Crises Worsen for Mexicanos
The liberal capitalist system is not working for most Mexicanos and Latinos, people of color, and most whites as well. Present political indicators suggest that regardless who is president of the United States, Democrat or Republican, little substantive change will ensue in the future, especially for people of color. Using present socioeconomic indicators, the status of Aztlán's colonized barrios and *colonias* in the future will decline and class stratification will become more pronounced. The social problems are so immense and complex that the "worst of times" crises, if unmitigated, will increasingly subject Aztlán's colonized barrios and *colonias* to a "South African apartheid syndrome" status. Yes, Mexicanos and Latinos will constitute demographically the new majority, but they will be an impoverished and marginalized majority. Yet without a doubt, a small percentage of Mexicano and Latinos will prosper. The growing egregious effects of the "South African apartheid syndrome" are clearly evident today in the prevalence of school segregation and numerous other education-related issues.

From the primary level to the graduate and professional schools, white power elites are deliberately reducing access to education for Mexicanos, Latinos, and other people of color. In response to the Latino population growth, the government is doing little to ameliorate the inferior education being provided to Mexicanos and Latinos at the primary and secondary levels. The present crisis they face in education requires the enactment of major educational reforms. Yet without adequate funding, adequate school facilities, a quality curriculum, bilingual/bicultural programs, quality texts and school materials, competent and committed teachers and administrators, and parental involvement, the barrio and *colonia's* primary schools will worsen and enter into a perpetual state of degradation. The same scenario applies to the secondary level of education, in order to stop the horrendous push out and drop out rates. Present political and educational indicators suggest that both primary and secondary schools will become increasingly more segregated, which translates into a pedagogical reality of the practice of a "neo-separate but unequal" doctrine.

If present trends continue, today's Mexicano and Latino students' already limited access to a four-year college or university or a graduate or professional education will worsen. Educating Mexicanos and Latinos or persons of color more than likely will not be a major priority for white power elites and their colonial agents that control the country's educational superstructure. After all, from their perspective to educate them could mean a serious threat to their hegemony. During the 1990s California's propositions 187, 209, and 227, and in 2003, Proposition 54, and in 2004 California's "Save Our State" neo-Proposition 187 initiative illustrated the growing nativist and racist crusade, which seeks to obviate the development and progress of people of color, especially that of Mexicanos and Latinos.

For most Mexicano and Latino poor and middle-class students today, it is already tough to get admitted into a four-year university. This is evident in the stringent admissions tests, and increasing tuition and book costs. Admission into graduate and professional schools is already low relative to the size of the Latino population, and present indicators suggest that in the future only a small percentage of Mexicanos and Latinos will have access. With affirmative action all but history and the lack of the federal and state government's resolve to create "equal opportunity," today's chronic shortage of Mexicano and Latino teachers, counselors, faculty, administrators, presidents, and chancellors will worsen in the future. Ethnic and Chicano Studies programs and departments as well as ethnic-oriented outreach, recruitment, and cultural programs are already under scrutiny today for the potential cuts and will increasingly come under siege by white power elites, especially nativists, as being superfluous and anachronistic. Current efforts to replace Ethnic or Chicano Studies with the "Eurocentric" American Studies are gaining ground as a way to slow down at least educationally the "re-browning of the United States."

If the above scenario prevails, most Mexicanos who reside in Aztlán's colonized barrios and *colonias* will be subject to what earlier in this work was referred to as a "South African apartheid syndrome." While Mexicanos and Latinos within the next three or four decades will constitute a majority of Aztlán's population, the educational institutions will be ostensibly controlled and administered by a non-Latino minority, mostly white, black, Asian, or Mexicano buffers and "want to be whites." Mexicanos in the future will not have sufficient numbers of educated and professionally trained people to administer their majority Latino cities, school districts, counties, or community colleges. One can deduce that based upon present trends white power elites will continue to use education as an instrument for their control and subordination.

Thus, if the above dismal scenario is to be prevented, Mexicanos and Latinos either by themselves or in coalition with people of color and disenchanted whites must initiate a relentless struggle for major educational change. In other words, education—the mental means of production—must be controlled by the people and become a vehicle for their liberation and not one for their continued oppression. Unfortunately, today among politicians, school officials, educational institutions themselves, and even most Mexicanos and Latinos no priority exists to alter this insidious trend.

Ominous Future Scenario: The Balkanization of the United States?

Ethnic and racial diversity have truly enriched and contributed to the progress and development of the United States. It will continue to do so providing ethnic/racial groups have greater access to the society's material benefits, have access to power sharing, and experience social mobility. Only then will the country's cohesion, stability, and tranquility be possible. Conversely, however, if ethnic groups are not given equal treatment and equal progress, the country's social equilibrium is in jeopardy. This ominous scenario following so many historical antagonisms could in the future precipitate the U.S. "balkanization," a breaking apart of the country.

Specifically, there are five major historical antagonisms that either individually or in combination could foster a possible balkanization of the country. One, the country's changing demographics are already heightening interethnic/racial conflicts and tensions, which are bound to worsen as people of color increase in population, particularly Mexicanos, and whites decline in number. Two, ethnic/ racial relations will worsen as interethnic/racial rivalry increases over the allocation of resources, political representation, and control of physical space, for example, neighborhoods and communities. Three, as the country's war economy fails to address the people's domestic socioeconomic conditions, interethnic/racial conflicts could dangerously escalate as each ethnic/racial group pursues its own interests. Four, a military defeat of the United States in some future war or its economic collapse could domestically unleash the historical forces of balkanization. Lastly, the white power elite's continued strategic use of "divide and conquer" tactics of pitting nonwhite ethnic groups against each other could fuel ethnic/racial tensions and act as a precondition for balkanization. Thus, because the country is comprised of divergent ethnic/racial groups and cultures these and other conditions could very well produce the unraveling or dissolution of the United States. What happened to *Pax Romana* could happen to *Pax Americana*.

The fact is that today interethnic conflicts are already occurring: in the schools, prisons, and numerous communities between Mexicanos/Latinos and blacks, whites and Mexicanos/Latinos, Asians and blacks, and so on. More specifically, tensions and conflicts between Latinos and blacks are commonplace, brought about by the Latino demographic transformation. At the crux of the growing rift is competition over power and resources. Because of Latinos' growing numbers, blacks perceive them to be a threat to their political, economic, and social gains.[3]

If the white power elite cannot satisfy the rising expectations of the country's diverse ethnic/racial groups, particularly Latinos and blacks, their levels of frustration and discontent could increase to a dangerous level. Any incident could ignite the fires of urban conflict, such as the 1992 South Central Los Angeles Riots. Like riots of the mid-1960s, for example, Watts, Detroit, Newark, they illustrate how the manifold effects of racism, relative deprivation, and poverty make every urban area susceptible. In response to numerous urban riots, the Kerner Commission Report in 1968 erroneously concluded that the United States was headed toward becoming two societies: one white, the other black, separate and unequal. Because of the changing demographics, today the United States has become a tripartite society: one white, the other brown or Latino, and the other black. However, the latter two are becoming increasingly separate and unequal. Asian Americans are in transition and will in time become the country's fourth major ethnic/racial force.

As farfetched as the above analysis might sound today one only has to look at Chechnya, Palestine, Kosovo, Iraq/Turkey (Kurds), Spain (Basques), and various other regions and countries throughout the world that are engulfed in separatist and irredentist struggles. Moreover, as historical empires have declined—from the Roman to the more recent Soviet Union—it is clear that the United States is not exempt from suffering the same fate. The impact of immigration, wars, struggles for autonomy, terrorism, poverty, conflicting religions, and repression, will continue to challenge the political boundaries of nation-states today and in the future. As the country enters the twenty-first century, the phrase *E Pluribus Unum* (Out of many, one) is becoming an anachronism.

A worsening of the country's socioeconomic crises could also precipitate fractious and contentious class conflict. This will be increasingly evident in the class polarization between the haves (the rich); the have-nots (poor); and the have a little, want more (middle class). Today a major disparity exists in which wealth is increasingly concentrated in the hands of the few, the plutocrats. The middle class is dwindling, and if the present economic crisis continues a greater number will join the ranks of the have-nots. Already today millions of people, especially Mexicanos and Latinos, live precariously, one paycheck away from being homeless. Overall, with the U.S. economy faltering and outsourcing millions of jobs overseas, poverty is increasing. In particular, Aztlán's colonized barrios and *colonias* and those beyond could evolve from islands of discontent, frustration, and alienation into great oceans of turbulence and upheaval within the next twenty to thirty years. This scenario is also applicable to the country's urban black ghettos and other oppressed peoples.

Today some militias and nativist groups propound the inevitability of the country's balkanization. They contend that sometime in the twenty-first century, Mexicanos in occupied Aztlán will secede from the United States and either form their own separate country or seek a reunification with México. This is a prevailing and pervasive view of ultra-xenophobic nativist paramilitary groups. Since 2000 they have acted as "domestic terrorists," including Glen Spencer's American Border Patrol, Chris Simcox's Civil Homeland Defense, and Jack Foote's Ranch Rescue, among others. From their racist perspective, re-Mexicanización de Aztlán will unleash a *Quebecois*-like separatist movement, and the migrant exodus is a full-fledged invasion and a conspiracy directed by México, involving Mexicano activists in the United States, to retake Aztlán. They vociferously claim that the country's sovereignty is being violated and that Mexicanos are a threat to the country's national security.

Today a powder keg situation particularly exists along the Arizona/México border. Beyond the hundreds of migrants that have died crossing the dangerously inhospitable desert of Arizona, several undocumented migrants have been reported killed, some suspicion falling on the white militias. One can deduce that if the white militias accelerate their "terrorism" against what they call "migrant invaders," Mexicanos might respond in kind. If attacked by the militias, México's army will surely respond. The results could be disastrous for both countries. Today with tensions running extremely high near a powder keg level, without any intervention and corrective policy action by both governments, particularly by the U.S. government, the tensions are bound to intensify and worsen in the future.

Beyond white nativist militias, a plethora of right-wing nativist organizations, newspapers, magazines, websites, and radio and television programs are a part of an ongoing vitriolic anti-Mexicano/Latino crusade. Even prominent white intellectuals and politicians are preaching the same xenophobic and nativist gospel of hate toward Mexicanos and Latinos. Former presidential candidate and television commentator Patrick Buchanan views La Reconquista just like the militias: an outright invasion of the United States by México. Critical of U.S. immigration policies, he states, "The United States lacks the fortitude to defend its borders and to demand, without apology, that immigrants assimilate into society."[4]

Renowned Harvard political scientist Samuel Huntington supports Buchanan's assertion. In his latest work, *Who Are We?*, he warns about the inherent dangers to the "Hispanization of the Southwest."[5] Furthermore, from a hypernegative futuristic perspective, Huntington argues that the influx of immigration from México and Latin America quite possibly will foster an end to the United States as we know it. "Mexican immigration is leading the demographic *reconquista* of areas Americans took from México by force in the 1830s and 1840s, mexicanizing them," writes Huntington.[6] In reference to the aforementioned developments, Huntington contends that "if continued, [they] could change America into a culturally bifurcated Anglo-Hispanic society with two national languages."[7] He also posits the argument that the United States is in the midst of "a crisis of national identity" that is a result of massive immigration. The United States' political culture that he describes as the "Creed," which is Anglo-Saxon and Protestant and accentuates individualism and usage of the English language, is under threat by other challenging cultures. He argues against "cultural diversity" and warns that the country's weakness in assimilating immigrants, particularly from México and Latin America, could create a dynamic of "two languages, two cultures, and two peoples."[8]

Through its militarization of the U.S./México border, the U.S. government itself has likewise acknowledged the prospects of the country's balkanization. Literally, the 2,000-mile-long U.S./México border has become a war zone. Today some Mexicano activists, organizations, and intellectuals in the United States ardently concur with their nemesis the white nativists on the inevitability of the country's balkanization. Frustrated by the Mexicano's colonial status, today some Mexicano activists and intellectuals preach the irredentist gospel of separatism.

As the demographic re-Mexicanización de Aztlán and Latinoización of the United States accelerates so will the debate on the country's possible balkanization. Presently the country's political climate is not propitious for the rise of a Mexicano insurgent secessionist movement in the United States. This is not to say, however, that sometime in the future it will not be.

Thus, the country's future progress and stability rests on its capacity to democratize and reform its political and socioeconomic systems. In particular, if Mexicanos and Latinos, among other ethnic/racial groups, do not experience major social change, gain greater access to power sharing, and significantly improve their quality of life, Aztlán's barrios and *colonias* and other parts of the country in the future could well be transformed into powder kegs of violence and insurgent politics. In short, the future prospects for balkanization will not be totally determined by Mexicanos or Latinos per se, but by the policies of the plutocratic white power elites themselves.

Changing Political Cultures

Struggle between Conflicting Generations Intensifies

Latinos and particularly Mexicanos in the twenty-first century are plagued by the continuing clash of divergent political subcultures and generational politics. As a result, politically and otherwise, Mexicanos and Latinos are both heterogeneous political communities. For the Mexicano, the existence of several political subcultures suggests that they are eclectic by-products of both México's and U.S. political cultures. Their existence has fomented the rise of various "political generations" that ultimately subscribe to these political subcultures and are reflected in their politics. The Mexican American Generation (MAG) with its emphasis on adaptation, integration, and assimilation, reflects more of an affinity to the U.S. political culture. While some middle-class Mexicanos still identified as *Mexican American*, the term was not in vogue or did not have massive appeal. The Chicano Generation (CG), as a political generation, with its essentially cultural pluralistic orientation, had a tenuous at best identification with U.S. political culture. Some adherents still propounded the virtues of "cultural pluralism"; while a few still propound an ultranationalist posture predicated on the notion of self-determination. Like the MAG, the CG too is in a decline mode, overshadowed by other competing political generations.

Outside Aztlán's barrios and *colonias*, the Hispanic Generation's (HG) ethos is still the most prevalent because of its compatibility with the white-dominated political culture. Governmental and corporate elites and their interests emphasize

Hispanicism, its political affinity to liberalism, and its economic adherence to capitalism. From corporate media to the country's manifold governmental structures, the term of choice for describing people of Spanish/Amerindian origin both from the United States and Latin America is *Hispanic*. With government, corporations, and media in particular acting as powerful socializing agents, the Hispanic's longevity in great part has been ascribable to their imposition of the HG mind-set. As an umbrella term, during the transition, however, the HG went into decline, yielding to the emergent Latino Generation (Lat-Generation—LG).

Increasingly the pan-ethnic term of choice is becoming *Latino*. As a political generation, the LG is still in its infancy but its growth is rapid because of its appeal and acceptability by many more subgroups. Today more and more persons of Spanish-Amerindian origin are rebuking *Hispanic* and opting for *Latino*. The usage of *Latino* is originating ostensibly from the people themselves rather than from the media, government, or corporations. While not yet a fully developed subpolitical culture, as a political generation the LG is developing its own political ethos based on acculturation and not assimilation, a sense of pan-Latino regional (Western Hemisphere) nationalism, a politic that is moderate to liberal, and while ideologically still liberal capitalist, is more open to change or reform. LG proponents adhere to the belief that for both Mexicanos and Latinos in the United States the future is inextricably tied to Latin America. Their future progress and change will be dependent on cooperatively working and struggling together, forming coalitions, and seeing each other as belonging to the same extended Latino family—Una Raza Unida de Bronce (A United People of Bronze).

The LG rejects assimilation and adheres to a more cultural pluralistic perspective. While still influenced by U.S. political culture, it is far more conducive to fostering solidarity, unity of action, and social change among the country's divergent Latino subgroups. For Mexicanos, the rise and development of the LG is politically an imperative, for it opens the door for greater collaboration. It is important, however, that as a subgroup, Mexicanos must "first" identify as Mexicanos and "secondly" as Latinos. This applies as well to other Latino subgroups, such as Puerto Ricans, Cubans, Central and South Americans, and others that are opting to maintain their own ethnic and cultural identity.

The Neo-Mex Generation (NMG) in the barrios and *colonias* of Aztlán were becoming the most dominant during the transition. From a political cultural perspective, it embodied its own political subculture, which was greatly predicated on México's semiauthoritarian parochial/subject political culture. Powerful U.S. socialization agents bombard Mexicanos who identified with the NMG to adhere to the country's liberal capitalist-based political culture; yet, most of them persevere, resist, and reject most of its values and maintain those endemic to their Mexicano political culture. Their cognitive, affective, and evaluative orientations acquired in México are strong enough to shield them from totally accepting U.S. political culture.

Throughout Aztlán, a political transition is occurring for Mexicanos. Demographically, as long as the re-Mexicanización de Aztlán continues to intensify, the hegemony of the NMG throughout Aztlán is inevitable. Today most Mexicano migrants, especially first generation, reject the ethos of the HG. They have neither the desire nor need to assimilate into the so-called white melting pot. Most adhere to a militant form of cultural pluralism, which allows them to preserve their traditional Mexicano cultural values and heritage and use of Spanish as their first language. Driven by a sense of Mexicano nationalism, most migrants are not willing to sever their cultural, political, economic, and historical ties to the motherland, México, particularly to their respective states and communities of origin. The factors contributing to the rise, maintenance, and growth of the NMG, are the "Mexicanización" of the barrios and *colonias*, the segregation of the barrios and *colonias*, the presence of a growing Mexicano/Latino electronic and print media, the proliferation of Mexicano/Latino businesses, the emergence of Mexicano-based organizations, the celebration of México's political and church holidays, the abundance of Spanish-speaking churches, and the outreach efforts of México's government to its nationals.

As time progresses, the NMG will also undergo a political cultural metamorphosis, from which a new and dynamic political culture will emerge. The reasons are primarily two: sooner or later dialectically the NMG will be affected by the power of U.S. political culture and the other existent political generations and their subpolitical cultures and some the NMG semiauthoritarian parochial/ subject-related values and orientations need to be replaced with participatory and progressive ones.

Mexicanos in the Midst of an Intellectual Crisis

Intellectually, the Mexicano political experience in the twenty-first century is at a critical juncture. Today no Mexicano intellectual renaissance exists. Instead there is a paralysis of ideas, especially at the universities and colleges, that is manifested by the chronic shortage of progressive scholarly work. One must not forget that intellect is a form of power and ideas are powerful weapons in the arsenal for social change. Intellectuals play an important role as agents of change in societies. They are the architects and purveyors of ideas, beliefs, symbols, and general knowledge. At the core of today's intellectual crisis is the adherence of too many

intellectuals to the ethos of the HG. CG scholars are disappearing due to retirement, old age, death, and co-optation, and are not being replaced; while those
who adhere to the HG have significantly increased. Those of the MAG, NMG,
and LG have yet to make their intellectual presence felt.

Instead most intellectuals today, especially within the academy, are mainstream-oriented and adherents of the liberal capitalist status quo. Few dare to
criticize the liberal capitalist system, its plutocratic power structure and two-party
dictatorship, and the Bush administration's heinous domestic and imperialist war
policies, or offer viable alternatives for social change. Being identified as liberals,
radicals, or worst nationalists or socialists is an anathema. To some scholarship
has become a business of receiving thousands of dollars for research that helps
prop up the existent social order. In fact, some scholars have placed the blame on
the victim rather than on the system. Some have been co-opted so completely
that they fail to recognize the continued existence of discrimination and racism
directed at Mexicanos and Latinos.

In particular, few of today's "young turk academicians" have the activist experience that characterized many of the CG. Products of postmodernism and the
HG, many lack the nationalist passion or *consciencia*. Too few have the direct linkages to the realities of the colonized barrios and *colonias* or the commitment to get
involved. Even fewer join with the masses in their struggles to decolonize Aztlán
or exercise leadership for social change; consequently, they reject the notion of
Gramsci's "organic intellectual." Too many adhere to a research, pedagogy, and
public service agenda that is essentially system-oriented and few. Most repudiate
a Marxist class or nationalist ideological perspectives, while those that do have
progressive propensities embrace postmodernism, with its emphasis on culture,
identity, and aesthetics. Hence, far too many are *acomodados* (accommodated ones)
and choose to play the colonial roles of either buffers or "want to be whites."
This assessment is tragic because without the existence of an enlightened, consci-
enticized, and involved intelligentsia, no social struggle for decolonization or
major social change can expect to triumph.

This trend is indeed politically deleterious to Mexicanos and needs to be
reversed. Whichever subpolitical culture becomes the most prevalent in the future
will determine in great part the direction of the Mexicano political experience. In
order to be able to guide or direct this trend, an intellectual renaissance is needed:
one that will reconfigure the NMG and LG into each adopting a progressive
ethos, that is ideologically committed to the creation politically of a truly democratic society, that is economically and socially egalitarian and just society, and
that seeks the "de-colonization of Aztlán."

Future Prospects for Latino Ballot Box Politics

Proliferation of Mexicano and Latino
Political Representation

Without a doubt, Mexicanos and Latinos have politically made significant progress. One can thus argue that from a political historical vantage point these are indeed the "best of times." Ballot box politics is alive and doing considerably well today. More Mexicanos and Latinos are being elected to public office and the future promises even greater strides in political representation at all levels of governance, from the local—school boards, city councils, special districts, and county—to the state and federal levels. It is an indisputable fact that as the Mexicano and Latino population increases so will the numbers of its elected officials. The trend is irreversible due to increased population, voter registrations, organization, political education, and greater financial resources.

At the federal level likewise, the future prospects for Mexicano and Latino increased political representation looks bright. Within the next fifty years or so, throughout Aztlán as well as in other parts of the country, Latino congressional representation based on demographic changes and a higher level of political development will close to double, from today's twenty-two to at least forty by 2040. This could forge a powerful legislative bloc that could well transform the present Congressional Hispanic Caucus (CHC) into a powerful and influential group, especially if the CHC includes Mexicano and Latino U.S. senators. This suggests that their number could increase from a minus zero or none today to a positive of at least six by 2040. The "brown presence" in Washington, D.C., will also be evident by the dramatic increase in the number of Mexicanos and Latinos who serve as secretaries for the various cabinet positions of future administrations. Moreover, it is not too far-fetched that in the ensuing years, the country could elect a Mexicano or Latino vice president or president to the White or "Brown" House. And of course, it is also politically inevitable that Mexicanos and Latinos will make up a growing percentage of the federal judges in the appellate courts and U.S. Supreme Court as well.

Throughout Aztlán, Mexicano and Latino political representation at the state levels will likewise increase significantly. From California to Tejas, it is only a matter of time before the number of Mexicano and Latino governors, lieutenant governors, secretaries of state, and other state posts in state governments increase dramatically. State Assemblies and State Senates will also reflect the incessant trend of Mexicano and Latino political empowerment. This means in some states Mexicano/Latino majorities will control the legislative superstructures and hold positions of leadership and control key committees. More Mexicano and Latino judges will be appointed to the state's hierarchy of courts, including state supreme courts. Thus, throughout Aztlán, at the state level, within a few decades, Mexicanos and Latinos throughout Aztlán will be in a position to control the reins of power and public policy. The key question is to what end?

At the local level of ballot box politics, Mexicano and Latino political representation will particularly ascend. Within the next thirty years or so, the present total of some five thousand Latino elected officials will more than double. The increase will be particularly evident at the school board, city council, county government, and special district levels of governance. Hence, the notion of "community control," which denotes a democratization of local government and control by the local citizenry could become increasingly attainable. Thus, through their elected officials, if organized, the people could have the capacity to make some limited local reforms and foster a decolonization movement. The cardinal question is will they have the vision and conviction to do so?

What is wrong with this "best of times" political scenario? Basically, increased Mexicano and Latino political representation will not necessarily translate to the decolonization of Aztlán's barrios and *colonias* or to meaningful policy change. Why? There are three major reasons, which stem from the actual political workings of the liberal capitalist system. First, the scope of policy change is limited since it is constrained by the political realities that change is allowable as long as it does not alter or threaten the superstructure's liberal capitalist political underpinnings. Second, social change in this country has been largely an involuntary process, which has followed the dictum, "power is never given, but taken." Lastly, as has been amply documented in this work, the role of most Mexicano and Latino *politicos* so far has been to act not as agents of social change, but as buffers or "want to be whites." Currently, at either the federal or state levels there are no "advocate transformers." As a result, this has contributed politically to major leadership crises, particularly among Mexicanos, that has its genesis in the two previous epochs.

The Leadership Crisis Intensifies

Today Mexicanos in occupied Aztlán find themselves in the midst of a deepening and devastating leadership crisis. The absence of nationally recognized Mexicano or Latino political leaders is not a rhetorical assertion, but a political fact. It was corroborated by a survey conducted in August 2002 by McLaughlin & Associates, which asked some one thousand Hispanic adults to name a "living national political leader." Fewer than one in ten did so: 3.7 percent named México's president Fox; 1.8 percent former HUD secretary Henry Cisneros, and 1.3 percent U.S. congressman Luis Gutierrez of Chicago, Illinois.[9] A year later, the same study was repeated, this time Jennifer Lopez was first, replacing México's president Fox with essentially the same percentage. While the previous epoch of militant protest produced a number of recognized leaders and organizers, such as Reies Lopez Tijerina, Cesar Chavez, Rodolfo "Corky" Gonzales, José Angel Gutiérrez, among others, no comparable leaders emerged during the previous two epochs and none exist today. Truly at this time, Mexicanos in Aztlán and the country as a whole find themselves without viable and recognized leaders.

At the national level, politically while blacks have a number of charismatic leaders such as Jesse Jackson, Al Sharpton, Congresswoman Maxine Waters, and Julian Bond, among others, Mexicanos have no leaders of similar or equal stature. None of the existent congressional *politicos* within the CHC are providing national leadership or are acting as proponents of a progressive change agenda. In other words, none fill the category of being "advocate transformers." Instead, their political roles are either one of a buffer or of a "want to be white." Mexicano migrants are dying crossing the treacherous deserts of Arizona/México border and are being hunted by white militias in Arizona as if they were prey, yet, in spite of several efforts to get congressional *politicos* and the CHC involved they have refused to do so. It is fair to deduce that if this was happening to blacks, the Black Congressional Caucus and every major black political and organizational leader would be in Arizona demanding federal and state intervention and action against these "domestic terrorist" militias.

Furthermore, today's leadership crisis also pervades state and local levels of politics. At the state level, a major vacuum of effective leadership exists. From Tejas to California, few Mexicano *politicos* enjoy or have the requisite name recognition among the majority of Mexicanos or Latinos. The level of cognition as to who a constituency's political representatives are is extremely low. Also, again with some exceptions, existent state *politicos* refuse to become engaged in issues that are controversial and specifically impact Mexicanos and Latinos. At the local level, the political leadership crisis is perhaps more pronounced. Too few local *politicos* are driven to effectuate major local reforms. In most cases, their political agenda seeks to advance their own particular interests or of those special interests that support them. Some become involved in illegal schemes for personal gain and get caught, consequently reinforcing the stereotype of some whites and others that Mexicanos cannot handle power and are basically corrupt. Unfortunately, the dependency of politics' money as a lubricant has fed into the corruption that permeates the political system as a whole.

The leadership crisis is so serious that if unresolved it threatens the future of Mexicano politics in the United States for a number of reasons. Few *politicos* today have the leadership skills to lead or the intellectual adroitness to offer ideas or legislation for change and reform. As is the case with white politicians, today far too many *politicos* are self-centered, more concerned about advancing their own selfish political interests or those of special interests than addressing the issues of their Mexicano and Latino constituencies. Often intoxicated with the acquisition of power, far too many *politicos* see elections as stepping-stones for higher office. Most are not willing to become involved in controversial issues for fear of alienating their special interest base or white voters or of jeopardizing their political career and mobility. Thus, even though there are more *politicos* today, up to now, they have yet to impact or change the colonized status of Aztlán's barrios and *colonias*. At the national and state levels, no charismatic Mexicano or Latino *politicos* exist who possess the requisite personality, image, or political clout to ignite a critical mass among Mexicanos and Latinos overall.

Recalling the Palestinian analogy, Mexicanos in occupied Aztlán today have no political leaders comparable to Yasir Arafat. As an occupied people, from the national to the local levels of politics, few if any *politicos* are consciously directing, guiding, inspiring, and leading people toward the decolonization of Aztlán's barrios and *colonias*. Overwhelmingly, most act as buffers, who shy away from controversy and are ardent exponents of accommodation politics.

Thus, the political challenge that lies ahead of creating massive social change, fostering the decolonization of Aztlán's barrios and *colonias*, and ending the occupation of Aztlán itself will come not from *politicos*, but from advocate transformer activists and intellectuals who are engaged with people themselves in their struggles. Conversely, "what must be done" is the development at all levels of political cadres of identifiable leaders from the divergent sectors of the community, including *politicos* when possible, who are committed to social change. Leadership must be collective, which means that it is an erroneous assumption to believe in the one greater leader or one hero theory of leadership. Leadership must be "organic," rooted in the struggles of the masses of the barrios and *colonias* of Aztlán.

The Crisis in Mexicano Political Participation

Beyond the political leadership crisis, Mexicanos and Latinos in the twenty-first century are concomitantly facing a crisis in voter and civic participation. Political apathy among the barrio and *colonia's* poor is acute as is complacency among the suburban middle class. While the number of Mexicanos and Latinos registered to vote was over eight million in 2003 and could reach some nine million nationally by the November 2004 presidential elections, the fact is, Mexicano and Latino voter turnout as previously documented has been rather low. Pundits are optimistically prognosticating that nearly seven million Latinos will vote. Yet the preceding numbers are not commensurate with the burgeoning population numbers. Too many Mexicanos and Latinos cannot vote for the ensuing three reasons: the number of Latinos who are undocumented, the scores of Latino documented migrants who are not citizens and consequently not registered to vote, and the omnipresence of "political alienation" among the residents of the colonized barrios and *colonias*.

This ominous reality suggests that Aztlán's future political landscape will increasingly see Mexicanos and Latinos as majority populations but will constitute a minority of the electorate. According to the U.S. Census Bureau, whites were 51 percent of California's voting age population during the 2000 elections, but were 70 percent of those who said they voted. In 2002, two political scientists from the Public Policy Institute of California, Benjamin Highton and Jack Citrin, reported that in California by 2040, whites will make up 31 percent of the population, but will comprise 53 percent of the voters. By contrast, Latinos will compose but 26 percent, Asians 12 percent, and blacks 8 percent of the voters.[10] Although a minority in population in several other states in Aztlán, whites could very well continue to constitute a majority of the voters for several decades to come. As a result, Aztlán politically will be subjected to a "South African apartheid syndrome," which will further aggravate the colonized status of its barrios and *colonias*.

The salient obstacles that Mexicanos particularly face in their quest for political representation and empowerment are several. One, while some Mexicanos are active locally, their activism tends to be apolitical. They participate in organizations and events that are social, cultural, sport, and religious-oriented, but shy away from political activity. Two, the growing NMG with its ethos imbedded in México's semiauthoritarian political culture coupled with the people's lack of experience in participatory and democratic liberal traditions does not prepare or encourage their political involvement in the United States. Three, the absence of committed leaders who lead effective grassroots political pressure organizations or advocacy groups at the barrio and *colonia* level has obviated political education and mobilization efforts. Four, in too many instances, Mexicanos do not coalesce behind their own candidates. This suggests that the electoral strategy of "bloc voting" is difficult to realize. Five, too often, they split their vote because several Mexicano candidates running for the same seat, allowing a non-Mexicano to get elected. Lastly, few Mexicano candidates develop a successful campaign strategy that energizes and awakens the people to actually get involved in the campaign or simply vote.

As a result, among Mexicanos today political mobilizations both conventional and unconventional are scarce. It is apparent that the "culture of poverty" described by Oscar Lewis and decades of colonialism have also stymied the people's civic participation and political efficacy. Few vote or become involved in change, and only when an issue acutely impacts their interest do they become engaged. Far too often, Mexicanos tend to be crisis-oriented and suffer from an acute lack of consistency of action and mass participation. If Mexicanos and Latinos do not become better organized politically and more unified; if Latino citizenship and voter registration rates do not increase; and if, from a political cultural perspective, the people do not adhere to a much more "civic participatory ethos" and vote and participate in greater numbers, then political underrepresentation will continue to be an acute problem in the future. Hence, in order to foster a greater sense of civic participation, what is needed is for Mexicanos and Latinos is to adopt a more consistent and far more aggressive direct action-oriented agenda that compliments the people's self-interests. Marches, rallies, vigils, and other forms of unconventional militant protest will enhance the people's conscientization and involvement. Action blended with the power of a new vision will be conducive to fostering a renaissance of activism.

During the epoch of militant protest, a renaissance of civic participation was produced, especially among youth. From the barrios and *colonias* to the universities and colleges an admixture of apathy and complacency characterizes the Mexicano political experience today. The barrios and *colonias* today are plagued by disorganization and a political leadership crisis. Within the universities and colleges only a miniscule number of students get involved and are not at the locus of civic participation. In particular, one can be hypercritical of the effectiveness of Ethnic or Chicano Studies programs and departments in engendering the requisite *consciensia* (consciousness) to activism. Literally since the epoch of militant protest, thousands of Chicano students have gotten involved in MEChA and have taken Chicano Studies classes from a number of prominent scholars, yet today no semblance of a social movement exists. What happens is that once activist students graduate only a few become engaged in community activism. Instead their primary focus is on getting a good-paying job, accumulate material goods, having a good time, and inevitably getting married and starting a family. In short, they are being reabsorbed and resocialized into the system.

Since the demise of the Chicano Movement in 1974, many Mexicanos have been rejecting the "UFW generation of activism (CG)" and have instead embraced the "Want to drive a BMW generation of material pursuit (HG)."

Mexicanos and Latinos in International Politics

Today Mexicanos and Latinos are becoming more involved at the international level of politics and undoubtedly will increase in the future. More Mexicano *politicos*, leaders, activists, intellectuals, and organizations in the United States are proponents of *la politica de acercamiento*. There is a growing consciousness among them that there is much to be gained by developing stronger political, economic, cultural, and educational relations with México and other Latin American countries and governments. Increasingly México's *politicos*, including President Fox's administration, and *partidos* (political parties), are also practicing *la politica de acercamiento* with Mexicanos in the United States. Unfortunately President Fox's relationship with President George W. Bush has been one of subordination and acquiescence on a number of issues, for example, immigration and relations with Cuba. In spite of a number of efforts by his administration to forge a nexus with Mexicanos in the United States, concretely, President Vicente Fox's administration has not been effective in protecting human rights or advancing the interests of Mexicanos in the United States. Nevertheless, collaborative efforts in a number of areas, for example, business, politics, and culture, between Mexicanos from both sides of the U.S./México border have been commonplace and are increasing.

As stated previously, México and Latin America are intrinsic to the future of Aztlán's Mexicano politics and to the creation of a decolonization movement. With their growing population and clout, Mexicanos in the United States must accelerate their efforts to become a political bridge to both México and the rest of Latin America. This requires a strengthening of their political, economic, cultural, educational, and social bonds not only with México and Cuba, but also with progressive struggles in Venezuela, Colombia, Brazil, Argentina, Bolivia, among others in Latin America. Relations between Mexicanos in the United States and Cuba must be strengthened, since it is a living laboratory of a society experiencing major social change, one from which Mexicanos could learn. Moreover, both Mexicanos and Latinos must politically be more proactive in pressuring the U.S. government to end its economic embargo of Cuba and to ensure it does not invade Cuba. In addition, Mexicanos must reach out to other emergent powers, such as Spain, France, the People's Republic of China, and Russia to form collaborative relationships. To garner support and advance their own interests, like the Palestinians, Mexicanos in the United States must become experienced in international politics.

Future Prospects for Organizational Politics

A General Critique of Today's Organizational Crisis

Today Mexicano political development is at a critical juncture. While Mexicanos by far are the largest Latino ethnic subgroup, few state or national Mexicano advocacy interest groups exist. At the national level, with the exception of MAL-DEF, all others examined in this work are pan-Latino or Hispanic-oriented with agendas that seek to bridge all the various ethnic subgroups. A crisis of organizational leadership permeates the Mexicano political experience. At the national and state levels, further exacerbating the existing individual political leadership crisis is the absence of viable organizational leadership among existent HG-oriented organizations. None of the leaders heading interest groups, regardless of the type, commands the power, influence, or following to claim to represent the people's interests. The weakness or absence of organizational leadership in many instances is impeding their respective organizational development and progress. At this time, not one HG interest group has the charismatic leadership to inspire and incite the people into direct action or to vote. No one organization has the power capability to create a critical mass. Not one has a power base or grassroots constituency in the colonized barrios and *colonias* of Aztlán.

Furthermore, not one is independent financially: all in varying degrees are dependent on corporate and foundation funding sources, which thwarts their ability to advocate and truly represent the interests of the masses. Moreover, because of their 501c3 nonprofit tax-exempt status, they are precluded from engaging in advocacy, pressure, or lobbying efforts. On the plus side, however, their noncorporate status allows them to secure funding from private and public sources. On the negative side, the moment they become too political or controversial because of their advocacy, they are susceptible to losing their nonprofit status and ultimately their funding. In trying to circumvent this problem, some old and new interest groups have established a number of research and educational institutes. Their purpose is to secure funding to conduct research, provide leadership training, and implement a number of social programs, while the mother organization, in this case the interest group, continues being involved in some aspect in policy change or social change activities.

With the exception of sectarian Left interest groups, not one HG-oriented interest group has a vision or a plan of action that ideologically purports effectuating major change of the liberal capitalist system. Like *politicos* they have no viable answers or solutions to the complex issues and problems confronting particularly the barrios and *colonias* of Aztlán and beyond. This suggests that as buffers or "want to be whites" at best they offer only Band-Aid approaches to change. Meta-phorically, it can be said that today national and state organizational leaders are like generals with little or no armies to command. Their memberships are small and internally suffer from an admixture of apathy and complacency. As a result, from an advocacy perspective, they operate as "paper tigers" emitting rhetorical roars at innocuous press conferences or preparing policy reports to attack their adversaries or address issues. In addition, most are purveyors of "cocktail activ-ism" rather than "direct action activism." Too often their responses to issues are calculated so as not to estrange or irritate their corporate donors or their white power elite connections. Their annual conferences and cultural and social events held at expensive hotels attract far too many "cocktail and conference activists," who seldom become engaged in direct action. For the people of the barrios and *colonias*, these conferences are financially largely out of reach and their agendas are seldom germane to their immediate interests or needs.

The acuteness of the organizational crisis is also apparent at the local levels of organizational politics, where there is a chronic scarcity of advocacy groups. The few that do exist are characterized as voluntary groups, have a limited mem-bership power base, lack resources, and in some cases lack competent leadership. Those that are politically inclined at times are plagued by internecine power struggles and schisms. With the exception of some of the Industrial Areas Foun-dation's "community power organizations," most Mexicano or Latino local orga-nizations are politically weak. They lack a mass power base and are limited in their capacity to influence public policy or the ballot box political arenas. Most local advocacy organizations operate as a result of the actions of a few zealots, which is problematic in that if something happens to its core activists, especially its leader, the organization can become moribund.

Today in many of Aztlán's barrios and *colonias* there are social service providers that are nonprofit, tax-exempt, corporate, foundation, state, or federally funded and outnumber advocacy or political organizations. While in most cases they pro-vide vital services and programs, they shy away from tackling issues. Because of their social service program emphasis, their scope of political engagement is lim-ited to lobbying for their funding or refunding. Also in abundance at the local level are cultural, church, recreational, sports, professional, and business organiza-tions that tend to be apolitical. They have an antipathy toward social change or electoral politics, which means that in actuality, they serve to maintain the system and do nothing to alter the barrio and *colonia's* colonized status.

Lastly, Latino coalitions are another form of organized advocacy activity that is particularly commonplace today at both the state and local levels. In most cases, coalitions are comprised of several groups that are loosely structured and come together on a commonly agreed issue; once the issue passes so does the coalition. In most cases, coalitions do little to build a permanent strong grassroots power base since they are transitory in nature. Also, most Latino-based coalitions adhere to a buffer role; some, however, with a sectarian Left slant do propound major social change. As transitory and structurally decentralized entities, they have yet to contribute to developing a viable power capability. Yet as the crises worsen, the future of Mexicano and Latino politics rests strategically with the ability of existent organizations and *politicos* to participate in coalitions that are going to advance not only their specific interests, but also the collective interests as Latinos. Also, whenever politically beneficial, coalition building must be pursued strategically with non-Latino groups as well.

Further exacerbating the present leadership crisis is the prevalence of low levels of organizational participation by the residents of Aztlán's barrios and *colonias*. Regardless of class status, as alluded to earlier, only a small percentage of Mexicanos actively participates in advocacy or political pressure interest groups or become involved in electoral politics. This is particularly true among Aztlán's poor, who are the victims of internal colonization. Their preoccupation is essentially on economic survival, not civic participation. The middle class is not exempt from the preceding characterization. Unless their interests are clearly impinged upon, as a class, today they suffer from a distorted complacency. There are pronounced class divisions that inhibit political efficacy and unified action or advocacy. Far too many Mexicano migrants who adhere to the ethos of the NMG view all politics with disinterest, cynicism, and distrust. With the masses of Mexicanos not organized at the barrio or *colonia* levels, future social change could very well be limited. Ultimately there can be no "de-colonization struggle" without the power of the organized masses.

Status of Existent Mexicano/Latino Organizations

Because of the country's changing socioeconomics, the *mutualistas* are fast becoming anachronisms. If they are to survive they must revive and replenish their dying membership. Especially with government cutbacks in social services, they are needed more than ever. Old interest groups, such as LULAC, must become even more assertive and effective in advocating for the interest of those in the barrios and *colonias*. They must connect with the barrios and *colonias* and be more consistent as buffers and not "want to be white" organizations. Their future greatly depends on the ability to adapt to the Mexicano's changing generational politics, political subcultures, and mode of activism. AGIF, if it is to have a future, must increase its shrinking veteran membership, secure sufficient resources, rework its goals and program, and become more proactive as an advocate.

Political pressure organizations as interest groups, with their electioneering and lobbying orientation, are not considered as effective and powerful when it comes to advocating for the interests of the poor and disenfranchised. MAPA in California for instance, for all intents and purposes, is tenuously surviving. Its future is in jeopardy because of internecine power struggles. It needs to get rid of the "politics of self-destruction" and prioritize the building of a new power base in the barrios and *colonias*. As NALEO, SVREP, and USHLI remain pro-system and continue to secure corporate and foundation funding, their future looks secure. As buffers they continue to register Latinos to vote, produce excellent reports on issues and election results, and ultimately with their adherence to the politics of the HG do an excellent job in propping up the existing superstructure. Other political pressure organizations, such the CHC, MAD, and the various caucuses examined, are in dire need of greater political unity, a change-oriented legislative agenda, and the leadership adroitness and assertiveness to advocate for the interests of both Mexicanos and Latinos.

The various new interest groups examined face the challenge of proving their credibility. They epitomize, for the most part, the traditional interest groups that work to influence public policy. In most cases, while they have the resources to do so, they lack the will or commitment or leadership to be more proactive in addressing the issues that affect Aztlán's barrios and *colonias*. At this point, it can be said that the one exception is MALDEF, which has been the most effective advocate for social change. In spite of its corporate funding, through litigation it has the power to continue being an effective instrument for moderate reform.

Other interest groups, such as the NCLR, USHCC, and HACER epitomize a buffer role and have yet to demonstrate a viable reform agenda. While they adhere to the traditional interest group function of influencing public policy, they have yet to be perceived in the barrios and *colonias* or by white power elites as major power brokers. Like other Mexicano and Latino organizations, they lack a "fear factor," and with their adherence to the HG politics, they act as "system maintenance buffers." The future of these new interest groups rests with their ability to demonstrate viable leadership, reach out and develop a power base among the Mexicano and Latino masses, and disassociate from the governing plutocratic interests of the white power elite.

Today protest organizations (PO) are few and those that do exist are in desperate need of revamping and reinvigoration both organizationally and ideologically. MEChA is one such PO that desperately needs to be refitted. If it does not get back to it original mission, it will be just another "cultural club." The Brown Berets too are in dire need of reorganization. Without a strong membership and a chapter base comprised of barrio youth, it will be short-lived. Herman Baca's

Committee on Chicano Rights needs to be resurrected and given new life. It has the leadership, but needs the structure, a renewed cadre, and a barrio membership base.

Mexicanos and Latinos in general are still committed to the maintenance of the country's two-political parties—two-party dictatorship. Some survey indicators, however, suggest a growing political alienation toward both the Democrat and Republican parties. This is occurring because neither party offers viable policy alternatives to the plethora of issues impacting Latinos. Furthermore, both are controlled by the same plutocratic interests and generally espouse the same liberal capitalist vision. Today there is no viable effort to organize a Mexicano or Latino-based third party that will seek to control via the ballot box. What does exist, under the aegis of the PNLRU, is the struggle to build a Mexicano-based sectarian/ideological cadre political party that is committed to the creation of Aztlán, a separate socialist Mexicano/Chicano nation. Like other sectarian Left groups, however, it lacks the power base or following of those living in the barrios and *colonias*.

Unions as labor interest groups continue to play an important buffer role for workers. The scope of change that unions advocate is limited. Most are adapted to liberal capitalism. They attain only subsistence wages and a few benefits, and only minor improvement for workers, leaving most to continue their impoverished status. Unions must revitalize their organizing efforts, and workers must fight to control the country's means of production and distribution.

This particularly applies to the various unions that cater to the Mexicano and Latino migrant workers. Within Aztlán, the UFW has the opportunity to reinvigorate itself into a powerful farmworker union, providing it goes back to the basics: organize agricultural workers, improve their living standards, and seek to control the land its workers cultivate. As to other labor organizing struggles in Aztlán such as the AFL-CIO, Teamsters, SEIU, OLAW, LACFL, and LCLAA, as buffers they are all in dire need of a major ideological injection of progressive social democratic ideas, strategies, and tactics.

Of all organizational models examined, the sectarian Left or advocate transformers, because of their antiliberal capitalist posture, face the toughest organizational challenges. They struggle to organize in a society with a powerful political culture that adulates liberal capitalism, demonizes Left sectarianism, and repudiates the liberal agenda of welfare capitalism. As a result the Mexicano and Latino working class has yet to be organized effectively into either a progressive reform or revolutionary movement. The cardinal reason for the failure is that they operate within the belly of the liberal capitalist superpower. As a result of 9/11 and the Bush administration's cold war mentality, characterized by an intrusive Big

Brother approach to governance, efforts by progressive organizations and individuals are difficult to carry.

As sectarian Left organizations, the Union del Barrio, Raza Rights Coalition, PNLRU, NCMC, among others, with their eclectic socialist-ultranationalist separatist agenda have difficulties in convincing barrio and *colonia* residents to support their progressive agenda. Another once sectarian Left organization, the HMN, since the death of its founder, Bert Corona, has been plagued by internecine conflict and in 2003 split into two competing entities. Few Mexicanos support the sectarian Left's separatist politics of self-determination, but this could change as the country's material conditions change and groups become better organized.

Women's organizations are not exempt from the problems facing the other organizations. MANA, Comisión Femenil, and HOPE are not mass-based and adhere to a conventional accommodation politics that embraces the HG and liberal capitalism. They lack a power base among Mexicanas and Latinas in the barrios and *colonias* and have no progressive, change-oriented agenda.

Mexicano-based organizations (MBOs) show promise for the future. Most MBOs are still at the incipient stage of organizational development, but they are fast becoming the largest Mexicano organizations within Aztlán and beyond. This is due in part because of their adherence to the NMG. They seem to be exempt from internal schisms, power struggles, apathy, and indifference among their memberships. MBOs such as La Coordinadora, MUSA, and La Federación de Clubes Zacatecanos del Sur de California are influencing politics in México, but not U.S. policy.

The future of the Mexicano political experience in occupied Aztlán rests with the people's ability to build a powerful mass-based organization or organizations that possess both a power capability and fear factor. A colonized people without organization will never create a viable social movement that will extricate them from their decolonization—Mexicanos in Aztlán are no exception.

What Needs to Be Done?

Politically, the most pressing question that Mexicanos and Latinos face is "What needs to be done?" In fact, this is the topic and title of a book I am currently working on, which quite appropriately has as its subtitle, "The Building of a New Movement."[11] Even though the people's frustration and discontent are increasing, no Mexicano or Latino social movement exists today. In spite of the continuing Latino demographic transformation, Mexicanos today and in the future will be challenged by the political reality that numbers per se do not constitute power or translate into major social change. It is a political truism that only organized people constitute a basis for power. The most pressing challenge then for Mexicanos and Latinos alike is to build a "decolonizing change" movement. The Mexicano community's potential for power and change is increasing day by day, while its actual power capability paradoxically has yet to be realized. While some political and socioeconomic parallels exist between the Palestinians in Israel and Mexicanos in occupied Aztlán, little else is comparable. Mexicanos are an occupied people in the United States, but they lack what the Palestinians have, which is the requisite leadership, organization, ideological and strategic vision and power resources, commitment and willingness to sacrifice and struggle, and international backing.

The future prospects for major change are dependent on the emergence of a Mexicano and Latino "New Movement." As a social movement, it must either adopt a reform or revolutionary posture: one that seeks to effect social change and put an end to Aztlán's occupation and colonial status. Its character will ultimately be shaped by endogenous and exogenous antagonisms and material conditions that permeate Mexicanos and Latinos in Aztlán, and also in the country and world as a whole. Inherent to both reform and revolutionary movements is the fundamental notion of change.[12] The salient difference between the two is the degree or scope of change and the methodology to attain it. Paul Wilkinson writes that a social movement is "a deliberate collective effort to promote change in any direction and by any means, not excluding violence, illegality, revolution or withdrawal into utopian community."[13] James Wood and Maurice Jackson define social movements "as unconventional groups that have varying degrees of formal organization and that attempt to produce or prevent radical or reformist type change."[14] For Mexicanos, resistance and change will be the key, the raison d'être of reform or a revolutionary movement.

The greatest political challenge facing Mexicanos in the twenty-first century is to build a New Movement that is focused on decolonization and social change. In order to do so, the change agents of such a movement must first adhere to what I call the three "Rs" of change: "recommit," "reorganize," and "remobilize."[15] The accentuation is on the "re" because Mexicanos need to recapture the zeal for a struggle that has been evident during past epochs, especially during the epoch of militant protest. This means a renaissance of political activism must reignite and once again pervade the Mexicano political experience. Therefore, first Mexicanos and Latinos must "recommit" themselves to the creation of Una Nueva Causa (A New Cause for Change). Second, they must "reorganize" because *organizacion es la base del poder* (organization is the basis of power). And third, they must "remobilize" based upon *un renaicimiento de activismo* (a rebirth of activism) in order to effect social change.

For a new movement to emerge, however, several interdependent variables must be present. First, a climate of change must exist that is permeated by the people's discontent and frustration, especially among the masses and intelligentsia. Second, a cadre of competent and committed leaders, intellectuals, and organizers must exist who possess the leadership skills and intellectual acumen to direct, inspire, and manipulate the people's worsening material conditions as well as their psychic fears and frustrations. Third, the leadership must be ideologically impelled by the power and clarity of a new vision that embodies a number of beliefs, ideas, and goals that provide alternatives to the existent liberal capitalist system and heighten the people's expectations for a better life and society. Fourth, new change-oriented mass-based organizations must be formed, existent ones revitalized, and a new Mexicano or Latino-based political party be established. Fifth, new strategic and tactical scenarios must be formulated that reflect the struggle's new vision and purpose, which incorporates the use of both conventional and unconventional methods. Lastly, the emergent New Movement must acquire a power capability, a mass base, and financial resources to foster a critical mass mobilization.

The core of the New Movement must be its ability to effect major change within the country's liberal capital system. Otherwise, Mexicanos and other Latinos within Aztlán and beyond will be doomed to a future of external colonization, worsening oppression, exploitation, and subordination. If Mexicanos and Latinos, particularly in Aztlán, are to control their destiny, the New Movement must be predicated on continued resistance and a relentless struggle for the decolonization of Aztlán. It must be guided by a vision that is based upon the pursuit of one of the following ideological/strategic options.

1. Struggle within the existent liberal capitalist system to effect change within the country's mode of politics, impelled by an economic agenda based upon welfare capitalism.
2. Struggle to coalesce with others to transform the existent liberal capitalist system into an egalitarian social democratic system where wealth and power are distributed equitably.
3. Struggle independently as Mexicanos or as Latinos collectively within Aztlán for the realization of a "nation-within-a-nation" to control as much as possible Aztlán's superstructure and substructure within the limits of the existent liberal capitalist system.
4. Struggle for the creation of a separate Chicano/Mexicano nation, Aztlán, or opt for Aztlán to be reannexed to the motherland México, the latter to depend on the ideological nature of its regime.

In short, because Aztlán's barrios and *colonias* today exist under the specter of colonialism, their political experience is at a crucial juncture. A new epoch and mode of Mexicano and Latino politics in the United States must emerge via a New Movement. The question is, Which of the above strategic options will the New Movement embrace? For Mexicanos to continue to support the existent social order without demanding major reforms suggests that Mexicanos throughout Aztlán will forfeit their future as a liberated and unoccupied people.

Notes

1. Ernest W. Lefever, "Confronting Unmeltable Ethnics," *Los Angeles Times*, May 20, 2003.

2. Ricardo Alonzo-Zaldivar, "Latinos Now Top Minority," *Los Angeles Times*, June 19, 2003.

3. For an excellent study on the unspoken overall growing Latino and Black conflict see Nicolas C. Vaca, *The Presumed Alliance: The Unspoken Conflict between Latinos and Blacks and What It Means for America* (New York: HarperCollins, 2004).

4. Patrick Buchanan, *The Decline of the West* (New York: Simon & Schuster, 2004), 127.

5. Samuel P. Huntington, *Who Are We? The Challenges to America's National Identity* (New York: Simon & Schuster, 2004), 221–56.

6. Huntington, *Who Are We?*, 221.

7. Huntington, *Who Are We?*, 221.

8. For a compendium of Huntington's hypercritical analysis on immigration see "The Hispanic Challenge," *Foreign Policy*, March/April 2004.

9. Martinez, "Poll Finds Latinos in Political Flux," *Hispanic Link Weekly Report*, August 26, 2002.

10. *The Press Enterprise*, "Whites to Retain Power at the Polls, Study Concludes," December 5, 2002.

11. The complete title of my fifth book is *What Needs to Be Done? The Building of a New Movement*. I anticipate its publication by late 2006. The focus of the work will be to examine in detail various ideological and strategic options available to Mexicanos and Latinos to extricate themselves from the continued clutches of internal colonialism. In this brief section, my intent is to present the reader with a cursory peek theoretically into some of the strategic and ideological options that will be dealt with in-depth in the context of the aforementioned study.

12. The literature on social movements is vast. The following are but a few to see: Sidney Tarrow, *Power in Movement: Social Movements and Contentious Politics*, 2nd ed. (New York: Cambridge University Press, 1998); Steve Breyman, *Movement Genesis: Social Movement Theory and the West German Peace Movement* (Boulder, Colo.: Westview, 1998); James L. Wood and Maurice Jackson, *Social Movements: Development, Participation, and Dynamics* (Belmont,

Calif.: Wadsworth, 1982); Charles Tilly, *From Mobilization to Revolution* (Menlo Park, Calif.: Addison Wesley, 1978); Roberta Ash, *Social Movements in America*, 2nd ed. (Chicago, Ill.: Rand McNally, 1977); and Norman I. Fainstein and Susan S. Fainstein, *Urban Political Movements: The Search for Power by Minority Groups in American Cities* (Englewood Cliffs, N.J.: Prentice Hall, 1974).

13. Paul Wilkinson, 1971, 27. Cited in Tilly, *From Mobilization to Revolution*, 3.

14. Wood and Jackson, *Social Movements*, 3.

15. For a more extensive examination of the question, "What needs to be done?" refer to my book *La Raza Unida Party: A Chicano Challenge to the Two Party Dictatorship* (Philadelphia: Temple University Press, 2000), 298–300.

Abbreviations and Acronyms

ABP   Alianza Bracero Proa
ACCPE   American Coordinating Council on Political Education
ACLU   American Civil Liberties Union
ACSSC   American Council of Spanish-Speaking People
ACWUA   Amalgamated Clothing Workers Union of America
AFL   American Federation of Labor
AFL-CIO   American Federation of Labor-Congress of Industrial Organizations
AGIF   American G.I. Forum
AIM   American Indian Movement
ALRA   Agricultural Labor Relations Act
ALRB   Agricultural Labor Relations Board
AMAE   Association of Mexican American Educators
ANMA   Asociación Nacional México-Americana (National Mexico American Association)
ATM   The August Twenty-ninth Movement
AWIL   Agricultural Workers Industrial League
AWOC   Agricultural Workers Organizing Committee
BB   Brown Berets
BBA   Brown Berets de Aztlán
CASA   Centro de Acción Social Autónoma (Center for Autonomous Social Action)
CASA-HGT   Centro de Acción Social Autónoma-Hermandad General de Trabajadores (Center for Autonomous Social Action-General Brotherhood of Workers)
CAWIU   Cannery and Agricultural Workers Industrial Union
CBPO   community-based power organization
CCE   civic-culture economic organization
CCR   Committee on Chicano Rights

CCRI   California Civil Rights Initiative
CDT   Coalition for Diversity on Television
CFLT   National Committee to Free Los Tres
CFR   Californios for Fair Representation
CG   Chicano Generation
CHC   Congressional Hispanic Caucus
CHCI   Congressional Hispanic Caucus Institute
CIA   Central Intelligence Agency
CIME   Coalicion Internacional de Mexicanos en el Exterior (International Coalition of Mexicanos in the Exterior)
CIO   Congress of Industrial Organizations
CISPES   Committee in Solidarity with the People of El Salvador
CIWA   California Immigrant Workers Association
CJ   Crusade for Justice
CLF   Chicano Liberation Front
CMMA   Council of Mexican American Affairs
COPS   Communities Organized for Public Service
CORE   Congress on Racial Equality
CP   Communist Party
CPA   Chicano Press Association
CPU   El Congreso para Pueblos Unidos (Congress for United Communities)
CPUSA   Communist Party of the United States of America
CROM   Confederación Regional de Obreros Méxicanos (Regional Confederation of Mexican Workers)
CSO   Community Service Organization
CTA   California Teachers Association
CUCOM   Confederación de Uniones Campesinos y Obreros Mexicanos (Confederation of Mexican Farmworker and Workers Unions)
CUOM   Confederación de Uniones Obreras Mexicanas (Confederation of Mexican Workers Unions)
DNC   Democratic National Committee
EEOC   Equal Employment Opportunity Commission
EGPPC   Ernesto Galarza Public Policy Center at the University of California
EGTTPP   Ernesto Galarza Public Think Tank on Public Policy
EICC   Educational Issues Coordinating Committee
EZLN   Ejercito Zapatista de Liberación Nacional (Zapatista National Liberation Army)
FALN   Fuerzas Armadas de Liberacion Nacional (Armed Forces of National Liberation)

FBI   Federal Bureau of Investigation COINTELPRO (Counter Intelligence Programs)

FEDMEX   Federaciónes Mexicanas

FEPC   Federal Employment Practices Commission

FLOC   Farm Labor Organizing Committee

FMLN   Farabundo Martí de Liberación Nacional (Farabundo Marti National Liberation Front)

FWA   Farm Worker Association

HACER   Hispanic Association on Corporate Responsibility

HACU   Hispanic Association of Colleges and Universities

HAD   Hispanic American Democrats

HCR   human civil rights (advocacy groups)

HERE   Hotel Employees and Restaurant Employees Union

HG   Hispanic Generation (Synonymous with the Viva Yo Hispanic Generation)

HMN   Hermandad Mexicana Nacional (National Mexican Brotherhood). Due to an internal split, HMN continued and a second HMN was renamed Hermandad Mexicana Latino Americana (HMLA).

HOPE   Hispanas Organized for Political Equality

HUD   Department of Housing and Urban Development

IAF   Industrial Areas Foundation

ILWU   International Longshoremen and Warehousemen's Union

IMAGE   Incorporated Mexican American Government Employees

IMF   International Monetary Fund

INS   Immigration and Naturalization Service

IRCA   Immigration Reform and Control Act

ISJ   Institute for Social Justice

IWW   Industrial Workers of the World

KKK   Ku Klux Klan

LACFL   Los Angeles County Federation of Labor

LADO   Latin American Defense Organization

LBA   Latino Business Association

LCLAA   Labor Council for Latin American Advancement

LG   Latino Generation or Lat-Generation

LLA   Latino Lawyers Association

LRS   League of Revolutionary Struggle

LULAC   League of United Latin American Citizens

MAD   Mexican American Democrats

MAG   Mexican American Generation

MALCS   Mujeres Activas en Letras y Cambio Social (Active Women in Letters and Social Change)

MALDEF   Mexican American Legal Defense and Education Fund

MAM   Mexican American Movement

MANO   Mexican American Nationalist Organization

MAPA   Mexican American Political Association

MAUC   Mexican American Unity Council

MAWNA   Mexican American Women's National Association

MAYO   Mexican American Youth Organization

MBOs   Mexicano-based organizations

MEChA   Movimiento Estudiantil Chicano de Aztlán [Chicano Student Movement from Aztlán]

MELA   Mothers of East Los Angeles

MG   Mexican Generation

MLEO   Mexicano and Latino elected officials

MNVREP   Midwest-Northeast Voter Registration Education Project (Previously MVREP)

MUSA   Mexicanos in the United States of America

MVREP   Midwest Voter Registration and Education Project (Became MNVREP in 1987 and USHLI in 1996)

NAACP   National Association for the Advancement of Colored People

NAAHP   National Association for the Advancement of Hispanic People

NACCS   National Association of Chicano/Chicana Studies Association (Formerly NACS—National Association of Chicano Studies)

NACSS   National Association of Chicano Social Scientists

NAES   National Annenberg Election Survey

NAFTA   North American Free Trade Agreement

NAHR   National Alliance for Human Rights

NALEO   National Association of Latino Elected and Appointed Officials (Initially called NALDO—National Association of Latino Democratic Officials)

NAWU   National Agricultural Workers Union

NCLR   National Council of La Raza (Formerly Southwest Council of La Raza)

NCMC   National Chicano Moratorium Committee

NFWA   National Farm Workers Association (Previously FWA—Farm Workers Association, later the UFW—United Farm Workers)

NFWU   National Farm Worker Union

NHLA   National Hispanic Leadership Agenda

NHLC   National Hispanic Leadership Conference

NHMC   National Hispanic Media Coalition
NICD   National Institute for Community Development
NLMC   National Latino Media Council
NMG   Neo-Mex Generation
NOW   National Organization of Women
OCR   Operation Corporate Responsibility
OLAW   Organization of Los Angeles Workers
OSA   Order of the Sons of America
PAC   Political action committee
PADRES   Padres Asociados para Derechos Religiosos, Educativos, y Sociales
   (Priests Associated for Religious, Education, and Social Rights)
PAN   Partido Acción Nacional (National Action Party)
PAN   Project Arizona Now
PAPA   Pan-American Progressive Association
PAS   Proyecto Acción Social (Project Social Action)
PASSO   Political Association of Spanish-Speaking Organizations
PCM   Partido Comunista Mexicano (Mexican Communist Party)
PLM   Partido Liberal Mexicano (Mexican Liberal Party)
PLO   Palestinian Liberation Organization
PNLRU   Partido Nacional de La Raza Unida (Previously Raza Unida Party—
   RUP)
PO   Protest organization
PPO   Political pressure organization
PRD   Partido de la Revolución Democratica (Democratic Revolutionary Party)
PRI   Partido Revolucionario Institucional (Institutional Revolutionary Party)
PST   Socialist Workers Party
RNHA   Republican National Hispanic Assembly
RUP   Raza Unida Party (later renamed Partido Nacional de La Raza Unida—
   PNLRU)
SCLC   Southern Christian Leadership Conference
SDS   Students for a Democratic Society
SEIU   Service Employees International Union
SER   Service, Employment, and Redevelopment
SLO   sectarian Left organization
SNCC   Student Nonviolent Coordinating Committee
SOS   Save Our State Initiative (Otherwise known as Proposition 187)
SPM   Sociedad Progrecista Mexicana (Mexicano Progressive Society)
SSP   social service provider
SVREP   Southwest Voter Registration Educational Project

SWP   Socialist Workers Party
TCCD   Trinity Concept of Community Development
TD   Tejano Democrats
TELACU   The East Los Angeles Community Union, established in 1970
TFWU   Texas Farm Workers Union
TODEC   Training Occupational Development Educating Communities
TUUL   Trade Union Unity League
UB   Union del Barrio [Union of Neighborhoods]
UCAPAWA   United Cannery, Agricultural, Packing, Allied Workers of America
UCLA   University of California, Los Angeles
UCR   University of California, Riverside
UFW   United Farm Workers (Previously FWA and NFWA)
UFWOC   United Farm Workers Organizing Committee (Later United Farm Workers—UFW)
UMAS   United Mexican American Students
UN   United Nations
UNO   United Neighborhood Organization
USAPA   USA Patriot Act
USHCC   U.S. Hispanic Chamber of Commerce
USHLI   United States Hispanic Leadership Institute (Previously MVREP then MNVREP)
VCT   Voices of Citizens Together
VISTA   Volunteers in Service to America
VOICE   Valley Organized in Community Efforts
WCVI   William C. Velasquez Institute
WFM   Western Federation of Miners
WPA   Works Progress Administration
YCCA   Young Citizens for Community Action (Became Young Chicanos for Community Action)
YMCA   Young Men's Christian Association
YSA   Young Socialist Alliance

Index

Page numbers in *italics* refer to tables and illustrations.

Burton, John, 611
Bush administration (GWB): border policies of, 590–93; Bush doctrine, 602–3; foreign policy of, 599–600, 601; Patriot Act and, 600–601, 680; runup to Iraq War and, 602–4; Vicente Fox and, 628; war on terrorism and, 680
Bush, George H. W., 404, 446, 476, 484, 525, 538
Bush, George W., AGIF and, 636; approval rating of (2002), 627; declaration of combat end, 604–5; doctrine of, 602–3; election of (2000), 580, 589, 599–600, 616–18; Vicente Fox and, 697
Bustamante, Cruz, 485, 621–22, 650
Bustillos, Ernesto, 516
Butler, Anthony, 69

Caballero, Ana, 486
Caballero, Ray, 623
Cabrera, Luis, 170
Cabrera, Martin, 211
Cabrera, Tomas, 110
Cadillo, Gil, 596–97
Cadiz Constitution of 1812, 60
Cahuenga, Treaty of, 76
Caldera, Louis, 484
Calderon, José, 494, 512, 538, 598, 606
Calderon, Julio, 537, 538
Caldron, Samuel, 272, 285
Calhoun, John C., 81
California: ballot box politics and, 131–37, 284–87; bilingualism in schools, 133, 451–52, 458–59; decline of armed resistance in, 107–8; laws passed, 133–34; Mexicano officeholders in, 135–36, 284–87; migrant population of, 178, 179, 251; mutualistas and, 149, 201–2; politics of armed resistance in, 103–7; RUP and, 351–52; Spanish colonization of, 58. See also California's nativist propositions; Chavez, Cesar
California Association of Scholars, 451

California Civil Rights Initiative (CCRI), 451
California Democratic Council, 272, 286
California Federation of Spanish-Speaking Voters, 241
California Immigrant Workers Association (CIWA), 504–5
California National Guard, 454
California SB60 (Senate Bill 60) issue, 596–97
California State Board of Education, 459
California Teachers Association (CTA), 458
Californians-for-Johnson campaign, 275
California's nativist propositions: growing racist crusade by, 682; Proposition 187 (1994), 449–50, 454, 455, 531; Proposition 209 (1995–96), 450–51, 457–58; Proposition 227 (1998), 451–52, 458–59
Californios for Fair Representation (CFR), 537, 555
Callahagan, Bryan, 130
Calles, Plutarco Elías, 173, 175, 195
Calloway, Larry, 331
Calvert, Robert A., 127, 279
Camacho, Amelia, 281
Camacho, Avila, 191
Camarillo, Albert, 124, 126–27
Camejo, Peter, 508, 621
Camín, Héctor Aguilar, 436
Camp, Roderic Ai, 12–13
Campa, Arthur I., 215, 258, 261
Campbell, Jack, 329
Campean, Mario, 367, 507
Campos, Marc, 546
Canales, Alma, 351
Canales, Don Antonio, 73–74
Canales, J. T., 121, 129
Cananea strike, 152–53
Cannery and Agricultural Workers Industrial Union (CAWIU), 214, 458
Cano, José R., 522–23
Canon, Lou, 477
capitalism, liberal. See liberal capitalism

About the Author

Armando Navarro is a professor of Ethnic Studies at the University of California, Riverside. He received his AA degree in political science from Chaffey College in 1968; BA in political science from Claremont KcKenna College in 1970; and his PhD in political science from the University of California, Riverside. His areas of teaching specialization include Mexicano/Latino politics, social movements, American politics, and contemporary issues.

Professor Navarro is the author of several books and articles. His books include *Mexican American Youth Organization: Avant-Garde of the Chicano Movements in Texas*, published by the University of Texas Press (1995); *The Cristal Experiment: A Chicano Struggle for Community Control*, published by University of Wisconsin Press (1998); and *La Raza Unida Party: A Chicano Challenge to the U.S. Two-Party Dictatorship*, published by Temple University Press (2000).

Professor Navarro is concurrently working on two books: *The U.S./Mexico Border Crisis: Militarization, Nativism, and the Militia Insurgency* and *What Needs to Be Done? The Building of a New Movement*. The former is scheduled for completion late 2005 and the latter late 2006. He also has authored several articles, monographs, and reports on Chicano/Latino politics, redistricting, community organizing, immigration, and the Los Angeles Eruption (riots) of 1992.

Professor Navarro is the founder and former director of the Ernesto Galarza Applied Research Center at the University of California, Riverside. He brings to academia some thirty-six years of activism and professional experience in community organizing, politics, and advocacy in dealing with a myriad of local, state, national, and international human rights and social justice issues that particularly affect Mexicanos and Latinos in the United States. Internationally he has led and facilitated numerous delegations to Latin America, specifically Mexico, Cuba, and Central America.

As a result of his scholarship and activism, Professor Navarro has gained widespread visibility and recognition both domestically and internationally.